PowerShell and WMI

PowerShell and WMI

RICHARD SIDDAWAY

MANNING
Shelter Island

For online information and ordering of this and other Manning books, please visit
www.manning.com. The publisher offers discounts on this book when ordered in quantity.
For more information, please contact

> Special Sales Department
> Manning Publications Co.
> 20 Baldwin Road
> PO Box 261
> Shelter Island, NY 11964
> Email: orders@manning.com

Manning Publications Co.   Development editor: Jeff Bleiel
20 Baldwin Road   Technical proofreaders: Aleksandar Nikolic
PO Box 261   Copyeditor: Andy Carroll
Shelter Island, NY 11964   Proofreader: Melody Dolab
                                    Typesetter: Gordan Salinovic
                                 Cover designer: Marija Tudor

ISBN 9781617290114
Printed in the United States of America
1 2 3 4 5 6 7 8 9 10 – MAL – 17 16 15 14 13 12

To my parents, June and Ron
Without your help, support, and encouragement
I'd never have been able to do this

brief contents

contents

ix

PART 3 THE FUTURE: POWERSHELL V3 AND WMI 421

foreword

I am glad that Richard Siddaway decided to sit down and write a book on WMI. I have had the privilege of working with Richard over the last several years since becoming the Microsoft Scripting Guy, and I have long been impressed by his technical prowess. Whether Richard is speaking at a user group or conference or writing a blog article, it does not take long before the topic of WMI crops up. When I am planning a guest series of articles for the Hey Scripting Guy! Blog, Richard is the first person I turn to if the subject is WMI. In short, Richard is the perfect person to write this book.

The book is not just about WMI. Richard begins with an overview of Windows PowerShell technology. In fact, the "Using PowerShell" chapter is an excellent overview of Windows PowerShell. In less than 40 pages he hits all the highlights—functions, modules, PSDrives, aliases, remoting, and jobs. But it is not simply a fly-by at 30,000 feet; he gets down to the nitty-gritty, boils down essential information, and surfaces a number of potential gotchas. Even if you already know Windows PowerShell, this chapter is worth a look; if you don't know Windows PowerShell, you should read this chapter a couple of times so you don't have problems with the remainder of the book.

WMI can be complicated—I know, I wrote a book on the subject for Microsoft Press a few years ago. Luckily, Richard has devoted an entire chapter to discussing not only the basics of WMI, but some of the more advanced concepts as well. I love his WMI documentation script in chapter 3. Of course, one of the nice things about WMI is that it is self-describing, which means that it is possible to write scripts to discover information about WMI. Well, now you do not need to write those scripts yourself, because Richard has done it for you.

But if the book were all esoteric academic minutiae, it would be of limited practical value to network administrators and to consultants in the field who are attempting to use this rather difficult technology to solve real world problems. Luckily, Richard lives in the real world and his book quickly begins to produce real value. His section on WMI in the enterprise covers system documentation, working with disk subsystems, the registry, and more.

Windows PowerShell is a powerful, cool technology. WMI is a powerful, cool technology. When you combine the two you have a flexible and powerful solution. When Richard Siddaway is the author of the book—you have an unbeatable combination. Buy this book! You will thank me later.

ED WILSON, MCSE, MCSD
MICROSOFT SCRIPTING GUY
AUTHOR OF
WINDOWS POWERSHELL 2.0 BEST PRACTICES

preface

I am very passionate about using PowerShell to automate the administration of Windows systems. This will become apparent very quickly if you talk to me, listen to me at conferences, or read my other books or blogs. WMI has a reputation for being powerful but hard to use. PowerShell is the way forward for system administrators, and WMI is that horrible, old technology that no one really knows how to use. So why do we need a book on PowerShell and WMI?

In reality, PowerShell and WMI are made for each other. They are both powerful, but put them together and you have low-level access to just about every facet of your Windows system. WMI is a first-class citizen in the PowerShell world, with a set of cmdlets to make using WMI easier and to provide the ability to work over WSMAN or DCOM protocols. The great strength of the pairing of PowerShell and WMI is that you can work with both local and remote systems. The other point to remember is that Microsoft is putting a lot of effort into WMI for the Windows 8 family of products. There are big changes coming regarding what you can do with WMI and how you can use it.

In short, it seemed that now was the time to bring WMI in from the cold and into mainstream administration where it belongs.

This book is written for system administrators, and it provides a suite of scripts to automate a large range of administration tasks. In most cases, these scripts are ready to use in your environment—I use many of them on a regular basis. In the chapters, those scripts are explained and the background to the tasks is discussed so you can put the script into context for your environment. This isn't a cookbook or a theoretical book on the PowerShell language—it's more. It's a practical guide to taking these two technologies and making them do what you need in order to solve the problems you have in your environment.

Best practices can be an emotive subject, but one of my goals in writing the book has been to supply best practice guidelines for using PowerShell and WMI and Windows administration in general. There is no point in automating bad practice—it just makes mistakes happen quicker.

The solutions presented in the book show the way that I solve various problems. Use the scripts to solve your problems, and if you find better solutions, please share them with the PowerShell community.

I've gained a number of things during the writing of this book:

- A deeper understanding of PowerShell and WMI
- Some wonderful opportunities to talk with very knowledgeable people
- New friends who share my interest in and passion for PowerShell and WMI

I hope you get a sense of that passion and interest from reading this book, and I hope that it both helps you in your role as an administrator and inspires you to investigate some of the areas of PowerShell and WMI that I haven't been able to cover. Who knows, we could be talking about it at a PowerShell Deep Dive sometime soon.

Use the techniques, join the PowerShell community, and most of all, enjoy what you do.

acknowledgments

Producing a book like this is never a solo effort. My name may appear on the cover, but a whole team of people was required to get this book into your hands. This is my opportunity to thank them for their efforts.

I have to start with the Microsoft PowerShell and WMI teams. Without their work, there wouldn't be anything to write about. The team members I have met and corresponded with have always tried their best to answer my questions, and without their input this book would be a very different animal. So a big thank you to current and former members of these teams, especially Jeffrey Snover, Kenneth Hansen, Bruce Payette, Lee Holmes, Jason Shirk, Osama Sajid, Wojtek Kozacynski, Lukasz Anforowicz, and James Brundage.

I would also like to thank the Microsoft Scripting Guy—Ed Wilson—for writing the foreword to this book and for some very stimulating and thought-provoking discussions on the subject of PowerShell and WMI.

The people at Manning continue to be superb. They are a very professional group who understand how to put a good book together and how to get the best from their authors. Many thanks to Marjan Bace, Michael Stephens, Sebastian Sterling, Maria Townsley, Jeff Bleiel, Andy Carroll, Melody Dolab, Karen Tegtmeyer, Ozren Harlovic, Mary Piergies, Maureen Spencer, and Christina Rudloff.

There were two reviews of this manuscript during its development. The individual reviewers took the time to read and comment, sometimes in great detail, on the contents. Without their contributions this would have been a poorer book. Thanks to

Jonathan Medd, James Berkenbile, Mike Shepard, Nikander Bruggeman, Margriet Bruggeman, Karsten Strøbæk, Amos Bannister, Adam Bell, and Peter Monadjemi.

Special thanks must go to Aleksandar Nikolic for performing the technical review of the final manuscript and code. My discussion in the Frankfurt airport with Ravikanth Chaganti, after the European PowerShell Deep Dive, was especially useful. As usual, any and all errors of omission or commission remaining in the book are mine and mine alone.

During the MEAP process, a forum exists for readers to post comments and ask questions. The comments and questions have all been read and incorporated into the book where appropriate. Thank you for taking the time to post.

The PowerShell community is very enthusiastic and willing to share. Thank you to those who have helped with example code, discussed topics with me, provided solutions to problems, listened to talks (I have been talking a lot about PowerShell and WMI over the last year, and will continue to do so), asked questions, and offered speaker slots. The PowerShell MVP community and UK PowerShell group deserve a special vote of thanks.

Final thanks must go to my family, friends, and colleagues who've supported me through the writing and production of this book.

about this book

This is a book for system administrators, those who manage administrators, those responsible for auditing systems, and anyone else who needs to discover information about Windows-based systems. PowerShell and WMI are powerful individually, but when they come together they supply an unrivalled way to access and administer your systems.

I have attempted to show the breadth of problems that PowerShell and WMI can solve. The depth of these technologies is also exposed by the detailed and practical examples. There are areas such as clustering and the System Center family that haven't been touched because of space considerations.

PowerShell versions

This book was written during the PowerShell v3 development and beta program. Except where otherwise stated, this book deals with PowerShell v2. Chapters 18 and 19 require PowerShell v3 as they use functionality only available in that version.

My development environment is Windows 7 and Windows Server 2008 R2, but I have also tested on Windows Server 2003 and Windows Server 2008 where possible.

Most of the code will also run on PowerShell 1.0, and I will point out where this is not the case and what alternatives are available.

This book isn't a pure cookbook of PowerShell-based scripts nor is it a book on Windows administration. It lies between these two points and provides insight into how to automate the administration of your Windows systems using PowerShell and WMI.

You may not choose to read this book from cover to cover, but I urge you to keep it on your desk. I hope you will find yourself referring to it on a frequent basis. Once you start automating, the possibilities are only limited by your knowledge, and this book's task is to supply you that knowledge along with appropriate examples so you can apply it to your environment.

The scripts are presented as techniques with problem, solution, and discussion sections. They should help you solve your particular problems. If they don't, a message on the Author Online forum will reach me, and I may be able to supply some pointers. But no promises, because I have a day job as well.

Who should read this book?

This book is primarily for that overworked, and undervalued, person—the IT administrator. As an administrator, you may well find yourself constantly bombarded with new requests, new technologies, and user problems, and you may want to automate some of those tasks but not know where to start. Even some simple tools that could discover the configuration of the server that your predecessor built but didn't document would be a help.

This book won't solve all of your problems, but it will help you start to automate some of those problem areas. Make sure your manager reads chapter 1. They will then see what you are trying to achieve and how using the techniques in this book will make them look good as well.

The sample code in the book is based on real-world examples—I use a lot of scripts based on these techniques in my job. I have combined many of the discovery scripts, for example, to create a script that completely documents my servers. Take the code, experiment (in a test lab), and discover how you can start automating now.

Roadmap

PowerShell and WMI is divided into three parts. The book starts with an overview of the PowerShell and WMI technologies in part 1, "Tools of the trade." This introductory section covers the overall problems you need to solve, provides an overview of Power-Shell and WMI, and offers some best practices.

Chapter 1 describes the challenges we face every day as administrators—increasingly complex environments, new applications, fewer staff, and tighter deadlines. A quick look at PowerShell and WMI shows how they can be used to solve these problems and recover at least some of the time we need to become proactive in our approach.

Chapter 2 provides an overview of PowerShell. The use of cmdlets at the Power-Shell prompt is described, followed by an introduction to how PowerShell uses .NET and how we can utilize some of the .NET functionality with PowerShell. Don't worry, this isn't going to become a developers' book! PowerShell also has a scripting language that supplies the framework for our code. Simple scripts are described, leading up to the advanced functions we'll be working with throughout the book. This chapter also supplies an overview of PowerShell remoting and jobs.

WMI is the other technology we'll be using, and it moves to center stage in chapter 3. This is the most theoretical chapter in the book, because we delve into the structure of WMI, discovering how to document providers, namespaces, and classes. Examples of using the five WMI cmdlets are presented, together with some of the issues that may cause problems (workarounds are also presented). WQL is an SQL subset that can be used to query the WMI repository. Using WQL may seem like an old fashioned way of working, but it's still required in a number of scenarios. A good working knowledge of WQL will help in the later chapters of the book. WMI maintains links, known as *associators* and *references* between many classes. These links can be used to make administration easier, so we'll spend some time discovering how to use them.

Part 1 closes with chapter 4. This chapter covers a number of topics that will help you get the most out of PowerShell and WMI. It starts with finding code examples and ensuring that they're safe to use. This leads into the topic of securing the PowerShell environment, including the digital signing of scripts. The section on optimizing PowerShell looks at data input and output, format files, simple debugging techniques, and error handling. WMI best practices, including the configuration of WMI-related settings, authentication within WMI, data filtering, and conversions bring the chapter to a close.

The bulk of the book is taken up by part 2, "WMI in the Enterprise." A number of the chapters in this section discuss using WMI events. By using events, you can perform actions such as these:

- Monitor for a USB pen drive being plugged in, and copy data to the drive
- Monitor changes to specific registry keys and values
- Monitor the filesystem for additions, deletions, or modification of the files in a given folder
- Monitor processes to block specific applications or to ensure that an application is restarted if it fails

WMI has traditionally been viewed as a method of gathering information about your system's configuration. Chapter 5 demonstrates how this can be achieved using PowerShell and WMI. Techniques for discovering system configuration information, including hardware, operating system, and installed software are presented.

This theme continues into chapter 6, where you'll discover how to investigate the storage systems installed in your servers. The WMI classes that enable you to work with, and discover information about, disk controllers, physical and logical disks, volumes, and mount points will be utilized and explained. Administering disks in terms of formatting and defragmenting disks will also be discussed.

In chapter 7, our attention turns to the registry. The usual warnings regarding registry modifications having the potential to destabilize your system still apply. Techniques to discover the registry size, administer registry keys and values, and work with security settings will be discussed.

The other major data store that administrators work with on a regular basis is the filesystem—this is the subject of chapter 8. WMI can't be used to create filesystem objects, but it can be used to search for files and folders on local and remote machines. This becomes especially useful when we want to discover files or folders with special attributes, such as being hidden. Techniques to compress (and uncompress) files and folders are presented before we move on to examining the security settings on filesystems. The chapter closes with a look at file shares, with code that can be used to automate their whole lifecycle.

A server isn't just a collection of hardware. In many cases, our main interest in a system is the applications that are running on that system. These are investigated in chapter 9, when we turn our attention to services and processes. The service health of a system (whether the correct services are running) and service load order are investigated. The whole process lifecycle from creation through administration to destruction can be managed with the PowerShell and WMI techniques presented in this chapter.

The one subject that's guaranteed to upset every administrator at some time in their career is printing. Chapter 10 discusses printers. It starts by showing how to discover printer configuration and status, followed by a look at printer drivers. The chapter then examines how to manage printers and print jobs. The final part of the chapter discusses troubleshooting printers and shows how to perform tests, such as sending a test page to the printer.

Networking is the subject of chapter 11. Discovering the physical configuration of the network adapters, their IP addressing configuration, and the protocols in use forms the first part of the chapter. This is followed by sections on managing the physical adapters, configuring IP addresses, and related information. The chapter closes by examining how to discover the IPv4 routing table.

IIS is a common component of the Windows infrastructure. The IIS WMI provider is the subject of chapter 12. The chapter demonstrates how to administer the web server configuration, the website lifecycle, application pools, and web applications. The IIS WMI provider requires us to use a number of specialized techniques, which are explained in detail.

Configuring new servers is the subject of chapter 13. We'll look at how to rename a server and perform the domain join operation. Network configuration using the techniques from chapter 11, setting the license key, and activating the operating system are all discussed. The final part of the chapter explains how to configure power plans.

Security should always be an important consideration, and in chapter 14 we'll consider the users who have access to our systems, together with a number of other security-related issues. After you've discovered how to work with the local users and groups on the system, we'll examine the antimalware status. The chapter closes with techniques for working with the firewall state and settings.

Windows is an event-driven operating system. In chapter 15, techniques for working with the event logs are presented. WMI can only work with the classic event logs, but we can discover event log sources and back up the event logs. Simple scheduled jobs and performance counters are discussed. In later versions of Windows, system assessments and a stability index can be produced, and these can be accessed by PowerShell and WMI. Accessing this information is an easy way to determine whether a particular system component isn't performing or is affecting system stability.

Chapter 16 is a bit different in that we use the Hyper-V PowerShell library, which is based on WMI, to work with virtual machines. Techniques to create and configure remote machines, control virtual machines, start a group of virtual machines in sequence, and administer virtual disks are presented. This chapter is a good example of what many administrators do automatically—take the tools that are provided and build a wrapper to do exactly what they need in their environment.

In part 3, "The future: PowerShell v3 and WMI," we take an in-depth look at some of the exciting new functionality associated with PowerShell and WMI; namely, using WMI over the WS-Management protocols and the introduction of CIM cmdlets and "cmdlets-over-objects" in PowerShell v3.

Chapter 17 examines the WSMAN cmdlets. Using these, it is possible to access the WMI provider from the WinRM service on the remote machine. This enables the retrieval of information and the configuration of the remote machine. It's possible to perform just about any task through the WSMAN cmdlets that you could using the WMI cmdlets. The advantage is that you bypass DCOM, become firewall friendly, and potentially can access CIMOM (other non-Windows WMI providers) instances on non-Windows systems. The disadvantage is that it involves a more complex coding syntax and that you're not dealing with live objects.

Chapters 18 and 19 should be read together, with the content in chapter 19 building directly on that in chapter 18. The starting point is new functionality in PowerShell v3 that enables you to wrap a WMI class in XML and use the resulting file as a PowerShell cmdlet—this is known by the catchy title of "cmdlets-over-objects." The cmdlet is loaded into PowerShell as a module, and parameters are added to the cmdlet to provide filtering and search options. Two or more WMI classes can be treated this way, and the resultant cmdlets are loaded by creating a module file that calls them as submodules. Format and type files are also added to the module to control the formatting of the output.

In chapter 19, WMI methods are added to the mix. These drive the creation of additional cmdlets that are again loaded as part of the module. The ability to "cmdlet-ize" WMI classes gives a huge boost to the ease of use. Much of the new PowerShell functionality in Windows Server 8 is produced in this manner.

Chapter 19 continues with the CIM cmdlets. These are analogous to WMI cmdlets but use a new API and new .NET objects. The CIM cmdlets are compared and contrasted to the WMI cmdlets to provide a context for their use. These CIM cmdlets combine the firewall friendliness of the WSMAN cmdlets and the ease of use of the WMI cmdlets. The chapter, and the book, closes with a review of CIM sessions, which can be thought of as similar to PowerShell remoting sessions. CIM sessions create a persistent connection to a remote machine to make multiple calls more efficient. They can work over WSMAN or DCOM to enable access to systems running PowerShell v3 or v2.

There are four appendices to the book. They supply a PowerShell reference guide, a WMI reference guide, a best practices guide, and a list of references that can be consulted for further information.

Source code downloads

The source code for this book can be downloaded from the publisher's website at www.manning.com/PowerShellandWMI.

> **WARNING** All downloaded code must be tested in your environment.

The code is provided as a zip file with a folder for each chapter, except that the nature of chapters 18 and 19 leads to a single folder spanning both of those chapters. A PowerShell file, .ps1, is provided to match each listing in the chapter. The files are named for the listings; for example, Listing3.1.ps1.

> **TIP** Each listing is presented as one or more functions. The most efficient way to load these is to use the chapter's module file.

Other files may be supplied occasionally, such as example output where the data is too big to include on the page or example input files. In all cases, they're referenced in the chapters.

Alternative coding styles are provided where I have used a report production style of script in the chapter. These can be found in subfolders of the relevant chapter, named "Alternative Non-Report Style".

In some cases, alternative scripts using the CIM cmdlets from PowerShell v3 are provided as examples of how to use this new functionality. The CIM alternatives are located in a subfolder of the chapter, named "CIM".

Code and typographical conventions

This is a book about using PowerShell, and there are a lot of examples provided throughout the book. A fixed-width font, `like this`, is used for short lines of code in the text. Listings and longer code examples embedded in the text also use a fixed width font:

```
like this.
```

Listings are annotated, where necessary, and full explanations are provided in the text. In many cases, the code statements have been split across multiple lines in order to fit the code on the page. These lines either terminate with a back tick (`` ` ``), which is the PowerShell continuation character, or the following line has a ➡ symbol to indicate that the line is a continuation.

If the code has been typed directly at a PowerShell prompt, it'll be displayed like this:

```
PS> 1kb
1024
```

I have followed a number of conventions when putting together the code for this book. Some of these are standard PowerShell best practices, and others are my personal coding style. I will usually refer to *servers* when discussing the types of machines we are administering, but many of the techniques covered in this book can be applied to desktop machines as well.

PowerShell commands (cmdlets and functions) can have shortcut names, known as *aliases*, defined. I don't normally use aliases in scripts, because I want to ensure that the scripts are readable, and are as easy to understand as possible. I also use the full parameter names in cmdlets. Cmdlet, parameter, property, and attribute names will be displayed like this.

There is one exception to my rule on aliases, and that's for the utility cmdlets, where I use the following conventions:

- `Where-Object` is aliased as `where` but never as `?`.
- `ForEach-Object` is aliased as `foreach` but never as `%`.
- `Select-Object` is aliased as `select`.
- `Sort-Object` is aliased as `sort`.

`Group-Object` and `Measure-Object` are used less frequently, but they're aliased to `group` and `measure` respectively. In the discussion around a script, I always use the full cmdlet name. I have adopted this convention for a number of reasons:

- It is advised by the PowerShell team.
- It represents accepted practice and usage.
- It's more readable.
- It saves some space on the page.

I use double quotes around strings unless I am sure that I don't want to substitute into the string. WMI filters and WQL use single quotes to delineate strings within the query. I also tend to leave keywords, such as `do` and `if` in lowercase. My function names and their parameters are usually lowercase—I'll make an exception to this if the name is long and some capitalization makes it more readable.

In some cases, the listings in the book are truncated. This is to save space and is always stated in the script's discussion. The download code for the book is complete. My goal has been to provide a balance between readability, conciseness, and completeness. Only you can tell if I have succeeded.

Author Online

Purchase of *PowerShell and WMI* includes free access to a private web forum run by Manning Publications where you can make comments about the book, ask technical questions, and receive help from the author and from other users. To access the forum and subscribe to it, point your web browser to www.manning.com/PowerShellandWMI. This page provides information on how to get on the forum once you are registered, what kind of help is available, and the rules of conduct on the forum.

Manning's commitment to our readers is to provide a venue where a meaningful dialog between individual readers and between readers and the author can take place. It is not a commitment to any specific amount of participation on the part of the author, whose contribution to the AO remains voluntary (and unpaid). We suggest you try asking the author some challenging questions, lest his interest stray!

The Author Online forum and the archives of previous discussions will be accessible from the publisher's website as long as the book is in print.

about the author

Richard Siddaway is a technical architect for Serco in the UK, working on transformation projects in the Local Government and Commercial arena. With more than 22 years of experience in various aspects of IT, Richard specializes in the Microsoft environment at an architectural level—especially around Active Directory (AD), Exchange, SQL Server, and infrastructure optimization.

Much of his recent experience has involved Active Directory migrations and optimizations, which often include Exchange. Richard has hands-on administration experience and is involved in implementation activity in addition to filling architectural and design roles. He has extensive experience specifying, designing, and implementing high-availability solutions for a number of versions of the Windows platform, especially for Exchange and SQL Server.

Richard is always looking for the opportunity to automate a process, preferably with PowerShell and WMI. Richard founded and currently leads the UK PowerShell User Group. Microsoft has recognized his technical expertise and community activities by presenting a Microsoft Most Valued Professional award. Richard has presented to The Technical Experts conference in the USA and Europe, the Directory Experts Conference, at various events at Microsoft in the UK and Europe, and for other user groups worldwide. Richard has a number of articles and technical publications to his credit, including *PowerShell in Practice* (Manning). He is a coauthor of the forthcoming *PowerShell in Depth: A system administrator's guide* (Manning).

about the cover illustration

The figure on the cover of *PowerShell and WMI* is captioned "The Bibliophile," which means a lover of books. The man on the cover may just be an avid reader or possibly he's a collector of rare editions or even a bookseller. The illustration is taken from a 19th-century edition of Sylvain Maréchal's four-volume compendium of regional and professional dress customs published in France. Each illustration is finely drawn and colored by hand. The rich variety of Maréchal's collection reminds us vividly of how culturally apart the world's towns and regions were just 200 years ago. Isolated from each other, people spoke different dialects and languages. In the streets or in the countryside, it was easy to identify where they lived and what their class, trade, or station in life was just by their dress.

Dress codes have changed since then and the diversity by region, so rich at the time, has faded away. It is now hard to tell apart the inhabitants of different continents, let alone different towns or regions. Perhaps we have traded cultural diversity for a more varied personal life—certainly for a more varied and fast-paced technological life.

At a time when it is hard to tell one computer book from another, Manning celebrates the inventiveness and initiative of the computer business with book covers based on the rich diversity of regional life of two centuries ago, brought back to life by Maréchal's pictures.

Part 1

Tools of the trade

Welcome to *PowerShell and WMI*. WMI is a mature administration technology that has been with us for a good number of years. PowerShell is the relatively new kid on the block that's bringing automation to administrators who haven't considered it in the past. PowerShell and WMI are a natural pairing, like Batman and Robin or fish and chips.

The book has three sections. In this first part of the book, we'll look at the technologies in isolation.

Chapter 1 provides a brief overview of the subject as well as some examples of the benefits that using PowerShell and WMI together will bring to your environment.

In chapter 2, we'll turn our attention to PowerShell, looking at its major elements and how to use them. This isn't intended to be a complete PowerShell tutorial, but taken together with appendix A, it will supply the information you need to get the most from this book.

WMI moves on stage in chapter 3, and you'll learn what it is and how to use it with PowerShell. We'll look at the WQL language along with some advanced topics, including using WMI and .NET together.

Finally, chapter 4 shows some ways to optimize your use of WMI and PowerShell. These suggestions are not intended to be prescriptions but are based on my accumulation of experience from using PowerShell and WMI. They will hopefully make using these technologies easier and more enjoyable. Learn from my mistakes, in other words.

Solving
administrative challenges

This chapter covers
- The administrator's headache
- Solving the challenge with automation
- PowerShell and WMI—the automation tools

Ask any Windows administrator about their biggest problems, and somewhere in the list, usually near the top, will be too much work and not enough time to do it. They know that automation is possible, will be at least aware of some of the technologies that could solve their problems, such as Windows Management Instrumentation (WMI) and PowerShell, but don't have the time to spend investigating the technologies. That's a shame because it's commonly accepted that 70 percent of an organization's IT budget is used to "keep the lights on." Automation can make a worthwhile contribution to reducing that percentage and freeing people and money to contribute to the business bottom line.

It's also possible that they've looked at WMI or PowerShell and decided they were too difficult. This is an understandable view, given the issues with WMI in VBScript—especially the amount of work involved in getting WMI to work in

VBScript, and the lack of usable examples that also explain the techniques that have to be used. Some horrendous examples of PowerShell have been posted on the web that put me off, never mind someone wanting to start with the subject! Unfortunately, administrators then miss out on the possibilities that automation provides to reduce their workload and accomplish more.

The aim of this book is to radically lower the entry bar to using WMI productively in your environment. The examples that are provided can be used with few or no, changes. You'll also gain a deeper understanding of WMI that can be used to work with areas we don't cover.

PowerShell itself is constructed to make WMI usage much easier and more intuitive. PowerShell is Microsoft's automation engine that, among other things, provides easy-to-use access to the rich management toolset available in WMI. Together, PowerShell and WMI provide a set of tested techniques that will enable you to administer your Windows environment more quickly and easily. You'll be able to automate many of the standard tasks that currently consume too much of your attention, freeing up time to do the more interesting things that otherwise couldn't be fitted into your normal working day.

The first thing I'll do in this chapter is define the problem we're trying to solve. There are a number of issues that affect any Windows environment of significant size:

- Number of systems
- Rising infrastructure complexity
- Rate of change

The second part of the chapter shows why PowerShell and WMI provide a great toolset for solving these problems. Getting the most out of PowerShell involves investing a little time in learning it, especially when using WMI. Automation is the key to making your life as an administrator easier. The benefits you can achieve with PowerShell and WMI automation provide an excellent return on the investment you make in learning to use the technologies.

The chapter closes with two examples showcasing the power this combination of technologies delivers to us. The first example shows how you can shut down all the servers in your data center with one command, and the second shows how you can test settings on many machines in one pass.

Let's start with a look at the responsibilities of a modern Windows administrator and the problems administrators face.

1.1 Administrative challenges

Administrators are very busy people. They seem to be continually asked to do more with fewer resources. Figure 1.1 illustrates this with a sketch graph that I'll refer to in the following sections. One thing the graph illustrates is the ever-decreasing cost, in real terms, of hardware. For example, I recently acquired a laptop with a quad-core processor (hyperthreading allows Windows to see eight cores) and 16 GB of RAM as a mobile lab. A few years ago, a machine with those specifications was a mid-range server, not a laptop!

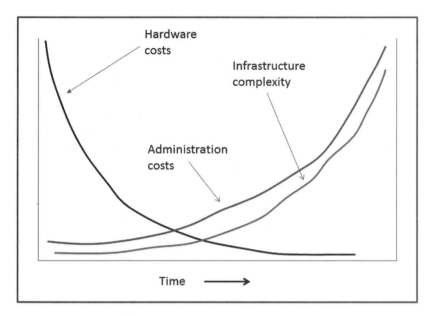

Figure 1.1 **The relationship between decreasing hardware costs, increasing infrastructure complexity, and the cost of administering the evolving infrastructure**

The same is true in the server market—4-, 8-, or even 10-core processors and lots of relatively cheap memory mean that we can afford to run applications and business processes that were previously only considered by large corporations with huge budgets.

This leads directly to the other components of the graph, which show the steep rise in infrastructure complexity and the even faster rise in administration costs. The continual upward growth of infrastructure complexity and cost isn't sustainable. PowerShell and WMI can help you break out of this growth curve. First, though, we need to examine the problem in a little more depth—where do the complexity and cost of administration come from?

1.1.1　Too many machines

This may seem to be an odd way to look at infrastructure, but do you really need every server you've created? Many, if not most, organizations have too many servers. This comes about for a number of reasons:

- *The decreasing cost of hardware*—This change leads to it being easier to add a new server than to think about using an existing one.
- *Department- or project-based purchasing*—This approach raises questions about server ownership and makes departments or projects unwilling to share resources.
- *The "one application—one server rule"*—Separating applications so that a problem in one doesn't affect others may still be valid for business-critical applications,

but it's not necessarily required for second- or third-line applications. It's definitely not required for testing and training versions.

- *Weak or reactive IT departments*—The lack of controls and processes in IT leads to departments and projects introducing systems that IT doesn't know about and has had no involvement with until the systems hit production.

An administrator's workload increases faster than the rate of increase of machines due to the time spent switching one's focus between machines (often requiring a new remote connection to be made) and the additional complexity each machine and its supported applications bring to the environment.

Virtualization is one of the hot topics in IT at present, with most organizations virtualizing at least part of their server estates. There are several advantages of virtualization:

- Reduced numbers of physical servers
- Reduced requirement for data center facilities, including space, power, and air conditioning
- Increased use of physical assets, giving a better return on investment

The organization as a whole benefits from virtualization, but the administrator's load is increased. If you have 100 servers to administer before virtualization, and you change to use 4 physical hosts and virtualize the 100 servers, you now have 104 systems to administer. The complexity may increase as well, because the virtualization platform may introduce a different operating system into the environment. The increase in the total (physical plus virtual) number of systems also means that there will be more change happening as the environment evolves.

1.1.2 Too many changes

Change can be viewed as an administrator's worst headache. Unfortunately environments aren't static:

- Operating system and application patches are released on a regular basis.
- New versions of software are released.
- Storage space needs to be readjusted to match usage patterns.
- Application usage patterns force hardware upgrades.
- Virtualization and other disruptive new technologies change the way environments are created and configured.

This level of activity, multiplied across the tens, hundreds, or even thousands of machines, builds on top of the day-to-day activity, such as monitoring and backups.

This situation isn't supportable in the long term. Organizations can't absorb ever-increasing administration costs, and today's economic realities prevent other mechanisms, such as increased revenue, from providing an escape. The situation has to be resolved by reducing the cost of administration. But administrators are hampered in doing this by the fact that many changes bring new technologies into the environment without ensuring they're supportable.

1.1.3 Complexity and understanding

Complexity is the real problem in many cases. It can arise due to a number of causes:

- Multiple operating systems bring different toolsets and terminology, even between versions of Windows.
- Different types of applications, such as databases, email, Active Directory, and web-based applications, require different skill sets, use different tools, and place different stresses on a server that the administrator must accommodate.
- Many machines perform the same or similar roles, but subtle, potentially undocumented, differences increase the likelihood of error.

Complexity is often compounded by incomplete knowledge and skill sets on the part of the administrators. Too often a project will introduce a new technology and administrators are expected to immediately pick up and manage the systems. Do the administrators have the skills? Do they have the time to learn the intricacies of the new technology? Sadly, the answer to both questions is often no.

This leads administrators to make best-guess decisions about how to do things. Sometimes, if the new technology is a version change from something already in use, administrators will continue to use the old methods even if there's now a better way to perform the task.

This lack of skills and knowledge leads to mistakes, and these mistakes cost money, often in terms of lost revenue for the organization. This puts more pressure on the administrators and leads to a lack of trust from the business. The IT department is often then excluded from discussions about new technologies until it's too late, and the cycle takes another spiral downwards.

Not only are major changes introduced by projects, administrators also face the host of minor changes required to keep their environments secure and running smoothly.

1.2 Automation: the way forward

The way to overcome these issues is to introduce automation. Get the machines to do the mundane, repetitive work—that's what we invented them for!

Automation means many things to many people. There's a hierarchy of automation activity that can be considered, as shown in figure 1.2.

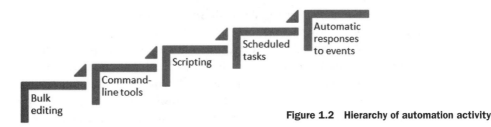

Figure 1.2 Hierarchy of automation activity

The question that needs to be answered by every organization is, "Where do I get the most benefit?" The answer depends on what you're trying to achieve and where you are now. I know of a number of organizations that are quite happy using the standard Windows tools and a few bulk-editing tools. Others attempt to schedule everything or even create automated responses to events. Automation, for most organizations, involves a mixture of command-line tools, scripting, and scheduled tasks.

That leads to the second big question, which is, "How do I automate my administrative tasks?" PowerShell provides a set of command-line tools (called cmdlets) that can be used interactively. As the commands become longer and more ambitious, there's a natural progression into scripting. One of the great strengths of PowerShell is that you can use exactly the same commands in a script or at the command prompt, so everything you've learned about commands is still usable in scripts.

PowerShell by itself is a wonderful tool (OK, I am fanatical about it), but you can take it a stage further and layer WMI on top. This opens a standards-based management toolset that you can use on local and remote machines and that can potentially include non-Windows systems when PowerShell v3 is used. The scripts can be run interactively or they can be scheduled to run at a specific time by using PowerShell and WMI. But before we get into those delights, let's have a look at automation in general.

In this book, we'll be concentrating on scripting as the primary automation activity. It could be argued that because you're using PowerShell, you could do much of your work from the command line. The benefit of scripting, though, is that you can reuse the code and save even more time by not having to rewrite the code each time you want to use it. This topic is covered in depth in chapter 4 of *PowerShell in Practice* (Manning 2010).

Scheduled tasks and automatic responses are too dependent on the particular environments for this book, so in chapter 3 we'll start to look at how you can automate responses to events that occur on your systems. We'll revisit this in later chapters as we consider specific areas of administration. We won't neglect the use of the command line, though. Many of the examples are short enough to use interactively.

Let's look at an example. Suppose you need to determine the amount of free space on the C: drive of a number of machines in your environment. One way is to go to the data center, assuming they're all in the same data center, and log onto the console of each machine. You'd then need to open Windows Explorer or another tool and find the free space on the C: drive. Write down the answer, and repeat for the next machine on the list.

A slightly easier option is to use Windows' Remote Desktop functionality to connect to each machine. Then you'd need to manually obtain the information. With this approach you don't have to move from your desk, but it still takes too much time.

My favorite solution is to use PowerShell as shown in listing 1.1. Don't worry if you don't understand the code right now. We'll return to this script in chapter 6 when we look at how to administer the disks in servers.

Scripting Conventions

I discussed these conventions in the introductory material but if you're like me you skipped that part of the book.

I will usually refer to servers when discussing the types of machines you're administering but many of the techniques covered in this book can be applied to desktop machines as well.

PowerShell commands (cmdlets and functions) can have shortcut names, known as aliases, defined. I don't normally use aliases in scripts as I want to ensure that the scripts are readable and as easy to understand as possible. I also use the full parameter names in cmdlets.

There is one exception to this rule and that's for the utility cmdlets where I use the following conventions:

- `Where-Object` aliased as `where` but never as `?`
- `ForEach-Object` aliased as `foreach` but never as `%`
- `Select-Object` aliased as `select`
- `Sort-Object` aliased as `sort`

In the discussion around a script I always use the full cmdlet name.

I have adopted this convention for a number of reasons:

- On the advice of the PowerShell team.
- Because it represents accepted practice and usage.
- Because it's more readable.
- It saves some space on the page.

In this PowerShell example you start with a list of server names taken from my lab setup. This list is piped into a `ForEach-Object` cmdlet (aliased as `foreach`) that calls `Get-WmiObject` for each server in the list in order to find the information on the logical disk used as the C: drive. You then format the information and output it as a table, as shown in the following listing.

Listing 1.1 Find free disk space

```
"dc02", "W08R2CS01", "W08R2CS02", "W08R2SQL08",
"W08R2SQL08A", "WSS08" | foreach {
    Get-WmiObject -Class Win32_LogicalDisk `
-ComputerName $_ -Filter "DeviceId='C:'" } |
Format-Table SystemName, @{Name="Free";
    Expression={[math]::round($($_.FreeSpace/1GB), 2)}} -auto
```

The free space is recalculated from bytes to GB to make the results more understandable. Notice that PowerShell understands GB, as well as KB, MB, TB, and PB. The results look like this:

```
SystemName      Free
----------      ----
W08R2CS01      119.04
W08R2CS02      118.65
W08R2SQL08     114.8
W08R2SQL08A    115.17
WSS08          111.41
DC02           118.53
```

NOTE   I don't intend to show output from every script we discuss in the book, but I will show output occasionally where it aids in the discussion of a particular issue.

There are a number of enhancements that you could apply to this script:

- Put the computer names into a CSV file (as we'll do in listing 1.4)
- Add the results to an Excel spreadsheet, or a database, so that trends can be seen
- Schedule the task to run on a periodic basis

I use a similar script, with the first two enhancements, to regularly report on disk space trends for the organization I'm currently working with. I now have a tool that takes seconds to run against each machine and provides vital information. It's also quickly and easily extensible to cover other machines that may become of interest. The script took me a few minutes to write and test, and there's an immediate payback every time I use it.

PowerShell is designed to provide this type of return. In the words of Jeffrey Snover, the architect of PowerShell, "I firmly believe that economics determine what people do and don't do so PowerShell is designed from the ground up to make composable, high-level task oriented abstractions be the cheapest things to produce and support." The full article, "The Semantic Gap," is available from the *Windows PowerShell Blog* at http://blogs.msdn.com/b/powershell/. A search for *semantic gap* will take you to the post.

The second part of this book will show many examples of this concept in action, but for now we'll have a closer look at PowerShell and discuss why it's the ideal platform for automating your administration.

1.3   *PowerShell overview*

In this section, I want to show you why PowerShell is the ideal platform for automating your Windows administration.

PowerShell is now on its second version (with the third in beta at the time of writing). It's part of the default installation of Windows 7 and Windows Server 2008 R2 (for Server Core it's an optional install). PowerShell v2 also can be installed on Windows Server 2008, Windows Server 2003, Windows Vista, and Windows XP. PowerShell v3 is an integral part of the Windows 8 family of operating systems. This level of support means you can use PowerShell to manage all of your Windows systems.

WINDOWS 2000 SUPPORT Windows 2000 is now out of support and won't be considered in this book. PowerShell doesn't have an option to install on Windows 2000.

There are also an increasing number of applications that have PowerShell support built into them. It's a requirement for all new versions of the major Microsoft products, and adoption by third-party vendors is steadily increasing the scope of PowerShell.

> **PowerShell resources**
>
> Chapter 2 provides an overview of PowerShell's features, the language, and how to use it. It isn't a full PowerShell tutorial, but it will explain what you need to understand the examples in the second part of the book.
>
> Bruce Payette's *Windows PowerShell in Action*, second edition (Manning 2011) provides the most detailed coverage of PowerShell from a language perspective. My *PowerShell in Practice* (Manning 2010) supplies many examples of using PowerShell to administer Windows systems.

The ability to access remote machines (which we'll look at in chapter 2) simplifies administration, because you can automate your whole Windows environment from a single administration console. This is how you can break the curve of rising infrastructure complexity. We'll look at how you can achieve this after we've examined Power-Shell's scope.

1.3.1 *PowerShell scope*

PowerShell enables you to administer a range of applications, from those having direct PowerShell support built into them to community-inspired and -provided additions that are available for download.

A number of major applications have direct PowerShell support:

- Exchange 2007/2010 (probably the poster child of PowerShell support)
- SQL Server 2008/2012
- SharePoint 2010
- Various members of the System Center family

Other elements of the Windows environment have PowerShell support available through Microsoft or third-party additions, including the following:

- Active Directory
- IIS
- Clustering
- Terminal Services
- Graphical presentation tools

The availability of functionality is good, but to get the most from it you need to get it into production use, and the sooner the better. One way to achieve this is to take advantage of the PowerShell community, which supplies sample code that can shorten the development cycle. PowerShell has a very strong and productive community that starts with the PowerShell team but also includes the following resources (links are provided in appendix D):

- Blogs, including mine
- Code repositories for community contributions, such as www.poshcode.org and www.powershell.com
- Forums, such as www.powershell.com

This provides a breadth and depth of support and additional functionality that almost guarantees you'll be able to find help with solving your problem.

1.3.2   *PowerShell and .NET*

Whenever PowerShell is discussed, the fact that it's .NET-based and can access most of the .NET Framework is brought up. At this point, I find that the eyes of many administrators begin to glaze over and they slide down into their seats. WAKE UP!

Yes, PowerShell is .NET-based and there are some really clever things that can be done by working directly with .NET code in PowerShell, some of which we'll see in later chapters. But you don't need to do this until you're ready to work at this level. There are a huge number of administration tasks you can perform without dipping your toes any further into the .NET waters than we did in listing 1.1. Just don't forget that .NET is there when you need it, and there are lots of great examples of how to work with .NET available from the PowerShell community.

> **WMI and .NET**
>
> It's possible to use WMI functionality through .NET code created and run in Power-Shell. This is an advanced technique that we'll look at in chapter 12, when we're working with IIS.
>
> There are generally alternatives to using .NET in this way, and I'll always choose those over a .NET-based solution. I'm an administrator, not a developer, and I'll present solutions for administrators.

As an example of how you can use .NET with PowerShell, let's look at the services running on a system. A subset of the installed services on my test system is shown in figure 1.3.

The `Get-Service` cmdlet (a PowerShell command) returns a list of the running services. I have restricted the output by using `wi*` to only return services starting with "wi." The results are piped into a `Format-Table` cmdlet that outputs the results as a nicely formatted table.

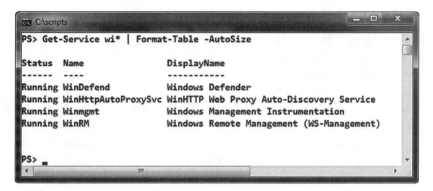

Figure 1.3 Using `Get-Service` to display a subset of the running services

> **NOTE** The PowerShell pipeline passes .NET objects rather than text as in with other shells. This supplies a large measure of PowerShell's power.

I deliberately chose to use `wi*` because it demonstrates two services we'll be seeing a lot more of later: WMI and Windows Remote Management (WinRM). (It also keeps the figure to a reasonable size.)

Underneath the hood, `Get-Service` is using a .NET class called `System.ServiceProcess.ServiceController`, which is fascinating but doesn't mean much to me without looking up the .NET documentation. The beauty is that you don't need to know this 99.99 percent or more of the time. PowerShell abstracts all of this, and you can perform your discovery with an easy-to-use command that has a descriptive name.

1.3.3 Breaking the curve

In figure 1.1 you saw that there's a continuous rise in the complexity of organizations and the cost of performing the administration in those organizations. This continuous increase isn't supportable in the long term, and we need a way to break the upward curve.

PowerShell can help us break that curve by providing the following:

- A set of tools to interactively administer servers and applications
- An automation engine that works across the entire Windows estate
- The ability to apply those concepts to a number of applications
- Remote administration engines that enable multiple machines to be administered with a single command
- Asynchronous and scheduled tasks to further enhance automation

PowerShell offers a productivity boost that will easily repay the time you spend learning to get the best from the technology. And using PowerShell and WMI together will further enhance your productivity gains.

1.4   *WMI overview*

In this section, we'll look at what WMI offers us as administrators. We'll examine WMI in much greater detail in chapters 3 and 4, where we'll drill into the details of how to use it to automate administration tasks.

WMI has been available to Windows administrators since the days of Windows NT 4, but it isn't a static technology. Each new version of Windows brings changes to the functionality available through WMI, usually by adding extra capabilities but occasionally by removing or radically changing functionality. New versions of other applications can have a similar impact. For instance, Exchange 2003 had WMI support, but that was removed in Exchange 2007/2010.

> **WMI AND OFFICE** Microsoft Office 2007 supplied a WMI provider in the shape of the root\MSAPPS12 namespace. This functionality was removed in Office 2010. Remnants of WMI classes will remain on a system if an upgrade from Office 2007 to 2010 is performed, but they won't be usable.

The only way to be sure that particular functionality is available on your version of Windows is to check the documentation on the Microsoft Developer Network (MSDN). The WMI functionality available on a particular system can be discovered in a number of ways using PowerShell and other tools. Chapter 3 supplies full instructions on this.

There are many automation scripts available using WMI, and most of them use VBScript due to the efforts of the people behind the Microsoft Script Center after Windows 2000 shipped. This gives the unfortunate impression that WMI requires a lot of coding for you to achieve any gains. This is no longer true, as you'll see in a little while, and it's slowly becoming apparent on the internet as the PowerShell community supplies example code using WMI.

To get started, let's look at what WMI actually is.

1.4.1   *What is WMI?*

Just what is WMI? The abbreviation stands for Windows Management Instrumentation and the functionality is automatically installed with Windows. The base functionality can be enhanced by adding features and roles to Windows or by installing additional applications.

At first glance, it may seem like a very large set of stuff that you might be able to use if you get lucky and someone has mapped out how to use the bit you're interested in. When we get to chapter 3, though, you'll see that there is a structure to WMI that you can exploit to discover what is available, and to some degree how to use it.

At this stage you need to be aware that WMI doesn't exist in a vacuum. It's Microsoft's implementation of the Common Information Model (CIM) that's produced by the Distributed Management Task Force (DMTF). The CIM (and WMI) defines a series of classes that supply information about Windows systems, and they may allow you to directly interact with aspects of local and remote systems.

You can look at the WMI classes available for working with disks by using `Get-WmiObject`:

```
Get-WmiObject -List *disk* | sort name | select name
```

This command will produce output like the following:

```
Name
----
CIM_DiskDrive
CIM_DisketteDrive
CIM_DiskPartition
CIM_DiskSpaceCheck
CIM_LogicalDisk
CIM_LogicalDiskBasedOnPartition
CIM_LogicalDiskBasedOnVolumeSet
CIM_RealizesDiskPartition
Win32_DiskDrive
Win32_DiskDrivePhysicalMedia
Win32_DiskDriveToDiskPartition
Win32_DiskPartition
Win32_DiskQuota
Win32_LogicalDisk
Win32_LogicalDiskRootDirectory
Win32_LogicalDiskToPartition
Win32_LogonSessionMappedDisk
Win32_MappedLogicalDisk
Win32_PerfFormattedData_PerfDisk_LogicalDisk
Win32_PerfFormattedData_PerfDisk_PhysicalDisk
Win32_PerfRawData_PerfDisk_LogicalDisk
Win32_PerfRawData_PerfDisk_PhysicalDisk
```

There are a number of classes that start with `CIM_` and others that start with `Win32_`. There isn't always a one-to-one pairing of the two types, but major object types such as logical disks are paired. The `CIM_` class is the parent, corresponding to the definition supplied by the DMTF; the `Win32_` classes are child classes that Microsoft has implemented. In some cases the classes are identical, and in others there is additional functionality in the Microsoft class. We'll usually be working with the `Win32_` classes.

POWERSHELL v3

Microsoft invested very heavily in WMI for PowerShell v3, and it offers several improvements:

- A new API and associated .NET classes
- Closer adherence to the CIM standards (so expect less deviation from the standard in Microsoft's implementations)
- Simplified creation of WMI providers (see chapter 3 for details on providers)
- The ability to create cmdlets directly from WMI objects (see chapters 18 and 19)

The scripts in chapters 2–16 will use the existing WMI cmdlets for compatibility between PowerShell v2 and v3. Annotated versions of the scripts using the new PowerShell v3 CIM cmdlets will be available in the book's source code.

There are also classes for working with performance counters that you'll experiment with in chapter 15. As you'll see in future chapters, you can work with many parts of your systems.

Technologies that have this level of power tend to seem very complicated when you're first introduced to them. WMI is no exception.

1.4.2 *Is WMI really too hard?*

In the years since its introduction, WMI has gained a poor reputation for a number of reasons:

- Many administrators don't think to look on MSDN for documentation. I know I didn't when I started using WMI.
- Discovering which classes are available isn't always easy. (Chapter 3 will show you how to discover detailed information on the WMI classes installed on a system.)
- Coding WMI can be time consuming. The examples in this book are ready to use, requiring few or no changes for your environment. They can also be used as templates for your own scripts.
- A lot of information is held in a coded form. For instance, the `Win32_LogicalDisk` class has a media type property that returns a numeric value—hard drives are type 3. If you don't know that, you can get into problems. The information about these values is available in the WMI documentation, and simple techniques are presented throughout this book to decode these values. The new CIM classes in PowerShell v3 also provide alternatives that simplify use.
- Class names aren't always consistent. For instance, there is a `Win32_LogicalDisk` class, but the physical counterpart is `Win32_DiskDrive` rather than a class called `Win32_PhysicalDisk`. This book's chapters are broken into topics that highlight the common classes you'll need to use, and this information is also gathered in appendix B.

WMI is a powerful technology that provides low-level access to the workings of your servers. It has been shunned by the administrator community because it's viewed as being too hard to use, but this need not be the case, as you've seen in this section. The rest of this book shows how you can make the most of this free power. Microsoft has also realized how much can be done with WMI and is providing a huge boost to the technology in the Windows 8 family.

But before we look at how to use WMI, we need to see how it works with PowerShell.

1.5 *Automation with WMI and PowerShell*

PowerShell v1 has good WMI support. You can use `Get-WmiObject` to access existing WMI objects, as you saw in listing 1.1. You can also create new WMI objects, perform searches, and manipulate the objects that are available. This is all explained in detail in chapter 3.

This capability is raised to a new level with PowerShell v2. The functionality of PowerShell v1 is at least maintained in v2, and it's often enhanced. For example, you can work directly with WMI security levels in the WMI cmdlets. PowerShell v2 also provides additional cmdlets to modify and even remove objects. You also get the capability to work directly with WMI events, as you'll see in a number of chapters, including 7, 8, and 15.

Internet code

You may not always have time to create a script to solve a problem, or you may not have the knowledge. Fortunately, there are a many scripts available on the Internet.

It's essential that you test any script that you downloaded from the internet or obtain from a book (including this one) in your environment to ensure that it works as advertised and doesn't any adverse effects. The original script writer is always working based on the assumptions inherent in their environment—they can't know any of the quirks in your environment that would cause the scripts to cause accidental damage.

This is a warning that I will repeat periodically throughout the book.

Let's look at a WMI example. The starting point is VBScript and WMI, which you'll translate into PowerShell. This will provide a template that can followed if you need to translate other scripts. The following code listing retrieves some information regarding the processes running on your system. The code is modified from Microsoft's Scripting Guide.

Listing 1.2 VBScript to retrieve process information

```
set objWMIService = GetObject("winmgmts:" _              ◁── Enable interrogation
    & "{impersonationlevel=impersonate}!\\" _         ❶  of WMI
    & ".\root\cimv2")

set colProcesses = objWMIService.ExecQuery _             ◁──  Select from
    ("SELECT * FROM Win32_Process")                   ❷  WMI class

for each objProcess in colProcesses                      ◁──
    WScript.Echo " "                                          Output
    WScript.Echo "Process Name : " + objProcess.Name    ❸  results
    WScript.Echo "Handle       : " + objProcess.Handle
    WScript.Echo "Total Handles: " + Cstr(objProcess.HandleCount)
    WScript.Echo "ThreadCount  : " + Cstr(objProcess.ThreadCount)
    WScript.Echo "Path         : " + objProcess.ExecutablePath
next
```

This example uses just a small subset of the available properties to keep the script manageable. The script starts by creating an object, `objWMIService`, to enable interrogation of the WMI service ❶. A list of active processes is retrieved by running a WQL query ❷. The collection of processes is iterated through, and you write a caption and the value of a particular property to the screen ❸.

Writing a script like this takes time, even with cut and paste in your editor. You have to set up the link to WMI, run a query, and then manually define the formatting of your display.

This code can be directly translated to PowerShell as shown in the next listing. The PowerShell commands are explained in more detail in later chapters, but their basic functions should be understandable by comparison to the VBScript example.

> **Listing 1.3   PowerShell translation**

```
$procs = Get-WmiObject -Query "SELECT * FROM Win32_Process"
foreach ($proc in $procs) {
    Write-Host "Name          :" $proc.ProcessName
    Write-Host "Handle        :" $proc.Handle
    Write-Host "Total Handles :" $proc.Handles
    Write-Host "ThreadCount   :" $proc.ThreadCount
    Write-Host "Path          :" $proc.ExecutablePath
}
```

You first run the WMI query to select the information you need and put the results into a variable. The variable is a collection of objects representing the different processes. You can then loop through the collection of processes (using the `foreach` command), and for each process in that collection use the `Write-Host` cmdlet to output a caption and the value of the properties you're interested in.

> **VBScript to PowerShell conversions**
>
> When you're working with WMI, it's inevitable that you'll end up translating VBScript code into PowerShell because of the sheer number of examples that are available from sites such as the Microsoft TechNet Script Center.
>
> The "VBScript-to-Windows PowerShell Conversion Guide" is available on the TechNet Script Center at http://technet.microsoft.com/en-us/scriptcenter/default.aspx. You'll need to find it through a search engine because it does move around on the site.
>
> Consult this guide if it isn't obvious how to change a particular piece of VBScript into PowerShell.

Using this approach will produce the results that you need, but it doesn't use Power-Shell to its full capabilities. You end up doing the formatting work yourself rather than leaving it to PowerShell. Your goal is to get the machines to do as much of the work as possible. You could just run `Get-WmiObject -Class Win32_Process`, but this displays a lot of information that you'd need to wade through, which is another manual process. You need to select the data you want to see and format it in a sensible way, which leads to the following PowerShell code:

```
Get-WmiObject Win32_Process |
Format-Table ProcessName, Handle, Handles,
ThreadCount, ExecutablePath -AutoSize
```

This final version uses the Get-WmiObject cmdlet directly. Get-WmiObject returns an object for each process, and you use the PowerShell pipeline to pass them into a Format-Table cmdlet. This combines the data selection and display functionality you saw earlier and produces neatly formatted tabular output. If you wanted the output in a list format, as in the previous two examples, you could substitute Format-List for Format-Table.

In these simple examples, you've progressed from a VBScript that requires a large amount of manual formatting to a one-line PowerShell version that does the formatting automatically. The final PowerShell version is small enough that you could type it and run it directly from the command line if required. But a better solution is to turn it into a script, or function, that can accept a machine name as a parameter, and you can use that across your server estate. You'll learn how to do this in chapters 2 and 3.

So far, the examples in this chapter have focused on day-to-day tasks we face as Windows administrators. We'll close the chapter with a couple of examples showing how PowerShell and WMI can help with some of the bigger tasks we might be asked to perform on a less frequent basis.

1.6 Putting PowerShell and WMI to work

The two examples we'll look at in this section are things that you may not need to perform on a frequent basis, but they'll involve a lot of work if you have to do them manually.

The first example involves shutting down all the Windows machines in your data center. This isn't an everyday task, but as an example of the power of PowerShell and WMI, it's difficult to beat.

The second example involves auditing a large number of machines to discover their capabilities. This can be especially useful when starting a new role or if you're performing any kind of investigation. In many cases you may have the base information but need other data to complete your knowledge. The techniques we develop in later chapters will build on this example.

Could you achieve these results without PowerShell and WMI? Yes, but it would not be as easy or efficient. You could shut down all the machines in your environment in a few different ways:

- Physically visiting each machine
- Using a remote desktop utility to access each system and shut it down
- Accessing an "out of band" management card in the server and forcing a shutdown
- Creating a script in another language to access a utility that forces a shutdown

All but the last one involve shutting down the system manually. That may be acceptable for a handful of servers, but not for tens or hundreds of machines.

Auditing can be achieved with a number of utilities, but they involve extra expense, infrastructure, and a learning curve. If you have PowerShell, WMI, and this book, you can perform these tasks for a fraction of the cost and time required to set up alternative systems.

Now, how can you shut down that data center?

1.6.1   *Example 1: Shutting down a data center*

Shutting down a data center isn't something that you want to do every day. At least, it isn't if you want to keep your job. But there are times when it's necessary, such as if there will be major work on the power supplies or air conditioning systems and it would be safer to have all the systems offline.

I first used this technique when I had to shut down all of the servers in a data center because we were moving them to a different location. Instead of having to travel 150 miles to supervise the shutdown, I did it all remotely and closed the gateway machines as I exited the environment.

> **NOTE**   I used this script on a regular basis to shut down the lab I used to develop the scripts presented in this book.

The `Win32_OperatingSystem` class has a method called `Win32Shutdown` that can be used to stop all your machines, as shown in the next listing.

Listing 1.4   Shut down a data center

```
Import-Csv computers.csv |
foreach {
 (Get-WmiObject -Class Win32_OperatingSystem  `
   -ComputerName $_.Computer ).Win32Shutdown(5)
}
```

This script uses a CSV file called computers.csv, which contains a list of computer names. The version that I use to shut down my lab contains the following lines:

```
Computer
W08R2CS01
W08R2CS02
W08R2SQL08
W08R2SQL08A
WSS08
DC02
```

The first line is a header, and each subsequent line has one computer name (computer names aren't case sensitive). You can generate this file manually for a small number of machines or create it with a script that queries Active Directory for a larger environment.

In some cases, you need to control the order in which machines shut down; for example a front end SharePoint server should be closed down before the back end database server. This is achieved by editing the order in which computer names appear in the CSV file.

In listing 1.4, `Import-Csv` is used to read the CSV file. The contents are piped into a `ForEach-Object` cmdlet (`foreach` is an alias). For each computer name that's passed along the pipeline, you use `Get-WmiObject` and the `Win32_OperatingSystem` class. The computer name is passed as `$_.Computer`, where the `$_` symbol refers to the current object on the pipeline and the `Computer` part comes from the CSV header.

The Get-WmiObject is contained in parentheses, (), so you can treat it as an object on which you can call the Win32Shutdown method. The value of 5 that's passed to the method forces a shutdown even if users are still logged on. This approach will be revisited in chapter 19 when we look at new ways to work with WMI in PowerShell v3.

In PowerShell v2, you could make this script even simpler by using the Stop-Computer cmdlet instead of a WMI call. Other possible enhancements included pinging the server prior to shutdown to ensure you can contact it and putting a delay between each machine you shut down to ensure that linked servers don't have problems.

The next example involves auditing servers. You can never have too much information about your servers' configuration.

1.6.2 Example 2: Auditing hundreds of machines

This example shows how you can gather basic information from many machines. You could get this same level of data by connecting to each machine in turn, running utilities on the system to get the information, and then recording it, but that's a lot of work for more than a few machines.

The audit should return the following information:

- Server make and model
- CPU data (numbers, cores, logical processors, and speed)
- Memory
- Windows version and service pack level

You can use a number of WMI classes, as shown in the following listing, to accomplish this task.

Listing 1.5 Computer audit

```
Import-Csv computers.csv |                            ←――❶ Computer list
foreach {
  $system = "" |                                             Create
  select Name, Make, Model, CPUs, Cores,               ←―― ❷ object
  LogProc, Speed, Memory, Windows, SP

  $server = Get-WmiObject -Class Win32_ComputerSystem `
  -ComputerName $_.Computer                            ←―― Computer
                                                         ❸ system
$system.Name = $server.Name
  $system.Make = $server.Manufacturer
  $system.Model = $server.Model
  $system.Memory = $server.TotalPhysicalMemory
  $system.CPUs = $server.NumberOfProcessors

  $cpu = Get-WmiObject -Class Win32_Processor `        ←――❹ Processor
  -ComputerName $_.Computer | select -First 1

  $system.Speed = $cpu.MaxClockSpeed
                                                        ❺ Operating
  $os = Get-WmiObject -Class Win32_OperatingSystem `      system
  -ComputerName $_.Computer                            ←――┘

  $system.Windows =  $os.Caption
```

```
    $system.SP =  $os.ServicePackMajorVersion

    if (($os.Version -split "\.")[0] -ge 6) {
      $system.Cores = $cpu.NumberOfCores
      $system.LogProc = $cpu.NumberOfLogicalProcessors
    }
    else {
      $system.CPUs = ""
      $system.Cores = $server.NumberOfProcessors
    }

    $system
}  |
Format-Table -AutoSize -Wrap                              ◁——❻ Output
```

As in listing 1.4, you again have a CSV file ❶ that contains a list of computer names. This file is read using `Import-Csv` and the results are piped into `foreach` (an alias of `ForEach-Object`).

The easiest way to present the final data is in a table, so you need to create an object ❷ to hold the results. One method of creating such an object is to pipe an empty string, `""`, into a `select` statement with the names of the properties you want the object to have. Note that this only works for properties that are strings. There are other ways of creating objects, which you'll see in later chapters.

Once you have your object, you can start gathering the data. The first data concerns the computer system itself, which you can find with the `Win32_ComputerSystem` class ❸. `Get-WmiObject` is used, and the results are put into a variable. You can then map the required properties across to the object you're using to store the results.

This process is repeated for CPU data ❹ and operating system details ❺ using the `Win32_Processor` and `Win32_OperatingSystem` classes respectively. You test the operating system version:

- If the major version number (the first part) is greater than or equal to 6, you're dealing with Windows Server 2008, Windows Vista, or later. In this case, the version of WMI will correctly return the number of cores and logical processors per physical CPU so you can populate the fields.
- If the major version number is less than 6, you're dealing with Windows Server 2003, Windows XP, or earlier, and you can only retrieve the total number of cores, so you show that and remove the number of processors.

The differences between the output for the two types of operating system are shown in the following output extract:

```
Make       Model         CPUs Cores LogProc Windows
----       -----         ---- ----- ------- -------
Dell Inc.  PowerEdge 1950   2     2       2 Windows Server® 2008
Dell Inc.  PowerEdge R710        16         Windows(R) Server 2003
Dell Inc.  PowerEdge 1950         8         Windows(R) Server 2003
```

When your object is fully populated, you can pipe it into `Format-Table` ❻. The `-Autosize` parameter will control the width of the columns to best display them on screen, and the -Wrap parameter will cause any data that's too long to fit in the column to wrap onto multiple lines to ensure you see all of the results.

This script could be enhanced in a number of ways:

- Ping the server to ensure it's reachable
- Add further information, such as disks, installed applications, hotfixes, and page file configuration
- Output the data to a file that could become the basis of your server documentation
- Add the data directly into a CMDB for configuration management

The first two points are covered in later chapters, whereas information on the second two can be found in *PowerShell in Practice* (Manning 2010).

These two examples show what can be achieved with the right knowledge and a few lines of very simple code. I don't know of any other combination of out-of-the-box tools that performs so much work for so little effort. WMI really does put the power in PowerShell.

1.7 Summary

As Windows administrators, we're under increasing pressure due to the rise in complexity of the environments we have to work in and the ever-rising costs of administration. On the one hand, we're being asked to take on more work and administrate a steadily increasing number of servers and applications. On the other hand, we're facing demands to cut costs.

The way out of this dilemma is to automate as much of our day-to-day work as possible. In a Windows environment, the pairing of PowerShell and WMI provides an unmatched set of capabilities:

- PowerShell is available on all currently supported Windows platforms except Windows Server 2008 Server Core.
- PowerShell support is built into an increasing number of Microsoft and third-party applications.
- WMI provides low-level access to hardware, operating systems, and applications enabling full lifecycle management.
- The ability to work with remote systems simplifies administration and stretches the envelope of automation.
- PowerShell enables WMI to be used much more easily and shortens the learning curve to productive use of the technologies.
- There is an existing body of knowledge regarding WMI that can be readily adapted for use in PowerShell.
- A thriving PowerShell community provides support for PowerShell and WMI usage.
- Both technologies will be available for the foreseeable future, ensuring that your investment will continue to show returns.

In the next chapter, we'll dive deeper into PowerShell to make sure you have all of the tools you need to get the most out of WMI.

Using PowerShell

2

You saw in chapter 1 that automation is the key to reducing pressure on Windows administrators and that it will also reduce the cost of managing IT environments. PowerShell is my preferred automation platform because it's available across the Windows environment, it's built into major Microsoft applications, and it's being adopted by an increasing number of third-party vendors. It's also the most powerful shell and scripting language available on the Windows platform, as it can leverage the .NET Framework.

In this chapter, we'll turn our attention to PowerShell. We'll focus on WMI in chapter 3. If you're familiar with PowerShell, you can skip this chapter or treat it as a refresher. It will also introduce some of the aspects of my style of using PowerShell and go over the terminology I'll be using. My PowerShell style is to use full names for cmdlets and parameters. I don't use aliases apart from the *object cmdlets, and I keep the names and parameters of my functions in lowercase so I can easily distinguish them. The full details of my coding style can be found in the "about this book" section at the beginning of the book.

If you're new to PowerShell this chapter, together with appendix A, will supply enough information for you to understand and use the rest of this book. This chapter will start by introducing PowerShell, explaining what it is and outlining its major features. The basic commands (cmdlets) will be explained and you'll see how to link them using the PowerShell pipeline. This is where .NET brings its power to bear. You'll learn how to use .NET directly, but just where you need to, because this is a book for administrators rather than developers.

> **NOTE** A full explanation of the PowerShell language can be found in Bruce Payette's *Windows PowerShell in Action*, second edition (Manning 2011). My *PowerShell in Practice* (Manning 2010) supplies many practical examples of administering Microsoft environments with PowerShell.

All modern scripting languages have a number of structures that can be used to control the scripts. These structures allow you to loop through the same commands a number of times and branch to execute different parts of the script depending on the outcome of a test. As you'll see, looping is performed using the Do, For, and While keywords; branching capabilities are supplied by the If and Switch statements. PowerShell also allows you to read from and write to files on your systems using the *-Csv, *-Content, and Out-File cmdlets. PowerShell is to a large degree self-describing, and it has a number of self-discovery mechanisms, including an extensive help system.

Using the PowerShell cmdlets from the command line will enable you to perform a lot of tasks, but to get the most from this automation engine you need to be able to reuse the code you devise. This is where scripts and modules earn their keep. They provide two mechanisms for storing your commands on disk so that you can use them as and when required without having to retype everything. Functions are a way of reusing code in scripts to make them more efficient, and they're the basic building blocks of PowerShell modules. Scripts, functions, and modules will be examined in depth in section 2.7 of this chapter.

Administering a single machine is straightforward. Administering tens, hundreds, or thousands of machines requires the ability to work remotely. PowerShell supplies several ways to accomplish this. Some cmdlets have the ability to access remote machines, which can save you time and effort when working interactively. PowerShell v2 enables remote administration via the industry standard Web Services–Management protocols.

One thing administrators never have enough of is time. Multitasking is much talked about but difficult to deliver with command-line or GUI-based tools. PowerShell jobs allow you to run tasks in the background while you get on with other activities. The results are then ready for you to access when you've finished your other activities.

Let's start our investigation by looking at PowerShell itself, and discussing just what it does.

2.1   *PowerShell in a nutshell*

Starting at the top, what does PowerShell give you for your money? Quite a lot, because it either comes as part of the operating system or it's a free download. Power-Shell v1 became available for download in November 2006. PowerShell v2 is part of the default installation of Windows 7 and Windows Server 2008 R2, and it's available as a download for older versions of Windows.

When you start PowerShell, you'll get a command prompt similar to the old DOS prompt. So what is special about PowerShell?

This is what you get:

- A shell
- A set of command-line tools (cmdlets)
- A scripting language
- An automation engine that allows for remote access, asynchronous processing, and integration between products

The shell is where things happen. It's a basic window with a prompt where you can type commands and get results. Shells have been available on operating systems for many years, and PowerShell is like other shells in that it allows you to do things such as these:

- Run PowerShell commands
- Run the standard Windows utilities, such as ipconfig or ping
- Work with the filesystem using standard commands
- Run Windows batch files (with some provisos around environmental variables)
- Run VBScripts

PowerShell gets more interesting when you move on and think about the command-line tools that ship with the product.

2.2   *Cmdlets*

PowerShell v2 ships with 236 command-line tools that are available as soon as it's installed (this number rises significantly in PowerShell v3). These are called *cmdlets* (I pronounce it as "command-lets," but other pronunciations are available). A cmdlet name consists of two words separated by a hyphen, such as Get-Process. The first part of the name is a verb, and the second part is a noun (which should be singular), which makes the cmdlet's function easy to guess. For example, Get-Process will get information about the processes running on the local, or a remote, machine.

> **NOTE** Not all PowerShell verbs are verbs in English. For example, New is a PowerShell verb; it's equivalent to "create a new" in English.

A consistent naming standard helps discovery. The PowerShell team introduced a standard set of verbs in PowerShell v2, and they can be discovered using the command

Get-Verb (which is a built-in function rather than a cmdlet). You can fetch a list of the cmdlets available in PowerShell using Get-Command:

```
Get-Command -CommandType cmdlet | group verb |
sort count -Descending | select name -First 20
```

This command groups the results by the verb in the cmdlet name and sorts the verbs on the number of occurrences (largest first). The top 20 verbs are then displayed, as shown in table 2.1.

Table 2.1 Top 20 verbs used in PowerShell

Get	Set	New	Remove
Out	Export	Invoke	Write
Import	Start	Add	Clear
Test	Enable	Stop	Format
ConvertTo	Disable	Register	Select

Much of what you'll be doing in this book can be accomplished with these verbs. The primary command in the preceding code example is Get-Command; the other commands are utility cmdlets that you'll be seeing a lot in later chapters, so it's worth understanding what they do.

2.2.1 Utility cmdlets

Utility cmdlets function as the glue that binds the working cmdlets together on the pipeline. They enable you to filter, sort, compare, and group data or even create new objects. They provide a suite of utility actions that you need to be able to perform when working with any data. PowerShell provides a set of such cmdlets that have the word object as their noun.

In many scripting languages you have to write these utilities yourself, but PowerShell supplies them out of the box. They're used so frequently that it's worth getting to know them before we dive deeper into PowerShell. The utility cmdlets, together with their purposes, are listed in table 2.2. You may have noticed that the only utility cmdlet verb that makes our top 20 list in table 2.1 is select. But if you change the previous script to discover the top 20 nouns, you'd see that object heads the list at number 1.

Table 2.2 Utility cmdlets, their aliases, and their purposes

Cmdlet	Alias	Purpose
Compare-Object	compare, diff	Compares two sets of objects.
ForEach-Object	foreach, %	Performs an operation against each member of a set of input objects.
Group-Object	group	Groups objects that contain the same value for specified properties.

Table 2.2   Utility cmdlets, their aliases, and their purposes *(continued)*

Cmdlet	Alias	Purpose
Measure-Object	measure	Calculates the numeric properties of objects, and the characters, words, and lines in string objects, such as files of text.
New-Object		Creates an instance of a Microsoft .NET Framework or COM object.
Select-Object	select	Selects specified properties of an object or set of objects. It can also select unique objects from an array of objects, or it can select a specified number of objects from the beginning or end of an array of objects.
Sort-Object	sort	Sorts objects by property values.
Tee-Object	tee	Saves command output in a file or variable and displays it in the console. This functions exactly like a T junction on a road. The stem of the T is the pipeline. When it reaches the top, it splits into two and the object is duplicated and sent to the variable or file in one direction and along the pipeline in the other.
Where-Object	where, ?	Creates a filter that controls which objects will be passed along a command pipeline.

Aliases are explained in more detail in the next section, but for now notice that New-Object doesn't have an alias and that some of the cmdlets have two possible aliases.

The code snippet in the previous section showed an example of using select, sort, and group. Their purposes are obvious from their names. Of the other utility cmdlets, where and foreach will be used the most.

2.2.2   *Where-Object*

The Where-Object cmdlet is used as a filter in that only objects that meet its criteria are passed along the pipeline. As an example, you can display the services running on a system like this:

```
Get-WmiObject -Class Win32_Service
```

An object is returned for each service and displayed in this format:

```
ExitCode  : 1077
Name      : WinRM
ProcessId : 0
StartMode : Manual
State     : Stopped
Status    : OK
```

This is probably a bit more information than you need, so you can trim it down using Select-Object, like this:

```
Get-WmiObject -Class Win32_Service |
select name, startmode, state
```

This time you get a nicely formatted table returned. At this point, you could sort on the service state to put all of the running and all of the stopped services together, or alternatively you could use a filter:

```
Get-WmiObject -Class Win32_Service |
select name, startmode, state  |
where {$_.state -eq "stopped"}
```

The objects are piped into a `Where-Object` cmdlet that has a filter of `where {$_.state -eq "stopped"}`.

The last code snippet could equally well be written as follows:

```
Get-WmiObject -Class Win32_Service |
where {$_.state -eq "stopped"} |
select name, startmode, state
```

If you're performing this action over the network, it may be better to filter out the objects that you don't want to bring back first, in order to reduce network traffic. When working against a single machine it probably doesn't matter, but against hundreds of machines, filtering as early as possible could improve performance.

> **SCRIPT BLOCK** The code inside the braces, {}, is known as a *script block*. You'll see other examples of script blocks throughout the book. A script block is a collection of statements or expressions that can be used as a single unit and that can accept arguments and return values. Script blocks are most often used as filters or unnamed functions.

In this case, the script block is comparing the value of the `state` property of the object on the pipeline (denoted by `$_`) to `"stopped"`. If they're equal, the object is passed; otherwise it's filtered out.

When I ran this on the machine I'm using to write this book, I noticed that a couple of services were set to automatically start but hadn't actually started. This is a scenario that could potentially cause problems if it's the Exchange or SQL Server service that's behaving in this manner. A little extra work will give you this code snippet, which displays the status of services set to start automatically on a particular computer:

```
$computername = "."
Get-WmiObject -Class Win32_Service -ComputerName $computername |
where {$_.state -eq "stopped" -and $_.startmode -eq "auto"} |
select name, startmode, state
```

The first line defines a variable to hold the computer name. In this case a period, `"."`, signifies the local machine (`localhost` or `$env:COMPUTERNAME` can also be used to denote the local system). By using the `-ComputerName` parameter, you can connect to a specific computer rather than the default local machine. A second filter is added to the script block to check whether the `startmode` is set to automatic. If both criteria are met, the object is displayed.

A few lines of PowerShell code have created a troubleshooting tool that you can use to test the state of important services on remote machines. In section 2.7, you'll see how to use this code in a script or function that can take the computer name as a parameter.

Data filtering

In the snippet we've been considering it doesn't matter if you perform the select or the filtering first, because all you're interested in is the data. In some cases, though, it will matter—especially if you're filtering a small number of results out of a large amount of data.

In most cases, it's best to assume that your scripts will have optimum performance if the data filtering is performed as soon as possible. This is very definitely true when you're returning data from a remote server. This topic is discussed further in chapter 4.

PowerShell always returns objects. Using `Select-Object` trims the object to only those properties of interest. If the full object is required for further use, such as to access a method, you'll need to use a different technique. One possible solution is presented in section 2.2.3.

2.2.3   *Foreach-Object*

The other utility cmdlet we need to consider is `ForEach-Object`. This performs one or more commands contained in a script block on each object on the pipeline. For instance, you could modify the previous code snippet to this:

```
$computername = "."
Get-WmiObject -Class Win32_Service -ComputerName $computername |
where {$_.state -eq "stopped" -and $_.startmode -eq "auto"} |
foreach { $_.StartService()}
```

The `select` statement has been dropped, and once you've filtered down to the services that you think should be started based on their start mode, you can use `ForEach-Object` to call the `StartService` method of the service object. WMI will provide a return code of `0` if the action was successful. Any other value means something went wrong, and you'll need to investigate. In chapter 4 you'll see how to test the return code in your scripts to detect errors and problems.

We've been discussing the utility cmdlets using their full names, but in the code snippets the alias has been used. Aliases have a place in your PowerShell usage, but you need to understand what they are and when you should and shouldn't use them.

2.2.4   *Aliases*

A PowerShell alias is a shortcut name for a command. The command can be a cmdlet or a function (you'll learn about functions later in the chapter when we look at code reuse). Table 2.2, earlier in this chapter, listed the aliases for the utility cmdlets. A list of currently defined aliases can be obtained by using `Get-Alias`.

You can reproduce the list in table 2.2 by filtering using `Where-Object` (alias where).

```
Get-Alias | where {$_.definition -like "*object"} |
Format-Table Name, Definition -AutoSize
```

You use where to filter on the definition of the alias, and only return those objects that have a definition ending in the characters "object".

Other cmdlets are available for working with aliases:

```
Get-Command *alias | select name

Name
----
Export-Alias
Get-Alias
Import-Alias
New-Alias
Set-Alias
```

If you're thinking there's gap in this list, you're right. There's no cmdlet to delete aliases. But there's a way round this, as you'll see shortly.

The import and export commands are for reading and writing the alias information to a file so you can reuse it in other PowerShell sessions. Unless you do this, or you set the alias in your profile, it's lost when you close PowerShell.

> **NOTE** Profiles are PowerShell scripts that run when you start PowerShell. Use the command `Get-Help about_profiles` for more details.

You can create an alias in two ways:

```
New-Alias -Name filter -Value Where-Object
Set-Alias -Name sieve -Value Where-Object
```

You can confirm the creation with the code snippet you used earlier to list the aliases of the utility cmdlets. You can also substitute your new alias into the snippet:

```
Get-Alias | filter {$_.definition -like "*object"} |
Format-table Name, Definition -AutoSize
```

Using sieve works just as well!

Alias problems

One of the main problems with custom aliases is that they're not necessarily available to other users. For example, suppose you've just created a new alias for Where-Object. If you prefer using that to the standard aliases, you could make it permanent on your system by adding the definition to your PowerShell profile.

You might later want to share your scripts with work colleagues, but if they don't have the alias defined in their profile, the script will fail. An even worse scenario occurs if they have the same alias but it's defined as something else. The best case outcome is that the script just fails, but it's possible that data will be lost or corrupted. The worst case scenario is that the system is severely damaged and needs rebuilding and the data needs restoring.

(continued)

You can test the effect of not having an alias defined by copying the snippet that uses the new alias into a new PowerShell window and trying to run it. You'll be told that the alias isn't recognized. Note that if you have defined the alias in your profile, you would need to use `powershell.exe -noprofile` before you test your snippet.

The other problem with aliases is readability. Our original code,

```
Get-Alias | filter {$_.definition -like "*object"} |
Format-table Name, Definition -AutoSize
```

is much more readable than this:

```
gal | ? {$_.definition -like "*obj*"} | ft name, definition -a
```

The bottom line is that aliases are fine at the command line, but don't publish code using them and don't include them in scripts.

`Set-Alias` can change an alias if required, but deleting an alias can be a little tricky. The defined aliases in a PowerShell session are exposed as the `alias:` drive, which means you can view them like this:

```
"filter", "sieve" | foreach {dir alias:\$_}
```

This will display your two aliases, and you can adapt it to delete them:

```
"filter", "sieve" | foreach {Remove-Item alias:\$_}
```

Checking the alias drive for your two aliases will now show that they're no longer present.

PowerShell drives

PowerShell exposes a number of data stores as if they were part of the filesystem. You can navigate them like a filesystem drive and use the `*-Item` and `*-ItemProperty` cmdlets in the same way you would against the filesystem.

The list of installed PowerShell drives can be found using `Get-PSDrive`.

For more information, see the help:

- `Get-Help about_Providers`
- `Get-Help Get-PSdrive`
- Help files for individual providers

Cmdlets provide the components that do things for you, but as you've seen in the examples so far, you can get more out of them when you link them on the PowerShell pipeline.

2.3   *Pipeline*

A lot is made of the PowerShell pipeline. Administrators who have used UNIX or DOS may say, "Oh yeah. We've had pipelines for years." Not like this one, you haven't.

The big difference is that DOS and UNIX commands produce (emit) text, whereas PowerShell cmdlets emit .NET objects. You're passing .NET objects along the Power-Shell pipeline. This gives you access to all of the methods on those objects, which massively increases the things you can do.

When we started discussing cmdlets in section 2.1.1, we used this piece of PowerShell:

```
Get-Command -CommandType cmdlet | group verb |
sort count -Descending | select name -First 20
```

This has a number of cmdlets linked on the pipeline. The | symbol is the pipe symbol, as in other shells. Figure 2.1 shows this pipeline as a process diagram.

The starting point is a request for a list of the cmdlets, which is implemented by `Get-Command`. The `-CommandType` parameter restricts the returned data to cmdlets.

The next step in the process is to group the cmdlets by verb. The grouped information is passed to the `Sort-Object` cmdlet, where the groups are sorted by count, which is the number of cmdlets in each group. They're sorted in descending order so that the groups with the largest number of cmdlets are at the top of the list.

The final action in this pipeline is to select the first 20 results passed by the sorting action and pick off their names.

TIP Always think of the pipeline as a set of processes being applied in this way. If you start at the top and work through each stage, it will soon become second nature to unravel complex-looking PowerShell statements.

The pipeline is a way to link PowerShell cmdlets together to create a series of actions where the sum is very definitely greater than the parts. I refer to PowerShell snippets like the one in the previous example as scripts. If I've saved it to a file with a .ps1 extension, it's definitely a script. There are people who will argue that when you type

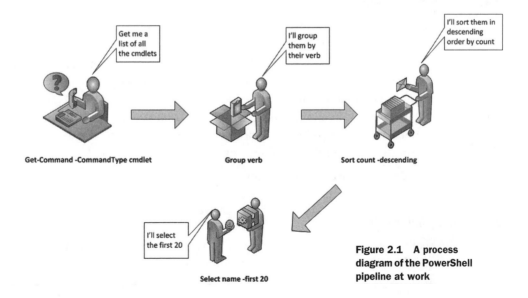

Figure 2.1 A process diagram of the PowerShell pipeline at work

them at the prompt they aren't scripts. But until someone comes up with a better name that everyone accepts, I'll keep calling them scripts.

We've stated several times that the PowerShell cmdlets emit .NET objects. The example in this section used properties of those objects to help in the processing. It's about time we had a closer look at .NET itself.

2.4   .NET for administrators

PowerShell is based on .NET. It makes extensive use of .NET under the covers, and as you saw in the previous section, pipeline processing is one way to work with those .NET objects. But this doesn't mean that you have to become a .NET developer in order to use PowerShell. It's possible to use the PowerShell cmdlets and language without delving into the murky depths of .NET code. The objective is to know enough to understand any scripts you may come across that use .NET classes directly.

PowerShell uses .NET objects, so your first task is to understand objects.

2.4.1   Objects

According to Bruce Payette (lead developer on the PowerShell team), "an object is a package that contains both data and the information on how to use that data" (*Windows PowerShell in Action*, p 11).

What this means is that an object is a thing, such as a process. It has a bunch of attributes, which are pieces of data (a name, an amount of CPU usage, or the number of handles used by the process). You can also do stuff to the thing, such as terminating a process.

Congratulations! You now know all that you need to know about objects to use them in PowerShell. However, there is a tiny complication in the way that PowerShell actually works with .NET objects.

2.4.2   PowerShell objects

PowerShell complicates things sometimes because it doesn't always work with pure .NET objects. Here are some examples:

- The .NET objects for Active Directory entities, such as users, have the VBScript type methods, but they aren't visible using `Get-Member`, which is a cmdlet you can use to discover information about objects (it's aliased as `gm`).
- PowerShell puts a wrapper around .NET objects. Sometimes properties and methods can be added or removed. The pure .NET object can be accessed by using a `.psbase` suffix. You'll see examples of this in later chapters.

You've seen how to access .NET objects created by cmdlets, but is there a way to create your own objects?

2.4.3   Creating .NET objects

I'm really glad you asked that question, because there's an easy way to create .NET objects. Back in table 2.1 there was a cmdlet called `New-Object`. That's what you use for creating objects.

Let's assume you want to work with some (pseudo) random numbers:

```
$rand = New-Object -TypeName System.Random -ArgumentList 42
$rand.Next()
```

It probably doesn't seem obvious, but this statement uses the `New-Object` cmdlet to create an object that's stored in the `$rand` variable. You use the `System.Random` .NET class to define the type of object you want to create, and you provide a value of `42` to the object, which acts as a seed value to the calculation of the random numbers. Using different seed values each time prevents a repetition of the numbers generated. Full details of the random class can be found on MSDN—search for `System.Random`.

NOTE PowerShell v2 has its own cmdlet for generating random numbers, `Get-Random`, but this is a nice simple example of using a .NET object.

As a test, you can use the `Next` method. This will generate a random number. Computers can't generate true random numbers, so I would expect your first answer to be 1434747710.

Using the standard .NET objects will satisfy many of your needs, but sometimes you'll need to create a brand new object of your very own.

2.4.4 Creating your own objects

You have three ways to create new objects that you've designed:

- Use the `select` method you saw in listing 1.5 in chapter 1.
- Use `New-Object` and the `PSObject` class.
- Create a new .NET class using C#.

Here's a recap of the first and simplest method:

```
$myobject = "" | select name, number, description
$myobject.Name = "Object1"
$myobject.Number = 100
$myobject.Description = "Simplest object creation"
```

If you run this code, you'll create an object called `myobject` that has three properties. The properties have the values defined in the script, which you can verify using `$myobject | gm`.

The drawback to this method is that the resultant object is a string, as are all of its properties. Technically, it's a `Selected.System.String`, but for all practical purposes it's a string.

The second method is a bit cleverer and uses `New-Object`:

```
$myobject = New-Object System.Management.Automation.PSObject   |
Add-Member -MemberType NoteProperty -Name "Name" `
    -Value "object2" -PassThru |
Add-Member -MemberType NoteProperty -Name "Number" `
    -Value 100 -PassThru |
Add-Member -MemberType NoteProperty -Name "Description" `
    -Value "More complicated" -PassThru
```

This approach uses `System.Management.Automation.PSObject` to create an object. The `Add-Member` cmdlet is used to add the properties. This allows you to use the PowerShell pipeline, but it still involves a reasonable amount of typing. It's easy to make a mistake in all of the `Add-Member` statements. The `Number` property will take an integer type, but if you decide to change that property to a string value, PowerShell will accept it. That could lead to problems further on in your script.

> **NOTE**   If you only want to add one or two extra properties to an existing object, such as a process object from `Get-Process`, using `Add-Member` is a good way to proceed.

You can simplify the second method slightly by using `New-Object PSObject` rather than the full .NET class name, but the other issues remain. It's possible to simplify the previous snippet like this:

```
$myobject = New-Object PSObject -Property @{
    Name = "object2a"
    Number= 100
    Description = "More complicated"
}
```

In this example, the `Property` parameter is used. It's a hash table of property names and values that are applied to the object as it's created. Some PowerShell users don't like this method, as the order of the parameters on the object can't be guaranteed because you're using a hash table.

The final method is to create a new object using a piece of C# code. This is an advanced technique, and if you're shuddering after reading it don't worry. It will be used in some scripts presented in later chapters, so by the end of the book you'll have a good idea how it works.

The following listing shows how you can convert the previous code snippet to create the object using C#.

Listing 2.1   Object creation

```
$source = @"
public class pawobject
{
    public string Description { get; set;}         ❶ C# code
    public string Name { get; set;}
    public int Number { get; set;}
}
"@

Add-Type $source -Language CSharpVersion3         ❷ Create
                                                      class

$myobject = New-Object -TypeName pawobject -Property @{   ❸ Create
    Name = "myobject3";                                      object
    Number = 200;
    Description = "More complicated again"
    }
```

The starting point for this adventure is a here-string (a multilined string that can be used to embed chunks of text into your script), $source, that holds your C# code ❶. The here-string starts with @" and ends with "@. The first line states that you want to create a new class called pawobject (PowerShell and WMI object, in case you're wondering). A class can be thought of as a template that you use to create an object. The three properties, Name, Number, and Description are defined, providing their names, data types, and whether they can be modified (get is used to read the property, and set is used to change the value of the property—I usually define both).

Add-Type, which is only available in PowerShell v2, and above, is then used to compile the class ❷. The class is created and held in memory ready for you to use when required.

> **NOTE** Listing 2.1 uses C# version 3, which allows for simpler C# code. Believe me, this is simplified! If earlier versions of C# are used, the code is much more verbose and involves defining variables that are only used inside the .NET class.

Now you're getting back to familiar territory. The class you created is used in New-Object to give you an object you can work with in PowerShell ❸. One nice feature of working this way is that you can define the properties of the object when you create it. This saves a bit of typing and looks impressive.

The main advantage of using this method is that the properties become strongly typed, which is developer-speak for saying that the Number property will only accept integer values and the Name and Description properties will only accept values that are strings or that can be converted to strings.

Objects are one of the keys to PowerShell. Once you understand that everything is treated as an object, it makes a lot more sense. As well as working with objects, you need to be able to create them. This is especially important when you combine data from a number of sources and want to output a single object. You'll be working with objects for the rest of the book, so this will be second nature by the time you're finished.

That's all I want to say about objects, and it's probably all you want to read about them for now, so let's move on and have a look at the features of the PowerShell scripting language.

2.5 PowerShell scripting language

In section 2.1, I said that PowerShell consists of four things: a shell, the command-line tools, a scripting language, and an automation engine. We've looked at the shell and the command-line tools (cmdlets); it's now time to look at the scripting language.

The PowerShell scripting language is the framework that binds the cmdlets, objects, and pipelines together. Two types of constructs—loops and branches—provide the majority of the framework structure. Loops and branches handle data inside the script, but scripts can't exist in isolation. You need to provide input so the script has data to work with, and you need to be able to access the output and save it to disk.

NOTE   I'll assume in this section that you have sufficient scripting background to be familiar with terms such as *array* and *variable*. If not, appendix A provides a brief introduction, but reading my *PowerShell in Practice* and Bruce Payette's *Windows PowerShell in Action*, second edition, is highly recommended.

Data input and output are important parts of any computer-based processing. There are a number of cmdlets that perform input and output, and when they're combined with other cmdlets and the scripting language they put the power into PowerShell.

We'll start by looking at the different ways you can create loops in PowerShell.

TIP   In many cases, PowerShell provides multiple methods of solving a particular problem. I'll present the ways that I think work best. If you find another way of doing things that you prefer, then by all means substitute it for what I do. The PowerShell language is based on the C# syntax, but unlike C# it's case insensitive. You'll see that demonstrated with my deliberately liberal view of the use of case in the PowerShell scripts later in the book.

2.5.1   Loops

You use a loop when you want to perform the same action a number of times. You've already seen one type of loop, in the shape of the ForEach-Object cmdlet, in section 2.2.1. There's also a foreach loop using a PowerShell keyword, and there are the usual for, do, and while types of loop structures. Foreach is the most confusing, so we'll get that one settled first.

FOREACH

The two flavors of the foreach statement can create confusion, but they can be distinguished because one is never part of a pipeline (the foreach keyword) whereas the other is always on the pipeline (foreach as an alias of ForEach-Object).

When you use the foreach keyword, you can write your script like this:

```
$lower = "a","b","c","d"
foreach ($letter in $lower){Write-Host $letter.ToUpper()}
```

An array (collection) of letters is defined. For each letter in the collection, you convert the letter to uppercase and use Write-Host to write it to the screen. This gives a display similar to that shown in figure 2.2.

Figure 2.2   Use of a foreach **keyword statement**

Figure 2.3 Use of a `foreach` alias

You can also use the `foreach` alias on the pipeline, as you've seen. In this example you're using the `ForEach-Object` cmdlet:

```
"a","b","c","d" | foreach {Write-Host $_.ToUpper()}
```

This is illustrated in figure 2.3.

In this case you're piping the array of letters into the `ForEach-Object` cmdlet (using its `foreach` alias). You don't need the (`$letter in $lower`) structure because it's implicit in the use of the pipeline. The other difference is that you use `$_` to represent the current object on the pipeline, which is the individual letters.

Both constructions give the same result. If `foreach` is on the pipeline, it's an alias for the `ForEach-Object` cmdlet. If `foreach` is followed by a (`$letter in $lower`) type of structure, it's a language statement.

FOR LOOP

A `for` loop is a simple counting loop that's present in most languages. You can turn the previous looping example into a `for` loop like this:

```
for ($i=65; $i -le 68; $i++){Write-Host $([char]$i)}
```

You define a variable, `$i`, to have a value of 65, and you define a limit where `$i` is less than or equal to 68. Starting at 65, you convert the value of `$i` into a character (using ASCII codes) and write it out. The value of `$i` is incremented until it reaches the limit. This will produce the same results as in figures 2.2 and 2.3.

As an example of PowerShell versatility, you could rewrite this loop as follows:

```
65..68 | foreach {Write-Host $([char]$_)}
```

The `..` or *range* operator is used to define a range of numbers. You pipe that range of numbers into a `ForEach-Object` cmdlet and display the character as before.

This isn't the end of the looping story for PowerShell though.

OTHER LOOPS

There are two other loop formats available in PowerShell.

The first of these is the `while` loop, which takes the following structure:

```
while (<condition>) {
    < PowerShell code>
}
```

This reads as "while this condition is true, execute the following code."

The other alternative is a do loop, with this syntax:

```
do {
    < PowerShell code>
} until (<condition>)
```

This one performs the condition checking at the end of the script block, rather than before it executes.

You won't see these loops in action in the scripts later in the book because these particular styles of loops aren't required in the tasks we'll be investigating. I've only mentioned them here for completeness. Their full details can be found using these help commands:

```
Get-Help about_While
Get-Help about_Do
```

That's about it for loops. We'll now branch out a bit and look at how to make decisions in PowerShell.

2.5.2   *Branching*

There will be many occasions where you'll run one batch of code if a particular condition is met, and otherwise you'll do something else. This decision-making process is called *branching*.

PowerShell provides two ways of making decisions. If you have one or a small number of possible outcomes, you can use an `if` statement. For the occasions when you have a larger number of potential outcomes, PowerShell offers the `switch` statement.

IF STATEMENT

An `if` statement has a simple structure that can be read as, "if this statement is true then do the commands in the following script block." Here's a straightforward example:

```
$date = Get-Date
if ($date.DayOfWeek -eq "Friday"){
  "The weekend starts tonight"}
elseif ($date.DayOfWeek -eq "Saturday" -or `
 $date.DayOfWeek -eq "Sunday"){"It's the weekend"}
else {"Still working!"}
```

The first line gets the current date. You then compare the day of the week to Friday. If it's Friday, you're happy because it's the end of the week, and the weekend starts tonight. There's an alternative that you want to check (`elseif`), just in case it's a Saturday or Sunday, in which case you're very happy because it's the weekend. The final choice is a catchall (`else`), in case the condition isn't true—in that case, you're still in the middle of the week and are possibly unhappy about it.

> **NOTE**   One thing to notice in the preceding example is that it doesn't use a cmdlet to write the data to screen. If you have a string all by itself on a line, PowerShell will treat it as something you want to output and will write it to the screen or whatever output mechanism you've defined.

This works very well for a small number of choices, but if you want to extend your choices and check for every day of the week, it would be more efficient to switch to another code structure.

SWITCH STATEMENT

The `switch` statement is used when you have more choices than can be sensibly managed using `if` statements. You can nest `if` statements, and it does work, but it's hard to read and can be very hard to maintain. You don't want to go looking for work—the idea is to reduce your workload.

A `switch` statement defines a statement or variable to check and then a number of possible outcomes. You can modify the previous example to use a `switch` statement instead:

```
switch ( (Get-Date).DayOfWeek ) {
    "Sunday"    {"It's the weekend but work tomorrow"; break}
    "Monday"    {"Back to work"; break}
    "Tuesday"   {"Long time until Friday"; break}
    "Wednesday" {"Half way through the week"; break}
    "Thursday"  {"Friday tomorrow"; break}
    "Friday"    {"It's the weekend tomorrow"; break}
    "Saturday"  {"It's the weekend"; break}
    default     {"Something's gone wrong"}
}
```

Here, you find the current day of the week and compare it to the possible outcomes. When one matches, you print out the message and use the `break` command to skip further processing in the `switch` statement. The `default` statement is there to catch any values that don't match one of the defined values—in that case you print a message to say something has gone wrong because you don't recognize the day of the week as reported by `Get-Date`. The scripts in later chapters will provide many examples of using `if` and `switch` statements.

In many cases, your scripts will need to have some kind of input and output. This means that you don't need to keep typing in data and that you can save results for further investigation.

2.5.3 Input and output

Input and output can be broken down into three main areas:

- Writing to the screen and accepting data typed in response to a prompt
- Writing to or reading from a file on disk
- Writing to or reading from a specialized data store, such as Active Directory, the registry, or SQL Server.

There are a number of input and output cmdlets you can use, as detailed in table 2.3. You've seen some of these cmdlets in action already, and you'll meet more of them in later examples.

XML support in PowerShell

I'm deliberately ignoring XML in this section, as I don't intend to use it in most of the scripts in the book. XML will be used in chapters 18 and 19 in a very specialized use. PowerShell has good XML support; for instance, it's used in the background when you use PowerShell remoting, but you see the results not the XML.

The full range of XML support can be seen by following the links obtained from this command: `Get-Help xml`.

Table 2.3   Common cmdlets that provide input and output functionality

Screen	Files	Specialized
Write-Host	Out-File	Write-Debug
Read-Host	Export-Csv	Write-Error
Out-Host	Import-Csv	Write-EventLog
Out-GridView	ConvertFrom-Csv	Write-Progress
Write-Output	ConvertTo-Csv	Write-Verbose
	Add-Content	Write-Warning
	Clear-Content	
	Get-Content	
	Set-Content	

This table is provided for reference. You'll learn how to use these cmdlets in the scripts in later chapters. If you want to learn more about a particular cmdlet right now, PowerShell's help system is available for just that purpose.

2.6   *Finding help*

PowerShell, like all good computer systems, has a way of supplying help to the user. The help information is contained in a series of XML files that are found in the PowerShell install folder, but don't worry about it being XML—PowerShell provides the `Get-Help` cmdlet to read it with, so you don't have to work out how to do so yourself. In addition, there's the `Get-Command` cmdlet for working with commands (including non-PowerShell commands) and `Get-Member` for investigating the objects that PowerShell uses.

The final part of the help system is the PowerShell community. This is an internet-based group of individuals who commit a lot of time and effort to helping others with PowerShell problems.

As with all IT products, the best place to start is with the help system.

2.6.1 *Get-Help*

You've seen that PowerShell uses a verb-noun convention for cmdlets. The obvious name for the cmdlet that reads help files is `Get-Help`. No aliases are defined for this cmdlet by default, but a built-in function called `Help` is available.

The function definition can be viewed in this way:

```
(Get-Item -Path function:\help).Definition
```

The working part of the function is the line

```
Get-Help @PSBoundParameters | more
```

which pipes the output of the `Get-Help` cmdlet into `more`, which produces a paged display. An alias, `man`, is defined on this function.

The standard way to use `Get-Help` is to follow it with the name of the cmdlet you want help for:

```
Get-Help Get-Command
```

This will supply basic help about the cmdlet, including a description and a basic view of the syntax. At the end of the display is a REMARKS section that takes this form:

```
REMARKS
    To see the examples, type: "get-help Get-Command -examples".
    For more information, type: "get-help Get-Command -detailed".
    For technical information, type: "get-help Get-Command -full".
```

I tend to use the `-Full` option as a matter of course, because I usually want to dig into the individual parameters to solve a problem or discover how to get something to work. Using `Get-Help Get-Help -Full` will give you the full information on using the help system.

One innovation in PowerShell v2 is that you can get access to online PowerShell help. This is useful because the PowerShell team corrects documentation bugs online, so this gives you access to the latest version. (In PowerShell v3, your local help files will be updateable.) If you want to see any changes, use this command:

```
Get-Help Get-Command -Online
```

Your browser will be opened at the appropriate TechNet page, providing access to the latest version of the documentation.

In addition to the information available about cmdlets, there's also a set of help files that give conceptual information about PowerShell. They cover specific language features, such as loops, or PowerShell features such as remoting. The range of help available in this category can also be viewed using `Get-Help`:

```
Get-Help about*
```

Text-based help files are good for quick lookups, but they're not very good for browsing. Graphical help files are available as a download from the TechNet Script Center for PowerShell v1 or as part of PowerShell ISE in v2. An updated CHM file for

PowerShell v2 is available for download from Microsoft. Details can be found at http: //blogs.msdn.com/b/powershell/—click the "Help file" tag.

2.6.2   *Get-Command*

`Get-Command` is another cmdlet that supplies information, though it focuses on the types of commands available on the system. `Get-Help` is restricted to supplying information from the help system, but `Get-Command` can look beyond PowerShell. As an example try running this:

```
Get-Command ipconfig | fl *
```

This will display information about the utility, including its path and version.

The difference between the PowerShell-related information returned by `Get-Help` and `Get-Command` can be illustrated by comparing the information supplied in their respective synopses:

```
SYNOPSIS - Get-Help
    Displays information about Windows PowerShell commands and concepts.

SYNOPSIS - Get-Command
    Gets basic information about cmdlets and other elements of Windows
    PowerShell commands.
```

`Get-Help` will tell you how to use a particular command, but `Get-Command` will discover what commands are available.

If you type `Get-Command *wmi*`, you'll find a long list of cmdlets, aliases, and applications is returned. If you just want to see the WMI cmdlets, you can use this command:

```
Get-Command *wmi* -CommandType cmdlet | select name

Name
----
Get-WmiObject
Invoke-WmiMethod
Register-WmiEvent
Remove-WmiObject
Set-WmiInstance
```

By the end of the book, you'll know a lot about working with these cmdlets.

The other use for `Get-Command` is finding the cmdlets that are loaded by a particular PowerShell snap-in or module:

```
Get-Command -Module BitsTransfer
```

You'll learn more about snap-ins and modules in section 2.7.4.

There are some other useful parameters to remember when using `Get-Command`:

- `-Syntax`—Displays a syntax list for a cmdlet. Useful for checking a parameter name or on parameter sets.
- `-Noun`—Displays all cmdlets with a particular noun. `Get-Command -Noun wmi*` is an alternative to the code you used to find the WMI cmdlets earlier.

- -Verb—Displays all cmdlets with a particular verb. If you know you need to *get* something but can't remember the noun, try Get-Command -Verb get.
- -CommandType—Returns particular types of commands. Valid values are Alias, Application, Cmdlet, ExternalScript, Function, and Script.

So far we've looked at getting help about PowerShell itself. The other area we need to consider is the objects you're working on in your PowerShell scripts.

2.6.3 Get-Member

PowerShell is based on .NET and uses .NET objects, as you've seen. When you're working with objects, you need to be able to look at the object to determine what properties and methods it has. This tells you what data the object holds and what you can do with it.

One option is to go to the MSDN website and browse the .NET documentation for the class used to create the object. But there are a couple of issues with this option:

- You need to find the object's type so you know which class to look up.
- It takes a long time.

A better way is to use the Get-Member cmdlet. The easiest way to use it is to pipe the object you want to investigate into the cmdlet:

```
Get-Process powershell | Get-Member
```

The object under investigation in this example is a process object (restricted to the PowerShell process). The first thing it returns is the type:

```
TypeName: System.Diagnostics.Process
```

You then get a list of the properties and methods. A very abbreviated example of the output from the preceding example code is as follows:

```
Name                  MemberType     Definition
----                  ----------     ----------
Handles               AliasProperty  Handles = Handlecount
Name                  AliasProperty  Name = ProcessName
OutputDataReceived    Event          System.Diagnostics...
WaitForInputIdle      Method         bool WaitForInputIdle...
__NounName            NoteProperty   System.String __NounName=Process
BasePriority          Property       System.Int32 BasePriority {get;}
Container             Property       System.ComponentModel..
WorkingSet64          Property       System.Int64 WorkingSet64 {get;}
PSConfiguration       PropertySet    PSConfiguration {Name...
PSResources           PropertySet    PSResources {Name..
Company               ScriptProperty System.Object Company...
CPU                   ScriptProperty System.Object CPU...
```

This shows that a wide range of property types is available. Using the -MemberType parameter you can select the type of information to return. The full list of options is shown in table 2.4.

Table 2.4   The options for `Get-Member -MemberType`

`AliasProperty`	`CodeProperty`	`Property`
`NoteProperty`	`ScriptProperty`	`Properties`
`PropertySet`	`Method`	`CodeMethod`
`ScriptMethod`	`Methods`	`ParameterizedProperty`
`MemberSet`	`Event`	`All`

You can also view static methods by using the `-Static` parameter. By default, these aren't returned. `Get-Member` also allows you to view the base object. PowerShell wraps objects, and it sometimes adds or removes methods and properties, and the `-View` parameter enables you to peel off these layers.

You've now seen the help available in PowerShell itself, but there's one other source of help that deserves a mention.

2.6.4   PowerShell community

PowerShell has a very strong, active, and passionate community. Two areas where the community excels are in answering questions on PowerShell forums and providing code examples, either in specific code repositories or on blogs. These examples can be very useful when you start writing your own code.

The heart of the PowerShell community is the PowerShell team members themselves. They can be found in various places:

- Posting on the team blog
- Answering questions on the Microsoft forums
- Providing code samples
- Commenting on blog posts by members of the community

Their participation can be intermittent, depending on their deadlines, but if you participate in the community long enough, you'll come across them. If you're ever lucky enough to be invited to a PowerShell community dinner at one of the major Microsoft conferences, you'll certainly get a chance to meet them.

The PowerShell team is backed up by the PowerShell MVPs. There are just over 40 of these individuals worldwide, and they're recognized by Microsoft for their technical expertise in PowerShell and their passionate (fanatical?) devotion to the product. Between them they

- Write blogs
- Write books and articles
- Create podcasts
- Answer questions on forums
- Maintain code repositories and other websites
- Run user groups
- Supply PowerShell code and functionality

They also make a lot of suggestions to the PowerShell team regarding new features for PowerShell and problems and bugs with the current version. They generally test it to destruction.

A third group is the vendors who build PowerShell into their products. In many cases, they offer free versions of PowerShell functionality from their websites. They also help push the boundaries of PowerShell by extending its control to other platforms.

There are many people interested in PowerShell who interact with the three groups already mentioned. They range from newcomers to experienced users who want to know more. Many of them make contributions to various parts of the PowerShell community.

> **TIP** I was a judge in the 2010 and 2011 Scripting Games organized by Microsoft (see their Script Center on TechNet). I was overwhelmed by the quality of some of the entries. People had really gone to town in creating production-quality code. These are superb learning exercises and they're well worth studying for ideas.

The PowerShell community is continually growing in strength because of the number of people who contribute. I strongly recommend getting involved. All you have to do is write some PowerShell code in a way that makes it reusable, as you're about to learn.

2.7 Code reuse

You've now had an introduction to PowerShell's scripting language and seen how it can be used with the cmdlets. But so far we've just looked at working interactively at the PowerShell prompt. A lot of work can be done that way, but for the longer pieces of code or functionality, you'll want to reuse the code. That means you need a way to save your PowerShell masterpieces. There are a number of editors that can be used to write and save your PowerShell scripts, including those supplied with Windows and PowerShell.

> **NOTE** I am deliberately excluding tools such as PowerGUI and PowerShell Plus from this discussion. Both products are excellent and have a role to play in *hosting* PowerShell code, but in this book I want to concentrate on *producing* code with PowerShell and WMI.

Setting PowerShell's execution policy

PowerShell won't allow you to run scripts when it's first installed. This is by design—it's a security policy designed to protect users from the execution of malicious code.

The ability to run scripts is controlled by the PowerShell execution policy, which you can examine using `Get-ExecutionPolicy`. This will be set to `Restricted` for a new installation. I recommend you change it like this:

```
Set-ExecutionPolicy -ExecutionPolicy RemoteSigned
```

The remote-signed setting allows scripts to run from the local drive but expects scripts on remote drives to be signed with a recognized code-signing certificate. You will need to be running PowerShell with elevated privileges (run as administrator).

I strongly recommend that you don't use the `Unrestricted` execution policy setting.

After a quick look at the editor provided with PowerShell, we'll focus on how to write scripts and functions. PowerShell v2 allows you to utilize a number of advanced capabilities in functions (they then become officially known as *advanced functions*). This enables your functions to work on the pipeline as first-class citizens alongside cmdlets.

PowerShell modules enable you to organize your code and load it into PowerShell very efficiently. They also provide an excellent method of storing code in an easily accessible manner, especially once you've built up a sizeable library of scripts and functions. You can also unload a module when it's no longer required, which allows maximum flexibility in your PowerShell configuration. PowerShell v3 modifies this behavior a little bit in that it will automatically load any module it finds on the module path.

But before you can do any of this good stuff, you need to be able to write the code, which means you need an editor.

2.7.1   *Editors*

There are a number of PowerShell editors available. I use several of them:

- Notepad
- PowerShell ISE
- PowerGUI Script Editor
- PowerShell Plus

Other editors are available, but these are the ones I use and am familiar with. They supply the functionality I need in the way, more or less, that I want to use it. I haven't examined all of the possible editors, and this isn't meant as a definitive list.

Notepad is available on all versions of Windows, but it only supplies text editing. There's no color syntax highlighting or PowerShell intelligence built into it. I find it very useful if I want to open a script and just read it. It has a fast response and low overhead.

The other three editors all provide a development environment of some kind, which includes the following:

- Editing capability with color highlighting and PowerShell intelligence
- Ability to run scripts within the environment
- Debugging features

I tend to use the PowerShell ISE most at the moment because it's supplied with PowerShell v2, so I know it will be available on whichever machine I am using. PowerShell ISE isn't installed by default on server operating systems, but it is an optional feature.

PowerGUI and PowerShell Plus need to be downloaded and installed. PowerGUI is a free tool from Quest, and PowerShell Plus is a commercial product from Idera.

The PowerShell ISE is illustrated in figure 2.4, showing the three main areas that each of the editors possesses.

The top pane is an editing pane where scripts can be created. It's possible to execute the whole script or to highlight a part of the script and run just that. The middle pane is an interactive PowerShell prompt that works exactly like a normal PowerShell

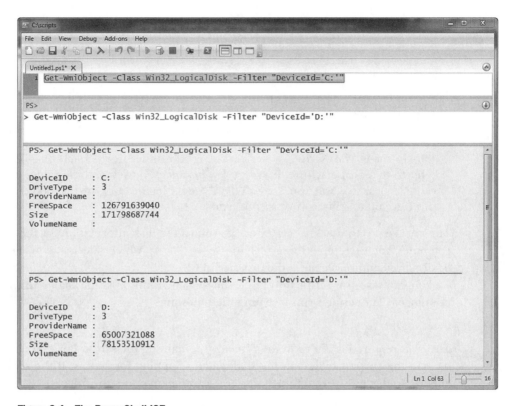

Figure 2.4   The PowerShell ISE

console. The bottom pane shows the code that was run and the results. The position of the various panes can be changed to a certain degree. In PowerShell v3, the interactive and result panes are combined into a single pane that mimics the PowerShell console.

You now know how to set your environment to run scripts, and you have an idea of the editors you can use. It's time to actually create a script.

2.7.2   Scripts

A script is simply a text file of PowerShell commands that has a .ps1 extension. The same extension is used for PowerShell v1, v2, and v3. (There was some discussion during the beta process of having a different extension for PowerShell v2, but it never happened.)

As an example, let's look at a script that discovers what disks are installed in your computers. The following listing shows the script.

Listing 2.2   Script to investigate physical disks

```
param (
  [string]$computername = "localhost"
)
  Get-WmiObject -Class Win32_DiskDrive -ComputerName $computername |
```

```
Format-List DeviceID, Status,
Index, InterfaceType,
Partitions, BytesPerSector, SectorsPerTrack, TracksPerCylinder,
TotalHeads, TotalCylinders, TotalTracks, TotalSectors,
@{Name="Disk Size (GB)"; Expression={"{0:F3}" -f $($_.Size/1GB)}}
```

The first line defines the input parameter for the script. You want a computer name, so to prevent any errors you define a default value of `localhost`. This means that if you don't enter a computer name, the disks in the local system will be evaluated.

> **TIP** In many WMI scripts, a period (`.`) Is substituted for `localhost`—both refer to the local machine. In a very few instances, however, these values can cause issues, so I will use `$env:COMPUTERNAME` in the bulk of the book. All three are valid as far as WMI is concerned.

The next step is to use `Get-WmiObject` to return the disk information for the selected computer. You then pipe the results into `Format-List`, which selects the properties to be displayed and recalculates the disk size in GB.

You can save this script into a file called Get-DiskInfo.ps1 (available in the code download). The script is run by typing the following:

```
.\Get-DiskInfo.ps1
```

The `.\` is required if you're in the directory containing the script. PowerShell doesn't include the current folder on the path when searching for scripts. If the script is in another folder, ensure that folder is on the search path or use the full path to the script.

> **NOTE** It isn't essential, but I tend to follow the PowerShell cmdlet naming conventions when naming scripts. PowerShell v2 will complain if you use a verb that isn't on the approved standard list.

Running the script in this manner produces a report for the local machine. To access another computer, you'd use something like this:

```
.\Get-DiskInfo.ps1 -computername "rslaptop01"
```

The parameter name you defined at the beginning of the script is used to pass the name of the machine to be investigated. You could leave the parameter name out, and PowerShell would assign your input to the `computername` parameter. One extra bonus is that tab completion works on the script name and parameter name.

I can guarantee that you'll build up a large collection of scripts over time. Some of these you'll want to run regularly, and some you'll want to keep together for other reasons. One way of doing this is to use a script file that contains a library of functions.

2.7.3   *Functions*

In PowerShell, a function is a set of code (a script block) to which you give a name. When you type that name at the prompt or include it in a script, you call the function, which will then execute its code. Functions can be very advanced, to the point of acting like cmdlets written in PowerShell, as you'll see later in the section.

You can produce a function from the script in listing 2.2. The body of code for that script becomes the function, and you can then wrap some code around it to read a CSV file of computer names and pass them to the function. This is shown in the following listing.

Listing 2.3 Function to investigate physical disks

```
function get-disk {
param (
  [string]$computername = "$env:COMPUTERNAME"
)
  Get-WmiObject -Class Win32_DiskDrive -ComputerName $computername |
  Format-List DeviceID, Status,
  Index, InterfaceType,
  Partitions, BytesPerSector, SectorsPerTrack, TracksPerCylinder,
  TotalHeads, TotalCylinders, TotalTracks, TotalSectors,
  @{Name="Disk Size (GB)"; Expression={"{0:F3}" -f $($_.Size/1GB)}}
}

Import-Csv computers2.csv | foreach {get-disk $_.computer}
```

This uses the previous code as a function within the script. A CSV file is used to input the computer names to the `get-disk` function.

An alternative method of using this code is to leave the last line of code out of this script and save it as listing2.3a.ps1. You can then run it as follows:

```
. .\Listing2.3a.ps1
```

It's very important to note that there are two dots in the command. The first tells PowerShell to keep any functions or variables in memory, rather than discarding them after execution. You'll see this referred to as *dot sourcing*. Once the function has been loaded into memory, you can use it as any other PowerShell command.

This means you can perform either of these actions at the prompt:

```
get-disk rslaptop01
Import-Csv computers2.csv | foreach {get-disk $_.computer}
```

The function has become part of PowerShell, and you can use it from the prompt or include in your scripts if desired. You can load this function into PowerShell by including it in your profile or running as you did earlier.

> **NOTE** You can use the `filter` command to use the function on the pipeline. This was a piece of PowerShell v1 functionality that has been superseded by the advanced function capabilities introduced in PowerShell v2.

This is good, but it isn't all you can do. You can make your function behave much more like a cmdlet. The following example will demonstrate how you can use this functionality.

I don't intend to discuss the full details of PowerShell's advanced function capabilities, because I want to concentrate on WMI. More details can be found in these help files:

- about_Functions
- about_Functions_Advanced
- about_Functions_Advanced_Methods
- about_Functions_Advanced_Parameters
- about_Functions_CmdletBindingAttribute

The books referenced in chapter 1 can also provide further information.

In order to turn the function from listing 2.3 into an advanced function that can behave like a cmdlet, you need to make the changes shown in the following listing.

Listing 2.4 Advanced function to investigate physical disks

```
function get-disk {                                         ➊ Act as
[CmdletBinding()]                                              cmdlet      ➋ Accept
param (                                                                       pipeline
    [Parameter(ValueFromPipelineByPropertyName=$true)]                       input
    [string]
    [ValidateNotNullOrEmpty()]                             ◄──➌ Perform validation
    $computername
)
PROCESS {                                                   ➍ Specify
    Write-Debug $computername                                  debugging
    Get-WmiObject -Class Win32_DiskDrive -ComputerName $computername |
    Format-List DeviceID, Status,
    Index, InterfaceType,
    Partitions, BytesPerSector, SectorsPerTrack, TracksPerCylinder,
    TotalHeads, TotalCylinders, TotalTracks, TotalSectors,
    @{Name="Disk Size (GB)"; Expression={"{0:F3}" -f $($_.Size/1GB)}}
}
}
```

The function starts with a name, as previously. The [CmdletBinding()] attribute ➊ is the clever piece that enables the function to behave like a cmdlet on the pipeline. It also provides access to the common parameters, such as debug (see Get-Help about_CommonParameters).

The other main alteration is that the parameter block gets a large number of options, some of which are used on the parameter in this function. These options are used individually on each parameter, which can make the parameter block rather large, but the functionality is worth the extra typing.

You can enable this parameter to accept input from the pipeline ➋. In this case, you're accepting it by property name. There are a number of validation techniques you can apply to the parameter, including checking it against a range or set of values. In this case, you're testing to see if it's null or empty ➌. If it's empty or null, an error is thrown and the function isn't executed.

The final change is to add some debugging capability to the function ➍. You can add the -Debug parameter to your use of the cmdlet, and you'll receive a printout of the computer name you're working with.

The function is loaded by dot sourcing the PowerShell file containing the code:

```
PS> . .\Listing2.4.ps1
```

After loading the function, you can try it without a computer name and it errors:

```
PS> get-disk
Get-WmiObject : Cannot validate argument on parameter 'ComputerName'. The
    argument is null or empty. Supply an Argument that is not null or empty
    and then try the command again.
```

Excellent. Another change you made was to add the -Debug parameter:

```
PS> get-disk rslaptop01 -Debug
DEBUG: rslaptop01

Confirm
Continue with this operation?
[Y] Yes  [A] Yes to All  [H] Halt Command  [S] Suspend  [?] Help (default is
    "Y"): y

DeviceID             : \\.\PHYSICALDRIVE0
Status               : OK
Index                : 0
InterfaceType        : IDE
Partitions           : 3
BytesPerSector       : 512
SectorsPerTrack      : 63
TracksPerCylinder    : 255
TotalHeads           : 255
TotalCylinders       : 30401
TotalTracks          : 7752255
TotalSectors         : 488392065
Disk Size (GB)       : 232.883
```

As you can see, the value of the variable is output, and you're also asked to confirm your continuation.

The last change was to enable pipeline input. You can make this work as follows:

```
Import-Csv computers3.csv | get-disk
```

The objects that are imported from the CSV file are piped into the function, and you can process a number of computers quite easily and simply.

Loading functions singly in this way is acceptable when you're creating and testing them, but it's a painful process if you have many to load. In PowerShell v1, you could put them into a library file and dot source that. PowerShell v2 supplies a superior alternative in the form of modules.

2.7.4 *Modules*

In PowerShell v1, you could extend PowerShell functionality by adding cmdlets via a snap-in. This method was used very successfully by Exchange 2007 and the Quest AD cmdlets, for instance. The one drawback to snap-ins is that they only allow for the addition of compiled cmdlets. You have to write your cmdlet in C# or another .NET language, compile it, and then install it. This isn't a technique that most administrators wish to embrace.

A PowerShell v2 module can contain a DLL with cmdlets in the same way as a snap-in. More importantly, it can contain module files (which have a .psm1 extension);

these are PowerShell files containing a set of PowerShell functions. You now have a way to load and unload PowerShell functionality very easily, and that functionality is created in PowerShell. This provides a way of organizing and delivering working code, and it's well within the reach of PowerShell-using administrators. Modules of useful functionality are also available from code repositories such as CodePlex. See, for example, the PowerShell Admin Modules at http://psam.codeplex.com/. I know these are safe—I wrote them.

You can discover the modules installed in your system like this:

```
Get-Module -ListAvailable
```

Modules, by default, are installed in two locations, which are stored in the PSModule-Path environmental variable. The variable content consists of a number of folder paths that are separated by semicolons. The -split operator can be used to make the variable contents easier to read. On my system, I get this result:

```
PS> $env:psmodulepath -split ";"
C:\Users\Richard\Documents\WindowsPowerShell\Modules
C:\Windows\system32\WindowsPowerShell\v1.0\Modules\
```

The first path is in my profile, and the second path is in the PowerShell install folder. I also store the modules I've written in C:\Scripts\Modules. This is achieved by adding this line to my PowerShell profile:

```
$env:PSModulePath = "C:\Scripts\Modules;" + $env:PSModulePath
```

If you examine any of these locations, you'll find a set of folders that match the module names. Each of these folders will contain a module file (.psm1), potentially a manifest file (.psd1, used to control which functions are visible and to ensure that any prerequisites are loaded), and possibly a number of script files (.ps1). If the module is supplying compiled cmdlets, it will also contain one or more DLLs.

Deploying a module is simple. Just copy the folder containing the required files into a folder on your module path.

> **NOTE** PowerShell v3 will, by default, automatically load all modules it finds on the module path when the console or ISE is started.

The module can then be imported into PowerShell like this:

```
Import-Module BitsTransfer
```

This is one of the standard PowerShell modules. You can discover the functions or cmdlets it has loaded as follows:

```
PS> Get-Command -Module BitsTransfer | select name

Name
----
Add-BitsFile
Complete-BitsTransfer
Get-BitsTransfer
```

```
Remove-BitsTransfer
Resume-BitsTransfer
Set-BitsTransfer
Start-BitsTransfer
Suspend-BitsTransfer
```

These commands can be used in scripts or at the prompt. Once you've finished with this task, you can remove the module:

```
Remove-Module BitsTransfer
```

Automating a process saves time and effort. In order to gain the maximum savings, you need to save the code you've produced so that you can reuse it. Scripts, functions, and modules are your tools for this task. Of the three, modules are the best way of organizing your PowerShell functionality. They're just one of the new features that PowerShell v2 offers.

The most requested feature for PowerShell v2 was the ability to work with remote machines.

2.8 PowerShell remoting

The examples we've discussed so far have been run against local, and in some cases remote, machines. An automation tool must be able to work easily and efficiently against a number of remote machines or you won't fully realize the benefits of developing scripts. There are a number of ways remote administration has been built into PowerShell:

- Some cmdlets can access remote machines.
- PowerShell can use the WS-Management protocols to create remote PowerShell sessions.
- You can access data directly through the WS-Management (WSMAN) cmdlets.
- PowerShell v3 allows you to use CIM sessions. These also use the WSMAN protocols and can be thought of as a cross between PowerShell remote sessions and the WSMAN cmdlets.
- You can access web services from within some PowerShell cmdlets.

We'll concentrate on using PowerShell remote sessions and the remoting features built into cmdlets in this chapter because they have the most impact on the functions you'll be working with in part 2 of the book. The WSMAN cmdlets are discussed in chapter 17, and the new CIM cmdlets and sessions are covered in chapters 18 and 19. The last option is used in Windows Server 2008 R2 Active Directory and Exchange 2010, though the implementations aren't identical. Neither of these technologies have a WMI component, so they won't be followed up in this work.

We'll start by looking at the cmdlets that can work remotely.

2.8.1 Remoting by cmdlet

A number of cmdlets have a -ComputerName parameter that enables them to access remote machines. Get-WmiObject had this ability in PowerShell v1, and others had the capability added in PowerShell v2. The full list of cmdlets that can work in this way can be discovered using `Get-Help`:

```
PS> Get-Help * -Parameter computername | Format-Wide -Column 3

Get-WinEvent              Get-Counter               Test-WSMan
Invoke-WSManAction        Connect-WSMan             Disconnect-WSMan
Get-WSManInstance         Set-WSManInstance         Remove-WSManInstance
New-WSManInstance         Invoke-Command            New-PSSession
Get-PSSession             Remove-PSSession          Receive-Job
Enter-PSSession           Get-EventLog              Clear-EventLog
Write-EventLog            Limit-EventLog            Show-EventLog
New-EventLog              Remove-EventLog           Get-WmiObject
Invoke-WmiMethod          Get-Process               Remove-WmiObject
Register-WmiEvent         Get-Service               Set-Service
Set-WmiInstance           Get-HotFix                Test-Connection
Restart-Computer          Stop-Computer
```

We'll be looking at working directly with the WSMAN cmdlets in chapter 17, but for now let's consider the other cmdlets. Most of them, such as `Get-Service`, `Get-WmiObject`, and `Get-EventLog`, don't require PowerShell to be installed on the remote machine. The `PSSession` cmdlets require PowerShell v2 to be installed and configured, but not necessarily running.

WMI remote access

All of the WMI cmdlets have a `-ComputerName` parameter. In order for these cmdlets to be able to work remotely, you need to configure the remote firewall. This can be performed using the firewall administrative tools or you can run the following commands from PowerShell or a command prompt.

```
Netsh firewall set service RemoteAdmin
Netsh advfirewall set currentprofile settings remotemanagement enable
```

On Windows Server 2008 R2, the second command will return a message saying that it's deprecated, but it will configure the firewall correctly.

Accessing data from one or more remote computers involves using the `-Computer-Name` parameter. For example, this is how you would check on a service on the local machine:

```
PS> Get-Service winrm

Status    Name                DisplayName
------    ----                -----------
Running   winrm               Windows Remote Management (WS-Manag...
```

It's just as easy to do this on remote machines:

```
PS> Get-Service -Name winrm -ComputerName w08r2sql08

Status    Name                DisplayName
------    ----                -----------
```

```
Running  winrm                  Windows Remote Management (WS-Manag...

PS> Get-Service -Name winrm -ComputerName w08r2sql08a

Status   Name                   DisplayName
------   ----                   -----------
Running  winrm                  Windows Remote Management (WS-Manag...
```

According to the help, you should be able to do this:

```
PS> Get-Service -Name winrm -ComputerName w08r2sql08, w08r2sql08a
```

Unfortunately, you'll only get the results for the first machine in the list. But you can fall back on WMI:

```
PS> $computers = @("localhost", "w08r2sql08", "w08r2sql08a")
PS> Get-WmiObject -Class Win32_Service -Filter "Name='winrm'" `
 -ComputerName $computers | ft SystemName, State, StartMode

SystemName          State          StartMode
----------          -----          ---------
SERVER02            Running        Auto
W08R2SQL08          Running        Auto
W08R2SQL08A         Running        Auto
```

This gives you a quick way to test whether the required services are running on remote machines. We'll be revisiting this idea in chapter 9.

Working within individual cmdlets is great, but it does have a couple of limitations. The biggest one is that not all cmdlets have a -ComputerName parameter, meaning you're confined to the local machine. The second issue is that working in this manner is slow because the connection to the remote machine has to be created, used, and destroyed for each use. What you need is a way, such as WinRM, to create a connection between the local and remote machines that remains open for as long as you need it.

2.8.2 *PowerShell remote sessions*

PowerShell can use the WinRM service to create a connection to a remote machine. WinRM is Microsoft's implementation of the industry standard Web Services for Management (WS-Management) protocol. In PowerShell v2, the installer includes PowerShell and WinRM.

The following requirements must be met for PowerShell remoting to work:

- The WinRM service must be installed on the remote systems.
- PowerShell v2 must be installed on both systems.
- The Enable-PSRemoting cmdlet must have been run on the remote machines with elevated privileges to configure WinRM, the firewall, and other necessary elements.

You can create a connection to one or more remote systems like this:

```
$s = New-PSSession -ComputerName W08R2SQL08, W08R2SQL08A
```

The available sessions can be viewed with Get-PSSession:

```
PS> Get-PSSession

Id Name        ComputerName  State    ConfigurationName    Availability
-- ----        ------------  -----    -----------------    ------------
 1 Session1    w08r2sql08    Opened   Microsoft.PowerShell Available
 2 Session2    w08r2sql08a   Opened   Microsoft.PowerShell Available
```

Now you need to be able to use these sessions:

```
PS> Invoke-Command -Session $s -ScriptBlock {Get-Service winrm}

Status   Name   DisplayName                PSComputerName
------   ----   -----------                --------------
Running  winrm  Windows Remote Management  w08r2sql08a
Running  winrm  Windows Remote Management  w08r2sql08
```

Your session currently consists of connections to a number of computers. You can access just one of the machines in the session as follows:

```
$sa = Get-PSSession -Id 2
Invoke-Command -Session $sa -ScriptBlock {Get-Service sql*}
```

This code creates a new session variable that points to the machine (session) you want to work with. When you have a number of sessions open, you can work with them in any desired combination to send the right commands to the server you want to work with.

The script block that `Invoke-Command` uses will be run against the remote machine. If you give a filename or path within the script block, it will be looked for on the remote machine. You can run a script from the local machine against a remote machine by using the `-FilePath` parameter of `Invoke-Command`.

When you've finished with the sessions, they should be removed:

```
Get-PSSession | Remove-PSSession
```

When you're working with WMI, you can use either the `-ComputerName` parameter built into the cmdlets or PowerShell remote sessions to access remote machines.

Both options have one thing in common, though. You can run them as background jobs.

2.9   *PowerShell jobs*

The objective of automating your work is to make the work easier and faster. You can start a script and let it perform the tasks rather than working through the tasks yourself. But there's one slight roadblock on the journey to the automation highlands. When you start a PowerShell script, it takes time to run. If you're connecting to a number of remote machines, this can take significant time. Your PowerShell prompt is unavailable for this time, which could impact other tasks. One way to avoid this problem is to start up another PowerShell session or, better still, you could use a background job.

PowerShell jobs run asynchronously. They return the prompt for immediate use while the job carries on running in the background. When the job has finished, the results are stored until you're ready to access them. Note that the results aren't persisted between PowerShell sessions, so they'll be lost if you close PowerShell.

Jobs can be created in two ways. First, there are a number of cmdlets specifically for working with jobs. Second, there are a number of cmdlets that have an -AsJob parameter that allows that cmdlet to be performed as a job. The two sets of cmdlets are listed in table 2.5.

Table 2.5 Cmdlets for working with PowerShell jobs

Cmdlets with AsJob parameter	Job cmdlets
Invoke-Command	Get-Job
Get-WmiObject	Receive-Job
Invoke-WmiMethod	Remove-Job
Remove-WmiObject	Start-Job
Set-WmiInstance	Stop-Job
Test-Connection	Wait-Job
Restart-Computer	
Stop-Computer	

A job can be created on the local machine using Start-Job:

```
Start-Job -Name PaW1 -ScriptBlock {
Get-WmiObject -Class Win32_Service -Filter "Name='winrm'"}
```

> **NOTE** It could be argued that the Start-Job cmdlet should be called New-Job. You can always create an alias, but remember the issues related to publishing scripts with your own aliases, as mentioned in section 2.1.1.

You can also create a job to run against remote machines:

```
Invoke-Command -ComputerName w08r2sql08, w08r2sql08a -ScriptBlock {
Get-WmiObject -Class Win32_Service -Filter "Name='winrm'"} -AsJob
```

Get-Job is used to see how your jobs are progressing, as shown in figure 2.5. Note that when you explicitly create a job, you give it a name, but when using the -AsJob parameter, the system will assign a name.

The important points in figure 2.5 are that both jobs have completed, as shown under the State column, and that HasMoreData is True. You can access data held in the jobs by using Receive-Job in a number of ways:

```
Receive-Job -Name PaW1 -Keep
Receive-Job -Name Job3 -Keep
Get-Job -Id 3 | Receive-Job -Location w08r2sql08a -Keep
```

In the first example, you get the information from the job you created with Start-Job. The second example retrieves data from the job created with Invoke-Command. The final example shows how you can access the data for one computer when the job has been

```
C:\scripts                                                                                    _ □ ×
PS> Start-Job -Name PaW1 -ScriptBlock {Get-WmiObject -Class win32_service -Filter "Name='winrm'"}

Id            Name          State      HasMoreData     Location        Command
--            ----          -----      -----------     --------        -------
1             PaW1          Running    True            localhost       Get-WmiObject -Class w...


PS> Invoke-Command -ComputerName w08r2sql08, w08r2sql08a -ScriptBlock {Get-WmiObject -Class win32_service -Filter "Name=
'winrm'"} -AsJob

Id            Name          State      HasMoreData     Location        Command
--            ----          -----      -----------     --------        -------
3             Job3          Running    True            w08r2sql08,w08r2s... Get-WmiObject -Class w...


PS> Get-Job

Id            Name          State      HasMoreData     Location        Command
--            ----          -----      -----------     --------        -------
1             PaW1          Completed  True            localhost       Get-WmiObject -Class w...
3             Job3          Completed  True            w08r2sql08,w08r2s... Get-WmiObject -Class w...

PS> _
```

Figure 2.5   Starting and viewing PowerShell jobs

run against a number of machines. In all cases, you use the -Keep parameter. If this isn't used, the data is deleted as it's accessed and won't be available for further analysis. I recommend always using -Keep unless you're sure you won't need to revisit the data.

The last job-related thing you need to think about is tidying up the environment by deleting jobs you don't need. You can use Get-Job to pipe specific jobs into Remove-Job, or for a complete and final cleanup, you can use this:

```
Get-Job | Remove-Job
```

PowerShell jobs created using the WMI cmdlets are slightly different from jobs created with Start-Job or Invoke-Command -AsJob. Each starts a child process, but they're different. In practical terms, this doesn't affect how you manage the jobs because the *Job cmdlets work on them all.

PowerShell jobs are one of the most overlooked features of PowerShell that can make life easier and add flexibility to the way you perform automated tasks.

2.10   *Summary*

PowerShell is a shell, a language, and a set of command-line tools that supply a framework for our automation work. It's .NET-based and its pipeline works on these objects rather than on text as is traditional in other shells.

The scripting language provides all of the features you require, including

- Different types of loops
- Branching via if or switch statements
- File input and output to use data and store results

There are a number of ways of finding help for PowerShell. There are cmdlets that read the XML help files and display information about cmdlets or the objects they're working with, and there's web-based help available. A final source of assistance is the PowerShell community.

When you create a piece of PowerShell code, you need to be able to store it so you can run it again in the future. The simplest way to do this is to create a script. If you have a lot of scripts that potentially interact or that need to be loaded together, you can rewrite them as functions to make code reuse a simpler proposition. PowerShell v2 offers you the option of creating modules of functions that ease the work in organizing and loading and unloading them much simpler.

Automation in the enterprise requires that you can work with remote machines. This can be achieved using the remote capabilities built into some cmdlets or by using PowerShell sessions to specific remote computers. You can also access remote machines and run PowerShell tasks as background jobs, making you more productive and more flexible.

PowerShell provides one way of performing administrative tasks. The other approach is to use WMI. In the next chapter, we'll turn our attention to WMI and see how it works with PowerShell.

WMI in depth 3

This chapter covers

- WMI structure
- WMI cmdlets and accelerators
- WMI Query Language
- Discovering links between WMI classes

Windows Management Instrumentation, known as WMI to its friends, isn't well understood by the majority of administrators. It appears to be a technology that's difficult to use and that isn't well documented, unless you want to go rummaging in the depths of TechNet and MSDN. Is this a fair assessment?

Until PowerShell appeared, this was my stance on WMI. I could make it work, but I didn't really understand it and certainly didn't feel I could get the best out of it. Code was difficult to produce and test in VBScript, using WMI interactively required a different set of tools with a cryptic syntax, and background information was very sparse and difficult to find. Now, though, I have the tools to make using it much easier, and I can also use those tools to investigate how WMI is put together. By the end of this chapter, you'll similarly have a good understanding of the underlying structure of WMI and how all the bits relate, and you'll know how to make it work for you.

In this chapter, we'll start by considering what WMI is, and we'll look at the major components that you need to understand in order to use it:

- Providers
- Namespaces
- Classes

PowerShell works with .NET objects, as you saw in chapter 2. In this chapter, you'll discover the makeup of the objects that WMI produces and learn how to use the methods and properties of those objects. You'll learn how to produce your own working documentation based on the information stored within WMI. This won't provide full explanations for WMI classes, but it will provide enough information to work productively with the classes. The linkages between classes enable a deep level of access to the information locked in WMI, and the techniques presented in this chapter will enable you to unlock that information.

The next item on the agenda is to explore what PowerShell can offer for working with WMI. We'll expand on the brief glimpse you had in chapter 1, and you'll see how much easier WMI becomes in PowerShell. You'll learn about each of the WMI cmdlets and about the type accelerators, which are shortcuts that make working with WMI objects via .NET much simpler.

The PowerShell cmdlets remove the need to write WMI queries, which was the only way to work with WMI in the past. But there are times when queries are the best way to get the information you need. This is when you'll want to turn to WMI Query Language (WQL), which is a subset of SQL. You can use WQL in complete queries or in filters.

WMI also enables you to discover the references and associations between different WMI classes and to work with WMI events. You'll see throughout the book that WMI exposes a wealth of information about the events occurring on your system. For example, would you like a specific task to occur when a USB memory stick is plugged into your system? Keep reading and you'll find out how to achieve this.

There are a small number of scenarios where the PowerShell WMI cmdlets can't solve your problem. The workaround is to access the .NET objects directly. One of the most common examples of this is the IIS WMI provider, which we'll look at in chapter 12.

But before you can do any of these things, you need a good understanding of WMI and how it works.

3.1 *The structure of WMI*

The first step in learning to use a technology involves understanding what it is and what it does. You learned in chapter 1 that WMI is Microsoft's implementation of the DMTF's Common Information Model (CIM). Microsoft has taken the basic CIM specification and often enhanced the classes or added new classes to produce WMI.

On modern Windows systems, WMI is part of the base operating system install. It's there automatically and you don't have to worry about it. When you extend the functionality of your systems, such as by installing the DNS role, additional WMI functionality is automatically installed. All you have to do is work out how to use it.

Run as administrator

WMI, in many cases, can be run and used without elevated privileges. But there are some namespaces, especially those related to security, that require PowerShell to be started using Run as Administrator.

If you're only pulling information, such as info about network cards, PowerShell can be started normally. If you're using the methods of a WMI class, you may need elevated privileges. Some of the work you'll do on IIS in chapter 12 will require you to start PowerShell using Run as Administrator.

The scripts in this chapter will complete without elevated privileges but you'll be denied access to some namespaces. I recommend using elevated privileges when trying the code.

We need to dive a bit deeper into the details before we get to the fun bits. On Windows systems there is a C:\Windows\System32\wbem folder that supplies the WMI functionality. WBEM stands for Web-Based Enterprise Management, and the architecture of WBEM is used in WMI. The DMTF supplies the standards for WBEM.

According to the DMTF website, WBEM is "a set of management and Internet standard technologies developed to unify the management of distributed computing environments. WBEM provides the ability for the industry to deliver a well-integrated set of standard-based management tools, facilitating the exchange of data across otherwise disparate technologies and platforms."

NOTE   For more information about WBEM, see the DMTF website: http://www.dmtf.org/standards/wbem.

What that means is that we have a standards-based way of managing distributed systems. The components that form the architecture of WMI are shown in figure 3.1.

Our starting point for understanding WMI's architecture is the Managed

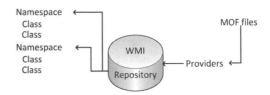

Figure 3.1   The structure of WMI

Object Format (MOF) files, which can be found in the WBEM folder. There are a large number of these files. The exact number will vary with the version of Windows you are using:

```
PS> (Get-ChildItem -Path C:\Windows\System32\wbem -Filter *.mof).count
207
```

The MOF files store the definitions of the WMI classes. It's possible to write your own MOF file and compile it to extend WMI. The details are available in the WMI SDK on MSDN. I don't intend to spend any time looking at the structure of MOF files or at how you can work with them. That topic is firmly outside the scope of this book. Good luck.

Associated with each of the MOF files is a provider. This is a DLL that's registered with Windows and WMI, giving you access to the classes you actually use. The class definitions are stored in the WMI repository. The instances of those classes are retrieved dynamically by a provider when requested by a consumer, such as a PowerShell cmdlet. The classes are arranged in namespaces to give a logical, hierarchical structure with the `root` namespace at the top.

> **NOTE** WMI is based on COM, not .NET. COM stands for Common Object Model and it's the programming model Microsoft used before .NET. It's slowly being replaced by .NET, but a lot of COM-based applications will be with us for many years. While COM uses classes, methods, and properties, these aren't identical to the .NET entities of the same name. We'll ignore these differences as long as they don't get in the way of using WMI with PowerShell.

Understanding the relationship between the components that make up WMI enables you to achieve a number of things:

- You can test the integrity of WMI and discover whether you need to rebuild. You'll know you need to rebuild if you get errors accessing an individual namespace, provider, or class (but remember to check that you're running with elevated privileges).
- You can discover the structure of WMI on your system. The WMI classes that are present change with the version of Windows, and of other applications, so it can be useful to determine whether a class or namespace is present.
- You can use WMI to its full capabilities.

The first item from figure 3.1 that can supply some useful help is the provider.

3.1.1 Providers

You won't use providers directly, but there are a couple of reasons for wanting to identify the provider:

- You know where the class was loaded from and if there are any associated classes.
- You know what it's providing.
- You know where to start looking if you need to repair WMI (this isn't something I'll cover, but instructions for recompiling WMI can be found on MSDN).

The providers can be found by using the WMI system class `__Win32Provider`.

All system classes are denoted by a prefix of two underscore characters, `__`. The class is available on a per namespace basis:

```
Get-WmiObject -Class __Win32Provider | select name
```

This lists all of the providers in the namespace that PowerShell uses as a default, root\cimv2. One thing to be aware of is that there's a namespace called root\DEFAULT. This isn't the same as PowerShell's default namespace, just to be confusing.

Up to now, I've implied that all providers are the same and that they just supply classes. Unfortunately things are a bit more complicated. There are a number of different provider types, as shown in table 3.1.

Table 3.1   WMI provider types

Provider type	Purpose	Registration type
Class	Supply applications with class definitions; rarely implemented	`__ClassProviderRegistration`
Event	Provide event notifications to WMI	`__EventProviderRegistration`
Event consumer	Consume WMI events	`__EventConsumerProviderRegistration`
Instance	Supply WMI classes, such as `Win32_Service`	`__InstanceProviderRegistration`
Method	Provide the methods of the relevant WMI classes	`__Method`
Property	Supply ways to work with property values, including reading and modifying	`__PropertyProviderRegistration`

A single provider can function as multiple, different provider types. The registry provider, for example, registers a number of WMI elements:

- Event
- Instance
- Method
- Property

Providers install classes into a namespace. Namespaces are the working part of WMI. You need to understand the namespaces that are installed and what they can do.

3.1.2   *Namespaces*

WMI namespaces are used to logically subdivide the available WMI classes. Some namespaces are installed by default on all Windows systems, and others are only available when specific applications or Windows features are installed.

The first question is what namespaces are installed on a system? You know that the namespace at the top of the hierarchy is called root and that your default namespace is root\cimv2. How can you find the other namespaces and their relationships?

DISCOVERING NAMESPACES

You saw earlier that WMI system classes are prefixed with a double underscore character. Take a look at the system classes for a namespace—in this case, root\cimv2:

```
Get-WmiObject -Namespace 'root\cimv2' -List "__*"
```

You'll see that there is a class called __NAMESPACE. You can now investigate that class and generate a list of the namespaces in the root\cimv2 namespace:

```
Get-WmiObject -Class __NAMESPACE | select name
```

You could generate a list of all namespaces by working from the root down and manually running the preceding code, but that would involve a lot of tedious manual work. The theme of the book is getting the machine to work for you, so you need a way to automate the discovery process. One way to achieve this is to use the code in the following listing.

Listing 3.1 Find WMI namespaces installed on a system

```
function get-namespace {
param ([string]$name)
    Get-WmiObject -Namespace $name -Class "__NAMESPACE" |
    foreach {
       "$name\" + $_.Name
       get-namespace $("$name\" + $_.Name)
    }
}
"root"
get-namespace "root"
```

The work engine of this script is the get-namespace function. (Functions are explained in chapter 2, if you skipped that chapter.) The function takes a namespace name as its only parameter. It then uses that name to retrieve the namespaces contained within that namespace using Get-WmiObject, as you saw previously. The results are piped into a ForEach-Object cmdlet that displays the name of the current namespace and the discovered namespaces using a backslash (\) as a divider. You can then use that full namespace path as the input to get-namespace. The script starts the whole discovery process by displaying *root* on screen and calling the get-namespace function.

Now I'm going to scare you. This process of getting a function to call itself is called *recursion*. I slipped the description into this discussion before telling you what it's called because recursion is one of those topics that causes grown administrators to run away. But it's not that bad, is it?

Now let's adapt listing 3.1 to not only show the namespaces but also show the providers.

TIP You need to run these scripts from an elevated shell to avoid the *access denied* messages, especially from the security-related namespaces.

If you take listing 3.1 and add the code from section 3.1.1 where we discussed providers, you'll end up with the following.

Listing 3.2 Find WMI providers in each namespace

```
function get-namespace {
param ([string]$name)
    Get-WmiObject -Namespace $name -Class "__NAMESPACE" |
```

```
    foreach {
      $ns = "$name\" + $_.Name
      "`nNameSpace: $ns"
      "providers:"
      Get-WmiObject -NameSpace $ns -Class __Win32Provider |
      select name

      get-namespace $("$name\" + $_.Name)
    }
  }
}
"root"
get-namespace "root"
```

The `get-namespace` function is still the work engine. You start off with the root namespace, as before, and call the function with the namespace name as a parameter. The function retrieves the namespaces and displays the namespace name, but this time it's prefixed with "`NameSpace: `". This enables you to distinguish namespaces from providers, which will make the output more meaningful. The namespace is used to get the list of providers. You then perform the recursion by calling `get-namespace` with the new namespace name.

This is a good start to the discovery process, but there are still a few more levels to dig into. When we were discussing providers, I mentioned that an individual provider can register itself into WMI in a number of different ways. You can also use PowerShell and WMI to discover how providers register themselves.

REGISTRATIONS

A provider will register itself within a namespace, and the types of registrations were detailed in table 3.1. As you might guess, there are a number of WMI system classes that deal with registrations. You can find a full list of the classes involved in dealing with registrations by using the `-List` parameter:

```
Get-WmiObject -Namespace 'root\cimv2'  -List "__*Registration*"
```

If you try this code,

```
Get-WmiObject -Namespace 'root\cimv2' -Class __ProviderRegistration
```

you'll get a long list of information. To see what the registration classes can tell you, you can look at one of each type of registration class:

```
Get-WmiObject -Namespace 'root\cimv2'  -List "__*Registration*" |
foreach {
    Get-WmiObject -Namespace 'root\cimv2' -Class $($_.Name) |
    select -First 1
}
```

Using `Select-Object` to just pick off the first of each type of class reduces the output to something you can work with. It's worth spending some time examining the output to discover what information is available. There are a number of properties that store WQL queries for returning information about events that you'll be meeting again.

It's also interesting to look at which providers perform which type of registration:

```
Get-WmiObject -Namespace 'root\cimv2' -List "__*Registration*" |
foreach {
    Get-WmiObject -Namespace 'root\cimv2' -Class $($_.Name) |
    Format-Table __CLASS, provider -AutoSize
}
```

This variation on the previous code displays the __CLASS (which tells you the type of registration) and the provider performing that registration.

Throughout the book, we'll keep returning to WMI events. A provider can register events, and one way you can discover the event classes you need to work with is to look at the __EventProviderRegistration class:

```
Get-WmiObject -Namespace 'root\cimv2' `
    -Class __EventProviderRegistration |
foreach {
    "`n"
    $_ | Format-Table EventQueryList, provider -Wrap
}
```

This will display the event classes you can use to discover events related to a specific provider. Better still, it shows the WMI query you have to run to get the information you want. Now that's something that makes life a lot easier.

We'll return to providers and namespaces when we put all of this together to document the WMI environment in section 3.3.

One of the things that providers can supply to namespaces is the WMI classes you need to work with. Classes are at the bottom of the hierarchy, but they're the most important component, because you'll work directly with them to perform your administration tasks.

3.1.3 Classes

A WMI class represents a specific item in your system. It could be a piece of hardware, such as a network card or CPU, or it could relate to software, such as the operating system, a hotfix, a feature like DNS, or any other installed software. It could even relate to an event or a data store, such as the registry. In the second part of the book, we'll look at a large number of WMI classes and see what they can do. For now, though, you need to understand how to work with the WMI classes.

The first thing to understand is the different types of classes available. CIM defines three class categories:

- *Core classes* represent managed objects that apply to all areas of management.
- *Common classes* represent managed objects that apply to specific management areas (these classes are prefixed with CIM_).
- *Extended classes* represent managed objects that are technology-specific—that is, classes that are created to manage the Windows platform and Microsoft applications. Examples would include the classes for managing IIS, Hyper-V, or DNS.

Within these categories there are a number of class types, as shown in table 3.2.

Table 3.2   WMI class types

Class type	Purpose	Example
System class (can be static or abstract)	Supports WMI configuration and operations.	`__NAMESPACE`
Abstract	Template used to define new classes. Identified by `Abstract` qualifier.	`__Provider` `CIM_Service`
Static	Defines data stored in WMI repository; usually used to define system classes. Identified by lack of `Abstract` or `Dynamic` qualifier.	`__Win32Provider`
Dynamic (typically extension classes)	Represents a WMI managed resource; the information is retrieved from a provider when requested. Identified by `Dynamic` qualifier.	`Win32_Service`
Association	Links two classes or resources. Identified by `Association` qualifier.	`Win32_SystemServices`

WMI classes can be divided into two groups. The first group is comprised of the system classes, which are present in each namespace. They provide information about the namespace, registrations, and security. They're also responsible for the processing of events created by other WMI classes.

The second group is more heterogeneous and includes the core CIM classes as well as the extension classes that Microsoft has created. These are the worker classes that you use to manage your Windows environment.

You've already seen some of the system classes in action. But what else can they do for you?

SYSTEM CLASSES

Each WMI namespace has an instance of each of the system classes, identified by a double-underscore prefix (__). The full list for the root\cimv2 namespace can be found by using the -List parameter in `Get-WmiObject`:

```
Get-WmiObject -Namespace 'root\cimv2' -List "__*"
```

The same system classes are present in each namespace. You can see this by comparing two namespaces at random:

```
$cimv2 = Get-WmiObject -Namespace 'root\cimv2' -List "__*" |
select name

$scent = Get-WmiObject -Namespace 'root\SecurityCenter' -List "__*" |
select name

Compare-Object -ReferenceObject $cimv2 -DifferenceObject $scent `
 -IncludeEqual
```

The preceding code generates a list of system classes for each namespace. The `Compare-Object` cmdlet is used to compare the two objects that are produced. If you don't use the -IncludeEqual parameter, you'll get nothing back, which indicates that the two objects are identical.

TIP This is a little gotcha with PowerShell: if it has nothing to return, it won't tell you that. It can be difficult to tell the difference between an error and a situation with no data to return. The only way to resolve the question is to test around the problem.

When you use the parameter, you'll get output with this form:

```
InputObject                         SideIndicator
-----------                         -------------
@{Name=__SystemClass}               ==
@{Name=__NAMESPACE}                 ==

Output truncated for brevity
```

You'll get one line of output per system class. Many of the system classes are involved in the production and consumption of events, and you won't work with them directly very often, though you do need to know that they exist.

When we were discussing providers, you saw that they register classes, but which provider registers which class?

CLASSES BY PROVIDER

In figure 3.1, you saw that providers install items into the WMI repository. This includes classes, but a number of other items are also installed by providers. It's useful to be able to document just what is being installed into WMI. This can be helpful when you're trying to troubleshoot a problem—discovering that a particular piece of WMI isn't installed may point to the problem.

For this example, you'll just work with a single namespace. The following listing takes what you know about WMI so far (oh yes, there's more to come) and demonstrates how you can use PowerShell and WMI to discover the classes installed by each provider.

Listing 3.3 Find WMI classes installed by a provider

```
$namespace = "root\cimv2"                                          ① Define
                                                                      namespace
Get-WmiObject -Namespace $namespace -Class __Win32Provider |
foreach {
  $provider = $_.Name
  "Provider: $provider"                                            ② List
                                                                      providers
  $refs = Get-WmiObject -Namespace $namespace `
  -Query "REFERENCES OF {__Win32Provider.Name='$provider'}"

  foreach ($ref in $refs) {                                        ③ Iterate
                                                                      references
    $type = $ref.__CLASS
    " Registration: $type"

    switch ($type) {                                               ④ Determine
                                                                      registration type
      "__PropertyProviderRegistration" {
            " does not have classes"                               ⑤ Process
            break                                                    registration
      }

      "__ClassProviderRegistration" {
```

```
            "  only provides class definitions"
            break
    }

    "__EventConsumerProviderRegistration" {
            "  uses these classes"
            "    $($ref.ConsumerClassNames)"
            break
    }

    "__EventProviderRegistration" {
            "  queries these classes:"
            foreach ($query in $ref.EventQueryList) {
              $a = $query -split " "
              "    $($a[($a.length-1)])"
            }
            break
    }
    default {
            "  supplies these classes:"
            Get-WmiObject -Namespace $namespace -List -Amended |
            foreach {
              if ($_.Qualifiers["provider"].Value -eq "$provider"){
                "    $($_.Name)"
              }
            } # class list
            break
        }
    } #switch
  } # refs
} # provider loop
```

This is quite a long script, but it can be broken down into a number of easy sections. You start by defining the namespace you want to work with ❶. As written, the script uses the default namespace. The __Win32provider system class returns all of the providers that contribute to the namespace.

A foreach loop iterates through the collection of providers. The provider name is displayed as the first action in the loop ❷. A piece of WMI Query Language (WQL) is used to get a list of the classes to which the provider is linked. These links are known as references. We'll examine WQL in more detail when we get to section 3.5.

Another foreach loop is used to work through each reference ❸. Notice that you have one foreach loop nested inside another. To help keep track of the braces, {}, I've put a comment on each of the closing braces to relate it to the appropriate starting point.

The type of registration is found in the __CLASS property of the reference. A switch statement ❹ uses the registration type to determine how to process the different registrations ❺:

- A __PropertyProviderRegistration will only provide properties, so you display a message that this provider doesn't supply classes.
- A __ClassProviderRegistration only provides class definitions, as explained by the message.

❺ Process registration

❻ Process method and instance registration

- An __EventConsumerProviderRegistration will use a number of event classes. The ConsumerClassNames property holds the class names.

- An __EventProviderRegistration queries one or more classes for WMI event information. The relevant classes are found in the EventQueryList property. This property is very helpful, as it lists the full query rather than just the class name.

The default clause in the switch statement ❻ enables processing of the __MethodProviderRegistration and __InstanceProviderRegistration types. These will sometimes appear to duplicate the registration in the list.

Running this script against the root\cimv2 namespace as you do here produces over a thousand lines of output. The output from running this script on my Windows 7 machine is included in a file called root_cimv2_providers_and_classes.txt, which is available in the script download package associated with the book.

You now know how to find the providers in a namespace and the classes linked to a provider. The last part of the puzzle is to find out which classes are available to work within a particular namespace.

CLASSES IN A NAMESPACE

You've used Get-WmiObject for much of your discovery work. It's the primary Power-Shell tool for retrieving WMI-related information. It's also useful for investigating the classes in a namespace.

Compared to the last script, this one is nice and simple:

```
Get-WmiObject -List
```

You've seen the -List parameter a few times already. You can use Get-Help to look at the parameter definition:

```
Get-Help Get-WmiObject -Parameter list
```

The output from this command is shown in figure 3.2.

The -List parameter can be thought of as the dir command of WMI. It shows you what is there so you can find the class you need to work with.

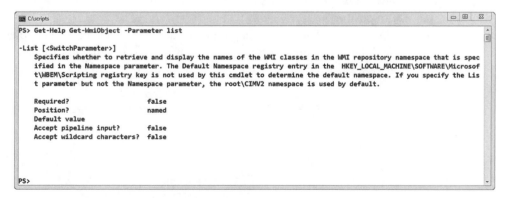

Figure 3.2 Using the -Parameter option with Get-Help

NOTE   In PowerShell v3, the Get-CIMClass cmdlet does a similar job. This is discussed in chapter 19. Versions of some of the scripts in this chapter written using Get-CIMClass are also available in the download.

The previous example will produce a list of all the classes in the root\cimv2 namespace. This is an impressive list of 1,045 classes.

A list of this length is a bit too big to keep scrolling through, so you need a way to filter the output. In PowerShell v2, you can add a filter to restrict the number of classes returned:

```
Get-WmiObject -List *network*
```

The filter will use the standard wildcards, as shown.

Unfortunately this doesn't work in PowerShell v1, so you'll need to do a bit more work in that case:

```
Get-WmiObject -List | where {$_.Name -like "*network*"}
```

The filtering is performed on the pipeline using Where-Object rather than in the Get-WmiObject cmdlet. The results are the same.

You aren't restricted to the default namespace when discovering the available classes. You can change the namespace to be interrogated by using the -Namespace parameter:

```
Get-WmiObject -Namespace "root\SECURITY" -List
```

Remember that the namespaces related to security require PowerShell to be run with elevated privileges; otherwise they enjoy giving you an error message and refusing to display the data.

You now know the class name that may help you with your task, but you don't know what it does or what information it provides. An overview of what the class does can be gained from its description. Unfortunately, the description is hidden by default.

QUALIFIERS

WMI classes have a number of hidden properties known as *qualifiers*. These properties are expensive, in processing time, to retrieve, due to the way the information is stored in the WMI repository.

PowerShell v2 added an -Amended parameter to Get-WmiObject that enables you to access these details. The qualifiers aren't directly displayed, but you can view them by treating them as a collection of properties:

```
PS> $q = Get-WmiObject -List Win32_Process -Amended
PS> $q.Qualifiers | Format-Table Name, Value -AutoSize -Wrap

Name           Value
----           -----
CreateBy       Create
DeleteBy       DeleteInstance
Description    The Win32_Process class represents a sequence of events
               on a Win32 system. Any sequence consisting of the
               interaction of one or more processors or interpreters,
```

```
                     some executable code, and a set of inputs, is a
                     descendent (or member) of this class.
                     Example: A client application running on a Win32 system.
DisplayName          Processes
dynamic              True
Locale               1033
provider             CIMWin32
SupportsCreate       True
SupportsDelete       True
UUID                 {8502C4DC-5FBB-11D2-AAC1-006008C78BC7}
```

In the preceding example, you use the -List parameter to generate the class information and use the class name as a filter to restrict the output. The -Amended parameter ensures the qualifiers are captured and piped into Format-Table, where the name and value of each qualifier are displayed. The -Wrap parameter is used to produce a display that wraps any text that's longer than the display line, making sure you don't miss any data.

One area where the qualifiers come in useful is when you have a number of related classes but aren't sure which one you really need to use. Network adapters are a good example. Suppose there are three classes of interest:

- Win32_NetworkAdapter
- Win32_NetworkAdapterConfiguration
- Win32_NetworkAdapterSetting

You have three choices. You could guess which one you need, but this could be frustrating and delay solving the problem. A second option is to use MSDN to look up the description of the class. This will give the correct result, but it will still take time. The third, and best, choice is to display the description of each class:

```
Get-WmiObject -List Win32*networkadapter* |
foreach {
  "`n$($_.Name)"
  ((Get-WmiObject -List $($_.Name) -Amended).Qualifiers |
  where {$_.Name -eq "Description"}).Value
}
```

You start by using Get-WmiObject to fetch a list of the WMI classes that are related to network adapters. This output is piped into a ForEach-Object cmdlet. The name of the class is displayed by putting it into a string on a line by itself. The new-line character (`n) forces the output of at least one blank line between data sets.

You reuse the class name in Get-WmiObject with the -Amended parameter to access the qualifiers. A Where-Object filter only allows the description qualifier through, and you only display the text of the description.

PowerShell treats the contents of the parentheses, (), as an object, so you can select the qualifiers and the description with minimal code. As an experiment, try building up the code in the foreach cmdlet one section at a time to see how the parentheses control the output. That's how I created it in the first place!

WMI has a structure. The WMI classes are created from providers and are organized in namespaces. Each namespace has a number of system classes that are always present, as well as WMI classes representing physical objects such as disks or logical objects such as processes. WMI objects are the instances of WMI classes present on a particular machine. The WMI objects have visible properties and methods, and sometimes a further set of invisible properties, and you need to explore them to get the most benefit from using WMI. As you do, you'll learn a little more about Get-Member.

3.2 *Methods and properties*

In chapter 2, you saw that Get-Member allows you to discover things about your PowerShell objects. This includes the available properties (the data describing and defining objects, such as the drive letter and size of a disk) and methods (which enable you to do things such as stop a process or format a disk).

All classes have a number of system properties (prefixed with a double underscore, __). A class also has a key property, which is the property that differentiates the instances of the class; for example, you can have multiple instances of Notepad open, each of which has its own unique Handle property. Handle is the key property for the Win32_Process class.

All Windows systems have processes, so they make ideal candidates for investigating WMI methods and properties. We'll start with methods.

3.2.1 *Methods*

If you want to work with processes using WMI, a quick look in the cimv2\root namespace will show that you want to use the Win32_Process class:

```
Get-WmiObject -List *process*
```

There are a large number of processes running on your system, so let's focus on the first one:

```
Get-WmiObject -Class Win32_Process |
select -First 1 | Get-Member
```

If you look at the help file of Get-Member, you'll find a parameter called -View.

```
PS> Get-Help Get-Member -Parameter View
```

This will produce the following output:

```
-View <PSMemberViewTypes>
    Gets only particular types of members (properties and methods). Specify
    one or more of the values. The default is "Adapted, Extended".

    Valid values are:
    -- Base:  Gets only the original properties and methods of the .NET
       Framework object (without extension or adaptation).
    -- Adapted:  Gets only the properties and methods defined in the
       Windows PowerShell extended type system.
    -- Extended: Gets only the properties and methods that were added in
       the Types.ps1xml files or by using the Add-Member cmdlet.
```

```
    -- All: Gets the members in the Base, Adapted, and Extended views.

  The View parameter determines the members retrieved, not just the display
    of those members.

  To get particular member types, such as script properties, use the
    MemberType parameter. If you use the MemberType and View parameters in
    the same command, Get-Member gets the members that belong to both sets.
    If you use the Static and View parameters in the same command, the View
    parameter is ignored.
```

The base option is equivalent to using psbase, which was mentioned back in chapter 2.

The best way to start examining the structure of the Win32_Process object is by looking at all of the methods and properties available:

```
Get-WmiObject -Class Win32_Process |
select -First 1 | Get-Member -View all
```

The methods available through this view are displayed in the Base column of table 3.3. I performed a similar exercise for the adapted and extended views to complete the table. There are no properties or methods in the extended view, so that column wasn't included in table 3.3.

Table 3.3 Win32_Process **methods**

Method	Base	Adapted
AttachDebugger		Y
Clone	Y	
CompareTo	Y	
CopyTo	Y	
CreateObjRef	Y	
Delete	Y	
Dispose	Y	
Equals	Y	
Get	Y	
GetHashCode	Y	
GetLifetimeService	Y	
GetMethodParameters	Y	
GetOwner		Y
GetOwnerSid		Y
GetPropertyQualifierValue	Y	
GetPropertyValue	Y	

Table 3.3 `Win32_Process` **methods** *(continued)*

Method	Base	Adapted
GetQualifierValue	Y	
GetRelated	Y	
GetRelationships	Y	
GetText	Y	
GetType	Y	
InitializeLifetimeService	Y	
InvokeMethod	Y	
Put	Y	
SetPriority		Y
SetPropertyQualifierValue	Y	
SetPropertyValue	Y	
SetQualifierValue	Y	
Terminate		Y
ToString	Y	

The relationship between an object's members is illustrated in figure 3.3.

If an object doesn't appear to have a method that you think it should, I recommend using either the psbase option or the -View parameter on Get-Member to investigate the base object. What appears when you do this can be very illuminating. The PowerShell-generated wrapper around the base .NET objects may be useful when

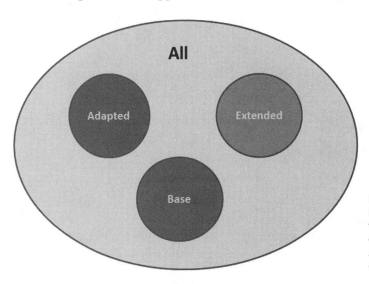

Figure 3.3   Relationships between the different views of a PowerShell object, showing that the All view is the sum of the other views

functionality is added, but it can become awkward when functionality is apparently removed! The same advice applies to properties—check the base object if you can't see what you think should be present.

One additional issue arises when you're investigating properties, and that's the PowerShell extensible type system. This is covered in detail in chapter 4, but for now we need to consider its impact on displaying WMI properties.

3.2.2 *Class properties*

Many newcomers are confused when they start trying to use WMI in PowerShell because they think they aren't getting all of the data they should. Consider the `Win32_OperatingSystem` class. When you request the class, you get the following information:

```
PS> Get-WmiObject -Class Win32_OperatingSystem

SystemDirectory : C:\Windows\system32
Organization    :
BuildNumber     : 7600
RegisteredUser  : Richard
SerialNumber    : 00426-065-1155216-86852
Version         : 6.1.7600
```

At this point, you might think "Is that all? Not worth bothering about!" The default display format has struck again. It's a simple matter to produce the full set of properties, neatly formatted in a list of property names and values.

```
Get-WmiObject -Class Win32_OperatingSystem | Format-List *
```

As an experiment, try producing a formatted list of all properties and their values in another scripting language. It's a frustrating exercise because of the many lines of code that have to be written just to format the output. In PowerShell you can use `Format-List *` to display all properties, as in the previous example, and

---

Format types

If you look in the PowerShell install folder, you'll see a number of files named *.format.ps1xml. These are the type files that control the default display for a significant number of the objects that the PowerShell cmdlets produce. The list of files can be found as follows:

```
Get-ChildItem -Path $pshome -filter *.format.ps1xml
```

There is some information about format types available through the PowerShell help system. Look up these cmdlets:

- `Get-FormatData`
- `Export-FormatData`
- `Update-FormatData`

And take a look at this file: about_format.ps1xml.

Reading this information before you get to chapter 4 will be good preparation.

Select-Object can be used to reduce the properties if further processing will be performed on the pipeline. Calculated fields can be used to look up numeric code values or convert sizes and dates to more readable formats.

Display errors

One issue to be aware of is that making a number of calls to Get-WmiObject in the same script and then attempting to format the results of each call individually can produce the following display error.

```
out-lineoutput : The object of type
 "Microsoft.PowerShell.Commands.Internal.Format.FormatStartData"
is not valid or not in the correct sequence. This is likely
caused by a user-specified "format-list" command which is
conflicting with the default formatting.
  + CategoryInfo          : InvalidData: (:) [out-lineoutput],
InvalidOperationException
  + FullyQualifiedErrorId : ConsoleLineOutputOutOfSequencePacket,
    Microsoft.PowerShell.Commands.OutLineOutputCommand
```

As it states, this error is due to the conflict between the coded display parameters and the default parameters. I have managed to overcome this by creating a variable that holds the output and then displaying that information, or by creating a new object to hold the required output data and using that for display purposes. You'll see these techniques in later chapters.

When you display the full set of an object's properties, you also get to see the system properties.

3.2.3   *System properties*

In section 3.1.2 (on namespaces), you saw that there are a number of system classes in each namespace. Each class has a number of system properties whose names start with a double underscore: __. The values for the system properties can be viewed separately using a format statement to restrict the output. This is illustrated in figure 3.4.

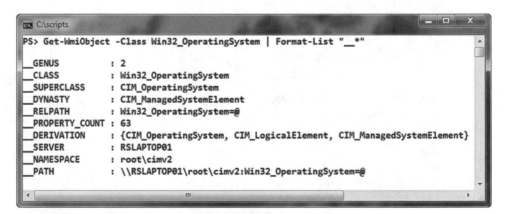

Figure 3.4   Viewing the system properties of a WMI class

The __PATH and __SERVER properties are probably the most useful, and you'll see them in later chapters. If you want to avoid displaying the system properties, they can also be filtered out:

```
Get-WmiObject -Class Win32_OperatingSystem |
select -ExcludeProperty __* -Property *
```

These system properties don't really add much, but you can't do anything about them. Unless you want to display all properties without the system properties, the best practice is to simply choose the properties you require.

One final thing you'll need to do with properties is discover which property functions as the key for a class.

3.2.4 Key properties

The key property is the property you need to supply a value for when you create a class using the [wmi] type accelerator (which you'll meet in section 3.4.2). If you don't know which property acts as a key for the class, you can't create an instance of that class.

You've seen that classes have qualifiers and, following the hierarchical nature of WMI, so do properties. The property that functions as the key can be discovered using the following code, which is adapted from a posting by Jeffrey Snover on the Power-Shell team blog.

Listing 3.4   Discover the key property of a WMI class

```
function get-key {
[CmdletBinding()]
param (
    [string]
    [ValidateNotNullOrEmpty()]
    $class
)
  $t = [WMIClass]$class
  $t.properties |
  select @{Name="PName";Expression={$_.name}} -ExpandProperty Qualifiers |
  where {$_.Name -eq "key"} |
  foreach {"The key for the $class class is $($_.Pname)"}
}
```

> **NOTE** The original script arose because an MVP reported an error using the type accelerators. It's in the "WMI Object Identifiers and Keys" article on the PowerShell blog and can be found at http://mng.bz/0JI2. The post explains why a key is required when creating an instance of a WMI class.

This function takes a single parameter—the name of the class. The ValidateNotNull-OrEmpty validation method is used to ensure that a value is passed into the function. This is then used to create an object representing that WMI class.

The properties are piped into a Select-Object cmdlet, where you create a calculated field for the name of the property and expand its qualifiers. Where-Object is used to filter out all of the properties except the key. The name of the property that functions as the key is written out using string substitution to create the output.

PowerShell can help you discover the information you need to successfully work with WMI classes. You may find it helpful to have a function that combines the code from this section to fully document a WMI class. I've included this combined code in the script download package as the `get-wmiclass` function.

You now know how to discover the properties and methods of WMI classes. It's time to move on and look at ways to document the specific WMI features on your system.

3.3 Documenting WMI

You've seen a number of pieces of the puzzle for documenting WMI in previous sections. In the following listing, they're put together to produce a script that will document WMI down to the class level. This is useful at this point in the chapter because the next sections deal with using the WMI functionality within PowerShell.

Listing 3.5 Document WMI on a machine

```
function main {
  "root"
  get-namespace "root"
}

function get-namespace {
param ([string]$name)
    Get-WmiObject -Namespace $name -Class "__NAMESPACE" |
    foreach {
        $ns = "$name\" + $_.Name
       "`nNameSpace: $ns"
        get-providerclass $ns
        get-namespace $ns
    }
}

function get-providerclass {
param ([string]$namespace)
 Get-WmiObject -Namespace $namespace -Class __Win32Provider |
 foreach {
  $provider = $_.Name
  "Provider: $provider"

  $refs = Get-WmiObject -Namespace $namespace -Query "REFERENCES OF
    {__Win32Provider.Name='$provider'}"

  foreach ($ref in $refs) {

    $type = $ref.__CLASS
    " Registration: $type"

    switch ($type) {

      "__PropertyProviderRegistration" {
            " does not have classes"
            break
      }
```

① **Main control function**

② **Namespace iteration**

③ **Provider iteration**

④ **Provider references**

⑤ **Provider types**

```
    "__ClassProviderRegistration" {
          "  only provides class definitions"
          break
    }

    "__EventConsumerProviderRegistration" {
          "  uses these classes"
          "    $($ref.ConsumerClassNames)"
          break
    }

    "__EventProviderRegistration" {
          "  queries these classes:"
          foreach ($query in $ref.EventQueryList) {
            $a = $query -split " "
            "    $($a[($a.length-1)])"
          }
          break
    }

    default {
            "  supplies these classes:"
            Get-WmiObject -Namespace $namespace -List -Amended |
            foreach {
              if ($_.Qualifiers["provider"].Value -eq "$provider"){
                "    $($_.Name)"
              }
            } # class list
            break
    }
  } #switch
 } # refs
} # provider loop
}
main
```

This code can be run on a system to determine the namespaces, providers, and classes available on the machine. The information produced by this script is a valuable resource for documenting your system. The script can also be used to test for problems with WMI—if it completes, there are no obvious problems.

The script starts on the very last line, where you call the controlling function, main ❶. This defines your starting point as the root namespace, and it calls get-namespace ❷. The work of documenting WMI starts here, as you recursively iterate through the namespaces installed on the system.

As each namespace is discovered you list out its name and call the get-providerclass function ❸. The instances of the Win32_Provider class for that namespace are returned, and for each of them you determine the references ❹. You can iterate through the references, determine the type of provider, and depending on the provider type ❺, display some or all of the following:

- Event classes that are used
- Event classes that are queried
- Classes that are supplied

I have commented the closing brace (}) of the major loops to aid understanding of the structure of the script.

This script produces over 2,550 lines of output on my Windows 7 system, which makes it a bit unwieldy to use when outputting to screen! One alternative is to send the output to a text file (I saved the listing to a script called `Get-WmiList`):

```
./Get-WmiList | Out-File wmidoc.txt
```

The text file can then be searched using `Select-String` or an editor to find the relevant information.

We've covered a lot of ground and delved into a lot of background material on WMI. In the course of this investigation, we've looked at how to use `Get-WmiObject`. But there are other PowerShell cmdlets for working with WMI that we need to consider.

3.4   *WMI cmdlets and accelerators*

PowerShell v1 provided the `Get-WmiObject` cmdlet—this was read-only access to WMI, though it could also be used to create an object from which you could call methods. This one cmdlet enabled you to work with WMI easily, compared to previous scripting languages. PowerShell v1 also offered some type accelerators for working with WMI through the .NET classes. Type accelerators are shortcuts for accessing .NET classes.

The delivery of PowerShell v2 expanded the list of cmdlets, as well as giving `Get-WmiObject` additional functionality. You now have additional cmdlets for invoking WMI methods, setting WMI property values, and removing WMI objects entirely.

> **TIP**   The CIM cmdlets available in PowerShell v3 are described in chapter 19.

The type accelerators are still available and provide an easier route to creating WMI classes and searching for WMI instances, if you have to resort to .NET code. But it's generally easier to work with the PowerShell cmdlets than the accelerators.

3.4.1   *Cmdlets*

You have a grand total of four cmdlets for working with WMI objects:

- `Get-WmiObject`
- `Set-WmiInstance`
- `Invoke-WmiMethod`
- `Remove-WmiObject`

A fifth cmdlet deals with WMI events, but we'll deal with that in section 3.7. `Get-WmiObject` is the one you'll be working with most, so we'll start there.

GET-WMIOBJECT
You've used `Get-WmiObject` a number of times already. Its help file synopsis states that it "Gets instances of Windows Management Instrumentation (WMI) classes or information about the available classes." It's the PowerShell method of discovery for WMI.

This cmdlet is normally used to define the namespace and class you want to work with. You can also supply credentials, authentication, and impersonation levels. You can use the cmdlet interactively or configure it to run asynchronously as a PowerShell job by using the `-AsJob` parameter. I'll explain these features as we need them.

SET-WMIINSTANCE

This cmdlet "Creates or updates an instance of an existing Windows Management Instrumentation (WMI) class." You'll mainly use this to modify existing instances of WMI objects.

> **WARNING** My experience with `Set-WmiInstance` suggests that using this cmdlet to create new WMI instances is of limited practical use. I don't recommend using `Set-WmiInstance` for anything but modifying the properties of existing objects.

WMI objects tend to have a long list of properties. Some properties are read-only, which means you can't change them. The property you're interested in should be checked to ensure that it can be modified before you attempt to change it. You can skip this step, but be prepared for the error messages when you hit a property that can't be changed.

You've seen that you can view an object's properties using `Get-Member`:

```
Get-WmiObject -Class Win32_NTEventLogFile `
-Filter "LogFileName='Scripts'" | Get-Member
```

You can view the property information, such as the maximum file size, of your log file:

```
MaxFileSize        Property  System.UInt32 MaxFileSize {get;set;}
```

The fact that it's modifiable is indicated by the presence of "set" in the curly braces after the data type: `{get;set;}`.

> **TIP** I've used an event log called Scripts in these examples to ensure that a mistake doesn't adversely affect your system. If you want to create an event log to experiment with, use the following syntax and change the source and log names as required: `New-EventLog -Source MyNewSource -LogName MyNew-Log`. This is discussed in more detail in chapter 15.

One thing this doesn't tell you is how to present the data. For example, a file size could be presented in bytes, KB, MB, or even GB. The two options are to guess from looking at the current setting or to check the documentation. The first is more exciting, but the second gets the job done faster. When you want to change the maximum file size of an event log, you need to present the size in bytes:

```
$log = Get-WmiObject -Class Win32_NTEventLogFile `
-Filter "LogFileName='Scripts'"

Set-WmiInstance -InputObject $log `
 -Arguments @{MaxFileSize=31457280}
```

You use `Get-WmiObject` to create an object representing the log file you're interested in (the Scripts file again, in this example). This object is used as input to `Set-WmiInstance`. The property or properties that you want to set are given as a hash table. The information could also be presented as follows:

```
-Arguments @{MaxFileSize=(30*1MB)}.
```

Note that `30*1MB` resolves to `31457280`, which is what was used in the preceding example. It has to be presented in this format, rather than as `30MB`, to ensure that the class accepts the value as bytes.

Objects have both properties and methods. You've seen how to manipulate WMI properties. Now let's look at how you can work with methods.

INVOKE-WMIMETHOD

PowerShell v2 supplies a brand new cmdlet especially for working with WMI methods. One of the tasks you'll need to do on a periodic basis is back up your event logs. Let's return to the Scripts log file and see how you can use methods.

`Get-WmiObject` is used to create a variable for the WMI object:

```
$log = Get-WmiObject -Class Win32_NTEventLogFile `
 -Filter "LogFileName='Scripts'"
```

`Get-Member` is then used to determine the methods on this object:

```
$log | Get-Member -MemberType method
```

The `-MemberType` parameter can take a number of options, one of which lists only the methods available on the object.

One of the methods is `BackUpEventLog`. A look at the documentation indicates that you only need to provide the name and path to the file that will be used as a target for your backup:

```
Invoke-WmiMethod -InputObject $log -Name BackupEventlog `
 -ArgumentList "c:\test\paw3.evt"
```

> **TIP** Remember to use PowerShell with elevated privileges or these commands will fail.

With `Invoke-WmiMethod`, you use the variable you've already created as the `InputObject`. The name of the method is supplied, and the file to be used is given as the argument.

It's also possible to do this in one pass using the pipeline:

```
Get-WmiObject -Class Win32_NTEventLogFile `
 -Filter "LogFileName='Scripts'" |
Invoke-WmiMethod -Name BackupEventlog `
 -ArgumentList "c:\test\paw4.evt"
```

This time you don't need to specify the object you're using because the pipeline manages that aspect of the processing. Note that I've changed the filename in this example. That's because the method will fail if the file already exists. In a production script, you'd use `Test-Path` to determine whether the file exists and throw an exception to stop processing if it did.

The three cmdlets we've looked at so far enable you to get information about WMI objects and work with the methods and properties. We'll look at how you can create new WMI objects in a while, but first we need to consider what happens when a WMI object is no longer required.

REMOVE-WMIOBJECT

Remove-WmiObject is a very easy cmdlet to understand. It removes WMI objects from your system. Be careful with it, though, as deleting the wrong objects could be a career-threatening action. There are many WMI objects, such as the computer system or disk drives, that it doesn't make sense to remove!

I have a very simple recommendation for working with Remove-WmiObject: use Get-WmiObject first. This is best illustrated with an example. Assume you have a process running on your machine (such as Notepad) that's misbehaving, and you need to shut it down. The first thing you have to do is identify the exact process, and this is best achieved with Get-WmiObject:

```
Get-WmiObject -Class Win32_Process |
where {$_.Name -like "Notepad*"}
```

A Where-Object filter is used to identify the exact process. Then, the simple way to delete the process is to pipe the resultant Win32_Process object into Remove-WmiObject:

```
Get-WmiObject -Class Win32_Process |
where {$_.Name -like "Notepad*"} |
Remove-WmiObject
```

Your misbehaving process is gone, and your system can settle back to its normal state. This way you've removed the process but you've put a check on the way you do it to ensure that you remove the correct process.

> **NOTE** This approach removes all instances of the process, in this example Notepad, from your system. When you're trying to remove a misbehaving process, this is exactly what you need. I once had to remove many (30+) instances of a cscript process from a system, and this technique would have saved me a lot of work.

Cmdlets provide the best way of working with WMI objects, but sometimes you need to get a bit closer to the underlying .NET code.

3.4.2 *Type accelerators*

In section 2.4 you saw how to use the New-Object cmdlet to create .NET objects. PowerShell also has *type accelerators*, which are shortcuts for creating .NET objects directly. WMI has three type accelerators, and they're listed in table 3.4 together with the .NET class they represent.

My experience is that the cmdlets are used much more than the accelerators. This is due to the additional WMI functionality introduced in PowerShell v2. The accelerators were more important in PowerShell v1 than they are now, but there are still a few

Table 3.4   WMI type accelerators

Accelerator	.NET type
Wmisearcher	System.Management.ManagementObjectSearcher
Wmiclass	System.Management.ManagementClass
Wmi	System.Management.ManagementObject

occasions when they come in handy. One task you'll always be performing is searching for information that WMI can make available.

[WMISEARCHER]

Get-WmiObject is used for retrieving WMI-based data. You've seen WQL queries used in the -Filter parameter and the -Query parameter. Section 3.5 will dive deeper into WQL, but you can get a taste of simple WQL queries by looking at the [wmisearcher] type accelerator.

These two PowerShell statements produce identical results:

```
Get-WmiObject -Class Win32_Process -Filter "Name='powershell.exe'"

Get-WmiObject `
-Query "SELECT * FROM Win32_Process WHERE Name='powershell.exe'"
```

In both cases, you're finding the WMI object that's the PowerShell process. You can also perform this using [wmisearcher]:

```
$query = [wmisearcher]
➥ "SELECT * FROM Win32_Process WHERE Name='powershell.exe'"
$query.Get()
```

All of these techniques will return the same information. The question now becomes which method to use. I use Get-WmiObject nearly 100 percent of the time. It's quicker to type and has the advantage of returning an object you can work with, rather than just the data. It's also easier to use against remote machines.

You've seen an accelerator for finding WMI information, but sometimes you'll need to create a WMI object. This can be done with the [wmiclass] accelerator.

[WMICLASS]

The [wmiclass] accelerator provides a shortcut for creating new instances of WMI classes. There isn't any New-WmiObject cmdlet or an easy way to work with WMI objects through New-Object. In PowerShell v1, the usual way to create a new WMI object was to use [wmiclass]. Invoke-WmiMethod has, at least partially, taken over this task in PowerShell v2.

Using the accelerator is straightforward:

```
$p = [wmiclass]'Win32_Process'
$p.Create("calc.exe")
```

TIP   If you're still using PowerShell v1, you'll need to change the second line of the preceding example to $p.psbase.Create("calc.exe").

There is one final accelerator to consider.

[WMI]

Table 3.4 shows that [wmi] works with the same .NET class as Get-WmiObject. When you're using the cmdlet, you can perform a task such as this:

```
Get-WmiObject -Class Win32_Process -Filter "Name='calc.exe'"
```

If you want to use the accelerator, you might try this:

```
[wmi]"root\cimv2:Win32_Process.Name='calc.exe'"
```

This will generate an error, because when using this accelerator you need to use the property that functions as the key for the class. The way to discover the key was covered in listing 3.4. Your code becomes

```
[wmi]"root\cimv2:Win32_Process.Handle='4456'"
```

This involves additional steps, and effort, to return the same information that you can get from the cmdlet. As with the [wmisearcher] accelerator, I recommend using the Get-WmiObject cmdlet rather than the accelerator.

Many of the WMI examples in this chapter have involved the use of a filter of some kind that has been created using WQL. You need to learn how WQL works in order to use the technology to its maximum potential.

3.5 Using WQL

You've seen WMI queries performed in a number of the examples in this chapter. If you thought that the syntax looked like SQL, you'd be correct. You've been using WMI Query Language (WQL). It's a subset of SQL that supplies only the functionality you need for working with the WMI repository. That means you're restricted to running simple SELECT statements without JOINs or any of the other complications you can expect in SQL.

> **TIP** It's important to note that the other SQL options—DELETE, UPDATE, and REPLACE—don't exist in WQL either.

You have a number of options available in the way you use WQL with PowerShell. These options are best explained with reference to the WQL keywords. A number of keywords are only used when working with WMI associations and references—those particular keywords will be discussed in section 3.6.

3.5.1 Keywords

WQL, like PowerShell, has a number of keywords that you need to understand if you're to use it properly. This is the basic structure of a WQL query:

```
SELECT <property list>
FROM <WMI class name>
WHERE <one or more conditions>
```

> **NOTE** I have deliberately used uppercase for the WQL keywords in this section for emphasis. WQL keywords aren't case sensitive.

There are two ways you can use WQL in PowerShell. The first follows the tradition established by VBScript of running a full query:

```
Get-WmiObject `
-Query "SELECT * FROM Win32_Process WHERE Name='PowerShell.exe'"
```

This runs a query that will select all of the data (properties) from a `Win32_Process` instance where the name of the process is `PowerShell.exe`. In WQL you can only specify a single class to query at a time. This restriction also applies to `Get-WmiObject` in that the `-Class` parameter only accepts a single class at a time.

You could restrict the properties returned by your query. For instance, the following query only returns the three properties you specify in the WQL statement:

```
Get-WmiObject -Query "SELECT Name, Threadcount, UserModetime FROM
    Win32_Process WHERE Name='PowerShell.exe'"
```

> **TIP**   If you need to work with an object that has a reduced property set, try using this approach: `Get-WmiObject -Class Win32_Process -Filter "Name= 'PowerShell.exe'" -Property Name, Threadcount, UserModetime`. It produces an object that has the system properties and the ones you defined only. This approach rarely seems to be adopted in practice for some unknown reason.

The second method of using WQL is to use the `-Filter` parameter rather than the `-Query` parameter:

```
Get-WmiObject -Class Win32_Process -Filter "Name='PowerShell.exe'"
```

The preceding code is similar to running the full query except that you select the class with the `-Class` parameter, and the `-Filter` parameter uses the part of the query that follows the `WHERE` keyword.

This approach can also restrict the properties you return:

```
Get-WmiObject -Class Win32_Process `
 -Filter "Name='PowerShell.exe'" |
Format-List Name, Threadcount, UserModetime
```

The advantage of this method is that the system properties aren't returned.

Is one approach better than the other? I tend to use a filter rather than a query because I find it easier to read and it involves less typing. I think it's also more flexible because I can easily change the properties selected for display without risking the syntax of the query.

Our queries so far have been based on simple `SELECT` statements, but WQL also enables us to perform other processing as part of the query.

3.5.2   *Operators*

There are three groups of WQL operators to consider:

- Logical operators which define how statements are combined
- Comparison operators which perform matching operations
- Wildcards which enable you to perform matching on a subset of data

The WQL queries you've seen so far have only had a single condition in the WHERE clause. That's a bit limiting, but there is a way to remove this limitation.

LOGICAL OPERATORS

The logical operators are used to combine statements. The logical operators available in WQL are detailed in table 3.5.

Table 3.5 WQL logical operators

Operator	Meaning
AND	Combines two expressions and returns TRUE if both expressions are TRUE
OR	Combines two expressions and returns TRUE if one expression is TRUE
TRUE	Boolean operator that evaluates to -1
FALSE	Boolean operator that evaluates to 0

The use of the first two operators in the table can be demonstrated as follows. I started two instances of PowerShell so that I had a choice of targets:

```
Get-WmiObject -Query "SELECT *
    FROM Win32_Process
    WHERE Name='PowerShell.exe'
    AND Handle='6036'"
```

In this example, the AND operator is used to link the two comparisons. Both comparison expressions must evaluate to TRUE for this query to work. On your system, the value of the Handle property will be different.

> **WARNING** It isn't possible to refer to a property name on both sides of the comparison operator in a WHERE clause. You'll receive an error if you try it.

An alternative way of using the criteria is to use an OR statement to link the two expressions:

```
Get-WmiObject -Query "SELECT *
    FROM Win32_Process
    WHERE Handle='6036'
    OR Name='PowerShell.exe'"
```

The Handle property is checked first, and if that evaluates to TRUE, your data is retrieved. If it evaluates to FALSE, the second expression is checked. These operators can also be used in a Get-WmiObject Filter statement.

The comparisons you've performed so far have involved checking equality. Other comparisons are also available.

COMPARISON OPERATORS

In this section, we'll consider numerical comparisons and how you can determine whether a property has a NULL value. The numerical comparison operators are listed in table 3.6.

Operator	Meaning
=	Equal to
<	Less than
>	Greater than
<=	Less than or equal to
>=	Greater than or equal to
!= or <>	Not equal to

Table 3.6   WMI comparison operators

You may recall the PowerShell comparison operators we discussed in chapter 2: -eq, -lt, -gt, -le, -ge, -neq. Using a PowerShell operator instead of the WMI operator in a WQL query will cause syntax errors. WMI is very unforgiving of syntax errors in WQL queries, so the script will fail rather than run and cause a problem with your systems.

These comparison operators can be used in a Query or Filter statement, and the syntax is similar for all of them. Starting with the -Query parameter, you can write this code:

```
Get-WmiObject -Query
➥ "SELECT Name, HandleCount FROM Win32_Process WHERE
HandleCount>=550" |
Format-Table Name, HandleCount -AutoSize
```

Alternatively, you can use a -Filter parameter as follows:

```
Get-WmiObject -Class Win32_Process -Filter "HandleCount>=550" |
 Format-Table Name, HandleCount -AutoSize
```

In the two preceding examples, you're discovering all of the processes that have more than 550 handles. In the first example, a full WQL query is used to return the data, whereas the second uses the -Filter parameter. Format-Table is used with the property names in both cases to screen out the system classes.

Using a full query allows you to trim down the amount of data you're dealing with as soon as possible. This is a good technique when accessing remote machines because it reduces network traffic.

You can, of course, perform the same filtering task in PowerShell:

```
Get-WmiObject -Class Win32_Process |
Where {$_.HandleCount -ge 550} |
Format-Table Name, HandleCount -AutoSize
```

Notice the difference in the comparison operator. They do the same job, but you need to write them differently. It's a pain, but you'll have to live with it because the technologies come from two separate teams.

A property may sometimes have a value of NULL. This doesn't mean that it's zero or that a string is empty. It's best thought of as meaning that a value hasn't been set. There are two comparison operators for working with NULL values. Try these two queries with and without a CD in the drive to really see the difference. If you can work out the results before running the query, you'll have this down solid:

```
Get-WmiObject -Query "SELECT *
➥ FROM Win32_CDRomDrive
➥ WHERE VolumeName IS NULL"

Get-WmiObject -Query "SELECT *
➥ FROM Win32_CDRomDrive
➥ WHERE Drive IS NOT NULL"
```

The first query returns all instances of the CD drive that don't have a volume name set. The second query returns instances of the CD drive that have a drive letter set.

In the examples of using WQL so far, you've used the full value of the property. Now let's consider the case where you aren't quite sure what the value should be.

WILDCARDS

Wildcards enable you to specify only part of the value you want to compare against. You need to use the LIKE operator and build expressions using wildcards.

> **TIP** You may see statements on the internet claiming that WMI can't use wildcards. This is incorrect. What those authors have done is tried to use the PowerShell wildcards and failed.

The WQL and PowerShell wildcard equivalents are given in table 3.7 for comparison purposes. Technically, the last two options in the table are beginning to get into regular expressions, but I'll deal with them here for completeness.

Table 3.7 Comparison of WQL and PowerShell wildcard characters

WQL	Meaning	PowerShell
_	Any single character	?
%	Zero or more characters	*
[a=c] [abc]	Any one character in the set or range	[]
[^a=c] [^abc]	Any one character *not* in the set or range	use -notmach operator or [^]

The expressions in table 3.7 can be used in a WMI query or with a -Filter parameter:

```
Get-WmiObject -Class Win32_Process -Filter "Name LIKE 'po%'"
```

In the preceding statement, all processes whose names start with the letters *po* will be returned. This is case insensitive, so PowerShell.exe will be returned. The same result could be obtained by using Where-Object:

```
Get-WmiObject -Class Win32_Process | where {$_.Name -like 'PO*'}
```

The matching can be made more sophisticated. For instance, you can test for different patterns of the name:

```
Get-WmiObject -Class Win32_Process -Filter "Name LIKE 'P_W%'"
Get-WmiObject -Class Win32_Process | where {$_.Name -like 'P?W*'}
```

In both of these cases, you're looking for a name that starts with *p*, that has any second character, and that has *w* as the third character.

If you want to get very sophisticated in your testing, you can start to match on groups of letters:

```
Get-WmiObject -Class Win32_Process `
-Filter "Name LIKE '%[sh][sh]%'" |
select name

Get-WmiObject -Class Win32_Process |
where {$_.Name -match '.[sh][sh].'} | select name
```

In this case, you're looking for processes that have some combination of the letters *s* and *h* somewhere together in their name.

It would be possible to fill the chapter with examples of using these expressions. I recommend experimenting with these options to get a good understanding of how they work. This is one area where some testing goes a long way to help understanding.

We've finished looking at using WQL for simple querying of data, but there are a few more WQL-related topics that we need to consider regarding the relationships between WMI classes—references and associators.

3.6   *WMI references and associators*

WMI classes supply information about a single discrete item in your system. Sometimes this granularity seems to have been taken too far, such as in the classes dealing with network adapters:

```
Get-WmiObject -List *Win32_NetworkAdapter*
```

This will return three results:

- `Win32_NetworkAdapter`
- `Win32_NetworkAdapterConfiguration`
- `Win32_NetworkAdapterSetting`

You need to understand the relationships between these classes, and you need to know how to use the relationships to make your work easier. This will involve looking at WMI references and WMI associators.

To investigate the relationship between the WMI classes, you need a starting point. We're using the network adapters as an example, so the obvious starting point is the physical adapter:

```
Get-WmiObject -Class Win32_NetworkAdapter |
where {$_.NetEnabled} | select name, deviceid
```

You're only interested in those adapters that are enabled. The name of the adapter and the `deviceid` are selected. The name is obvious, but why the `deviceid`? The particular adapter you're investigating needs to be identified in such a way that it can be used to determine relationships with other classes. There are many possible identifiers, but the property that acts as the key for the class is a good place to start; you can find the key by using listing 3.4. It's possible to determine relationships using the WMI documentation, but that takes longer.

You'll work with a single adapter, as that keeps the examples simple. You can start by looking at the references of the adapter. I chose the wireless adapter in my development system, based on the results of the previous code snippet:

```
Get-WmiObject `
 -Query "REFERENCES OF {Win32_NetworkAdapter.DeviceId='11'}"
```

Notice the use of { } to define the WMI instance for which you need the references.

A number of WMI classes will be returned. They're classes that show the links between two other classes. The links are described by a pair of properties. Unfortunately the names of the properties can vary. These are some common pairs of names:

- `SameElement, SystemElement`
- `GroupComponent, PartComponent`
- `Element, Setting`
- `Antecedent, Dependent`

In some classes, a third property is available, called `device`.

The links can be better displayed by using the `__PATH` system property of each class:

```
Get-WmiObject `
 -Query "REFERENCES OF {Win32_NetworkAdapter.DeviceId='11'}" |
foreach {
 ""
 $_.__CLASS
 $($_.__PATH -split ",")
}
```

This will show the class and the instance that links to your particular adapter. If you only want to see the classes involved, you can simplify the code by using the `ClassDefsOnly` keyword:

```
Get-WmiObject -Query "REFERENCES OF
 ➥ {Win32_NetworkAdapter.DeviceId='11'}
 ➥ WHERE ClassDefsOnly" |
Format-Table Name, Properties -AutoSize

Name                            Properties
----                            ----------
Win32_PnPDevice                 {SameElement, SystemElement}
Win32_NetworkAdapterSetting     {Element, Setting}
Win32_SystemDevices             {GroupComponent, PartComponent}
Win32_AllocatedResource         {Antecedent, Dependent}
Win32_ProtocolBinding           {Antecedent, Dependent, Device}
```

An additional benefit of starting with the classes is that you can see the properties involved in the links. The information that's returned can be controlled by using the other keywords that are available for use with references and associators. They're described in table 3.8.

Table 3.8   Keywords for references and associators queries

Keyword	Meaning	References	Associators
ClassDefsOnly	Returns class definition instead of class instances	Y	Y
RequiredQualifier	Specifies a qualifier that returned classes must meet	Y	Y
ResultClass	Restricts results to one class	Y	
AssocClass	Restricts association to a single class		Y
RequiredAssocQualifier	Only returns instances that are linked through a class with a specific qualifier		Y

A reference supplies the linking, or associating, WMI classes. In many cases, it's more productive to jump straight to the endpoint of the link. This is where you'll find the information you need. You can find the endpoints by using ASSOCIATORS OF instead of REFERENCES OF.

You can start with the associated classes:

```
Get-WmiObject -Query "ASSOCIATORS OF
{Win32_NetworkAdapter.DeviceId='11'} WHERE ClassDefsOnly" |
select Name
```

This supplies a list of WMI classes, one of which is the Win32_NetworkAdapterConfiguration class:

```
Get-WmiObject -Query "ASSOCIATORS OF
 {Win32_NetworkAdapter.DeviceId='11'} WHERE RESULTCLASS =
Win32_NetworkAdapterConfiguration"
```

You now have a method of linking two related classes and ensuring that you can find all of the required information about the system component. You'll see more examples of performing these types of queries in later chapters.

Windows is an event-driven operating system. Everything you do, from pressing a key to working in your applications, causes events to be generated. Many of these events are WMI-based, and you need to be able to utilize this functionality.

3.7   *WMI events*

PowerShell v2 provides access to the Windows event engine through a number of mechanisms:

- WMI
- .NET
- PowerShell engine

The cmdlets that you can use to work with events are outlined in table 3.9.

Table 3.9 Cmdlets for working with events

Cmdlet	Purpose
Get-Event	Gets the events in the event queue
Get-EventSubscriber	Gets the event subscribers in the current session
New-Event	Creates a new event
Register-EngineEvent	Subscribes to events that are generated by the Windows PowerShell engine and by the New-Event cmdlet
Register-ObjectEvent	Subscribes to events that are generated by a Microsoft .NET Framework object
Register-WmiEvent	Subscribes to a Windows Management Instrumentation (WMI) event
Remove-Event	Deletes events from the event queue
Unregister-Event	Cancels an event subscription
Wait-Event	Waits until a particular event is raised before continuing to run

As an example, consider plugging in a USB device. There's a WMI class, Win32_VolumeChangeEvent, that you can use to discover when something changes:

```
$query = "SELECT * from Win32_VolumeChangeEvent WITHIN 5"
Register-WmiEvent -Query $query -SourceIdentifier 'USBEvent'
```

The first part of this query is a standard select from the class. Within 5 means that the class is checked every 5 seconds to determine whether an event has occurred. The event is then registered using USBEvent as an identifier. You can use Get-EventSubscriber to see the subscription.

When you plug in a USB device, the VolumeChangeEvent will be triggered. You can see the results by using Get-Event:

```
$e = Get-Event | select -First 1
```

The drive that was added can be identified using this code:

```
$e.SourceEventArgs.NewEvent
```

A corresponding event is raised when the USB drive is removed.

You can also work with other events, such as a process being started:

```
$process = "calc.exe"
$WMIQuery = "SELECT * FROM __InstanceCreationEvent WITHIN 5 WHERE
 TargetInstance ISA 'Win32_Process' AND TargetInstance.Name =
```

```
'$Process'"
Register-WmiEvent -Query $WMIQuery `
 -SourceIdentifier "Process $Process"
```

This will trigger an event when the Windows calculator is started but not when other processes such as Notepad are started.

This is good, in that you can find out what has happened, but you'll want more. You'll want to be able to perform some action when a particular event is triggered. Suppose you have a process that should only run out of normal business hours. If it starts during business hours, you want to immediately shut it down. You can adapt the last example to accomplish this, as follows.

Listing 3.6   Trigger an action through a WMI event

```
$process = "calc.exe"
$action = {                                                    ◁──┐  Action
  Write-Host "Calculator is running and must be stopped"          │  script
  Get-WmiObject -Class Win32_Process -Filter "Name='$process'" |  ❶  block
  Invoke-WmiMethod -Name Terminate
  Write-Host "Calculator has been stopped"
}                                                              ❷  WMI
$WMIQuery = "SELECT * FROM __InstanceCreationEvent            ◁──  query
WITHIN 5 WHERE TargetInstance ISA 'Win32_Process' AND
TargetInstance.Name = '$Process'"
                                                             ❸  Register
Register-WmiEvent -Query $WMIQuery `                          ◁──┐  event
-SourceIdentifier "Process $Process" -Action $action
```

The script starts by defining the process you want to prevent running. A script block ❶ is created that will perform the processing. You produce a message to say that the process is running, you stop the process using the `Terminate` method of the `Win32_Process` class, and you write out another message to say it has happened.

> **NOTE**   I know I could have used `Stop-Process` to kill the Calculator process, but this is a WMI book after all.

The WMI query to check for the process starting is defined ❷, and the event is registered ❸, adding the `-Action` parameter with the script block as its value. One thing to note is that when the event is registered in this manner, it creates a PowerShell job that runs in the background. The data produced by this job isn't accessible by the `*-Job` cmdlets.

When the Windows calculator is started, the event will trigger and close it down. This is illustrated in figure 3.5. Once you've finished with the event, it should be unregistered.

```
Unregister-Event -SourceIdentifier "Process $Process"
```

The job created by the event can be safely removed at this point. Always unregister the event before deleting the job. Otherwise, you won't be able to remove the event! You'll see further examples of WMI events in the second part of the book.

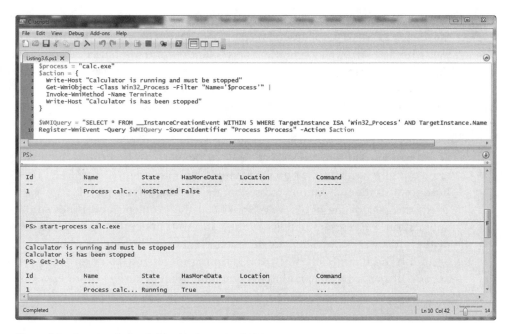

Figure 3.5   Running listing 3.6 in the PowerShell ISE

We've covered a lot of ground in this chapter. It provides the basic information that you'll need to perform the management tasks you'll see in the second part of the book.

3.8   Summary

WMI is one of the most powerful tools available to Windows administrators. It's a misunderstood and underused technology due to the perceived complexity, the lack of documentation, and the difficulty in using it in the past. PowerShell corrects this and brings an ease of use to WMI that should make it the tool of choice for all administrators.

WMI is a standards-based management toolset that's installed by default in modern Windows systems. It supplies a large number of classes that correspond to physical entities in your systems, such as CPU, operating system, or installed application. The classes contained in namespaces are arranged into a logical hierarchy.

PowerShell delivers ease of use through four cmdlets:

- `Get-WmiObject`
- `Set-WmiInstance`
- `Invoke-WmiMethod`
- `Remove-WmiObject`

There are also three type accelerators that are shortcuts for working with the .NET classes PowerShell uses to access WMI data. The most useful of these is `[wmiclass]`, which you can use to create new WMI objects.

WMI information resides in the WMI repository (or database). There's a SQL-like language called WQL for querying the repository. This can be used in a number of ways with `Get-WmiObject`, but it's easiest to understand when used in conjunction with the `-Filter` parameter.

WQL also enables you to work with the links between WMI classes. These are created and maintained automatically by WMI, so all you have to do is tap into the information. An example of this is the link between the network adapter and its configuration.

Windows is an event-driven operating system, and WMI and PowerShell provide access to the event engine so that you can be alerted when things happen. You can also configure an action to be performed when an event is triggered. This starts to head towards the fully automated system we discussed in chapter 1.

In this part of the book, we've looked at the problems and issues you'll solve by automation. We've examined PowerShell and WMI in depth to gain an understanding of the tools you'll be using. In the next chapter, we'll look at some best practices around using PowerShell, WMI, and scripting in general, to ensure that your scripts are as efficient as possible and that you maintain the security of your environment.

Best practices
and optimization

4

This chapter covers

- Finding code samples
- Securing the PowerShell environment
- PowerShell best practices
- WMI best practices

We've had a good look at PowerShell and WMI in the last two chapters. In this chapter, we'll start to examine how you can use them to solve your administrative problems. We're not quite at the point of jumping into lots of scripts, though. That treat is reserved for part 2 of the book, which starts with the next chapter.

As the title suggests, this chapter is about best practices. There are a lot of views on what constitutes best practices, ranging from a loose collection of tips and tricks to a rigid set of commandments that should be followed to the letter. My approach falls somewhere between those two extremes, but closer to the loose collection of ideas. I'll be presenting a collection of techniques that I've used or collected over the last five or six years of using PowerShell (that's going back into the early Power-Shell v1 betas). I'll also present a number of advanced techniques. You can adopt these as and when required; they can be of great benefit in streamlining the production of your PowerShell scripts. The idea is that at the end of the chapter, you'll know how to produce a good script.

> **NOTE** I have a very simple definition of a *good script*. It's a script that works correctly and does the intended job in a reasonable time frame. Sometimes better performance is required, in which case I'll revise the script. It takes 90 percent of the estimated development time to perform 90 percent of the task of creating the best script to do a job. It takes another 90 percent of the time to get that last 10 percent of polish. Spend the time on another script!

The first thing we'll look at in this chapter is security. You'll often need to find sample code on the internet to help you solve your problems. This raises a number of issues:

- Where can you find the code?
- Can you trust the code?
- Which code sample supplies the correct answer?

When you utilize the automation techniques described in this book, there are a number of security concerns related to the code: who can access and run it, and how can you audit that usage. These questions will be answered in the first part of the chapter.

Second, PowerShell has a very wide scope. There are a number of areas where it's possible to script solutions that don't take full advantage of PowerShell's strengths and features. In this chapter, we'll examine a number of areas where this is common, including

- Data input and output (including working with strings)
- Calculated fields, types, and members
- Error handling

You saw in chapter 3 that PowerShell uses format files to determine how the data from PowerShell objects should be displayed by default. This default behavior can be modified to enable better control of the output, and we'll also look at that in this chapter.

Next, it's inevitable that bugs and mistakes will creep into your scripts, and PowerShell v2 provides a number of simple techniques for finding and eliminating bugs. Errors will also occur when you're running your scripts. In some cases, you can ignore them and continue processing your data, but other times the errors could cause significant problems if you don't deal with them properly.

Finally, WMI has its own set of best practices that you need to understand. You've seen some of the underlying WMI structure, but you also need to understand the way WMI is configured and what you can modify.

Automation usually implies accessing remote machines, which in turn means that you need to be able to authenticate yourself on that machine. Your default credentials may often be enough, but sometimes you'll need that little bit more, and we'll look at that in this chapter.

WMI will often return data in its own internal format, especially for dates. Luckily, there's a very simple way to convert them to a readable format. You also need to be aware that WMI will return sizes (of files, disks, and so on) in bytes, so you need to be able to convert them to more usable forms. PowerShell can do some formatting for us but we can also perform some simple formatting in our scripts—especially where we want to make things more readable.

We'll get to all of these topics in turn. Our first port of call on this journey to good scripting is security. PowerShell is too powerful to leave unsecured.

4.1 Security

PowerShell has a number of security features built into it:

- It doesn't run scripts by default—you must modify the execution policy to enable this.
- It doesn't allow scripts to run by double-clicking—don't modify this.
- It doesn't run scripts from the current folder—don't modify this.

Those features were covered in chapter 2.

In this section, we'll extend our security thinking and look at how you can make sure that code you download is safe. Beyond that, we'll look at how you can keep your code safe and restrict access to PowerShell scripts. (You also need a way to monitor who is using your code, and this final point will be covered in chapter 15.)

The internet is a great resource for PowerShell code, but how can you use it safely?

4.1.1 Using internet code

PowerShell is all about solving problems—your administration problems. Ideally, you would have all the time you require to

- Properly define the problem
- Research possible solutions
- Decide on the best approach
- Write and test the solution
- Apply it in production

But in reality, you generally have a problem to solve *now*. There isn't time to go through a full cycle of developing the ideal solution. You need something to use immediately. You have to find some sample code, and this usually means the internet.

The first thing you need to do is find the code you need. One method is to enter some search criteria into your favorite search engine (no, I'm not getting involved in that debate, thank you) and see what you get back.

It's highly probable that you'll get a number of hits, including some of the sites I'll discuss shortly. One group of hits will be question and answer threads on the various forums that support PowerShell. These sources may be useful depending on who is supplying the answer. If you get lucky and find that someone else has posted a question that's similar to your problem, you'll have a potential answer.

TRUST

Do you trust code you download from the internet?

I generally don't, and I know many people who supply code on their blogs or on the sites they run.

If I know the person who actually wrote the code, and I trust them, I will be confident that the code isn't deliberately malicious. But I can't be sure that it will run error free in my environment. I will perform a read-through of the code at a minimum. If it's for a production environment, I will test it under controlled conditions.

If I don't know the code author, I am much more careful about the code. I will perform a painstaking examination of the code, especially if a lot of aliasing or cascading function calls have been used. I will test the code extensively in a sandbox before it hits the production environment.

Care should be applied to any code received as part of a download package with a book, including this one, or on a CD accompanying a book. The code won't be deliberately malicious, but it hasn't been tested in your environment. Test before use must be the approach.

A second group of hits will include PowerShell-related blogs, several of which are very good. The ones I regularly read are listed in appendix D. Many of these blogs are maintained by PowerShell MVPs. I know I'm laboring the point, but you still need to test any scripts you take to use in your environment, even the ones from my blogs.

The third group of hits will likely include the various PowerShell repositories that are available:

- *CodePlex*—Contains over 400 PowerShell-related projects, including the Hyper-V library, PowerShell Community extensions, and my administration modules
- *Microsoft TechNet Script Center*—Has lots of WMI examples, but many of the older ones are direct translations of VBScript and so may need reformatting
- *MSDN code gallery*—Contains some PowerShell-related projects, including the CIM IDE used in chapters 18 and 19
- *PowerShell Code Repository (PoshCode.org)*—The site of the Scripting Games and a large code repository; many MVPs deposit code here
- *PowerGUI.org*—Mainly PowerGUI related, but the ideas can be reused
- *PowerShell.com*—A large code repository and that has excellent forums, including one dedicated to PowerShell and WMI

There are others, but I've either used these ones or I know the people who run the sites. Guess what? You still need to test the code!

One thing that shocks many newcomers to PowerShell is that when they look for code to solve a particular problem, they find two or three different approaches to the solution instead of the single definitive answer they were hoping for. By the time you get to the end of this book, you'll be able to look back and say, "You could have solved that one by doing ..." for any of the examples in the book.

There is no right answer. If your solution solves the problem in a reasonable time, it's a good script. Pick the answer you feel most comfortable with and that you understand. Get the problem solved rather than spending time puzzling out some complicated piece of code. You can always unravel the complicated code at your leisure for reuse in the future. Remember the KISS principle: Keep It Simple Scripter.

Let's suppose you've found some code that sort of answers your question. Unless you're really lucky, it won't be a complete answer, so you'll need to do some work on it. You also need to consider how you'll ensure that the code you create hasn't been modified to produce a harmful result.

4.1.2 Code security

In chapter 2, I recommended that your execution policy should be set to `Remote-Signed`. This will run unsigned scripts from your local disk, but it requires that downloaded scripts, including scripts on network drives, be signed. This eases development but enables you to protect the code you've developed. The only question remaining is what is *code signing* and how do you do it?

> **Developers and signers**
>
> How many PowerShell developers are you going to have? Many organizations will have a single person doing the majority of the development. Other users may do some of the code writing, but the one guru is the person who approves the code. At most, an organization will have a small number of people producing code.
>
> Keeping the number of PowerShell developers small enables better control over the code. Even with a single person doing all of the work, using a version-control system ensures that you can track the changes made to scripts. If your application developers have a system for doing this, ask them nicely and see if they can let you use a little bit of it. Otherwise a simple script-naming convention that incorporates a version number would allow you to identify current script versions.
>
> Code signing should be restricted to one or two individuals. If your application developers already have a process, I recommend that you join it. Otherwise, adopt a method that will achieve the security goals outlined in this section.

Code signing is the act of applying a code certificate to your code. This will put a lot of seemingly random characters at the end of your PowerShell scripts. An example of this can be seen if you open any of the XML files in the PowerShell install folder. They're all signed. *Don't modify them or PowerShell won't load them.*

There are three steps to code-signing a PowerShell script:

1 Obtain a code-signing certificate.
2 Install the certificate.
3 Apply the certificate.

Easy! You can obtain a code-signing certificate from a number of places:

- You can create a self-signed certificate using the makecert utility. This is usable if the scripts will only run on your machine.
- Your enterprise's Public Key Infrastructure (PKI), if you have one, can generate a certificate for you. Talk to the PKI administrators. This is a good solution if the scripts will only be used inside the organization.
- You can buy a code-signing certificate from a commercial certificate authority (CA). This is the best solution if scripts will be shared beyond a single organization.

You can install the certificate with the Certificates management tool. This isn't readily available, so open the MMC and add the Certificates snap-in. Select Personal. Right-click and select Import. A wizard will guide you through importing the certificate. This GUI tool can also be used to request a certificate from your PKI or a commercial authority.

It's generally a good idea to secure the certificate by exporting the private key. This can be performed using Internet Explorer. Alternatively Quest supplies tools to work with the certificate store in their AD cmdlets (search for *AD cmdlets* at http://www.quest.com). There is also a PowerShell module for administering certificates developed by one of the PowerShell MVPs, which you can download from http://pspki.codeplex.com/.

The last step is the most straightforward. The following code can be used to apply the certificate. Change the name of the certificate and script to work in your environment. This code can be used interactively or can become part of a script if you have a lot of signing to perform:

```
$cert = Get-ChildItem -Path cert:\CurrentUser\my -CodeSigningCert
Set-AuthenticodeSignature myscript.ps1 $cert
```

Once you've signed the script, any modifications to it will cause it to fail unless it's re-signed.

Now you know how to secure your code against tampering. How can you ensure that only the right people can access your scripts?

4.1.3   Access to code

PowerShell scripts do a wonderful job of automating the administration of Windows machines. But like all powerful tools, they have the potential to cause a lot of damage if they're misused. You need to ensure that only authorized personnel can access your scripts.

There are two basic solutions to the problem of controlling who has access to your administration scripts. The first depends on them being on your personal workstation. This ensures that you're the only person who has access. With this approach, you need to follow the normal security guidelines:

- Lock the machine when you aren't using it.
- Possibly encrypt the folder, or drive, that contains the scripts.
- Don't share the folder containing the scripts.
- Don't divulge your password.

This will work unless someone gains access to the machine. At that point, unless there's a further layer of protection, such as encryption, the scripts are accessible.

The second approach is more common and must be adopted if multiple people are using the scripts. This involves putting the scripts on a network share. Access can be controlled by only allowing the group of administrators who need to use the scripts permissions to the network share containing the scripts. An Active Directory group can be assigned the appropriate permissions. Make sure that the group membership is under change control or is treated as a Restricted Group in Group Policy to maintain the security. Check the group membership periodically, just to be sure.

An essential part of any administrator's job is maintaining security on the data and resources in their area of responsibility. Using PowerShell and WMI to administer that environment doesn't remove the need for security procedures and awareness. In fact, a few extra security requirements come into play:

- Be careful with code downloaded from the internet. Always ensure that you understand how it works and always, always test it very carefully.
- Use code-signing techniques to ensure that your code hasn't been changed.
- Restrict access to production code. Only those who need to use it should have access. Be even more careful about who has permissions to modify production code.

PowerShell has a number of areas where adherence to best practices can save time and effort when writing and testing scripts. Optimized code will run more efficiently and be easier to maintain.

4.2   *Optimizing PowerShell code*

Using PowerShell effectively is about getting the job done with the minimum amount of code. And within your PowerShell code, there are a number of areas where you can be more productive:

- Data handling (input, output, string substitution, and so on)
- Format files
- Debugging
- Error handling

Notice that I'm not including the standard best practices, such as

- Commenting code
- Using functions
- Code formatting
- Using naming conventions for scripts, variables, and the like

I'll assume that you know the basics and want to progress to getting the best out of PowerShell. The first area to consider is how you get data into PowerShell.

4.2.1   *Data input*

There are two aspects to getting data into your PowerShell scripts (assuming you aren't going off to another data store, such as Active Directory or SQL Server—that would be a completely different problem). The first is the bulk use of data through reading a file. The second is getting single values for the main variables into PowerShell.

READING FILES

There are two cmdlets that you can use to read the content of files:

- `Import-CSV`
- `Get-Content`

Which one you should use tends to be dictated by the type of data. If it's a CSV file, you use `Import-CSV`, and if its text, you use `Get-Content`. This covers the majority of situations. The important part is what you do with the data after you've read it.

Let's create a CSV file to work with:

```
Get-Service | select Status, Name, DisplayName |
Export-CSV chapt4.csv -NoTypeInformation
```

If you want to read this file, you can simply use

```
Import-CSV chapt4.csv | Format-Table -AutoSize -Wrap
```

The choice comes when you want to do something with the data. Consider a little script that checks the status of each service; if the service is stopped, the information is written out in red, and otherwise the normal foreground color is used. You need to access each service to test its status. As you'll recall from chapter 2, you have two options. You can use the `foreach` PowerShell keyword as in figure 4.1.

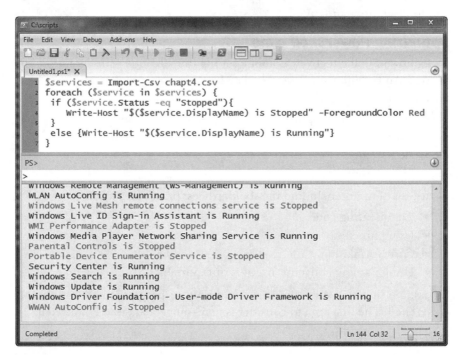

Figure 4.1 Using the `foreach` keyword

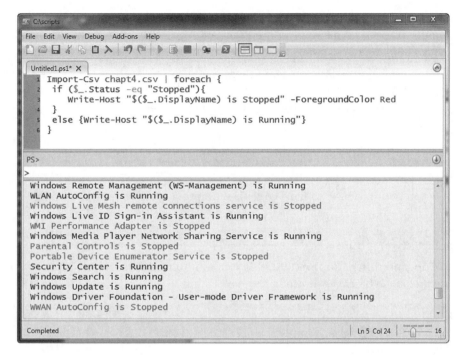

Figure 4.2 Using the `ForEach-Object` **cmdlet**

The other alternative is to use the `ForEach-Object` cmdlet (aliased as `foreach`) as in figure 4.2.

The contents of the loop are the same. The variation is in how you set up the loop. If you use the pipeline, you can start processing immediately, but if you use a loop you have the option of doing more with the data later in the script.

`Import-CSV` doesn't demand that a file have a .csv extension. You can use .txt or anything else sensible. The delimiter can be defined, and you can even force a header onto the data if one doesn't exist.

`Get-Content` can be used in a similar manner except that you use it to read text files. These files are either structureless or the data needs to be handled on a row by row basis.

You've now seen how to perform a bulk read from a file, but what about getting values for individual variables?

PARAMETERS

I've mentioned several times that WMI can access remote computers. This is one of the big selling points for WMI. We need to get the computer name into a variable so that we can use it in the script. But the bigger problem is getting the computer name into the script in the first place.

Imagine for a moment that you've been tasked with gathering information on the amount of physical memory in the PC estate. You could go round and visit them all, but it would be much easier to use WMI and the Win32_ComputerSystem class:

```
Get-WmiObject -Class Win32_ComputerSystem |
Select Name, @{Name="RAM"; Expression={$_.TotalPhysicalMemory / 1GB}}
```

Great. That works on the local machine, but you need the -ComputerName parameter to work with remote machines:

```
$computer = "rslaptop01"
Get-WmiObject -Class Win32_ComputerSystem -ComputerName $computer |
Select Name, @{Name="RAM"; Expression={$_.TotalPhysicalMemory / 1GB}}
```

You don't want to have to hard-code the computer name, so you might do this:

```
$computer = Read-Host "Computer name?"
Get-WmiObject -Class Win32_ComputerSystem -ComputerName $computer |
Select Name, @{Name="RAM"; Expression={$_.TotalPhysicalMemory / 1GB}}
```

No, no, and thrice no! Don't do it! If you want to pass data into a script (or function) use the param block, as shown in the next listing.

Listing 4.1   Using the param block

```
function get-ram {
[CmdletBinding()]
param (
 [parameter(Mandatory=$true)]
 [string]$computername
)
 Get-WmiObject -Class Win32_ComputerSystem -ComputerName $computername |
 Select Name, @{Name="RAM"; Expression={$_.TotalPhysicalMemory / 1GB}}
}
```

You can use the [parameter(Mandatory=$true)] advanced parameter. It forces a prompt for a value if you don't supply one. This technique prevents a number of potential errors that would stop the script from running and forces you to present the computer name to the script. All of this value from a simple line of code.

Advanced parameters and methods

Advanced parameters enable you to add static and dynamic parameters to functions that use the [CmdletBinding()] attribute. Dynamic parameters are parameters that are only available in a particular PowerShell provider—see about_Providers and the individual provider help files.

Static parameters include the following:

- Mandatory
- Position
- ValueFromPipeline
- HelpMessage
- Alias

(continued)

There are a number of parameters that can be used to validate the data input to a function, including testing for null values or empty strings. The data can also be tested against a set or range of data.

Advanced methods include the following:

- Input-processing methods that compiled cmdlets use to do their work
- The ShouldProcess and ShouldContinue methods, which are used to get user feedback before an action is performed
- The ThrowTerminatingError method for generating error records
- Several Write methods that return different types of output

Full details are available in the following PowerShell help files:

- about_Functions_Advanced
- about_Functions_Advanced_Methods
- about_Functions_Advanced_Parameters
- about_Functions_CmdletBindingAttribute

The function in listing 4.1 can be used within your scripts as an additional piece of PowerShell functionality. You can call it from loops or any other script block.

Now that you know how to get data into a script, let's look at what you can do with it. Many of your scripting actions will revolve around creating and manipulating the contents of strings.

4.2.2 *String substitution*

I was a judge in Microsoft's Scripting Games in 2010 and 2011, and one of the things that I noticed was that many of the entries spent a lot of effort building up elaborate strings when they could have done it in a single line of PowerShell.

String substitution is one of my favorite bits of PowerShell. If you've not seen it before, the idea is that you can substitute a variable into a double-quoted string. Note that single-quoted strings won't work. As an example, consider this piece of PowerShell:

```
$colour = "red"
"The balloon is $colour"
```

That code will produce this output:

```
The balloon is red
```

However, this line,

```
'The balloon is $colour'
```

will produce this output:

```
The balloon is $colour
```

One place where this breaks down is when substituting properties of an object. Consider something you might pull back with WMI, such as the output from accessing the `Win32_OperatingSystem` class:

```
PS> $os = Get-WmiObject -Class Win32_OperatingSystem
PS> $os

SystemDirectory : C:\Windows\system32
Organization    :
BuildNumber     : 7600
RegisteredUser  : Richard
SerialNumber    : 00426-065-1155216-86852
Version         : 6.1.7600
```

You can pick off a couple of properties, like this:

```
PS> $os | select Caption, ServicePackMajorVersion | Format-List
Caption                 : Microsoft Windows 7 Ultimate
ServicePackMajorVersion : 0
```

Then you can use `Write-Host`,

```
PS> Write-Host $os.Caption, $os.ServicePackMajorVersion
Microsoft Windows 7 Ultimate  0
```

and even expand it a bit:

```
PS> Write-Host $os.Caption, "Service Pack", $os.ServicePackMajorVersion
Microsoft Windows 7 Ultimate  Service Pack 0
```

But if you try string substitution,

```
PS> Write-Host "The OS is $os.Caption with Service Pack
    $os.ServicePackMajorVersion"
The OS is \\RSLAPTOP01\root\cimv2:Win32_OperatingSystem=@.Caption with
    Service Pack
    \\RSLAPTOP01\root\cimv2:Win32_OperatingSystem=@.ServicePackMajorVersion
```

Oops—that's not what you want. The problem is that you're getting the object rather than the value. You need to use a subexpression:

```
PS> Write-Host "The OS is $($os.Caption) with Service Pack
    $($os.ServicePackMajorVersion)"
The OS is Microsoft Windows 7 Ultimate  with Service Pack 0
```

All this does is say, "give me the result of the expression in the parentheses and substitute that in the string." Easy and neat. No need to concatenate strings to create the display line in your scripts.

> **NOTE**   The double space in the previous result is due to there being a space as the last character of the `Caption` property. I have never seen a reason presented for its presence, but be aware that it exists—especially if you try filtering on the `Caption` value.

There's one further point on building strings to consider, and it has to do with building file paths. How many times have you seen this type of code?

```
$path = "C:\Test" + "\" + "proc1.txt"
Get-Content $path
```

You could use string substitution and change the code to this:

```
$file = "proc1.txt"
Get-Content "C:\test\$file"
```

Better still, you could use Join-Path:

```
$file = "proc1.txt"
Get-Content (Join-Path -Path c:\test -ChildPath $file)
```

Join-Path, and the other cmdlets for working with paths, will also work on Power-Shell drives such as the registry. They save a lot of typing and save you from having to remember to add the dividers.

Any automation techniques involving scripting will need to access data at some point. You'll either get it in bulk by reading from a file, or as single values via the parameters used with functions and cmdlets. Handling the data inside the scripts can be made much simpler by using the string substitution functionality and the *Path cmdlets.

The data you produce in your scripts can be used as is, but in many cases you need to perform further calculations or change the way the data is formatted.

4.3 *Calculated fields, types, and formatting*

PowerShell provides a very good set of presentation opportunities via the Format-* cmdlets. Sometimes these aren't quite enough, though, and you'll need to create your own values to display. This is done by creating a *calculated field*—an expression that involves one or more properties of the object you're displaying. You could, alternatively, modify the PowerShell type system to always add this calculated field to the object you want to work with. This is more work in the short term, but it provides a more powerful and easier-to-use solution. Just keep in mind that you need to distribute the new format file to every machine that will run the script requiring that format.

Many of the PowerShell cmdlets and WMI classes have a default set of properties that are displayed. Compare the output from these two PowerShell examples:

```
Get-WmiObject -Class Win32_ComputerSystem
Get-WmiObject -Class Win32_ComputerSystem | Format-List *
```

The first example displays a total of six properties (the default display), whereas the second displays all of the properties on the object.

These default displays are controlled by PowerShell format files. The bad news is that they're XML. The good news is that the format system is easy to change.

First, though, let's look at how you can use calculated fields.

4.3.1   *Calculated fields*

A calculated field can be used in a number of ways:

- *To recalculate a value*—For example, to change a file size from bytes to GB
- *To reformat a value*—For example, to change a date from WMI's format to a format commonly used
- *To calculate a new value*—For example, to calculate a value based on two or more existing values

> **TIP**   A *calculated field* in PowerShell is analogous to a *calculated column* in a SQL Server database table.

The `Win32_LogicalDisk` class can be used to return information about the logical disk volumes in a computer. This WMI class returns the disk size and free space in bytes. In many cases it may be simpler, and more meaningful, to report the percentage of free space remaining on the disk. A system that has a disk that's 80 percent full needs attention, irrespective of the size of the disk. The following listing shows how you can achieve this.

Listing 4.2   Calculated field in `Format-Table`

```
function calcfree {
param (
 $disk                                        Function with ❶
)                                             parameter
 $free = ($disk.FreeSpace / $disk.Size) * 100
 "{0:F2}" -f $free                            Calculate ❷
}                                             free space
Get-WmiObject -Class Win32_LogicalDisk |
Format-Table DeviceId,                                  ❸ Calculated
@{Name="PercFree"; Expression={calcfree $_}}               field
```

This script starts by defining a function that will calculate the percentage of free space on the disk ❶. It takes a single parameter. I haven't typed this parameter for two reasons. First, the function only exists in this simple script, so there's no risk of sending the wrong type of data. Second, the type doesn't have a shortcut, so it would be rather overwhelming in terms of the space taken.

The function then calculates the percentage of free space on the disk in the usual manner, rounding the result to two decimal places to make it more presentable ❷. It uses the .NET format string—the bit in the braces, {}—and the PowerShell format operator, `-f`. This line is worth spending a little time understanding as this method of formatting is very simple once you understand it, and very powerful.

A .NET formatted string consists of one, or more, fields defined in a string. The individual fields are defined by curly braces, {}. Within the curly braces, the number to the left of the semicolon provides an index for the field; in this case, it's the first field. The `F2` tells PowerShell to format the data as a floating-point number with two decimal places. Other formats are available.

The line then continues with the PowerShell format operator `-f`, which will take the data to its right and format it into the fields on the left ❷. Individual items on the right side of the operator are separated by commas. This is a string on a line by itself, so the function returns the formatted string.

The function needs to be called somehow, and you do that by piping the results of a `Get-WmiObject` call using the `Win32_LogicalDisk` class. The results are piped into `Format-Table` ❸ where you display the `DeviceId` that denotes the drive and a calculated field that gives you the percentage free space.

The calculated field is a hash table—denoted by `@{}`. The hash table has two entries. The first entry provides a name for the calculated field. The second provides an expression that calculates its value, and in this case it's a call to the `calcfree` method. You could put a calculation in the expression itself, but that can make it more difficult to read and maintain. You'll be seeing this technique in a lot more scripts as you progress through the book.

A calculated field can be used with `Select-Object` as well as the `Format-*` cmdlets. When used in `Select-Object`, it becomes part of the object, so it can be used in further processing. This enables you to modify listing 4.2 to give the next listing.

Listing 4.3   Calculated field in `Select-Object`

```
function calcfree {
param (
 $disk
)
 $free = ($disk.FreeSpace / $disk.Size) * 100
 "{0:F2}" -f $free
}
Get-WmiObject -Class Win32_LogicalDisk |
select DeviceId,
@{Name="PercFree"; Expression={calcfree $_}} |
sort perfree -Descending |
Format-Table -AutoSize
```

The main change here is that you replace `Format-Table` with `Select-Object`. You can then continue the pipeline by sorting on the `PercFree` property you've created and finally displaying the results with `Format-Table`.

> **NOTE** In the first version of PowerShell, the calculated fields used in the `Select-Object` and `Format-*` cmdlets were slightly different. `Select-Object` used `Name` and `Expression`, as demonstrated in the previous example, but the `Format` cmdlets used `Label` and `Expression` instead. The `Format` cmdlets will still accept `Label`, so old scripts won't break, but I recommend standardizing on `Name` in PowerShell v2 and above.

I use a technique based on listing 4.3 to monitor the fullest disks in my customers' server estate. I'll show you how to do that in chapter 6.

You've just seen how to use calculated fields to modify the data that's presented. It's also possible to alter the default data that's displayed by using the type and format files. These files are created when PowerShell is installed and they're loaded every time PowerShell is started.

4.3.2   *Type files*

Type files enable you to add properties and methods to the Windows PowerShell objects. *Format files* define the default display of objects in Windows PowerShell. Both sets of files are XML and can be modified to add further customization to PowerShell. We'll start by looking at how you can use type files to extend an object, and you'll get to format files in the next section.

> **WARNING**   Don't overwrite the format and type files in the PowerShell install folder because any future PowerShell updates will destroy your changes. Also, the files are digitally signed and will stop working if you modify them!

PowerShell type files can be found in the PowerShell install folder with a .ps1xml extension:

```
Get-ChildItem $pshome\*types.ps1xml
```

The majority of the information is stored in the `types.ps1xml` file.

> **NOTE**   On a 64-bit machine, PowerShell installs both 32- and 64-bit versions of PowerShell in separate folders. If you need changes to type or format files to apply to both, you have to explicitly apply them in both folders.

You've seen how to create a calculated field that identifies the percentage of free space on a disk. Let's look at how you can add that as a property that will always be produced.

We'll start by looking at what PowerShell is already doing to the `Win32_LogicalDisk` class. You haven't seen much of `Select-String` so far, but it's a great tool for poking into the contents of text files. It will display the lines of a file that contain the pattern you define. You can also display the lines before and after the ones you're searching for to put your match into context. Use `Get-Help Select-String` for full details.

In this case, you want to discover the type and format files that modify the way the `Win32_LogicalDisk` class is processed by PowerShell:

```
Select-String -Path $pshome\*.ps1xml -Pattern "Win32_Logicaldisk"
```

On my machine, this gives three references to the types.ps1xml file, of which the last looks most likely. If you open up the file, you'll see XML that defines a property set and the standard members. It's the standard members you see when you use the default display.

> **TIP**   A quick way to open a file from the PowerShell prompt is to use `Invoke-Item` (aliased as `ii`). This is one place where the alias is worth remembering, as it means you can quickly type `ii $pshome\types.ps1xml` to open the file. It also works for CSV, Excel, and Word files—any file that has a file association defined.

Your mission, and you don't get an option about accepting it, is to add a property to the default set that shows the percentage of free space on the disk. Don't try to modify types.ps1xml, because it's digitally signed and will stop working. It's much better practice to create a type file with the changes, if for no other reason than that you can just restart PowerShell to make your changes go away if you get something wrong. Listing 4.4 shows the XML you need. Details of the XML structure can be found in `Get-Help about_Types.ps1xml`.

> **TIP** The name about_Types.ps1xml may seem odd, but it's what is returned if you try `get-help about_t*`. This help file can be accessed with `get-help about_types` or `get-help about_types.ps1xml`. That's just one of the oddities of PowerShell.

Listing 4.4   Win32_LogicalDisk type file

```
<?xml version="1.0" encoding="utf-8" ?>
<Types>
  <Type>
    <Name>System.Management.ManagementObject#
                  root\cimv2\Win32_LogicalDisk</Name>
    <Members>
     <ScriptProperty>
       <Name>PercFree</Name>
         <GetScriptBlock>
           "{0:F2}" -f
               $(($this.FreeSpace/$this.Size)*100)
         </GetScriptBlock>
     </ScriptProperty>
    </Members>
  </Type>
</Types>
```

Note that the name of the type should on a single line. It's only split here to fit into the page width.

The important part of the type definition starts with the `<ScriptProperty>` tag. You define the name of the new property and provide a script block that calculates the value of the property. The script block is taken directly from the `calcfree` function you used in listing 4.3.

The XML is saved to a file called listing4.4.ps1xml, and this new type information needs to be loaded into PowerShell. The `Update-TypeData` cmdlet forces a reload of type data, including any extras you want to add.

```
Update-TypeData -PrependPath listing4.4.ps1xml
```

The `-PrependPath` parameter instructs PowerShell to load your type data ahead of the default data. This ensures that your new type structure is used.

Figure 4.3 shows this occurring. If the load is successful, no messages are returned (as in this case). Unfortunately, on some occasions PowerShell doesn't return any feedback if the command hasn't worked either. This is a feature of PowerShell that can cause

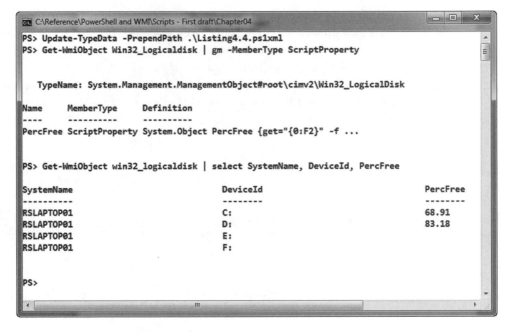

Figure 4.3   Extending the PowerShell type system

issues sometimes, in that you're never quite sure if something has worked or not. In this case, you can use Get-Member to prove that the script property has been added.

```
Get-WmiObject Win32_Logicaldisk | gm -MemberType ScriptProperty
```

The information produced by Get-Member is also shown in figure 4.3.

The final test is to try and use the new property:

```
Get-WmiObject Win32_LogicalDisk |
select SystemName, DeviceId, PercFree
```

Figure 4.3 shows the results. The C: and D: drives have a percfree value calculated. The E: and F: drives are DVD drives that don't contain disks at present.

The first time I used a script like this across my server estate, I found two disks that had zero free space! A quick check showed that they were both CD drives where an engineer had left the disk in the drive! In chapter 6, you'll see how you can filter the output so that you can cut down on the number of shocks you get.

In the meantime, we need to look at how you can control the default formatting of PowerShell's output.

4.3.3   *Format files*

Format files define how objects are displayed in Windows PowerShell by default. The PowerShell format files have a .ps1xml extension and are also found in the PowerShell install folder:

```
Get-ChildItem $pshome\*format*
```

The WMI classes don't use the format file very much. Most of the formatting is handled by the type files you've already seen. You can perform a search of the format files using `Select-String`:

```
Select-String -Path $pshome\*format*ps1xml -Pattern "Win32_"
```

You'll see results returned for the `Win32_PingStatus` and `Win32_QuickFixEngineering` classes. You'll use `Win32_PingStatus` for this exercise. The first part of figure 4.4 shows how to use this class and the results you can expect. I don't use IPv6, so I'm going to drop that result from the default display.

The first task is to extract the format data for the `Win32_PingStatus` class:

```
Get-FormatData -TypeName `
System.Management.ManagementObject#root\cimv2\Win32_PingStatus |
 Export-FormatData -Path chapt4_ping_status.ps1xml
-IncludeScriptBlock -Force
```

This pulls the XML out of the current format file and creates a file for you to use. You can examine the file like this:

```
ii chapt4_ping_status.ps1xml
```

At this point, you'll discover that it isn't formatted. In fact it's horrible to try and read through. To be kind, I've created a nicely formatted version that is also included in the download file for the book. Access the file by typing this command at a Power-Shell prompt:

```
ii prettychapt4_ping_status.ps1xml
```

If you examine the file, you'll notice that you need to remove the following sections:

```
<TableColumnHeader>
      <Label>IPV6Address</Label>
      <Width>40</Width>
</TableColumnHeader>

        <TableColumnItem>
          <PropertyName>IPV6Address</PropertyName>
        </TableColumnItem>
```

The file can then be saved as Win32_PingStatus.format.ps1xml.

Once you have a new format file, you need to apply it:

```
Update-FormatData -PrependPath Win32_PingStatus.format.ps1xml
```

As with the type file, using the `-PrePendPath` parameter ensures that your formatting is used in preference to the default. Figure 4.4 shows that you don't get any response if the format data is successfully updated.

The final test is to use `Win32_PingStatus` again. This time you won't get the IPv6 address showing in the output.

Note that this change also works for the `Test-Connection` cmdlet. The reason for this can be discovered if you try the following:

```
Test-Connection 127.0.0.1 | Get-Member
```

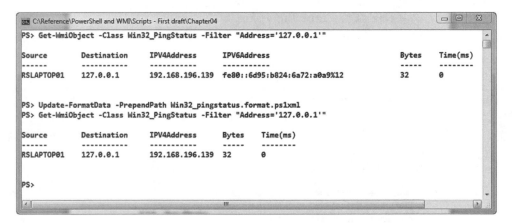

Figure 4.4   Modifying the default display format

Calculated fields or type/format files

This and the previous sections have shown how you can modify the way PowerShell outputs objects:

- Create a calculated field.
- Add a script property by modifying the type files.
- Modify the default formatting to include or exclude a field.

The best approach to use depends on what you're doing. My personal approach is to use calculated fields, because they only apply to the script in which they're defined, and they make the scripts more portable, which is an important consideration for a consultancy role. Calculated fields are also easier to implement.

In a situation where these scripts will only be used by you, or possibly by a small number of users, modifying the format or type files is a good approach. This is also a good approach if you're delivering the functionality through a module, though loading format files through a module requires care to ensure they are prepended. The Hyper-V management module from CodePlex (see chapter 16) provides a good example.

At some point when creating a script, you'll find that the thing won't work. "Thing" is the politest name you'll use for the offending script. You need to track down what is causing your script to fail. This is known as debugging.

4.4   *Debugging and error handling*

As you progress with PowerShell, your scripts will become more complex. This increases the possibility of bugs, or errors, creeping into the code. An error terminating a script may not be too bad if you're only gathering information, but it could cause your system to become unstable if you're performing changes. An error that doesn't terminate the script but that makes the wrong change could have drastic consequences. You need to be able to cope with potential errors and discover the bugs in your scripts.

Using the [CmdletBinding()] attribute in your functions provides access to the -Debug and -Verbose parameters. By using Write-Debug and Write-Verbose in your functions, you can produce output as the function executes, which enables you to perform simple debugging techniques.

> **TIP** PowerShell provides very good debugging functionality—see Get-Help about_Debuggers. I've never found it necessary to use this functionality when debugging my PowerShell code. If you're interested in this sort of thing, feel free to investigate.

The best-written function will come across situations where errors occur. This is often, if not usually, due to the data being passed to the function. PowerShell includes try-catch functionality to ensure that these errors can be handled gracefully if required.

The last part of error handling we'll deal with is the return codes supplied by WMI. There is a simple rule—zero is good and everything else is bad—but what do you do when you get a nonzero return code?

Debugging is the art of finding problems in the code syntax (often typing mistakes) that prevent the code from running or produce the wrong results. We'll start by looking at how you can remove these bugs.

4.4.1 Debugging

A bug is something that prevents a script from running correctly. It may be a coding or typographic error, or it may be an error in the logic of your script. How can you find bugs? One way is to read through the code until you spot the error. But this can take a bit too much time. A quicker way is to put some debug statements into your script. These statements will show you the values of particular variables, which will enable you to track what is happening. The problem with this approach is remembering to remove them after you've finished debugging. Ideally, you could switch them on and off. The advanced functions capabilities you've already seen give you this capability.

> **NOTE** If you would like to practice debugging on a script with known errors, search for "Beginners PowerShell Event 7" on my blog at http://richardspow-ershellblog.wordpress.com/. It was posted on 2 March 2008 and was a commentary on one of the events from the Microsoft 2008 Scripting Games.

Let's create and debug a script. The script in the following listing ensures that your systems are up and running. It does this with a list of computers passed into a ForEach-Object cmdlet.

Listing 4.5 Script debugging

```
function test-status {
    Import-Csv computers4.csv |
    foreach {
        Get-WmiObject -Class Win32_PingStatus
            -Filter "Address='$($_.Computer)'"
    }
}
function test-status2 {
 [CmdletBinding()]
 param()
    Import-Csv computers4.csv |
    foreach {
        Write-Debug $_.Computer
        Get-WmiObject -Class Win32_PingStatus `
        -Filter "Address='$($_.Computer)'"
    }
}
```

❶ Initial function

❷ Add debug capability

❸ Debug statement

You can start with a simple function ❶ that reads the contents of a CSV file and uses `Win32_PingStatus` to test if the system is responding. This function is used in the same way as `test-status`. It will return one ping per computer.

If you start having problems with this script, you may want to check that the computer name is being passed correctly. The second version of the function adds the `[CmdletBinding()]` attribute ❷. This brings the advanced function capability into play. You also need the `param()` statement, or PowerShell will throw an error. A `Write-Debug` statement is added to write out the computer name when you require it ❸.

This second function is used from the PowerShell command prompt as `test-status2`. As before, you get a single ping returned per computer. If you want to invoke the debugging functionality, you simply add the debug switch:

```
test-status2 -Debug
```

This allows you to switch debug reporting on or off as required, without the need to modify your code, which could introduce other errors.

Most of the time, I find that simple instrumentation of the script is sufficient to discover any bugs—especially if the script is tested in sections as it's written. If you have more complicated debugging needs, PowerShell ISE provides a debug capability that allows you to step through the code one line at a time and discover where it's going wrong. This functionality can be invoked from the PowerShell prompt using the cmdlets listed in table 4.1. A good example of using these cmdlets can be found in the `about_Debuggers` help file.

Now that you have an idea of how to track down bugs in your code, it's time to think about handling errors when the script is running.

Table 4.1 PowerShell debugger cmdlets

Cmdlet	Purpose
Set-PSBreakpoint	Sets breakpoints on lines, variables, and commands
Get-PSBreakpoint	Gets breakpoints in the current session
Disable-PSBreakpoint	Turns off breakpoints in the current session
Enable-PSBreakpoint	Re-enables breakpoints in the current session
Remove-PSBreakpoint	Deletes breakpoints from the current session
Get-PSCallStack	Displays the current call stack

4.4.2 Error handling

PowerShell has a number of ways to handle errors. There are a number of PowerShell automatic variables that deal with errors that are summarized in table 4.2.

Table 4.2 PowerShell error handling variables

Variable	Description
$ErrorActionPreference	Determines response to a non-terminating error. Values: Stop, Inquire, Continue, SilentlyContinue
$ErrorView	Displays format of error information. Values: NormalView, CategoryView
$error	Contains an array holding recent error messages. $error[0] is the latest.
$?	Tests if last command completed successfully (True) or produced an error (False).
$lastexitcode	Contains the exit code of the last command run. It only works for Windows commands and PowerShell scripts. It doesn't capture the WMI return code.

The $ErrorActionPreference setting can be overridden by using the ErrorAction parameter on an individual cmdlet basis.

The $error variable contains a collection of the recent errors that have occurred, with the most recent error being in the first element—$error[0]. The easiest way to see the error contents is to generate an error! You can do this by trying to access a process that isn't running (make sure Notepad isn't running before trying this):

```
Get-Process notepad
$?
$error[0]
```

This command generates an error that can be viewed using $error. The contents of the error messages can be separated out (to a certain extent) by using the individual parameters of $error.

Instead of working out why an error has occurred, it may be a better proposition to catch the error as it happens. You can do this with a new feature in PowerShell v2—the try-catch block.

We'll start by considering a simple function that performs arithmetic on two integers:

```
function div {
 param ([int]$a, [int]$b )
$a+$b
$a/$b
}

div 10 2
div 3 2
div 7 0
```

The function accepts the integers as parameters. Then it produces the sum of the integers and divides the first integer by the second. All will go well until your third call to the function, when the divide fails with a divide-by-zero exception.

An *exception* is a .NET term for a terminating error, which is one that will cause your script to stop. This may be a bad thing if you have a script performing many actions. One way to handle this situation is to rewrite the function to use try-catch-finally script blocks, as shown in the next listing.

Listing 4.6   Using `Try-Catch-Finally`

```
function div {
 param (
   [int]$a,
   [int]$b
 )
  try {
   $a+$b
   $a/$b
 }
 catch [Exception] {"It's gone wrong" }
 finally {"end"}
}

div 10 2
div 3 2
div 7 0
```

When you run this script, you'll get the following output:

```
12
5
end
5
1.5
end
7
It's gone wrong
end
```

The first two calls to the function produce the results you'd expect. The integers are summed and divided correctly. Everything within the `try` block has worked. Notice, however, that after each set of results the word *end* is printed out. This is because the `finally` block has performed its job. The `finally` block is an optional extra that will always execute irrespective of what happens in the `try` block.

Your third and final call to the function performs the sum as expected, but when the divide goes wrong you get a message stating, `It's gone wrong` rather than the failure report you'd expect. The `finally` block then executes.

The job of the `catch` block is to catch exceptions. .NET exceptions are defined in the documentation, such as MSDN. Be warned—there are a lot of them. I used the most generic exception in the preceding example, but there's also a specific divide-by-zero exception. The best way to find the specific exception is to look in `$error[0].exception` and then perform an internet search to track down the specific exception. The preceding script could be altered so it reads as follows:

```
catch [DividebyZeroException] {"oops - divide by zero"}
catch [Exception]{"It's gone wrong" }
```

An attempt is made to catch the specific exception first. If that doesn't match, the generic exception functions as a catchall statement. When using multiple `catch` statements, always start with the most specific one first as PowerShell will use the first catch statement that can handle the exception. The download code contains this additional line of code. Try commenting out the different catch statements to see the effect.

One question remains: how much code should you put in the `try` block? This depends on what your script is trying to achieve. Ideally it should be minimal, so that every individual exception that could occur can be caught. But this increases the amount of code you need to type and makes the script more cumbersome. A better result is gained by putting the more critical code into individual `try` blocks. The safer code can be contained in larger blocks. Only experience, together with knowledge of the problem you're solving and the data involved, can produce the correct answer. Your approach to exception-handling will change over time as you become more accustomed to PowerShell.

The `try-catch-finally` blocks are designed to work with .NET exceptions. But WMI isn't .NET-based—it's a COM-based technology. This means you need another approach.

4.4.3 *WMI return codes*

When you invoke a WMI method, a numeric code is returned to report on the outcome of the action. The rule when dealing with WMI return codes is very simple:

0 = Good
Anything else = bad

The return code is normally displayed on screen, but you can capture it in a variable, as the following listing shows.

Listing 4.7   WMI return codes

```
Start-Process notepad
Start-Sleep -Seconds 5

$ret = Get-WmiObject -Class Win32_Process `
    -Filter "Name='notepad.exe'" |
    Invoke-WmiMethod -Name terminate

if ($ret.ReturnValue -eq 0) {Write-Host "Worked OK"}
else {Write-Host "FAILED"}
```

The script starts by opening Notepad. I recommend you close any open instances of Notepad before running the script, or they will be shut down as well. "Oops, I didn't mean to shut that one down" isn't a recognized PowerShell statement.

Start-Sleep pauses the script for five seconds. The cmdlet also has a -Milliseconds parameter for shorter pauses. After the pause, the script finds the Win32_Process class corresponding to Notepad and pipes it to Invoke-WmiMethod, which kills the process.

> **WARNING**   WMI methods don't have any -WhatIf or -Confirm parameters. You call it, and it works. Remember this—it may just save some valuable data. (I'll repeat this warning at various points throughout the book.)

The $ret variable catches the output of the pipeline. The pipeline ends by invoking a WMI method, so the return information includes the return code. A generic way of dealing with the return code is shown in the script. The contents of the if-else script blocks are totally dependent on the WMI classes being used, the script, and the data involved. A full list of the return codes is available in the WMI documentation for each method. One option is to use a switch statement for the most important return codes and lump the rest into the default bucket.

That's it for debugging. Next, WMI has a few areas you need to consider to ensure you're getting the best out of it.

4.5   *Getting the most from WMI*

WMI, like all technologies, has some issues. In this section, we'll look at common problems and how to overcome them. Along the way, we'll cover some best practices that you can take forward into the rest of the book.

> **NOTE**   The previous part of the chapter covered a number of points, such as the format files, that apply to PowerShell in general as well as to WMI in particular.

The primary issue with WMI is the number of classes available and, in many cases, the lack of documentation for those classes. The WMI cmdlets can extract information on the classes, as you saw in chapter 3. There are also some internet sources you can utilize. In this section, we'll look at some things that can be done to mitigate these deficiencies.

There are also a number of configuration settings you need to set on your systems to ensure that WMI will work correctly. WMI doesn't require PowerShell remoting to access remote machines, but the WSMAN and CIM cmdlets require the WinRM service to be running on the remote machine. If you make enabling PowerShell remoting a part of your configuration checks, you'll have covered all eventualities. The techniques to test that these settings are configured correctly, as well as how to perform the configuration changes, will be covered later in this section.

Controlling access to resources is an important part of system administration, and WMI is no exception. The cmdlets will negotiate authentication whenever possible, but occasionally you'll have to override the defaults. The WMI cmdlets provide a way to do this. When, and how to, change the default authentication mechanisms will be explained.

> **TIP** Run PowerShell with elevated privileges when working with WMI. It's the only way to access some classes.

The final parts of this section cover data filtering and conversions. Reducing the amount of data you work with will make your scripts more efficient. WMI doesn't always return data in the best of formats, so you need to know how to convert the results into a format you can work with.

We'll look first at how you can overcome WMI's imperfections.

4.5.1 Issues with learning to use WMI

Two major issues stand out when working with WMI:

- Inadequate documentation
- The large number of classes available

These issues sometimes overlap, in that some classes aren't documented, or the documentation hasn't been brought up to date as changes have been made.

The primary issue with WMI is one of documentation. For example, the root\cimv2 namespace is well documented, but the classes in the root\wmi namespace are undocumented. In chapter 5 I'll introduce the `BatteryStatus` class, but I haven't been able to discover any documentation on this class. Attempting to read the class description isn't much of a help:

```
(Get-WmiObject -Namespace 'root\wmi' -List BatteryStatus `
  -Amended).Qualifiers |
Format-Table Name, Value -AutoSize -Wrap
```

This will return the class description, among other information, but unfortunately all you get is the rather terse `BatteryStatus`. You can make some guesses based on the class name and the property names you can find as follows:

```
Get-WmiObject -Namespace 'root\wmi' -Class BatteryStatus |
Get-Member
```

An internet search doesn't reveal much more useful information. There appear to be a number of potentially useful classes in this namespace, but their usage is hampered by the lack of documentation.

The available classes aren't always very well publicized. Did you know that there are a set of WMI classes for working with failover clusters? They're still present in Windows Server 2008 R2, even though there are PowerShell cmdlets for working with clusters as well! On your nearest cluster, try this:

```
Get-WmiObject -Namespace 'root\cluster' -List
```

The cluster properties can be discovered with

```
Get-WmiObject -Namespace 'root\cluster' -Class MSCluster_cluster
```

If you have any clusters in your organization, it's worth checking out.

Another issue is that some WMI classes don't return any data. PowerShell has one habit that I find annoying and confusing—this lack of return messages. If a PowerShell statement is wrong, sometimes there's no return message. If a WMI class doesn't return data, there's no return message. How do you know whether your PowerShell statement has failed or there isn't any data to return? All you can do is try other ways of formatting the statement.

The second major issue with WMI is the sheer number of classes available. No one can know them all. We'll look at some of the most commonly used classes in the following chapters, but we'll only be scratching the surface. Furthermore, WMI functionality is constantly changing as Microsoft products evolve, but some of the documentation doesn't evolve as quickly. In chapter 5, we'll look at the devices that can be carried on a system's motherboard. The documented list of devices hasn't been updated recently, so one of the machines I was testing against had a device that wasn't recognized.

Next, WMI works out of the box on the local system, as long as the `Winmgmt` service is running, but you need to do a little bit of work to enable access to remote systems.

4.5.2   *WMI configuration settings*

There are a number of settings you need to check and configure before you start working with WMI:

- Required services are running
- Windows firewall is configured for remote access to WMI
- PowerShell remoting is enabled

I recommend that installing and configuring these items should be a part of the setup procedure for all new servers.

> **NOTE**   Among other things, enabling PowerShell remoting ensures that the WinRM service is configured and running. This isn't required for WMI but it is required for using the WSMAN cmdlets and the CIM cmdlets in PowerShell v3, so you should ensure it's configured with the other requirements.

The first thing you need to do is make sure that the services you need are running. This includes the WMI service:

```
Get-WmiObject -Class Win32_Service -Filter "Name LIKE 'win%'" |
select Name, State
```

You're interested in the Winmgmt (WMI) and WinRM services. If they're running, you're in good shape. On machines that will be accessed remotely, also check that the DCOM Launcher is running because WMI uses DCOM for remote access.

The introduction of the Windows firewall in the more recent server versions has impacted WMI. You need to open the firewall to allow WMI access. This can be achieved through the GUI, a GPO, or by using the following `Netsh` commands (I haven't found a way to configure the firewall using PowerShell directly yet):

```
Netsh firewall set service RemoteAdmin
Netsh advfirewall set currentprofile settings remotemanagement enabled
```

This gives you a route to connect to remote machines using WMI. You can now work with your remote machines whether or not they have PowerShell installed.

If you're performing a significant number of actions on a remote machine, you'll be accessing it frequently and you're better advised to enable PowerShell remoting. This is a simple case of ensuring that the WinRM service is running on both machines and that you've run the `Enable-PSRemoting` cmdlet to perform the configuration.

> **TIP** Technically you only need PowerShell remoting enabled on the remote machine, but if you have it enabled on both machines you can use the WSMAN provider (see chapter 17) because enabling remoting ensures that the WinRM service is configured correctly.

If a PowerShell WMI cmdlet can't connect to a remote server, it will time out eventually. This can take a significant amount of time and will significantly delay the results if you're testing a number of remote machines. This process can be accelerated by testing the connection to the remote machine first:

```
$computer = "server02"
if (Test-Connection -ComputerName $computer -Count 1) {
 Get-WmiObject -Class Win32_Service -Filter "Name LIKE 'win%'" |
 select Name, State
}
else {Write-Host "Cannot connect to $computer"}
```

You can use the `Test-Connection` cmdlet, which uses `Win32_PingStatus` to test if your machine can be reached. If it can be, you perform your actions; otherwise you write a message stating that you couldn't contact the machine.

The next step is to make sure that you have the required permissions to access the WMI data on the remote machine.

4.5.3 *Authentication*

PowerShell v2 introduced a number of new parameters for `Get-WmiObject`, one of which was the `-Authentication` parameter. This parameter is available on the four cmdlets you use with WMI:

- `Get-WmiObject`
- `Invoke-WmiMethod`

- Remove-WmiObject
- Set-WmiInstance

This may seem confusing because there is also a -Credential parameter available on these cmdlets. The -Credential parameter deals with passing a userid and password to access the remote system. If credentials aren't supplied, the cmdlets use the credentials of the user.

> **NOTE**   WMI only needs credentials for remote machines. The WMI cmdlets won't accept a credential when accessing the local system.

This is best done by using Get-Credential to create the credential rather than trying to create it using the -Credential parameter, which has been known to cause errors because Get-WmiObject attempts the connection before it has used the credential to prompt for the password. The connection doesn't have a credential and so fails:

```
$cred = Get-Credential
Get-WmiObject Win32_ComputerSystem `
-Credential $cred -ComputerName dc02
```

The -Authentication parameter deals with DCOM authentication. WMI is COM-based and uses DCOM to access remote systems. There are a number of possible settings, as shown in table 4.3.

Table 4.3   WMI authentication

Value	Meaning
-1	Unchanged—authentication remains as it was before.
0	Default COM authentication level. Authentication is negotiated. WMI uses default Windows Authentication setting. An authentication level of 1 (none) will never be negotiated.
1	None. No COM authentication is performed.
2	Connect. COM authentication is performed only when the client establishes a relationship with the server. No further checks are performed.
3	Call. COM authentication is performed only at the beginning of each call when the server receives the request. Only packet headers are signed. No data is encrypted.
4	Packet. COM authentication is performed on all the data that's received from the client. Only packet headers are signed. No data is encrypted.
5	PacketIntegrity. All the data that's transferred between the client and the application is authenticated and verified. All packets are signed. No data is encrypted.
6	PacketPrivacy. The properties of the other authentication levels are used, and all the data is encrypted.

Under normal circumstances, the -Authentication parameter doesn't need to be specified. The default value is applied and negotiates the correct level of authentication. There aren't many WMI providers that require an authentication level above default.

The one you're most likely to meet is the ISS provider, where the `PacketPrivacy` level is needed. This will be explained in more detail in chapter 12.

Once you're authenticated to the remote server, you can retrieve your data.

4.5.4 *Data filtering*

We've already touched on the fact that WMI can return a lot of data. This can slow down your scripts, especially if you're returning data from remote machines, because of the amount of data returned across the network.

You have a number of ways to filter your data. All three of the following code snippets will return the same results:

```
Get-WmiObject -Class Win32_Service |
where {$_.ExitCode -ne '0'} |
select Name, ExitCode, StartMode, State

Get-WmiObject -Query "SELECT Name, ExitCode, StartMode, State FROM
    Win32_Service WHERE ExitCode <> 0"

Get-WmiObject -Class Win32_Service -Filter "ExitCode <> '0'" | select Name,
    ExitCode, StartMode, State
```

The first option uses the `Win32_Service` class and then filters with `Where-Object` and `Select-Object` to restrict the output. This works, but it has the drawback of returning all of the `Win32_Service` properties before you start filtering. When you're working remotely, it means you extract all of the data, return it to base, and then start filtering.

Technically the second option will return a bit more, because it also returns the system properties, but all of the filtering is performed as you extract the data from the WMI database. This means you only transport the objects and properties you're interested in (plus the overhead of the system properties). You could perform another select once you get the data back to filter out the system properties.

The third approach uses a WMI filter to only return the services showing the exit codes that aren't zero. You then use `Select-Object` to filter down to the properties of interest.

Which is the best approach? As always, it depends. I would probably go for the third option because it filters out the objects of no interest and is more easily modified than the second option. I also don't need to worry about the system properties getting in the way.

Returning just the subset of data you need is good, but you'll find that some of the data isn't in a format that you can easily use.

4.5.5 *Data conversions*

One of the things about computer systems that prevents us from getting bored is that every technology seems to have at least a couple of quirks in the way data is stored and handled. WMI is no exception. Most sizes, such as disk capacities, are measured in bytes, and dates are stored in a format that's readable but difficult to work with (for example, `20101020191535.848200+060`).

Both of these can cause problems, but there are fairly simple ways to cope with them.

SIZES

There are a number of places you need to deal with sizes, including memory size, file and folder sizes, and disk sizes. WMI nearly always returns sizes in bytes, which isn't the most understandable of formats. If you're presented with a disk that has 118530666496 bytes of free space, how quickly can you work out what that means? A lot slower than understanding 110.39 GB, I'll bet.

PowerShell understands the same sizes that administrators do, from kilobytes to petabytes. You can see this by running the following code:

```
1kb, 1mb, 1gb, 1tb, 1pb |
foreach {"{0,16}" -f $_ }
```

You pipe a collection of the size constants into a `foreach` command, where you display the value in right-justified fields using .NET string formatting and the `-f` operator. Notice that you can't just use `kb` and the like—you have to put a numeric value in front of the constant. The value doesn't have to be an integer; `1.5mb` is understood as 1572864.

A calculated field can be used to display the result of changing a value in bytes to one in another unit, such as gigabytes. Compare the output produced by the two options presented in the following snippets:

```
Get-WmiObject -Class Win32_ComputerSystem |
Format-List Manufacturer, Model, TotalPhysicalMemory
```

The first option uses the `Win32_ComputerSystem` class and produces a list including manufacturer, model, and the total amount of memory. This is in bytes. If you're testing machines to ensure that they have sufficient RAM for a new piece of software, you need to compare against the vendor specifications, which will be in megabytes or gigabytes:

```
Get-WmiObject -Class Win32_ComputerSystem |
Format-List Manufacturer, Model,
@{Name="RAM(GB)";
Expression={$([math]::round(($_.TotalPhysicalMemory / 1gb),2))}}
```

The second option provides a more usable display. The manufacturer and model are displayed as before. This time you use a calculated field to divide the memory by 1 GB and round the result to two decimal places. This is much easier to understand and compare against the specifications. I'm in the middle of checking the specifications on 150 machines as I write this section, and I'm using the second approach. It does work!

The other area where WMI causes problems with data is when you consider dates.

DATES

WMI has its own format for dealing with dates. This can be seen in figure 4.5, where the `Win32_OperatingSystem` class is used to determine the last time the machine was booted. There are other ways of measuring the time when a machine was started, including checking when the event log service was started, but I find this technique

```
C:\scripts                                                        ─ □ ⊠
PS> Get-WmiObject Win32_OperatingSystem | Select LastBootUpTime

LastBootUpTime
--------------
20101020180910.359600+060


PS> Get-WmiObject Win32_OperatingSystem | select @{Name="BootTime"; Expression={$_.ConvertToDateTime($_.LastBootUpTime)}
}

BootTime
--------
20/10/2010 18:09:10


PS>
```

Figure 4.5   Using the WMI date conversion methods

more accurate. The date is returned as year, month, day, hours, and seconds. This is followed by a value indicating the number of microseconds and the time zone.

I can read it and figure it out, but I can't easily work with it.

Use `Get-Member` on the `Win32_OperatingSystem` class and you'll find two script methods added to the object (they are automatically added to all WMI objects):

- `ConvertToDateTime`
- `ConvertFromDateTime`

You'll be converting WMI values to normal date formats most often, so let's start with that. The second line of code in figure 4.5 shows how this works:

```
Get-WmiObject Win32_OperatingSystem |
select @{Name="BootTime";
 Expression={$_.ConvertToDateTime($_.LastBootUpTime)}}
```

Call the method on the object on the pipeline, and use the object's `LastBootUpTime` as the argument. It looks a bit messy, but if it's something you're going to use a lot, put it into a function that's loaded into PowerShell from your profile.

I use the `ConvertToDateTime` method much more than the `ConvertFromDateTime` method. But as the method is available, it would be rude not to show how it works:

```
$date = [datetime]"8 October 2010 19:46:00"
Get-WmiObject -Class CIM_DataFile -Filter "Path='\\Test\\'" |
where {$_.LastModified -gt ($_.ConvertFromDateTime($date))}
```

A .NET DateTime object is created. The format used to present the date and time is usable in any locale, which makes it the safest option if your code is likely to be used in different countries. If you post it to the internet, expect it to be used in different countries.

The `CIM_DataFile` class is used to retrieve the files from the c:\test folder. Note how you have to use a double backslash (\\) to represent a single backslash (\) in the folder path. This is because the backslash symbol is an escape character in WMI. More on this topic in chapter 8.

A PowerShell filter is used to test the `LastModified` property against your date. You have to convert the date into WMI format for each test.

> **TIP** Combining the information about data filtering and data formatting that has been presented in this chapter leads to a simple rule of thumb: filter as soon as possible and format as late as possible.

There is always more to learn about WMI, but we've reached the point where it's time to stop looking at the theory and see how you can use it in practice to make your administrative tasks easier.

4.6   *Summary*

You've seen three broad areas of best practices. These can be applied in any environment to help maximize the return from your investment in learning PowerShell and WMI.

Security is a major issue in any organization. The internet is a great source of PowerShell examples, but you should use a trusted source and always, without fail, test any code you download.

Keeping the code secure once you've created your scripts involves a number of steps:

- Sign code to reduce the risks of tampering.
- Restrict access to the shares containing the code.
- Audit the use of administrative scripts.

When you're using PowerShell, there are some best practices you can employ to make your code more efficient and easier to write:

- Use the pipeline when reading from files if possible.
- Use parameters instead of prompting for values.
- Use string substitution to save a lot of typing.
- Use calculated fields to change the data you output.
- Use type and format files to add new properties to PowerShell objects.
- Use the PowerShell debugging and error handling to find and fix problems in your code.

WMI adds another handful of items to consider:

- WMI documentation may be out of date or nonexistent.
- It can be difficult to discover what classes are available.
- The Windows firewall must be configured to allow WMI access.
- Use `Test-Connection` rather than waiting on multiple timeouts.
- Some providers such as IIS and Microsoft Clustering require authentication for remote access.
- Filter early and format late.
- Size and date conversions are simple with PowerShell

We've now completed our look at PowerShell and WMI theory. It's time to start using these tools to administer your systems. Chapter 5 starts this process by showing what you can discover about your systems with some simple WMI scripts.

Part 2

WMI in the enterprise

This is where the fun starts. You've learned how to use PowerShell and WMI in part 1 of the book. In this second part, we'll concentrate on solving administrative problems using PowerShell scripts. Lots and lots of scripts.

WMI has been traditionally been used to gather information about computer systems. This where we'll start with chapter 5, looking at system hardware, peripherals, the operating system, and installed software. Chapter 6 extends this theme by examining the storage systems attached to our computers. We'll look at performing actions such as defragmentation as well as discovering the disk configuration.

Chapters 7 and 8 examine the registry and filesystem respectively. The management of these two data stores is essential to the well-being of your servers. In chapter 9 we'll look at how to manage the services and processes you have running.

Chapter 10 looks at printers and chapter 11 focuses on discovering and configuring network adapters and performing other network-related tasks. IIS has a WMI provider that you'll use in chapter 12; it enables you to configure websites and applications.

In chapter 13, we'll bring these topics together to configure a server's name, network, domain, and power plan, among other items.

Chapter 14 looks at security, focusing on what WMI has to offer regarding users and the firewall. Chapter 15 extends the security aspect with a look at event logs. We'll also consider performance counters.

Virtualization is a hot topic, and Hyper-V has its own WMI provider, which is covered in chapter 16.

Throughout these chapters, you'll see examples of discovery and management scripts that are immediately usable in your environment.

System documentation 5

Using WMI to discover information about your systems is the traditional role of the technology. Many of the WMI-based scripts that you'll find will show how to perform these tasks. Documenting systems is a necessary task, but one that most administrators put off until they're forced into it. It's a long, tedious, and boring process.

Not anymore! The scripts you'll work with in this chapter won't necessarily make documenting your systems interesting, but they will make it a quick and relatively painless process. Run the functions from this chapter and output the results to a file. Instant documentation! I recently had to update the documentation for several hundred servers ahead of an audit, and the scripts I used were based on this chapter. It ran as an overnight task. A quick check the next morning, and that activity was marked as complete. Compare that to how long the documentation would take to prepare manually, and the savings in time and effort available through PowerShell and WMI soon become apparent.

TIP   Notes on the structure of the scripts and on how to use the functions are given in the "about this book" section at the start of this book. Remember also that the functions can be quickly rewritten if you only need a subset of the data, such as if you only need the operating system version and service pack.

This chapter opens with a look at system hardware, covering topics such as the computer itself, its role in the domain, the processor, the motherboard, and memory configuration. At the end of section 5.1, you'll know how to retrieve information about the computer hardware that comprises your system. I use these scripts to create server documentation whenever I build a new server. It's so easy that it doesn't really register as a task. Updating documentation becomes a simple matter.

NOTE   In this chapter, we'll concentrate on information-gathering, but the methods available with these WMI classes won't be forgotten. They'll be discussed in later chapters, especially chapter 13.

You also need to discover the peripherals attached to your systems. The basic set is the monitor, keyboard, and mouse. USB ports play an important part in computer peripheral usage, so discovering what is available through them is an important task. Parallel and serial ports may have declined in popularity, but are still present on many systems. These peripherals may be more orientated toward your desktop estate, but understanding the capabilities of your systems is a requirement for upgrades. I once had to determine if we could roll out a new piece of software to a number of machines in a remote site. This software interacted with a USB device, so I had to check if the machines had USB ports. I used the USB-related scripts in section 5.2 and easily discovered the answer.

Computers all have one thing in common. They need power. Understanding a computer's power supply, battery status, and power plans are important configuration items. These items also form part of the computer's documentation. Being able to access them remotely makes producing documentation easier and quicker. Testing the battery status is also a useful diagnostic step. All these and more are covered in section 5.3.

After the hardware, the operating system is the next most important item. The scripts in section 5.4 show how you can discover the operating system configuration, installed hotfixes, boot and recovery configurations, as well as the system time and time zone. I regularly need to report on when my servers were last rebooted to prove my uptime statements. I use a script based on this section to easily check the time synchronization on domain controllers.

Systems in the enterprise are usually running a suite of applications. We'll close the chapter by looking at the installed software and registered COM applications. This completes our documentation requirements.

You may have noticed that the preceding hardware lists don't include disks and network cards. Don't worry, I haven't forgotten them. Chapter 6 is devoted to disk systems, and network cards are covered in chapter 11. Before we get to those items, you need to know how to discover your basic hardware.

5.1   System hardware and configuration

The starting point for any investigation of your computer estate has to be the basic system hardware. In this section, you'll learn how to retrieve information about the configuration of your servers from local and remote systems. This information will allow you to document your servers as well as test for specific situations. I've used subsets of these scripts to test whether a system meets the requirements for installing or running a particular piece of software.

We'll start by examining the basic computer system, including the make and model. Don't worry if you're running virtual systems, as WMI will report them as virtual servers. The type of computer can be important when determining what else can be done with the machine, and the role of the machine in the domain can similarly be important. Simple scripts enable you to discover this information remotely.

One of the most important parts of the system is the CPU. Determining how many and what types there are can help you balance loads across the server estate. With Windows Server 2008 and above, you also get an easy way to discover the number of processor cores in each physical processor.

The BIOS controls how the system starts. A recent project I was working on had a problem because of bugs in a particular version of the BIOS. Using WMI, you can easily check the BIOS versions of all the servers involved.

Memory is often one of the main areas of concern. If you don't have enough, your applications won't run properly. As well as discovering how much memory is in your machines, you can discover how many banks of memory are in use and hence whether you can upgrade these systems to prolong their life and reduce costs for the organization. The final script of section 5.1 presents a technique for discovering this information.

The WMI classes used in this section are listed in table 5.1. These classes cover the major pieces of hardware you'll meet in your systems. Some of the classes will be used in more than one script, and some scripts use multiple classes, but the table presents them in the order you'll meet them in this section. I normally start with the basics of the computer system and then work down to the fine details.

Table 5.1   System hardware classes

Component	WMI class
Computer make and model, Computer type, Domain role	`Win32_ComputerSystem`
Chassis type	`Win32_SystemEnclosure`
Motherboard	`Win32_BaseBoard`
Devices on motherboard	`Win32_OnBoardDevice`
CPU	`Win32_Processor`
BIOS	`Win32_BIOS`
Memory	`Win32_PhysicalMemoryArray` `Win32_PhysicalMemory`

Code samples

The scripts in this chapter are designed to be used as the basis of a system-documentation process. I've treated the scripts as report-generation tools, and in some instances, usually where multiple WMI classes have been called, I've inserted strings that will be output as headers. They also function as reminders of the data we are retrieving when multiple WMI classes are accessed in one script.

PowerShell purists may view this as a cardinal sin, because these scripts aren't outputting pure objects. But these scripts are written to fulfill a purely reporting function and aren't designed to be used in any further processing.

If you prefer not to have the headers produced, I've created alternative scripts in the Chapter05\Alternative Non-Report Style folder of the download code. These alternatives use `Write-Verbose` to control whether or not the header is produced when the script runs. A further possibility would be to use `Write-Warning` to display the messages.

Alternative code will be provided at other points in the book where similar reporting styles are used.

TECHNIQUE 1   **Get computer system information**

Ideally organizations should possess an asset database or, better still, a configuration-management database. The database would detail the configuration of the computers and other parts of the IT infrastructure. Unfortunately, many organizations don't have this information.

There are a number of WMI classes you can use to find this information.

PROBLEM

You need to discover the configuration of the computers in your organization. This may be to determine if the computers meet the requirements for a new software installation. Alternatively, the information could be used to form the initial load of your asset database or as a check on the currently loaded data.

SOLUTION

The WMI used in the following listing will supply the basic data you require, including make and model of the computer.

Listing 5.1 Basic system information

```
$chassis = DATA {ConvertFrom-StringData -StringData @'
3 = Desktop
5 = Pizza Box
7 = Tower
10 = Notebook
'@}

$obd = DATA {ConvertFrom-StringData -StringData @'
3 = Video
```

❶ Data lookups

```
5 = Ethernet
'@}

function get-computersystem {
[CmdletBinding()]
param (
 [parameter(ValueFromPipeline=$true,
   ValueFromPipelineByPropertyName=$true)]
 [string]$computername="$env:COMPUTERNAME"
)
PROCESS {
  "Computer System"
  Get-WmiObject -Class Win32_ComputerSystem `
  -ComputerName $computername|
  select Name, Manufacturer, Model,
  SystemType, Description,
  NumberOfProcessors, NumberOfLogicalProcessors,
  @{Name="RAM(GB)";
  Expression={[math]::round($($_.TotalPhysicalMemory/1GB), 2)}}

  "System Enclosure:"
  Get-WmiObject -Class Win32_SystemEnclosure `
  -ComputerName $computername |
  select Manufacturer, Model,
  @{Name="Chassis"; Expression={$chassis["$($_.ChassisTypes)"]}},
  LockPresent,SerialNumber, SMBIOSAssetTag

  "Base Board:"
  Get-WmiObject -Class Win32_BaseBoard `
  -ComputerName $computername |
  select Manufacturer, Model, Name,
  SerialNumber, SKU, Product,
  Replaceable, Version

  "On Board Devices:"
  Get-WmiObject -Class Win32_OnBoardDevice `
  -ComputerName $computername |
  select Description,
  @{Name="Device";
  Expression={$obd["$($_.DeviceType)"]}}
}}
```

2 Computer system

3 Chassis type

4 Motherboard

5 Onboard devices

This script follows the basic pattern you'll see throughout the book. You define some hash tables **1** as lookup tables and use Get-WmiObject to retrieve the required data. Convert-FromStringData is a PowerShell v2 cmdlet that converts a here-string (a PowerShell multiline string) into a hash table. If PowerShell v1 is being used, the hash table will need to be defined from scratch (see appendix A). The Win32_ComputerSystem class supplies data **2**, such as the make and model, the number of processors, and the amount of RAM. The RAM is recalculated from bytes to gigabytes (GB) to make a more readily understood display.

The system enclosure **3** and the motherboard (baseboard) **4** are returned by the appropriate classes. They both have properties labeled manufacturer, which won't necessarily be the same. It's always interesting to compare the manufacturers given here with the manufacturer of the whole system.

Motherboards may possess a number of components, such as video controllers or network cards, that are additional devices on the board. These can be discovered by the `Win32_OnBoardDevice` class ❺. The list of available devices in the WMI documentation is a little out of date, but the description of the device will usually supply sufficient information.

DISCUSSION

A calculated field in `Select-Object` uses the lookup tables. The type of onboard device is a good example of using the lookup tables ❺:

```
@{Name="Device"; Expression={$obd["$($_.DeviceType)"]}}
```

A name is defined as a string, and the lookup is performed by the expression. In this case, the `$obd` variable holds the hash table and the `DeviceType` property is used as the lookup. A subexpression is used to ensure the value of the property is obtained.

> **NOTE**   The full hash tables may not be given in the listings. Selected values are used to illustrate the scripts in the book, but the full list of values is in the code download.

The function can be used from the command line:

```
".", "127.0.0.1" | foreach {get-computersystem}
```

Alternatively, a list of computers could be supplied in a CSV file and piped to the function.

As an example of the evolving nature of WMI, the `NumberofLogicalProcessors` property on the `Win32_ComputerSystem` class ❷ is only available on Windows Vista/2008 and above.

One of the things about WMI that may cause confusion is that there can be multiple answers to the same question, such as the computer type.

TECHNIQUE 2   **Get computer type**

In listing 5.1 you saw that the `Win32_SystemEnclosure` class returned the chassis type. This data is also available on the `Win32_ComputerSystem` class.

PROBLEM

You've been tasked with discovering which machines in your environment are desktops and which are servers.

SOLUTION

The data can be discovered using the `Win32_ComputerSystem` class. The next listing shows how this class can be used.

Listing 5.2   Computer type

```
$comptype = DATA {
ConvertFrom-StringData -StringData @'
0 =   Unspecified
1 =   Desktop
2 =   Mobile
```

```
3 =  Workstation
4 =  Enterprise Server
5 =  Small Office and Home Office (SOHO) Server
6 =  Appliance PC
7 =  Performance Server
8 =  Maximum
'@
}
function get-computertype {
[CmdletBinding()]
param (
 [parameter(ValueFromPipeline=$true,
   ValueFromPipelineByPropertyName=$true)]
 [string]$computername="$env:COMPUTERNAME"
)
PROCESS {
  Get-WmiObject -Class Win32_ComputerSystem `
  -ComputerName $computername |
  select Name,
  @{Name="ComputerType"; Expression={$comptype["$($_.PCSystemType)"]}}
}}
```

The imaginatively named `$comptype` hash table is created using `ConvertFrom-StringData` and defines the computer types. This is then used in a calculated field to return the computer type.

DISCUSSION

The computer types produced by listings 5.1 and 5.2 are similar but not identical. An example is shown in figure 5.1. Note that you can use `Select-Object` on the results of these functions. Remember that you're dealing with objects.

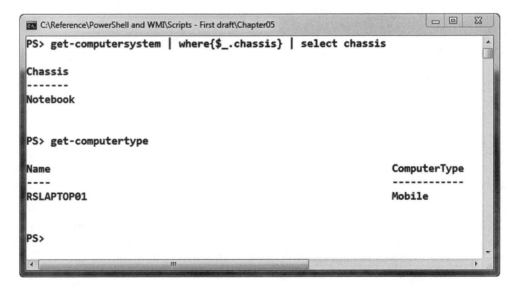

Figure 5.1   Results of running the functions from listings 5.1 and 5.2

In addition to determining its physical type, you can view a computer in the light of its role in a domain.

Get domain role

A Windows machine can be in a domain or a work group. It can be a workstation or a server. If it's in a domain, it could be a domain controller. You can find your domain controllers in a number of ways using .NET, ADSI, or the AD cmdlets from Microsoft or Quest. If you're retrieving computer information using WMI, you can also find domain controllers.

PROBLEM

You need to determine if your systems are in the domain and what role they play in the domain. You specifically want to know if any machines are domain controllers.

SOLUTION

The script in the next listing follows the pattern established in previous scripts.

Listing 5.3   Domain role

```
$domrole = DATA {
ConvertFrom-StringData -StringData @'
0 = Standalone Workstation
1 = Member Workstation
2 = Standalone Server
3 = Member Server
4 = Backup Domain Controller
5 = Primary Domain Controller
'@
}
function get-domainrole {
[CmdletBinding()]
param (
 [parameter(ValueFromPipeline=$true,
   ValueFromPipelineByPropertyName=$true)]
 [string]$computername="$env:COMPUTERNAME"
)
PROCESS {
  Get-WmiObject -Class Win32_ComputerSystem `
  -ComputerName $computername |
  select Name, Domain,
  @{Name="DomainRole";
  Expression={$domrole["$($_.DomainRole)"]}}
}}
```

The hash table defines the possible outcomes for the domain role. The function accepts a string containing a computer name as a parameter, and the parameter has a default of $env:COMPUTERNAME, which means the local system name. Win32_ComputerSystem is used to return the information using a calculated field to decode the domain role.

DISCUSSION

The default value on the parameter enables you to use just the function name to get the information on the local machine. One of the really great things about the advanced functions is that tab completion works on the parameter names. It just happens—no coding required!

If you don't want to use a default parameter, I suggest you use a mandatory parameter. This will force PowerShell to prompt for the computer name. You can do this by changing the parameter statement to the following syntax:

```
[parameter(Mandatory=$true, ValueFromPipeline=$true,
   ValueFromPipelineByPropertyName=$true)]
```

If a default value and mandatory parameter are used together, the default is ignored.

You've now learned about as much as you can at the machine level. It's time to dive into the computer hardware and configuration. We'll start by looking at the processor.

TECHNIQUE 4   Get processor information

The computer's processor performs the computational effort in your systems that enable you to play games or even write a book. The number of cores in a physical CPU continues to rise, but you still need to understand what your servers are capable of processing.

As a consultant, I've often ended up on new sites where no one can tell me the configuration of a particular machine. Now I can find out for myself in much less time.

PROBLEM

Will your server support an increased workload? The answer depends on two things: First, how busy is the server at the moment? You'll learn how to discover this in chapter 15. Second, what size processors do you have, and how many of them are in your computer?

Another thing you need to know is whether the processor can support 64-bit applications.

SOLUTION

Discovering the speed and type of the processors in a computer can be achieved with the `Win32_Processor` class, as shown in the following listing. Be careful when typing, as the `Win32_Process` class will give you unexpected results if it's selected by an editor with IntelliSense on WMI class names.

Listing 5.4   CPU type

```
$arch = DATA {ConvertFrom-StringData -StringData @'
0 = x86
9 = x64
'@}

$fam = DATA {ConvertFrom-StringData -StringData @'
29 = AMD Athlon™ Processor Family
112 = Hobbit Family
131 = AMD Athlon™ 64 Processor Family
132 = AMD Opteron™ Processor Family
'@}

$type = DATA {ConvertFrom-StringData -StringData @'
```

❶ Lookup hash tables

```
3 = Central Processor
4 = Math Processor                                              Lookup hash
6 = Video Processor                                          ❶ tables
'@}

function get-cputype {
[CmdletBinding()]
param (
 [parameter(ValueFromPipeline=$true,
   ValueFromPipelineByPropertyName=$true)]                      Parameter
 [string]$computername="$env:COMPUTERNAME"                   ❷ block
)
PROCESS {
 Get-WmiObject -Class Win32_Processor `
  -ComputerName $computername |                                 Processor
 Select DeviceID,                                            ❸ properties
 @{Name="Processor Type";
 Expression={$type["$($_.ProcessorType)"]}},
 Manufacturer, Name, Description,
 @{Name="CPU Family";
 Expression={$fam["$($_.Family)"]}},
 @{Name="CPU Architecture";
 Expression={$arch["$($_.Architecture)"]}},
 NumberOfCores, NumberOfLogicalProcessors, AddressWidth,
 DataWidth,  CurrentClockSpeed, MaxClockSpeed,
 ExtClock,  L2CacheSize, L2CacheSpeed, L3CacheSize,
 L3CacheSpeed,  CurrentVoltage, PowerManagementSupported,
 ProcessorId, SocketDesignation, Status
}}
```

Executing the listing creates a function called get-cputype and some hash tables ❶ to be used as data lookups. The function takes a computer name as a parameter ❷ and performs a call to Win32_Processor ❸. Where applicable, Select-Object uses a calculated field to convert the numeric codes into meaningful values using the hash tables. The results are displayed as a list. A separate listing will be created for each CPU. Note that the CPU device IDs start numbering at zero.

DISCUSSION

A limited number of hash table members are shown for brevity. The full type listings are available in the download version of the script. In case anyone is wondering, the Hobbit processor is genuine.

If this function is run against a Windows Server 2008/Vista or later system, the number of logical processors and number of cores are reported correctly. Earlier operating systems won't report values for these properties and will report logical processors as physical processors.

Next, the BIOS controls how a system starts up. The version can have an impact on your systems.

TECHNIQUE 5   **Get BIOS information**

The Basic Input/Output System (BIOS) runs when the computer starts. It initializes certain system devices and then loads the operating system. On modern systems, the

BIOS can be upgraded. This may need to happen before other firmware can be upgraded.

PROBLEM

What version of the BIOS is being used to start your system? This information has to be recovered so that you can determine if an upgrade is required to work with a new device.

SOLUTION

The following listing shows how you can create a function to return the BIOS information. You need to use the class twice in order to unravel the BIOS characteristics.

Listing 5.5 Listing 5.5 BIOS

```
$bioschar = DATA {ConvertFrom-StringData -StringData @'          Hash ❶
7 = PCI is supported                                             table
8 = PC Card (PCMCIA) is supported
9 = Plug and Play is supported
11 = BIOS is Upgradable (Flash)
15 = Boot from CD is supported
33 = USB Legacy is supported
'@}
function get-biosinfo {                                          Function ❷
[CmdletBinding()]                                                definition
param (
 [parameter(ValueFromPipeline=$true,
   ValueFromPipelineByPropertyName=$true)]
    [string]$computername="$env:COMPUTERNAME"
)
PROCESS {
 Get-WmiObject -Class Win32_Bios `                               Main ❸
-ComputerName $computername |                                    data
 Select  BuildNumber, CurrentLanguage, InstallableLanguages,
 Manufacturer, Name, PrimaryBIOS,
 @{Name="Release Date";
 Expression={ $_.ConvertToDateTime( $_.ReleaseDate) }},
 SerialNumber, SMBIOSBIOSVersion, SMBIOSMajorVersion,
 SMBIOSMinorVersion, SMBIOSPresent, Status, Version            Expand BIOS ❹
                                                               characteristics
 "BIOS Characteristics:"
 Get-WmiObject -Class Win32_Bios -ComputerName $computername |
 Select -ExpandProperty BiosCharacteristics |
 foreach {$bioschar["$($_)"]}

}}
```

The BIOScharacteristics property is an array of integers that you'll need to expand so that you can decode the meaning of the integer. These values are defined in the hash table called $bioschar ❶. The characteristics are a good guide to the devices that the system can support.

The get-biosinfo function ❷ is used to get the BIOS information ❸. This data is displayed as a list, as shown in figure 5.2. A data conversion using the ConvertToDateTime method is performed on the BIOS release date.

```
PS> get-biosinfo


BuildNumber          :
CurrentLanguage      :
InstallableLanguages :
Manufacturer         : Hewlett-Packard
Name                 : PhoenixBIOS 4.0 Release 6.1
PrimaryBIOS          : True
Release Date         : 23/12/2008 00:00:00
SerialNumber         : 2CE9029SFT
SMBIOSBIOSVersion    : F.34
SMBIOSMajorVersion   : 2
SMBIOSMinorVersion   : 4
SMBIOSPresent        : True
Status               : OK
Version              : HPQOEM - 6040000

BIOS Characteristics:
ISA is supported
PCI is supported
PC Card (PCMCIA) is supported
Plug and Play is supported
APM is supported
BIOS is Upgradable (Flash)
BIOS shadowing is allowed
ESCD support is available
Boot from CD is supported
ACPI is supported
USB Legacy is supported
AGP is supported
```

Figure 5.2 Expanding the BIOS characteristics

A second call to `Win32_Bios` is made ❹ to access the `BIOS` characteristics. It would be possible to slightly improve the function by making a single call to `Get-WmiObject` and putting the results into a variable. The variable would then be used twice to display the data.

The `BiosCharacteristics` property is expanded by `Select-Object`, and each integer code is looked up in the hash table to determine its meaning. Figure 5.2 shows the output.

DISCUSSION

There are a number of WMI classes that use arrays of values as a property. In some cases, you don't need to worry about them because the information is available from other properties. When the information can only be recovered from an array, you have to use `Select-Object` and `ExpandProperty` to access the data.

The drawback to `ExpandProperty` is that you can't display other properties at the same time as you're expanding a property. You have to use two individual calls to `Select-Object`.

The last object on our tour of the main computer system is memory.

TECHNIQUE 6 Get memory configuration

The amount of memory in computer systems has rocketed. I remember having arguments with management ten years ago because I wanted to put 256 MB in some PCs.

Now you wouldn't really consider a new full-size machine that has less than 2 GB. Netbooks currently tend to come with 1 GB of RAM, but the Windows 7 Starter Edition is configured to run with a low memory footprint.

> **NOTE**   Just in case you were thinking of jumping to using 1 GB of RAM and Windows 7 Starter Edition for your main machines, remember that Starter Edition can't join a domain.

PROBLEM

Memory is normally arranged on one or more chips. You need to know the arrangement so that you can determine if the system can be upgraded in a cost-effective manner. You also need to know the amount of RAM in the system.

SOLUTION

Listing 5.1 showed how to use the `Win32_ComputerSystem` class to find the total system memory. If you need that information as part of the memory information, the following line of PowerShell can be utilized:

```
get-computersystem | where{$_."RAM(GB)"} | select "RAM(GB)"
```

Your functions can be used on the pipeline just like cmdlets. The rest of the memory information is obtained from the `get-memory` function defined in the following listing.

Listing 5.6   Memory configuration

```
$memuse = DATA {ConvertFrom-StringData -StringData @'
3 = System memory
'@}

$memcheck = DATA {ConvertFrom-StringData -StringData @'
3 = None
4 = Parity
'@}

$memform = DATA {ConvertFrom-StringData -StringData @'
7 = SIMM
8 = DIMM
'@}

$memtype = DATA {ConvertFrom-StringData -StringData @'
2 = DRAM
20 = DDR
21 = DDR-2
'@}

function get-memory {
[CmdletBinding()]
param (
 [parameter(ValueFromPipeline=$true,
   ValueFromPipelineByPropertyName=$true)]
 [string]$computername="$env:COMPUTERNAME"
)
PROCESS{
 Get-WmiObject -Class Win32_PhysicalmemoryArray `
```

❶ Hash tables

❷ Memory array

```
 -ComputerName $computername |
 Select @{Name="Location"; Expression={
  if ($_.Location -eq 3){"System Board"}
  else {"Other"}
 } },
 @{Name="Use";
 Expression={$memuse["$($_.Use)"]}},
 MemoryDevices, HotSwappable,
 @{Name="MaxRAM(GB)";
 Expression={[math]::round($($_.MaxCapacity/1mB), 2)}},
 @{Name="CheckType";
 Expression={$memcheck["$($_.MemoryErrorCorrection)"]}}

""
 Get-WmiObject Win32_Physicalmemory `
-ComputerName $computername  |
 select BankLabel,
 @{Name="Size(GB)";
 Expression={[math]::round($($_.Capacity/1gb), 2)}},
 DataWidth, DeviceLocator,
 @{Name="Form";
 Expression={$memform["$($_.FormFactor)"]}},
 @{Name="Type";
 Expression={$memtype["$($_.MemoryType)"]}},
 Speed, TotalWidth,
 @{Name="Detail";
 Expression={$memdetail["$($_.TypeDetail)"]}}
}}
```

❸ Memory chips

After defining the hash tables ❶, this script makes use of two WMI classes. The first class, `Win32_PhysicalMemoryArray` ❷, displays the basic information, including where the memory is located and how many memory devices can be fitted. The `MaxRAM(GB)` is important for determining if further RAM can be fitted.

The second class is `Win32_Physicalmemory` ❸, which is used to display information about each individual memory device. This will include the memory size in GB, the type of memory, and its speed.

DISCUSSION

If only the number of devices and the total size is required, you can use `Measure-Object` to determine the results:

```
get-memory | Measure-Object -Sum "Size(GB)"
```

Comparing the results of this code with using `get-computersystem` (shown at the beginning of the solution) can very quickly identify whether any memory has been diverted for graphics or other uses.

Memory is the last of the basic computer system components we'll consider. It's time to look at the peripherals attached to your computers.

5.2   *Peripherals*

Computer systems aren't self-contained boxes—you have to attach other devices to them, such as a monitor, keyboard, and mouse. You also need to think about the hardware ports that are available on the system. Parallel and serial ports are often still available, even though they're being superseded by USB ports in many systems.

The WMI classes we'll be dealing with in this section are summarized in table 5.2.

Table 5.2   Computer peripheral classes

Component	WMI Class
Display settings	Win32_DesktopMonitor Win32_VideoController
Input device	Win32_Keyboard Win32_PointingDevice
Hardware ports	Win32_ParallelPort Win32_SerialPort Win32_USBHub Win32_USBController

The monitor is the primary peripheral you need to consider.

TECHNIQUE 7   Get display settings

Every client machine will have a monitor. Servers may not have a monitor physically attached if they're virtual machines or connected to a KVM to allow screen sharing.

PROBLEM

You need to determine the display characteristics of your system.

SOLUTION

There are two WMI classes you need to consider to solve this problem. `Win32_DesktopMonitor` will provide information on the monitor that's attached to the system. There's also the video controller to take into consideration; this information is discovered using the `Win32_VideoController` class. The following listing shows how these can be combined into a single function.

Listing 5.7   Display settings

```
function get-display {
[CmdletBinding()]
param (
 [parameter(ValueFromPipeline=$true,
   ValueFromPipelineByPropertyName=$true)]
 [string]$computername="$env:COMPUTERNAME"
)
PROCESS{
 "Monitor"
 Get-WmiObject -Class Win32_DesktopMonitor `
 -ComputerName $computername |
 select Name, Description, DeviceId,
 MonitorManufacturer, MonitorType,
 PixelsPerXLogicalInch,
 PixelsPerYLogicalInch,
 ScreenHeight, ScreenWidth
```

```
"Video"
Get-WmiObject -Class Win32_VideoController `
-ComputerName $computername |
select Name,
@{Name="RAM(MB)"; Expression={$_.AdapterRAM/1mb}},
VideoModeDescription,
CurrentRefreshRate,
InstalledDisplayDrivers,
@{Name="DriverDate";
Expression={$_.ConvertToDateTime($_.DriverDate)}},
DriverVersion
}}
```

This function is very straightforward. It starts with the standard parameter of a computer name. This could also be an IP address. The `Win32_DesktopMonitor` class is used first, and the required properties are selected.

The `Win32_VideoController` class is called. Two calculated fields are used: the first calculates the video RAM into megabytes from bytes, and the second converts the driver date to a readable format.

DISCUSSION

The `Win32_DesktopMonitor` class was introduced with Windows Vista to replace the `Win32_DisplayConfiguration` class. The `Win32_VideoController` class was introduced at the same time to replace the `Win32_DisplayControllerConfiguration` class. The old classes are still available in Windows up to at least Windows 7. The new classes may misreport on devices using old drivers on older operating systems. It may be worth trying the older classes in that case.

The situation is much simpler when you consider input devices.

TECHNIQUE 8 Get input devices

The standard input devices are a keyboard and mouse. You'll usually only have a single keyboard, but you may have multiple mice, especially on laptops.

PROBLEM

The keyboard and mouse attached to your computer need to be determined to complete the documentation of your system.

SOLUTION

Listing 5.8 shows how you can retrieve this information. The `Win32_Keyboard` class will return the information on the keyboard. I've selected the properties that I think are most useful, but as with all of the listings in the book, I encourage you to examine the full list of available properties to determine if there are any others you require to meet your particular needs.

Listing 5.8 Input devices

```
function get-input {
[CmdletBinding()]
param (
 [parameter(ValueFromPipeline=$true,
```

```
    ValueFromPipelineByPropertyName=$true)]
  [string]$computername="$env:COMPUTERNAME"
)
PROCESS {
 "Keyboard"
 Get-WmiObject -Class Win32_Keyboard `
 -ComputerName $computername |
 select Name, Description, DeviceId,
 Layout, NumberOfFunctionKeys

 "Mouse"
 Get-WmiObject Win32_PointingDevice `
 -ComputerName $computername |
 select Manufacturer, Name, DeviceID,
 DeviceInterface
}}
```

The information on the mouse is provided by the `Win32_PointingDevice` class, which isn't exactly an intuitively named WMI class. If other, more exotic, input devices are used on a particular system, I'm afraid you'll need to experiment to determine if they're detected by this class.

DISCUSSION

The `Win32_PointingDevice` class will return multiple devices, especially on a laptop. On the laptop I'm using to write this book, I have the touchpad and a Bluetooth-attached wireless mouse, both of which are recorded. On IBM/Lenovo laptops, the touchpad is recorded as well as the red mouse button in the middle of the keyboard.

The last category of devices we need to consider in this section is the hardware ports to which you attach other peripherals. Printers, disks, and other devices that may be attached through these ports will be covered in the relevant chapters.

TECHNIQUE 9   Get ports

The standard hardware ports, for many years, were the parallel port and the serial port. These are being replaced by USB ports, and many laptops only have USB ports. There are also FireWire (1394) ports that may have to be considered.

PROBLEM

A new service is being introduced into your organization. This service requires a device to be attached to some of the computers used in the organization. Do those machines have a suitable hardware port?

SOLUTION

The parallel and serial ports can be discovered using the appropriately named port, as shown in listing 5.9. Each of the relevant WMI classes is called and the appropriate properties displayed. The `Win32_SerialPort` class has a number of properties that indicate what is supported and settable. These can be quickly viewed using

```
Get-WmiObject Win32_SerialPort | select Support*, Settable*
```

These properties could be incorporated into the script if you deem it necessary.

Listing 5.9 Hardware ports

```
function get-port {
[CmdletBinding()]
param (
 [parameter(ValueFromPipeline=$true,
   ValueFromPipelineByPropertyName=$true)]
 [string]$computername="$env:COMPUTERNAME"
)
PROCESS {
"Parallel Port"
Get-WmiObject -Class Win32_ParallelPort `
  -ComputerName $computername |
select Name, OSAutoDiscovered, PNPDeviceID

"Serial Port"
Get-WmiObject -Class Win32_SerialPort `
  -ComputerName $computername |
select Name, OSAutoDiscovered,
PNPDeviceID, ProviderType, MaxBaudRate

 "USBHub"
 Get-WmiObject -Class Win32_USBHub `
  -ComputerName $computername | select Name, PNPDeviceID

 ""
 "USB Controller"
 Get-WmiObject -Class Win32_USBController `
  -ComputerName $computername | Select Name, PNPDeviceID
}}
```

Accessing the information about the USB ports is more problematic. There are two classes you can use: `Win32_USBHub` and `Win32_USBController`. Neither of the classes directly show the number of USB ports that are available, and there is no apparent way to determine this. All you can do is show that USB connectivity is available.

DISCUSSION

As with all of the functions in this chapter, you can use it in a number of ways. If you just need information on the local machine, you can use `get-port`. If you're accessing a remote machine, then `get-port -computer server02` or `get-port -computer 10.10.54.201` will work.

If required, the `Win32_1394Controller` and `Win32_1394ControllerDevice` classes can be added to listing 5.9 to supply information on FireWire (1394) ports.

Laptops are replacing desktop machines as the client of choice in many organizations. If you use laptops, you need to consider the state of their batteries.

5.3   *Power supplies*

Discovering information about the battery and its state is an interesting task. You need to look beyond the default root\cimv2 namespace to discover the information. Table 5.3 summarizes the classes you need to work with and the namespaces you need to use. We'll start simply with the default namespace.

Table 5.3   Computer power classes

Component	WMI class
Battery	`Win32_Battery`
Battery status Test power source	`root\wmi   BatteryStatus`
Power plans	`root\cimv2\power   Win32_PowerPlan`

TECHNIQUE 10   Get battery details

Our starting point is the battery itself. What type is it, and what is it doing?

PROBLEM

How can you discover the battery type installed in your system?

SOLUTION

The `Win32_Battery` class in the root/cimv2 namespace is used in the following listing
to determine the battery type.

Listing 5.10   Battery details

```
$status = DATA {ConvertFrom-StringData -StringData @'
1 = Discharging
2 = On AC. No battery discharge. Not necessarily charging.
6 = Charging
'@}

$chem = DATA {ConvertFrom-StringData -StringData @'
6 = Lithium-ion
'@}

function get-battery {
[CmdletBinding()]
param (
 [parameter(ValueFromPipeline=$true,
   ValueFromPipelineByPropertyName=$true)]
 [string]$computername="$env:COMPUTERNAME"
)
PROCESS {
 Get-WmiObject -Class Win32_Battery    `
  -ComputerName $computername |
 select DeviceID, Name, Description,
 @{Name="Status";
  Expression={$status["$($_.BatteryStatus)"]}},
  @{Name="Chemistry";
  Expression={$chem["$($_.Chemistry)"]}},
 @{Name="Voltage(V)";
  Expression={$($_.DesignVoltage / 1000)}},
 @{Name="PecentChargeLeft";
  Expression={$($_.EstimatedChargeRemaining)}},
 PowerManagementSupport
}}
```

Some lookup tables are created at the beginning of the listing. These are truncated for brevity, but the full lists are available in the download code. The `Win32_Battery` class is used with a number of calculated fields, decoding the integers to meaningful values.

The voltage is reported in millivolts which we divide by 1000 to produce the display in volts.

DISCUSSION

`EstimatedRunTime` on Windows 7 (and Windows Server 2008 R2) always seems to return 71582788, which is approximately 136 years if the documentation is correct. Talk about a lifetime guarantee!

Knowing how long the battery will last may be important to you. There is an indirect way of discovering this.

TECHNIQUE 11   Get battery status

There's another way to get information on your battery status. This involves using an undocumented WMI class from the root\wmi namespace. There are many classes in this namespace that appear as if they should be useful, but when investigated they don't return any data. You're interested in the `Batterystatus` class:

```
Get-WmiObject -Namespace 'root\wmi' -Class Batterystatus
```

PROBLEM

How can you determine the status of your battery and use that to determine how long it will take to discharge the battery?

SOLUTION

There isn't a simple solution to this problem, so you need to approach it in a roundabout fashion. Your starting point is to determine the battery status, as shown in the following listing. I have left the voltage in millivolts in this script. The appropriate calculated field from listing 5.10 can be utilized in this script to convert it to volts if required.

Listing 5.11   Battery status

```
function get-batterystatus {
[CmdletBinding()]
param (
 [parameter(ValueFromPipeline=$true,
   ValueFromPipelineByPropertyName=$true)]
 [string]$computername="$env:COMPUTERNAME"
)
PROCESS {
 Get-WmiObject -Namespace 'root\wmi' -Class BatteryStatus `
  -ComputerName $computername |
  Select Active, ChargeRate, Charging,
 Critical, DischargeRate, Discharging,
 PowerOnline, RemainingCapacity,
 Tag, Voltage
}}
```

The key to determining the time left on the battery is the RemainingCapacity property. If you measure this while the battery is discharging, you can calculate the time to discharge. As an example, you can let the battery discharge for approximately one hour. At the start of the discharge period, run these lines of code:

```
$c1 = (get-batterystatus).RemainingCapacity
$d1 = Get-Date
```

After sufficient time has elapsed, repeat the measurements using $c2 and $d2 for the variables. The difference between $d1 and $d2 creates a timespan object that will have a totalminutes property. The difference between $c1 and $c2 shows how much capacity has been used in the period. Divide that number by the totalminutes property to determine capacity used per minute. Divide that into $c1 to determine how long the battery will take to discharge. Finally, now that you know the discharge rate, you'll be able to calculate the time remaining on the battery for any RemainingCapacity value.

This approach assumes that the rate of discharge is always the same. You may need to repeat this experiment under different loads to determine the complete battery usage pattern.

DISCUSSION

I saw a post that stated the value of RemainingCapacity divided by 252 gave the time to discharge. This doesn't seem to hold on the systems I've tested under Windows 7 and Windows Server 2008 R2 Datacenter edition. (Yes, I run Datacenter on my laptop. It runs Hyper-V very nicely.)

You can also use the Batterystatus class to give a quick indication of whether the laptop is running on battery or external power.

TECHNIQUE 12   Test power source

I was recently giving a talk using two laptops for the demonstration. I had an RDP link from one to the other that repeatedly disconnected toward the end of the demonstration. It wasn't until I'd finished that I realized that I'd left the second laptop on battery power!

PROBLEM

How can you determine if a laptop is running on battery power or external power? This question could arise for the reason given in the introduction, or a user could complain that their screen is dull, which could indicate being on battery.

SOLUTION

The following listing provides a simple test to determine the state of the power supply.

Listing 5.12 Test power source

```
function test-powersource {
[CmdletBinding()]
param (
 [parameter(ValueFromPipeline=$true,
   ValueFromPipelineByPropertyName=$true)]
 [string]$computername="$env:COMPUTERNAME"
```

```
)
PROCESS {
 $status = Get-WmiObject -Namespace 'root\wmi' -Class BatteryStatus `
  -ComputerName $computername

 if ($status.PowerOnLine) {"System on External Power"}
 else {"System on Battery Power"}
}}
```

The `BatteryStatus` class is interrogated as shown. You then use the `PowerOnLine` property as the condition in the `if` statement. It returns a Boolean (`true` or `false`), so you can use it directly rather than testing the value. If the property returns `true`, you're on external power and you print the appropriate message. Otherwise you're on battery power.

DISCUSSION

In the example I gave at the beginning of this section, the power had been switched to battery because the power switch had been knocked off. It would be possible to use the techniques we'll discuss in chapter 15 to create a scheduled job that tests the power source during the presentation. If it's running on external power, nothing is returned, but if the system switches to battery power, a warning is given to the presenter. Alternatively, a WMI event could be used to detect the change using the `BatteryStatusChange` class.

The last power-related item to be investigated is the power plan.

TECHNIQUE 13   Get power plans

Windows 7 and Windows Server 2008 R2 introduced a new WMI namespace called root\cimv2\power for working with power plans. A power plan controls how the machine reacts to being on external or battery power. This includes the control of items such as screen brightness or hibernation after a period of inactivity.

You can view the classes in this namespace:

```
Get-WmiObject -Namespace 'root\cimv2\power' -List
```

The documentation for these classes can be found on MSDN in the WMI section under "Power Policy classes." The classes involve a number of associations, as you'll see when you discover how to use them.

PROBLEM

The active power plan needs to be checked and its settings displayed.

SOLUTION

The script in the following listing makes use of a number of the WMI and PowerShell features you saw in chapters 2 and 3. Refer to those chapters if you need a refresher.

Listing 5.13   Power plan

```
function get-powerplan {
[CmdletBinding()]
param (
 [parameter(ValueFromPipeline=$true,
```

```
   ValueFromPipelineByPropertyName=$true)]
  [string]$computername="$env:COMPUTERNAME"
)
PROCESS {                                                                    ❶ Identify active
 Get-WmiObject -Namespace 'root\cimv2\power' `                                  power plan
  -Class Win32_PowerPlan -ComputerName $computername |
 sort IsActive -Descending |
 Format-List ElementName, Description, InstanceID, IsActive

"'nActive Plan Details"
$plan = Get-WmiObject -namespace 'root\cimv2\power' `
-Class Win32_PowerPlan -ComputerName $computername |                         ❷ Separate
 where {$_.IsActive}                                                            active plan

$id = ($plan.InstanceID).Replace("\","\\")

$query = "ASSOCIATORS OF {Win32_PowerPlan.InstanceID=""$id}""}"
$psIndexes = Get-WmiObject -ComputerName $computername `                     ❸ Get Powersetting-
-namespace 'root\cimv2\power' -Query $query                                     Dataindex

"Battery Power"
foreach ($psIndex in ($psIndexes | where {$_.InstanceID -like "*DC*"})){
 $inxid = ($psIndex.InstanceId).Replace("\","\\")
 $query = "ASSOCIATORS OF                                                    ❹ Discover
    ➡ {Win32_PowerSettingDataIndex.InstanceID=""$inxid}""}                      power settings
    ➡ WHERE RESULTCLASS = Win32_PowerSetting "                                   for battery
 Get-WmiObject -ComputerName $computername `
 -namespace 'root\cimv2\power' -Query $query |
 Add-Member -MemberType Noteproperty -Name "SettingIndexValue"`              ❺ Display
 -Value $($psIndex.SettingIndexValue) -PassThru |                              results
  Format-List InstanceId, Description, SettingIndexValue
}                                                                            ❻ Discover power
                                                                               settings for
"External Power"                                                               external power
foreach ($psIndex in ($psIndexes | where {$_.InstanceID -like "*AC*"}) ) {
 $inxid = ($psIndex.InstanceId).Replace("\","\\")
 $query = "ASSOCIATORS OF                                                    ❼ Discover
    ➡ {Win32_PowerSettingDataIndex.InstanceID=""$inxid}""}                      WMI
    ➡ WHERE RESULTCLASS = Win32_PowerSetting "                                   asociator
 Get-WmiObject -ComputerName $computername `
 -namespace 'root\cimv2\power' -Query $query |
 Add-Member -MemberType Noteproperty `
-Name "SettingIndexValue" `
 -Value $($psIndex.SettingIndexValue) -PassThru|                             ❽ Display
  Format-List InstanceId, Description, SettingIndexValue                       results
}
}}
```

The function starts by obtaining a list of the current power plans on the system ❶.
This is sorted in descending order to ensure that the active plan is at the top of the
list. The information about the plans is displayed.

The details of the active plan are obtained by creating a variable that represents
the active plan ❷. WMI uses the backslash (\) as an escape character, so you need to
replace single instances with double occurrences of the character. A WMI query ❸ is
constructed and run to find the power setting indexes associated with the power plan.

The settings for battery power are discovered first. The indexes are filtered in the `foreach` condition to only pass those referring to battery power (DC). A query to find the associators is constructed, with the results limited to the power settings ❹. The query is executed ❺ and the results are passed on to the pipeline. `Add-member` is used to add the value of the setting, and the results are displayed.

The process is repeated for external power (AC) ❻, with the associators being discovered via a query ❼ and the correct value ❽ being added again.

DISCUSSION

This is the most complicated script we've looked at so far. If you can follow the logic, then congratulations! You're well on the way to being a PowerShell and WMI expert.

The `Win32_PowerPlan` class can be used to change the active plan. You'll learn how to perform this task in chapter 13 when we consider server configuration.

The power plan classes are only available on Windows 7 and Windows Server 2008 R2. You could refine listing 5.13 by testing that you're running against the correct operating system. But first you need to learn to discover the operating system in use on your computers.

5.4   *Operating system*

The operating system is fundamental to your system. It determines what applications can run and how you administer the system. Table 5.4 lists the main WMI classes you'll use when you're working with the operating system.

Table 5.4   Operating system classes

Component	WMI class
Operating system Service pack Boot time	Win32_OperatingSystem
Hotfix	Win32_QuickFixEngineering
Boot-up configuration	Win32_BootConfigurations
Recovery configuration	Win32_OSRecoveryConfiguration
	Win32_LocalTime
System time	Win32_UTCTime
	Win32_TimeZone

In many cases the operating system determines what you can do with the system, which often makes it the best place to start.

TECHNIQUE 14   **Get operating system version**

You need to document the operating system for a number of reasons. The obvious reason is to complete the system documentation, but you also need to be able to

answer questions such as when did the system last restart, how long has it been running, and what is the latest service pack that's been applied.

PROBLEM

The system documentation on your servers is incomplete, and you need to add information about the operating system. You've also been tasked with finding a way to measure the up-time of your servers as a measure of their reliability.

SOLUTION

The `Win32_OperatingSystem` class has a large number of properties that can help
answer these questions. Listing 5.14 shows the output of the apparently useful properties of this class. I say "apparently" because you may well discover a use for one of the
other parameters.

The script starts by defining a set of lookup tables. Extracts from some of the more
interesting ones are shown here. The full set is available in the download listing.

Listing 5.14   Operating system

```
$sku = DATA {ConvertFrom-StringData -StringData @'
1 = Ultimate Edition
8 = Datacenter Server Edition
'@}

$lang = DATA {ConvertFrom-StringData -StringData @'
1033 = English US
2057 = English UK
'@}

$code = DATA {ConvertFrom-StringData -StringData @'
1252 = Latin I
'@}

$fboost = DATA {ConvertFrom-StringData -StringData @'
0 = None
1 = Minimum
2 = (Default) Maximum
'@}

function get-operatingsystem {
[CmdletBinding()]
param (
 [parameter(ValueFromPipeline=$true,
   ValueFromPipelineByPropertyName=$true)]
 [string]$computername="$env:COMPUTERNAME"
)
PROCESS {
 Get-WmiObject -Class Win32_OperatingSystem `
  -ComputerName $computername |
 select CSName, Caption,
 @{Name="Operating System SKU";
 Expression={$sku["$($_.OperatingSystemSKU)"]}},
 SerialNumber, ServicePackMajorVersion,
 ServicePackMinorVersion, BuildNumber, Version,
 OSArchitecture, SystemDevice, SystemDrive,
```

```
WindowsDirectory, SystemDirectory,
@{Name="OS Language";
Expression={$lang["$($_.OSLanguage)"]}},
@{Name="OS Type";
Expression={$os["$($_.OSType)"]}},
@{Name="Code Set";
Expression={$code["$($_.CodeSet)"]}},
@{Name="Country Code";
Expression={$country["$($_.CountryCode)"]}},
EncryptionLevel,
@{Name="Foreground Application Boost";
Expression={$fboost["$($_.ForegroundApplicationBoost)"]}},
DataExecutionPrevention_32BitApplications,
DataExecutionPrevention_Available,
DataExecutionPrevention_Drivers,
@{Name="Data Execution Prevention Support Policy";
Expression={$depsupport["$($_.DataExecutionPrevention_SupportPolicy)"]}},
@{Name="Installation Date";
Expression={$_.ConvertToDateTime($_.InstallDate)}},
@{Name="Last Bootup time";
Expression={$_.ConvertToDateTime($_.LastBootUpTime)}},
@{Name="Local Date Time";
Expression={$_.ConvertToDateTime($_.LocalDateTime)}},
@{Name="Offset from GMT";
Expression={"$($_.CurrentTimeZone) minutes"}},
@{Name="Locale "; Expression={$loc["$($_.Locale)"]}},
MaxNumberOfProcesses,
@{Name="Max Process Memory Size (GB)";
Expression={"{0:F3}" -f $($_.MaxProcessMemorySize*1kb /1GB)}},
PAEEnabled,
@{Name="Free Physical Memory (GB)";
Expression={"{0:F3}" -f $($_.FreePhysicalMemory/1GB*1kb)}},
@{Name="Size Stored In Paging Files (GB)";
Expression={"{0:F3}" -f $($_.SizeStoredInPagingFiles *1kb /1GB)}},
@{Name="Free Space In Paging Files (GB)";
Expression={"{0:F3}" -f $($_.FreeSpaceInPagingFiles *1kb /1GB)}},
@{Name="Total Visible Memory Size (GB)";
Expression={"{0:F3}" -f $($_.TotalVisibleMemorySize *1kb /1GB)}},
@{Name="Total Virtual Memory Size (GB)";
Expression={"{0:F3}" -f $($_.TotalVirtualMemorySize *1kb /1GB)}},
@{Name="Free Virtual Memory (GB)";
Expression={"{0:F3}" -f $($_.FreeVirtualMemory*1kb /1GB)}}
}}
```

Csname is the first property selected; it returns the name of the computer. The majority of the script is comprised of calculated fields in the Select-Object, and the majority of them use the lookup hash tables to decode integer values into more meaningful output. Dates are changed from WMI format into the more normal format you're used to by the ConvertToDateTime method. Service pack information includes a major and minor version number, though usually only the major version number is populated.

The memory-related properties at the end of the script are converted from kilobytes to gigabytes by a simple calculation using the PowerShell constants. They're then formatted to three decimal places using .NET formatting.

DISCUSSION

The system uptime can be calculated from the "Last Bootup Time" property you calculate in the script:

```
(Get-Date) - (get-operatingsystem)."Last Bootup time"
```

The current date and time is retrieved by using Get-Date. It's wrapped in parentheses so that it's treated as an object.

The "Last Bootup Time" property is used from the get-operatingsystem function from listing 5.14. Notice how PowerShell happily accepts property names with spaces—just wrap them in quotes. Subtracting the two dates creates a TimeSpan object that will give the uptime, as shown in figure 5.3. The TotalDays property is the most appropriate to use for reporting purposes.

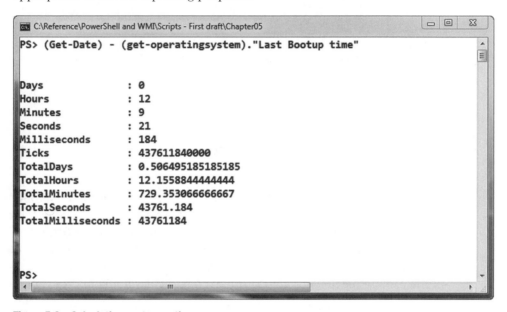

Figure 5.3   Calculating system uptime

One thing to note is that time zone and daylight saving time offsets will be included in the "Offset from GMT" property. You'll learn more about time zones soon, but first we need to consider hotfixes.

TECHNIQUE 15   Discover hotfixes

Patching is a fact of life for Windows administrators. The speed of evolution of new threats to Windows systems means you have to keep them up to date. There are a number of mechanisms for applying patches to your servers, and they all report in slightly different manners.

PROBLEM

You need to interrogate your systems to determine which patches have been applied. You'd also like to be able to test if a particular hotfix has been applied.

SOLUTION

PowerShell v2 introduced a cmdlet that can perform this task—Get-HotFix. In Power-Shell v1, you can use the underlying WMI class, Win32_QuickFixEngineering, that the Get-HotFix cmdlet uses. The only problem is how to determine if you're running PowerShell v2 or v1. The following listing shows how you can resolve this.

Listing 5.15   Hotfixes

```
function get-hf {
[CmdletBinding()]
param (
 [parameter(ValueFromPipeline=$true,
   ValueFromPipelineByPropertyName=$true)]
 [string]$computername="$env:COMPUTERNAME"
)
PROCESS {
if ($psversiontable.PSversion.Major -qe 2) {
 $fixes = Get-HotFix -ComputerName $computername }
 else {
  $fixes = Get-WmiObject -Class Win32_QuickFixEngineering `
    -ComputerName $computername
 }

 $fixes | select CSName, HotFixID, Caption,
 Description, InstalledOn, InstalledBy
}}
```

DISCUSSION

The PowerShell automatic variable $psversiontable only exists in PowerShell v2. You start by testing for its existence (the Major property will have a value of 2 for Power-Shell vs2 and 3 for PowerShell v3. If it exists, you can use the cmdlet; otherwise you can use the WMI class directly. You could just use WMI, but this is a simple example of how you can test for PowerShell versions, so it's worth doing this way.

You can use the function to test whether a particular hotfix has been applied.

```
get-hf | where {$_.Hotfixid -eq "KB982799"}
```

There may be some hotfixes that can't be discovered by this mechanism. These should be found in the registry under these keys:

```
HKEY_LOCAL_MACHINE\SOFTWARE\Microsoft\Windows NT\CurrentVersion\Hotfix
HKEY_LOCAL_MACHINE\SOFTWARE\Microsoft\Updates
```

You'll learn how to look at this information in chapter 7. In the meantime we need to consider how the system is configured to boot up.

TECHNIQUE 16   **Get boot configuration**

When a Windows system boots up, it needs to find the files it needs in order to boot. If the directory with these files is incorrectly stored, the system won't boot. Checking that the boot configuration is correct can save a lot of troubleshooting effort and potentially save you having to rebuild the system.

PROBLEM

You need to check the boot configuration on your systems to ensure that the machines will start up correctly.

SOLUTION

The following listing shows how you can use the `Win32_BootConfiguration` class to solve this problem.

Listing 5.16   Boot configuration

```
function get-bootconfig {
[CmdletBinding()]
param (
 [parameter(ValueFromPipeline=$true,
   ValueFromPipelineByPropertyName=$true)]
 [string]$computername="$env:COMPUTERNAME"
)
PROCESS {
 Get-WmiObject -Class Win32_BootConfiguration `
 -ComputerName $computername |
 select ConfigurationPath, BootDirectory,
 Caption, LastDrive,
 ScratchDirectory, TempDirectory
}}
```

There are no surprises in this script. It retrieves the information from the WMI class and displays the required properties. Note that the `ScratchDirectory` and `Temp-Directory` properties relate to the folders that are used during startup, not the user's temp folder.

DISCUSSION

If you explore the root/cimv2 namespace, the `Win32_SystemBootConfiguration` class should be ignored, as it only links the `Win32_ComputerSystem` class with the `Win32_BootConfiguration` class.

Closely related to the boot configuration is the recovery configuration.

TECHNIQUE 17   **Find recovery configuration**

In an ideal world, your servers would be started and would keep running until you shut them down or until you initiate a restart due to a change, such as the application of patches. Unfortunately, this isn't always true, and your servers will sometimes fail for no apparent reason. Windows can supply you with information related to the failure if it's configured correctly.

PROBLEM

Windows has a number of options for determining what happens if a crash occurs. You need to ensure that they're set consistently across the server estate. You also need to be able to check on any exceptions enabled for servers that need a different configuration.

SOLUTION

This information is recovered using the `Win32_OSRecoveryConfiguration` class, as the following listing shows.

Listing 5.17   Recovery configuration

```
$dump = DATA {ConvertFrom-StringData -StringData @'
1 = Complete Memory Dump
2 = Kernel Memory Dump
'@}

function get-OSrecovery {
[CmdletBinding()]
param (
 [parameter(ValueFromPipeline=$true,
   ValueFromPipelineByPropertyName=$true)]
 [string]$computername="$env:COMPUTERNAME"
)
PROCESS {
 Get-WmiObject Win32_OSRecoveryConfiguration `
  -ComputerName $computername |
 select Name, AutoReboot, DebugFilePath,
 @{Name="Debug Info";
 Expression={$dump["$($_.DebugInfoType)"]}},
 ExpandedDebugFilePath, ExpandedMiniDumpDirectory,
 KernelDumpOnly, MiniDumpDirectory,
 OverwriteExistingDebugFile,
 SendAdminAlert, WriteDebugInfo,
 WriteToSystemLog
}}
```

A hash table is constructed to store the lookup information for the type of memory dump produced during a failure. Think carefully about this, because a full memory dump of a 64-bit machine could take a lot of disk space. The properties are displayed as shown in figure 5.4.

DISCUSSION

The `DebugFilePath` and the `MiniDumpDirectory` contain the environmental variable `%SystemRoot%`. The value of this variable can be discovered using

```
$env:SystemRoot
```

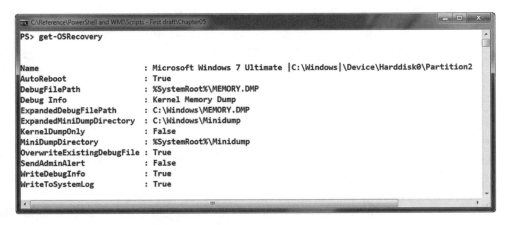

Figure 5.4 Output of running the `get-OSrecovery` **function in listing 5.17**

On my systems, it returns C:\Windows. This is the standard value if Windows has been installed with the default installation path. The function could be modified to replace the full variable with its value if you suspect that a nondefault installation path has been used.

One last configuration item needs to be considered: the system time.

TECHNIQUE 18	**Test system time**

In an Active Directory environment, the system clocks are only allowed a maximum difference of five minutes from the domain controllers, by default. If this allowable difference is exceeded, the machine can't authenticate to the domain and nothing works properly. This is generally viewed as a bad thing to happen.

PROBLEM

The local time on the system has to be checked to ensure that it's correct. In an organization that spans time zones, you need to check the UTC (GMT) time to ensure that the time settings across the organization are correct. Twice yearly, you have an additional issue with the changes to and from daylight saving time.

SOLUTION

There are a number of classes you can use to work with the system time, as shown in the following listing. It starts by using the Win32_LocalTime and the Win32_UTCTime classes to determine the respective time values.

Listing 5.18   System time

```
function test-systemtime {
[CmdletBinding()]
param (
 [parameter(ValueFromPipeline=$true,
   ValueFromPipelineByPropertyName=$true)]
 [string]$computername="$env:COMPUTERNAME"
)
PROCESS {
 $now = Get-WmiObject -Class Win32_LocalTime `
 -ComputerName $computername

 $now2 = Get-WmiObject -Class Win32_UTCTime `
 -ComputerName $computername

 $local = Get-Date -Year $($now.Year) -Month $($now.Month) `
        -Day $($now.Day) -Hour $($now.Hour) `
        -Minute $($now.Minute) -Second $($now.Second)

 $utc = Get-Date -Year $($now2.Year) -Month $($now2.Month) `
        -Day $($now2.Day) -Hour $($now2.Hour) `
        -Minute $($now2.Minute) -Second $($now2.Second)

 $tz =  Get-WmiObject -Class Win32_TimeZone `
        -ComputerName $computername

$daylton = Get-Date -Month $tz.daylightmonth -Day $tz.daylightday `
          -Hour $tz.daylighthour -Minute $tz.daylightminute `
```

```
              -Second $tz.daylightsecond
$stndon = Get-Date -Month $tz.standardmonth -Day $tz.standardday `
          -Hour $tz.standardhour -Minute $tz.standardminute `
              -Second $tz.standardsecond
if (($local -ge $daylton) -and ($local -le $stndon)){
  $timename = $tz.DaylightName
}
else {$timename = $tz.StandardName}
 "Server      : $($now.__SERVER)"
 "Time Zone   : $($tz.Description)"
 "Time Setting: $timename"
 "Local Time  : $local"
 "UTC   Time  : $utc"
}}
```

The information isn't returned in a format that enables simple conversion to a datetime format, so you use Get-Date to create the objects you need. You can then retrieve the time zone information. The information on when the change to and from daylight saving time occurs can be used to determine which time setting you display. The data is displayed at the end of the function, where the dates will display as MM/DD/YYYY.

DISCUSSION

It isn't possible to use the IsDaylightSavingTime method of Get-Date because that will only apply to the local machine, not the remote machine. This could lead to errors where you cross time zones and localities with different dates for changing the daylight saving time settings.

Win32_CurrentTime will display both Win32_LocalTime and Win32_UTCTime. In my experience it's easier to deal with them separately.

This completes our investigation of the operating system configuration. The last area we need to explore is the installed software.

5.5   Software

Computers are great, but they can't do much without software. The main task when you're working on the system configuration is discovering what software has been installed.

TECHNIQUE 19   **Discover installed software**

Software can end up on machines for a number of reasons, including a corporate decision to install it and a user taking an arbitrary decision to install the software. When you're troubleshooting issues with a client machine or server, you need to know what has been installed.

PROBLEM

The software that has been installed on your computers can affect their performance. In some cases, the installed versions need to be checked before an upgrade to other software can occur. You need to be able to determine what software is installed on a system.

SOLUTION

Software can be installed in a number of ways. If the software was installed by the Windows installer, you can use the `Win32_Product` class to discover what has been installed. The following listing shows how this class is used, following the standard pattern we've adopted throughout the chapter.

Listing 5.19 Installed software

```
function get-software {
[CmdletBinding()]
param (
 [parameter(ValueFromPipeline=$true,
   ValueFromPipelineByPropertyName=$true)]
 [string]$computername="$env:COMPUTERNAME"
)
PROCESS {
"Installed Software"
 Get-WmiObject -Class Win32_Product `
 -ComputerName $computername |
 select Name, IdentifyingNumber,
 InstallLocation, Vendor, Version

"Installed COM Applications"
 Get-WmiObject -Class Win32_COMApplication `
 -ComputerName $computername |
select Name, AppID
}}
```

`Win32_Product` supplies information on application and version, which is probably the most important data that you need. Many applications also register COM components. You can use `Win32_COMApplication` to discover this aspect of the data.

DISCUSSION

The `get-software` function will return the majority, if not all, of the installed software. There is always the possibility that an odd application is installed in some manner that doesn't register correctly, so you can't find it with these classes. In chapter 7, we'll look at the information held in the registry on installed software.

This concludes our journey around system configuration. Applying these techniques will enable you to derive information about your systems. One issue to think about is how you'll store it. An easy way is to pipe the output from these functions into text files as follows:

```
get-software | out-file c:\reports\software.txt
```

5.6 *Summary*

Understanding your system configuration is the first step toward controlling the environment and being able to automate your administration. The techniques in this chapter enable you to discover configuration settings for each of the following:

- The computer system, including make, model, form factor, motherboard, onboard devices, processors, and memory
- The peripheral devices including keyboard, mouse, and hardware ports
- The battery and power plan active on the system
- The operating system, including service packs, hotfixes, boot and recovery options, and the time settings
- The installed software

These techniques, in isolation, enable you to discover information about specific aspects of your servers.

I use these functions, on a regular basis, to document new servers as they come into production. The production of the documentation is fully automated because my PowerShell script writes the data directly into a Microsoft Word document. (An explanation of this is beyond the scope of this chapter, but details can be found in my *PowerShell in Practice*, page 214.) All I have to do is complete the front cover of the document. Producing the documentation takes at least a day per server if performed manually; automating the task allows it to run as a background task and takes about five minutes of my time.

We haven't covered storage systems yet. We'll look at them in the next chapter, where you'll learn how to discover the disk configuration and perform some administration tasks on your disks.

Disk systems 6

This chapter covers

- Discovering the physical disks in your systems
- Relating physical and logical disks
- Managing disk volumes

Disk systems, along with CPU and memory, are the primary system resources we're interested in as administrators. We looked at how to explore CPU and memory configurations in chapter 5. In this chapter, we'll turn our attention to the disk systems.

Working with the disk system on a local machine is easy. Administering the disks on remote machines gets more difficult. As a real-world example consider the 200 virtual servers I have running. Virtual disks become fragmented just like physical disks, leading to poor performance. The techniques you'll learn later in this chapter will show you which disks need defragmenting and could be used to perform the defragmentation overnight. All from a single script. This is a classic of example of how PowerShell and WMI can save you time and effort—quicker, easier administration, and you get the benefits.

We'll start by considering physical disks and their controllers. Disk controllers can be IDE- or SCSI-based. You can easily test for both in the same script. PowerShell and WMI don't return error messages if there's no data, so you can use that feature to test both types of controllers without worrying if they're both present.

A physical disk can contain one or more partitions. Discovering the partitions and how they relate to the physical disks starts to build the picture of your disk systems. There are a good set of relationships defined in WMI between the various components of the disk system, so you can look forward to getting lots of practice finding associated classes. Now would be a good time to review WQL if you skipped chapter 3.

> **NOTE** This information is all viewed from within Windows. If your disk system consists of five disks in a RAID 5 array on your SAN that's presented to Windows as a single disk, WMI will report it as a single disk. WMI can't drill down into the structure of external disk arrays.

Partitions are the stepping stone to logical disks. You can have multiple partitions and logical disks defined for a single physical disk, and discovering the relationships is a quick and easy way to discover any unallocated space on your physical disk. The last link in the chain is the volumes to be found on a system. These are the real point where you work with the disks on a day-to-day basis. At the volume level, you can monitor changes to the disk system as well as perform management tasks, such as formatting, running chkdsk, or defragmenting a volume. PowerShell and WMI enable you to perform this as easily on a remote machine as on a local machine.

The chapter closes with a quick look at CD/DVD drives to complete your exploration of working with disks through WMI.

Physical disks are the starting point of any investigation into disk management.

6.1 *Physical disks*

The hardware involved in disk systems consists of the physical disks themselves and the disk controllers used by the operating system to communicate with the disks. The relationships between the various components we'll deal with in this chapter are illustrated in figure 6.1.

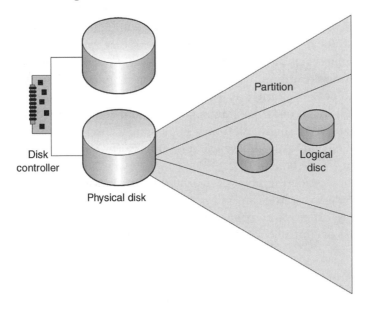

Figure 6.1   The components of disk systems

A disk controller can work with one or more physical disks. A physical disk can have one or more partitions, and a partition can contain one or more logical disks. The WMI classes that correspond to these physical entities are listed in table 6.1.

WMI changes

As an example of how the IT infrastructure landscape is changing I've deliberately decided to not include any content on floppy disks. These drives aren't standard on modern servers and are rapidly disappearing from our environments. If information is required on these devices use the `Win32_FloppyController` and `Win32_FloppyDrive` classes.

WMI itself is constantly changing and evolving in addition to hardware changes. If you have worked with WMI before you may notice that the `Win32_PhysicalMedia` class isn't mentioned. It gives inconsistent results on Windows 7 and it appears this class is being replaced by `Win32_DiskDrive`. I recommend only using `Win32_DiskDrive`.

Table 6.1 Disk-related WMI classes

Component	WMI class
Disk controller	`Win32_IDEController`
	`Win32_IDEControllerDevice`
	`Win32_SCSIController`
	`Win32_SCSIControllerDevice`
Physical disk	`Win32_DiskDrive`
	`Win32_DiskDriveToDiskPartition`
Partition	`Win32_DiskPartition`
	`Win32_LogicalDiskToPartition`
Logical disk	`Win32_LogicalDisk`
Mount point	`Win32_MountPoint`
Volume	`Win32_Volume`
CD drive	`Win32_CDROMDrive`

Notice the names of `Win32_LogicalDisk` and `Win32_DiskDrive` for working with logical and physical disks respectively. This is one place where the logical naming of WMI classes breaks down. Don't try to search for `Win32_PhysicalDisk`, or you'll have the same frustrating experience I did.

Disk controllers are at the head of the line for the physical side of disk systems.

TECHNIQUE 20   **Discover disk controllers**

Figure 6.1 shows that storage systems consist of a number of items that all need to be connected and working properly. Disk controllers can be split into two main types:

- IDE—Generally used in PCs, laptops and low-end servers
- SCSI—Generally used in servers

But this isn't a hard and fast division, especially when you're dealing with virtual machines.

PROBLEM

The disk controllers in your systems need to be enumerated so that you know how the storage solution is configured. Ideally you also want to be able to discover the physical disks that are connected to the controllers.

SOLUTION

There are two WMI classes for working with disk controllers: `Win32_IDEController` and `Win32_SCSIController`, as shown in table 6.1. You can use both classes in your discovery script, as shown in the following listing.

Listing 6.1   Disk controllers

```
$dprot = DATA {
ConvertFrom-StringData -StringData @'              Define data
9 = SCSI Parallel Interface                    ①  values
10 = SCSI Fibre Channel Protocol
11 = SCSI Serial Bus Protocol
42 = Enhanced ATA/IDE
'@
}

function get-diskcontroller {
[CmdletBinding()]
param (
 [parameter(ValueFromPipeline=$true,
   ValueFromPipelineByPropertyName=$true)]
 [string]$computername="$env:COMPUTERNAME"
)
PROCESS{
  $ide = $null                                    ②  Get IDE
  $scsi= $null                                        controllers

  $ide = Get-WmiObject -Class Win32_IDEController `
  -ComputerName $computername
                                                  ③  Get SCSI
  $scsi = Get-WmiObject -Class Win32_SCSIController `   controllers
  -ComputerName $computername

  if ($ide){                                          Display IDE
    "IDE Controllers"                            ⑤  data
    $ide | select Name, Status, Manufacturer,
    MaxNumberControlled,
    @{Name="Protocol"; Expression={$dprot["$($_.ProtocolSupported)"]}}
  }
```

```
    if ($scsi){
      "SCSI Controllers"
      $scsi | select Name, Status, Manufacturer,
       MaxNumberControlled,
       @{Name="Protocol"; Expression={$dprot["$($_.ProtocolSupported)"]}}
    }
}}
```

◄─┐ **Display**
  ❺ **SCSI data**

The script follows the pattern established in chapter 5. The script starts by defining
the lookup values for the supported protocols ❶. The function takes a computer
name as a parameter with a default of ".", which signifies the local host. Two variables
are created to represent the controller information and are deliberately set to `null`.

The `Win32_IDEController` ❷ and `Win32_SCSIController` ❸ classes are called to
get the required information. In this function, you're returning the information to the
previously defined variables rather than directly to the user. The variables are checked
individually to determine if they have a value. If IDE controllers exist ❹, the appropriate
data is displayed. Similarly, the SCSI controllers ❺ are checked and displayed.

DISCUSSION

This script relies on the way the `null` values are handled by PowerShell to determine whether data should be displayed. A `null` value isn't equal to `$false`. Try this
experiment:

```
$test = $null
if ($test){"hello"}
if (-not $test){"hello"}
```

You'll get a result from the last line. Now try this:

```
$test -eq $false
```

It will return `False`. When testing variables, if the value is `$null`, it will react as if it's
`$false`, but it doesn't carry a value of `$false`.

Now that you know which disk controllers are in your system, you need to understand how the controllers are linked to the physical disks. This can be achieved by
using the appropriate associating class:

```
Get-WmiObject Win32_IDEControllerDevice |
Format-List Antecedent, Dependent
```

And for SCSI controllers, you use this:

```
Get-WmiObject Win32_SCSIControllerDevice |
Format-List Antecedent, Dependent
```

You know what controllers you have, and you know which disks are attached to them.
What can you discover about the disks themselves?

TECHNIQUE 21   **Physical drive information**

The physical drives in your computers control how much data you can store. Even
with compression, there is a finite limit to the amount of data you can cram onto a

disk. Understanding the capacity limits of your disk systems is the first step toward a realistic capacity management plan.

> **NOTE** `Win32_DiskDrive` doesn't include information on CD drives, but `Win32_LogicalDisk` does. This can lead to confusion when matching logical to physical disk information.

The `Win32_DiskDrive` class only works with disks that Windows counts as being internal. Any disks in the computer and in external storage systems that are allocated to the computer will be included. Mapped drives won't be included.

PROBLEM

The physical disks in your machines need documenting, including their capacity.

SOLUTION

The following listing shows a function that uses `Win32_DiskDrive` to solve this problem. The function takes a computer name as a parameter and then accesses the WMI class.

Listing 6.2   Disk drives

```
function get-diskdrive {
[CmdletBinding()]
param (
  [parameter(ValueFromPipeline=$true,
    ValueFromPipelineByPropertyName=$true)]
  [string]$computername="$env:COMPUTERNAME"
)
PROCESS{
  Get-WmiObject -Class Win32_DiskDrive `
  -ComputerName $computername |
  select DeviceID, InterfaceType,
  Manufacturer, Model, FirmwareRevision,
  SerialNumber, Signature,
  StatusInfo, Partitions,
  TotalHeads, BytesPerSector, TotalSectors,
  SectorsPerTrack, TotalTracks, TracksPerCylinder,
  TotalCylinders,
  @{Name="Disk Size (GB)";                            ❶ Calculate
    Expression={"{0:F3}" -f $($_.Size/1GB)}},            capacity
  SCSIBus, SCSILogicalUnit, SCSIPort, SCSITargetId

  "Capabilities:"                                     ❷ Determine
  Get-WmiObject -Class Win32_DiskDrive `                 capabilities
  -ComputerName $computername |
  select  -ExpandProperty CapabilityDescriptions
}}
```

`Select-Object` is used to choose the properties you want to display. The ones selected in this script are the ones I've found most useful, but as with all of these scripts, it's worth checking if there are other properties that may be of use to you in your specific circumstances.

The majority of the properties can be just displayed, but the disk size is returned in bytes. This gives you a number that's more than a bit unwieldy. A simple calculated field ❶ is used to divide the returned size by 1 GB to give a more meaningful result. The result is formatted to three decimal places.

The `Win32_DiskDrive` class returns a collection of capability descriptions as well as the numeric code representing those descriptions. You can work directly with the capability descriptions by using the `-ExpandProperty` parameter of `Select-Object` ❷. This provides a neatly formatted display of the disk capabilities.

DISCUSSION

The disk capabilities will include some of the following:

- Random access
- Supports writing
- Encryption
- Compression
- Supports removable media

Expect the first two on all physical hard drives.

TECHNIQUE 22   ## Link partitions to disk drives

Figure 6.1 shows that a physical disk can contain a number of partitions. Assuming that you're using master boot record (MBR) partitioning, you can create either

- Up to four primary partitions on a physical disk
- Up to three primary partitions and an extended partition that can be divided into multiple logical partitions

A primary partition is bootable.

PROBLEM

The disk systems on a number of remote servers need to be examined to determine the relationship between the physical disks and the disk partitions. The boot partition also needs to be determined.

SOLUTION

A quick list of the partitions on each physical disk can be obtained using the `Win32_DiskDriveToDiskPartition` class. This class associates the disk drive and its partitions. The information can be found with this simple PowerShell script:

```
Get-WmiObject -Class Win32_DiskDriveToDiskPartition |
Format-List Antecedent, Dependent
```

This just supplies the partition identifiers. You really need to find more detailed information. You can use the `Win32_DiskPartition` class, but you have to relate it to the physical drive. The physical drives will always be numbered from 0, so you can discover if disk partitions can be directly associated with disk drives:

```
$query = "ASSOCIATORS OF
{Win32_DiskDrive.DeviceID=""\\\\.\\PHYSICALDRIVE0""} WHERE
ClassDefsOnly"
Get-WmiObject -Query $query
```

This WMI query will produce the following output:

- `Win32_PnPEntity`
- `Win32_ComputerSystem`
- `Win32_DiskPartition`
- `Win32_PhysicalMedia`

This leads to the following listing, which allows you to discover the partitions that are associated with each disk drive.

Listing 6.3   Link disk drives to partitions

```
function get-drivetopartition {
[CmdletBinding()]
param (
 [parameter(ValueFromPipeline=$true,
   ValueFromPipelineByPropertyName=$true)]
[string]$computername="$env:COMPUTERNAME"
)
PROCESS{
  Get-WmiObject -Class Win32_DiskDrive -ComputerName $computername |
  foreach {
    $_.DeviceId
    $inxid = ($_.DeviceID).Replace("\","\\")
    $query = "ASSOCIATORS OF {Win32_DiskDrive.DeviceID=""$inxid""}
      ➥ WHERE RESULTCLASS = Win32_DiskPartition"
    Get-WmiObject -ComputerName $computername -Query $query

  }
}}
```

The function accepts a computer name as a parameter. The `Win32_DiskDrive` class is used to discover the physical drives. These are piped into a `ForEach-Object` cmdlet that displays the device ID of the physical disk.

Single backslash (\) characters are replaced by doubles (\\) because the backslash is a WMI escape character and you need to ensure that the device ID is read correctly. Alternatively, the `__RELPATH` property could be used.

A query is created to find the associated partitions and is executed.

DISCUSSION

The display produced by running this script uses the default display of `Win32_DiskPartition`. This produces something similar to the following display for each of the partitions present on the disk:

```
NumberOfBlocks    : 204800
BootPartition     : True
Name              : Disk #0, Partition #0
PrimaryPartition  : True
Size              : 104857600
Index             : 0
```

I've deliberately left the size in bytes in this display. It would be possible to combine listing 6.3 with the next listing to give more information and to recalculate the partition size.

TECHNIQUE 23　**Enumerating disk partitions**

We've seen how to discover the disk partitions created on a specific physical disk drive. There's more information available about the partition that may be of use to us.

PROBLEM

In many organizations there's a tendency to over partition the physical disks. This is especially true on the C: drive which is used to boot Windows. Many systems are configured with small partitions which can lead to them running out of disk space. Can we determine the size distribution of the partitions to discover if this will be a problem?

SOLUTION

We've seen in listing 6.3 that the `Win32_DiskPartition` class can be used to investigate the disk partitions on our system. The next listing extends the use of this class to determine more information including the size of the partition.

Listing 6.4　Disk partitions

```
function get-partition {
[CmdletBinding()]
param (
 [parameter(ValueFromPipeline=$true,
   ValueFromPipelineByPropertyName=$true)]
[string]$computername="$env:COMPUTERNAME"
)
PROCESS{
  Get-WmiObject -Class Win32_DiskPartition -ComputerName $computername |
  select DeviceID, Description, Bootable,
  BootPartition, PrimaryPartition,
  BlockSize, NumberOfBlocks,
  @{Name="Partition Size (GB)";
   Expression={"{0:F3}" -f $($_.Size/1GB)}},
  StartingOffset
}}
```

The function follows our usual pattern with the `Win32_DiskPartition` class being used to return the partition data. The required properties are selected for display. A calculated field is used to display the size in gigabytes rather than bytes.

DISCUSSION

The device id is of the form "`Disk #0, Partition #0`" which means that you can link the partition information directly to the physical disk information. Figure 6.1 shows that partitions form the link between physical disks and logical disks. The next step is to link the partition information to the logical disks you've defined in the system.

TECHNIQUE 24   **Link partitions to logical disks**

The logical disks are the ones that you're used to working with. They're identified by drive letters and are where you're used to storing your files.

PROBLEM

You need to enumerate the logical disks that are contained within your partitions. Ideally you want to start at the partition and discover the logical disks.

SOLUTION

If you search for WMI classes that refer to disk partitions using

```
Get-WmiObject -List *partition*
```

you'll find a class called `CIM_LogicalDiskBasedOnPartition`. This appears to give you what you want, but the information is the same as what you'd find with `Win32_Logical-DiskToPartition`. The following listing uses `Win32_LogicalDiskToPartition` to determine the relationships between partitions and logical disks.

Listing 6.5   Partitions to logical disks

```
function get-logicaltopartition {
[CmdletBinding()]
param (
 [parameter(ValueFromPipeline=$true,
   ValueFromPipelineByPropertyName=$true)]
[string]$computername="$env:COMPUTERNAME"
)
PROCESS{
 Get-WmiObject -Class Win32_LogicalDiskToPartition `
 -ComputerName $computername |
 Format-List Antecedent, Dependent, StartingAddress, EndingAddress
}}
```

The `Antecedent` and `Dependent` properties show the partition and logical disk respectively. On machines with a separate system partition, where they've been configured for dual boot, the small partition configured to control bootup may not be displayed.

DISCUSSION

You can perform a similar exercise to the one in technique 22 to discover the WMI classes associated with `Win32_LogicalDiskToPartition`. The following three classes will be returned:

- `Win32_DiskDrive`
- `Win32_ComputerSystem`
- `Win32_LogicalDisk`

Using these classes and the examples in listings 6.2 to 6.5, it's possible to construct a script that starts with the physical disks and discovers the partitions and logical disks in one pass. I'll leave that as an exercise for you. (There's a solution in the download code—it's called get-disk.ps1 and it can be found in the Extras folder for this chapter.) In the meantime, let's turn our attention to logical disks.

6.2   *Logical disks*

Logical disks are where you start to get close to the data. These are the disks that you see when you look in Windows Explorer. There are two items of interest related to logical disks.

First, all logical disks have a root directory. While the name of the root directory is of obvious interest, its other properties also reveal interesting information. We'll look at root directories first.

The second item of interest is mount points, where you mount another disk into a directory on your disk. Before we look at mount points, you need to discover the logical disks you have in the system.

TECHNIQUE 25   **Logical disk information**

The `Win32_LogicalDisk` class returns both local as well as mapped logical disks. Use this class for obtaining information on local disks, and use the `Win32_MappedLogicalDisk` class for information on mapped disks.

PROBLEM

Some of your servers are running out of disk space. You need to be able to check the free space left on the disks in your servers.

SOLUTION

You've already seen that that the `Win32_LogicalDisk` class returns information about your local disks. This is the class you want to use, because you're interested in the disks that belong to the server, and not anything that's mapped. The following listing shows how you can use the `Win32_LogicalDisk` class.

Listing 6.6   Logical disks

```
$dtype = DATA {ConvertFrom-StringData -StringData @'
3 = Local Disk
4 = Network Drive
'@}

$media = DATA {ConvertFrom-StringData -StringData @'
11 = Removable media other than floppy
12 = Fixed hard disk media
'@}

function get-logicaldisk {
[CmdletBinding()]
param (
 [parameter(ValueFromPipeline=$true,
   ValueFromPipelineByPropertyName=$true)]
[string]$computername="$env:COMPUTERNAME"
)
PROCESS{

 Get-WmiObject -Class Win32_LogicalDisk `
 -ComputerName $computername |
 select DeviceID, Compressed, Description,
```

❶ **Define lookups**

❷ **Call WMI class**

```
@{Name="Drive Type";
  ➦ Expression={$dtype["$($_.DriveType)"]}},
@{Name="Media Type";
  ➦ Expression={$media["$($_.MediaType)"]}},
FileSystem,
@{Name="Disk Size (GB)";
  ➦ Expression={"{0:F3}" -f $($_.Size/1GB)}},
@{Name="Free Space (GB)";
  ➦ Expression={"{0:F3}" -f $($_.FreeSpace/1GB)}},
SupportsDiskQuotas, SupportsFileBasedCompression,
VolumeName, VolumeSerialNumber
}}
```

❸ Use lookups

❹ Calculate fields

You start by defining some lookups ❶; the listing is truncated for brevity. The Win32_LogicalDisk class is called ❷, and the results are piped into Select-Object. You can select the properties in which you're interested.

The lookups are used to determine the drive type and the media type ❸. The disk size and free space are returned in bytes. Calculated fields are used to change these numbers to gigabytes ❹.

DISCUSSION

This listing can be adapted to only return the size information. This makes it easier to see servers with disk issues. Alternatively, you could use Select-Object on the output:

```
get-logicaldisk | select "Disk Size (GB)", "Free Space (GB)",
@{Name="% Free"; Expression={"{0:F3}" -f `
$(($_."Free Space (GB)"/$_."Disk Size (GB)")*100)}}
```

You take the output from the function and select the two properties related to disk size. Remember that they're calculated fields. You need to use quotes around the property names because they have spaces and special characters. You can then use those two properties to calculate the percentage of free space. How flexible is that?

Now that you know about the logical disks installed in your system, what can you discover about their root directories?

TECHNIQUE 26   Root directory data

You can get a view of the root directory by using Win32_LogicalDiskRootDirectory like this:

```
Get-WmiObject Win32_LogicalDiskRootDirectory |
select GroupComponent, PartComponent
```

This will return the logical disk device ID and the associated root directory.

But discovering that C:\ is the root directory of C: probably doesn't come as much of a surprise. You need to be able to dig a bit deeper than this.

PROBLEM

You need to determine if the root directory of a logical disk is hidden, compressed, or encrypted, as these can have an impact on how the folder structure system is used and seen.

SOLUTION

The root directory controls a number of properties of its child directories. If you look at the root directory in detail, you can discover how it affects the folder structure. The WMI class `Win32_Directory` can be used to discover the properties of your folders, as you'll see in chapter 8. If you check the classes associated with `Win32_LogicalDisk`, like this,

```
Get-WmiObject -Query "ASSOCIATORS OF
  {Win32_LogicalDisk.DeviceID='C:'} WHERE CLASSDEFSONLY"
```

you'll see that `Win32_Directory` is one of them and returns the root directory. You can use this information, as in the following listing, to discover the directories associated with a logical disk.

Listing 6.7 Root directory

```
function get-rootdirectory {
[CmdletBinding()]
param (
 [parameter(ValueFromPipeline=$true,
   ValueFromPipelineByPropertyName=$true)]
[string]$computername="$env:COMPUTERNAME"
)
PROCESS{
Get-WmiObject -Class Win32_LogicalDisk `
  -ComputerName $computername |
  foreach {
   $_.DeviceId
   $inxid = ($_.DeviceID).Replace("\","\\")
   $query = "ASSOCIATORS OF {Win32_LogicalDisk.DeviceID=""$inxid""}
   WHERE RESULTCLASS = Win32_Directory"
   Get-WmiObject -ComputerName $computername -Query $query  |
   select Name, Hidden, Archive, Compressed, Encrypted,
   Readable, FSName, EightDotThreeFileName,
   FileSize, LastAccessed, LastModified
  }
}}
```

The function uses `Win32_LogicalDisk` to return the logical disks on the computer. The device ID of each disk is printed, and the device ID is then modified by doubling the backslash (\) characters (the backslash is a WMI escape character that needs to be doubled to use it literally).

You can find the `Win32_Directory` instances associated with that logical disk and select the properties you want to display.

DISCUSSION

The important properties are `Hidden`, `Compressed`, and `Encrypted`. You can always select just those properties using this line:

```
get-rootdirectory | select Name, Hidden, Compressed, Encrypted
```

The other way that directories interact with logical disks is through mount points.

TECHNIQUE 27   Mount points

When you create a logical disk (volume), you can choose to give it a drive letter and make it accessible as g:\, for instance. Alternatively, you can take an empty folder, such as c:\data, and mount the volume in the folder. This makes the volume's disk space appear as part of the c: drive, but it's only accessible through the c:\data folder.

I often use the latter technique for big Exchange or SQL Server systems where I have more volumes than drive letters available. It also makes configuring Exchange replication easier, because creating the same folder structure becomes a simple proposition.

You can use `Get-WmiObject Win32_MountPoint` to discover the active mount points on your system, but this class only returns the directory and the volume that are associated through a mount point.

PROBLEM

You've inherited a large Exchange server with multiple mount points defined. You need to discover the volumes associated with those mount points.

SOLUTION

We'll assume that you have a single root folder that holds the folders used for mount points. We'll also assume, for the sake of brevity, that you know the path to this folder. The usual function structure is modified in the following listing by the addition of a second parameter.

Listing 6.8   Mount points

```
function get-mountpoint {
[CmdletBinding()]
param (
 [parameter(ValueFromPipeline=$true,
   ValueFromPipelineByPropertyName=$true)]           ❶ Create
 [string]$computername="$env:COMPUTERNAME",              parameters
 [string]$path ="C:\Data*"
)
 $test = 'Win32_Directory.Name="' +                  ❷ Set folder
 ➥ $path.Replace("\","\\") + '"'                        for WMI

Get-WmiObject -Class Win32_MountPoint `
-ComputerName $computername |                        ❸ Test
where {$_.Directory -like $test} |                      folder
foreach {
 $vol = $_.Volume
 Get-WmiObject -Class Win32_Volume `
 -ComputerName $computername |                       ❹ Test
 where {$_.__RELPATH -eq $vol} |                        volume
 Select @{Name="Folder";
  Expression={$_.Caption}},
 @{Name="Size (GB)";
  Expression={"{0:F3}" -f $($_.Capacity / 1GB)}},
 @{Name="Free (GB)";
  Expression={"{0:F3}" -f $($_.FreeSpace / 1GB)}},
```

```
  @{Name="%Free";
    Expression={"{0:F2}" -f $(($_.FreeSpace/$_.Capacity)*100)}}
  }
}}
```

The second parameter enables you to input the folder you want to test against ❶. The folder name must be changed from a Windows format to a WMI format ❷. This is achieved by doubling the backslash (\) characters. You can find the mount points that match your folder ❸. This script uses `Where-Object` rather than a WMI filter because the `-like` operator gives you an easier way to code the test, and I think it's more flexible.

The mount points are piped into `ForEach-Object`, where you display the volume name and use the `Win32_Volume` class to retrieve the volume data. A filter is placed on the volume using `Where-Object` ❹ to compare the volume name to the `__RELPATH` (relative path) property returned by WMI.

When a volume is mounted in a folder, `Win32_Volume` returns the folder name in the `Caption` property. You can display the folder and use three calculated fields to display the volume size, free space, and percentage free space. This provides instant space monitoring for your Exchange systems with mount points.

DISCUSSION

The script could be extended by using `Test-Path` to ensure that the folder you're testing against is in existence.

In practical terms, there isn't a great deal of difference between volumes and logical disks. In WMI terms there's a big difference, because the `Win32_Volume` class has some methods for doing good things to your volumes.

6.3   *Volumes*

Volumes are the most useful of the disk structures we'll deal with. They can be regarded in the same light as logical disks, though there are technical differences. Volumes are where you can directly administer your disks through the methods of the `Win32_Volume` class. The classes that we dealt with for physical and logical disks don't have useful methods, so you can only use them to discover information. The situation changes with volumes, as you'll see in this section and the next.

In this section, you'll learn how to enumerate the volumes in your system. It's worth comparing listing 6.9 (coming up next) with listing 6.6 (which used `Win32_LogicalDisk`) to see the similarities and differences in the data you can get about logical disks and volumes. This section closes with a look at managing change events related to your volumes.

TECHNIQUE 28   **Enumerate volume information**

The main class for working with volumes is `Win32_Volume`. It has a large number of properties and some very useful methods. A quick look at the available methods and properties can be obtained with

```
Get-WmiObject Win32_Volume | Get-Member
```

You can view the arguments needed by a particular method like this:

```
$v = Get-WmiObject Win32_Volume -Filter "DriveLetter='C:'"
$v.AddMountPoint
```

In this case, the method takes a directory path as an argument. An example of using this method is supplied in section 6.4.

> **TIP** This technique can be used for any method. Use the method name without any arguments or parentheses, and you'll get information on the method, including the arguments that are required.

PROBLEM

You need to enumerate the volumes in your system. This will enable you to manage the disk space.

SOLUTION

The following listing shows the solution to this problem. You can use the Win32_Volume class to directly find the information you need.

Listing 6.9 Enumerate volumes

```
$dtype = DATA {ConvertFrom-StringData -StringData @'        ← Lookup ❶ data
2 = Removable Disk
3 = Local Disk
5 = Compact Disk
'@}

function get-volume {
[CmdletBinding()]
param (
 [parameter(ValueFromPipeline=$true,
   ValueFromPipelineByPropertyName=$true)]              ← ❷ Function parameter
[string]$computername="$env:COMPUTERNAME"
)
PROCESS{                                                    ❸ WMI call
 Get-WmiObject Win32_Volume -ComputerName $computername|   ←
 select Caption, Label, Automount, Blocksize,
 BootVolume, SystemVolume,
 @{Name="Drive Type"; Expression={$dtype["$($_.DriveType)"]}},
 @{Name="Disk Size (GB)";
   Expression={"{0:F3}" -f $($_.Capacity/1GB)}},
 @{Name="Free Space (GB)";
   Expression={"{0:F3}" -f $($_.FreeSpace/1GB)}},
 Compressed, FileSystem, IndexingEnabled,
 MaximumFileNameLength, PageFilePresent,
 QuotasEnabled, QuotasIncomplete, QuotasRebuilding,
 SerialNumber, SupportsDiskQuotas,
 SupportsFileBasedCompression
}}
```

The script starts by defining a lookup hash table to supply the information on the disk types ❶. Note that the Win32_Volume class does show information about CD/DVD drives. There won't be much returned if the drive is empty.

The function takes a computer name as a parameter ❷ and uses the `Win32_Volume` class to retrieve the data ❸. Calculated fields are used to make the disk size and free space values more presentable.

DISCUSSION

The `Win32_Volume` class is of most value for the methods it provides.

But before you jump into managing the disks with those methods, you need to consider how you can manage events related to volumes.

TECHNIQUE 29   Using volume change events

We discussed using WMI events in chapter 3. Events are triggered when something happens on your system. If you try looking for WMI classes related to events,

```
Get-WmiObject -List *Event*
```

you'll find a long list of classes, including `Win32_VolumeChangeEvent`. The name suggests that it deals with events involving changes to a volume. But if you try to access the class directly using

```
Get-WmiObject Win32_VolumeChangeEvent
```

you get nothing back! The event-handling cmdlets have to be used before you can access the event engine.

PROBLEM

You've been tasked with copying a folder full of files onto a large number of USB memory sticks. In order to speed the operation and spread the work across a number of people, you want to automate the process.

SOLUTION

The solution depends on you detecting a USB memory stick being plugged in. WMI treats the USB device as another volume. Run this PowerShell statement:

```
Get-WmiObject Win32_Volume |
Format-Table DriveLetter, DriveType, FileSystem, `
SerialNumber -AutoSize
```

Insert a USB device and repeat. You should see that the new volume is recognized.

Note that the new drive type is given as 2, which is a removable drive (see listing 6.9) but existing volumes are type 3 (hard drive) or type 5 (CD). This enables you to test for the addition of a USB drive, as shown in listing 6.10.

> **WARNING**   This script is presented as a standalone script, rather than being incorporated into the PowerShell module for the chapter. It's presented in this manner to avoid issues with variable scope. Feel free to rename the script if that's more convenient.

The script is run as follows:

```
. ./listing6.10 c:\teszzt2
```

You dot-source the script to ensure that the functions and variables remain in memory. The path to the folder you wish to copy to the USB sticks is passed to the script as a parameter. Use quotes around the folder path if it contains spaces or other special characters.

Listing 6.10   Automatic copy to USB memory stick

```
param (
 [string]$folder
)
if (-not (Test-Path $folder)){                              ❶ Test folder
 Throw "Folder $($folder) not found"                            existence
}

function add-drive {                                        ❷ Perform on
param (                                                        USB addition
 [string]$drive
)
 Write-Host "Drive $($drive) Added"
 Write-Host "Copying Files to Drive $($drive) "

 Copy-Item -Path $folder -Destination $drive -Recurse -Force -Verbose
 Write-Host "Finished Copying Files to Drive $($drive)"
}

function remove-drive {                                     ❸ Perform on
param (                                                        USB removal
 [string]$drive
)
 Write-Host "Drive $($drive) Removed"
}

if (Get-EventSubscriber |
 where {$_.SourceIdentifier -eq "usb plug in"}) {
 Unregister-Event -SourceIdentifier "usb plug in"
}                                                           ❹ Clean up
                                                               events
if (Get-EventSubscriber |
 where {$_.SourceIdentifier -eq "usb plug out"}) {
 Unregister-Event -SourceIdentifier "usb plug out"
}                                                           ❺ Define
                                                               queries
$queryIn = "SELECT * FROM __InstanceCreationEvent
WITHIN 2 WHERE  TargetInstance ISA 'Win32_Volume'
AND TargetInstance.DriveType=2"
$queryOut = "SELECT * FROM Win32_VolumeChangeEvent WHERE EventType=3"

$actionIn = {
    add-drive $($event.SourceEventArgs.NewEvent.TargetInstance.DriveLetter)
}                                                           Define actions ❻
$actionOut = {
   remove-drive $($event.SourceEventArgs.NewEvent.DriveName)
}

Register-WmiEvent -Query $queryIn `                         ❼ Register
-SourceIdentifier "usb plug in" -Action $actionIn              events
Register-WmiEvent -Query $queryOut `
-SourceIdentifier "usb plug out" -Action $actionOut
```

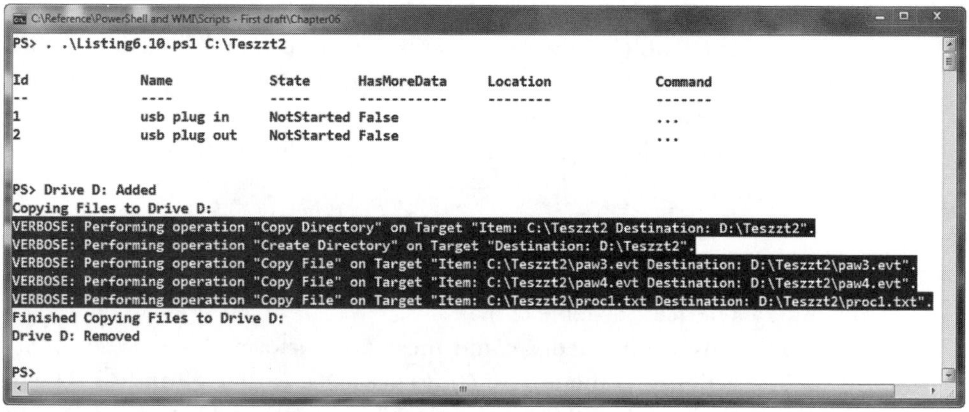

Figure 6.2   Running the automatic copy of files when a USB stick is plugged in

The script will test to see if the folder exists ❶. If Test-Path doesn't return True, the script will throw an error and stop. The test only determines if the folder exists—it doesn't test to see if the folder has any content!

Two functions are defined. The first function provides the actions that will occur when a USB stick is plugged into the system ❷. It takes the device's drive letter as a parameter and copies the folder to the drive with appropriate messages. The -Recurse and -Force parameters on Copy-Item ensure that the folder contents are copied and that an existing copy of the folder on the USB device is overwritten. The -Verbose parameter displays a message as each file is copied, as shown in figure 6.2.

The second function is executed when the USB stick is removed. In this case, it provides a message to say that the drive has been removed ❸.

If the script is run multiple times, the existing events need to be removed before new events are created ❹. A test is performed to determine whether an event subscriber exists with the specific source identifier. If it does exist, it's removed. The event subscriptions will also be deleted when PowerShell is shut down.

You've determined what you're going to do when a USB device is plugged in, but how do you recognize that event? There are two methods you can use to determine if a change has occurred to your volumes. These are defined in the WMI queries the script uses ❺.

The first method uses the __InstanceCreationEvent class, which is a system class defined in each WMI namespace:

```
$queryIn = "SELECT * FROM __InstanceCreationEvent
➥ WITHIN 2 WHERE    TargetInstance ISA 'Win32_Volume'
➥ AND TargetInstance.DriveType=2"
```

This query selects all of the data from the __InstanceCreationEvent class, which looks for the events related to the creation of an instance of a WMI class. The WITHIN 2 statement means that it checks every two seconds to determine if an event has occurred. The events are filtered by using WHERE TargetInstance ISA 'Win32_Volume', which only passes events related to volume creation. A further filter, TargetInstance.DriveType=2, ensures that the volume has to be a removable one before you take any notice of it.

The second method checks for the removal of the drive. This uses a much simpler query:

```
$queryOut = "SELECT * FROM Win32_VolumeChangeEvent WHERE EventType=3"
```

It uses the Win32_VolumeChangeEvent class and tests for event type 3, which is the removal of a device (see table 6.2).

Two actions are defined ❻, and these are performed when the events are triggered. The actions call the two functions discussed earlier, ❷ and ❸. The script's last action is to register the WMI events using the queries and actions you've defined ❼. Suitable identifiers are used so that you can distinguish the events.

DISCUSSION

Two different methods have been presented to work with volume-related events. If you prefer, a single method could be used to access the events. This involves changing the queries to use either the Win32_VolumeChangeEvent class or the system classes.

When using the Win32_VolumeChangeEvent class, you need to modify your queries to detect the relevant events. Event type 2 is used for a device arrival (USB device plugged in) and event type 3 is used when it's removed. The full list of event types is given in table 6.2.

Value	Meaning
1	Configuration changed
2	Device arrival
3	Device removal
4	Docking

Table 6.2 Win32_VolumeChangeEvent event types

This would make the relevant portions of the script read as follows:

```
$queryIn = " SELECT * FROM Win32_VolumeChangeEvent WHERE EventType=2"

$queryOut = "SELECT * FROM Win32_VolumeChangeEvent WHERE EventType=3"

$actionIn = {
    add-drive $($event.SourceEventArgs.NewEvent.DriveName)
}

$actionOut = {
    remove-drive $($event.SourceEventArgs.NewEvent.DriveName)
}
```

Notice that the event type is different in the two queries and that the way the drive letter of the USB stick is accessed is now identical in both action statements.

Alternatively, you could use the system classes, which would change those portions of the script as follows:

```
$queryIn = "SELECT * FROM __InstanceCreationEvent WITHIN 2 WHERE
    TargetInstance ISA 'Win32_Volume' AND TargetInstance.DriveType=2"

$queryOut = " SELECT * FROM __InstanceDeletionEvent WITHIN 2 WHERE
    TargetInstance ISA 'Win32_Volume' AND TargetInstance.DriveType=2"

$actionIn = {
    add-drive $($event.SourceEventArgs.NewEvent.TargetInstance.DriveLetter)
}

$actionOut = {
  remove-drive `
$($event.SourceEventArgs.NewEvent.TargetInstance.DriveLetter)
}
```

Your query to detect the removal of the drive has to be changed to use the `__InstanceDeletionEvent` class, and the drive letter access is also changed to be consistent.

The most difficult task when working with events is determining how to access the information produced by the event. The examples in this script show two of the major WMI-related methods.

At the first meeting of the UK PowerShell User Group, two of us sat and copied the PowerShell downloads onto USB sticks. I think we did about 50 of them. I could have used this script at that time. Now I would use listing 6.10 and be able to control the process just by plugging in the USB stick. With most laptops having three USB ports, that speeds up the process.

You've now used a number of disk-related WMI classes to discover information about your disks. It's time to discover how you can manage the disks in your systems.

6.4 Managing disks

The `Win32_Volume` class presents a number of methods for managing disks, including formatting, performing a `chkdsk`, and defragmenting the data on the disk. But before we get to that, let's see how you can work directly with the volumes by modifying the properties.

The two properties you're most likely to change are the drive letter and the volume label. Changing the drive letter is a matter of altering the `DriveLetter` property:

```
Get-WmiObject -Class Win32_Volume -Filter "DriveLetter='D:'" |
Set-WmiInstance -Arguments @{DriveLetter='K:'}
```

You can remove the drive letter completely by using `@{DriveLetter=$null}` as the argument for `Set-WmiInstance`. If you try to set the drive letter to be the same as one in use, an error will occur.

Changing the volume label follows a similar pattern:

```
Get-WmiObject -Class Win32_Volume -Filter "DriveLetter='K:'" |
Set-WmiInstance -Arguments @{Label='PaWtest'}
```

You use `Get-WmiObject` and filter on the drive letter. This is piped into `Set-WmiInstance` where you can change the label.

> **WARNING**   This technique can't be used to change properties such as the volume block size. That involves reformatting the volume.

One issue that you meet in Windows is that drives have to be allocated letters, and there are only 26 letters in the alphabet. This can mean that on very big systems you run out of drive letters. Exchange systems with a dozen or so databases with separate drives for the data and logs will soon reach this limit. You can overcome this problem by using mount points. Listing 6.8 showed how to discover mount points. Creating them is performed using the `AddMountPoint` method:

```
Get-WmiObject -Class Win32_Volume -Filter "DriveLetter='D:'" |
Invoke-WmiMethod -Name AddMountPoint -ArgumentList "C:\\pawtest"
```

This example uses a drive letter for simplicity, but it's also possible to use the device ID of the volume:

```
Get-WmiObject -Class Win32_Volume | where
➥ {$_.DeviceId -eq "\\?\Volume{d203ba64-8654-11de-add0-
    ➥ 001f1663f5df}\"}|
Invoke-WmiMethod -Name AddMountPoint -ArgumentList "C:\\pawtest"
```

In both cases, the result is piped into `Invoke-WmiMethod` to call the `AddMountPoint` method. The folder to be used as the mount point has to be presented in WMI format with double backslashes (\\) rather than a single one.

One of the first management tasks you'll have to perform on your volume is formatting it so that it becomes usable.

TECHNIQUE 30   Formatting a disk

The disks have to be formatted when you first install a new server. You also need to format them when you're rebuilding the system so that it can be repaired or repurposed. Occasionally, reformatting may be necessary if a machine has been infected with a virus. Formatting is a destructive process, so it's a good way of clearing the disks of all data prior to reuse.

PROBLEM

You're rebuilding a server because you're changing its purpose. You need to format the data drives. The C: drive will be reformatted during the installation of Windows.

SOLUTION

In the following listing, you use the `Format` method of the `Win32_Volume` class to reformat the disk.

Listing 6.11   Formatting a disk

```
function format-drive {
[CmdletBinding()]
param (
```

```
[parameter(ValueFromPipeline=$true,
  ValueFromPipelineByPropertyName=$true)]
[string]$computername="$env:COMPUTERNAME",

[parameter(Mandatory=$true)]
[string]$drive,

[ValidateSet("NTFS", "FAT", "FAT32")]
[string]$filesys = "NTFS",
[boolean]$quick = $true,
[int]$cluster = 4096,
[string]$label = ""
)
PROCESS{
  if (-not $drive.EndsWith(":")){$drive = "$drive:"}
  $v = Get-WmiObject -Class Win32_Volume `
  -Filter "DriveLetter='D:'" -ComputerName $computername
  $ret = $v.Format($filesys, $quick, $cluster, $label, $false)

  if ($ret.ReturnValue -eq 0){"Drive $drive formatted"}
  else {"Formatting of drive $drive failed" }
} }
```

❶ Set parameters

❷ Format drive

Display results ❸

The function accepts a number of parameters ❶. You've seen the computer name and drive before. There are a limited number of choices available for the filesystem. You should be using NTFS for the filesystem, so you set that as the default. The ValidateSet() method is used on the parameter to check that only acceptable values can be passed.

If the drive doesn't end with a colon (:), you add one. Get-WmiObject is used to create a variable to represent the volume you want to format ❷.

> **WARNING** Remember that you don't get -Whatif or -Confirm with WMI. Be careful when using this function. I've included a version of this function that implements –Whatif using functionality from PowerShell's advanced functions. It's in the Chapter06\Extras folder of the code download.

The Format method is invoked on the volume object using the parameters you've passed into the function.

If a result of 0 is returned, the formatting has succeeded ❸; otherwise a message is displayed to say that it has failed.

DISCUSSION

One surprise while researching this technique was that using Invoke-WmiMethod and formatting arguments didn't work. For instance, this code should work:

```
Get-WmiObject -Class Win32_Volume -Filter "DriveLetter='D:'"  |
Invoke-WmiMethod -Name Format `
-ArgumentList "NTFS", $true, 4096, "Test", $false
```

In fact, it returns an error stating, "Input string was not in a correct format." Luckily, you have more than one way to format a disk, and the method described in listing 6.11 works.

MVPs find the answer

I discussed the problem of `Invoke-WmiMethod` and how it takes arguments with the other PowerShell MVPs, and after some investigation Shay Levy discovered that this would work:

```
Get-WmiObject Win32_Volume -Filter "DriveLetter='D:'" |
Invoke-WmiMethod -Name Format `
 -ArgumentList @(4096,$false,'NTFS','King',$true,$null)
```

where the arguments are in the order of:

- `ClusterSize`
- `EnableCompression`
- `FileSystem`
- `Label`
- `QuickFormat`
- `Version`

He looked at the parameters that were returned by

```
([wmiclass]"Win32_Volume").GetMethodParameters('Format')
```

These are in the order given in the code in this sidebar, whereas the order given on MSDN matches what I used in the listing and what is produced by using

```
(Get-WmiObject Win32_Volume -Filter "DriveLetter='D:'").Format
```

Very odd.

Now that your disk has been formatted, you can put it into use. During the lifetime of the system, you may have to perform routine maintenance on the disk.

TECHNIQUE 31   **Performing Chkdsk**

Chkdsk performs a low-level check on the disk. It's especially useful for detecting whether sectors on the disk have become corrupted. Unfortunately, it's often users complaining that they can't access a file that alerts you to a potential disk problem.

PROBLEM

A user has complained that they can't access a file. It won't open, even though other files in the same folder are usable. You need to perform a `chkdsk` operation on the volume to determine if there is any corruption of the media.

SOLUTION

The `Win32_Volume` class has a `Chkdsk` method. If you have used the command-line `chkdsk` utility, you'll find it very similar. The advantage of using WMI is that you can work on the disks of remote machines.

I have called this function `invoke-chkdsk`, following the PowerShell naming conventions. It's shown in the following listing. The function can be used as

```
invoke-chkdsk mycomputer f:
```

Listing 6.12 Performing a `chkdsk`

```
function invoke-chkdsk {
[CmdletBinding()]
param (
 [parameter(ValueFromPipeline=$true,
   ValueFromPipelineByPropertyName=$true)]
 [string]$computername="$env:COMPUTERNAME",
 [string]$drive ="D:",
 [boolean]$fixerrors = $false,
 [boolean]$vigorousIndexCheck = $true,
 [boolean]$skipFolderCycle = $true,
 [boolean]$forcedismount = $false,
 [boolean]$recoverbadsectors = $false,
 [boolean]$oktorunatbootup = $false
)
PROCESS {
 if (-not $drive.EndsWith(":")){$drive = "$drive:"}

 Get-WmiObject Win32_Volume -Filter "DriveLetter='$drive'" `
 -ComputerName $computername |
 Invoke-WmiMethod -Name ChkDsk `
 -ArgumentList $fixerrors, $vigorousIndexCheck,$skipFolderCycle, `
 $forcedismount, $recoverbadsectors, $oktorunatbootup
}}
```

The function takes the usual computer and drive parameters. It also takes a number of Boolean (`true` or `false`) parameters. The default values will perform a `chkdsk` but won't attempt to repair any errors. If you want that to happen, the function should be used as follows:

```
invoke-chkdsk mycomputer f: -fixerrors $true `
-recoverbadsectors $true
```

DISCUSSION

Performing a `chkdsk` in this manner will work on all drives except the C: drive (assuming C: is the boot drive). On the boot drive, the `chkdsk` will be performed the next time the system is restarted.

The other maintenance activity you need to consider is how you deal with file fragmentation.

TECHNIQUE 32 **Analyzing and removing fragmentation**

When a file is deleted from a volume in a Windows system, the remaining files aren't shuffled around to use the space that has been made. New files will start to be written into the first available space on a disk. If there isn't enough space for the file to fit in a single piece, it will be written into whatever space is next available.

As this process proceeds and more files are deleted, the resulting space gets broken up into small pieces, meaning that files can be spread across multiple areas of the disk. This is *fragmentation*. If the level of fragmentation becomes too high, performance can be affected.

Modern Windows systems perform a certain amount of defragmentation automatically, but it isn't always enough. Sometimes you have to step in and do the job yourself.

PROBLEM

The users are complaining (again) that one of your servers is slow to respond when files are requested. You need to analyze the volume for its fragmentation state and, if necessary, perform a defragmentation on the disk.

SOLUTION

The following listing shows how you can use the `DefragAnalysis` and `Defrag` methods of the `Win32_Volume` class to solve this problem.

Listing 6.13 Analyzing and performing defragmentation

```
function invoke-defraganal {
[CmdletBinding()]
param (
 [parameter(ValueFromPipeline=$true,
   ValueFromPipelineByPropertyName=$true)]
 [string]$computername="$env:COMPUTERNAME",      ❶ Set
 [string]$drive ="D:",                              parameters
 [switch]$defrag
)
PROCESS
if (-not $drive.EndsWith(":")){$drive = "$drive:"}   ❷ Perform
                                                       analysis
if (-not $defrag) {
 "Analysing drive $drive"
 $dfa = Get-WmiObject Win32_Volume `
 -Filter "DriveLetter='$drive'" -ComputerName $computername |
 Invoke-WmiMethod -Name DefragAnalysis
  if ($($dfa.ReturnValue) -eq 0){
    "Defrag Recommended: $($dfa.DefragRecommended)"
  }                                                 ❸ Perform
} else {                                              defragmentation
   "Defraging drive $drive"
   $dfa = Get-WmiObject Win32_volume `
   -Filter "DriveLetter='$drive'" -ComputerName $computername |
   Invoke-WmiMethod -Name Defrag -ArgumentList $false
}                                                   ❹ Display
                                                       results
if ($($dfa.ReturnValue) -eq 0){
 $dfa.DefragAnalysis |
 select AverageFileSize, AverageFragmentsPerFile,
 @{Name="AverageFreeSpacePerExtent (GB)";
  Expression={"{0:F3}" -f $($_.AverageFreeSpacePerExtent/1GB)}},
 ClusterSize, FragmentedFolders,
 ExcessFolderFragments, FilePercentFragmentation,
  @{Name="FreeSpace (GB)";
  Expression={"{0:F3}" -f $($_.FreeSpace/1GB)}},
 FreeSpacePercent, FreeSpacePercentFragmentation,
 @{Name="LargestFreeSpaceExtent (GB)";
  Expression={"{0:F3}" -f $($_.LargestFreeSpaceExtent/1GB)}},
 MFTPercentInUse, MFTRecordCount, PageFileSize,
 TotalExcessFragments, TotalFiles, TotalFolders,
```

```
TotalFragmentedFiles, TotalFreeSpaceExtents,
TotalMFTFragments, TotalUnmovableFiles,
@{Name="TotalMFTSize (GB)";
  Expression={"{0:F3}" -f $($_.TotalMFTSize/1GB)}},
TotalPageFileFragments,  TotalPercentFragmentation,
@{Name="UsedSpace (GB)";
  Expression={"{0:F3}" -f $($_.UsedSpace/1GB)}},
VolumeName,
@{Name="VolumeSize (GB)";
  Expression={"{0:F3}" -f $($_.VolumeSize/1GB)}}
}
else {"Error occurred - return code: $($dfa.ReturnValue)"}
}}
```

The function accepts the computer and drive parameters as usual for this chapter ❶, but you also have another parameter, defrag. This is a switch that's set to False by default. If you use it, a defragmentation occurs, and if you don't, you just get the analysis.

The script checks the formatting of the drive parameter and corrects it if required.

If the defrag switch isn't set ❷, then an analysis is performed using the Defrag-Analysis method. Get-WmiObject is used to retrieve the volume, and then it's piped into Invoke-WmiMethod.

A similar process is used if the defrag switch is set ❸, except that the Defrag method is used.

In both cases, the results are output to a variable, $dfa. If the return code is 0, the results are displayed ❹; otherwise an error message is displayed. The results are similar to those obtained from running the analysis in the GUI tools. The sizes are all recalculated as gigabytes for ease of use.

DISCUSSION

The defrag switch makes the function easy to use:

```
Invoke-defraganal mycomputer f:
```

This line will test the F: drive on the stated computer. If the results come back suggesting that defragmentation is required, you simply add the defrag parameter:

```
Invoke-defraganal mycomputer f: -defrag
```

This then performs the defragmentation and returns the results so you can see the progress.

Sometimes you'll need to run multiple defragmentation passes to remove the maximum amount of fragmentation. This can be achieved with a slight modification:

```
1..5 | foreach {Invoke-defraganal mycomputer f: -defrag}
```

That completes our look at the system's hard drives, but before we close the chapter we need to consider CD drives.

6.5   *CD drives*

CD/DVD drives (for simplicity, I'll refer to them as CD drives throughout this section) are often the forgotten component when you're discussing disks. They're included by

Win32_LogicalDisk and Win32_Volume but are excluded by Win32_DiskDrive. You've seen how to deal with them as logical disks and volumes earlier in the chapter. All that remains is to discover the data you need on the physical drive.

TECHNIQUE 33   **Enumerating CD drives**

Most modern systems have a CD drive. Virtual machines can gain access to the physical drive of the host or can attach an ISO file through a virtual CD drive.

PROBLEM

In order to complete the documentation of your servers you have to enumerate the CD drives that are present in the system.

SOLUTION

The listings presented earlier in the chapter will provide information on the volumes present because of the CD drive. You can discover the required information on the physical aspect of the CD drive using Win32_CDROMDrive. This class also works for DVD drives.

> **WARNING**   Be careful with the name of this class. It's easy to get it wrong, especially if you're in a hurry and just type Win32_CDROM as many people do. (Yep, done that.) It's a pity we can't establish aliases for WMI classes.

The following listing shows how you can use this class.

Listing 6.14   Enumerating CD drives

```
function get-cdrom {
[CmdletBinding()]
param (
 [parameter(ValueFromPipeline=$true,
   ValueFromPipelineByPropertyName=$true)]
 [string]$computername="$env:COMPUTERNAME"
)
PROCESS{
  Get-WmiObject -Class Win32_CDROMDrive `
  -ComputerName $computername |
  foreach {
    ""
   $_ | select Drive, MediaLoaded, Status, Name,
   MediaType, SCSIBus, SCSILogicalUnit,
   SCSIPort, SCSITargetId, TransferRate

   "Capabilities:"
   Get-WmiObject -Class Win32_CDROMDrive `
   -ComputerName $computername -Filter "Drive='$($_.Drive)'" |
   select  -ExpandProperty CapabilityDescriptions
 }
}}
```

The function takes a computer name as a parameter. The default is the local machine, as usual.

You can then use `Win32_CDROMDrive` to return the information on the physical aspects of the drive. A further call is made to the class to determine the capabilities. You can use the capability descriptions via the `ExpandProperty` parameter of `Select-Object` to create a formatted list of the capabilities. The capabilities are things like

- Random access
- Supports removable media

Notice that the call `Win32_CDROMDrive` to determine the capabilities uses the drive letter as a filter to ensure that the capabilities are linked to the correct drive.

DISCUSSION

This script could be adapted to determine whether a CD drive is present in the machine by testing to see if `Win32_CDROMDrive` returns data. If it doesn't, there isn't a CD drive present.

This brings our tour of the disk-related WMI classes to a close.

6.6 *Summary*

The functionality presented in this chapter and chapter 5 will provide most, if not all, of the information you require about the physical aspects of your systems. It's how I document my systems.

This chapter has worked through the WMI classes that enable you to work with

- Physical disks and disk controllers
- Partitions
- Logical disks and volumes
- CD drives

You've also seen how to work with events raised by the disk systems. This technique also can be used to format drives and perform other management activities.

Disks, like all aspects of your systems, need managing occasionally. You can use the techniques in this chapter to format your disks, run disk-checking routines, and perform defragmentation.

Chapters 5 and 6 have covered the hardware aspects of our systems. In the next chapter, we'll start to investigate some other aspects, starting with the registry.

Registry administration

7

This chapter covers

- Discovering the registry's size
- Manipulating registry keys and values
- Discovering security settings on registry keys
- Monitoring changes on keys and values

The registry is used to contain configuration information about your Windows systems. It's entirely separate from the information maintained by the WMI providers we discussed in chapter 3, though some of the information may overlap.

> **WARNING** This is the point where I issue the traditional warning about being careful with the registry. If you damage the registry, you may have to rebuild your system. I'm assuming that if you're reading this, you aren't going to deliberately wreck your system, but do be careful. Creating a system restore point before experimenting with the registry is highly recommended—use Checkpoint-Computer on a client system.

Working with the registry on your local computer is easy because you have the registry provider. This means you can use the standard cmdlets (*-Item, *-ItemProperty, and so on) to perform your administration tasks. If you have PowerShell v2 installed on all of your machines, you could use PowerShell remoting to access the registry provider on your servers. But many organizations aren't in that position, so you'll need to use WMI to work with remote registries. There's similar .NET functionality, but I'm not going to cover it here.

We'll start the chapter by looking at how you can access the registry. The registry size can be checked to ensure you don't have a problem. Also, you'll probably spend more time reading registry values compared to other activities, so you need to understand the data types available in the registry. Techniques to read, create, modify where applicable, and delete registry keys and values are presented in turn to enable you to manage the whole lifecycle.

> **TIP** When working with the registry, the *paths* are known as *keys*, and the actual *entries* are known as *values*, even though a registry value will have a name and a value.

Security is always a concern. The registry needs to be protected from rogue actions, so you need to be able to check access permissions on particular keys. If an untoward action has occurred, you may need to reset the ownership of a registry key so that you can perform further actions on the key and its values.

There are some keys and values that you may need to protect further. You can use the WMI registry events to monitor for changes to a key or its values.

Before you can do anything, though, you need to learn how to access the registry and what data types are available.

7.1 Accessing the registry

The registry consists of a number of areas known as *hives*. Each hive has a number of *keys*. When you look at these in regedit.exe (see figure 7.1), they appear to be arranged in a hierarchy similar to the filesystem. The keys can have *subkeys*. A key or subkey can act as a container for *values*. A registry value has a *name* and an *actual value*. Figure 7.1 displays these various elements.

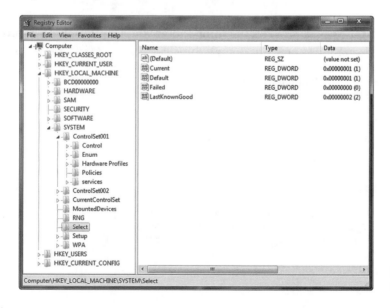

Figure 7.1 The structure of the registry

WMI uses a constant numeric value to identify each hive, as you'll see in the later sections. These constants are listed in table 7.1, together with the variables I'll use in this chapter's scripts.

Table 7.1 Constants for accessing registry hives

Variable	Value	Hive
$HKCR	2147483648	HKEY_CLASSES_ROOT
$HKCU	2147483649	HKEY_CURRENT_USER
$HKLM	2147483650	HKEY_LOCAL_MACHINE
$HKUS	2147483651	HKEY_USERS
$HKCC	2147483653	HKEY_CURRENT_CONFIG

Before we dive into reading and writing in the registry, let's look at a couple more things about it.

TECHNIQUE 34   **Test registry size**

Do you know how big the registry is on your systems? The registry is created at machine startup from a number of files on the hard drive. If these files become full of rubbish, then server startup time will be slower and performance will potentially suffer.

PROBLEM

You need to be able to test the current and maximum sizes of the registry to ensure that it isn't becoming bloated, which could cause problems. You need to be able to perform this test on local and remote machines.

SOLUTION

The `Win32_Registry` class provides the information you need to solve this problem. The following listing shows how you can use this class.

Listing 7.1 Discovering the registry size

```
function get-registrysize {
[CmdletBinding()]
param (
  [parameter(ValueFromPipeline=$true,
    ValueFromPipelineByPropertyName=$true)]
  [string]$computername="$env:COMPUTERNAME"
)
PROCESS {
Get-WmiObject -Class Win32_Registry -ComputerName $computername |
Select CurrentSize, ProposedSize, MaximumSize, Status,
@{Name="InstallationDate";Expression={$_.ConvertToDateTime($_.InstallDate)}}
}
```

This function is similar in structure to the functions you saw in the previous chapter. If you're automating the documentation of your systems, you may want to include this function. I do!

The function takes a computer name as a parameter and calls the `Win32_Registry` class. The appropriate properties are displayed by piping the WMI object into `Select-Object`.

DISCUSSION

Converting WMI dates into a readable format was covered in detail in chapter 4.

One potential enhancement to this function would be to add a calculation of registry size as a percentage of the maximum size of the registry, as configured for that system. This gives a more immediate indicator of the size and potential issues. After the `Status` property in listing 7.1, add this line of code:

```
@{N="PercSize"; E={"{0:F3}" -f $(($($_.CurrentSize)/
    $($_.MaximumSize))*100)}},
```

The comma at the end is required so that the date conversion is still part of the statement. In this snippet, I used N and E as abbreviations for `Name` and `Expression` respectively. This is valid PowerShell, but I generally use the full versions for clarity.

Now that you know the registry size, you need to think about reading the registry itself. In figure 7.1 the values are shown with data types such as `REG_SZ`. You need to know the type before you can read the data on a particular value.

| TECHNIQUE 35 | **Discovering registry data types** |

The registry can store multiple data types, including strings, numbers, and binary data. Table 7.2 lists the data types you'll meet most commonly.

Table 7.2 Registry data types

Method	Data type	Comments
GetBinaryValue	REG_BINARY	Returns an array of bytes
GetDWORDValue	REG_DWORD	Returns a 32-bit number
GetExpandedStringValue	REG_EXPAND_SZ	Returns expanded references to environmental variables, such as %SYSTEMROOT%
GetMultiStringValue	REG_MULTI_SZ	Returns multiple string values, such as "A","B","C","D"
GetQWORDValue	REG_QWORD	Returns a 64-bit number
GetStringValue	REG_SZ	Returns a string

One of the difficulties when working with the registry is that you need to use a different WMI method to access each data type. These methods are listed in the first column of table 7.2. A similar set of methods exists to write to the registry (for example, `SetDWORDValue`).

Before you can successfully read the registry you have to understand the data types you're dealing with.

PROBLEM

You need to check on a registry value across many machines in your environment to ensure that they're configured correctly. Unfortunately, you don't know the correct data type to access the value.

SOLUTION

The WMI registry provider supplies a method known as `EnumValues`. Listing 7.2 shows how you can utilize this method. The function accepts a number of parameters including hive type, registry key, and computer name. The computer name defaults to "$env:COMPUTERNAME", which is the local machine.

The parameters for the hive and the key both carry a mandatory tag. This means that if you don't supply them, you'll be prompted for them. That's a lot of functionality for adding one line of code to the parameter definition! The hive parameter is also tested against the set of valid hive types. PowerShell is the perfect doorman—if it isn't on the list it doesn't get in.

Listing 7.2   Discovering registry value types

```
function get-regvaluetype {
[CmdletBinding()]
param(
 [parameter(Mandatory=$true)]
 [string]
 [Validateset("HKCR", "HKCU", "HKLM", "HKUS", "HKCC")]
  $hive,

 [parameter(Mandatory=$true)]
 [string]$key,

 [parameter(ValueFromPipeline=$true,
   ValueFromPipelineByPropertyName=$true)]
 [string]$computername="$env:COMPUTERNAME"
)
PROCESS {                                              ❶ Set hive
switch ($hive) {                                          constant
 "HKCR" {$rh = 2147483648}
 "HKCU" {$rh = 2147483649}
 "HKLM" {$rh = 2147483650}
 "HKUS" {$rh = 2147483651}
 "HKCC" {$rh = 2147483653}
}
$regtype = DATA {                                      ❷ Lookup table
ConvertFrom-StringData -StringData @'                     for data types
1 = REG_SZ
2 = REG_EXPAND_SZ
3 = REG_BINARY
4 = REG_DWORD
7 = REG_MULTI_SZ
'@
```

```
}
$reg = [wmiclass]\\$computername\root\default:StdRegprov
$data = $reg.EnumValues($rh, $key)
$x = ($data.snames).Length
for ($i=0; $i -le $x; $i++){"{0,-30} {1}" -f
  $($data.snames[$i]), $regtype["$($data.types[$i])"] }
}}
```
❸ WMI registry provider

❹ Display values

A switch statement ❶ is used to set the hive constant based on the input parameter. A hash table is created, holding the possible data types ❷. This is the same technique you saw in chapters 5 and 6.

The registry provider can't be accessed using `Get-WmiObject` ❸. You have to use `[wmiclass]` to create an instance of the class that you can then populate. Chapter 3 covers the `[wmiclass]` type accelerator in detail.

> **NOTE** I deliberately used the `StdRegprov` class from the `root\default` namespace. In Windows Vista, Windows 2008, and later, the registry classes are also available in the `root\cimv2` namespace. I've used `root\default` for consistency with earlier versions of Windows.

The `EnumValues` method is used with the hive and key as parameters to retrieve the registry values associated with that particular key. The names and data types are displayed in a formatted string ❹. This listing also uses an extra line of code to get the number of values, to keep the loop coding simpler.

DISCUSSION

The function is loaded as part of the chapter module, or the individual listing can be run. Remember to dot-source the listing!

Advanced functions are used in the same way as cmdlets, as you can see in the following example:

```
get-regvaluetype -hive HKLM `
-key "SOFTWARE\Microsoft\Windows\CurrentVersion"
```

The results of running this example are shown in figure 7.2.

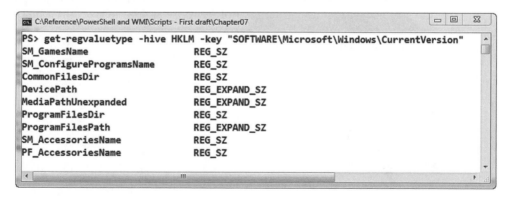

Figure 7.2 Displaying registry value types

In this particular case, you have strings (REG_SZ) and expanded strings (REG_EXPAND_SZ).

> **NOTE** Setting the hive constant in each function is inefficient. In the next listing you'll move this functionality into a separate function so that it can be reused easily.

Now that you know how to discover data types, you can move on to reading the registry.

7.2   *Reading the registry*

Reading the registry comprises two separate actions:

- Reading a registry key to find subkeys
- Reading registry values

We'll start by reading a registry key.

TECHNIQUE 36   **Reading registry keys**

One nice thing about working with the registry through WMI is that the same pattern of code is repeated. You'll see this and you'll also see the function for setting the hive constant that I promised earlier.

PROBLEM

An application requires a particular subkey to be present. You need to be able to test remote systems to determine whether this key is present to troubleshoot a problem.

SOLUTION

The solution to this problem is shown in listing 7.3. It consists of two functions: set-HiveValue and get-regkey. The set-HiveValue function accepts a hive, such as HKLM, as a parameter and returns the appropriate constant using the switch statement you saw in listing 7.2. You don't need to test the hive name because it's tested in the parent function.

> **TIP** If you load the chapter module, the set-HiveValue function will be automatically loaded for you. If you use the listings individually, cut and paste the set-HiveValue function into another script and be sure to run it first.

Listing 7.3 Reading registry keys

```
function set-HiveValue {
param([string]$hive)
switch ($hive) {
 "HKCR" {$rh = 2147483648}
 "HKCU" {$rh = 2147483649}
 "HKLM" {$rh = 2147483650}
 "HKUS" {$rh = 2147483651}
 "HKCC" {$rh = 2147483653}
}
 $rh
}
```

```
function get-regkey {
[CmdletBinding()]
param (
 [parameter(Mandatory=$true)]
 [string]
 [Validateset("HKCR", "HKCU", "HKLM", "HKUS", "HKCC")]
  $hive,

 [parameter(Mandatory=$true)]
 [string]$key,

 [parameter(ValueFromPipeline=$true,
   ValueFromPipelineByPropertyName=$true)]
 [string]$computername="$env:COMPUTERNAME"
)
PROCESS {
$rh = set-HiveValue $hive
$reg = [wmiclass]"\\$computername\root\default:StdRegprov"
$subkeys = $reg.EnumKey($rh, $key)
switch ($subkeys.ReturnValue) {
 0 {$subkeys.snames; break}
 2 {"Key $key not found"; break}
 default {"Error has occurred"; break}
}
}}
```

The get-regkey (remember the PowerShell verb-noun naming conventions) takes a hive and key as mandatory parameters. The computer name is an optional parameter. A call is made to set-HiveValue to get the hive constant.

An instance of StdRegprov (the registry provider) is created so that you can retrieve the subkeys using the EnumKey method. This takes the hive constant and key as parameters, as do most of the registry methods.

The switch statement is an example of the type of error handling that can be used with these functions. It tests the return value, and if the value is 0 it prints the subkeys; otherwise an error message is shown. I haven't done this in all the examples in the chapter for brevity.

DISCUSSION

Being able to read registry keys is fundamental to working with the registry. It's worth experimenting with this function. As well as returning subkeys, the function can also be used to test whether a key is present. Try the following code after loading the function:

```
get-regkey -hive HKLM -key "SYSTEM\CurrentControlSet\Services"
```

The output will be a list of services. If the key doesn't exist, however, an error message will be displayed. This can be illustrated by trying this version which has deliberately misspelled the final part of the registry key:

```
get-regkey -hive HKLM -key "SYSTEM\CurrentControlSet\Servicez"
```

You'll receive a message stating that the key doesn't exist. Two purposes fulfilled with one function—that's productivity!

Reading the registry keys is step one. Step two is to drop down a level and read the values.

Reading registry values

Reading registry values is where the real administrative effort lies. These are the entries that control the configuration of your systems and can potentially cause problems, especially if they are wrong.

PROBLEM

You need to be able to read registry values for an arbitrary key. The function must work across a number of hives and with the standard registry data types. A generic function of this sort will save you from having to recreate scripts.

SOLUTION

You've seen how to work with multiple hives in previous listings in this chapter. You need to add the ability to read multiple data types. The following listing shows how you can perform this task.

Listing 7.4   Reading registry values

```
function get-regvalue {
[CmdletBinding()]
param (
 [parameter(Mandatory=$true)]
 [string]
 [Validateset("HKCR", "HKCU", "HKLM", "HKUS", "HKCC")]
  $hive,

 [parameter(Mandatory=$true)]
 [string]$key,

 [parameter(Mandatory=$true)]
 [string]$value,

 [parameter(Mandatory=$true)]
 [string]
 [Validateset("DWORD", "EXPANDSZ", "MULTISZ", "QWORD", "SZ")]
 $type,

 [parameter(ValueFromPipeline=$true,
   ValueFromPipelineByPropertyName=$true)]
  [string]$computername="$env:COMPUTERNAME"
)
PROCESS {
$rh = set-HiveValue $hive
$reg = [wmiclass]"\\$computername\root\default:StdRegprov"switch ($type) {
"DWORD"      {$data =
    ➥ ($reg.GetDwordValue($rh, $key, $value)).uvalue}
"EXPANDSZ"   {$data =
    ➥ ($reg.GetExpandedStringValue($rh, $key, $value)).svalue}
"MULTISZ"    {$data =
    ➥ ($reg.GetMultiStringValue($rh, $key, $value)).svalue}
"QWORD"      {$data =
    ➥ ($reg.GetQwordValue($rh, $key, $value)).uvalue}
```

```
"SZ"        {$data =
    ➥ ($reg.GetStringValue($rh, $key, $value)).svalue}
}
$data
}}
```

The `get-regvalue` function builds on listing 7.3. The parameters for the hive, key, and computer name work as described earlier. You add a parameter (`$type`) to describe the data type. This parameter will automatically validate the data it's given against the set of acceptable values.

The hive constant and WMI registry provider are configured. A `switch` statement is used to perform the hard work. The registry data type is tested, and the appropriate method is used to read the data.

The code extracts the value from the data returned by WMI. An `svalue` indicates a string and a `uvalue` indicates a numeric. The data is returned to the user.

DISCUSSION

This function may seem complicated, given the variety of data that can be entered for the hive and the data type. The following examples will show how it works.

This first example retrieves a `DWORD` value:

```
get-regvalue -hive HKLM `
-key "SOFTWARE\Microsoft\Windows\CurrentVersion\BITS" `
-value "LogFileMinMemory" -type DWORD
```

This reads the `LogFileMinMemory` value and returns a result of 120 on my system.

The second example reads a string value—in this case, the Common Files directory:

```
get-regvalue -hive HKLM -key "SOFTWARE\Microsoft\Windows\CurrentVersion" `
-value "CommonFilesDir" -type SZ
```

This returns the expected result of C:\Program Files\Common Files.

Our final example reads an expanded string. The path for program files is a good example:

```
get-regvalue -hive HKLM -key "SOFTWARE\Microsoft\Windows\CurrentVersion" `
-value "ProgramFilesPath" -type EXPANDSZ
```

It returns C:\Program Files, and it's stored in the registry as `%ProgramFiles%`. Its value can be checked using `$env:ProgramFiles`.

Often you'll want to read a number of keys at the same time.

TECHNIQUE 38   **Enumerating keys and values**

There are times when reading a single value is insufficient. You must read multiple keys and extract a value from each of them. This is known as *enumeration*.

PROBLEM

You need to discover what software is installed on your servers. This is to determine what they're doing and will help complete the documentation of the servers.

SOLUTION

You can restrict the number of parameters you need for the function in the following listing because you know exactly what you want to read. The computer name defaults to the local system, which is always good for testing. In this type of case, I tend to develop a script to give a specific result rather than try to be too generic. The registry key could be made a parameter to provide a more generic approach.

Listing 7.5 List installed software

```
function get-software {
[CmdletBinding()]
param (
 [parameter(ValueFromPipeline=$true,
   ValueFromPipelineByPropertyName=$true)]
   [string]$computername="$env:COMPUTERNAME"
)
PROCESS {
$rh = set-HiveValue "HKLM"
$key = "SOFTWARE\Microsoft\Windows\CurrentVersion\Uninstall"
$reg = [wmiclass]"\\$computername\root\default:StdRegprov"$subkeys =
     $reg.EnumKey($rh, $key)
$subkeys.snames |
 foreach {
  if ($_ -notlike "{*}") {
  $key2 = "$key\$_"
  $value = "DisplayName"
  $name = $reg.GetStringValue($rh, $key2, $value)
  if (($name.sValue -ne "") -and
      ($name.sValue -notlike "*(KB*)*")){
    $name.sValue
   }
  }
 }
}}
```

You can use the `set-HiveValue` function to set the hive constant. You give an explicit value rather than a variable. The key is also set. You can enumerate the subkeys of a key by using the `EnumKey` method.

> **TIP** This code doesn't show all installed software. The `Win32_Product` class should be used as well as this code to retrieve a fuller list of installed software.

The names of the keys are returned. Each name is tested to ensure it isn't a value in braces. The original key and the subkey names are joined and used to retrieve the display name of the software, which is displayed.

DISCUSSION

This may seem complicated if you have used the PowerShell registry provider. You can accomplish the same task with this code:

```
Get-ChildItem `
-Path HKLM:SOFTWARE\Microsoft\Windows\CurrentVersion\Uninstall |
where {$_.Name -notlike  "*{*" } |
foreach { Get-ItemProperty -Path $($_.PSPAth) -Name DisplayName |
select DisplayName}
```

The drawback here is that you can't use provider-based code on remote machines.

Being able to read registry values is a good thing. Being able to create or modify them is even better.

7.3 *Creating and modifying registry keys and values*

Making modifications to systems is an essential part of being able to administer them. You can make bulk changes to the registry by using Group Policies (GPOs), but in many cases you only need to modify a single value or create a single key. A PowerShell function is a simpler, easier, and safer proposition.

> **WARNING**   You'll need administrator privileges to be able to write to the registry or to perform deletions. Run PowerShell with elevated privileges for these examples.

Before you can create a value, you need to create a key.

TECHNIQUE 39   **Creating registry keys**

At this point, I need to emphasize my warning from the beginning of the chapter. You'll be making changes to the registry, so be careful. It's a good idea to create a system restore point before working with these examples.

> **WARNING**   These examples worked on my test system. There's no guarantee that they'll work on your system. Please test them thoroughly in your environment.

PROBLEM

You need to create a registry key on one or more machines.

SOLUTION

There is a `CreateKey` method on the registry provider that will perform the key-creation task. The use of this method is shown in the following listing.

Listing 7.6   Create registry key

```
function new-regkey {
[CmdletBinding()]
param (
 [parameter(Mandatory=$true)]
 [string]
 [Validateset("HKCR", "HKCU", "HKLM", "HKUS", "HKCC")]
  $hive,

 [parameter(Mandatory=$true)]
 [string]$key,

 [parameter(ValueFromPipeline=$true,
```

```
        ValueFromPipelineByPropertyName=$true)]
    [string]$computername="$env:COMPUTERNAME"
)
PROCESS {
$rh = set-HiveValue $hive
$reg = [wmiclass]"\\$computername\root\default:StdRegprov"$reg.CreateKey($rh,
    $key)
}}
```

The usual hive, key, and computer parameters are input to the function. In this case, the key doesn't exist. The hive constant is obtained and an instance of the WMI registry provider is created. A call to the CreateKey method using the hive and key completes the function and creates the new key.

DISCUSSION

You could extend the script by incorporating the code from listing 7.3, testing the output from that portion of code, and creating the key if it doesn't exist.

The function is used like this:

```
new-regkey -hive HKLM -key "SOFTWARE\PAW"
```

This example creates a key on the local machine. You can test whether it has worked by using the PowerShell registry provider:

```
Test-Path HKLM:\SOFTWARE\PAW
```

If we use something like this,

```
new-regkey -hive HKLM -key "SOFTWARE\PAW\Ch7"
```

the full path will be created (the PAW subkey will be created with its own subkey of Ch7).

That's how you create keys, but what about setting values?

TECHNIQUE 40   **Setting registry values**

When you want to set or create registry values, you're faced with the same problem you had in technique 37, in that you have to be able to deal with multiple data types. It would be possible to create one function per data type, but that sounds like a lot of repetitious coding to me. It's also harder to maintain. When creating scripts, always think about how you're going to maintain them.

> **TIP**   I recommend that you always add comments to your scripts, even if they're simple reminders of what the script does. I haven't used them in the scripts in this book for brevity and because I'm explaining the scripts in the text.

PROBLEM

You have to modify, or create if it isn't present, a registry value on a number of servers.

SOLUTION

You can amend listing 7.4 to provide the solution, as demonstrated in the following listing. The set-regvalue function (notice I'm using approved verbs) takes the hive, key, value, type, and computer parameters you saw in listing 7.4. Remember that the value parameter takes the value name. In addition, you have three parameters you can use to supply the data to be written into the registry.

Listing 7.7 Set registry value

```
function set-regvalue {
[CmdletBinding()]
param (
 [parameter(Mandatory=$true)]
 [string]
 [Validateset("HKCR", "HKCU", "HKLM", "HKUS", "HKCC")]
  $hive,

 [parameter(Mandatory=$true)]
 [string]$key,

 [parameter(Mandatory=$true)]
 [string]$value,

 [parameter(Mandatory=$true)]
 [string]
 [Validateset("DWORD", "EXPANDSZ", "MULTISZ", "QWORD", "SZ")]
 $type,

 [string]$svalue,

 [int32]$dvalue,

 [int64]$qvalue,

 [parameter(ValueFromPipeline=$true,
   ValueFromPipelineByPropertyName=$true)]
 [string]$computername="$env:COMPUTERNAME"
)
PROCESS {   switch ($type) {
"DWORD"     {$data = ($reg.SetDwordValue($rh, $key, $value, $dvalue))}
"EXPANDSZ"  {$data = ($reg.GetExpandedStringValue($rh, $key, $value,
     $svalue))}
"MULTISZ"   {$data = ($reg.GetMultiStringValue($rh, $key, $value, $svalue))}
"QWORD"     {$data = ($reg.SetQwordValue($rh, $key, $value, $qvalue))}
"SZ"        {$data = ($reg.SetStringValue($rh, $key, $value, $svalue))}
}
if ($data.ReturnValue -eq 0) {"Setting $key\$value was successful"}
else {"Setting $key\$value was unsuccessful"}
}}
```

The hive constant and registry provider are set. A switch statement is used to call the appropriate method based on the data type. If the registry value exists, it's updated; otherwise it's created and the data written into it. A test of the WMI return code determines whether the registry value was updated successfully.

DISCUSSION

Here are two examples (for a string and a DWORD respectively) that show how to use the function. These are the value types you'll deal with most often:

```
set-regvalue -hive HKLM -key "SOFTWARE\PAW" `
-value "stringvalue" -type SZ -svalue "This is a string"
get-regvalue -hive HKLM -key "SOFTWARE\PAW" `
-value "stringvalue" -type SZ
set-regvalue -hive HKLM -key "SOFTWARE\PAW" `
-value "integervalue" -type dword -dvalue 98
get-regvalue -hive HKLM -key "SOFTWARE\PAW" `
-value "integervalue" -type DWORD
```

Each example of using `set-regvalue` is followed by the equivalent `get-regvalue` to show that it has been set.

The last part of our registry lifecycle is to delete keys and values.

7.4   *Deleting registry keys*

All good things come to an end, and that includes the registry keys you've come to know and love. Sooner or later you're faced with the task of deleting registry keys and values. This section will show you the most painless way to perform this task.

The order of play is reversed, compared to the earlier sections, and we'll start with registry values.

TECHNIQUE 41   **Deleting registry values**

You first created keys and then values, and here you'll reverse this to delete values and then keys. If you delete the key, you delete all subkeys and associated values, which may be a bit heavy-handed.

PROBLEM

A registry value has become obsolete because software versions have changed or because some other aspect of your system has been modified. You need to be able to delete this value across one or more machines.

SOLUTION

You can use the pattern established in earlier scripts. The following listing illustrates how this will work. The usual parameters are accepted—hive, key, value, and computer. The hive is tested to ensure it's part of the accepted set of values.

Listing 7.8   Delete registry value

```
function remove-regvalue {
[CmdletBinding()]
param (
 [parameter(Mandatory=$true)]
 [string]
 [Validateset("HKCR", "HKCU", "HKLM", "HKUS", "HKCC")]
  $hive,

 [parameter(Mandatory=$true)]
 [string]$key,

 [parameter(Mandatory=$true)]
 [string]$value,
```

```
  [parameter(ValueFromPipeline=$true,
    ValueFromPipelineByPropertyName=$true)]
  [string]$computername="$env:COMPUTERNAME"
)
PROCESS {
$rh = set-HiveValue $hive
$reg = [wmiclass]"\\$computername\root\default:StdRegprov"
$reg.DeleteValue($rh, $key, $value)
}}
```

The hive constant and registry provider instance are created. The WMI registry provider supplies a method called `DeleteValue`, which takes the hive, key, and value as arguments.

DISCUSSION

The function follows the same standards as the rest of the functions in the chapter. It's used as follows:

```
remove-regvalue -hive HKLM -key "SOFTWARE\PAW" -value "stringvalue"
```

This will remove the `stringvalue` from the `SOFTWARE\PAW` key in the `HKLM` hive.

> **WARNING** Remember that with WMI methods, you don't get the standard PowerShell `-Confirm` or `-WhatIf` options. Deletion will occur immediately.

It's now time to bring out the big guns to delete registry keys. Given that you use the `DeleteValue` method to remove registry values, can you guess what you'll use to delete registry keys?

TECHNIQUE 42   Deleting registry keys

Deleting registry keys removes the key, all subkeys, and all associated values. Re-creating a value that has been deleted in error is a relatively simple task. Re-creating a registry key can be a lot more work. I recommend exporting the key on a test machine prior to any widespread deletion activity. This will make it available for restore operations.

PROBLEM

A piece of software has been removed from your machines. Unfortunately it didn't perform a clean uninstall and left a registry key behind. You need to remove that registry key.

SOLUTION

You can adapt listing 7.8 to use the `DeleteKey` method. This is shown in in the following listing.

Listing 7.9   Delete registry key

```
function remove-regkey {
[CmdletBinding()]
param (
 [parameter(Mandatory=$true)]
 [string]
```

```
[Validateset("HKCR", "HKCU", "HKLM", "HKUS", "HKCC")]
 $hive,

[parameter(Mandatory=$true)]
[string]$key,

[parameter(ValueFromPipeline=$true,
   ValueFromPipelineByPropertyName=$true)]
[string]$computername="$env:COMPUTERNAME"
)
PROCESS {
$rh = set-HiveValue $hive
$reg = [wmiclass]"\\$computername\root\default:StdRegprov"
$reg.DeleteKey($rh, $key)
}}
```

The difference between listings 7.8 and 7.9 is that in 7.9 you don't have a parameter to get the value, and you use the `DeleteKey` method of the WMI registry provider.

DISCUSSION

The function is used as follows:

```
remove-regkey -hive HKLM -key "SOFTWARE\PAW"
```

On a local machine, you can test that the deletion has worked by using the PowerShell registry provider:

```
Test-Path HKLM:\SOFTWARE\PAW
```

This should return a value of `False`, indicating that the key can't be found.

Security is extremely important, and the registry needs to be protected. Do you know who has permission to access your registry keys?

7.5   *Registry access rights*

In a Windows environment, security permissions, or access rights, are set on the object. These permissions control what you, as an individual, can do with that object—read, write, delete, and so on.

Permissions on registry keys are usually set when the key is created. These permissions are then normally sufficient for the lifetime of the object. Occasionally a problem will occur that can be traced back to permissions on registry keys. At that time, you need to be able to discover the permissions on a particular key.

If the permissions on a key become corrupted for any reason, you may need to take ownership of the key so that the problem can be corrected.

TECHNIQUE 43   **Reading access rights**

You have two potential methods of reading the access rights on a registry key. You can discover all of the rights of all of the users, or you can discover the rights that you have. In the tradition of the little boy in the sweetshop, when you're faced with a choice, grab both.

PROBLEM

A particular registry key appears to be giving problems and is preventing a piece of software from working. You need to check the access rights on the key to determine whether they need changing. The rights of all users need to be checked, as well as your individual rights.

SOLUTION

When you're faced with two choices, as in this case, you have a number of options:

- Create two scripts
- Return both sets of data, even though you may only need one set in most situations
- Use a mechanism to switch between the options

You'll use the latter choice in the following listing and switch between the options. PowerShell provides the [switch] data type for just this situation. The switch parameter defaults to false, but when you supply it to the function, its value is set to true and a different branch of the code is executed.

Listing 7.10 Discovering registry key security settings

```
$regmask = DATA {                                                    ┌──   ❶ Lookup
ConvertFrom-StringData -StringData @'                                ◄─┘      data
1 = Query the values of a Registry key.
2 = Create, delete, or set a Registry value.
4 = Create a subkey of a Registry key.
8 = Enumerate the subkeys of a Registry key.
32 = Create a Registry key.
65536 = Delete a Registry key.
524288 = Write Ownership
'@
}
                                                                         ❷ Function
function get-regsecurity {                                       ◄─┐       parameters
[CmdletBinding()]                                                  ─┘
param (
 [parameter(Mandatory=$true)]
 [string]
 [Validateset("HKCR", "HKCU", "HKLM", "HKUS", "HKCC")]
  $hive,

 [parameter(Mandatory=$true)]
 [string]$key,

 [parameter(ValueFromPipeline=$true,
   ValueFromPipelineByPropertyName=$true)]

 [string]$computername="$env:COMPUTERNAME",

 [switch]$all
)
PROCESS {
$rh = set-HiveValue $hive
$reg = [wmiclass]"\\$computernamename\
```

```
➡ root\default:StdRegprov"                                    Registry
                                                          ③  provider
if ($all) {
$sd = $reg.GetSecurityDescriptor($rh, $key)                   All
                                                          ④  permissions
 "Owner "
$sd.Descriptor.Owner | Format-Table Domain, Name -AutoSize

 $sd.Descriptor.DACL | foreach {
  "`n$($_.Trustee.Domain)/$($_.Trustee.Name)"
  $accessmask = $_.AccessMask                                 Display
                                                          ⑤  permissions
  $regmask.GetEnumerator()| sort Key |
  foreach {
   if ($accessmask -band $_.key){
    "$($regmask[$($_.key)])"
   }
  }
 }
}
else {                                                        Your
 "You have the following permissions:"                    ⑥  permissions

 $regmask.GetEnumerator()| sort Key |
 foreach {
  $test = Invoke-WmiMethod -InputObject $reg `
   -Name CheckAccess -ArgumentList $rh, $key, $($_.Key)
  if ($test){
   " $($regmask[$($_.key)])"
  }
 }
}

}}
```

The script starts by defining a hash table ❶ as lookup data.

If you're familiar with the permissions set on files, you'll notice that these are different. The function defines a number of parameters ❷. The [switch] parameter defaults to false, remember. The hive constant and registry provider are also set ❸.

Now you get to the decision point. If the $all parameter is true (the switch has been set) ❹, you retrieve the security descriptor of the registry key.

NOTE   The security descriptor structure is described in the documentation for the Win32_SecurityDescriptor class.

The object owner can be displayed using the Owner property of the descriptor. The access mask is held as a collection. For each member of the collection, you display the user (or group) and get the access mask.

You need to get the enumerator of your lookup table and sort it by the key ❺. That way you can compare each value in order against the access mask to determine if that permission is set.

If the -all switch isn't set ❻, you're looking for your own permissions. This is a simpler proposition. You sort the lookup table as before, but you use each hash table key in turn as an argument to the CheckAccess method. If the test is passed, you print the permission.

DISCUSSION

The function is used as follows:

```
get-regsecurity -hive HKLM -key "SOFTWARE\Microsoft\Windows\CurrentVersion"
```

If all permissions are required, the -all parameter is added to the end.

We'll be working more with security descriptors in chapters 8 and 14. Being able to read access permissions is a useful skill, but you'll sometimes need to go further and take control of the key.

TECHNIQUE 44   **Taking ownership of a registry key**

Once you have ownership of an object, such as a registry key, you can do anything with it.

> **TIP**   The WMI SetSecurityDescriptor method can only be used on Windows Vista and above or Windows Server 2008 and above. Downlevel operating systems won't be able to use this method and will return an error. In that case, you'll have to use a .NET-based solution. I will post a .NET version on my blog. It's also included in the source code as listing 7.11a.

PROBLEM

The permissions on a registry key have become corrupted. You need to take ownership of the key so that you can resolve the issue.

SOLUTION

This solution is based on an answer provided by PowerShell MVP Vadims Podans to a question on the PowerShell MVP mailing list.

The following listing shows how you can use PowerShell and WMI to take ownership of a registry key. If you compare it to listing 7.10, you'll notice that you're still working with the security descriptor.

Listing 7.11   Take ownership of a registry key

```
function set-regkeyowner {
[CmdletBinding()]
param (
 [parameter(Mandatory=$true)]
 [string]
 [Validateset("HKCR", "HKCU", "HKLM", "HKUS", "HKCC")]
  $hive,

 [parameter(Mandatory=$true)]
 [string]$key,

 [parameter(ValueFromPipeline=$true,
   ValueFromPipelineByPropertyName=$true)]
 [string]$computername="$env:COMPUTERNAME"
)
PROCESS {
$rh = set-HiveValue $hive
```

① Set parameters and constants

```
$reg = [wmiclass]"\\$computername\root\default:StdRegprov"
$Trustee=([WMIClass]"Win32_Trustee").CreateInstance()
$sd=([WMIClass]"Win32_SecurityDescriptor").
  ➥ CreateInstance()

$user = New-Object -TypeName Security.Principal.NTaccount `
-ArgumentList "Administrators"

$sid=$user.Translate([Security.Principal.SecurityIdentifier])
[byte[]] $SIDArray = ,0 * $sid.BinaryLength
$sid.GetBinaryForm($SIDArray,0)

$Trustee.Name = "Administrators"
$Trustee.SID = $SIDArray
$sd.Owner = $Trustee
$sd.ControlFlags = 524288

$reg.Scope.Options.EnablePrivileges = $true
$reg.SetSecurityDescriptor($rh,$key, $sd)
}}
```

❷ Create objects

Create administrator account

❸

❹ Set SID

Set
❺ properties

❻ Take ownership

The function commences by taking the usual parameters ❶ and setting the hive constant and registry provider. You then create two WMI objects ❷. The first is from the `Win32_Trustee` class, which you use to hold the information about the new owner of the registry key. The second is from the `Win32_SecurityDescriptor` class, which you use to take ownership.

> **TIP**   I have assumed that this script will be run on the local machine. Accessing the registry remotely to perform these changes adds an additional layer of risk. In that situation, use PowerShell remoting to create the connection, and use the `-FilePath` parameter to run a local script with this function embedded.

The security descriptor has to be populated with information. You start by creating an object representing the new owner ❸. This uses a .NET class, because you can't perform this task in WMI. The user's Security Identifier (SID) is created in binary form ❹ and used with the name to create the trustee information ❺. The trustee and the control flags are used to create the security descriptor. The value of 524288 for the control flag indicates that the account (or group in this listing) you have created will be taking ownership of the registry key.

You need to enable all of your privileges on the registry provider ❻. This has to be performed even if you've started PowerShell with elevated privileges. The final act of the function is to apply the security descriptor, which transfers ownership of the registry key to the Administrators group.

DISCUSSION

Using this function is a lot easier than describing it. The hive and key are provided as follows:

```
set-regkeyowner -hive HKLM -key software\PAW
```

These two parameters are mandatory, so you'll be prompted for them if they aren't supplied. The function uses the built-in local Administrators group as the new owner. This could be modified, but I recommend leaving it in place.

One last topic and then we're finished with the registry. You can be more proactive with your registry administration by monitoring the WMI events related to registry changes.

7.6 Registry events

You've seen how the PowerShell and WMI eventing engines combine in chapter 6. You use a WMI query to interrogate the appropriate event class. The `Register-WmiEvent` cmdlet is used to register this query with the PowerShell event engine and define the actions to be taken when the event is triggered. The registry WMI provider supplies similar functionality using the classes listed in table 7.3.

Table 7.3 Registry event handling classes

Class	Purpose
RegistryKeyChangeEvent	Represents changes to a specific key (*not* its subkeys)
RegistryTreeChangeEvent	Represents changes to a key *and* its subkeys
RegistryValueChangeEvent	Represents changes to a singular value of a specific key

Notice the difference between `RegistryKeyChangeEvent` and `RegistryTreeChange-Event`. The first one monitors only a specific key, but the second also monitors subkeys and values.

> **WARNING** `HKEY_CLASSES_ROOT` and `HKEY_CURRENT_USER` hives aren't supported by the registry event classes listed in table 7.3. In most cases, this won't impact you because you're not likely to work directly with these hives.

This technique can be useful for determining which keys are modified during a software install.

TECHNIQUE 45   **Monitoring registry events**

It has been stated many, many times that the registry is a potential source of problems in Windows environments. You have to protect it, and you need to know what's happening and, in some cases, when changes are made. A registry change that sneaks through and takes down the organization's email server won't look good on a resume.

PROBLEM

The registry is being changed on a server. How can you monitor when the changes are occurring and which subkeys are affected?

SOLUTION

Listing 7.12 provides a template that you can modify as required to monitor registry events. This listing shows you how to monitor change events at the tree and value levels. Key event changes could be added using the same structure. Notice that I haven't parameterized this script. I think this activity should be explicitly set up rather than using generic code, because it's not something you're likely to be doing every day.

Listing 7.12   Monitor registry events

```
function valuechange {
param ($e)
 Write-Host "The following value has changed"
 $e.SourceEventArgs.NewEvent |
 Format-Table Hive, KeyPath, ValueName,
 @{N="Time";
 E={$([datetime]::FromFileTime($_.TIME_CREATED))}} |
 Out-Host
}

function treechange {
param ($e)
 Write-Host "The following tree has changed"
 $e.SourceEventArgs.NewEvent |
 Format-Table Hive, RootPath,
 @{N="Time";
 E={$([datetime]::FromFileTime($_.TIME_CREATED))}} |
 Out-Host
}

if (Get-EventSubscriber |
where {$_.SourceIdentifier -eq "regvalue"}) {
Unregister-Event -SourceIdentifier "regvalue" }

if (Get-EventSubscriber |
where {$_.SourceIdentifier -eq "regtree"}) {
Unregister-Event -SourceIdentifier "regtree" }

$vquery = "SELECT * FROM RegistryValueChangeEvent WHERE
➥ Hive='HKEY_LOCAL_MACHINE' AND KeyPath='SOFTWARE\\PAW' AND
➥ ValueName='stringvalue'"

$tquery = "SELECT * FROM RegistryTreeChangeEvent WHERE
➥ Hive='HKEY_LOCAL_MACHINE' AND RootPath='SOFTWARE\\PAW'"

$vaction = {valuechange $($event)}
$taction = {treechange $($event)}

Register-WmiEvent -Query $vquery `
-SourceIdentifier "regvalue" -Action $vaction
Register-WmiEvent -Query $tquery `
-SourceIdentifier "regtree" -Action $taction
```

❶ Define event-handling functions

❷ Clean event subscribers

❸ Create event queries

❹ Create event actions

❺ Register events

You start by defining two functions to handle the events that are produced ❶. The functions for value changes and tree changes are similar in that they're passed the event as an argument and then write out the registry object that has been changed and the time the change occurred. Other activities could be included in these functions, including checking the data in particular values and resetting it if required. The event-handling functions use N and E as abbreviations for Name and Expression for brevity. The script will run, but this abbreviation makes it slightly less readable.

WMI events return the time in file time format, which is a 64-bit value that represents the number of 100-nanosecond intervals that have elapsed since 12:00 A.M. on 1 January 1601 Coordinated Universal Time (UTC). The .NET DateTime class provides a simple way to convert this value to a more readable format.

When registering events, you have to supply a source identifier. If a particular source identifier exists, you need to delete it to enable the script to run ❷. WMI queries are created ❸ to retrieve the events. You have to supply the key and value you want to monitor in the query. It's possible to monitor the root of the hive to get all changes.

Two simple actions are created to pass the event into your event-handling functions ❹. The script then registers the events, supplying the query and the actions ❺.

DISCUSSION

This script isn't included in the chapter module. It can be invoked as

```
. ./Listing7.12.ps1.
```

Feel free to change the name to something more meaningful if you desire.

The PowerShell and WMI functionality provided in this chapter will allow you to become an expert in administering the registry in a safe and productive manner. I must emphasize again that registry changes must be tested before using them in production.

7.7 *Summary*

In this chapter you've learned several things about working with the registry:

- The structure of the registry
- How to read, write, and create registry keys and values
- How delete objects from the registry
- How the security on registry objects works and how to change it
- How to monitor changes to the registry

This functionality will help protect your environment and allow you to safely administer a fundamental part of your Windows systems.

In chapter 8, we'll look at the filesystem and how you can work with files, folders, and shares.

Filesystem administration 8

This chapter covers

- Working with files
- Working with folders
- Administering shares
- Filesystem events

Filesystem administration is probably one of the most neglected aspects of our jobs. You create a disk volume and then set up some folders and shares. The area is turned over to the users, and they proceed to fill it up with their files.

You'll have areas on specific servers for SQL Server databases or Exchange mail stores, but much of your storage space is still taken up by files of one sort or another. These files are often referred to as unstructured data and can include Microsoft Word documents, spreadsheets, pictures, and output produced by the many applications in your organization.

Files are the basic building blocks of your filesystem. As an administrator, you need to understand what files are stored and how you can find them. Files can be hidden, compressed, and possibly encrypted (but not all three at once). Being able to easily discover which files have gone through this process increases your ability to administer the system.

PowerShell and WMI provide tools to perform these management tasks, as you'll see in the first section of this chapter. In addition to discovering information about your files, you'll see how to use WMI to perform actions on the files. You'll create techniques to compress, encrypt, and hide files. You'll also learn techniques to copy files and remove unwanted files.

TIP One thing that's true of both files and folders when working through WMI is that you can't create these objects. You can analyze, manipulate, and delete them, but you can't create new ones.

Folders are used to organize files. You arrange them in hierarchies and often forget about files in the bottommost layers. I have a vague memory of creating the files in figure 8.1 when I was working on a problem posted on one of the forums. I don't really need them, but I haven't got around to deleting them. Multiply this by several other folders in a similar situation, and then by the hundreds, or thousands, of users in your environment, and you'll soon see where your disk space is going.

Discovering the folders on your system is the first step to controlling the filesystem. You then need to examine the files in those folders. If the files aren't needed, the folder can be deleted—reclaimed and reused disk space means reduced costs to your organization because you don't need to buy more disks! You'll also see how to work with folders that are compressed or encrypted. You'll learn about all of these subjects in the folder administration section of this chapter (section 8.2).

Another important part of administering the filesystem is controlling access to files and folders. Do you know who has access to a particular folder? You'll learn to use PowerShell and WMI to discover this information via the folder's security access mask (also in section 8.2).

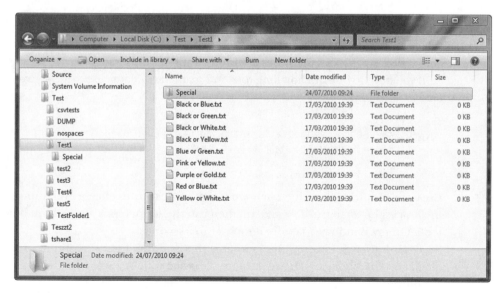

Figure 8.1 The hierarchy of folders and files

Folders are made available across the network by creating shares on the folders. This is an area where you can, and will, manage the whole lifecycle (creation, discovery, modification, and deletion) through PowerShell and WMI. Shares are always on a remote machine to you, so being able to use WMI to manage the lifecycle is beneficial. Shares are discussed in section 8.3.

Do you know what the users are doing to your filesystem? Are they changing or deleting files that they shouldn't? In section 8.4 you'll see how to use the PowerShell eventing system to discover WMI events related to the filesystem and then to create a monitoring system that can be applied to your important and confidential files.

Our final stop when exploring the filesystem is the page file. This is used to swap information from memory to disk, and it's essential for the wellbeing of your systems. Some applications, such as SQL Server, shouldn't be using the page file much. If they do, it's an indication that something is not quite right with the machine's setup. You'll see how to use PowerShell and WMI to manage the page file, once you've learned how to take control of it from the system.

Our starting point is the place where we store our data—the files themselves.

8.1   Working with files

Files are where you store your data. They may be valuable or they may be worthless a few hours after they're written. Users become frustrated when they can't find a file, and administrators become frustrated when the users don't clean up their old files. You can use the file management capabilities of WMI to remove both of these frustrations.

> **NOTE** One oddity of WMI is that you work with the `CIM_DataFile` class rather than a `Win32` class. I've never seen a reason for this when nearly everything else has a `Win32` class.

On a large remote system, PowerShell and WMI may not be the fastest solution. They will, however, be one of the cheapest. These technologies will work for you at a reasonable speed unless your file stores are in the multi-terabyte range.

If you need to find out how long your commands are taking, use the `Measure-Command` cmdlet as follows:

```
$sb = {
$query = "SELECT * FROM CIM_DATAFILE WHERE Extension='ps1'"
Get-WmiObject -Query $query | select Name
}
Measure-Command -Expression $sb
```

Create a script block of the commands you want to run—that's everything between the braces: {}. `Measure-Command` will then run the script block and tell you how long it took. On my Windows 7 laptop, it took 21.577 seconds.

One drawback to using this cmdlet is that you don't get the output of the script block, just the timings. Replace `Measure-Command` with `Invoke-Command` and you'll get the output.

Now it's time to return to our main topic and start looking at the other ways you can find files. Once you've found your files, you'll usually want to do something with them. The usual suspects include copying, renaming, and deleting. You could also change the compression or encryption state of the files. All of these activities are based on finding the files in the first place.

TECHNIQUE 46   **Finding files**

One common scenario you'll need to deal with is finding a file or group of files. If you're connected directly to the system you can use the search capabilities built into Windows, but if you're working across multiple machines, you'll need a remote capability. You saw one possible way to search for files in the introduction to this section. Other filter options are available.

PROBLEM

You need to start tidying up the filesystem on a server. Unfortunately the person responsible for administering this server has left, and the documentation is inadequate. No one really knows what's on this server or what should be on it. Your job is to start investigating the files stored on this system.

SOLUTION

There isn't a single technique you can use to investigate the files on a machine. We'll look at a number of ways that you can use WMI to provide information about the files. The code in the following listing provides a series of code snippets that you can use as the basis of scripts to access files based on various criteria.

Listing 8.1 Investigating files with WMI

```
$query = "SELECT * FROM CIM_DATAFILE           ◁─┐ Select from
  ➥ WHERE Drive='C:' AND Path='\\Test\\'"       ❶ folder
Get-WmiObject -Query $query |
select Name

$query = "SELECT * FROM CIM_DATAFILE           ◁─┐ Select specific
  ➥ WHERE Extension='log'"                      ❷ extension
Get-WmiObject -Query $query |
select Name

$query = "SELECT * FROM CIM_DATAFILE           ◁─┐ Select
  ➥ WHERE Writeable='$false'"                   ❸ read-only
Get-WmiObject -Query $query |
select Name

$query = "SELECT * FROM CIM_DATAFILE           ◁─┐ Select
  ➥ WHERE Hidden='$true'"                       ❹ hidden
Get-WmiObject -Query $query |
select Name

$query = "SELECT * FROM CIM_DATAFILE           ◁─┐ Select
  ➥ WHERE Drive='C:' AND Path='\\Test\\'        ❺ encrypted
  ➥ AND Encrypted = '$true'"
Get-WmiObject -Query $query |
```

```
select Name
```

6 Select on creation date

```
$test = (Get-Date).AddDays(-60)
$query = "SELECT * FROM CIM_DATAFILE
WHERE Drive='C:' AND Path='\\Test\\' "
Get-WmiObject -Query $query |
foreach {
 $date = $_.ConvertToDateTime($_.CreationDate)
  if ($date -lt $test ) {
    $_ | select Name
  }
}
```

The easiest way I've found to use the `CIM_DataFile` class is to write a query. You could use the `-Filter` parameter of `Get-WmiObject`, but I find it gets a bit complicated. Separation adds a line of code, but it makes things easier to read.

One of the first things you may want to do is look at the contents of a particular folder ❶. You can use this query:

```
$query = "SELECT * FROM CIM_DATAFILE WHERE
   Drive='C:' AND Path='\\Test\\'"
Get-WmiObject -Query $query | select Name
```

The query looks clumsy because you have to specify the drive and folder path independently, but it gives you the flexibility to parameterize the query if you need to check the same folder on multiple drives. Another common issue is that the drive letters aren't common across machines. If you can parameterize the query, it makes life easier.

When you use `Get-ChildItem` to search the local filesystem, you can recurse through the subfolders, but there's no built-in recursion facility in WMI. If you want to search subfolders as well, you need to do it yourself. We'll come back to this when we look at folders later in the chapter.

You may have noticed that I haven't used the `-Computername` parameter in any of the code in this section. This was a deliberate decision to simplify the discussion. When you do add the `-Computername` parameter, remember to use it *before* the query. I've seen problems when the computer name is specified after the query. This is an intermittent failure that can be difficult to reproduce.

A frequent task is to search the filesystem for a particular type of file. You saw an example of this at the beginning of the section. When searching for particular files, you'll often search for a particular extension ❷. You saw how to find all of the .ps1 files earlier. A common need is to discover the .mp3 and .jpg files your users have managed to squirrel away on your servers.

Many applications hide log files in odd places. The extension property supplies the means to discover files of a particular type such as log files:

```
$query = "SELECT * FROM CIM_DATAFILE WHERE Extension='log'"
Get-WmiObject -Query $query | select Name
```

It's possible to use multiple extensions in the query, or you can simply run multiple queries. The latter option is more flexible and maintainable.

There are other criteria you can use when searching for files. Normally your files can be modified, but in some cases you may want the files to be read-only ❸. Do you know which files on your system are set to be read-only? This is how you find out:

```
$query = "SELECT * FROM CIM_DATAFILE WHERE Writeable='$false'"
Get-WmiObject -Query $query | select Name
```

The oddity here is that you're testing whether the file is writable rather than whether it's read only—you're looking for confirmation of the negative case. You use the PowerShell Boolean value $false to provide the test value.

> **NOTE** If you think back to chapter 4 where we discussed string substitution, you'll remember that you can only substitute in strings bounded by double quotes. In this case, it may look like you're substituting into a string bounded by single quotes, but you really aren't, because the single quotes form part of the overall string.

A similar situation holds when you want to test for hidden files ❹. The users that sneaked their MP3s, photos, or other personal and inappropriate files onto your server may know just enough to hide them.

```
$query = "SELECT * FROM CIM_DATAFILE WHERE Hidden='$true'"
Get-WmiObject -Query $query | select Name
```

In this case, you're testing for a positive outcome. If you want to see the full range of properties, you can retrieve a file and pipe it into Get-Member, as for any other object.

Another area you might think of testing is encrypted files ❺. If your users use EFS and one such user leaves, you may want to ensure that they haven't left any encrypted files behind before they actually exit the organization:

```
$query = "SELECT * FROM CIM_DATAFILE WHERE Drive='C:'
➥ AND Path='\\Test\\' AND Encrypted = '$true'"
Get-WmiObject -Query $query |select Name
```

The change on this query is that you include a test to determine whether the Encrypted property is set to true. You can test for compressed files in this way as well—just change Encrypted to Compressed in the query.

In many cases, you may want to put an end-of-life date on your documents ❻. If you buy a document management system this is a feature you'd expect, but organizations that aren't in a position to implement such a system can use a simple WMI query to test the age of a particular document:

```
$test = (Get-Date).AddDays(-60)
$query = "SELECT * FROM CIM_DATAFILE WHERE Drive='C:'
➥ AND Path='\\Test\\' "
Get-WmiObject -Query $query |
foreach {
 $date = $_.ConvertToDateTime($_.CreationDate)
  if ($date -lt $test) {
    $_ | select Name
  }
}
```

You start by creating a test date. This example uses a date 60 days in the past to be sure you catch something. It uses the AddDays method with a negative number of days to get a date in the past. There are a number of methods you can use to create a test date:

- AddDays
- AddHours
- AddMilliseconds
- AddMinutes
- AddMonths
- AddSeconds
- AddTicks
- AddYears

Once you've created your test date you can create a query to discover the files in a particular folder. (You could test the whole drive, but that would take a lot longer to run.) A test is performed against each file to determine whether the creation date is less than the test date, and you display the filenames that pass the test. Alternatively, you could just as easily delete them or move them to an archive. It's also possible to test on InstallDate, LastAccessed, and LastModified dates.

DISCUSSION

It may seem that it would be possible to perform these searches by pulling all of the files back and then using Where-Object to perform your filtering. This is an option, and on the local machine it probably doesn't matter which you do. If you're performing the queries against a remote machine, though, it's definitely a best practice to perform the filtering on the source machine, in the query. This restricts the amount of data that's returned across your network.

Now that you know how to discover files that meet certain criteria, what can you do with them?

TECHNIQUE 47   **Performing actions on files**

WMI doesn't provide a mechanism for creating files or modifying the contents of a file. You can, however, manage other aspects of the file's lifecycle, including deletion, copying, and renaming.

PROBLEM

A group of files are created on a regular basis in a particular folder, with the same names each time. Those files are copied to another folder, and any files with matching names have to be deleted from the second folder before the copy occurs. The original files have to be renamed to preserve them against future processing.

SOLUTION

This solution may seem a bit odd, but I've seen similar activities where files are created and then copied to a working folder. The original folder acts as an archive. It makes the most sense to delete the files in the target folder, perform the copy action, and then rename the original files.

The following listing presents a WMI based solution to this problem.

Listing 8.2   File actions

```
$query = "SELECT * FROM CIM_DATAFILE WHERE Drive='C:'
  ⇒ AND Path='\\Test\\' AND FileName LIKE 'file_'"
Get-WmiObject -Query $query | foreach {                        ❶ Delete
  $_.Delete() | Out-Null                                          files
}

$query = "SELECT * FROM CIM_DATAFILE WHERE Drive='C:' AND
        ⇒ Path='\\Teszzt2\\' AND FileName LIKE 'file_'"
$files = Get-WmiObject -Query $query
foreach ($file in $files){
  $newcopy = "C:\Test\$($file.FileName).$($file.Extension)"    ❷ Copy
  $file.Copy($newcopy) | Out-Null                                 files

  $name = $file.FileName -replace "file", "test"
  $ext = $file.Extension -replace "txt", "csv"
  $newname = "C:\Teszzt2\$name.$ext"                            ❸ Rename
                                                                  files
  $file.Rename($newname) | Out-Null
}
```

The script starts by creating a query to find all of the files in the target folder that match the pattern you're working with. In this case, you're looking for files that start with the characters "file" and have a single other character in the name.

TIP   The underscore character (_) is the WQL wildcard equivalent of a question mark (?); it represents a single character. If you think you might have multiple wildcard characters to deal with, change the query to be "FileName LIKE 'file%'"

Get-WmiObject is used to run the query. The results are piped into ForEach-Object where the Delete method of the WMI file object is used to perform the deletion ❶. Out-Null is used to absorb the return code information from the multiple deletions and prevent its display on screen. Alternatively, you could capture the return code and display warning messages for files that fail to delete.

The second query selects the files from the source folder. This time you create a collection for the files, and each file in the files collection is processed in turn. A new file path is created ($newcopy) and the file is copied ❷.

The filename and extension are modified using the -replace operator, and the file is renamed ❸. The return codes from the copy and the rename actions are again suppressed by using Out-Null.

DISCUSSION

There are alternatives to using Out-Null. The following three lines of code all perform the same action in suppressing the output:

```
$file.Rename($newname) | Out-Null
$null = $file.Rename($newname)
[void]$file.Rename($newname)
```

Which one should you use? Whichever one you like best. They all perform the same job. It really comes down to which fits best with the way you like to work and the way you think about the code. I tend to use `Out-Null` mainly because it's easiest to add on to the line of code when I've finished testing that section and want to clean up the output.

You may come across a `Win32_MoveFileAction` class during your investigations of WMI. It won't really help you in this case because it's one of a series of classes associated with installing software.

In technique 46 you saw how to discover files that had been compressed. PowerShell and WMI provide you with a method of performing file compression and decompression.

TECHNIQUE 48 **Compressing files**

The amount of data stored by organizations seems to be on a continuous upward spiral. Disk space is comparatively cheap, so one strategy is to keep buying more disk space. This works for a while, but eventually you'll run out of space in your SAN racks or data center. An alternative is to use file compression to reduce the size files occupy. This can save up to 80 or 90 percent of the space a file occupies, depending on the file type.

PROBLEM

Your file server drives are running out of space. There isn't any money in the budget to acquire extra storage. The larger files on the disk need to be compressed to reclaim some space.

SOLUTION

The solution presented in listing 8.3 follows the pattern established in technique 47: you discover the files you need to work with, and then you perform the required actions. This is a common approach to developing administration scripts because you can test that you've discovered the correct files before you perform any actions on them.

Listing 8.3 Compress a file

```
function compress-file {
[CmdletBinding()]
param (
 [parameter(ValueFromPipeline=$true,
   ValueFromPipelineByPropertyName=$true)]
 [string]$computername="$env:COMPUTERNAME",     ❶ Set
 [string]$path="c:\test",                            parameters
 [int]$size = 2MB
)
PROCESS {
$drive = Split-Path -Path $path -Qualifier        ❷ Specify drive
$folder = $path.Remove(0,2).Replace("\","\\") + "\\"   and path

$query = "SELECT * FROM CIM_DATAFILE WHERE Drive='$drive' AND Path='$folder'
    AND Filesize > $size"
Get-WmiObject -ComputerName $computername -Query $query |    ❸ Run WMI
 foreach {                                                      query
  $_.Compress()                              ❹ Compress file
 }
}}
```

The function starts by setting out the parameters it will accept ❶. The computer name has been a common parameter in many of the scripts presented to date, and you'll see a lot more of that. The path to the folder you want to test is presented as a string and the file size is presented as an integer. CIM_DataFile handles file sizes in bytes, and PowerShell translates 2MB to 2097152 bytes automatically.

Split-Path is used on the path to get the drive letter (including the colon) by using the -Qualifier parameter ❷. The path is then modified to work in WMI queries. The query is created and run through Get-WmiObject ❸. Your results are piped into ForEach-Object, where you use the Compress method on the file ❹.

This script could be converted to encrypt the files by replacing Compress() with Encrypt(). Remember that you can't do both to the same file!

DISCUSSION

This script compresses files above the size of 2 MB. If you want to use larger sizes you may run into the limits of the int32 data type. The maximum file size you can present as a parameter is

```
PS> [int]::MaxValue / 1gb
1.99999999906868
```

If you want to use a larger value as your test point, the data type will have to be changed to [int64]. This allows much larger file sizes to be used:

```
PS> [int64]::MaxValue /1gb
8589934592
```

In case you're curious (I know I was), this translates to a large amount of storage:

```
PS> [int64]::MaxValue / 1pb
8192
```

If you have files this big, you may need to look at other techniques.

Compressing files is a good thing when you're short on disk space. If at a later date you manage to acquire more storage, you may want to uncompress these files so that the overhead of uncompressing the data to work on it and then compressing it again is removed.

> **WARNING** Don't compress, or encrypt, SQL Server data files, Exchange databases, or similar files with high I/O levels. The overhead can have a severe impact on performance.

The function to perform the uncompression is shown in the following listing. I've called it expand-file, using the recommended verb, which stops Import-Module from throwing up warning messages about unapproved verbs.

Listing 8.4 Uncompress a file

```
function expand-file {
[CmdletBinding()]
param (
 [parameter(ValueFromPipeline=$true,
```

```
  ValueFromPipelineByPropertyName=$true)]
 [string]$computername="$env:COMPUTERNAME",
 [string]$path="c:\test"
)
PROCESS {
$drive = Split-Path -Path $path -Qualifier
$folder = $path.Remove(0,2).Replace("\","\\") + "\\"

$query = "SELECT * FROM CIM_DATAFILE
  ➥ WHERE Drive='$drive' AND Path='$folder'
  ➥ AND Compressed = '$true'"
Get-WmiObject -ComputerName $computername -Query $query |
 foreach {
  $_.UnCompress()
 }
}}
```

If you compare listing 8.4 to listing 8.3, you'll see that the file size parameter has been removed. This query looks for compressed files in the folder and then uses the Uncompress method.

The scripts have been deliberately restricted to a single folder for ease of use. They could be modified to work against the whole drive by changing the query to test just the drive. The query would then read

```
$query = "SELECT * FROM CIM_DATAFILE
  ➥ WHERE Drive='$drive' AND Compressed = '$true'"
```

Files don't exist in isolation. Let's step up the hierarchy a level and see what can be done with folders.

8.2   *Folder administration*

Folders provide the organizational components of your filesystem. You can create folder hierarchies to control the filesystem and help you find your files. Sometimes, though, the hierarchy gets a bit too deep and you forget where you put things. At this point you need to start searching for folders.

A simple WMI call will list all of the folders on a machine:

```
Get-WmiObject -Class Win32_Directory | select Name
```

You'll be surprised by the number of folders that are listed. Remember that NTFS file paths are limited to 260 characters when creating folders. If you exceed this length, most of your programs won't be able to access the folder. And no, you can't pass this off as a security measure.

You can easily retrieve data on a single folder:

```
Get-WmiObject -Class Win32_Directory `
-Filter "Name = 'C:\\Teszzt2'"
```

The PowerShell formatting files control what is displayed for the WMI class, so if you want to see all of the information you need to bypass the default display:

```
Get-WmiObject -Class Win32_Directory `
-Filter "Name = 'C:\\Teszzt2'" | Format-List *
```

`Win32_Directory` only displays information about the folder itself. Listing the files and subfolders of a particular folder is covered in technique 49. The other techniques in this section look at folders with specific attributes (compressed or encrypted) and how you can decode the security settings on a folder.

TECHNIQUE 49   **Discovering the files in a folder**

In technique 46 you saw how to discover the files in a particular folder. Unfortunately, if you're working from the folder and want to get to its contents there's no direct association between a `Win32_Directory` object and the files contained within the folder, but the `CIM_DirectoryContainsFile` class is a WMI association class providing some linkage information you can use.

PROBLEM

You need to be able to access the files in one or more folders based on the folder name. Your filesystem contains a number of folders with similar names that you've discovered using the code in the introduction to this section. You now need to look at the files in those folders.

SOLUTION

The most direct route to solving this problem is to use the code in the introduction to section 8.1 and access each folder individually. If you need to work through the relationship between a folder and its files, you can use the following listing to discover how this works.

Listing 8.5   Folder contents

```
function get-foldercontent {
[CmdletBinding()]
param (
 [parameter(ValueFromPipeline=$true,
   ValueFromPipelineByPropertyName=$true)]
 [string]$computername="$env:COMPUTERNAME",        ❶ Take
 [string]$path                                          ownership
)
PROCESS{
 $target = $path.Replace("\", "\\\\")
 $filter = "GroupComponent = '" +
'Win32_Directory.Name="' + $target + '"' + "'"      ❷ Parameters

 Get-WmiObject -ComputerName $computername `
-Class CIM_DirectoryContainsFile -Filter $filter |     File
foreach {                                              and folder
    $ff =                                          ❸ relationship
➥ ($_.PartComponent -split "CIM_DATAFile.")[1].Replace('"',"'")

    Write-Debug $ff
    Get-WmiObject -ComputerName $computername
    -Class CIM_DataFile -Filter $ff |              ❹ File
    select Name, FileSize, AccessMask                  information
  }
}}
```

The `get-foldercontents` function takes a computer name and folder path as parameters ❶. The path is used to create a filter for accessing the `CIM_DirectoryContainsFile` class ❷. This is an association class that contains two properties per instance. The first property is the `GroupComponent`, which maps to the folder. The second is the `PartComponent`, which maps to the file. I built the filter string using concatenation rather than string substitution because I found it simpler—getting the different sets of quotes correct became more trouble than it was worth. Sometimes you just have to go with the simple approach.

The filter is used to find the files associated with the folder ❸. Each instance of the `CIM_DirectoryContainsFile` class that's returned is piped through `ForEach-Object`, where `PartComponent` is split and modified for use in `CIM_DataFile` ❹.

The name, file size, and access mask (security permissions) are displayed for each file. The file size is left in bytes in the listing, but this could be converted to MB or GB if required. Other properties are available for display, as discussed in section 8.1.

DISCUSSION

You use the `PartComponent` property from the `CIM_DirectoryContainsFile` class in listing 8.5. The value of this property is of this form:

```
\\RSLAPTOP01\root\cimv2:CIM_DataFile.Name="c:\\teszzt2\\paw4.evt"
```

On the left side of the equal sign you have the WMI path, and on the right side you have the folder path in the correct format for WMI. The quotes aren't correct for use in further WMI processing, so you need to work on this.

You need to extract sufficient information from the `PartComponent` to create the filter in this form:

```
Name='c:\\teszzt2\\paw4.evt'
```

The `PartComponent` string is split at `"CIM_DATAFile."`. The period (.) is effectively removed by including it in the split operator (it's possible to retain the patterns used for deciding where to split, but that's beyond the scope of this book). The string `Replace()` method can be used on the second element produced by the split to produce the filter you need. Creating multi-operation string-processing code like this may seem complicated, but it's straightforward if you build it up one bit at a time and test each stage as you add it to the process.

While we're looking at folders, consider how you'd copy a folder and all its contents:

```
$d = Get-WmiObject -Class Win32_Directory -Filter "Name='c:\\teszzt2'"
$d.Copy("d:\test")
```

Simply use `Get-WmiObject` to create the WMI object for the relevant folder, and then use the `Copy` method to create the copy. Notice that the path to which the folder should be copied only uses single backslashes (\). Consistency isn't one of WMI's strong points. If you're copying to the root of a drive, you only need the single backslash, as shown in the previous example.

Listing 8.5 generates a list of the files within a folder. It doesn't include subfolders. You can create a list of subfolders in a couple of ways. First, you can use `Win32_Directory` and use the `Path` property as a filter:

```
Get-WmiObject -Class Win32_Directory -Filter "Path='\\Test\\'"
```

This will generate a list of the first-level subfolders. It won't recurse through those folders to find their subfolders.

The second option is to use a wildcard in the WMI filter:

```
Get-WmiObject -Class Win32_Directory `
-Filter "Drive='C:' AND Path LIKE '\\Test\\%'" |
select Name
```

Adding the percent character (`%`) to the path and using `LIKE` means that you're testing for all folders whose path starts with `\Test\`. This will generate all subfolders to whatever depth is present.

Now that you've found your folders, what can you discover about them?

TECHNIQUE 50   **Discovering folders with specific attributes**

In section 8.1 we looked at how you could discover files that were hidden, encrypted, or compressed. But it's more likely that you'll need to deal with these issues at a folder level than at a file level.

PROBLEM

A number of machines need to be tested to discover if there are any hidden, compressed, or encrypted folders.

SOLUTION

You could write a total of three functions to solve this problem—one to test each attribute. The only part that changes is the filter that decides the type of folder for which you're searching. But it's more efficient to write a single function, as in the following listing. It also gives you a chance to practice using the `switch` statement.

Listing 8.6 Folders with specific properties

```
function test-folder {
[CmdletBinding()]
param (
 [parameter(ValueFromPipeline=$true,
   ValueFromPipelineByPropertyName=$true)]
 [string]$computername="$env:COMPUTERNAME", [string]
 [Validateset("Hidden", "Compressed", "Encrypted")]
 $test
 )
PROCESS{
 switch($test){                                              ❶ Create
  "Hidden"    {$filter = "Hidden='$true'"; break}                filter
  "Compressed" {$filter = "Compressed='$true'"; break}
  "Encrypted"  {$filter = "Encrypted='$true'"; break}

 }
```

```
 Get-WmiObject -ComputerName $computername `           ❷  Run
-Class Win32_Directory -Filter $filter |                  query
 select Name
}}
```

The function takes the usual computer name parameter. A second parameter determines the type of folder. The possible values that can be input are limited by the `ValidateSet()` attribute on the parameter. The results of inputting an incorrect value to the `-test` parameter are shown in figure 8.2.

The function throws an error, but more importantly it supplies feedback to the user informing them of the correct values. Using the validation attributes in this manner can supply a lot of error checking with minimal effort. They also make your scripts look more professional and ready for production.

The `switch` statement ❶ takes the type of folder you're testing and creates the appropriate WMI filter. `Get-WmiObject` can then be used to retrieve the data ❷.

DISCUSSION

You can perform a number of actions on `Win32_Directory` objects. Hiding, encrypting, or compressing are the actions in the script in listing 8.6. Compressing a folder is straightforward:

```
$d = Get-WmiObject -Class Win32_Directory -Filter "Name='c:\\teszzt2'"
$d.Compress()
$d.UnCompress()
```

The other methods available on folder objects include the following:

- `ChangeSecurityPermissions`
- `Compress`
- `Copy`
- `Delete`
- `GetEffectivePermission`
- `Rename`
- `TakeOwnerShip`
- `Uncompress`

When creating folders using Windows Explorer, I sometimes get finger trouble and end up with folders called "New folder." You can clean out these mistakes like this:

```
Get-WmiObject -Class Win32_Directory -Filter "Name Like '%New folder%'" |
Invoke-WmiMethod -Name Delete
```

```
PS> test-folder -test Uncompressed
test-folder : Cannot validate argument on parameter 'test'. The argument "Uncompressed" does not belong to the set "Hid
den,Compressed,Encrypted" specified by the ValidateSet attribute. Supply an argument that is in the set and then try th
e command again.
At line:1 char:18
+ test-folder -test <<<<  Uncompressed
    + CategoryInfo          : InvalidData: (:) [test-folder], ParameterBindingValidationException
    + FullyQualifiedErrorId : ParameterArgumentValidationError,test-folder

PS> _
```

Figure 8.2   Result of inputting an incorrect value when using `ValidateSet()`

Use `Get-WmiObject` to show the folders that meet the criteria and then invoke the delete method on the folder. This can only be performed if you have the correct level of permissions on the folder.

TECHNIQUE 51   **Decoding the access mask**

Windows, unlike some other operating systems, sets permissions on the object—in this case a folder. You have to interrogate the object itself (the folder) to discover the permissions that have been set.

PROBLEM

A user is complaining that they can't access the files in a particular folder. You need to discover the permissions set on the folder to determine if they've been granted access.

SOLUTION

You can solve this problem by decoding the access mask. Back in technique 43 (in chapter 7) you did this for registry keys. You can adopt a similar approach, as shown in the next listing.

Listing 8.7 Folder access mask

```
$fmask = DATA {
ConvertFrom-StringData -StringData @'
4 = Grants the right to append data to the file.
  ➡ For a directory, this value grants the right
  ➡ to create a subdirectory.
8 = Grants the right to read extended attributes.
65536 = Grants delete access.
524288 = Assigns the write owner.
'@
}

function get-foldermask {
[CmdletBinding()]
param (
 [parameter(ValueFromPipeline=$true,
   ValueFromPipelineByPropertyName=$true)]
 [string]$computername="$env:COMPUTERNAME",
 [string]$path
)
PROCESS{
$path = $path.Replace("\","\\")
$sd = Get-WmiObject -Class Win32_LogicalFileSecuritySetting `
 -ComputerName $computername -Filter "Path='$path'" |
 Invoke-WmiMethod -Name GetSecurityDescriptor

 "Owner "
 $sd.Descriptor.Owner | Format-Table Domain, Name -AutoSize

 $sd.Descriptor.DACL | foreach {
  "`n$($_.Trustee.Domain)/$($_.Trustee.Name)"
  $accessmask = $_.AccessMask

   $fmask.GetEnumerator()| sort Key |
   foreach {
```

```
    if ($accessmask -band $_.key){
      "$($fmask[$($_.key)])"
    }
  }
 }
}}
```

The script starts by creating a hash table of the permissions and the values associated with them. The listing doesn't show the full set for brevity, but it's available in the code download. The `get-foldermask` function takes a computer and path as parameters.

The `Win32_LogicalFileSecuritySetting` class is used to get the security descriptor. This class works with files and folders, even though it has file in the name! The security descriptor stores the permissions data in which you're interested.

The data you want is in the `Descriptor` property of the security descriptor. You start by displaying the owner of the folder and then work through each DACL in the descriptor. The keys in the hash table are compared to the access mask using the binary AND (`band`) operator. Where there is a match, the appropriate permissions are displayed.

DISCUSSION

Once you have the set of permissions on the folder, you can determine whether the user has any rights assigned on the folder. File and folder permissions are usually assigned to groups rather than individual users, so you need to discover the user's group membership. That's an ADSI task rather than a WMI task, so it isn't included here.

If the permissions have been set incorrectly, you may need to take ownership of the folder to rectify the problem:

```
Get-WmiObject -Class Win32_Directory -Filter "Name='c:\\teszzt2'" |
Invoke-WmiMethod -Name TakeOwnership
```

In a network environment, folders are normally made available as shares. You can also work directly with shares using WMI.

8.3   *Listing, creating, and modifying shares*

Shares are an important part of administering Windows systems. They control how you make resources available to the user population. You'll normally think in terms of file shares, but you can also share printers and other devices.

If you want to view the available shares on the local system try this command:

```
ls hklm:\system\currentcontrolset\services\lanmanserver\shares |
select -ExpandProperty property
```

This will provide a list of the available shares.

It would be possible to use the techniques you saw in chapter 7 to read the registry of a remote machine, but shares on a cluster are a slightly different proposition. Details can be found in KB article 971403 from http://support.microsoft.com.

You can access share information directly using WMI. The `Win32_Share` class enables you to manage the share lifecycle, including creation and deletion.

TECHNIQUE 52   **Listing shares**

As a consultant I often need to discover how a machine is configured before I can work on it. I've used many of the techniques you've seen so far in the book when presented with a new set of machines to work with.

PROBLEM

A file server is in the process of failing. You need to list the shares so that you can recreate them on another machine when you move the data.

SOLUTION

WMI provides the `Win32_Share` class which you can use to answer this question. Listing 8.8 shows how you can use it. The function has two parameters: `-name` and `-computername`, which supply a share name and computer name respectively. The name parameter defaults to `%`, which is the standard WMI wildcard for any character. This means that by default information on all shares is displayed. The parameter can also accept standard Windows wildcard characters. A check is performed to change the Windows wildcard `*` to `%`, which is the WMI equivalent.

Listing 8.8   Listing shares

```
function get-share {
[CmdletBinding()]
param (
 [string]$name="%",
 [parameter(ValueFromPipeline=$true,
   ValueFromPipelineByPropertyName=$true)]
 [string]$computername="$env:COMPUTERNAME"
)
PROCESS{
$name = $name -replace "\*","%"
if ($name -eq "%") {
 Get-WmiObject -Class Win32_Share -ComputerName $computername
}
else
{
 Get-WmiObject -Class Win32_Share -ComputerName $computername `
 -Filter "Name LIKE '$name'"
 }
}}
```

If a name is given, you search for a specific share that contains the value given to the -name parameter. Otherwise you dump information for all available shares. The default display includes the path to the folder.

DISCUSSION

This script will display all share types as written. You could just produce output related to file shares or printer shares by adding a type parameter that takes the value of 0 for file shares and 1 for printer shares. The WMI filters could be altered to add the type as a search parameter. I've included that option as listing 8.8a in the download code.

Jumping back to the share lifecycle, you need to be able to create shares before you can do anything with them.

TECHNIQUE 53   Creating shares

The data-access requirements of organizations are constantly changing, and you'll need to create and remove shares to accommodate these changes. The changes can occur due to reorganizations, mergers and acquisitions, or the setting up of major project areas. Add the occasional need to move data between servers, and a large organization can have a very fluid environment.

PROBLEM

A major new project has started within your organization. It needs its own separate data area, and this data area has to be shared for access across the network.

SOLUTION

The `Win32_Share` class has a `Create` method that you'll use to create the share. The function in listing 8.9 has been deliberately written to only create file shares, but I left the share type as a parameter in case you wish to extend this script to cover creating other types of shares.

The other parameters are the computer name, the name of the share and the folder you're sharing, a description, and the maximum number of connections you're allowing to the share. A value of `0` means the number of users simultaneously able to access the share is unlimited.

Listing 8.9   Creating shares

```
function new-fileshare {
[CmdletBinding()]
param (
 [string]$name,
 [string]$path,
 [int]$type=0,
 [int]$maxcon,
[Alias("Description")]
[string]$desc,
 [parameter(ValueFromPipeline=$true,
   ValueFromPipelineByPropertyName=$true)]
[string]$computername="$env:COMPUTERNAME"
)
PROCESS{  if (!(Test-Path -Path $path)){Throw "Folder does not exist"}
 $s = [WmiClass]"\\$computername\root\cimv2:Win32_Share"
 $ret = $s.Create($path, $name, $type, $maxcon, $desc)

 if ($ret.ReturnValue -ne 0){
    Write-Host "Share $name was not created"
 }
 else {Write-Host "Share $name was created"}
}}
```

An instance of the `Win32_Share` class is created using the `[wmiclass]` type accelerator and is put into the variable `$s`. The `Create` method is called on this object. The folder path, share name, share type (0 for a file share), maximum connections, and description are used as arguments to the method.

The return value is tested, and if the value is 0 a success message is displayed. Any other value causes the display of a failure message.

DISCUSSION

It would be nice to be able to create the underlying folder structure and then create the share on top, but WMI doesn't give you a way to create folders. One possible solution is to use PowerShell remoting. The folders could be created using New-Item, and then your new-fileshare function could be used to create the share. If the function is used through PowerShell's remote administration capabilities, the computer name should be left as $env:COMPUTERNAME to represent the local machine.

The opposite end of the share's lifecycle is deleting the share. It's an activity that sometimes gets forgotten because of more pressing work. WMI can be used to delete a share:

```
Get-WmiObject -Class Win32_Share -Filter "Name='Test'" |
Remove-WmiObject
```

The share is identified by using Get-WmiObject. The resultant object is piped into Remove-WmiObject. Adding the -computername parameter to Get-WmiObject enables you to work with shares on remote machines.

Creation and deletion form the endpoints of a share's lifecycle. In the middle, you may need to modify the share.

TECHNIQUE 54   **Modifying shares**

There aren't many aspects of a share that you can modify. The maximum number of connections and the description are the only properties you can sensibly change. Anything else involves recreating the share.

PROBLEM

During an audit of your fileservers you discover that none of the shares on your fileservers have descriptions set. It will be easier for your junior administrators to work with the shares if descriptions are set.

SOLUTION

The following listing demonstrates how you can use the SetShareInfo method to modify a share's properties. The function takes the share name, maximum connections, description, and computer name as parameters.

Listing 8.10   Modifying shares

```
function set-share {
[CmdletBinding()]
param (
 [string]$name,
 [int]$maxcon,
[Alias("Description")]
```

```
 [string]$desc,
 [parameter(ValueFromPipeline=$true,
   ValueFromPipelineByPropertyName=$true)]
[string]$computername="$env:COMPUTERNAME"
)
PROCESS{          $share = Get-WmiObject -Class Win32_Share `
    -Filter "Name='$name'" -ComputerName $computername

    if (!$maxcon){$maxcon = $share.MaximumAllowed }
    if (!$desc){$desc = $share.Description}

    $share.SetShareInfo($maxcon, $desc, $null)
}}
```

A variable is created to hold the object created when `Get-WmiObject` retrieves the share information. The variables for the maximum connections and description are tested. If they haven't been created because values haven't been passed into the parameters, then the existing values from the share are used.

The `SetInfo` method is used to apply the modification to the share. The maximum connections and description are set simultaneously. This is why you need to pick up the existing values if they aren't being changed.

DISCUSSION

I suspect that most shares are created and not touched again until they're deleted, but you still need to be aware of how to modify shares for the times when it becomes necessary.

You've seen that Windows is an event-driven system. In previous chapters we've looked at disk events and registry events. It's time to turn our attention to filesystem events.

8.4   *Filesystem events*

When we talk about events affecting the filesystem, we're really discussing events that impact the files themselves. There are three possible actions that could affect our files:

- Creation
- Deletion
- Modification

There are techniques available to monitor these events using WMI or .NET. In this section, we'll look at how to use the WMI filesystem events.

TECHNIQUE 55   **Working with filesystem events**

There are a number of reasons for wanting to monitor parts of your filesystem. The files could contain sensitive information that you don't want changed or deleted. Perhaps the files perform a function in one of your critical applications and you can't afford to have them deleted. Alternatively, a third-party organization may deliver a file to a certain location, and you need to be made aware of any new files being created so that you can trigger further processing.

PROBLEM

You need to monitor part of the filesystem for creation, deletion, and modification events. Each of these events needs to trigger a separate action.

SOLUTION

The solution presented in the following listing sticks with the pattern established in previous chapters. You have a separate function for handling the events, and the main body of the script defines the queries and actions you'll use when registering the events.

Listing 8.11   Filesystem monitoring

```
function eventhandler {                                            ❶ Event
param ($e)                                                            handler
 $time = $e.TimeGenerated                                         ❷ Event
 if (!($e.SourceIdentifier -eq "modfile")){                          type
  $pc = $e.SourceEventArgs.NewEvent.TargetInstance.PartComponent
  $data = $pc -split "="
  $file = $data[1].Replace("\\","\").Replace("""","")
 }
 else {
  $file = $e.SourceEventArgs.NewEvent.PreviousInstance.Name
 }                                                                ❸ Event
                                                                    processing
 switch ($e.SourceIdentifier) {
   "newfile" {Write-Host "$time : File $file has been created"
              break}

   "delfile" {Write-Host "$time : File $file has been deleted"
              break}

   "modfile" { Write-Host "$time : File $file has been modified"
    Write-Host "Original"
    $e.SourceEventArgs.NewEvent.PreviousInstance | fl AccessMask,
    Archive, Encrypted, Extension, FileName, FileSize, Hidden,
    Readable, Status, System, Writeable | Out-Host

    Write-Host "Modified"
    $e.SourceEventArgs.NewEvent.TargetInstance | fl AccessMask,
    Archive, Encrypted, Extension, FileName, FileSize, Hidden,
    Readable, Status, System, Writeable | Out-Host
    break}
 }
}                                                                ❹ Clean
if (Get-EventSubscriber |                                            up
where {$_.SourceIdentifier -eq "newfile"}) {
Unregister-Event -SourceIdentifier "newfile" }

if (Get-EventSubscriber |
where {$_.SourceIdentifier -eq "delfile"}) {
Unregister-Event -SourceIdentifier "delfile" }

if (Get-EventSubscriber |
where {$_.SourceIdentifier -eq "modfile"}) {
Unregister-Event -SourceIdentifier "modfile" }        ❺ Define
                                                         queries
$nquery = "SELECT * FROM __InstanceCreationEvent
```

```
⇒ WITHIN 5 WHERE TargetInstance ISA
⇒ 'CIM_DirectoryContainsFile'
⇒ AND TargetInstance.GroupComponent =
    ⇒ 'Win32_Directory.Name=""C:\\\\Teszzt2""'"

$dquery = "SELECT * FROM __InstanceDeletionEvent
⇒ WITHIN 5 WHERE TargetInstance ISA
⇒ 'CIM_DirectoryContainsFile'
⇒ AND TargetInstance.GroupComponent =
    ⇒ 'Win32_Directory.Name=""C:\\\\Teszzt2""'"

$mquery = "SELECT * FROM __InstanceModificationEvent
⇒ WITHIN 5 WHERE TargetInstance ISA
⇒ 'CIM_DataFile' AND TargetInstance.Name =
⇒ 'C:\\Teszzt2\\proc1.txt'"

$action = {eventhandler $($event)}                          ❻ Define
                                                              action

Register-WmiEvent -Query $nquery `                          ❼ Register
-SourceIdentifier "newfile" -Action $action                   events
Register-WmiEvent -Query $dquery `
-SourceIdentifier "delfile" -Action $action
Register-WmiEvent -Query $mquery `
-SourceIdentifier "modfile" -Action $action
```

The event handler function ❶ is called when one of the registered events is triggered. It takes the event information as a parameter. The time the event was generated is picked out of the event object.

The file that has been affected by the event is recovered from the event object ❷. The recovery method depends on whether you're dealing with a file modification event or a file creation or deletion event.

A `switch` statement is used to perform the bulk of the event processing ❸. The `switch` criterion is the event source identifier (the type of event). If the file has been created or deleted, you display the time the event occurred, the name of the file, and whether the file was created or deleted.

File modification is a bit more complicated. You display a number of properties of the file in its original state and in its modified state. The change in file size could indicate that data has been added to the file or has been removed. Changes to the encryption, compression, and hidden states are also immediately obvious.

You need to register for the file events before your function can receive and process them. The main body of the script starts by deleting the registration of any previously defined instances of these events ❹. The WQL queries that are used to discover the events are defined next ❺.

There are two types of queries in this script. The first type is for the creation and deletion events. You use the `CIM_DirectoryContainsFile` class and look for the `__InstanceCreationEvent` and `__InstanceDeletionEvent` events respectively. There is a five second window in which you test for events, and the search is further restricted to the defined folder. This query works because the `CIM_DirectoryContainsFile` class maintains the link between a folder and its constituent files. A new instance of the class is created when a file is created, and an instance is removed when a file is deleted.

Unfortunately this approach won't work for file modifications, because the WMI instance linking the file to the folder hasn't been changed—only the file contents have been changed. You can overcome this by using the second type of query. The CIM_DataFile class is used to look for instances of __InstanceModificationEvent. You have to monitor individual files rather than a whole folder with this approach.

> **TIP** It's important to remember that you can monitor a whole folder for creation and deletion events but you have to monitor individual files for modification events.

The action ❻ is a simple statement that calls the eventhandler function. The event is passed to the function. Registration of the events occurs as the last action of the script ❼. One registration is made for each type of event using the appropriate query and source identifier. The action is identical across all registrations.

DISCUSSION

Discovering the information that's available within the event object can be a time-consuming task, because it will vary depending on the type of event that's triggered. One way to find out what you're working with is to use a modified version of listing 8.11 to discover this information. You can test any event by putting these lines in the eventhandler function:

```
$e | fl * | Out-Host
$e.SourceEventArgs.NewEvent | fl * | Out-Host
```

They can either replace what is there, or they can just be added to the function.

The first line displays the basic event information. The following example is from a file deletion event:

```
ComputerName     :
RunspaceId       : fef8fee4-2113-4b99-8471-a2513e1c4dbc
EventIdentifier  : 1
Sender           : System.Management.ManagementEventWatcher
SourceEventArgs  : System.Management.EventArrivedEventArgs
SourceArgs       : {System.Management.ManagementEventWatcher,
    System.Management.EventArrivedEventArgs}
SourceIdentifier : delfile
TimeGenerated    : 10/02/2011 21:54:44
MessageData      :
```

The second line displays the contents of the SourceEventArgs.NewEvent property. The same file deletion event produced this output:

```
__GENUS          : 2
__CLASS          : __InstanceDeletionEvent
__SUPERCLASS     : __InstanceOperationEvent
__DYNASTY        : __SystemClass
__RELPATH        :
__PROPERTY_COUNT : 3
__DERIVATION     : {__InstanceOperationEvent, __Event,
    __IndicationRelated, __SystemClass}
```

```
__SERVER             : RSLAPTOP01
__NAMESPACE          : //./root/CIMV2
__PATH               :
SECURITY_DESCRIPTOR  :
TargetInstance       : System.Management.ManagementBaseObject
TIME_CREATED         : 129418484845666000
Properties           : {SECURITY_DESCRIPTOR, TargetInstance, TIME_CREATED}
SystemProperties     : {__GENUS, __CLASS, __SUPERCLASS, __DYNASTY...}
Qualifiers           : {abstract}
ClassPath            : \\.\root\CIMV2:__InstanceDeletionEvent
Site                 :
Container            :
```

Once you have this information, you can add further lines to drill down deeper into the event information. It's worth looking at the description of the System.Management .EventArrivedEventArgs class on MSDN. It will help explain what is happening.

This is the technique that I used to discover the TargetInstance and PreviousInstance properties on the file modification event. A cut-down version of listing 8.11 configured to test an event can be found in the source code for this chapter. It's the script called test-event.ps1.

The last lap of our race around the filesystem involves a quick look at the page file.

8.5   *Page file management*

The page file is used to swap data out of memory and onto disk when the system is busy. It's also known as virtual memory. The page file is usually created during the installation of the operating system and often is just left to get on with its job. The Windows operating system does a good job of managing the page file.

Nevertheless, the page file can take up a lot of space on disk, and you may want to make modifications to the way the file works, such as moving it to another disk. There are some WMI classes for working with the page file. If we try this,

```
Get-WmiObject -Namespace root\cimv2 -List *pagefile*
```

the following classes will be returned:

- Win32_PageFileUsage
- Win32_PageFile
- Win32_PageFileSetting
- Win32_PageFileElementSetting

On Windows 7 or Windows Server 2008 R2, you won't get any output if you try any of these PowerShell commands:

```
Get-WmiObject -Class Win32_PageFile
Get-WmiObject -Class Win32_PageFileSetting
Get-WmiObject -Class Win32_PageFileElementSetting
```

The Win32_PageFileUsage class will return information:

```
Get-WmiObject -Class Win32_PageFileUsage |
Format-Table Name, CurrentUsage, PeakUsage,
AllocatedBaseSize, TempPageFile
```

If you substitute `Format-List` for `Format-Table`, the output may be easier to present (if you want to pipe to a file for saving in a report). You'll get something like this:

```
Name              : C:\pagefile.sys
CurrentUsage      : 146
PeakUsage         : 146
AllocatedBaseSize : 2814
TempPageFile      : False
```

The sizes are in megabytes.

Don't panic. Your machine isn't broken, even though some of the classes don't return information. The problem is that the system is configured to automatically manage the page file. You need to revert to manual management before you can work with it. If you look back at the `Win32_ComputerSystemClass` that we used in chapter 5,

```
Get-WmiObject -Class Win32_ComputerSystem | select *pagefile*
```

you'll find that the `AutomaticManagedPageFile` property is set to `true`. The way to modify this is to run PowerShell with elevated privileges and use the `-EnableAllprivileges` parameter on `Get-WmiObject`:

```
Get-WmiObject -Class Win32_ComputerSystem -EnableAllPrivileges |
Set-WmiInstance -Arguments @{AutomaticManagedPageFile=$false}
```

> **TIP** This combination of running with elevated privileges and using the `-EnableAllPrivileges` parameter forces the system to accept that you have the permissions to perform this action. The combination is essential. Using only one of the options will generate an access-denied message.

The three reluctant page file classes are now accessible, and you can now work with the page file to modify the maximum size, as follows:

```
$pf = Get-WmiObject -Class Win32_PageFileSetting
$pf.InitialSize = 5120
$pf.MaximumSize = 5120
$pf.Put()
```

Alternatively, having discovered the information you need, you can return the page file to automatic management:

```
Get-WmiObject -Class Win32_ComputerSystem -EnableAllPrivileges |
Set-WmiInstance -Arguments @{AutomaticManagedPageFile=$true}
```

Most of the time you're better off leaving the system to manage the page file.

8.6 Summary

The filesystem is fundamental to the operation of your Windows systems. Files are responsible for storing your valuable data, and they're grouped into folders for ease of management. You can perform a number of actions on files and folders:

- Discovery
- Compression, encryption, and hiding (plus their reversal)

- Copying and moving
- Deleting
- Setting permissions

You can monitor files and folders for creation, deletion, and modification events. This can help you protect your most critical files.

Shares are used to make the server's filesystem accessible across the network. You can manage the full share lifecycle through WMI.

The page file is used by the system as virtual memory. Information is swapped to disk as required to meet an application's requirements. You can usually allow the page file to be managed automatically, but it's possible to override this to fine tune its performance.

In chapter 9 we'll start to look at the applications running on our systems and turn our attention to services and processes.

Services and processes

Operating system components and applications run as processes on Windows systems. Examples of operating system processes include the Local Security Authority Process (lsass.exe), Windows Explorer (explorer.exe), and the Desktop Window Manager (dwm.exe). Processes created by applications could include Word, Notepad, or PowerShell.

A service is a process that's controlled by the Service Control Manager, such as DNS, Net Logon, Exchange, or SQL Server. Services usually start when the system boots up and runs in the background.

> **TIP** Run the scripts in this chapter from PowerShell, or the ISE, when it has been started with elevated privileges. You'll get partial information returned or errors if you run with PowerShell started as normal.

251

This chapter opens by examining how you can interact with the services on local and remote machines. WMI enables you to discover information about services that you can't get through the PowerShell cmdlets, and configuration can be simpler when working through WMI. Services, and their dependencies, have to be loaded in a particular order—the order and the list of dependencies form a useful troubleshooting tool when services won't start.

Processes potentially provide more opportunities for automation than services, as they tend to be more volatile. Discovering who has started a process on your server that's eating resources can enable you to stop the process to return the resources to the critical applications that need them and prevent that user from performing other actions that degrade the system's performance. PowerShell and WMI also enable you to manage the process lifecycle for local and remote systems. The creation and termination of processes provides an extra level of control over your systems.

PowerShell enables you to utilize the WMI event system easily and efficiently. You'll see how to use WMI events to discover when processes are stopped or started. You've already seen WMI events in some of the earlier chapters, and in this chapter you'll learn how to investigate WMI events of any kind. This is a generic technique that you can apply in any situation—we'll look at a practical example that shows you how to monitor processes. This will be extended to restart process that shouldn't stop, and to stop processes that shouldn't be started.

Before we dive into these events, though, we need to go back and look at the services on our systems.

9.1   Services

Services start when the system starts. They can be part of the base system functionality or host important infrastructure components, such as DNS or DHCP. Services also provide a way for applications such as Exchange or SQL Server to function.

Managing the services on your systems is an important administrative task. Power-Shell supplies a number of cmdlets for working directly with services, as listed in table 9.1.

Table 9.1   PowerShell service cmdlets

Get-Service	New-Service	Restart-Service	Resume-Service
Set-Service	Start-Service	Stop-Service	Suspend-Service

Get-Service and Set-Service can work remotely because they have a -ComputerName parameter. The other cmdlets can only work on the local system.

There are some differences between the way the cmdlets work with services and the way WMI works with services. You can see this by running these two lines of code and comparing the output:

```
Get-Service -Name W32Time | Format-List *
Get-WmiObject -Class Win32_Service -Filter "Name='W32Time'" |
Format-List *
```

TIP Use two PowerShell consoles to compare the results directly. It's often a good plan to have a couple of consoles open to dip into help or to test something.

WMI adds some interesting and useful properties:

- `Description`—The description seen in the Services GUI
- `StartName`—The account used to start the service
- `PathName`—The path to the service executable
- `DesktopInteract`—Whether the service can interact with the desktop

Table 9.2 lists the methods available for use through WMI. Many of the methods listed in table 9.2 have cmdlet equivalents listed in table 9.1. A very important difference is that the WMI methods don't have access to the `-WhatIf` and `-Confirm` parameters that are present on the cmdlets. This means you need to be very careful when testing scripts involving methods that can change the state of your systems.

Table 9.2 Methods of the `Win32_Service` class

Change	ChangeStartMode	Delete	GetSecurity-Descriptor
InterrogateService	PauseService	ResumeService	SetSecurity-Descriptor
StartService	StopService	UserControlService	

On the other hand, the `Get-Service` cmdlet supplies an easy way to discover dependent services (`Win32_DependentService` can also be used, but it's more cumbersome) and the services a particular service depends on. `Set-Service` can be used to modify some properties of a service, including the following:

- Description
- Display name
- Status—running, stopped ,or paused
- Start mode

At this point, you may be thinking that you don't need WMI at all when working with services. It may not be the only way to work with remote services, as it once was, but it still supplies some valuable and unique functionality.

When troubleshooting a problem, one of the first diagnostic techniques is to determine whether the services related to a particular application are running. This is a very straightforward technique, as you'll see shortly, especially when you use it to compare those services that are running against those services that should be running.

There are also a number of service-related configuration items you can modify with PowerShell and WMI, such as the service account and the start mode. Changing a service account password on many machines is a painfully slow process, but it's essential at times, such as when an administrator leaves the organization. The technique we'll use later brings automation and efficiency to this task, making it easy to accomplish (don't forget the change-control process though).

Many services (and other parts of the operating system) are loaded as the machine starts. The loading has to occur in a precise order to ensure that all system dependencies are honored. The final service-related technique we'll examine enables you to determine the load order, which is very useful for troubleshooting startup errors on your systems.

Before we can get to the deep technicalities of service loading, you need to understand the services that are running and the services that should be running.

TECHNIQUE 56　Listing services

You saw in the section introduction that WMI adds access to some properties over and above those returned by the `Get-Service` cmdlet. You can use this to find out more information about the services running on your systems.

PROBLEM

`Get-Service` will tell you if a particular service is running or not. It can't tell you if the service should be running. You need a method of comparing the running services against those that should be running (those that are set to start automatically).

SOLUTION

This problem can be solved by comparing the status of the service (running or stopped) against the mode of starting. The following listing shows how to obtain the information required for this comparison.

Listing 9.1　Listing services

```
function get-servicestatus {
[CmdletBinding()]
param (
 [parameter(ValueFromPipeline=$true,
   ValueFromPipelineByPropertyName=$true)]
 [string]$computername="$env:COMPUTERNAME",
 [string]$name
)
PROCESS{
if (-not $name) {
$services = Get-WmiObject -Class Win32_Service `
-ComputerName $computername }
else {
$services = Get-WmiObject -Class Win32_Service `
-Filter "Name='$name'"  -ComputerName $computername
}

$services | select DisplayName, StartMode,
 State, Description
}}
```

The get-servicestatus function takes an optional computer name as a parameter. It can also take a service name as a parameter. Be careful with this parameter as it's the service name rather than the display name that's required.

If a service name isn't supplied, the function returns all instances of the Win32_Service class from the required computer. Supplying a service name restricts the information to the particular service of interest.

The service information is then piped into Select-Object to restrict output to the required information. The StartMode property shows how the service should start—automatically or manually.

DISCUSSION

The combination of the start mode and the current state of the service shows you which services are running and which services should be running.

The function emits objects and can be used as follows:

```
get-servicestatus |
where {$_.StartMode -eq "Auto" -and $_.State -ne "Running"} |
Format-Table -Autosize
```

Notice that the start mode is Auto and not Automatic! This information could be used to force a restart of a service that hasn't started.

When applying patches to the server estate I work with, occasionally some services won't restart. I need to check them and force them to start if required.

> **TIP** There is a school of thought that says that PowerShell best practice is to always return objects. A lot of the work I do is investigative rather than direct administration. I have found it quicker to write scripts and functions that return the results directly. As with many other aspects of PowerShell, I end up taking a pragmatic view to solve the immediate problem.

Step one is always discovering what is happening. You've just done that. Step two is to do something about it. You need to be able to configure services to complete step two, and it just happens that's our next topic.

TECHNIQUE 57   **Configuring services**

In many cases, you'll install your services and leave them alone, especially if they're major applications such as Exchange or SQL Server. A service account is created with a password that doesn't expire, and you never get around to changing it. This could be a security vulnerability, exploitable by a rogue administrator, if the password is known and the service needs a high level of privilege.

PROBLEM

You have a number of servers running a service that has a high level of privilege. The password used by the service account has been compromised and needs to be changed. You've been instructed to use a new account to be extra sure.

SOLUTION

One possible solution is to do this manually. It would work for a few machines, but you can automate this activity, as shown in the following listing.

Listing 9.2 Configure services

```
function set-serviceaccount {
[CmdletBinding()]
param (
 [parameter(ValueFromPipeline=$true,
   ValueFromPipelineByPropertyName=$true)]
 [string]$computername="$env:COMPUTERNAME",

 [parameter(Mandatory=$true)]
 [string]
 [ValidateNotNullOrEmpty()]
 $servicename,

 [parameter(Mandatory=$true)]
 [string]$account,
 [parameter(Mandatory=$true)]
 [string]$password
)
PROCESS{
 $service = Get-WmiObject -Class Win32_Service `
 -ComputerName $computername -Filter "Name='$servicename'"

 $service.StopService()

 $service.Change($null,$null,$null,$null,$null,$null,
   ➥ $account,$password,$null,$null,$null)

 $service.StartService()
} }
```

The set-serviceaccount function has the service name as a mandatory parameter. A validation test is performed to ensure that the name given isn't null or empty. The account and password to use for the service are deliberately left as optional. If they aren't given, all that happens is that the service is stopped and restarted. Sometimes that's all you need to do.

Get-WmiObject is used to create an object for the service in question. The StopService method is called, and while the service is in a stopped state, the Change method is used to make the required changes to the account and password.

The function then restarts the service.

DISCUSSION

The Change method takes a long list of arguments, and their meaning is given in table 9.3.

Table 9.3 Options for the Change method of the Win32_Service class

Argument name	Comment
DisplayName	Display name of the service; maximum of 256 characters
PathName	Full file path to the service executable
ServiceType	Type of service—usually set as $null to indicate no change

Table 9.3   Options for the `Change` method of the `Win32_Service` class *(continued)*

Argument name	Comment
ErrorControl	Severity of error if service fails to start; accepts `0–4`
StartMode	Start mode of service—usually `automatic` or `manual`
DesktopInteract	Set to `true` if service can communicate with window on desktop
StartName	Service account name
StartPassword	Password for service account
LoadOrderGroup	Group in which service loads—see technique 58
LoadOrderGroupDependencies	Load order groups that must start before this service starts
ServiceDependencies	List of services that must start before this service starts

It's possible to not give the three arguments after the password because they will default to a NULL value. I have given them for completeness. The function is used like this:

```
set-serviceaccount -servicename BITS `
-account RSLAPTOP01\BITSTEST -password Pa55w0rd
```

> **WARNING**   The service won't restart on Windows 7. If you try to start the service manually, you'll get an error stating that it can't start because the service isn't using the same account as other services running in the same process. I have used this service as a safe example, even though it will fail. It also gives an opportunity to show how to reset to system accounts.

You'd better put it back like it was:

```
set-serviceaccount -servicename BITS `
 -account LocalSystem -password ""
```

Notice that you're using an empty string for the password. This is the correct way to reset to using the system type accounts. If you use $null you'll generate an error.

You now know how to discover the running services and configure them as required. The last aspect of service administration to cover is how they're loaded at system startup.

TECHNIQUE 58   Discovering the service load order

Most services are loaded when the system starts. There is a defined order in which services and their dependencies must be loaded. Many services are loaded in groups, but not all services are members of a group and not all groups have members. System startup involves the loading of other functionality, such as drivers, and is a complex process that can occasionally exhibit problems.

PROBLEM

There are intermittent problems with one of your servers. You need to discover the services, drivers, and other things that are loaded at system startup to determine whether the problem is related to a malfunction of the load process.

SOLUTION

The solution involves some repetitive processing, because the WMI associations don't work in the direction that you require. You can start with a service and associate a load group, but you can't start with the load group and discover the associated services. This is illustrated in the following listing.

Listing 9.3   Service load order

```
function get-serviceloadorder {
[CmdletBinding()]
param (
 [parameter(ValueFromPipeline=$true,
   ValueFromPipelineByPropertyName=$true)]
 [string]$computername="$env:COMPUTERNAME"
)
PROCESS{
 $LOGSM = Get-WmiObject -Class Win32_LoadOrderGroupServiceMembers `
  -ComputerName $computername

 Get-WmiObject -Class Win32_LoadOrderGroup -ComputerName $computername |
 foreach {
  $name = $_.Name
  "{0,2} {1}" -f $_.GroupOrder, $name

  $LOGSM |
  where {$_.GroupComponent -like "*$name*"} |
  foreach {
   "  $((($_.PartComponent).Split(':'))[1]) "
  }
 }
}}
```

The get-serviceloadorder function only requires a computer name as a parameter, because you want to know the information for all the services.

The processing starts by retrieving all instances of the Win32_LoadOrderGroupServiceMembers class. The parts you're interested in are the GroupComponent, which supplies the load order group, and the PartComponent, which supplies the name of the service or driver. Here's an example:

```
GroupComponent :\\RSLAPTOP01\root\cimv2:
   ➥ Win32_LoadOrderGroup.Name="Boot Bus Extender"
PartComponent  :\\RSLAPTOP01\root\cimv2:Win32_SystemDriver.Name="ACPI"
```

You could try to sort and group based on the GroupComponent, but the output is easier to understand if you approach the problem slightly differently. The instances of the Win32_LoadOrderGroup class are retrieved and piped into a ForEach-Object. Each group has the group order and name displayed.

The Win32_LoadOrderGroupServiceMembers that you've loaded into the $LOGSM variable are filtered on the name of the load order group. The PartComponent of each of the accepted instances is split on the colon (:) and the result is displayed.

DISCUSSION

The resultant display is too large to include in the book, but here's a small portion:

```
53 Cryptography
   Win32_SystemDriver.Name="KSecPkg"
54 PNP_TDI
   Win32_SystemDriver.Name="AFD"
   Win32_SystemDriver.Name="NDProxy"
```

The WMI class is deliberately left as part of the display to aid in discovering further information about the item.

We didn't cover the `Win32_SystemDriver` class in chapter 5, but you can use it as follows:

```
Get-WmiObject -Class Win32_SystemDriver |
sort State, DisplayName |
Format-Table DisplayName, State, Status -AutoSize
```

Adding a function to the chapter 5 module to return driver information is a good exercise to test your understanding. A possible solution is available in the download code—see get-systemdriver.ps1.

Services tend to be static when compared to processes. New processes can be started by users or by other processes, and you need to turn your attention to processes to determine whether this volatility is having an adverse effect on your systems.

9.2   *Processes*

Do you know and understand the full list of processes running on your systems? PowerShell provides a set of cmdlets for working with processes, as listed in table 9.4.

Debug-Process	Get-Process
Start-Process	Stop-Process
Wait-Process	

Table 9.4   Process-related cmdlets

Only `Get-Process` has the ability to work against remote machines.

Using Start-Process

One little known use for the `Start-Process` cmdlet is accessing websites and opening them directly in your browser:

```
Start-Process http://www.manning.com/siddaway2
```

You can make this easier to use if you create an expression for the command and put it into your profile:

```
$meap = "Start-Process http://www.manning.com/siddaway2"
```

You can then execute it like this:

```
Invoke-Expression -Command $meap
```

Better still, from the command line you can use the alias:

```
iex $meap
```

This is a nice easy way to get to your favorite websites.

Many processes are started by the system, but you also need to understand the processes that users are starting. Processes have a limited lifecycle in that users tend to start them, let them do their work, and then close them down. There is little need to modify processes.

TECHNIQUE 59   ## Listing process owners

You can use the Get-Process cmdlet to discover which processes are running on your local and remote systems. Unfortunately this cmdlet doesn't tell you who is the owner of the process—it doesn't tell you who started it. This is a limitation of the .NET class used by Get-Process rather than a PowerShell issue.

PROBLEM
A remote server is running slowly because extra processes are being started on it that use badly needed resources. You need to determine who is starting these processes.

SOLUTION
The Win32_Process class can be used as shown in the following listing. The function only requires a computer name as a parameter, which defaults to the local system, as usual.

Listing 9.4   List process owners

```
function get-processowner {
[CmdletBinding()]
param (
 [parameter(ValueFromPipeline=$true,
   ValueFromPipelineByPropertyName=$true)]
 [string]$computername="$env:COMPUTERNAME"
)
PROCESS{
Get-WmiObject -Class Win32_Process `
-ComputerName $computername |
select Name,
@{Name="Domain";Expression={($_.GetOwner()).Domain}},
@{Name="User";Expression={($_.GetOwner()).User}}

}}
```

The call to Get-WmiObject will return running processes. The Win32_Process class has a method to find the process owner—GetOwner(). You can't access this information directly, but you can use Select-Object to create two calculated fields that display the domain and userid of the process owner by calling the GetOwner method.

DISCUSSION
This technique can also be used to check that processes such as Exchange, Share-Point, and SQL Server are being started with the correct account.

> **TIP** You won't get system processes, such as winlogon.exe, unless you run this function in PowerShell started with elevated privileges. This mimics the behavior of the Task Manager utility, which only shows your own processes by default.

Usually you'll start processes interactively, but there are times when you need to create a process on a remote machine.

Creating a process

The "Using Start-Process" sidebar earlier in this section showed you how to start a process on the local machine using the Start-Process cmdlet. If you look at the help file for Start-Process, you can see that it doesn't have a -ComputerName parameter. Alternatively, you can use Get-Command to check the available parameters:

```
Get-Command Start-Process -Syntax
```

PROBLEM

You need to be able to start a process on a remote machine. This will enable you to run programs on the remote machine as well as put additional load on that machine's resources to simulate additional load on the existing processes.

SOLUTION

The Win32_Process class has a Create method that you can use to start a new process on a remote machine, as shown in listing 9.5. This will start the process in a default manner.

You can take this a stage further and use the Win32_ProcessStartUp class to refine how the processes are started. This class can accept a number of options, as listed in table 9.5.

Table 9.5   Win32_ProcessStartUp options

CreateFlags	EnvironmentVariables	ErrorMode	FillAttribute
PriorityClass	ShowWindow	Title	WinstationDesktop
X	XCountChars	XSize	Y
YCountChars	YSize		

The X and Y properties refer to the position on screen of the top left corner of the window in which the application runs.

Listing 9.5   Create process

```
function new-process {
[CmdletBinding()]
param (
 [parameter(ValueFromPipeline=$true,
   ValueFromPipelineByPropertyName=$true)]
 [string]$computername="$env:COMPUTERNAME",

 [parameter(Mandatory=$true)]
 [string]$name
)
PROCESS{
 $prcstart1 = [wmiclass]"\\$computername\root\cimv2:Win32_ProcessStartup"
```

```
$prcstart1.Properties["ShowWindow"].Value = 2

$prcstart2 = [wmiclass]"\\$computername\root\cimv2:Win32_ProcessStartup"
$prcstart2.Properties["PriorityClass"].Value = 128

$proc = [wmiclass]"\\$computername\root\cimv2:Win32_Process"
$proc.Create($name, $null, $prcstart1)

$proc.Create($name, $null, $prcstart2)
}}
```

TIP   This function is written to demonstrate how to use these classes and options. If you need this in your own environment, I suggest rewriting it to meet your requirements.

The function takes two parameters. The first is the usual computer name parameter that accepts the name of the remote machine you're going to work with. The second parameter is the name of the process you intend to start. The process name is mandatory. Remember that with WMI, you need to include the extension if you're starting an application, such as notepad.exe.

This demonstration function then creates two instances of the Win32_ProcessStartup class. The [wmiclass] type accelerator is the easiest way to achieve this, as shown. The first instance is used to set the ShowWindow property to a value of 2, which forces the application to start with a minimized window.

The second instance has the PriorityClass property set to 128, which forces the application to start with its priority set to High.

A single instance of the Win32_Process class is created. You can then call the Create method twice using the name of the process and the relevant startup properties, as shown. The middle parameter that's set to $null is the current drive and directory for the process. If left as $null, it has the same path as the calling process, which is PowerShell.

DISCUSSION

Windows supplies a few utilities that are ideal for testing this type of functionality, most notably Notepad and the Calculator. In this case we'll use Notepad to perform our tests. The function is used as follows:

```
new-process -name notepad.exe
```

The WMI return information includes the ProcessIds of the new processes. This information could be captured in a variable if required for future processing.

You can test that the processes start with different priorities by using this code:

```
Get-WmiObject Win32_Process -Filter "Name='notepad.exe'" |
Format-Table Name, ProcessId, Priority -AutoSize
```

It will return a result similar to this:

```
Name         ProcessId Priority
----         --------- --------
notepad.exe       5980        8
notepad.exe       5520       13
```

You'll get visual confirmation that one of the instances of Notepad starts in a minimized window.

This function was tested using `Invoke-WmiMethod` as a variant. If I was just creating the process, it would have worked as shown in this example:

```
$proc = [wmiclass]"\\.\root\cimv2:Win32_Process"
Invoke-WmiMethod -InputObject $proc -Name Create `
-ArgumentList "notepad.exe"
```

Extending the code to utilize the startup options produces this code:

```
$proc = [wmiclass]"\\.\root\cimv2:Win32_Process"
Invoke-WmiMethod -InputObject $proc -Name Create `
-ArgumentList "notepad.exe", $null, $prcstart2
```

Unfortunately this code throws an invalid operation error and won't work. I've determined that `Invoke-WmiMethod` expects the parameters in the order that was used, but it still fails. In any case, you have a method that works, using listing 9.5, which is the important point.

Creating processes and checking ownership of processes leads you to the situation where you'll need to terminate a process.

TECHNIQUE 61   **Terminating a process**

Stopping a process on the local machine can be achieved in many ways:

- Close the application window with a mouse click
- Right-click the minimized application and select Close Window.
- Use the Task Manager utility
- Use `Stop-Process`

But none of these can be used when you're dealing with a remote machine, so you need a different approach.

PROBLEM

You've determined that there are processes running on a remote machine that need to be terminated in order to conserve the resources used by that machine.

SOLUTION

If this is an ad hoc activity, you could perform the action at the PowerShell prompt. But it's likely that you'll need to perform this action more frequently, so you can wrap it in a function that you call as required and use easily against multiple machines. The following listing shows how you can solve this problem.

Listing 9.6   Terminate process

```
function stop-remoteprocess {
[CmdletBinding()]
param (
 [parameter(ValueFromPipeline=$true,
   ValueFromPipelineByPropertyName=$true)]
 [string]$computername="$env:COMPUTERNAME",
```

```
      [parameter(Mandatory=$true)]
      [string]$name
)
PROCESS{
  Get-WmiObject -Class Win32_Process `
  -ComputerName $computername -Filter "Name='$name'" |
  Remove-WmiObject
}}
```

This function is derived directly from listing 9.5. The computer name and process name are input as parameters. Get-WmiObject is used with the Win32_Process class to discover the relevant processes, based on the computer name and a filter created from the process name. The results of that search are piped to Remove-WmiObject, which deletes the instances of the Win32_Process class, which thus terminates the process and closes the application.

DISCUSSION

This function takes a heavy-handed approach in that it stops all processes with a given name. If you want to be more selective, substitute the ProcessId for the name. Better still, you can write a function that will take a name or a ProcessId and either terminate all processes of that name or the individual process by ID. This is shown in the following listing.

Listing 9.7 Terminate process by name or `ProcessId`

```
function stop-remoteprocessid {
[CmdletBinding()]
param (
 [parameter(ValueFromPipeline=$true,
   ValueFromPipelineByPropertyName=$true)]
 [string]$computername="$env:COMPUTERNAME",

 [parameter(ParameterSetName="Procname")]
 [string]$name,

 [parameter(ParameterSetName="Procid")]
 [int]$procid

)
PROCESS{
  switch ($psCmdlet.ParameterSetName) {
   "Procname" {
      Get-WmiObject -Class Win32_Process `
      -ComputerName $computername -Filter "Name='$name'" |
      Remove-WmiObject
    }
   "Procid" {
      Get-WmiObject -Class Win32_Process `
      -ComputerName $computername -Filter "ProcessId=$procid" |
      Remove-WmiObject

  }
  }
}}
```

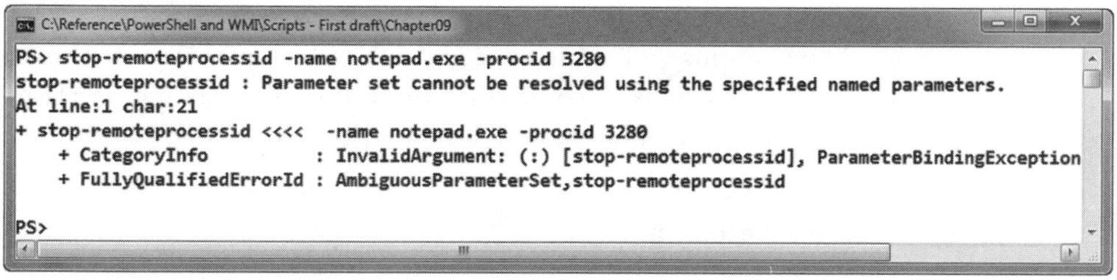

Figure 9.1 Error message when mixing parameter sets

You start with listing 9.6 and add a new parameter—$procid—to hold the ProcessId. The goal is to use either the process name or ProcessId to identify the processes to terminate. These two options can be separated by using parameter sets. The process name is put into a parameter set called ProcName whereas the ProcessId is in a parameter set called ProcId. The computer name parameter isn't put into an explicit parameter set and is therefore in both.

This can be illustrated by displaying the syntax of the function:

```
Get-Command stop-remoteprocessid -Syntax
stop-remoteprocessid [-computer <String>] [-name <String>]...
stop-remoteprocessid [-computer <String>] [-procid <Int32>] ...
```

Get-Command displays two different syntaxes, one for each parameter set. The "..." represents the common parameters, which I removed for brevity. The good thing about parameter sets is that they're mutually exclusive. If you start to use the parameters in one set, you can't mix them with the parameters from another. Both of the following examples will work:

```
stop-remoteprocessid -name notepad.exe
stop-remoteprocessid -procid 3280
```

If You tried to use name and ProcessId, like this,

```
stop-remoteprocessid -name notepad.exe -procid 3280
```

you'd get an error, as shown in figure 9.1.

Processes consume resources on your systems. Sometimes you may want to prevent particular processes from running to ensure that valuable resources are available for your critical processes. Alternatively, you may need to ensure that a critical process is restarted in the event of failure. You can accomplish both of these goals through the WMI events related to processes.

9.3 *Process-related events*

An event is triggered on your systems when something happens or something changes state. The two most common events related to processes are

- New processes starting up
- Processes shutting down

These events are similar to events you've seen previously in that they produce information in a known format. The difference is in the exact information returned.

You know from previous chapters that the following WMI system classes can be used to monitor process creation and deletion:

- `__InstanceCreationEvent`
- `__InstanceDeletionEvent`

WMI spoils you for choice with process-related events because you also get the classes listed in table 9.6.

Table 9.6   Process event classes

Class	Purpose
`Win32_ProcessTrace`	Base class for process events
`Win32_ProcessStartTrace`	Indicates a new process has started
`Win32_ProcessStopTrace`	Indicates a process has stopped

Events relating to the registry and filesystem have been discussed in previous chapters, and a pattern of working with events has been established. Processes provide an easy, and *safe*, way of investigating the WMI event engine in more detail. After we look at that, we'll look at using the WMI classes to monitor process events and to add further controls to your systems.

TECHNIQUE 62   **Investigating an event**

You've seen, for instance in listing 8.11, that `Register-WmiEvent` is used to register a WMI event so you can work with it. When the event is triggered an object is created using the `System.Management.Automation.PSEventArgs` .NET class. You need to understand the anatomy of this object if you want to get the most from working with events.

PROBLEM

The objects produced by a WMI-based event need to be investigated so that you can determine the optimum method of processing events.

SOLUTION

Listing 9.8 will create an event object that you can work with at the command line.

> **WARNING** This code should *not* be run as a script because you won't see the output due to the script being in a different scope. Paste each line into the PowerShell console and run it. I also recommend opening a new PowerShell console to run this code. That will ensure that there are no other events registered that could interfere with the investigation.

Listing 9.8 Investigate process events

```
$query = "Select * FROM __InstanceCreationEvent
➥ within 3 WHERE TargetInstance ISA 'Win32_Process'"

Register-WmiEvent -Query $query `
-SourceIdentifier "WMI process start"

Get-EventSubscriber

Start-Process notepad

Get-Event
$e = Get-Event | select -First 1

$e.SourceEventArgs

$e.SourceEventArgs.NewEvent

$e.SourceEventArgs.NewEvent.TargetInstance
```

The first step is to define a query. This will extract all instance-creation events where the target is a member of the `Win32_Process` class. The next step is to register the WMI event. In this case, you aren't registering an action, so the event information is accessible from the event queue. The event queue is simply the collection of events that have occurred, to which the current PowerShell session has subscribed via the registration cmdlets, and for which no processing action is registered. Events created using `New-Event` will also appear on the queue if an action isn't registered.

You can test the registration by using `Get-EventSubscriber` which will confirm the `SourceIdentifier` you've chosen. An instance of Notepad is started using the `Start-Process` cmdlet. You could use the WMI function in listing 9.5 as an alternative to this line. The event information can be displayed using `Get-Event`, but this only works if an action hasn't been defined when registering the event. If an action is defined, the action handles the event and the event doesn't appear on the event queue. A display similar to figure 9.2 should result at this point.

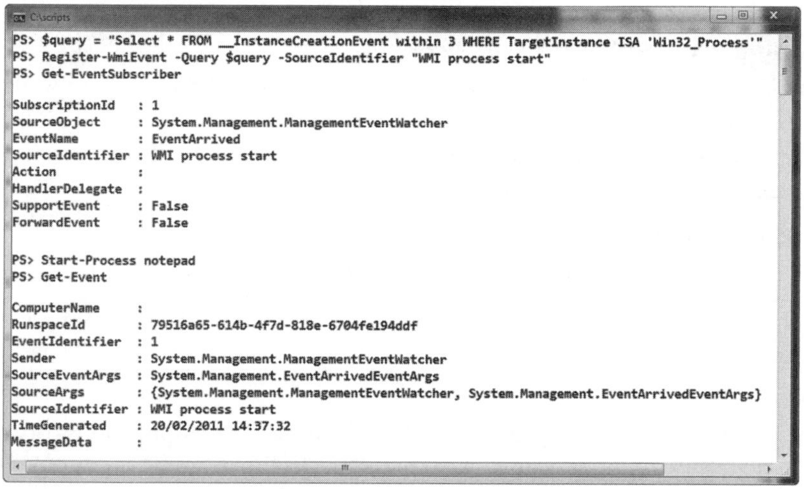

```
PS> $query = "Select * FROM __InstanceCreationEvent within 3 WHERE TargetInstance ISA 'Win32_Process'"
PS> Register-WmiEvent -Query $query -SourceIdentifier "WMI process start"
PS> Get-EventSubscriber

SubscriptionId   : 1
SourceObject     : System.Management.ManagementEventWatcher
EventName        : EventArrived
SourceIdentifier : WMI process start
Action           :
HandlerDelegate  :
SupportEvent     : False
ForwardEvent     : False

PS> Start-Process notepad
PS> Get-Event

ComputerName     :
RunspaceId       : 79516a65-614b-4f7d-818e-6704fe194ddf
EventIdentifier  : 1
Sender           : System.Management.ManagementEventWatcher
SourceEventArgs  : System.Management.EventArrivedEventArgs
SourceArgs       : {System.Management.ManagementEventWatcher, System.Management.EventArrivedEventArgs}
SourceIdentifier : WMI process start
TimeGenerated    : 20/02/2011 14:37:32
MessageData      :
```

Figure 9.2 Event processing

A variable, $e, can be created to hold the event. In this example, I forced the selection of the first event, in case any other events occurred while working through the previous steps. The various components of the event object can be displayed using the syntax provided.

The final step is to recover the name of the process that has been started:

```
$e.SourceEventArgs.NewEvent.TargetInstance.name
```

DISCUSSION

The event information in figure 9.2 includes a `ComputerName` property. This is useful when events are being forwarded to you. You can easily determine which machine is generating the event.

The `Sender` property contains three items:

- Scope
- Query
- Options

They're worth investigating to completely understand the `event` object, though there is no information you need to access for the purposes of this example.

This gives you two different methods of analyzing events. You can use the manual steps given in listing 9.8, or you can adopt the test harness described in technique 55 (chapter 8).

> **TIP** I strongly recommend experimenting with the information presented by the event object. Event handling is one of those subjects that can seem incomprehensible until you've experimented enough to get to the Eureka! moment.

You've learned a lot about administering processes and process-related events in this chapter. Let's close out the chapter by putting it all together: you'll create a method of monitoring your processes.

TECHNIQUE 63   Monitoring processes

You saw event-handling scripts at the end of chapters 7 and 8 where you were working with the registry and filesystem respectively. In both cases, you used the `__InstanceCreation` system class as you did in technique 62. There are two alternative classes you can use when working with process events:

- `Win32_ProcessStartTrace`
- `Win32_ProcessStopTrace`

The same information can be retrieved, whether you work with the system class or the trace classes.

PROBLEM

You have a server that's running a critical application. The application's process must be immediately restarted if it stops. Resources are in short supply on the server, so you want to prevent some other processes from starting and using those resources.

SOLUTION

The following listing shows one possible solution to this problem. I used the Solitaire and Calculator applications as examples in this listing so that you can experiment in safety. Other applications can be substituted as required.

Listing 9.9 Process monitoring

```
function eventhandler {
param ($e)
 $proc = $e.SourceEventArgs.NewEvent.ProcessName
 if ($e.SourceIdentifier -eq "Process Start") {
  Write-Host "$proc has started"

  if ($proc -eq "Solitaire.exe") {
    Write-Host "Solitaire is not allowed. It is stopping"
    Get-WmiObject Win32_Process -Filter "Name='solitaire.exe'" |
    Remove-WmiObject
  }
 }
 else {
  Write-Host "$proc has stopped"
  if ($proc -eq "calc.exe") {
   Write-Host "Calc.exe must be restarted."
   $np = [wmiclass]"Win32_Process"
   $np.Create("calc.exe")
  }
 }

}

if (Get-EventSubscriber |
where {$_.SourceIdentifier -eq "Process Start"}) {
 Unregister-Event -SourceIdentifier "Process Start" }
if (Get-EventSubscriber |
where {$_.SourceIdentifier -eq "Process Stop"}) {
Unregister-Event -SourceIdentifier "Process Stop" }

$queryStart = "SELECT * FROM Win32_ProcessStartTrace"
$queryStop = "SELECT * FROM Win32_ProcessStopTrace"

$action = {eventhandler $($event)}

Register-WmiEvent -Query $queryStart `
-SourceIdentifier "Process Start" -Action $action
Register-WmiEvent -Query $queryStop `
-SourceIdentifier "Process Stop" -Action $action
```

The script starts by defining the `eventhandler` function. Notice that you only need a single function to handle the events from two different registrations. The process name is immediately recovered from the event information. The examples in listing 9.8 illustrated how you get to this structure.

A test on the `SourceIdentifier` property determines whether you're dealing with a process that's starting or stopping. If the process is starting, you display the appropriate message and then test if it's the Solitaire application. When using WMI, you have to include the program's extension (.exe). In the event that Solitaire has been started, you get the WMI object corresponding to its process and remove it, which closes down the application.

If you're dealing with a process that has been stopped, you display the message, test if it's calculator.exe, and start it up again if necessary.

The body of the script is similar to previous event handling scripts in that it cleans up the registrations if you're rerunning it, creates the queries and action, and then registers the events.

DISCUSSION

This example uses two applications that are safe to experiment with. In reality, you may want to stop a number of applications from running—I never have understood why Windows server editions include the games. A small number of applications (six or so) could be managed by creating an array and testing the newly started application against the array using the -contains operator. A larger number of applications would require using a file and comparing the newly started process against the file contents. The whole concept could be extended to include the time of day. For example, perhaps some applications could only be run out of business hours.

It's worth leaving the script running for a while to watch the processes that stop and start automatically during the normal running of your system—it's quite educational. And on that note, our coverage of services and processes is brought to a close.

9.4   *Summary*

Services and processes enable you to work with the applications running on your systems. You can use WMI to work with these objects to perform efficient management and troubleshooting, including

- Service discovery and configuration
- Service load order and dependency diagnosis
- Process owner discovery (who is running what)
- Process lifecycle management
- Process events, enabling you to control which applications can be run and when

Managing services and processes ensures that you concentrate your computer resources where they're required—running your critical applications.

In chapter 10, we'll move on to the favorite topic of many administrators, namely printers and printing.

Printers

10

This chapter covers

- Discovering printer configuration and status
- Discovering and comparing printer drivers
- Managing printers and print jobs
- Testing printers

Printers are probably the second most common cause of issues in Windows environments (password resets are the first). In many cases, these are logistical issues involving toner, paper, and mechanical problems that administrators can't control directly, but we can control the printer and its associated print jobs. PowerShell and WMI enable us to perform the control tasks on remote or local systems.

> **NOTE** A *printer* in Windows terminology is the queue to which a print job is sent. It's linked to one or more physical print devices.

The first two parts of this chapter are concerned with discovering information about printers. Our starting point will be to determine what printers are connected to a particular computer. The capabilities of those printers are very important; for example, can a particular printer print in color? This information is available through WMI, but you have to deal with collections of properties to determine the answers. We'll then look at printer drivers and printer ports. Many printer issues can be traced to using an incorrect driver, and having a quick way to determine the exact driver can save time when troubleshooting.

Users tend to be more interested in the status of the printer and their print jobs than in the technicalities of the printer configuration. PowerShell and WMI techniques for retrieving this information are presented in the second section of the chapter.

The third section of the chapter is concerned with managing printers. Setting the default printer for users can save them, and you, a lot of effort in determining what's happening to their printouts. You can force a test page to be printed to determine whether the connection is working correctly. The printer can be paused for maintenance work and then resumed to allow the accumulated print jobs to be printed. You can, if necessary, cancel all print jobs associated with a particular printer. Printers, like many objects you deal with, can be renamed with more suitable and descriptive names to make it easier for users to select the printer they need. The combination of PowerShell and WMI enables you to perform these tasks on remote systems, enhancing your service to your users without any additional spending or effort.

First, you need to discover your printer configurations before you can start managing them.

10.1   *Printer configuration*

WMI provides a number of classes for dealing with printers. You can discover these classes using the -List parameter of Get-WmiObject, as you've seen previously:

```
Get-WmiObject -List *print*
```

The amended qualifiers of the WMI class will yield a description. You have to retrieve this information specifically, as it's relatively expensive to produce. This example expands on the simple list to display the description of each class:

```
Get-WmiObject -List *print* | sort name |
foreach {
"`n$($_.Name)" (( Get-WmiObject -List $_.Name  -Amended ).Qualifiers |
 Where {$_.Name -eq "Description"}).Value
}
```

The two main classes we'll consider are Win32_Printer and Win32_PrintJob. In this section, you'll use these two classes to discover your printers, printer status, and capabilities, together with the print jobs, ports, and drivers associated with the printers. The first task is to discover the printers to which a particular machine is connected.

TECHNIQUE 64   **Discovering printers**

Some organizations have simplified printer management by using third-party software. This enables the users to all print to the same printer, but delivery is controlled by the user physically accessing the device to "pull" their prints from a central queue.

Many, if not most, organizations work with a mixture of printers distributed throughout the organization. Some of these will manage their own print queues, and some will utilize a dedicated printer server. Users can be allocated printers via logon scripts, GPOs, or even as part of the base build of their PC. The situation is further complicated by some applications and other technologies, such as faxes appearing as printers. Discovering which printer a particular user is accessing can be problematical.

PROBLEM

A user calls the help desk saying, "My printer is not working." You need to discover to which printers the user is connected before any action can be taken to resolve the call.

SOLUTION

The function presented in the following listing solves this problem. It has a single parameter that accepts a computer name. The local machine is the default, as usual.

Listing 10.1   Discover available printers

```
function get-printer {
[CmdletBinding()]
param (
 [parameter(ValueFromPipeline=$true,
   ValueFromPipelineByPropertyName=$true)]
 [string]$computername="$env:COMPUTERNAME"
)
PROCESS {
  Get-WmiObject -Class Win32_printer `
  -ComputerName $computername |
 select Name, Default, Direct, DoCompleteFirst,
 HorizontalResolution, VerticalResolution,
 KeepPrintedJobs, Local, Network, PortName, PrintJobDataType,
 PrintProcessor, Priority, Published, Queued, RawOnly, Shared,
 WorkOffline
}}
```

The working part of the function uses the `Win32_Printer` class on the required system. This will pull back the properties defined to `Select-Object`, which are then displayed.

The function outputs an object that the PowerShell engine then displays in the default manner. This enables you to use the function at the prompt and perform further filtering if required, as shown in figure 10.1, where the printer name and whether it's the default or shared are listed.

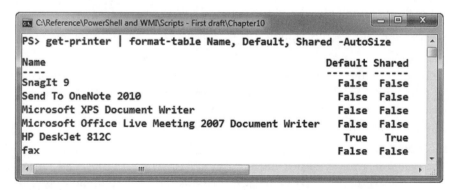

Figure 10.1   Filtering the output of the `get-printer` function

DISCUSSION

One common requirement is to determine the default printer on a system. You could use the get-printer function as shown in figure 10.1, or you can access the information directly:

```
Get-WmiObject -Class Win32_Printer -Filter "Default='$true'" |
Select Name
```

The properties defined to Select-Object can be modified to suit your particular purposes.

It can be useful to examine the WMI classes associated with your printer:

```
Get-WmiObject -Query "ASSOCIATORS OF
➥ {Win32_Printer.DeviceId='HP DeskJet 812C'} WHERE CLASSDefsOnly"
```

> **TIP** You have to use the DeviceId parameter rather than the name to find the associations in this case. If you're in doubt about which property to try, look at the Path property and use that syntax.

The Win32_PrinterDriver and Win32_PrinterConfiguration classes are the only results that look to be of interest:

```
Get-WmiObject -Query "ASSOCIATORS OF
➥ {Win32_Printer.DeviceId='HP DeskJet 812C'}
➥ WHERE ResultClass = Win32_PrinterConfiguration"
```

The results show that the Win32_PrinterConfiguration class doesn't add much to your knowledge of printers because it contains the same information as the Win32_Printer class. We'll return to the Win32_PrinterDriver class in technique 67.

The other thing you need to be able to determine is what your printers can do.

TECHNIQUE 65   **Testing printer capabilities**

Printers come in all shapes and sizes. They have a large number of possible capabilities, such as

- Printing to specific paper sizes
- Printing in color
- Printing on both sides of the paper (duplex)

The printer name or description usually doesn't carry this information.

PROBLEM

Common questions from users include, "Which printer can I use to produce color output?" and "Which printers will print on both sides of the paper?" There are also requests to determine which printers support specific paper sizes. You need to be able to answer these questions easily and quickly.

SOLUTION

The solution involves unraveling the CapabilityDescriptions and PrinterPaper-Names properties of the Win32_Printer class, as shown in the following listing. These properties are collections that WMI doesn't deal with very well. You can use the Power-Shell -contains operator to solve this. You can also use the PowerShell advanced function capabilities to validate your input.

Listing 10.2   Test printer capabilities

```
function test-printercapabilities {
[CmdletBinding(DefaultParameterSetName="Pcap")]
param (
 [parameter(ValueFromPipeline=$true,
   ValueFromPipelineByPropertyName=$true)]
 [string]$computername="$env:COMPUTERNAME",

 [parameter(ParameterSetName="Pcap")]
 [string]
 [ValidateSet("Duplex", "Color", "Collate")]
 $capability="Color",

 [parameter(ParameterSetName="Paper")]
 [string]
 [ValidateSet("Letter", "Legal", "Executive", "A4", "A3")]
 $paper

 )
PROCESS {
$printers = Get-WmiObject -Class Win32_Printer  `
-ComputerName $computername

switch ($psCmdlet.ParameterSetName) {
  "Pcap" {
    "$capability printers on $computername"
    $printers |
    Where {$_.CapabilityDescriptions -contains $capability} |
    select Name
  }
  "Paper" {
    "$paper printers on $computername"
    $printers |
    Where {$_.PrinterPaperNames -contains $paper} |
    select Name
  }

 }
}
}
```

❶ Define parameter sets

❷ Switch statement

Two parameters are defined in addition to the usual computer name parameter ❶. In both cases, you use the ValidateSet() advanced function parameter to restrict the input to predefined paper sizes and printer capabilities. The examples presented in the code are the common sizes and capabilities and can easily be changed to items that meet your particular requirements.

The -capability and -paper parameters are presented as two parameter sets. The -computername parameter isn't labeled as being a member of an individual parameter set, so it's a member of both. Parameter sets restrict the parameters that can be used together so you can test for paper size or printer capability but not both together. The use of a default parameter set and default values means that you can run the function without using any parameters and it won't fail.

Get-WmiObject is used to fetch the WMI objects representing all of the printers on the target machine. A switch statement based on the parameter set name is used to display the printers that match either the desired capability or printer size ❷. This is achieved by using the -contains operator to test if the capability or paper type is a member of the collection returned by the relevant property.

DISCUSSION

Ideally, filtering should be performed as soon as possible, but in this particular case it's easier to use Where-Object. The full range of possible paper types a printer supports can be found by using the -ExpandProperty parameter of Select-Object:

```
Get-WmiObject -Class Win32_Printer -Filter "Default='$true'" |
select -ExpandProperty PrinterPaperNames
```

If you introduce ForEach-Object into the code, you can get a nice output where you display the printer name and then the paper types it supports:

```
Get-WmiObject -Class Win32_Printer |
foreach {
"`n $($_.Name)"
$_ | select -ExpandProperty PrinterPaperNames
}
```

A similar activity can be performed for printer capabilities:

```
Get-WmiObject -Class Win32_Printer -Filter "Default='$true'" |
select -ExpandProperty CapabilityDescriptions
```

On my system, using an HP DeskJet 812C, the following capabilities are reported:

- Copies
- Color
- Collate

Servers connect to printers via printer ports. You need to be able to discover the printer ports to further your understanding of the printing environment.

TECHNIQUE 66   Discovering printer ports

Most of the information about printer ports can be found by using the Win32_Printer class:

```
Get-WmiObject -Class Win32_Printer | select Name, PortName
```

This works well for USB, old-style parallel ports, and the ports created for the fax system or applications such as Microsoft OneNote. It doesn't work for TCP/IP ports.

PROBLEM

Many of your printers are networked rather than being directly attached to a server. You need to discover the relevant TCP/IP ports used to connect to these servers.

SOLUTION

Listing 10.3 presents a solution for this problem using the `Win32_TCPIPPrinterPort` class. There are two possible protocols used to print to networked devices: the original LPR protocol or the newer RAW protocol. The protocol is stored as a numeric value. The listing starts by defining a hash table to be used as a lookup for the protocol meaning.

Listing 10.3   List TCP/IP printer ports

```
$pp = DATA {
ConvertFrom-StringData -StringData @'
1 = RAW Printing directly to a device or print server.
2 = LPR Legacy protocol, which is eventually replaced by RAW
'@
}

function get-tcpport {
[CmdletBinding()]
param (
 [parameter(ValueFromPipeline=$true,
   ValueFromPipelineByPropertyName=$true)]
 [string]$computername="$env:COMPUTERNAME"
)
PROCESS {
Get-WmiObject -Class Win32_TCPIPPrinterPort    `
  -ComputerName $computername |
select Name, HostAddress, PortNumber,
@{N="Protocol"; E={$pp["$($_.Protocol)"]}},
SNMPCommunity, SNMPDevIndex, SNMPEnabled

}}
```

The `get-tcpport` function has a single parameter for a computer name. It then uses the `Win32_TCPIPPrinterPort` class to retrieve data about the ports. The properties are filtered using `Select-Object`, including the lookup of the printing protocol.

DISCUSSION

The last three properties are important in that they define the Simple Network Management Protocol (SNMP) configuration of the port. SNMP is a protocol for managing devices on IP networks. The `SNMPCommunity` property shouldn't be set to `Public` or any other well-known setting. If it's configured in that way, you need to talk to your network administrators.

The last configuration item to investigate is printer drivers.

TECHNIQUE 67   **Discovering printer drivers**

Printers, like all computer peripherals, need drivers to enable the computer operating system to communicate with the printer. Printer drivers seem to be more prone to causing problems than other drivers. A simple way of checking the driver version can be very useful.

PROBLEM

You have a number of printers, of the same type, scattered throughout the organization. Most of them are functioning correctly, but one or two are causing problems. You need to check that the drivers are the same across all of the printers.

SOLUTION

You could use the `Win32_PrinterDriver` class to get information about the printer drivers installed on the system. This, however, isn't the best way to solve the problem because you want to associate the driver with the printer. WMI associations can enable you to do this, as shown in the following listing.

Listing 10.4   Discover printer drivers

```
function get-printerdriver {
[CmdletBinding()]
param (
 [parameter(ValueFromPipeline=$true,
   ValueFromPipelineByPropertyName=$true)]
 [string]$computername="$env:COMPUTERNAME",

 [string]$printer
)
PROCESS {
$query = "ASSOCIATORS OF {Win32_Printer.DeviceId='$printer'}
  ➥ WHERE ResultClass = Win32_PrinterDriver"

$driver = Get-WmiObject -ComputerName $computername -Query $query

"Driver for $printer"
$driver | select Version, SupportedPlatform, OEMUrl,
DriverPath, ConfigFile, DataFile, HelpFile

" Dependent Files"
$driver | select -ExpandProperty DependentFiles

}}
```

The `get-printerdriver` function accepts a computer and a printer name as parameters. Both parameters are optional. A WMI query is created by substituting the printer name into the string. Notice that you need to use the `DeviceId` property to identify the printer, instead of the `Name` property.

The query is run against the printer, and the results are held in the `$driver` variable because you want to access them twice. The driver information is selected and displayed, including the driver version. The dependent files property is then expanded to show the other files that are loaded with this driver.

DISCUSSION

The `-printer` parameter in this function could be made mandatory to ensure that it's entered. At present the function throws an error if a printer name isn't supplied. You've seen how to make parameters mandatory in several functions already. Modifying this script will be a good test of your understanding.

In theory, you could use PowerShell and WMI to install printer drivers, as this code from PowerShell MVP Aleksandar Nikiloc shows:

```
$server = "PrintServer"
$printdriver = [wmiclass]"Win32_PrinterDriver"
$driver = $printdriver.CreateInstance()

$driver.Name="HP2420"
$driver.DriverPath = "\\$server\drivers\printers\hp\lj2420"
$driver.Infname = "\\$server\drivers\printers\hp\lj2420\hpc24x0c.inf"

$printdriver.AddPrinterDriver($driver)
$printdriver.Put()
```

Personally, in an enterprise, I prefer to install drivers via a software distribution mechanism such as System Center, as I find there is more flexibility. It's interesting that Microsoft has added an `Add-PrinterDriver` cmdlet in Windows 8, but it's based on a new `MSFT_PrinterDriver` class rather than the `Win32_PrinterDriver` class.

You know how to find the printers that are available and their capabilities. Now you need to consider whether the printer is available to the user.

10.2 Printer status

Printer status can be split into two parts. The first part is the printer itself: Is it online and available to the user? The second part is the print jobs sent to the printer: Is there anything stopping a print job being produced? This section will answer both questions, starting with the status of the printer.

TECHNIQUE 68 Testing printer status

When considering the status of printers, you may see references to a `PrinterState` property. This property has been deprecated by Microsoft, which means it will be removed in a future version of Windows.

PROBLEM

A user is having difficulties printing. You need to check on the status of the printer to determine if the problem is confined to a single user or will affect many users because the printer is unavailable.

SOLUTION

The following listing presents a quick function that will return the status of the printers connected to a particular machine.

Listing 10.5 Test printer status

```
$pstatus = DATA {
ConvertFrom-StringData -StringData @'
1 = Other
2 = Unknown
3 = Idle
4 = Printing
5 = Warming Up
```

```
6 = Stopped printing
7 = Offline
'@
}

function get-printerstatus {
[CmdletBinding()]
param (
 [parameter(ValueFromPipeline=$true,
   ValueFromPipelineByPropertyName=$true)]
 [string]$computername="$env:COMPUTERNAME"
)
PROCESS {
  Get-WmiObject -Class Win32_printer `
  -ComputerName $computername |
 select Name,
 @{N="Status"; E={$pstatus["$($_.PrinterStatus)"]}}
} }
```

A hash table is used to define the meanings of the numeric status codes returned by
WMI. The function only takes a computer name as a parameter. `Get-WmiObject`
returns the printer objects. The printer name and a descriptive version of the status
are displayed. The numeric status value is converted to the description using the hash
table lookup defined at the beginning of the listing.

DISCUSSION

This listing could be combined with listing 10.1 if a single function to investigate
printers is required.

The calculated field uses `N` and `E` as abbreviations for `Name` and `Expression` respectively. You've seen the full names used in previous listings; they'll be abbreviated in
future listings to save space where necessary.

Printers are just the devices you use to print. Users are often much more interested
in the jobs they've submitted to the printer, especially if those jobs haven't appeared.

TECHNIQUE 69   **Listing print jobs**

Printers can find many ways to go wrong. The paper jams, they run out of toner, or the
maintenance warnings start to flash. Many of these issues can stop the user's printout
from appearing.

PROBLEM

Users are complaining that their printout isn't appearing. You need to check the print
jobs associated with the printer to determine if there is a backlog that could indicate a
problem.

SOLUTION

It isn't unknown for users to send print jobs to the wrong printer and then complain
that they can't find them. You can use the `Win32_PrintJob` class to determine which
print jobs are still outstanding for a particular printer. The following listing shows how
you can test a single printer or all of the printers on a server.

Listing 10.6 List print jobs

```
function get-printjob {
[CmdletBinding()]
param (
 [parameter(ValueFromPipeline=$true,
   ValueFromPipelineByPropertyName=$true)]
 [string]$computername="$env:COMPUTERNAME",
 [string]$printer
)
PROCESS {
  if (-not $printer ){
    $pjobs = Get-WmiObject -Class Win32_PrintJob `
     -ComputerName $computername
  }
  else {
    $pjobs = Get-WmiObject -Class Win32_PrintJob `
     -ComputerName $computername -filter "DriverName='$printer'"
  }

  $pjobs | select Document, JobId, Name, PagesPrinted,
  Status, Color, DataType, DriverName, Owner,
  PaperSize, Size, TotalPages,
  @{N="SubmissionTime"; E={$($_.ConvertToDateTime($_.TimeSubmitted))}}
}}
```

The get-printjob function takes the usual computer name as a parameter. It also has an optional parameter of a printer name. If the -printer parameter isn't supplied, Get-WmiObject is used with the Win32_PrintJob class to return all of the print jobs on the designated computer. Inputting a printer name causes a filter to be used that restricts the output to the print jobs for the designated printer. Notice that the filtering is performed on DriverName not printer name. This is an artifact of WMI in the way the classes are coded. WMI associations can't be used to link the Win32_Printer class and the Win32_PrintJob class.

The collection of print jobs is piped into Select-Object. A calculated field is used to determine the time the print job was submitted.

DISCUSSION

The function is used as follows:

```
get-printjob
get-printjob -printer "HP DeskJet 812C"
```

The first example will display all of the print jobs on the local machine, and the second will display those for the "HP DeskJet 812C" printer.

Remove-WmiObject can be used to delete print jobs:

```
Get-WmiObject Win32_PrintJob | Remove-WmiObject
```

Where-Object could be used to restrict the jobs being deleted. It isn't easy to filter a print job on its name as it's a combination of the printer name and the JobId, as shown in figure 10.2.

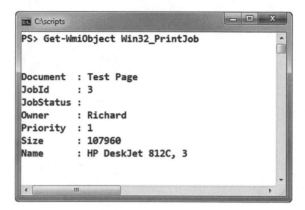

Figure 10.2 `Win32_PrintJob`
output

The `Owner` property would be a useful filter if you needed to find all of the print jobs for a single user.

The `Pause` and `Resume` methods on `Win32_PrintJob` can be used to control print jobs. For example, this code will halt all print jobs on a server:

```
Get-WmiObject Win32_PrintJob | Invoke-WmiMethod -Name Pause
```

The `Resume` method can be used to restart printing. This is discussed further in technique 72.

That concludes our investigation of the printer configuration and status. The next step is to look at how you can manage printers using WMI.

10.3   *Managing printers*

Printer management tasks can be split into two broad groups. The first group comprises mundane tasks such as adding paper, changing toner or ink supplies, and clearing jams. Unfortunately WMI can't help with this sort of activity.

> **TIP** A bonus function, `get-printersecurity`, is available in the download code for this chapter. It can be used to determine the security permissions set on a shared printer.

The second group of tasks comprises activities such as printing a test page, pausing and restarting the printer, and renaming a printer. The act of setting a default printer also falls into this group, and it's the first task we'll examine.

TECHNIQUE 70   **Setting a default printer**

All users have a default printer defined if they have any printers installed. The default printer is the one an application will print to if the print icon is clicked and then the Print button is clicked. It's also the printer used by the `Out-Print` cmdlet if a printer isn't specified.

This example will send the output to the default printer:

```
Get-WmiObject -Class Win32_Printer |
select Name, PortName | Out-Printer
```

PROBLEM

A significant number of users have moved location within your organization. Their new printer has been configured. Now you need to set the new printer as their default printer.

SOLUTION

The following listing shows how you can use the `Win32_Printer` class to solve this problem.

Listing 10.7 Set default printer

```
function set-defaultprinter {
[CmdletBinding()]
param (
 [parameter(ValueFromPipeline=$true,
   ValueFromPipelineByPropertyName=$true)]
 [string]$computername="$env:COMPUTERNAME",

 [string]$printer
)
PROCESS {
Get-WmiObject -Class Win32_Printer `
-ComputerName $computername -Filter "Name='$printer'" |
Invoke-WmiMethod -Name SetDefaultPrinter

}}
```

The function accepts the usual computer name and printer parameters. The appropriate printer instance is retrieved using `Get-WmiObject` with the printer name as the filter. It's piped to `Invoke-WmiMethod`, where the `SetDefaultPrinter` method of the `Win32_Printer` class is called.

DISCUSSION

The default printer can be discovered using the `get-printer` function from listing 10.1. This is demonstrated in figure 10.3, where the following code is used:

```
get-printer | where{$_.Default
   -eq $true}
```

Alternatively, the `Win32_Printer` class can be used at the prompt, as explained in the discussion of technique 64.

Once you've set the default printer, you'll probably want to print a test page from it to ensure that it works for the user.

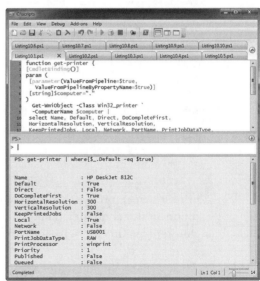

Figure 10.3 Discovering the default printer

| TECHNIQUE 71 | **Printing a test page** |

Most printers have the ability to print a test page. This is often done to prove connectivity, that the printer is configured correctly, or that the printer hardware is working. Talking a user through producing a test page can be difficult.

PROBLEM

Printing a test page is a good diagnostic technique. You need to be able to perform this task, remotely, for a user on their machine.

SOLUTION

The `Win32_Printer` class can also solve this problem for you as the following listing demonstrates.

Listing 10.8   Print test page

```
function send-testpage {
[CmdletBinding()]
param (
 [parameter(ValueFromPipeline=$true,
   ValueFromPipelineByPropertyName=$true)]
 [string]$computername="$env:COMPUTERNAME",

 [parameter(ParameterSetName="NonDefPrint")]
 [string]$printer,

 [parameter(ParameterSetName="DefPrint")]
 [switch]$default
)
PROCESS {
 switch ($psCmdlet.ParameterSetName) {
  NonDefPrint {$filt = "Name='$printer'"}
  Defprint {$filt = "Default='$true'" }
 }

 $device = Get-WmiObject -Class Win32_printer `
 -Filter $filt -ComputerName $computername

 if ($device) {
  $device | Invoke-WmiMethod -Name PrintTestPage
 }
 else {
  "Printer not found"
 }
}}
```

A printer name and switch parameter that selects the default printer are defined, in addition to the computer name parameter. The printer and default parameters are in different parameter sets, with the computer name parameter being a member of both.

A `Switch` statement creates a WMI filter based on the parameter set selected. It will either create a filter based on the printer name or on the fact that the target printer is the default printer.

The WMI object representing the printer is retrieved and put into the $device variable. If a printer is found that matches the filter criteria, the object represented by $device is piped into Invoke-WmiMethod where the PrintTestpage method is called. A message stating that the printer couldn't be found is produced if the $device variable is NULL (empty).

DISCUSSION

On my development system, these will both work:

```
send-testpage -printer "Send To OneNote 2010"
send-testpage -default
```

The following command will fail because the printer doesn't exist:

```
send-testpage -printer "Send To OneNote 2001"
```

You can also use a simple loop to send multiple test pages:

```
1..5 | foreach {send-testpage -default}
```

> **TIP**   This is an easy way to build up a number of print jobs to experiment with for listing 10.6 and technique 72.

There are times when you need to control the printer, pause, and resume, so that essential maintenance can be performed. It's recommended that you inform the users before this happens to avoid a lot of irate callers.

TECHNIQUE 72   **Controlling printers**

Remote control of the printer could involve working at the individual job level or at the printer level. You saw in technique 69 that you can pipe Win32_PrintJob objects into Remove-WmiObject to delete print jobs individually or in groups.

The Win32_PrintJob class has Pause and Resume methods that can be used to control print jobs. Pausing the print job is performed in this manner:

```
Get-WmiObject Win32_Printjob -Filter "JobId=7" |
Invoke-WmiMethod -Name Pause
```

The job is started again by using the Resume method:

```
Get-WmiObject Win32_Printjob -Filter "JobId=7" |
Invoke-WmiMethod -Name Resume
```

You can pause all of the jobs destined for a particular printer by filtering on the printer name. You have to use the DriverName property to perform the filtering:

```
Get-WmiObject Win32_Printjob `
-Filter "DriverName='HP DeskJet 812C'" |
Invoke-WmiMethod -Name Pause
```

The state of the print jobs can be tested using the get-printjob function from listing 10.4, or you can use the WMI class directly:

```
Get-WmiObject Win32_Printjob `
-Filter "DriverName='HP DeskJet 812C'" |
select name, JobStatus
```

You can also control the printer rather than the print jobs.

PROBLEM

You have a printer that needs some maintenance work. You have to stop jobs that have been submitted from printing but still allow new jobs to be submitted and queued until the printer is ready.

SOLUTION

The following listing demonstrates a solution to this problem.

Listing 10.9   Pause and resume printer

```
function set-printer {
[CmdletBinding()]
param (
 [parameter(ValueFromPipeline=$true,
   ValueFromPipelineByPropertyName=$true)]
 [string]$computername="$env:COMPUTERNAME",

 [string]$printer,

 [parameter(ParameterSetName="Pause")]
 [switch]$pause,

 [parameter(ParameterSetName="Resume")]
 [switch]$resume,

 [parameter(ParameterSetName="Cancel")]
 [switch]$cancelall

)
PROCESS {
$device = Get-WmiObject -Class Win32_Printer `
-ComputerName $computername -Filter "Name='$printer'"

 switch ($psCmdlet.ParameterSetName) {
  Pause {$device | Invoke-WmiMethod -Name Pause}
  Resume {$device | Invoke-WmiMethod -Name Resume }
  Cancel {$device | Invoke-WmiMethod -Name CancelAllJobs }
  }

}
}
```

The computer and printer parameters are joined by three switches that pause printing, resume printing, or cancel all print jobs. The printer object is put into the `$device` variable, which, depending on the parameter set being used, is piped into an instance of `Invoke-WmiMethod` that calls the correct method to perform the task.

DISCUSSION

The function is used like this (assuming it has already been loaded):

```
set-printer -printer "HP DeskJet 812C" -cancelall
```

If a printer isn't supplied, an error is thrown. Error checking similar to that performed in listing 10.8 could be added to the function.

The final management task we need to consider in this chapter is renaming a printer.

Renaming a printer

Renaming a printer isn't a task that you'll need to perform every day, but it does become useful when you're changing the way you do things in the organization. Another potential reason for changing printer names is that you have to change the printer.

PROBLEM

A printer has been changed, and you need to rename it to match user expectations and your organization's naming standards. You can also reduce the level of help desk calls if the users are able to find printers themselves.

SOLUTION

It would be possible to send instructions to the users so they could perform this task themselves, but that would potentially introduce another source of error into the environment. Instead, you can use the `Win32_Printer` class to solve this problem as shown in the following listing.

Listing 10.10   Rename a printer

```
function rename-printer {
[CmdletBinding()]
param (
 [parameter(ValueFromPipeline=$true,
   ValueFromPipelineByPropertyName=$true)]
 [string]$computername="$env:COMPUTERNAME",

 [string]$printer,
 [string]$newname
)
PROCESS {
Get-WmiObject -Class Win32_Printer `
-ComputerName $computername -Filter "Name='$printer'" |
Invoke-WmiMethod -Name RenamePrinter -ArgumentList $newname

}}
```

Three parameters are required by the `rename-printer` function, namely computer name, printer, and its new name. The WMI object representing the printer is retrieved using `Get-WmiObject`. The object's `RenamePrinter` method is called by piping the printer object into `Invoke-WmiMethod`.

DISCUSSION

The function is used in this way:

```
rename-printer -printer fax -newname test21
```

Neither parameter checking nor error recovery has been included in the function. There are sufficient examples in the other listings in the chapter to illustrate how this could be achieved.

This concludes our use of WMI to manage printers.

10.4   *Summary*

Printers may be viewed as a necessary evil, but until the day of the paperless office really arrives they're something you have to live with and manage. WMI is an excellent tool for discovering information about your computing and printing environment.

The functions in this chapter supply the capability of remotely managing printers across your organization but are customizable to meet your exact requirements. With them, you're able to

- Discover printers and their configuration
- Test printer capabilities and status
- Discover existing print jobs
- Find printer ports and drivers

You can also use PowerShell and WMI to actively manage your printers by

- Setting the default printer
- Printing a test page
- Controlling printers and print jobs
- Renaming printers

Being able to perform these tasks in a more efficient manner won't change your view of printers, but it will make life easier when you have to manage them.

In chapter 11 we'll look at networking and you'll see how PowerShell and WMI enable you to manage network cards across the environment.

11
Configuring network adapters

This chapter covers

- Network adapters, configuration, and protocols
- Managing network adapters
- Configuring DHCP and static addresses
- Managing entries for DNS and WINS servers
- Displaying the IPv4 routing table

Networking is the glue that holds your infrastructure together. If the network isn't working or configured correctly the users can't connect to the applications and you can't administer the systems. Your primary concern is the configuration of the network adapters in your servers. This chapter presents a number of techniques you can use to test the configuration and configure the network adapters.

NOTE The WMI networking classes, and especially their methods, discussed in this chapter only work with IPv4. As of Windows 7 and Windows Server 2008 R2, WMI isn't able to configure IPv6 settings.

Table 11.1 presents the WMI classes that you can use to work with network adapters. You'll be using many of them in this chapter. The `Win32_NetworkAdapter` and `Win32_NetworkAdapterConfiguration` classes can cause some confusion. The first one deals with the physical adapter and the second with the configuration of the device.

Table 11.1   WMI networking-related classes

Class	Use
`Win32_NetworkAdapter`	Works with physical adapters
`Win32_NetworkAdapterConfiguration`	Works with adapter settings
`Win32_NetworkAdapterSetting`	Associates `Win32_NetworkAdapter` and `Win32_NetworkAdapterConfiguration`
`Win32_NetworkConnection`	Displays information about the active network connections on a Windows system
`Win32_NetworkProtocol`	Displays the network protocols and their characteristics associated with an adapter
`Win32_NetworkClient`	Displays information regarding the network client software installed on the system
`Win32_IP4RouteTable`	Displays information about IP routing from the system

> **NOTE**   `Win32_NetworkConnection` doesn't seem to work on Windows 7 SP1. It does work on Windows Server 2008 R2.

This chapter begins with a section that explains how you can discover information about the network adapters in your systems. We'll look at techniques to discover the physical adapters and their configuration and then consider the network protocols associated with an adapter. The section closes with a look at the connections mapped from a machine.

The second section shows how you can configure a computer's adapters. This includes enabling, disabling, and renaming the adapters. Once you have the network adapters enabled, you need to configure the IP addresses.

The third section illustrates how you can configure the adapters to accept addresses from DHCP or to have static addresses set for the adapter. You need to be able to view the DHCP configuration and control the lease. If a static address is set it's important that you set a default gateway as well.

In the fourth section of the chapter, we'll look at setting the Domain Name System (DNS) and Windows Internet Name Service (WINS) servers your systems will use, and you'll see how to display the routing table.

Regardless of what you're doing you need to be able to discover the network adapters in your systems before you can work with them.

11.1 Discovering network adapters

Network adapters are the physical devices you rely on to link your computers to the network. In this section, we'll start by looking at how you can discover the physical network adapters that are installed in your system. Those adapters have a configuration that you need to be able to access to determine if their settings are correct. Discovering the adapter configuration is the second task you'll learn to perform.

Network protocols are used to perform the communication between systems, and communication can break down if the protocols associated with an adapter aren't configured correctly. This section's third technique demonstrates how protocols can be related to a network adapter.

Computers can have connections defined that enable access to resources on other machines. These connections may be critical to the continued performance of your applications and need to be checked. This section closes by examining the connections a machine makes and, where appropriate, discovering information about the remote disk accessed through that connection.

Until you've determined what network adapters are installed in your system you can't do anything else.

TECHNIQUE 74   Identifying network adapters

Network adapters (also known as *network interface cards* or NICs) are the starting point for our discussion. They're also the foundation for administering network-related issues. There are a number of different types of adapters—the laptop I'm using to write this has these adapters:

- 1 wireless adapter
- 1 Ethernet adapter
- 1 Bluetooth adapter
- 3 Microsoft ISATAP adapters (provides ability to transmit IPv6 on IPv4 networks)
- 1 RAS async adapter
- 1 Teredo tunneling adapter
- 8 WAN miniport adapters

That's a lot of adapters, and many of them won't be used the majority of the time. You need to be able to determine which adapters are carrying useful traffic on your systems.

PROBLEM

You need to identify the network adapters in your system so that you can determine which ones are carrying the traffic to your applications. This will also enable you to identify the adapters with which you'll be working.

SOLUTION

Using table 11.1 or `Get-WmiObject -List *network*`, you can determine that the `Win32_NetworkAdapter` class will satisfy your needs. The following listing shows how you can use this class in a PowerShell function.

Listing 11.1   Listing network adapters

```
function get-nic {
[CmdletBinding()]
param (
 [parameter(ValueFromPipeline=$true,
   ValueFromPipelineByPropertyName=$true)]
 [string]$computername="$env:COMPUTERNAME",
 [int]$device
)
PROCESS {
if ($device) {
 $nics = Get-WmiObject -Class Win32_NetWorkAdapter `
 -ComputerName $computername -Filter "DeviceID='$device'"
}
else {
 $nics = Get-WmiObject -Class Win32_NetWorkAdapter `
 -ComputerName $computername
}
 $nics | select NetConnectionID, Name, DeviceID,
 AdapterType, AutoSense, GUID, Index, Installed,
 InterfaceIndex, MACAddress, Manufacturer, MaxSpeed,
 NetConnectionStatus, NetEnabled, PhysicalAdapter,
 ProductName, ServiceName, Speed
}}
```

The usual computer name parameter is used so you can access remote machines, and it's joined by a -device parameter. This takes an integer value that's the DeviceId of a particular adapter.

> **NOTE**   Most if not all of the functions in the remaining part of the book will have a -computername parameter. It will be shown in the code but not necessarily mentioned in the text to avoid repetition.

Get-WmiObject is used with the Win32_NetworkAdapter class to return data on all adapters or a single adapter to a variable called $nics. Whether it returns data for one or all adapters is controlled by the use of the -device parameter. The contents of the $nics variable are piped into Select-Object, where the required properties are selected. These are then displayed by the PowerShell engine.

DISCUSSION

A Selected.System.Management.ManagementObject type is output by the function. This means that you can use your function as the start of a pipeline. If you only wanted to see information on physical adapters, you could use this snippet:

```
get-nic | where{$_.PhysicalAdapter}
```

This would include the wireless and Ethernet adapters but exclude the WAN miniport adapters if applied to the list of adapters on my laptop.

There are a number of properties that could be used to identify a network adapter, including the following:

- NetConnectionID
- DeviceId
- GUID
- MACAddress
- ProductName

So why use the DeviceId? Because it's the key parameter for the class. In a number of techniques earlier in the book, I mentioned looking at the Path property to determine the property you can use to test for WMI associations. In the case of a network adapter you'd get something like this:

```
\\RSLAPTOP01\root\cimv2:Win32_NetworkAdapter.DeviceID="11"
```

You can also get the key property by using the following function (which I borrowed from the PowerShell Team blog—I promise to give it back when I've finished with it):

```
function Get-WmiKey
{
  $class = [wmiclass]$args[0]
  $class.Properties |
  Select @{Name="PName";Expression={$_.name}} -Expand Qualifiers |
  Where {$_.Name -eq "key"} | foreach {$_.Pname}
}
```

The get-nic function can be used to return the Name and DeviceId of all adapters in a machine, as shown in figure 11.1.

The physical configuration of the network adapter is only half the story. You also need data about the IP address and other items that relate to actual communication through the adapter.

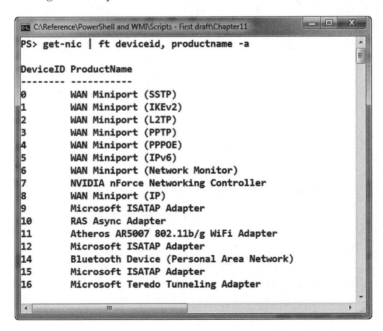

Figure 11.1 Using the get-nic function to discover network adapter DeviceIDs

TECHNIQUE 75   ## Discovering adapter configurations

The network adapters for your system have been located using listing 11.1. Unfortunately, the `Win32_NetworkAdapter` class doesn't supply IP addressing information, which is an essential item if you're to administer your servers.

PROBLEM

Users are reporting issues communicating with a particular server. The network adapter appears to be functioning, but you need to check that the IP addressing is configured correctly.

SOLUTION

The following listing shows how this problem can be solved. The code is similar to listing 11.1, with the main difference being the use of the `Win32_NetworkAdapter-Configuration` class.

Listing 11.2 Display the network adapter configuration

```
$nbstatus = DATA {
ConvertFrom-StringData -StringData @'
0 = EnableNetbiosViaDhcp
1 = EnableNetbios
2 = DisableNetbios
'@
}

function get-nicsetting {
[CmdletBinding()]
param (
 [parameter(ValueFromPipeline=$true,
   ValueFromPipelineByPropertyName=$true)]
 [string]$computername="$env:COMPUTERNAME",
 [int]$index
)
PROCESS {
if ($index) {
 $nics = Get-WmiObject -Class Win32_NetWorkAdapterConfiguration `
 -ComputerName $computername -Filter "Index='$index'"
}
else {
 $nics = Get-WmiObject -Class Win32_NetWorkAdapterConfiguration `
 -ComputerName $computername
}

 $nics | select ServiceName, Description, Index,
DHCPEnabled, DHCPServer,
@{N="DHCPLeaseStart"; E={$_.ConvertToDateTime($_.DHCPLeaseObtained)}},
@{N="DHCPLeaseEnd"; E={$_.ConvertToDateTime($_.DHCPLeaseExpires)}},
IPEnabled, IPAddress, IPSubnet, DefaultIPGateway,
IPConnectionMetric,  IPFilterSecurityEnabled,
DNSDomain, DNSDomainSuffixSearchOrder, DNSEnabledForWINSResolution,
DNSHostName, DNSServerSearchOrder, DomainDNSRegistrationEnabled,
FullDNSRegistrationEnabled, WINSEnableLMHostsLookup,
WINSHostLookupFile, WINSPrimaryServer, WINSScopeID,
```

```
WINSSecondaryServer, DatabasePath, DeadGWDetectEnabled,
DefaultTOS, DefaultTTL, ForwardBufferMemory, GatewayCostMetric,
IGMPLevel, InterfaceIndex, IPPortSecurityEnabled,
IPSecPermitIPProtocols, IPSecPermitTCPPorts, IPSecPermitUDPPorts,
IPUseZeroBroadcast, KeepAliveInterval, KeepAliveTime, MACAddress,
MTU, NumForwardPackets, PMTUBHDetectEnabled, PMTUDiscoveryEnabled,
SettingID,
@{N="NetBIOSOption"; E={$nbstatus["$($_.TcpipNetbiosOptions)"]}},
TcpMaxConnectRetransmissions, TcpMaxDataRetransmissions,
TcpNumConnections, TcpUseRFC1122UrgentPointer,
TcpWindowSize
}}

}
```

A hash table is defined to enable the lookup of the TCPIPNetBios setting value. This function uses -index as the parameter, instead of -device as in listing 11.1. Index is the key value for the Win32_NetworkAdapterConfiguration class, which can be confusing because it takes the same numeric value as the Win32_NetworkAdapter DeviceId property when referring to the same adapter. This can be illustrated on your system by running this code.

```
Get-WmiObject -Class Win32_NetworkAdapterSetting |
Format-Table Element, Setting -AutoSize
```

> **TIP** I recommend running the previous code using PowerShell ISE rather than a PowerShell console as the output is rather wide.

By default, information is returned on all adapters in the system unless the -index parameter is used. This parameter takes an integer value as input. The resultant information, held in the $nics variable, is piped into Select-Object. A number of calculated fields are defined. Two convert the start and end dates of the DHCP lease from WMI format to a more readable format. The third calculated field resolves the TCPIP-NetBIOS property from its integer value to an understandable description.

DISCUSSION

The script may look ugly with the large set of properties in the Select-Object, but if you compare it to the information put out by the WMI class you'll see that the function is filtering out a lot of nonessential or empty properties. A lot of the information presented by the get-nicsetting function will be very familiar if you've used ipconfig.exe. The function could just as easily have been called get-ipconfig!

> **NOTE** The IPX protocol settings have been deliberately excluded. If you require them, please check the WMI documentation for details and add the properties into the function.

There is a WMI association between the Win32_NetworkAdapter and Win32_NetworkAdapterConfiguration classes:

```
Get-WmiObject -Query "ASSOCIATORS OF
    ➥ {Win32_NetworkAdapter.DeviceID=7} WHERE
    ➥ ResultClass=Win32_NetworkAdapterConfiguration"
```

Alternatively, the two functions in listings 11.1 and 11.2 could be used like this:

```
7,11 | foreach {get-nic -device $_; get-nicsetting -index $_}
```

The preceding line of code will display the adapter information and the configuration information for network adapters whose `DeviceId` is 7 or 11.

You could even use these functions in other PowerShell functions, like this:

```
function get-ipconfig {
[CmdletBinding()]
param (
 [parameter(ValueFromPipeline=$true,
   ValueFromPipelineByPropertyName=$true)]
 [string]$computername="$env:COMPUTERNAME",
 [parameter(ValueFromPipeline=$true,
   ValueFromPipelineByPropertyName=$true)]
  [int]$device
)
PROCESS{
 get-nic -computername $computername -device $device
 get-nicsetting -computername $computername -index $device
}}
```

> **NOTE**   This function is available in the code download. See get-ipconfig.ps1.

The physical and IP addressing configuration information needs to be supplemented by the protocols bound to the individual adapters.

TECHNIQUE 76   **Listing an adapter's network protocols**

You're mainly interested in the TCP/IP protocol suite being available on the Ethernet adapters for the servers in your enterprise environment. Other protocols may be of interest at the workstation level.

The network protocols are associated to adapters by WMI as can be shown by testing an individual adapter:

```
gwmi -Query "ASSOCIATORS OF {Win32_NetworkAdapter.DeviceId=7}
   ➥ WHERE ClassDefsOnly"
```

When you look at the `Win32_NetworkProtocol` class, you'll see that there isn't a property such as `DeviceId` or `Index` that enables you to identify the adapter to which the protocol is bound. You need to approach the problem in a slightly different way.

PROBLEM

The network protocols bound to your adapters need to be checked to ensure that the required protocols are available and that they're configured correctly.

SOLUTION

The following listing builds on what you know about network adapters and uses WMI associations to link the protocols to the adapter.

Listing 11.3   List an adapter's associated protocols

```
function get-protocol {
[CmdletBinding()]
param (
 [parameter(ValueFromPipeline=$true,
   ValueFromPipelineByPropertyName=$true)]
 [string]$computername="$env:COMPUTERNAME"
)
PROCESS {
 Get-WmiObject -Class Win32_NetWorkAdapter `
 -ComputerName $computername | sort DeviceId |
 foreach {
    "$($_.NetConnectionID) - $($_.Name)"

 Get-WmiObject -ComputerName $computername -Query
 ➥ "ASSOCIATORS OF
 ➥ {Win32_NetworkAdapter.DeviceId=$($_.DeviceId)}
 ➥ WHERE Resultclass=Win32_NetworkProtocol" |
 select Name, ConnectionlessService, Description,
 GuaranteesDelivery, GuaranteesSequencing,
 MaximumAddressSize, MaximumMessageSize,
 MessageOriented, MinimumAddressSize,
 PseudoStreamOriented, Status,
 SupportsBroadcasting, SupportsConnectData,
 SupportsDisconnectData, SupportsEncryption,
 SupportsExpeditedData, SupportsFragmentation,
 SupportsGracefulClosing, SupportsGuaranteedBandwidth,
 SupportsMulticasting, SupportsQualityofService,
 @{N="InstallDate"; E={$($_.ConvertToDateTime($_.InstallDate))}}
 }
}}
```

You use `Get-WmiObject` twice in this function. The first time you retrieve the network adapters in a computer using `Win32_NetworkAdapter`. The results are sorted by `DeviceId` and then piped into `ForEach-Object`. String substitution is used to display the network connection (the connection name in Windows) and the adapter name.

The second call to `Get-WmiObject` uses an association query to determine the instances of `Win32_NetworkProtocol` associated with the particular adapter. The results are piped through `Select-Object` to filter the display to show the properties of interest and to convert the protocols' installation date to a readable format.

DISCUSSION

This function could be modified to take a network adapter's `DeviceId` as a parameter. This would enable checks to be made on single adapters if required. The other potential modification would be to add some of the network adapter's properties to the protocol object using `Add-Member`. This would then output a single object for further analysis.

Network adapters, adapter configurations, and protocols define how communications take place. You need to create explicit network connections between systems to facilitate the functioning of particular applications.

TECHNIQUE 77   ## Listing network connections

The connections between your servers would look like a ball of spaghetti if you traced them. No, I'm not talking about the network cables! There are various mappings made between systems to enable applications to work. These connections are often made when an application is installed and then forgotten about. Do you know all the network mappings made from your servers?

PROBLEM

You need to move an application to a new server. It has become so popular that usage has exceeded the original assumptions and the current hardware is proving to be insufficient. There are some connections between the server and other systems that need to be analyzed so that they can be reproduced on the new server.

SOLUTION

The get-networkconnection function in listing 11.4 looks a little different from previous functions. After the param block, there are three script blocks:

- Begin
- Process
- End

When Begin, Process, and End blocks aren't defined, the code is treated as an End block.

Listing 11.4   List the network connections from a machine

```
function get-networkconnection {
[CmdletBinding()]
param (
 [parameter(ValueFromPipeline=$true,
   ValueFromPipelineByPropertyName=$true)]
 [string]$computername="$env:COMPUTERNAME"
)
BEGIN {$data = @()}

PROCESS {
 Get-WmiObject -Class Win32_NetWorkConnection `
 -ComputerName $computername | foreach {

  $connection = New-Object -TypeName PsObject `
   -Property @{
     Local       = $_.LocalName
     Remote      = $_.RemoteName
     Type        = $_.ConnectionType
     Description = $_.Description
     Display     = $_.DisplayType
     Provider    = $_.ProviderName
     Resource    = $_.ResourceType
     User        = $_.Username
     DiskSize    = 0
     FreeSpace   = 0
  }
```

```
    if ($_.ResourceType -eq "Disk"){
      $disk = Get-WmiObject -Class Win32_MappedLogicalDisk `
      -ComputerName $computername -Filter "DeviceId='$($_.LocalName)'"

      $connection.Disksize  = [math]::round($($disk.Size / 1GB), 3)
      $connection.FreeSpace = [math]::round($($disk.FreeSpace / 1GB), 3)
    }

  $data += $connection
  }
}

END {$data}
}
```

The Begin block is executed once, and only once, when the first object on the pipe-line enters the function. If there are multiple instances of the function on the pipe-line, the Begin block will execute once for each instance of the function as the objects on the pipeline reach that instance. In this case, the Begin block initializes an array that will be used to accumulate your results.

The Process block executes once for each object on the pipeline that enters the function. This function's Process block retrieves the network connections using the Win32_NetworkConnection class. The results are piped into ForEach-Object. A new PowerShell object is created and the properties are set using the information in the WMI object on the pipeline ($_). The DiskSize and FreeSpace properties are set to 0.

The WMI object's ResourceType parameter is tested to determine whether you're dealing with a disk connection (the other connection type that may be of interest is print). The Win32_MappedLogicalDisk class is used to return information on the remote disk. The DiskSize and FreeSpace properties on your connection object are populated after the results have been converted to gigabytes.

The last act of the Process block is to add the connection object you created into the array. Remember that in PowerShell everything is an object, so arrays can happily contain objects.

When the last object on the pipeline has been processed, the End block is exe-cuted once. The data in the array is pushed onto the pipeline, where the default dis-play processes take over and display the data.

DISCUSSION
The function accepts computer names on the pipeline, so it can be used like this:

```
"server02", "10.10.54.201" | get-networkconnection
```

One extension to the function would be to use the functionality developed in chap-ter 10 to add information about whether the connection is to a printer. Extra properties would need to be added to the object in $connection to accommodate this information.

You've now gathered information on your adapters and their configuration. In the next section, we'll look at configuring the adapters.

11.2 *Configuring network adapters*

Most of the network adapter configuration activity will be around IP addresses and the related properties, which we'll look at in the next section. In this section, we'll look at configuring the adapters themselves.

You can work directly with the adapters to enable or disable them. These two techniques are presented separately to give a little more safety in their use. The whole function has to be called, rather than choosing a switch on a single function.

> **WARNING** The WMI methods presented in this chapter don't have a safety net like PowerShell cmdlets. There are no -WhatIf or -Confirm parameters.

The other task you can perform is renaming the adapter. We'll refer back to this technique in chapters 13 and 16.

First up is enabling an adapter.

TECHNIQUE 78   **Enabling network adapters**

Network adapters are no use to you if you can't get network traffic through them. You need to ensure that your adapters are enabled. Disabled adapters can be discovered using listing 11.1.

```
get-nic | where {!$_.NetEnabled}
```

If all of the network adapters are disabled, you'll need to issue this command when physically logged on to the server.

PROBLEM

Communication has been broken with the server because the network adapter has been disabled while you performed some maintenance on the server. You have to enable the adapter so that users can reconnect to their applications.

SOLUTION

The enable-connection function in the following listing has parameters that will identify a network adapter by device (DeviceId) or connection (NetConnectionid). These are kept mutually exclusive by being in different parameter sets.

Listing 11.5 Enable a network adapter

```
function enable-connection {
[CmdletBinding()]
param (
 [parameter(ValueFromPipeline=$true,
   ValueFromPipelineByPropertyName=$true)]
 [string]$computername="$env:COMPUTERNAME",

 [parameter(ParameterSetName="Device")]
 [int]$device,

 [parameter(ParameterSetName="Connection")]
 [string]$NetConnectionID

)
```

```
PROCESS {
 switch ($psCmdlet.ParameterSetName) {
  Device {$filt = "DeviceID=$device"}
  Connection {$filt = "NetConnectionID='$NetConnectionID'"}
 }
Get-WmiObject -Class Win32_NetWorkAdapter `
-ComputerName $computername -Filter $filt   |
Invoke-WmiMethod -Name Enable

}}
```

A Switch statement is used to create a WMI filter. The filter is used with Win32_NetworkAdapter to select the adapter you want to enable. Invoke-WmiMethod accepts the WMI object and calls the Enable method. A return code of 0 indicates success.

DISCUSSION

The following two examples show how you can use the function with either a device identity (first) or a connection (second):

```
enable-connection -computer win7 -device 11
enable-connection -computer win7 -NetConnectionID "VWireless"
```

How did your adapter become disabled in the first place? That's answered in the next technique.

TECHNIQUE 79   **Disabling network adapters**

Disabling a network adapter may seem like an odd thing to do, but there are times when it becomes necessary, such as when you're doing the following:

- Performing maintenance on an application
- Investigating a problem
- Updating the Active Directory schema

The disablement in these cases is expected to be a temporary measure. There are also times when an almost permanent disabling of the adapter is required.

PROBLEM

You have two adapters in all of the virtual machines in a test environment. The first is an Ethernet adapter that enables normal communication. The second is a link to the wireless adapter in the host that enables Internet access for activation and so on. You want this wireless link to be disabled.

SOLUTION

You can adapt listing 11.5 to provide a way of disabling network adapters. The function shown in the following listing differs in the method that's called.

Listing 11.6   Disable a network adapter

```
function disable-connection {
[CmdletBinding()]
param (
 [parameter(ValueFromPipeline=$true,
```

```
    ValueFromPipelineByPropertyName=$true)]
  [string]$computername="$env:COMPUTERNAME",

  [parameter(ParameterSetName="Device")]
  [int]$device,

  [parameter(ParameterSetName="Connection")]
  [string]$NetConnectionID
)
PROCESS {
 switch ($psCmdlet.ParameterSetName) {
  Device {$filt = "DeviceID=$device"}
  Connection {$filt = "NetConnectionID='$NetConnectionID'"}
 }
Get-WmiObject -Class Win32_NetWorkAdapter `
-ComputerName $computername -Filter $filt  |
Invoke-WmiMethod -Name Disable

}}
```

The network adapter's WMI object is retrieved using the appropriate filter based on the parameter choice. This object is then piped into `Invoke-WmiMethod`, where the `Disable` method is called.

DISCUSSION

The function can be used with either a device identifier or the network connection identifier, as shown in these two examples:

```
disable-connection -computer win7 -device 11
disable-connection -computer win7 -NetConnectionID "VWireless"
```

> **WARNING** Be careful not to disable the network adapter you're connecting through. You'll need to visit the machine to re-enable it.

When you add network adapters, especially in a virtual environment, they're given names that don't help you in distinguishing them. You need to be able to change the name given to the adapter.

TECHNIQUE 80   **Renaming network adapters**

There are a number of situations in which you may want to rename network adapters:

- In clusters, where you want to differentiate the public and private networks
- In virtual environments, where your adapters are called "Local Area Connection *n*" (where *n* is a digit)
- In a server that has connections to multiple networks (multihomed server), such as where public and management networks exist

As you'll see in chapter 13, you want to be able to do this as part of a server setup routine.

PROBLEM

A new server has been commissioned with multiple network adapters. The adapters have to be renamed to differentiate their purposes.

SOLUTION

There isn't a method to perform the renaming, but you can change the value of a property to perform this action, as shown in the following listing.

Listing 11.7   Rename a network adapter

```
function rename-connection {
[CmdletBinding()]
param (
 [parameter(ValueFromPipeline=$true,
   ValueFromPipelineByPropertyName=$true)]
 [string]$computername="$env:COMPUTERNAME",

 [parameter(ParameterSetName="Device")]
 [int]$device,

 [parameter(ParameterSetName="Connection")]
 [string]$NetConnectionID,

 [parameter(Mandatory=$true)]
 [string]$newname
)
PROCESS {
 switch ($psCmdlet.ParameterSetName) {
  Device {$filt = "DeviceID=$device"}
  Connection {$filt = "NetConnectionID='$NetConnectionID'"}
 }

Get-WmiObject -Class Win32_NetWorkAdapter `
-ComputerName $computername -Filter $filt |
Set-WmiInstance -Arguments @{NetConnectionID=$newname}

}}
```

The adapter to be renamed is identified by the device identifier or the current name (NetConnectionId). The new name is a mandatory parameter, so you'll be prompted for it if you forget. A Switch statement is used to create a WMI filter from the input parameters.

Get-WmiObject pipes the object representing the adapter to Set-WmiInstance. The adapter's new name is used in a hash table as the value, and the property name you're changing—NetConnectionId—is the key. Set-WmiInstance uses the hash table as input to its Arguments parameter and makes the change.

DISCUSSION

It's possible to perform multiple changes with one call of Set-WmiInstance by providing the required number of key-value pairs in the hash table. In this case you only need the one pair.

The function is used as follows:

```
rename-connection -computer win7 `
-NetConnectionID "Local Area connection 2" -newname "VWireless"
```

The new name will be prompted for, even if you run the function in ISE or another editor environment instead of from the console.

Your adapters are now enabled and named. The next step is to set the IP address information so that users can communicate with the server.

11.3   *Enabling and setting network addresses*

Networks identify computers so that they can communicate (that's a gross simplification, but it's sufficient for this book). Addresses can be supplied automatically by Dynamic Host Configuration Protocol (DHCP) or you can manually set a static address, which is the preferred solution for servers.

Enabling DHCP is a quick way to clear the old address from an adapter. The first technique in this section shows how to perform this task. If your system should use DHCP you need to be able to view the DHCP configuration, which you'll learn to do in the second technique. This is followed by a method you can use to control DHCP leases through WMI. No more `ipconfig.exe` for you!

> **NOTE**   One of the major pieces of functionality missing from WMI and Power-Shell is the ability to manage DHCP servers. This is addressed in Windows Server 8.

The alternative to DHCP is to set a static address, which means that the other properties also have to be set manually. This section also covers techniques to set a static IP address and other properties, such as the default gateway. You'll have to dip into using regular expressions for these techniques but it's relatively painless.

DHCP is simpler to configure, which makes it the ideal place to start.

TECHNIQUE 81   **Enabling DHCP**

Life used to be simple. We used static addresses for servers and DHCP for client machines. The rules have changed a bit with Windows Server 2008, where using DHCP for servers isn't so bad. You can even use them in cluster scenarios.

IP addresses and related settings are configured using the `Win32_NetworkAdapterConfiguration` class. This is an important point to remember and can save lots of frustration when scripts don't work because you're using `Win32_NetworkAdapter`!

PROBLEM

You need to change the configuration on a network adapter to use DHCP addresses rather than a static address.

SOLUTION

The `enable-dhcp` function in the following listing solves this problem.

Listing 11.8   Enable DHCP on an adapter

```
function enable-dhcp {
[CmdletBinding()]
param (
 [parameter(ValueFromPipeline=$true,
   ValueFromPipelineByPropertyName=$true)]
```

```
[string]$computername="$env:COMPUTERNAME",
[int]$index

)
PROCESS {
 Get-WmiObject -Class Win32_NetWorkAdapterConfiguration `
 -ComputerName $computername -Filter "Index=$index" |
 Invoke-WmiMethod -Name EnableDHCP

}}
```

The `-index` parameter is used to identify the adapter you want to configure. `Win32_NetworkAdapter` uses `DeviceID` and `Win32_NetworkAdapterConfiguration` uses `Index`. They both have the same numeric value for a given adapter.

`Get-WmiObject` pipes the adapter's object to `Invoke-WmiMethod`, which calls the object's `EnableDHCP` method.

DISCUSSION

In some cases you may find that not all manually configured settings are removed when DHCP is enabled. If the DHCP scope doesn't set DNS servers they'll retain the static settings.

You may want to extend this function by using the `SetTCPIPNetBIOS` method with an argument of `0` to control the setting through DHCP. See technique 85 for the details of using the method.

When DHCP is enabled there are a number of configuration settings you may want to investigate.

TECHNIQUE 82   Displaying DHCP configuration

How can you test that an adapter is configured for DHCP? This code snippet shows how:

```
Get-WmiObject Win32_NetworkAdapterConfiguration `
-ComputerName win7 | where {$_.DHCPEnabled}
```

When troubleshooting, you may want to test the DHCP configuration of a system.

PROBLEM

Users are reporting that they can't connect to a server. You've discovered that the network adapter is configured to use DHCP. You need to display the DHCP configuration.

SOLUTION

Listing 11.2 could be used to perform this task, but it examines all adapters and produces a lot of information you don't need at this point. The following listing produces just the output you need.

Listing 11.9   Display DHCP configuration

```
function get-dhcpsetting {
[CmdletBinding()]
param (
 [parameter(ValueFromPipeline=$true,
```

```
   ValueFromPipelineByPropertyName=$true)]
  [string]$computername="$env:COMPUTERNAME"
)
PROCESS {
 Get-WmiObject -Class Win32_NetWorkAdapterConfiguration `
 -ComputerName $computername -Filter "DHCPEnabled='$true'" |
 select ServiceName, Description, Index,
 DHCPEnabled, DHCPServer,
 IPAddress, IPSubnet,
 @{N="DHCPLeaseStart"; E={$_.ConvertToDateTime($_.DHCPLeaseObtained)}},
 @{N="DHCPLeaseEnd"; E={$_.ConvertToDateTime($_.DHCPLeaseExpires)}}
}}
```

You apply a filter of "DHCPEnabled='$true'" to the Win32_NetworkAdapter-Configuration class. This will only return information for those adapters that have DHCP enabled. Filtering data at the remote system speeds up your processing by reducing the data that's returned.

The Select-Object cmdlet then filters the properties you want to see. The DHCP lease start and end times are converted to a readable format. An example of the output from this function is shown in the discussion of technique 83.

DISCUSSION

If the adapter is configured for DHCP and an address of the form 169.254.x.x is returned, this means your server couldn't communicate with the DHCP server. The IP address and subnet should be checked to ensure that the adapter has been assigned an address from the correct scope.

DHCP leases don't last forever (usually), and it may be necessary to control the leases.

TECHNIQUE 83   Controlling DHCP leases

IT administrators learn to use ipconfig.exe to release and renew DHCP leases. This is great for the local machine, but doesn't work remotely.

PROBLEM

You need to be able to control DHCP leases on local and remote systems. This could involve releasing a DHCP lease when you want to put a static address on an adapter, or it may require you to force the renewal of a lease.

SOLUTION

Listing 11.10 provides a solution for this problem. The network adapter you need to work with is identified by the -index parameter. Two switch parameters are used to determine whether you are releasing or renewing a lease. They're in different parameter sets, so the release and renew choices are mutually exclusive.

Listing 11.10   Release or renew DHCP lease

```
function set-dhcp {
[CmdletBinding()]
param (
 [parameter(ValueFromPipeline=$true,
   ValueFromPipelineByPropertyName=$true)]
```

```
[string]$computername="$env:COMPUTERNAME",
[int]$index,

[parameter(ParameterSetName="Release")]
[switch]$release,

[parameter(ParameterSetName="Renew")]
[switch]$renew
)
PROCESS {
 $nic = Get-WmiObject -Class Win32_NetWorkAdapterConfiguration `
 -ComputerName $computername -Filter "Index=$index"

 switch ($psCmdlet.ParameterSetName) {
  Release {$nic | Invoke-WmiMethod -Name ReleaseDHCPLease}
  Renew {$nic | Invoke-WmiMethod -Name RenewDHCPLease}
 }
}}
```

The `Win32_NetworkAdapterConfiguration` object is stored in the `$nic` variable. A `Switch` statement based on the parameter set name is used to determine whether you're releasing or renewing. `$nic` is piped to `Invoke-WmiMethod`, which calls the appropriate method to perform the desired action.

DISCUSSION

After releasing a DHCP lease you can test the results using the `get-dhcpsetting` function from technique 82:

```
PS> get-dhcpsetting -computer win7

ServiceName     : netvsc
Description     : Microsoft Virtual Machine Bus Network Adapter #2
Index           : 11
DHCPEnabled     : True
DHCPServer      : 255.255.255.255
IPAddress       : {169.254.201.55, fe80::bc37:dcdf:70f7:c937}
IPSubnet        : {255.255.0.0, 64}
DHCPLeaseStart  : 14/03/2011 20:29:00
DHCPLeaseEnd    : 15/03/2011 20:29:00
```

Notice the `DHCPServer` and `IPAddress` values. They indicate that DHCP is disabled even though the lease start and end times appear valid.

The alternative to using DHCP is to manually set a static IP address.

TECHNIQUE 84 **Setting an IP address**

A server will have its IP address set when it's first created. Servers don't normally change their IP addresses. Very occasionally you may have to perform this task, and when you do, you need to be able to perform the task remotely rather than visit the hundreds or even thousands of servers in the estate.

PROBLEM

Your network team has decided that the IP addressing scheme needs to change due to company growth requiring many more servers than originally thought. You need to be able to change the IP addresses of your servers remotely.

SOLUTION

You'll be using the `Win32_NetworkAdapterConfiguration` class again to solve this problem. The PowerShell function to perform this is supplied in the following listing.

Listing 11.11   Set an IP address

```
function set-IPAddress {
[CmdletBinding()]
param (
 [parameter(ValueFromPipeline=$true,
   ValueFromPipelineByPropertyName=$true)]
 [string]$computername="$env:COMPUTERNAME",

 [parameter(Mandatory=$true)]
 [int]$index,

 [parameter(Mandatory=$true)]
 [string]
 [ValidatePattern("\b\d{1,3}\.\d{1,3}\.\d{1,3}\.\d{1,3}\b")]
 $ipaddress,

 [parameter(Mandatory=$true)]
 [string]
 [ValidatePattern("\b\d{1,3}\.\d{1,3}\.\d{1,3}\.\d{1,3}\b")]
 $subnet
)
PROCESS {
$nic = Get-WmiObject -Class Win32_NetWorkAdapterConfiguration `
-ComputerName $computername -Filter "Index=$index" -EnableAllPrivileges
$nic.EnableStatic($ipaddress, $subnet)

}}
```

The first point to note about the parameters is that all but the `-computer` are mandatory. You can't set the address if the new address isn't supplied. You could have left the subnet as non-mandatory but it's better to think about both together to ensure consistency.

   The second point is that you're using the `ValidatePattern` advanced parameter with the `-ipaddress` and `-subnet` parameters. This uses a regular expression to validate the input. If you aren't a regular expression expert (I don't like them myself), the regular expression breaks down as follows:

- Four groups of 1–3 digits
- A dot separator
- `\b` to indicate that the first and last matches must occur on the boundaries of the string

   NOTE   Thanks to PowerShell MVP Tobias Weltner for the regular expression.

The WMI object representing the network adapter configuration is put into the `$nic` variable. The `EnableStatic` method is called on the object with the IP address and subnet as parameters.

I tried using `Invoke-WMImethod`, but it failed to work with this method. There's a lot of discussion surrounding `Invoke-WmiMethod` in the PowerShell community, as we haven't been able to completely understand its quirks. There's a bug that causes it to fail sometimes with multiple parameters, which is what I suspect was happening in this situation.

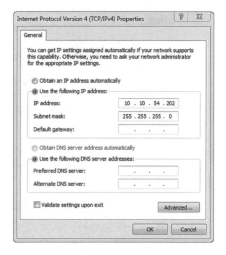

DISCUSSION

The addresses you're changing are the ones shown in the IP address dialog box from the IPv4 properties of a network adapter, as shown in figure 11.2.

The function can be used as follows:

Figure 11.2   IPv4 Properties dialog box

```
set-IPAddress -computer win7 -index 13 `
-ipaddress "100.99.98.97" -subnet "255.255.255.0"
```

WARNING   The regular expression can check that the string follows the correct pattern for an IP address. It can't validate that a correct address is presented. If you used "700.99.98.97" in the previous example, it would pass validation even though it isn't a valid address.

There are a few other properties that you need to think about setting as well.

TECHNIQUE 85   **Setting other properties**

This technique could be combined with technique 86 and the techniques in section 11.4 if you want to create a super-script that enables you to set all of the IP address properties in one go. The mandatory property would need to be removed from the input parameters unless you want to perform a lot of typing.

PROBLEM

The default gateway and the use of NetBIOS over TCP/IP need to be configured to complete the settings on your network adapter.

SOLUTION

Listing 11.11 can be modified to produce Listing 11.12. This is a common technique in administration scripting. Take something that works and modify it to perform another similar task.

In this case, the parameters supply the default gateway (`$gateway`), which is validated against a regular expression pattern and the value for `tcpnetbios`, which can be 1 (Enable) or 2 (Disable).

Listing 11.12   Set default gateway and TCP/IP NetBIOS setting

```
function set-IPdetails {
[CmdletBinding()]
param (
 [parameter(ValueFromPipeline=$true,
   ValueFromPipelineByPropertyName=$true)]
 [string]$computername="$env:COMPUTERNAME",

 [parameter(Mandatory=$true)]
 [int]$index,

 [parameter(Mandatory=$true)]
 [string]
 [ValidatePattern("\b\d{1,3}\.\d{1,3}\.\d{1,3}\.\d{1,3}\b")]
 $gateway,

 [parameter(Mandatory=$true)]
 [int]
 $metric,

 [int]
 [ValidateRange(1,2)]
 $tcpnetbios
)
PROCESS {
$nic = Get-WmiObject -Class Win32_NetWorkAdapterConfiguration `
-ComputerName $computername -Filter "Index=$index"
$nic.SetGateways($gateway, $metric)
$nic.SetTcpipNetbios($tcpnetbios)

}}
```

$nic is the variable that holds the configuration object for your adapter. The Set-Gateways method is called to set the default gateway and the SetTcpipNetbios method is used to set NetBIOS over TCP/IP.

DISCUSSION

The default gateway needs to be configured correctly to ensure that the system can communicate with machines on other subnets. Any organization with more than 200 computers is probably running on multiple subnets, which make it essential that you get this setting correct.

The remaining configuration items you need to consider are the addresses of the DNS and WINS servers.

11.4   *Configuring network services*

The primary network services in a Windows environment are DNS and DHCP. You can't do anything about DHCP, but you can configure the DNS servers that will be used, which is what you'll do in the section's first technique. Then you'll configure WINS in the second technique. WINS is an older name-resolution method that's used in many organizations with legacy applications.

A final check on the networking configuration can be supplied by looking at the IP routing table to see which networks your system is connecting to and the routes it tries to apply to reach those networks. The function to perform this is presented in the section's last technique.

You can use WMI to configure DNS servers directly as discussed in chapter 9 of *PowerShell in Practice*. On the client side, you need to configure the DNS servers your systems will contact.

TECHNIQUE 86 Setting DNS servers

DNS is the name resolution method of choice for modern Windows environments. You need to make sure the DNS and DHCP client services are running and that you've configured the correct DNS servers in your network adapter's properties.

PROBLEM
The DNS servers have changed due to an upgrade to your domain controllers (you're running integrated DNS). You need to modify the DNS server that your systems use.

SOLUTION
Workstations will usually have their DNS server settings controlled by DHCP. Servers and those workstations with static addresses can be modified using the following listing. The -index parameter identifies the network adapter whose properties you'll modify. The -dnsserver parameter takes an array of strings representing the IP addresses of the DNS servers.

Listing 11.13 Configure DNS server

```
function set-DNSsserver {
[CmdletBinding()]
param (
 [parameter(ValueFromPipeline=$true,
   ValueFromPipelineByPropertyName=$true)]
 [string]$computername="$env:COMPUTERNAME",

 [parameter(Mandatory=$true)]
 [int]$index,

 [parameter(Mandatory=$true)]
 [string[]]
 [ValidatePattern("\b\d{1,3}\.\d{1,3}\.\d{1,3}\.\d{1,3}\b")]
 $dnsserver
)
PROCESS {
$nic = Get-WmiObject -Class Win32_NetWorkAdapterConfiguration `
-ComputerName $computername -Filter "Index=$index"
$nic.SetDNSServerSearchOrder($dnsserver)

}}
```

The $nic variable holds the adapter configuration object. The object's SetDNSServer-SearchOrder method is used to set the DNS server list. The array of addresses must hold one or more addresses.

DISCUSSION

The SetDNSServerSearchOrder method can also be used to clear the DNS server settings:

```
Get-WmiObject Win32_NetworkAdapterConfiguration `
-ComputerName win7 -Filter "Index=13" |
Invoke-WmiMethod -Name SetDNSServerSearchOrder
```

Listing 11.8 could be modified to incorporate this code, because calling the Enable-DHCP method clears the IP address, subnet, and default gateway. It doesn't clear the DNS servers.

As stated earlier, WINS is an older name-resolution method, but you still need to know how to configure the addresses of your WINS servers.

TECHNIQUE 87   **Setting WINS servers**

You can set a number of WINS servers if you use the IPv4 Properties dialog box, but you're limited to setting a primary and secondary WINS server if you use WMI. This would normally be considered sufficient.

PROBLEM

You need to set the WINS servers that your server will access because it has to communicate with a legacy application that demands the presence of WINS.

SOLUTION

The set-WINSserver function presented in listing 11.14 will solve this problem for you. The -winsprimary parameter uses the ValidatePattern advanced parameter to check the address. You may not want to set a secondary WINS server, so that parameter isn't mandatory in this function.

Listing 11.14 Configure WINS server

```
function set-WINSserver {
[CmdletBinding()]
param (
 [parameter(ValueFromPipeline=$true,
   ValueFromPipelineByPropertyName=$true)]
 [string]$computername="$env:COMPUTERNAME",

 [parameter(Mandatory=$true)]
 [int]$index,

 [parameter(Mandatory=$true)]
 [string]
 [ValidatePattern("\b\d{1,3}\.\d{1,3}\.\d{1,3}\.\d{1,3}\b")]
 $winsprimary,

 [string]
 $winsseconndary
)
PROCESS {
if ($winsseconndary -and $winsseconndary -notmatch
    "\b\d{1,3}\.\d{1,3}\.\d{1,3}\.\d{1,3}\b") {
  throw "Invalid WINS Secondary address $winsseconndary"
}
```

```
$nic = Get-WmiObject -Class Win32_NetWorkAdapterConfiguration `
-ComputerName $computername -Filter "Index=$index"
$nic.SetWINSServer($winsprimary, $winsseconndary )

}}
```

If an address for a WINS secondary server is presented through the -winssecondary parameter, you use a regular expression to test that a string of the correct pattern is presented. The SetWINSServer method is used to set the addresses.

DISCUSSION

This function will accept one or two addresses, as shown in these examples:

```
set-WINSserver -computer win7 -index 13 -winsprimary "10.10.10.200"
```

```
set-WINSserver -computer win7 -index 13 `
-winsprimary "10.10.10.200" -winssecondary "10.10.89.51"
```

You can clear the WINS server settings like this:

```
Get-WmiObject Win32_NetworkAdapterConfiguration `
-ComputerName win7 -Filter "Index=13" |
Invoke-WmiMethod -Name SetWINSserver -ArgumentList "", ""
```

You use a string to define the original WINS server settings, and empty strings are used to remove the WINS servers that are configured. Remember that an empty string, defined as "", is different from a NULL value defined by $null.

The last stop on our journey around networking is to look at the routing table.

TECHNIQUE 88　Displaying the routing table

The routing table shows how your server is communicating with the outside world. An example is shown in figure 11.3 (in the following discussion). One point to note is that WMI can't provide information on IPv6 routing, at present.

PROBLEM

You need to examine the IP routing table to determine whether network connectivity is configured correctly on your server.

SOLUTION

The following listing uses Win32_IP4RouteTable to solve this problem. The function is presented as a single block of code, but it could be divided into Begin, Process, and End blocks as in listing 11.4.

Listing 11.15　Display routing table

```
function get-routetable {
[CmdletBinding()]
param (
 [parameter(ValueFromPipeline=$true,
   ValueFromPipelineByPropertyName=$true)]
 [string]$computername="$env:COMPUTERNAME"
)
BEGIN {
```

```
$source=@"
public class WmiIPRoute
{
  public string Destination {get; set;}
  public string Mask {get; set;}
  public string NextHop {get; set;}
  public string Interface {get; set;}
  public int    Metric {get; set;}
}
"@
Add-Type -TypeDefinition $source -Language CSharpversion3
}
PROCESS {
$data = @()
Get-WmiObject -Class Win32_IP4RouteTable -ComputerName $computername |
foreach {
 $route = New-Object -TypeName WmiIPRoute
 $route.Destination = $_.Destination
 $route.Mask        = $_.Mask
 $route.NextHop     = $_.NextHop
 $route.Metric      = $_.Metric1

 $filt = "InterfaceIndex='" + $_.InterfaceIndex + "'"
 $ip = (Get-WmiObject -Class Win32_NetworkAdapterConfiguration
   ➥ -Filter $filt -ComputerName $computername).IPAddress

 if ($_.InterfaceIndex -eq 1) {$route.Interface = "127.0.0.1"}
 elseif ($ip.length -eq 2){$route.Interface = $ip[0]}
 else {$route.Interface = $ip}

 $data += $route
}
$data | Format-Table -AutoSize
}}
```

A here-string (a multiline PowerShell string whose structure is @"..."@) is used to define the C# code for a new class, WmiIPRoute, that you create for this function. This is compiled using Add-Type. An empty array, $data, is created to store the data prior to display.

Get-WmiObject puts all of the instances of Win32_IP4RouteTable on the pipeline. ForEach-Object is used to create a new instance of the WmiIPRoute class and populate its properties from the WMI object.

The InterfaceIndex is used in a WMI filter to retrieve the IP address via Win32_NetworkAdapterConfiguration. The IP address is set and the new route object is added to the collection in $data.

When all of the routes have been processed, the data is displayed using Format-Table.

DISCUSSION

The data takes the form shown in figure 11.3. The Interface property corresponds to the IP address on the network adapter. The NextHop property is the default gateway you've configured on the adapter.

```
C:\Reference\PowerShell and WMI\Scripts - First draft\Chapter11
PS> get-routetable

Destination      Mask              NextHop         Interface          Metric
-----------      ----              -------         ---------          ------
0.0.0.0          0.0.0.0           192.168.196.1 192.168.196.140        25
10.10.54.0       255.255.255.0     0.0.0.0         10.10.54.202         286
10.10.54.202     255.255.255.255 0.0.0.0           10.10.54.202         286
10.10.54.255     255.255.255.255 0.0.0.0           10.10.54.202         286
127.0.0.0        255.0.0.0         0.0.0.0         127.0.0.1            306
127.0.0.1        255.255.255.255 0.0.0.0           127.0.0.1            306
127.255.255.255 255.255.255.255 0.0.0.0            127.0.0.1            306
192.168.196.0    255.255.255.0     0.0.0.0         192.168.196.140      281
192.168.196.140 255.255.255.255 0.0.0.0            192.168.196.140      281
192.168.196.255 255.255.255.255 0.0.0.0            192.168.196.140      281
224.0.0.0        240.0.0.0         0.0.0.0         127.0.0.1            306
224.0.0.0        240.0.0.0         0.0.0.0         10.10.54.202         286
224.0.0.0        240.0.0.0         0.0.0.0         192.168.196.140      281
255.255.255.255 255.255.255.255 0.0.0.0            127.0.0.1            306
255.255.255.255 255.255.255.255 0.0.0.0            10.10.54.202         286
255.255.255.255 255.255.255.255 0.0.0.0            192.168.196.140      281
```

Figure 11.3 An IPv4 routing table

This finishes our look at working with network adapters using WMI.

11.5   Summary

Configuring servers to communicate on the network is an essential activity. You can use WMI to accomplish a variety of networking tasks:

- Display information about network adapters and their IP configuration
- Discover network protocols and connections
- Enable, disable, and rename adapters
- Examine the DHCP configuration, enable DHCP, and manage the leases
- Set static IP addresses and default gateway properties
- Configure the DNS and WINS servers that will be used by the server
- Display the IP routing table

WMI only allows you to work with IPv4 at the moment, but as only a small fraction of organizations have moved to IPv6 this likely won't be an issue. The techniques presented in this chapter, together with cmdlets such as Test-Connection, provide a good foundation for a PowerShell-based network administration toolkit.

Chapter 12 is a little different in that we'll look at using WMI to administer IIS.

Managing IIS

12

This chapter covers

- IIS WMI providers
- Configuring web servers
- Website lifecycle and management
- Application pools and web applications

Internet Information Server (IIS) is used in many situations in Windows-based environments. It's used directly as a web server and it's also used in the background in products such as Windows Server Update Services (WSUS), Exchange 2007/2010, and SharePoint. IIS may not be the first application that comes to mind when you think of using PowerShell and WMI to administer remote servers, but it provides a lot of functionality. You need to be able to administer IIS remotely the same as any other application.

IIS 7   This chapter will only consider working with IIS 7 (Windows Server 2008 and 2008 R2). A WMI provider is available for IIS 6 on Windows Server 2003, but it isn't identical. The techniques in this chapter can be used as a guide for working with the older version.

There are a number of ways you can administer IIS using PowerShell, as listed in table 12.1.

Method	Remote working
.NET	No
WMI	Partial
WMI with .NET	Yes
IIS cmdlets	No
IIS provider	No

Table 12.1   Methods of accessing IIS through PowerShell

When you install IIS on a system, a .NET assembly is installed that provides administration access to IIS. The WMI provider is also installed.

NOTE   Remember that a version of IIS is available on client versions of Windows, including Vista and 7, as well as the server versions.

You can access the WMI provider directly through the standard PowerShell cmdlets, but you'll encounter a few issues, which we'll look at later. It's possible to wrap the use of WMI in the .NET objects you create in PowerShell, and we'll also look at this technique.

Windows Server 2008 R2 supplies an IIS provider and cmdlets. An optional download from www.iis.net (check the Manage category on the Download page) is available to install this functionality on Windows Server 2008. These cmdlets can't work remotely, but you can use PowerShell remoting to work with them on a remote system.

The focus of this chapter is on using WMI, so we'll start by examining the WMI provider, its features, and its limitations. This leads to working at the web server level, where we'll investigate the server configuration and use WMI to restart the web service.

Websites are covered in section 12.2, including discovering their properties, controlling them (restarting is the usual control option you'll need), and creating new sites. In the final section of this chapter, we'll look at how you can discover web applications and application pools. The recycling of application pools is an important topic that we'll cover at the end of the chapter.

First, you need to learn a bit more about the IIS WMI provider, because it has some quirks that you haven't seen before.

12.1   *IIS WMI provider*

You access the functionality to administer your IIS servers through the IIS WMI provider. It installs its classes into the root\webadministration namespace. Everything you've seen so far would suggest that you can discover the classes in this namespace like this:

```
Get-WmiObject -Namespace 'root\webadministration' -List -ComputerName web01
```

Afraid not, as figure 12.1 shows.

```
C:\scripts                                                          _ □ ×
PS> Get-WmiObject -Namespace 'root\webadministration' -List -ComputerName web01
Get-WmiObject : Access denied
At line:1 char:14
+ Get-WmiObject <<<<  -Namespace 'root\webadministration' -List -ComputerName w
eb01
    + CategoryInfo          : NotSpecified: (:) [Get-WmiObject], ManagementExc
  eption
    + FullyQualifiedErrorId : System.Management.ManagementException,Microsoft.
  PowerShell.Commands.GetWmiObjectCommand
PS> ▄
```

Figure 12.1   Error message when accessing the IIS WMI provider remotely

You need to use Packet Privacy to encrypt the traffic to a remote web server for this to work, which changes the code as follows:

```
Get-WmiObject -Namespace 'root\webadministration' `
-List -ComputerName web01 -Authentication 6
```

We'll investigate Packet Privacy authentication and how you can work with it, and then we'll look at how you can discover your web server configuration and how you can control the IIS service to restart the web server.

12.1.1 *Packet Privacy authentication*

The various WMI authentication levels were explained in section 4.5.3. Table 12.2 is presented as a recap.

Table 12.2   WMI authentication

Value	Meaning
-1	Unchanged—authentication remains as it was before.
0	Default COM authentication level. Authentication is negotiated. WMI uses the default Windows Authentication setting. The None setting (1) is never the result of a negotiated authentication.
1	None. No COM authentication is performed.
2	Connect. COM authentication is performed only when the client establishes a relationship with the server. No further checks are performed.
3	Call. COM authentication is performed only at the beginning of each call, when the server receives the request. Only packet headers are signed. No data is encrypted.
4	Packet. COM authentication is performed on all the data that's received from the client. Only packet headers are signed. No data is encrypted.
5	Packet Integrity. All the data that's transferred between the client and the application is authenticated and verified. All packets are signed. No data is encrypted.
6	Packet Privacy. The properties of the other authentication levels are used, and all the data is encrypted.

The IIS WMI provider insists on level 6 authentication (Packet Privacy), which ensures the data is encrypted. In order to use this level of authentication, you need to be logged on to the domain, have the correct level of permissions, and run PowerShell from an elevated prompt. In a non-domain situation, you'd need to supply explicit credentials for the remote machine as well as using Packet Privacy.

Use Get-Credential to create the credential rather than attempting to create it in the -Credential parameter. The latter option will fail because Get-WmiObject attempts to contact the server before resolving the credential.

> **NOTE** PowerShell v1 can't be used for these techniques because its version of Get-WmiObject can't set the level of authentication to be used. But you could wrap the WMI in .NET code, which would enable you to use Packet Privacy.

Now you know how to use WMI authentication. It's time to look at accessing the WMI classes and see what you can discover about your web server.

TECHNIQUE 89 Displaying web server defaults

One issue with the provider is that many of the properties you'll want to work with are returned as embedded objects. They can't be accessed directly. This is illustrated in figure 12.2, where the results of retrieving the Server class are displayed.

The Server class returns four properties of interest:

- ApplicationDefaults
- ApplicationPoolDefaults
- SiteDefaults
- VirtualDirectoryDefaults

All that you see is a System.Management.ManagementBaseObject object. It consists of other WMI classes that are held as embedded objects in the parent object. Many of the

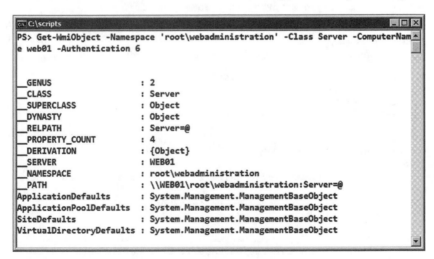

Figure 12.2 Embedded objects returned by Server class

other classes you'll meet in this chapter also behave in this manner. You need to be able to drill down further into the properties to discover how your web server is configured.

PROBLEM

There are a number of web servers in your internal environment that have been managed by different people over a period of time. You suspect that the default configuration of some of these servers has drifted from their desired state. You need to retrieve the default configuration so comparisons can be made to determine which servers need reconfiguring.

SOLUTION

Listing 12.1 demonstrates how you can solve this problem. The get-webserverdefault function takes a computer name as its only parameter.

> **NOTE**   The expand-property function used in this script is described in the discussion section that follows.

Listing 12.1   Display web server default settings

```
function get-webserverdefault {
[CmdletBinding()]
param (
 [parameter(ValueFromPipeline=$true,
   ValueFromPipelineByPropertyName=$true)]
 [string]$computername="$env:COMPUTERNAME"
)
PROCESS{
 $server = Get-WmiObject -Namespace 'root\webadministration' `
-Class Server -ComputerName $computername -Authentication 6      ❶ Create
                                                                     object
 $webdata = New-Object -TypeName PSobject
 $webdata |
 Add-Member -MemberType NoteProperty -Name "Server" `
-Value $server.__SERVER
                                                                 ❷ Add application
                                                                     data
 expand-property
  ➥ $server.ApplicationDefaults.Properties "Application"

 $apdproperties = $server.ApplicationPoolDefaults.Properties |
 where {$_.type -ne "Object"}
 expand-property
  ➥ $apdproperties "ApplicationPoolDefaults"

 expand-property
  ➥ $server.ApplicationPoolDefaults.CPU.Properties "APD_CPU"
 expand-property
  ➥ $server.ApplicationPoolDefaults.Failure.Properties "APD_Failure"
 expand-property
  ➥ $server.ApplicationPoolDefaults.ProcessModel.Properties
     ➥ "APD_ProcessModel"

 $apdproperties =
  ➥ $server.ApplicationPoolDefaults.Recycling.Properties |
 where {$_.type -ne "Object"}
```

```
expand-property $apdproperties "APD_Recycling"

expand-property
    ➥ $server.ApplicationPoolDefaults.Recycling.PeriodicRestart.
➥ Properties "APD_Recycle_Periodic"

$webdata |
Add-Member -MemberType NoteProperty -Name "SiteAutoStart" `
-Value $server.SiteDefaults.ServerAutoStart

expand-property
➥ $server.SiteDefaults.Limits.Properties "SiteLimits"
expand-property
➥ $server.SiteDefaults.Logfile.Properties "SiteLogfile"
expand-property
➥ $server.SiteDefaults.TraceFailedRequestsLogging.Properties
    ➥ "SiteTraceFailedRequestsLogging"

expand-property
➥ $server.VirtualDirectoryDefaults.Properties
➥ "VirtualDirectoryDefaults"

$webdata
}}
```

❸ **Add site data**

❸ **Add virtual directory data**

The `Server` class from the root\webadministration namespace holds the data you need. The object needs to be held in a variable, `$server`, because you need to use it several times as you unravel the embedded data.

The next step is to create a PowerShell object to store the results ❶. The object is initially created without any properties. `Add-Member` is used to extend the object by creating additional properties. The first one is the server name, which you retrieve from the __SERVER system property.

You can then step through the four properties you saw in figure 12.2 to add additional data to the object. You start with the application defaults ❷ and move on to the application pool data. At this point, you meet another level of embedded objects, necessitating more explicit expansion. Each time you expand an embedded object to retrieve its properties, you ensure that you can identify the resultant data by passing a title into the `expand-property` function, which acts as a prefix to the property name.

The final property sets are the site defaults ❸ and the virtual directory defaults ❹. The function returns the `$webdata` object, which can be filtered using the standard PowerShell utility and formatting cmdlets.

DISCUSSION

The workhorse of listing 12.1 is the `expand-property` function. This function is part of the module of functions for this chapter. It has two parameters. The first is a property set that you expand, and the second is a string that is used as a prefix for the property name:

```
function expand-property {
 param ($properties, $title)

 foreach ($property in $properties) {
  Add-Member -InputObject $webdata -MemberType NoteProperty `
```

```
    -Name "$title-$($property.Name)" `
    -Value $property.Value
  }
}
```

You loop through the properties and use `Add-Member` to create a property on your `$webdata` object that will hold the property you're working with. You can use `$webdata` directly in this way because `expand-property` is executing in a child scope of `get-webserverdefault`—that's because it was called by that function. A child scope can access variables created in the parent scope. The `expand-property` function will also be used in other scripts in the chapter.

Compared to the description, using the function is very simple. Assuming the module is loaded the syntax is as follows:

```
get-webserverdefault -computername web01
```

IIS servers tend not to need a lot of looking after once they're set up and running. There are a few things, though, such as patching, that you need to do on a regular basis. One task you may need to perform is restarting the IIS service on your web server.

TECHNIQUE 90   Restarting the web server

The one task we seem to have to keep doing is restarting the IIS service on our web servers. This need can arise for a number of reasons, including an issue with a website or application, or introducing a change to a website or to the web server configuration.

Being able to restart IIS quickly and efficiently minimizes the downtime of the service and ensures that the system's users suffer the minimum of inconvenience. It's also a good way to help maintain availability service-level agreements (SLAs).

PROBLEM

An application that's installed on a number of web servers is undergoing a series of upgrades. After each upgrade, the IIS service must be restarted to ensure that the changes are brought online immediately.

SOLUTION

You could write a function that restarts the IIS service on a local, or remote, system, but if you break down the problem a little further, the underlying issue is that you need to stop and then restart the web server.

Listing 12.2 shows how you can deliver a granular solution that provides for the three possible situations that arise:

- Stop the IIS service
- Start the IIS service
- Restart the IIS service

The following solution consists of three functions that perform the tasks of stopping, starting, and restarting the service.

Listing 12.2 Restart web server

```
function restart-webserver {                                    ❶ Restart-webserver
[CmdletBinding()]                                                  function
param (
 [parameter(ValueFromPipeline=$true,
   ValueFromPipelineByPropertyName=$true)]
 [string]$computername="$env:COMPUTERNAME"
)
PROCESS{                                                         ❷ Call worker
 stop-webserver -computer $computername                            functions
 start-webserver -computer $computername
}
}
function stop-webserver {                                        ❸ Stop-webserver
[CmdletBinding()]                                                  function
param (
 [parameter(ValueFromPipeline=$true,
   ValueFromPipelineByPropertyName=$true)]
 [string]$computername="$env:COMPUTERNAME"

)
PROCESS{                                                         ❹ Get WMI
 $www = Get-WmiObject -Class Win32_Service `                       object
-ComputerName $computername -Filter "Name='W3SVC'"

 if ($www.State -eq "Running") {                                 ❺ Stop
  $ret = $www.StopService()                                        service
  if ($ret.ReturnValue -ne 0) {
    Write-Host "$($computername): IIS did not stop correctly"
    $return
  }
 }
 else {Write-Host "$($computername):                             ❻ Display error
 ➥ IIS service not started"}                                      message
}
}
function start-webserver {                                       ❼ Start-webserver
[CmdletBinding()]                                                  function
param (
 [parameter(ValueFromPipeline=$true,
   ValueFromPipelineByPropertyName=$true)]
 [string]$computername="$env:COMPUTERNAME"

)
PROCESS{
 $www = Get-WmiObject -Class Win32_Service `
-ComputerName $computername -Filter "Name='W3SVC'"

 if ($www.State -ne "Running") {
  Write-Host "$($computername): IIS Stopped. Attempting restart"
  $ret = $www.StartService()
  if ($ret.ReturnValue -ne 0) {
    Write-Host "$($computername): IIS did not start correctly"
    $return
```

```
    }
  }
  else {Write-Host "$($computername): IIS is running" }
}}
```

The `restart-webserver` function ❶ accepts a computer name as the input parameter and then calls the functions ❷ to stop and start the service. The computer name is passed through to the child functions.

The `stop-webserver` function ❸ performs the task of stopping the web server. The computer name is accepted and then used in the WMI call to `Win32_Service` ❹. A check on the state of the service is performed, and if the service is running, an attempt is made to stop it ❺; otherwise an error message is issued. The return code is tested to determine whether the service shut down correctly ❻. An error message is returned if the service didn't close properly.

The `start-webserver` function ❼ has a similar construction, except that the `StartService` method is used. The error messages are modified to reflect the task this function is performing.

DISCUSSION

The tasks performed by this technique are straightforward, common administrative chores that you'll need to perform on a regular basis, making them ideal candidates for automation. Similar functions could be created for other important services. Approaching the solution in the most granular way ensures that you achieve the maximum flexibility and reuse in your use of PowerShell. The time spent developing a solution at this scale is repaid, because you gain the flexibility to perform three tasks out of the solution.

Administering web servers is the high-level task for this chapter. We'll now drill down a level and look at the websites that are hosted on those servers.

12.2 *Websites*

Websites are where your user's interests are concentrated because this is where they'll be accessing the server and performing their work. They won't care whether the server is running if the website itself is unavailable.

The first technique in this section will look at retrieving a list of the websites on a particular server, together with their properties. Subsequent techniques will examine the website lifecycle—specifically creation and deletion—and how you can control websites.

You need the ability to discover which websites exist on a particular server before you can administer those sites.

TECHNIQUE 91   Listing websites

You can list the sites on a server by using the `Site` class, as this code snippet demonstrates:

```
Get-WmiObject -Namespace 'root\webadministration' -Class Site `
  -ComputerName web01 -Authentication 6 `
-Filter "Name='Default Web Site'"
```

Packet Privacy authentication is used by passing a value of 6 to the -Authentication parameter, and a WMI filter ensures that only the information for the default website is returned.

You still have the problem of embedded objects to overcome, as figure 12.2 demonstrated.

PROBLEM

Web servers can be configured in a farm, where multiple servers host the same set of sites and access is load-balanced across the farm to provide scalability and resiliency. Comparing the configuration of the various websites across the farm can be a time-consuming and error-prone task if performed manually. You need to be able to generate the site configuration so that an automatic comparison can be performed.

SOLUTION

The comparison operation can be performed using Compare-Object, as you saw in chapter 2, if you can get the configuration into a suitable format. The following listing shows how you can obtain the data you need.

Listing 12.3   Listing websites

```
function get-website {
[CmdletBinding()]
param (
 [parameter(ValueFromPipeline=$true,
   ValueFromPipelineByPropertyName=$true)]                    ❶ Input
 [string]$computername="$env:COMPUTERNAME",                      parameters
 [string]$site

)
PROCESS{                                                       ❷ Get site
if ($site) {                                                     data
 $sites = Get-WmiObject -Namespace 'root\webadministration' `
-Class Site -ComputerName $computername -Authentication 6 `
-Filter "Name='$site'"
}
else {
 $sites = Get-WmiObject -Namespace 'root\webadministration' `
-Class Site -ComputerName $computername -Authentication 6
}
$data = @()
                                                              ❸ Add site
foreach ($site in $sites){                                      properties
 $webdata = New-Object -TypeName PSobject                       to output
 $webdata |
 Add-Member -MemberType NoteProperty -Name "Name" `
-Value $site.Name -PassThru |
 Add-Member -MemberType NoteProperty -Name "Id" `
-Value $site.Id -PassThru |
 Add-Member -MemberType NoteProperty -Name "ServerAutoStart" ` ❹ Add
-Value $site.ServerAutoStart                                    application
                                                                defaults to
 expand-property                                                output
 ➥ $site.ApplicationDefaults.Properties "Application"
```

```
$i = 0
foreach ($binding in $site.Bindings) {
 $webdata |
 Add-Member -MemberType NoteProperty `
-Name "Binding$i-BindingInformation" `
    -Value $binding.BindingInformation -PassThru |
  Add-Member -MemberType NoteProperty -Name "Binding$i-Protocol" `
    -Value $binding.Protocol

 $i++
}
expand-property $site.Limits.Properties "Limits"
expand-property $site.Logfile.Properties "Logfile"
expand-property $site.TraceFailedRequestsLogging.
 Properties "TraceFailedRequestsLogging"
expand-property $site.VirtualDirectoryDefaults.
 Properties "VirtualDirectoryDefaults"

$data += $webdata
}
$data
}}
```

⬅ **⑤ Add binding data to output**

⬅ **⑥ Add other properties to output**

A good design practice for PowerShell cmdlets and functions is to return all of the objects in question by default. An optional parameter is then used to filter the data down to a specific subset of the possible objects. The get-website function follows this practice by using the -Site parameter to allow a single site to be selected ❶.

A WMI call is made to retrieve the data for a single desired site or for all sites on the server ❷. The presence of a WMI filter determines whether one or all sites are returned. In either case, the data is returned to the sites variable, which enables you to use a single set of code for the remainder of the function's processing.

The foreach keyword loop is used to iterate through the sites ❸. The processing in this loop uses a similar technique to listing 12.1. An empty object is created and Add-Member is used to extend the object by adding the properties that define the site.

You can deal with embedded objects, such as ApplicationDefaults ❹, by calling the expand-property function from technique 89. This will drill down into the given object and add the appropriate properties and their values to your object.

A website can have multiple bindings ❺. Each binding defines a unique combination of protocol, IP address, and port that are used to communicate with the website. Bindings are a common source of problems. This technique provides an easy way to determine their current settings.

Additional embedded objects have to be expanded ❻. In some cases, these are identical to those discussed in relation to listing 12.1.

DISCUSSION

The function can be used in two modes. The first mode requires a website name to be supplied, as shown in the following example:

```
get-website -computername web01 -site "Default Web Site"
```

This option will only return the details for the website, as discussed in the solution.

If information relating to all websites is required, you can use the second mode, as shown in this snippet:

```
get-website -computername web01
```

The only parameter you need is the computer name if you're dealing with a remote computer.

Knowing which sites exist on a server provides you with a starting point for managing the website lifecycle.

TECHNIQUE 92   **Creating a website**

You can create websites using the WMI provider, but there are some issues with performing this action due to Packet Privacy being enforced by the provider. This means you need to be a little bit sneaky in the way you approach this problem. I don't recommend this approach for all use of WMI, but it's a useful fallback technique if you can't work directly with the WMI cmdlets.

PROBLEM

You have to create a website on a number of servers in your web farm. Once the site is created, you can copy in the data and web pages. Some of the web servers are in a remote location, so you can't physically get to them without travelling.

SOLUTION

Your immediate thought might be to use the `[wmiclass]` type accelerator to create an instance of the `Site` class and then configure its properties. Unfortunately, this won't work because the accelerator can't work with Packet Privacy when working with a remote machine.

You can solve this problem, as shown in the following listing, by working directly with the WMI-related .NET classes and therefore bypassing the restrictions in the `[wmiclass]` accelerator.

Listing 12.4 Create website

```
function new-website {
[CmdletBinding()]
param (
 [parameter(ValueFromPipeline=$true,
   ValueFromPipelineByPropertyName=$true)]
 [string]$computer="$env:COMPUTERNAME",
 [parameter(Mandatory=$true)]
 [string]$site,
 [parameter(Mandatory=$true)]
 [string]$domain,
 [parameter(Mandatory=$true)]
 [string]$dirpath
)
PROCESS{
$conopt = New-Object System.Management.ConnectionOptions
```
 ① Create options

```
$conopt.Authentication =
  ➥ [System.Management.AuthenticationLevel]::
  ➥ PacketPrivacy
```

❷ **Create scope**

```
$scope = New-Object System.Management.ManagementScope
$scope.Path = "\\$computer\root\WebAdministration"
$scope.Options = $conopt

$path = New-Object System.Management.ManagementPath
$path.ClassName = "Site"
```

❸ **Create site object**

```
$website = New-Object System.Management.ManagementClass(
  ➥ $scope, $path, $null)

$path2 = New-Object System.Management.ManagementPath
$path2.ClassName = "BindingElement"
```

❹ **Create binding**

```
$bind = New-Object System.Management.ManagementClass(
  ➥ $scope, $path2, $null)
$BInstance = $bind.CreateInstance()

$Binstance.BindingInformation = "*:80:$site.$domain"
$BInstance.Protocol = "http"
```

❺ **Create site**

```
$website.Create($site, $Binstance, $dirpath, $true)
}}
```

The standard computer name parameter is joined by parameters for the new site name, the domain, and the directory path used by the site. These are made mandatory to ensure that they have to be input. You don't set a default value when using mandatory parameters, because the default is never accessed.

The .NET classes you need are in the System.Management namespace (.NET namespaces aren't connected to WMI namespaces). You start with the Connection-Options class ❶ which enables you to configure the connection WMI is making. In this case you're setting the authentication level. Other options include a timeout, userid, and password to be used on the connection. The timeout is especially useful, as you'll see in the next chapter.

Your next step is to set the scope in which you're working ❷. This defines the WMI namespace you'll be using. The connection options become the options of the scope.

The ManagementPath class is used to define the WMI class you're using, which in this case is Site. At this point there isn't a check to determine that the class exists in the namespace! You can then create a .NET ManagementClass object that represents the site ❸. This is equivalent to using [wmiclass]. The final parameter represents other options, which in this case are nonexistent, so you use $null.

You then have to repeat your use of ManagementPath and ManagementClass to create the binding for the site ❹. The binding is set to port 80, and you're only using the HTTP protocol.

After all that's accomplished you can create the site using the Create method ❺. This takes the site and binding objects as parameters. You also supply the path to the virtual directory associated with the site. If this doesn't exist you can perform a simple copy to create an instance of it on the remote machine as a precursor step in your script. The final parameter is set to $true, which means the site will automatically start when IIS is started. Set this parameter to $false if you don't want this behavior to occur.

DISCUSSION

If you can remote desktop, or establish a PowerShell remote connection, to the system, the website creation code can be simplified to the following:

```
$Site = [WMIClass]'root\webadministration:Site'
$Binding = [WMIClass]'root\webadministration:BindingElement'

$BInstance = $Binding.CreateInstance()
$Binstance.BindingInformation = "*:80:testwmi.manticore.org"
$BInstance.Protocol = "http"

$Site.Create('NewSiteWMI', $Binstance, 'C:\Inetpub\TestWMI', $true)
```

The [wmiclass] accelerator is used to create instances of the Site and BindingElement classes. The binding information is created, and then the Create method on the site object is used as previously. This version is available in code download for this chapter as new-site.ps1.

Once you've created your site you need to be able to determine if it's running. It should start automatically, but you shouldn't rely on that happening. Being able to test if a site is running is also a good troubleshooting technique.

TECHNIQUE 93   **Testing website status**

Like any applications, websites require a number of other components, such as the network and the operating system, in order to function. In the case of a problem you need to isolate the component causing the problem. One quick test is to see if the website is running. If you can confirm that it shows that the network and other components are functioning.

PROBLEM

The phone rings. "The website isn't available," shouts the user. You need to check whether the website is up before performing other diagnostics.

SOLUTION

The following listing enables you to retrieve the website status, either for a single site if the -site parameter is used, or for all sites if it's omitted.

Listing 12.5   Get website status

```
$ws = DATA {
ConvertFrom-StringData -StringData @'
1 = Started
2 = Starting
3 = Stopped
4 = Stopping
5 = Unknown
'@
}
function get-websitestatus {
```

```
[CmdletBinding()]
param (
 [parameter(ValueFromPipeline=$true,
   ValueFromPipelineByPropertyName=$true)]
 [string]$computername="$env:COMPUTERNAME",
 [string]$site

)
PROCESS{
if ($site) {
 $sites = Get-WmiObject -Namespace 'root\webadministration' `
-Class Site -ComputerName $computername `
-Authentication 6 -Filter "Name='$site'"
}
else {
 $sites = Get-WmiObject -Namespace 'root\webadministration' `
-Class Site -ComputerName $computername -Authentication 6
}
$data = @()

foreach ($site in $sites){
 $wsdata = New-Object -TypeName PSobject
 Add-Member -InputObject $wsdata -MemberType NoteProperty
 ➥ -Name "Name" -Value $site.Name

 $state = $site.GetState()
 Add-Member -InputObject $wsdata -MemberType NoteProperty
 ➥ -Name "Status" -Value $ws["$($state.ReturnValue)"]

 $data += $wsdata
}
$data
}}
```

The function will use `Get-WmiObject` to return the site information for all sites or for the specified site. A WMI filter is used to restrict the output to a single site.

The collection of sites (one or all of them) is processed to create a new object representing each site containing just the information you need. The first property is the site name. You then have to use the `GetState` method to find out if the site is running.

> **NOTE** It would have been so much easier if the site status had been maintained as a property on the site object.

`GetState` returns an integer code to describe the site status. You can use a hash table lookup to decipher the code when you add the status member to your object. The object you created is then added to your storage array.

The array of objects is output to the pipeline when you've finished looping through the sites.

DISCUSSION

The function emits a collection of objects. This means that you can perform further processing of the output:

```
get-websitestatus | sort Name -descending
get-websitestatus | sort status | Format-Table -GroupBy status
```

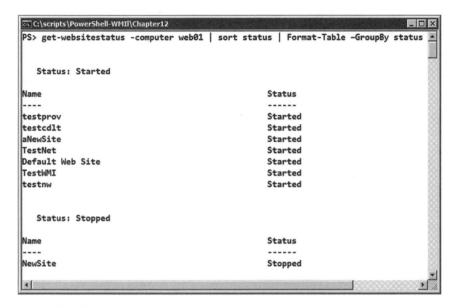

Figure 12.3   Website status reporting using `Format-Table` **and** `GroupBy`

The first example sorts the sites into alphabetical order. The second example is more interesting in that it sorts on the website status and then uses the `-GroupBy` parameter on `Format-Table` to create a more report-like display, as shown in figure 12.3.

If a website is showing problems you may need to restart it to resolve the issue.

TECHNIQUE 94   **Restarting a website**

Restarting a website is a common administrative task. Many websites are started on a nightly basis, which makes the task an ideal candidate for automation. The `Site` class doesn't have a `Restart` method, but it does have `Start` and `Stop` methods.

PROBLEM

A website needs to be restarted on a regular basis as well as on demand. The web server is in another location and you need to be able to schedule a task to perform the action.

SOLUTION

A little thought produces the three functions in the following listing. You have a stop and a start function, which you then combine to produce the restart function. This provides maximum flexibility for administering the website.

Listing 12.6   Restart website

```
function stop-website {
[CmdletBinding()]
param (
 [parameter(ValueFromPipeline=$true,
  ValueFromPipelineByPropertyName=$true)]
```

◁─┐ **Stop**
❶   **website**

```
    [string]$computername="$env:COMPUTERNAME",
    [parameter(Mandatory=$true)]
    [string]$site

)
PROCESS{
Get-WmiObject -Namespace 'root\webadministration' `
-Class Site -ComputerName $computername -Authentication 6 `
-Filter "Name='$site'" |
Invoke-WmiMethod -Name Stop

}}

function start-website {
[CmdletBinding()]
param (
 [parameter(ValueFromPipeline=$true,
   ValueFromPipelineByPropertyName=$true)]
 [string]$computername="$env:COMPUTERNAME",
 [parameter(Mandatory=$true)]
 [string]$site

)
PROCESS{
Get-WmiObject -Namespace 'root\webadministration' `
-Class Site -ComputerName $computername -Authentication 6 `
-Filter "Name='$site'" |
Invoke-WmiMethod -Name Start

}}

function restart-website {
[CmdletBinding()]
param (
 [parameter(ValueFromPipeline=$true,
   ValueFromPipelineByPropertyName=$true)]
 [string]$computername="$env:COMPUTERNAME",
 [parameter(Mandatory=$true)]
  [string]$site

)
PROCESS{
Write-Verbose "Stopping Website $site on $computername"
stop-website -computer $computername -site $site
get-websitestatus -computer $computername -site $site

Write-Verbose "Starting Website $site on $computername"
start-website -computer $computername -site $site
get-websitestatus -computer $computername -site $site

}}
```

◁— **❷ Start website**

◁— **❸ Restart website**

The script begins with the stop-website function ❶. The -site parameter is mandatory—you can't stop a site if you don't know its name. You use the name in the WMI filter
to retrieve the object representing the site. This is then piped into Invoke-WmiMethod,
which calls the Stop method.

A site is started using the start-website function ❷. It works in exactly the same
way, but it calls the Start method.

You can then use the two functions together to perform a restart of the site in the restart-website function ❸. The site name is passed in to stop-website, and the site status is checked using get-websitestatus from listing 12.5. Start-website is then called and another check on the website status is performed.

DISCUSSION

The use of [CmdletBinding()] provides a suite of functionality for free. This includes adding the -Debug and -Verbose common parameters to the function. If the -Verbose parameter is used with the function, the Write-Verbose commands embedded in the function will output extra informational messages.

Websites are the outward facing portion of an IIS server—they are the parts that the users see and interact with. You've seen how to list the websites on a server and how to create, test, and restart individual websites. That covers the major administration tasks at the site level.

Next we'll turn our attention to the internals of IIS—the parts that users don't see directly. You need to learn to work with application pools.

12.3 *Application pools and applications*

An IIS server can host multiple websites. Each website can host multiple applications. An application is a group of files delivering specific content or services. An application pool defines a set of applications that share worker processes.

Using multiple worker processes isolates applications ensuring that a problem in one doesn't leak into all of the applications on the server. This increases stability and reliability of the IIS server.

Your first technique is to discover the web applications hosted on the server. That leads us to the application pools defined on the server and finally we'll look at how you can recycle them. This is analogous to a server reboot but doesn't cause downtime.

TECHNIQUE 95   Listing web applications

Web applications are the reason we have web servers. They're the only part in which users have an interest. The web applications are linked to sites and application pools. Understanding web applications means that you can understand what is happening on the servers.

PROBLEM

Users are reporting issues with the web server. It hosts a number of web applications. You suspect that one particular application is causing the problem. The applications and their related application pools need to be tested to determine their configuration.

SOLUTION

The following listing provides a view of the relationship between the websites, web applications, and application pools. You're looking at this at a server level so there's no parameter to select an individual application pool. This could be added using listing 12.5 as a template.

Listing 12.7   List web applications

```
function get-application {
[CmdletBinding()]
param (
 [parameter(ValueFromPipeline=$true,
   ValueFromPipelineByPropertyName=$true)]
 [string]$computername="$env:COMPUTERNAME"

)
PROCESS{
Get-WmiObject -Namespace 'root\webadministration' `
-Class Application -ComputerName $computername `
-Authentication 6 |
select SiteName, ApplicationPool, Path, EnabledProtocols
}}
```

The body of the function consists of a call to the Application WMI class. Select-Object is then used to deliver the properties you need to see. In this case, you get the site and application pool that are related to the application.

DISCUSSION

This is probably the simplest script in the chapter, but it's the one that probably has the most impact. The secret of a happy IIS server is to ensure that each application is isolated in its own application pool with its own worker processes. The get-application function provides an easy way to discover whether applications are sharing application pools and could therefore interfere with each other.

Now that you know that application pools exist you need to investigate them a bit more.

TECHNIQUE 96   Listing application pools

When an IIS server is created a default application pool is created. Application pools are the way you can control the worker processes on your IIS server. Other application pools can be created as required to host your applications, but they aren't created automatically.

If the application pool associated with an application isn't responding then the application won't work.

PROBLEM

After checking the web applications defined on the server you notice that a number of the applications are sharing an application pool. This could be the source of the problem, so you need to dig deeper into the application pool configuration.

SOLUTION

Listing 12.8 provides a solution to this problem. You can either look at all of the application pools on a server, or you can examine a single application pool.

> **NOTE**   This script displays the properties that I think are most useful. There are a significant number of other properties available, and I strongly urge you to experiment with the ApplicationPool class to discover if there's any other information you need for your particular environment.

The script starts by defining a hash table lookup of the possible application pool states. These are subtly different from the list of states for websites (see listing 12.5). Don't you just love consistency!

Listing 12.8   List application pools

```
$as = DATA {
ConvertFrom-StringData -StringData @'
0 = starting
1 = started
2 = stopping
3 = stopped
4 = unknown
'@
}

function get-apppool {
[CmdletBinding()]
param (
 [parameter(ValueFromPipeline=$true,
   ValueFromPipelineByPropertyName=$true)]
 [string]$computername="$env:COMPUTERNAME",
 [string]$apppool

)
PROCESS{
if ($apppool) {
 $apppools = Get-WmiObject -Namespace 'root\webadministration' `
-Class ApplicationPool -ComputerName $computername `
-Authentication 6 -Filter "Name='$apppool'"
}
else {
 $apppools = Get-WmiObject -Namespace 'root\webadministration' `
-Class ApplicationPool -ComputerName $computername `
-Authentication 6
}
$data = @()

foreach ($apppool in $apppools){

 $state = $apppool.GetState()

 $webdata = New-Object -TypeName PSobject
 $webdata |
 Add-Member -MemberType NoteProperty -Name "Name" `
     -Value $apppool.Name -PassThru |

 Add-Member -MemberType NoteProperty -Name "Status" `
    -Value $as["$($state.ReturnValue)"]    -PassThru |

 Add-Member -MemberType NoteProperty -Name "AutoStart" `
-Value $apppool.AutoStart    -PassThru |

 Add-Member -MemberType NoteProperty -Name "RunTime" `
 -Value $apppool.ManagedRunTimeVersion -PassThru |

 Add-Member -MemberType NoteProperty -Name "CPULimit" `
 -Value $apppool.CPU.Limit    -PassThru |
```

❶ Input parameters

❷ Get application pools

❸ Add properties

```
Add-Member -MemberType NoteProperty -Name "RapidFailprotection"    `
-Value $apppool.Failure.RapidFailProtection

 $data += $webdata
}
$data
}}
```

The function parameters are the computer name and an optional application pool ❶. All application pools, or a single application pool, depending on the use of the parameter, are retrieved and stored in the $apppool variable using a WMI call to the ApplicationPool class ❷. The foreach loop then iterates over the collection of application pools.

   The state of the application pool is placed into the $state variable. A new object is created and populated with the desired properties ❸.

> **NOTE**   The Add-Member statements are shown with a line between them to make the code more readable. The function will still run like this because PowerShell ignores the white space. The version in the code download doesn't have these gaps.

The -PassThru parameter passes the newly extended object to the pipeline, which enables you to simplify the code required to add multiple properties to an object. The object is added to the array you defined to act as a holding collection. At the end of the script the array is passed to the pipeline for further processing and display.

DISCUSSION

An alternative method of setting the properties is as follows:

```
$webdata = New-Object -TypeName PSobject -Property @{
  Name = $apppool.Name
  Status = $as["$($state.ReturnValue)"]
  AutoStart = $apppool.AutoStart
  RunTime = $apppool.ManagedRunTimeVersion
  CPULimit = $apppool.CPU.Limit
  RapidFailprotection  = $apppool.Failure.RapidFailProtection
  }
```

This is a lot less typing and is preferred when you understand what's happening, whereas the Add-Member approach is more meaningful for newcomers to PowerShell. Regardless of your experience, I still recommend using Add-Member when you need to add a single property to an existing object.

   One activity that occurs with some regularity is recycling application pools. This enables you to achieve a finer level of control over the activities on your web server.

TECHNIQUE 97   **Recycling an application pool**

You've seen that application pools are directly related to the worker processes within IIS. There are times you'll need to restart the IIS server, times you'll need to restart a website, and times you'll need to restart an application within a website. You can accomplish the latter task by recycling the application pool. This limits the impact to the minimum number of applications rather than the whole site or server.

PROBLEM

A web application is intermittently exhibiting strange behavior. There are a number of websites on the server, each with several applications. It isn't possible to restart the server or the website due to the needs of other users. You need to recycle the application pool of the application to effectively restart the application.

SOLUTION

The following listing demonstrates how you can use the `ApplicationPool` class to recycle an application pool. The `-apppool` parameter is mandatory. You don't want to recycle every application pool on the IIS server at this stage.

Listing 12.9 Recycle application pool

```
function restart-apppool {
[CmdletBinding()]
param (
 [parameter(ValueFromPipeline=$true,
   ValueFromPipelineByPropertyName=$true)]
 [string]$computername="$env:COMPUTERNAME",
 [parameter(Mandatory=$true)]
 [string]$apppool

)
PROCESS{
Get-WmiObject -Namespace 'root\webadministration' `
-Class ApplicationPool -ComputerName $computername `
-Authentication 6 -Filter "Name='$apppool'" |
Invoke-WmiMethod -Name Recycle

}}
```

This function follows a pattern you've seen a number of times in that you get a WMI object that represents the application pool you're working with. You then pipe this into `Invoke-WmiMethod` and call the `Recycle` method.

> **TIP** This piece of WMI code, like many in the book that deal with performing actions, could be executed at the PowerShell prompt. Wrapping it in a function reduces the amount of typing and increases productivity. When you find yourself using the same code repeatedly it's time to wrap it in a function.

DISCUSSION

The `ApplicationPool` class has `Stop` and `Start` methods. It's possible to create `stop-apppool` and `start-apppool` functions using listing 12.6 as a template. I suspect that the functions to restart a website and to recycle an application pool will be the most-used ones from this chapter.

This concludes our work with the IIS WMI provider, though we haven't covered everything it can do. The techniques presented in this chapter will enable you to dig further into the provider to make your IIS administration easier and more productive.

12.4   *Summary*

PowerShell and WMI provide a robust mechanism to administer local and remote IIS servers. There's an issue with using the provider in that it expects to use Packet Privacy authentication. You've seen how to use that to retrieve information, create new objects on the server, and perform administrative actions on the server.

IIS has a number of components. You've learned to administer

- The web server itself
- Websites
- Applications
- Application pools

In addition, you must remember the other WMI techniques you've seen in previous chapters that enable you to administer the operating system, networking, and other aspects of the system as a whole. One of the great strengths of WMI is that it works from the hardware to the application and enables you to use the same types of techniques to perform administration at all levels.

The next chapter looks at how you can use WMI to configure a brand new server. This will combine some of the techniques that you've already seen with some new techniques.

Configuring a server

This chapter covers

- Renaming a server and joining it to a domain
- Configuring network adapter settings
- Setting the license key and activating a server
- Setting the power plan

I add servers to my test domain on a regular basis. An organization of any size could be adding many servers over the course of a year, especially if they're undertaking a major piece of infrastructure work, such as server consolidation or the introduction of a thin client environment using Terminal Services or Citrix. The key premise of this chapter is that you're adding a new server to a domain. Many of the techniques are still valid in a workgroup environment, but most organizations with more than a handful of computers will be using a domain.

> **TIP** I've assumed in this chapter that the new server has a usable IP address (possibly via DHCP) and that the Windows Firewall is either off or configured to allow remote WMI-based management.

There are a number of tasks you'll need to perform after the operating system has been installed and prior to the installation of applications. These tasks are common across most servers, providing a good reason for automating them. As you'll see, the automation of these tasks builds on some of the PowerShell and WMI functions you've seen in earlier chapters.

> **NOTE**   The order of the tasks described in this chapter isn't the order in which you have to perform them. I prefer to rename the server and set the correct IP address before joining it to the domain. You may prefer a different approach. The techniques can be applied in whatever order is required to satisfy your process.

Modern Windows systems don't supply an option to provide a name for the machine during the installation process. It's unlikely that you'll want to use the name the install routine invents, so your first task will be to rename the server. This technique can also be used at other times in a server's life, such as if it's being repurposed. Once it's renamed, you can then join the machine to the domain to ensure the correct security policies are applied and that you can administer the system more efficiently.

You'll need to restart the server several times during the overall process. You may also need to shut it down to perform a cold start. We'll look at how these tasks can be performed using PowerShell and WMI-based functions.

> **TIP**   If you ever need to shut down a whole data center, the shutdown function presented in this chapter can be used as the basis of that process (or you could use listing 1.4). It works—I've done it. Compare that to logging on to several hundreds of machines to close them down.

I usually configure the network settings next. You saw how to configure network adapters in chapter 11, and you'll use those functions with a wrapper to overcome the issue of resetting the address on the adapter you're connecting through. You'll also see how to reuse the chapter 11 functions to set the DNS servers and other network-related configuration items.

Microsoft's system activation process means that a license key needs to be set for the machine. You'll set the license key through PowerShell and WMI (though this only works for the latest version of Windows). The same WMI classes will be used to activate the machine. This can be always performed at a later date, as you have a number of days grace after installation before you have to activate the server.

Power plans are usually more important for managing client machines than servers. But there are occasions when you may need to set a plan to reduce your server's power consumption. We'll finish the chapter by looking at a technique to perform this task using PowerShell and WMI.

> **NOTE**   You can't use these techniques to configure Windows components such as creating a DNS server or installing IIS. Those actions need to be performed using PowerShell remoting to access the ServerManager module in Windows Server 2008 R2.

The first task on our list is renaming the server.

13.1   Initial tasks

When creating a new server, I normally rename it and then join it to the domain. This avoids having the temporary name in DNS. I also get the time-consuming reboots out of the way by performing these two tasks up front.

TECHNIQUE 98   **Renaming a server**

PowerShell v2 doesn't supply a cmdlet to rename a computer. You can find cmdlets to rename Active Directory objects, but that doesn't change the name of the server.

> **TIP**   You may see references on the internet to a `Rename-Computer` cmdlet. This was available during part of the PowerShell v2 beta process but was withdrawn before version 2 was finalized. The `Rename-Computer` cmdlet has been reinstated in PowerShell v3 (at least as far as the beta version).

This gap in the functionality provides us another opportunity to dip into our WMI bag of tricks.

PROBLEM

An operating system has been installed on a new server. The name assigned to the computer by the Windows install process isn't suitable for your domain, so you need to change it.

SOLUTION

Listing 13.1 shows how you can use the `Win32_ComputerSystem` class to perform this task. The `rename-computer` function has the current computer name and the new name as mandatory parameters. It's important to remember that an IP address can be supplied as the current computer name, as shown in figure 13.1 later in the discussion.

Listing 13.1   Rename server

```
function rename-computer {
[CmdletBinding()]
param (
 [parameter(ValueFromPipeline=$true,
   ValueFromPipelineByPropertyName=$true,
   Mandatory= $true)]
 [string]$computername,
 [parameter(Mandatory= $true)]
 [string]$newname

)
BEGIN{
 $cred = Get-Credential
}
PROCESS {
 $comp = Get-WmiObject Win32_ComputerSystem
 ➥ -ComputerName $computername -Credential $cred
 $ret = $comp.Rename($newname, $null, $null)
 if ($ret.ReturnValue -eq 0){
  Write-Host "Rename of $computer succeeded. Restarting $computer"
```

```
  Restart-Computer -ComputerName $computername -Credential $cred -Force
 }
 else {Write-Host "Rename of $computer failed"}
}}
```

If you've renamed a computer using the manual process, then you know that it requires administrator privileges on the system. The machine isn't part of the domain yet, so you can't use your domain accounts (these techniques are a real-life "chicken and egg" situation—which do you perform first?). You can use Get-Credential to supply the password in a secure manner for the Administrator account on the server, as illustrated in figure 13.1. In my test it wasn't necessary to supply the machine name as part of the credential. It's an available option if required.

> **TIP**   I put Get-Credential into the BEGIN block in listing 13.1 so it executes once if a number of machine names are piped to the function. This may not be appropriate if the same password hasn't been used for all Administrator accounts (ideally they should all be different, but it rarely happens). In that case, move it into the PROCESS block, and you'll be prompted for credentials for each machine.

The Win32_ComputerSystem class is used to create a WMI object for the machine. The credential you created in the previous step is used during the WMI call. This ensures that the object is assigned the correct permissions. The Rename method is used with

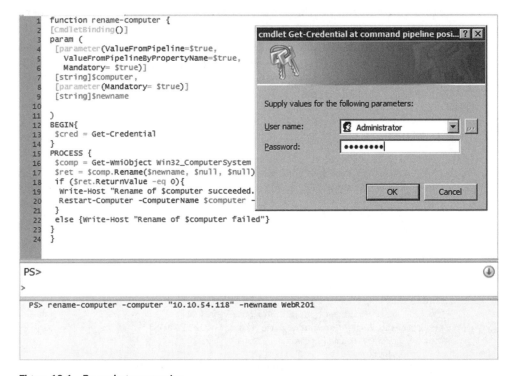

Figure 13.1   Renaming a computer

the value of the script's `newname` parameter. The second and third possible parameters on this method are set to `$null` as they represent an account and password that has permission to perform the rename. You've already supplied this information when you created the WMI object.

The return code is tested, and if it's `0` (success), a message is displayed and the computer is restarted. If any other value is returned, a message stating that the rename action was unsuccessful is displayed.

> **TIP** The vast majority of rename failures can be traced to mistyping the credentials or using the wrong credentials.

DISCUSSION

This function uses the `Restart-Computer` cmdlet from PowerShell v2. This could be replaced by a call to the `Reboot` method of `Win32_ComputerSystem` as shown in section 13.2.2.

This function could also be used if a computer is being repurposed and you need to rename the machine. You can't use WMI to move the server to an Organizational Unit (OU) within Active Directory, but that capability could be added to the script, if required, by utilizing the `[adsi]` type accelerator.

An organization with multiple servers will find that administering those computers through an Active Directory domain is more efficient. You'll need to join your new server to the domain before you can administer it in this way.

TECHNIQUE 99   Joining a computer to a domain

You can use GUI tools to join a computer to the domain, but that means creating a remote desktop connection to the server. It's more efficient to send a command from a script to enable this action.

> **NOTE** The `Add-Computer` cmdlet can be used to join a computer to the domain, but it only works on the local machine. You can't use it to join a remote machine to the domain.

PROBLEM

You need to join your new server to the domain. The correct credentials are available and you need to perform this action in the most efficient manner possible.

SOLUTION

You're joining computers to domains, as shown in the following listing, which means you'll find the WMI method for this on the `Win32_ComputerSystem` class. The important point to note about this script is that two sets of credentials are required.

Listing 13.2 Join computer to domain

```
function join-domain {
[CmdletBinding()]
param (
 [parameter(ValueFromPipeline=$true,
```

```
   ValueFromPipelineByPropertyName=$true,
   Mandatory= $true)]
 [string]$computername
)
BEGIN {
$cred = Get-Credential -Credential Administrator

$domcred = Get-Credential
$domain = $domcred.GetNetworkCredential().Domain
$user = $domcred.UserName
$password = $domcred.GetNetworkCredential().Password
}
PROCESS {
$comp = Get-WmiObject Win32_ComputerSystem
  ➥ -ComputerName $computername -Credential $cred
  ➥ -Authentication 6
$ret = $comp.JoinDomainOrWorkgroup($domain, $password, $user, $null, 3)
if ($ret.ReturnValue -eq 0){
 Write-Host "Joining $computer to $domain succeeded. Restarting $computer"
 Restart-Computer -ComputerName $computername -Force
}
else {Write-Host "Joining $computer to $domain failed"}
}}
```

You start by getting the administrator credential for the new server—it wasn't necessary in my testing to give the machine name as part of the credential. When you join a machine to the domain, you have to provide the credentials of a domain account that has permissions to perform this act.

A second `Get-Credential` call is performed to allow input of the domain credential—the domain name must be part of the credential. The domain is determined from the credential information and the password is also retrieved. The password has to be in a clear string for this technique to work—it's encrypted within the credential. Figure 13.2 shows the encrypted and unencrypted versions of the password in a credential object. Obtaining the password in this way means that you don't store it anywhere for it to be compromised, and it can't be read as you input it.

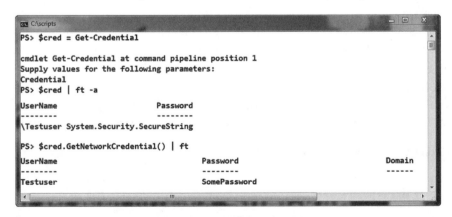

Figure 13.2   Accessing a password from a network credential

A WMI object based on the `Win32_ComputerSystem` class is obtained from the remote machine. The administrator credential for the server is used in this call.

NOTE You have to use Packet Privacy (by using `-Authentication 6` as parameter and value) on the WMI call. The connection has to be encrypted for this action; otherwise an error is thrown by the WMI engine.

The `JoinDomainOrWorkgroup` method is used to add the computer to the domain. The argument given a value of `$null` represents the OU you want the machine to be placed in (`$null` indicates that you're using the default), and the final parameter indicates that you're joining the machine to the domain and creating an account.

A final check on the return value indicates whether the attempt to join the machine to the domain was successful or not. You can then restart the server. If the attempt to join the domain fails for any reason it may be necessary to restart the server before reattempting the action.

DISCUSSION

One of the major reasons for failure when attempting to join a machine to a domain is that the server can't find a domain controller in the domain because DNS isn't configured correctly. This technique assumes that at least one DNS server is configured via DHCP, as is usual in most organizations. If for some reason there isn't one you should perform the tasks in section 13.3 before attempting to join the server to the domain.

I always put new systems into the default Computers container when joining them to the domain. This ensures that Group Policies (GPOs) don't affect the system until I've finished configuring it. If you want to put the machine directly into an OU add a line something like this to define the OU to the script:

```
$ou = "OU=MyOU,DC=Mydomain,DC=COM"
```

The call to the `JoinDomainOrWorkgroup` method is then changed to this:

```
$ret = $comp.JoinDomainOrWorkgroup($domain,
    ➥ $password, $user, $ou, 3)
```

A computer restart is required when you rename the computer or join it to a domain, but you also need to be able to perform these actions at other times. When you use the GUI tools to configure a new server the reboot is triggered by the GUI. When using WMI you need to trigger server shutdown and restarts within the script. Controlling server restarts with WMI is the topic we'll cover next.

13.2 *Controlling server restarts*

There are two actions you need to consider when you want to control a new server. You either want to shut it down completely, or you want to perform a restart so that your configuration changes will be committed and used.

PowerShell v2 supplies cmdlets to perform these actions:

- `Stop-Computer`
- `Restart-Computer`

It's useful to be able to perform these actions directly from WMI.

Shutting down a server

A server may need to be shut down for a number of reasons:

- It's a system that isn't needed at present.
- Configuration hasn't been completed, and you don't want people accessing it until it's ready.
- It's a virtual machine, and the host resources are needed for something else.
- Hardware maintenance has to be performed.

PROBLEM

There's an issue with the power supply in your data center. The power supply will be switched off for safety reasons while this issue is rectified. This requires that all of the systems be shut down during the period of the work.

SOLUTION

The following listing shows how you can shut down one or more servers. This will also work with client machines.

Listing 13.3   Shut down server

```
function stop-server {
[CmdletBinding()]
param (
 [parameter(ValueFromPipeline=$true,
   ValueFromPipelineByPropertyName=$true)]
 [string]$computername="$env:COMPUTERNAME"

)
BEGIN{
$cred = Get-Credential
}
PROCESS {
$comp = Get-WmiObject Win32_OperatingSystem
  ➡ -ComputerName $computername -Credential $cred
$ret = $comp.Shutdown()
if ($ret.ReturnValue -eq 0){
 Write-Host "Shutting down $computername succeeded."
}
else {Write-Host "Shutting down $computername failed"}
}}
```

The computername parameter can be supplied on the command line for a single machine or via the pipeline for a number of machines. You get credentials that give you permission to shut down the server (usually the local administrator on non-domain machines or the domain administrator if in a domain).

The Win32_OperatingSystem class is used on the remote machine and the Shutdown method is called. A test of the return value can be used to check for a successful shutdown.

DISCUSSION

If the same credentials can't be used to shut down all computers you can move the content of the BEGIN block into the start of the PROCESS block.

```
PROCESS {
$cred = Get-Credential
...
}
```

In the perimeter network you may have different administrator passwords on the separate machines.

You can also use the Stop-Computer cmdlet for this action. When in a domain, you'd use this:

```
Stop-Computer -ComputerName web01
```

Otherwise you'd use this:

```
$cred = Get-Credential
Stop-Computer -ComputerName 10.10.54.246 -Credential $cred -Force
```

Stopping the server is a bit drastic and not something you'd want to do on a regular basis. It's more common, especially when configuring a new server, to have to restart the server multiple times.

TECHNIQUE 101   ## Restarting a server

There's a school of thought that states that "Windows servers should be restarted on a regular (often nightly or weekly) basis." I haven't found this to be necessary with modern versions of Windows. The idea is left over from the Windows NT days when the operating system and applications were not as reliable (there are still a few applications that need a regular restart, but this is definitely application driven rather than operating system driven). But you still need to reboot the server after specific tasks have been performed.

PROBLEM

A server has to be restarted due to a problem with an application. That particular application is business critical at this time of year, so you need to initiate the restart as quickly as possible.

SOLUTION

A minor change to technique 99 produces the following listing. The comments in the discussion of listing 13.2 regarding the positioning of the Get-Credential command also apply to this listing.

Listing 13.4 Restart server

```
function restart-server {
[CmdletBinding()]
param (
 [parameter(ValueFromPipeline=$true,
   ValueFromPipelineByPropertyName=$true)]
```

```
  [string]$computername="$env:COMPUTERNAME"
)
BEGIN{
$cred = Get-Credential
}
PROCESS {
$comp = Get-WmiObject Win32_OperatingSystem `
-ComputerName $computername -Credential $cred
$ret = $comp.Reboot()
if ($ret.ReturnValue -eq 0){
 Write-Host "Restarting $computername succeeded."
}
else {Write-Host "Restarting $computername failed"}
}}
```

The change from listing 13.2 is that the Reboot method is used rather than the Shutdown method. The return value is tested to determine whether the restart has succeeded.

DISCUSSION

It would be possible to combine listings 13.2 and 13.3 and use switches to indicate whether a restart or shutdown is required. That was my initial approach, but I decided that it was less confusing to have the granularity of two functions. It also reduces the chances of error!

> **TIP**   When designing your functions I recommend that you build the maximum amount of granularity into your code. Make many small functions, each performing a single job, rather than a small number of large functions. Maintenance will be much easier.

When giving credentials be careful if you use Administrator as the user account. If the machine is a member of a domain it will attempt to use the domain administrator account which may not have rights to the system. It's safest to always fully define the account that's being used:

- Domain\user_name for an Active Directory account
- Computer\user_name for a local account

> **NOTE**   One thing to remember is that restarting the server doesn't necessarily ensure that the applications and services restart. In some cases you'll need to test whether specific services have restarted. You can use the Get-Service cmdlet or listing 9.1 to perform this task.

When I create a new server I normally use DHCP to configure it with an IP address. It's a best practice to use a static IP address for servers. Setting the networking configuration is the next task.

13.3   *Configuring network adapter settings*

When you configure a server's network adapter two main groups of tasks need to be performed:

- Set the IP address and subnet.
- Configure the DNS servers that the server will use and set the connection name.

If you've read these chapters in order you'll remember that you created functions to do this in chapter 11. Setting the DNS servers and connection name can be performed using the functions directly. There's a problem with setting the IP address, but you can find a way around that.

You need to know which adapter you're working with before you start. In this section, I'm assuming you're working with a single adapter. Network adapter teaming can't be performed by WMI and will need to be configured manually.

You can find the adapters using technique 74 in chapter 11:

```
get-nic -computer webr201 |
ft DeviceId, NetConnectionID -a
```

The results for my system show that I need to work with the adapter that has a `DeviceID` of `7` and a `NetConnectionID` of `Local Area Connection`. Your results will probably be different.

Now that you've established which adapter you need to configure we'll look at setting the IP address and then the other information.

TECHNIQUE 102   Setting an IP address

The function in technique 84 (chapter 11) will set an IP address. It works fine when you're modifying the adapter on the local machine or an adapter on a remote machine that's *not* the adapter through which you're connecting to the system. But when you try to modify the IP address of an adapter on a remote machine, which is also the adapter you're attached to, you'll find the following:

1 The IP address will be changed immediately.
2 PowerShell will appear to hang.
3 The server doesn't immediately reset its information in DNS.

Item 1 is good. Item 3 isn't a problem because you can work with the new IP address instead of the name. Item 2 is a problem. What happens is that the IP address on the remote machine is changed, and PowerShell and WMI immediately lose their connection to the machine because the address has changed. You can set WMI to time out, but the network connection doesn't time out as quickly, so PowerShell doesn't regain control of the prompt.

The only way around this that I've discovered, apart from restarting PowerShell, is to wrap the change in a PowerShell job. This immediately returns the prompt, which means you can keep on working while the job waits for the timeout. It's an ugly workaround but it does work. This is the essence of administration scripting—doing what's necessary to get the job done. There are no points for style and artistic interpretation in this game.

PROBLEM

You need to change the IP address on a remote machine. It has a single network adapter and you don't want to wait for the timeout to occur.

SOLUTION

Listing 13.5 is a script rather than a function mainly because using a function added some unnecessary layers of complexity. I've called it set-ipaddress as can be seen in the discussion section. The script takes a computer name, IP address, subnet, and network adapter index as parameters (see technique 74 in chapter 11 for details on discovering the index value).

Listing 13.5   Set IP address

```
[CmdletBinding()]
param (
 [string$computername="$env:COMPUTERNAME",
 [string]$address,
 [string]$subnet,
 [int]$index
)

$script = @"
`$tspan = New-TimeSpan -Seconds 20              ❶ Create timespan
`$conopt = New-Object System.Management.ConnectionOptions
`$conopt.TimeOut = `$tspan

`$scope = New-Object System.Management.ManagementScope   ❷ Set WMI scope
`$scope.Path = "\\$computername\root\cimv2"
`$scope.Options = `$conopt                      ❸ Set WMI path

`$path = New-Object System.Management.ManagementPath
`$path.Path = "Win32_NetworkAdapterConfiguration.Index=$index"

`$nic =
   ➥ New-Object System.Management.ManagementObject(
   ➥ `$scope, `$path, `$null)                   ❹ Create object
`$nic.EnableStatic('$address', '$subnet')
"@
$script | Set-Content -Path setnic.ps1
$path = Join-Path -Path (Get-Location) -ChildPath "setnic.ps1"   ❺ Start job

Start-Job -Name setnic -FilePath $path
```

The next step is to create a here-string (a PowerShell structure for multiline strings) that holds PowerShell code. The backticks (`` ` ``) are used to escape the dollar symbols ($) so that variable substitution is *not* attempted. This script uses the .NET classes to wrap the WMI functionality as an example of how they can be used.

The code starts by creating a timespan object of 20 seconds ❶ and applying it to the timeout property of the WMI connection. The scope defines the WMI namespace and includes the connection options ❷.

The path to the WMI instance you need is defined ❸, and a WMI object is created representing that network adapter configuration ❹. The EnableStatic method is used to set the IP address and subnet.

The contents of the here-string are written to a file using Set-Content. The full path to the file is created, and the final act is to start a job ❺ using the file you've created as the item to action. It's important to remember that the file is on your local system but because of its contents will run against the remote machine.

DISCUSSION

The script can be used as follows. This assumes that you've discovered the index of the adapter you need to modify:

```
set-ipaddress -computername webr201 -address "10.10.54.118" `
 -subnet "255.255.255.0" -index 7
```

That's the hard part out of the way. Setting the DNS servers and the connection name is a piece of cake by comparison.

TECHNIQUE 103   ## Configuring other settings

You need to set the DNS servers so that the machine can find a domain controller for its domain. The network connection name on the adapter should be changed so that it's consistent with your other servers.

PROBLEM

You need to complete the configuration of your network adapter by setting the DNS servers and connection name.

SOLUTION

Listing 13.6 shows how you can do this at the command line. You start by loading the module you created in chapter 11 (it's OK to rename the module if you want, but remember that the .psm1 file needs to be renamed as well).

Alternatively, you could use this line:

```
Import-Module ./Chapter11.psm1 -Force
```

This will reimport the module if it's already loaded. You may need to give the full path on your machine.

The second act is to define the network address of the machine (this assumes you've just changed the IP address, so the name isn't available because DNS hasn't caught up).

Listing 13.6   Set network information

```
if (-not(Get-Module -Name Chapter11)){
  Import-Module ./Chapter11.psm1
}
$computername = "10.10.54.118"

"Set Connection Name"
rename-connection -computername $computername `
-NetConnectionID "Local Area Connection" -newname "Virtual LAN"

"Set DNS Servers"
$dnssvr = "10.10.54.201","10.10.54.98"
set-DNSserver -computername $computername -index 7 -dnsserver $dnssvr
```

You can then use the `rename-connection` (technique 80) and `set-DNSserver` (technique 86) functions from chapter 11. I've added a couple of strings as comments that will be displayed to show progress.

DISCUSSION

This section on configuring the network addresses has illustrated two key points you should keep in mind regarding the use of PowerShell (or any other automation tool):

- Look for reuse when you create your scripts and functions. Technique 103 is all about reuse in that you're using preexisting functions to do the job.
- Concentrate on getting the task completed. The solution in technique 102 isn't elegant but it works. At some stage in the future you may discover a different way of performing the task, but for now your time is better spent on solving other problems.

The remaining major problem to solve is how to activate the servers.

13.4 *Activating a server*

Product activation for Windows servers may seem to be a pain, but it's a fact of life. You have to do it for two reasons:

- To ensure the software is properly licensed and you remain legal
- To keep the servers working

How can you do it in the most efficient manner?

My friend James O'Neill answered this in a blog post. Check http://jamesone111.wordpress.com/ and search for "SoftwareLicensingProduct." You'll find references to two WMI classes:

- `SoftwareLicensingProduct`
- `SoftwareLicensingService`

NOTE   These classes are new in Windows 7 and Windows Server 2008 R2. They're *not* available on earlier versions of Windows.

This section is derived from James' post. You can test the license status of Windows like this:

```
Get-WmiObject SoftwareLicensingProduct |
select Name, LicenseStatus
```

`LicenseStatus` will return an integer value where `0` = Unlicensed and `1` = Licensed. A number of results are returned that represent the various ways Windows can be licensed or activated. The important result is the one with a partial product key:

```
Get-WmiObject SoftwareLicensingProduct |
where {$_.PartialProductKey} |
ft  Name, ApplicationId, LicenseStatus -a
```

This indicates the licensing situation you're dealing with. It would be nice, though, if you could get a little bit more information about the licensing state of your system.

| TECHNIQUE 104 | **Testing license state** |

Has your IT environment ever been audited? Can you prove that all of your servers are properly activated? This section will help you answer that second question. As well as being a useful test while you're building a new server, you can also use it to test the setup of your whole estate.

PROBLEM

You need to test the activation and license state of your servers for auditing purposes. Some of the servers are in remote locations and you don't have the time or resources to physically visit them all.

SOLUTION

You've seen that the license status information is available through the `Software-LicensingProduct` class. The following listing shows how you can use that class to generate a meaningful statement about the license status of your server.

Listing 13.7   Test license status

```
$lstat = DATA {
ConvertFrom-StringData -StringData @'
0 = Unlicensed
1 = Licensed
2 = OOB Grace
3 = OOT Grace
4 = Non-Genuine Grace
5 = Notification
6 = Extended Grace
'@
}
function get-licensestatus {
param (
[parameter(ValueFromPipeline=$true,
   ValueFromPipelineByPropertyName=$true)]
  [string]$computername="$env:COMPUTERNAME"
)
PROCESS {
 Get-WmiObject SoftwareLicensingProduct -ComputerName $computername |
 where {$_.PartialProductKey} |
 select Name, ApplicationId,
 @{N="LicenseStatus"; E={$lstat["$($_.LicenseStatus)"]} }
}}
```

A hash table, `$lstat`, is defined at the beginning of the script. You can then call the `SoftwareLicensingProduct` class against the computer passed as a parameter to the function. The results are filtered on the `PartialproductKey` property to ensure you only get the results you need. There are three pieces of data you need:

- The name of the product
- The `ApplicationId`, which is a GUID
- The decoded license status

Figure 13.3   Testing the license status

The decoding of the license status is managed by the calculated field in the `Select-Object` statement.

DISCUSSION

Figure 13.3 shows the results of running the function. The `ApplicationId` is fixed for versions of Windows. You should get the same result returned on all versions.

The results in figure 13.3 show that you're still in the grace period after installation of the operating system. You need to set the license key before you can activate the server.

TECHNIQUE 105   **Setting the license key**

A Windows license key consists of five groups of five alphanumeric characters. A valid license key is required for each instance of Windows. The key is usually found with the media. Keys are specific to the version of Windows and the source of the media. For instance, you can't use an MSDN key on a commercial version of Windows.

PROBLEM

The license key needs to be set before you can activate the system. You need to perform this act remotely and ensure that the license key is in the correct format.

SOLUTION

Windows 7 and Windows Server 2008 R2 have a WMI class—`SoftwareLicensing-Service`—that you can use to solve this problem, as shown in the following listing. The license key and computer name have been made mandatory parameters. This removes the need for default values. The license key pattern is evaluated using a regular expression and the `ValidatePattern` method. This won't guarantee that the key is correct, but it will ensure it's in the right format.

Listing 13.8   Set license key

```
function set-licensekey {
param (
[parameter(Mandatory=$true)]
[string]
[ValidatePattern("^\S{5}-\S{5}-\S{5}-\S{5}-\S{5}")]
$Productkey,

[parameter(Mandatory=$true)]
[string]$computername="$env:COMPUTERNAME"
```

```
)
  $product = Get-WmiObject -Class SoftwareLicensingService `
-computername $computername
  $product.InstallProductKey($ProductKey)
  $product.RefreshLicenseStatus()
}
```

You use the `SoftwareLicensingService` class to create a WMI object. You can use the `InstallProductKey` method with the license key as an argument. The last line of the function refreshes the license status information.

DISCUSSION

The function is used as follows:

```
set-licensekey -Productkey "XXXXX-XXXXX-XXXXX-XXXXX-XXXXX" `
-computername "10.10.54.118"
```

The `"XXXXX-XXXXX-XXXXX-XXXXX-XXXXX"` represents the license key. You didn't really think I'd use my real key? The computer on which you're installing the key can be designated by IP address as here or by its name.

> **TIP**   One additional possibility is to use WMI to read the operating system type (see technique 14 in chapter 5), retrieve the key from a secure store, and apply it. Ideally, the script would then activate the server as well (technique 106, coming up next).

The server is now properly licensed. All you have to do is activate the license.

TECHNIQUE 106   **Activating a server**

Product activation can be accomplished in a number of ways. In this section, we'll assume that the server has a connection to the internet so that direct activation can occur. It's possible to activate manually via a phone call, but you can't get PowerShell and WMI to do that for you—yet.

> **TIP**   Reactivation will be required if you move a virtual server between hosts that have different CPU architectures.

Activation is based on the hardware configuration of your server. If it changes too much be prepared to reactivate.

PROBLEM

Your server needs to be activated. Activation is required because you've just created a new server and you need to ensure that it remains usable beyond the grace period.

SOLUTION

You can use the `SoftwareLicensingProduct` class to solve this, as shown in the next listing. Your `invoke-activation` function has a mandatory parameter for the computer name. I wasn't sure which PowerShell verb to use in the name of this function—"invoke" seems to be the closest match.

Listing 13.9   Activate server

```
function invoke-activation {
param (
  [parameter(Mandatory=$true)]
  [string]$computername="$env:COMPUTERNAME"
)

 $product = Get-WmiObject SoftwareLicensingProduct `
-ComputerName $computername |
 where {$_.PartialProductKey}

 $product.Activate()
}
```

You create a WMI object using the SoftwareLicensingProduct class. The results are filtered down to a single instance by using the PartialProductKey property. The Activate method is called to perform the task.

You should be aware that it takes a little while for the activation to complete, as the system has to link to the Microsoft website to register the activation.

DISCUSSION

Once you've completed the activation process, you should double-check that everything has worked by using get-licensestatus from technique 104. The results should be similar to those shown in figure 13.4. Notice how the LicenseStatus has changed to read Licensed, as compared to Grace in figure 13.3.

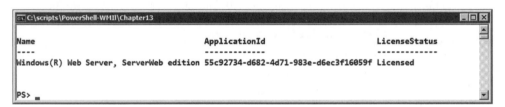

Figure 13.4   A licensed server

Your server is now renamed, licensed, activated, and joined to the domain. You've configured the network adapters. The server is ready for the installation of the appropriate applications.

One last optional task is to set the power plan for the server.

TECHNIQUE 107   **Setting a power plan**

Windows power plans control how your system consumes power. You can view the existing power plans using the Win32_PowerPlan class:

```
Get-WmiObject -Namespace 'root\cimv2\power' `
-Class Win32_PowerPlan -ComputerName "10.10.54.118" |
select ElementName, IsActive
```

A new Windows Server 2008 R2 or Windows 7 system will have three power plans defined:

- Balanced
- High performance
- Power saver

The Balanced plan is usually the active one on new installs.

> **NOTE** Power plans are arguably less important when you're dealing with a
> virtualized server, because it's the power plan of the host that controls the
> power consumption. You may be able to save some power by configuring the
> virtual server's power plan, but it would be very difficult to quantify.

Most organizations have a number of physical servers and you can make an impact by
configuring the power plans on those systems.

PROBLEM
You need to be able to configure the Windows power plans across your server estate to
ensure that all servers are consuming the minimum amount of power that's consistent
with them being able to perform their functions correctly.

SOLUTION
There's a root\cimv2\power namespace tucked away inside WMI. It's often overlooked
because it's a child of the more important root\cimv2 namespace. In that namespace
you'll find a `Win32_PowerPlan` class. This is the core of the solution to the problem, as
shown in the following listing.

Listing 13.10 Set power plan

```
function set-powerplan {
param (
[string]$plan="Balanced",

[parameter(Mandatory=$true,
   ValueFromPipeline=$true,
   ValueFromPipelineByPropertyName=$true)]
[string]$computername
)
PROCESS {
 Get-WmiObject -Namespace 'root\cimv2\power'
 -Class Win32_PowerPlan  -ComputerName $computername `
 -Filter "ElementName='$plan'" |
 Invoke-WmiMethod -Name Activate
}
}
```

A string representing the power plan name and a computer name are the only parameters you need for this function. You call the `Win32_PowerPlan` class (notice that you
need to give the namespace because you're not working in the default). The plan
name is used as a filter on `Get-WmiObject`.

The resultant object is piped into `Invoke-WmiMethod`, where you call the `Activate`
method. This will replace any existing active plan with the one you want.

DISCUSSION

It's possible to create power plans using the WMI classes in the root\cimv2\power namespace. In my experience the plans that are built into Windows are sufficient for servers. The classes in the namespace are listed in table 13.1.

Table 13.1   Classes in the root\cimv2\power namespace

Win32_PowerMeter	Win32_PowerMeterConformsToProfile
Win32_PowerMeterEvent	Win32_PowerPlan
Win32_PowerSetting	Win32_PowerSettingCapabilities
Win32_PowerSettingDataIndex	Win32_PowerSettingDataIndexInPlan
Win32_PowerSettingDefine-Capabilities	Win32_PowerSettingDefinition
Win32_PowerSettingDefinition-PossibleValue	Win32_PowerSettingDefinitionRangeData
Win32_PowerSettingElementSetting-DataIndex	Win32_PowerSettingInSubgroup
Win32_PowerSettingSubgroup	Win32_PowerSupply

This quick look at power plans concludes our look at configuring a new server. This isn't necessarily the complete list of things you need to do to a server, but the techniques in other chapters will supply ways to complete those other tasks, such as creating registry keys (chapter 7) or creating shares (chapter 8).

13.5 *Summary*

Configuring a new server is a task that occurs on a regular basis in most organizations. There are a number of steps to be completed after the operating system is installed:

- Rename the server to something more meaningful.
- Stop and restart the server as required.
- Set the IP address and DNS servers.
- Rename the network connection.
- Join the server to the domain.
- Install the license key.
- Activate the server.
- Set the power plan.

All of these activities take time. You can use PowerShell functions to perform these tasks remotely so you don't need to spend time accessing the server directly.

That completes our look at server configuration. In the next chapter you'll discover how you can work with users and groups. You'll also learn how to work with the security configurations of your servers.

Users and security

14

This chapter covers

- Working with local users and groups
- Discovering antimalware software status
- Testing firewall state
- Listing firewall settings

If it wasn't for the users we wouldn't have our jobs. Sometimes it may seem that the users cause all our problems, but they're an essential part of the IT environment. Honest! In this chapter, we'll focus on administrating user accounts and also on security, related both to user accounts and external threats.

The majority of the user administration in a Windows environment occurs through Active Directory. The WMI connector for Active Directory is deprecated in Windows Server 8. Active Directory administration is best performed using the PowerShell cmdlets. However a significant amount of administration is still required for accounts local to a specific machine, and this is where WMI and PowerShell can be of assistance.

TIP Chapters 5, 10, and 11 of my *PowerShell in Practice* book cover using PowerShell to administer Active Directory in great detail.

Most organizations have a set of procedures that are followed when people join or leave. This can include setting up user accounts, adding users to groups, creating mailboxes, and setting permissions on data shares. The WMI classes associated with users don't really lend themselves to being involved in this activity, apart from the setting of permissions on file shares, as we discussed in chapter 8.

Do you know what local accounts have been created on your servers and why they were created? Do you know who is a member of the local Administrators group on your SQL Server machine? You had better be able to answer these questions, especially the last one, because it can leave a serious security hole if the wrong people have too much access.

> **WARNING**   The reason for asking specifically about local administrators on SQL Server systems is that the group is automatically given sysadmin (full) rights to SQL Server. Oops.

WMI enables you to view the list of user accounts on the server. You can also investigate which users are logged onto the system. In addition you can delve into the user accounts and discover their membership in local groups, their desktop and profile, and their logon session.

You can work with local groups to discover the members of a particular group. This is great for checking who has been granted membership in the local Administrators group. The techniques discussed for discovering user and group information will also work on client machines. In some respects they may be more useful when applied to client machines because many organizations have to grant administrator privileges to users to ensure that their applications work, and some users like to tinker. You can use the WMI techniques presented in this chapter to undo some of those changes without having to visit the machines.

Security has many aspects. In this chapter we'll concentrate on the steps you need to take to protect your systems directly against external threats. This involves checking the status of the antivirus and antispyware software. Windows provides some WMI classes to perform these tasks, and there are other classes introduced by specific products that can help. We'll examine both.

The last aspect of security we'll examine is the firewall on the machine. Modern versions of Windows ship with a software firewall built into the system. This can be replaced by a third-party offering if desired. You can use WMI to discover the firewall status and settings.

We'll start by looking at the local user accounts.

14.1   *User accounts on the local system*

Local user accounts can be defined for a number of reasons, such as allowing a third-party organization access to a system to maintain the application or even giving a user access to work with a specific part of an application. We'll work on the principle that there's a good reason for creating local accounts.

The first item on the agenda in this section is to discover which accounts are present on your local system. Creating accounts using WMI isn't something I recommend as there are easier methods of performing the task. But WMI is useful for auditing purposes—for determining what accounts have been created.

The usual outcome of an audit of this sort is that some user accounts will be found to be no longer required. We'll look at a function to delete those unwanted accounts. This will also provide you with an opportunity to discover how to use the PowerShell utility cmdlets to link functions that work with different object types and parameters.

While the list of user accounts is useful for housekeeping, when it comes to troubleshooting you need to know which accounts are actually logged on. This technique aids in determining whether the accounts linked to services are configured correctly.

This section closes with a technique to discover information associated with a user, such as the desktop and profile. The profile information is especially useful if you suspect profile corruption is causing problems for the user.

All objects in a Windows environment have a Security Identifier (SID). This is what Windows uses under the covers to work with objects, assign permissions, manage group membership, and so on. Table 14.1 lists the SID types you're likely to encounter. Most of the time you'll be working with types 1 or 2—users and groups respectively.

Value	Meaning
1	SidTypeUser
2	SidTypeGroup
3	SidTypeDomain
4	SidTypeAlias
5	SidTypeWellKnownGroup
6	SidTypeDeletedAccount
7	SidTypeInvalid
8	SidTypeUnknown
9	SidTypeComputer

Table 14.1   SID types

Once you know what users have been created on your system you can determine which accounts are valid and which should be removed.

TECHNIQUE 108   Listing user accounts

Windows has a simple model for granting permissions. Put the users into a group and apply the permissions to the group. In many of the organizations I've worked with this model has been ignored either through lack of knowledge or for expediency. This can lead to the situation where a lot of accounts are defined on local systems that you don't need. In a domain environment all permissions should be managed through domain-level accounts rather than local accounts.

PROBLEM

You need to investigate the user accounts that have been created on your local systems to ensure that your security model isn't being bypassed. Ideally you need an efficient method of removing unrequired local user accounts.

SOLUTION

The following listing illustrates how you can solve this problem. The `Win32_UserAccount` class was created to supply this information.

Listing 14.1 List user accounts on the local machine

```
function get-useraccount{
[CmdletBinding()]
param (
 [parameter(ValueFromPipeline=$true,
   ValueFromPipelineByPropertyName=$true)]
 [string]$computername="$env:COMPUTERNAME"
)
PROCESS{
 Get-WmiObject -Class Win32_UserAccount -ComputerName $computername |
 select AccountType, Description, Disabled, Domain, FullName,
 InstallDate, LocalAccount, Lockout, Name, PasswordChangeable,
 PasswordExpires, PasswordRequired, SID, SIDType
}}
```

The function has a computer name as a parameter, and then it accesses the `Win32_UserAccount` class to discover the users. The properties of immediate interest are chosen using `Select-Object`.

DISCUSSION

Figure 14.1 illustrates the output from this function. I've applied a further restriction to the output using `Format-Table` (aliased to `ft`). The domain, name, and description are displayed. The `-a` is a shortened form of `-AutoSize`.

> **TIP** PowerShell will accept the minimum number of characters in a parameter name to unambiguously identify the parameter. It's a great idea at the command line but shouldn't be used in scripts.

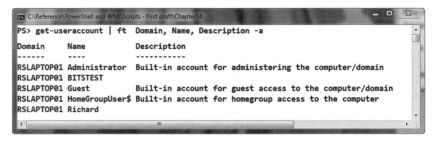

Figure 14.1 Discovering local user accounts

One property that isn't shown in the figure is `AccountType`. You'd generally expect the `AccountType` property to have a value of 512, which indicates a normal user account.

The `Win32_UserAccount` class enables you to rename a user account but you can't do much else with it directly. The WMI provider doesn't support deleting accounts which means you need to drop out of WMI to perform that task. Let's take a little side trip. I happen to have a function that you can use to delete local accounts, as the next listing shows.

Listing 14.2 Delete local user account

```
function remove-user {
[CmdletBinding(SupportsShouldProcess=$true)]
param (
 [parameter(ValueFromPipeline=$true,
   ValueFromPipelineByPropertyName=$true)]
 [string]$computername,

 [parameter(ValueFromPipeline=$true,
   ValueFromPipelineByPropertyName=$true)]
 [string]$id
)
BEGIN {Add-Type -AssemblyName System.DirectoryServices.AccountManagement}

PROCESS {
 switch ($computername){
  "."       {$computername = $env:COMPUTERNAME}
  "localhost" {$computername = $env:COMPUTERNAME}
 }

 $ctype = [System.DirectoryServices.AccountManagement.ContextType]::Machine

$context = New-Object -TypeName
 ➥ System.DirectoryServices.
 ➥ AccountManagement.PrincipalContext
 ➥ -ArgumentList $ctype, $computername

$user = [System.DirectoryServices.AccountManagement.
 ➥ UserPrincipal]::FindByIdentity($context, $id)

if ($psCmdlet.ShouldProcess("$id", "Will be deleted")) {
    $user.Delete()
  }
}}
```

The function takes a computer name and ID as parameters. It uses the `System.DirectoryServices.AccountManagement` classes to specify that you're dealing with a local account (machine context type) and then find the account of interest. The account is then deleted. Just to be safe, I've added the ability to use the `-WhatIf` parameter.

Ideally you'll want the WMI function that discovers the local user accounts to be able to talk to the function that deletes them. Unfortunately, the WMI function outputs all user accounts and it doesn't output a property called `computername` or `id`. Not good. Will you have to rewrite one of the functions or write a brand new function?

If you remember back to chapter 2, we discussed the utility cmdlets, such as `Where-Object` and `Select-Object`. These are designed to be the glue between your processing cmdlets or functions.

You can use `Where-Object` to restrict the output of `get-useraccount`:

```
get-useraccount |
where {$_.Name -eq "BITSTEST"}
```

You now have a single user account on the pipeline. You can use calculated fields in `Select-Object` to redefine the names of the properties:

```
get-useraccount |
where {$_.Name -eq "BITSTEST"} |
select @{N="computer"; E={$_.Domain}},
@{N="id"; E={$_.Name}}
```

Your object now consists of two properties—computer (name) and id (user account name). This can be piped into the `remove-user` function to perform the deletion:

```
get-useraccount |
where {$_.Name -eq "BITSTEST"} |
select @{N="computer"; E={$_.Domain}},
 @{N="id"; E={$_.Name}} |
remove-user -WhatIf
```

I used the `-Whatif` parameter during testing. It's always a good idea to experiment with it present, just to avoid unpleasant surprises. This PowerShell pipeline could now be put into a function to make an admin tool for deleting local user accounts on remote machines.

This exercise demonstrates a very important point about using PowerShell. You'll acquire functionality from a number of sources. The output and property names you need won't always match up and you have two choices:

- Rewrite everything to produce a unified set of properties and parameters
- Use the utility cmdlets to integrate the various cmdlets and functions

The second option maximizes your return from the time spent doing the integration. You end up being able to automate more in a shorter time and so get the maximum benefit from the time you spend working on the problem.

You can now find the user accounts that exist on the server, but can you find the users that are currently logged on to the system?

TECHNIQUE 109   Finding logged on users

The list of user accounts defined on a system gives you one part of the jigsaw, but it doesn't tell you if those users are active. When you're troubleshooting a problem, you may need to determine whether an account has established a logon session with the system. As an example, if SQL Server won't start, it may be because the service account hasn't successfully connected to the server.

PROBLEM

You need to discover which accounts are logged on to a system. This may include individual user accounts as well as service accounts.

SOLUTION

You don't have any direct way to determine this information, but WMI maintains links between classes using association classes. The following listing uses an association class to discover the information you need to solve this problem.

Listing 14.3   Discover logged on users

```
function get-loggedonuser{
[CmdletBinding()]
param (
 [parameter(ValueFromPipeline=$true,
  ValueFromPipelineByPropertyName=$true)]
 [[string]$computername="$env:COMPUTERNAME")

PROCESS{
 Get-WmiObject -Class Win32_LoggedOnUser -ComputerName $computername |
 foreach {
   $ud = $_.Antecedent -split ","
   $user = New-Object -TypeName PSObject -Property @{
    Domain = (($ud[0] -split "\.")[2] -split "=")[1] -replace '"', ''
    User = ($ud[1] -split "=")[1] -replace '"', ''
    Id = (($_.Dependent -split "\.")[2] -split "=")[1] -replace '"', ''
   }
   $user.PSTypeNames[0] = "LoggedOnUser"
   $user
 }
}#process
}
```

The function uses the `Win32_LoggedOnUser` class to retrieve data from the system of interest. An instance of the class is returned for every user account that's logged on to the system. Each instance associates a user account with a logon session. The `Antecedent` property stores the user account. Here's an example:

`\\.\root\cimv2:Win32_Account.Domain="RSLAPTOP01",Name="SYSTEM"`

The `Dependent` property stores the logon session, like this:

`\\.\root\cimv2:Win32_LogonSession.LogonId="999"`

You pipe each of the returned WMI objects into `ForEach-Object`. The first task is to split the `Antecedent` property on the comma. A new PowerShell object is created to store the output and the properties are populated.

The `Domain` property is found by taking the first element of the array created by splitting the `Antecedent` property. That's then split again on the period (`.`). The slash (`\`) is an escape character to ensure you split on the literal character, which gives you `Domain="RSLAPTOP01"` as the third element (index 2). That's split on the equal sign

(=)and the double quotes are removed. The domain should be the machine name for a local user.

The `User` name is also present in the `Antecedent` property. You go back to your original split of this property and use the second element (index 1). This is split on the equal sign (=)and the double quotes are removed.

The session `Id` can be found on the dependent property. You can split on the period (.) and then split the third element on the equal sign (=) and remove the double quotes.

> **TIP**   Work through this example to ensure that you fully understand how to arrive at the answer. PowerShell is object-based but that doesn't mean you can avoid string handling completely.

The object type is renamed and output to complete the processing.

DISCUSSION

Renaming the type of the output object is very useful if you intend on creating default display formats for your output. You've seen default display formats in action when you use `Win32_ComputerSystem`—compare the six properties displayed by default with the full set of properties.

Default display formats are based on the .NET type name of the object to be formatted (you'll see an example of a format file in chapter 18). You can't create a default display format for a `PSObject` because that type is used for numerous different sets of data. But if you rename the type you can then create individual default formats as required. The original type name can be seen like this:

```
New-Object PSObject | gm
```

It returns a type of `System.Management.Automation.PSCustomObject`. When you change the object type and test again

```
get-loggedonuser | gm
```

you get a type name of `LoggedOnUser`.

You can also access other information regarding user accounts on your system.

TECHNIQUE 110   Discovering user information

You've seen the concept of associations between WMI classes a number of times throughout the book. The concept applies to the `Win32_UserAccount` class too. There are a number of classes associated with users, as you'd expect.

You can display the associated classes using this piece of PowerShell.

```
Get-WmiObject -Query "ASSOCIATORS OF
    {Win32_UserAccount.Domain='RSLAPTOP01',Name='Richard'} WHERE
    ClassDefsOnly"
```

This takes a while to run, but it produces the following list:

- `Win32_Desktop`
- `Win32_ComputerSystem`
- `Win32_LogonSession`
- `Win32_Group`
- `Win32_SID`
- `Win32_NTLogEvent`

You can ignore `Win32_ComputerSystem`, `Win32_SID`, and `Win32_NTLogEvent` for our current purposes. The computer system you already know, the SID is also delivered by `Win32_UserAccount`, and the event log entries will be investigated further in the next chapter.

When you're investigating issues that users may be having, you need to look beyond the account. You need to consider other aspects related to users, such as the profile, desktop, and group membership.

PROBLEM

A full investigation into the user configuration on a system is required. You need to be able to retrieve as much information on the configuration of the user account and associated items as is practicable.

SOLUTION

Listing 14.4 may seem to be a very long script to solve this problem. A lot of the length comes from the use of `Add-Member` to add properties to the object you're creating.

> **NOTE** The following listing is truncated for brevity. A number of properties are added that aren't shown in the listing. The listing in the code download has the full property set.

The goal of this function is to output a single object that includes all of the information you need. This will enable you to put the data onto the PowerShell pipeline for further processing.

Listing 14.4 Get user information

```
function get-userinfo{
[CmdletBinding()]
param (
 [parameter(ValueFromPipeline=$true,
   ValueFromPipelineByPropertyName=$true)]
 [string]$computername="$env:COMPUTERNAME",
 [parameter(Mandatory=$true)]
 [string]$user
)
PROCESS{
 if ($computername -eq "." -or
 ➥ $computername -eq "localhost"){
   $domain = $env:COMPUTERNAME}
 else {$domain = $computername}
```

 1 Set domain

```
$userfilt = "Name='$user'"
$userinfo = Get-WmiObject -Class Win32_UserAccount `
-ComputerName $computername -Filter $userfilt |
select Name, Domain, FullName, Description,
LocalAccount, Disabled, Lockout,
PasswordChangeable, PasswordExpires,
PasswordRequired, SID

if (!$userinfo){Throw "User NOT found"}

$qdesktop = "ASSOCIATORS OF
➥ {Win32_UserAccount.Domain='$domain',Name='$user'}
➥ WHERE ResultClass = Win32_Desktop"
$desktop =
➥ Get-WmiObject -ComputerName $computername -Query $qdesktop

$userinfo |
Add-Member -MemberType NoteProperty -Name DeskScreenSaverActive `
-Value $desktop.ScreenSaverActive     -PassThru |

Add-Member -MemberType NoteProperty -Name DeskScreenSaverExecutable `
-Value $desktop.ScreenSaverExecutable -PassThru |

Add-Member -MemberType NoteProperty -Name DeskScreenSaverSecure `
-Value $desktop.ScreenSaverSecure     -PassThru |

Add-Member -MemberType NoteProperty -Name DeskScreenSaverTimeout `
-Value $desktop.ScreenSaverTimeout    -PassThru |

Add-Member -MemberType NoteProperty -Name DeskWallpaper `
-Value $desktop.Wallpaper

$profilt = "SID='$($userinfo.SID)'"
Write-Debug $profilt
$profile = Get-WmiObject -Class Win32_UserProfile `
-Filter $profilt -ComputerName $computername

$userinfo |
Add-Member -MemberType NoteProperty -Name ProfileLastUseTime `
-Value $($profile.ConvertToDateTime($profile.LastUseTime))  -PassThru |

Add-Member -MemberType NoteProperty -Name ProfileLocalPath `
-Value $profile.LocalPath -PassThru |

Add-Member -MemberType NoteProperty -Name ProfileSpecial `
-Value $profile.Special

$qlogon = "ASSOCIATORS OF
➥ {Win32_UserAccount.Domain='$domain',Name='$user'}
➥ WHERE ResultClass = Win32_LogonSession"
$logons = Get-WmiObject -ComputerName $computername -Query $qlogon

$ls = 1
foreach ($logon in $logons) {
   $userinfo |
   Add-Member -MemberType NoteProperty `
   -Name "Logon$ls-AuthenticationPackage"  `
   -Value $logon.AuthenticationPackage -PassThru |

   Add-Member -MemberType NoteProperty `
   -Name "Logon$ls-LogonId"  -Value $logon.LogonId -PassThru |
```

2 **Get user**

3 **Get desktop data**

4 **Get profile**

5 **Get logon session**

```
    Add-Member -MemberType NoteProperty -Name "Logon$ls-StartTime"   `
      -Value $($logon.ConvertToDateTime($logon.StartTime))

    $ls++
}
$qgroups = "ASSOCIATORS OF
  ➡ {Win32_UserAccount.Domain='$domain',Name='$user'}
  ➡ WHERE ResultClass = Win32_Group"
$groups = Get-WmiObject -ComputerName $computername -Query $qgroups

$groupnames = @()
foreach ($group in $groups){$groupnames += $group.Name}
$userinfo |
Add-Member -MemberType NoteProperty -Name Groups -Value $groupnames

$userinfo

}#process
}
```

6 Get group membership

The function commences by taking a computer name and user name as parameters. The user name is a mandatory parameter to ensure you have something to work with. You need to ensure that the computer name is in a format you can work with; converting it to the actual computer name ensures that you can also use it as the domain name when required **1**.

The next step is to get the Win32_UserAccount object representing the user **2**. The output object ($userinfo) is created by selecting the properties you want. If the user account can't be found an error is thrown and the function stops processing.

A WQL query is created and run to get the Win32_Desktop associated with the user **3**. Properties are added to the $userinfo object using Add-Member.

The user profile information is added in a similar manner, except this time you create a WMI filter based on the SID of the user **4**. There isn't a direct association between the user account and the profile. This is just one of WMI's little mysteries.

You're back to using an "ASSOCIATORS OF" type WQL query when you want to retrieve the logon sessions associated with the user account **5**. There may well be more than one logon session associated with an account, so you need to use foreach to iterate through the sessions. Add-Member continues to be used to add more properties to the $userinfo object, but you differentiate each logon session using an integer counter.

The function ends by getting the groups the user is a member of by associating the Win32_Group class **6**. In this case you only need the group names. You can iterate through the groups, add the group name to an array, and then add the array as the value of a new property. The $userinfo object is then output to the PowerShell pipeline.

DISCUSSION

This technique returns a lot of information. There are a few options for restricting the data returned:

- Break the script into a number of smaller functions. This has the drawback of losing the ability to retrieve all information in one pass.
- Add more parameters to switch functionality on or off.
- Use `Where-Object` to restrict the output.

These options show PowerShell at its best—very flexible and able to meet your particular needs.

You saw at the end of listing 14.4 how you can discover the groups associated with a user. We need to investigate local groups a little bit more.

14.2   Groups on the local system

I've mentioned groups several times in the chapter. Groups are an important concept in Windows environments. Without them we'd have to administer each user account individually, which would increase our workload significantly.

Groups are important for allocating permissions, but there are only two things you really need to consider in this section—discovering which groups are present on the system, and then discovering the membership of those groups.

TECHNIQUE 111   **Listing local groups**

Active Directory groups are used for the majority of administration needs, but there are a number of scenarios where you'll need to investigate local groups and their membership. The first task is to discover what local groups are present on the system.

PROBLEM

The list of local groups on your servers has to be determined so that you can properly audit the security settings on the system. You need to ensure that additional groups haven't been created to bypass your Active Directory–based security.

SOLUTION

The following listing shows how you can obtain a list of groups. You only need a computer name as a parameter.

Listing 14.5   List local groups

```
function get-group{
[CmdletBinding()]
param (
 [parameter(ValueFromPipeline=$true,
   ValueFromPipelineByPropertyName=$true)]
 [string]$computername="$env:COMPUTERNAME"
)
PROCESS{
 Get-WmiObject -Class Win32_Group -ComputerName $computername |
 select Description, Domain, InstallDate, LocalAccount,
 Name, SID, SIDType
}}
```

The `Win32_Group` class supplies everything you need to solve the problem. A call to `Get-WmiObject` with the `ComputerName` parameter, ensuring you target the correct system, is followed by `Select-Object` to filter the properties you wish to output.

DISCUSSION

One point that must be remembered when looking at local users and groups with
WMI is that the Domain property will have a value of the local computer name, but for
domain-level accounts, the Domain property will carry the name of the domain. This
can appear confusing if the results are just skimmed.

It's one thing to know what groups are on the system. It's more important, though,
to understand the membership of those groups.

TECHNIQUE 112　　**Listing group membership**

There are some local groups, such as the Administrators group, for which it's very
important that you keep a tight control on membership. You could use Restrictive
Groups in GPOs, but that can lead to administrative overhead. It can also lead to
group membership being wiped out if you get the GPO wrong. I prefer to audit the
group membership on a regular basis.

PROBLEM

You need to determine the group membership for the local groups on a specified system. This ensures that too many privileges haven't been granted.

SOLUTION

The following listing demonstrates how to solve this problem. The computer name is
the only parameter again.

Listing 14.6　List group membership

```
function get-groupmembership{
[CmdletBinding()]
param (
 [parameter(ValueFromPipeline=$true,
   ValueFromPipelineByPropertyName=$true)]
 [string]$computername="$env:COMPUTERNAME"
)
PROCESS{
 Get-WmiObject -Class Win32_Group -ComputerName $computername |
 foreach {
  $group = $_.Name
  $domain = $_.Domain
  $query = "ASSOCIATORS OF {
➥ Win32_Group.Domain='$domain',Name='$group'}
➥ WHERE ResultClass = Win32_UserAccount"
  Get-WmiObject -ComputerName $computername -query $query |
  foreach {
    $member = New-Object -TypeName PSObject -Property @{
       GroupName = $group
       GroupDomain = $domain
       UserName = $_.Name
       UserDomain = $_.Domain
    }
    $member
  }
 }
}}
```

You retrieve the list of groups on the system using `Win32_Group` (alternatively, it would have been possible to use a call to the `get-group` function from listing 14.5). You then iterate through the groups, and for each of them you find the associated users.

An object is created that contains the user name, the group name, and their respective domains. The function outputs the object as its last act.

DISCUSSION

If you only want to check the membership of one or two groups you could modify the function to filter out the other groups using `Where-Object`. The local Administrators group should always be included in any audit activity.

The other aspect of the computers that you need to consider is their security settings. This includes the antimalware and the firewall installed on the server.

14.3 *Security*

Security is a massive subject, and I could fill the book just on that topic. In this book, we'll touch on various security-related topics as we progress because I prefer to deal with security as something that everyone needs to consider, whatever they're doing, rather than as something that those funny guys in the corner do.

In this section we'll look at some security products that are likely to be present on your Windows systems, including

- Antivirus
- Antispyware
- Firewall

NOTE   Antivirus and antispyware will be grouped together as antimalware in parts of this section.

You've already seen a number of times that WMI documentation is a bit sparse in places—well, OK, it's nonexistent in many places. As there doesn't seem to be much documentation available for these areas I tried a bit of digging, like this:

```
Get-WmiObject -Namespace root -Recurse -List *firewall*
```

I started at the top of the WMI tree and worked through the namespaces. I ended up with four namespaces to consider, as listed in table 14.2. These namespaces are only accessible if PowerShell is running with elevated privileges.

Table 14.2 WMI security namespaces

Namespace	Notes
ROOT\SecurityCenter	Windows Vista and earlier
ROOT\SecurityCenter2	Windows Vista SP1 and later
ROOT\Microsoft\SecurityClient	Forefront Endpoint Protection 2010
ROOT\Microsoft\PolicyPlatform\WindowsFirewallConfiguration	Forefront Endpoint Protection 2010

Two of the namespaces are standard for Windows. There are three active classes in the ROOT\SecurityCenter* namespaces:

- AntiSpywareProduct
- AntiVirusProduct
- FirewallProduct

The specific namespace to use is dependent on the version of Windows, as shown in table 14.2. You can use the Windows build numbers to quickly determine the version, as shown in table 14.3. An example of how to apply this is shown in listing 14.7.

Build number	OS version
6000	Windows Vista RTM
6001	Windows Vista SP1
6002	Windows Vista SP2
7600	Windows 7 RTM
7601	Windows 7 SP1

Table 14.3 Windows build numbers

The other two namespaces are installed with my antivirus software. Similar classes may be present with other such products.

Now that you know the WMI classes that are available, what are you going to do with them? The obvious starting point is to ensure that the various types of antimalware software are working. You'll work with these WMI classes to create techniques that test that the antivirus, antispyware, and antimalware software is working correctly and that the files are up to date.

Modern Windows systems incorporate a firewall to increase the security of the system. You'll use PowerShell and WMI to test the firewall status and determine the firewall settings so you know which applications are being blocked and which are allowed through the firewall.

The standard Windows namespaces enable you to test your antivirus software.

TECHNIQUE 113   Testing antivirus status

Viruses are a fact of life. Cleaning up an enterprise after it has suffered a major virus infection isn't a pleasant task; even cleaning up a single machine can be a painfully tedious procedure, as I discovered recently. You need to ensure that your antivirus software is working. Many enterprise level antivirus products have a central reporting console, but being able to test individual systems can supply a quicker answer.

PROBLEM

A test needs to devised that will quickly show if the antivirus software on one or more systems is working and up to date. Ideally this should work across multiple antivirus products.

SOLUTION

Listing 14.7 illustrates the solution to this problem. The difficult part is deciding which of the WMI namespaces to use. This is resolved by using the `Win32_OperatingSystem` class—you test the `BuildNumber` property to determine the operating system version, and hence which namespace to use.

Listing 14.7   Get antivirus status

```
function get-antivirus{
[CmdletBinding()]
param (
 [parameter(ValueFromPipeline=$true,
   ValueFromPipelineByPropertyName=$true)]
 [string]$computername="$env:COMPUTERNAME"
)
PROCESS{
 $os = Get-WmiObject -Class Win32_OperatingSystem `
 -ComputerName $computername

 if ($os.BuildNumber -ge 6001 ) {
   $av = Get-WmiObject -Namespace 'ROOT\SecurityCenter2' `
   -Class AntiVirusProduct -ComputerName $computername
 }
 else {
   $av = Get-WmiObject -Namespace 'ROOT\SecurityCenter' `
   -Class AntiVirusProduct -ComputerName $computername
 }
 $av | select displayName, instanceGuid, pathToSignedProductExe,
     pathToSignedReportingExe, productState

}}
```

The `AntiVirusProduct` class of the appropriate namespace is interrogated. You can then pipe the object into `Select-Object` to restrict the display to the properties of interest.

DISCUSSION

Product state is a numeric value—I get 397312 on my system. I'm assuming that this is OK, as the GUI shows that my antivirus software is up to date and working. There doesn't seem to be a definitive statement I can find that describes how the product state value is produced. I've seen a lot of speculation but little corroborated data. What little information there is supports the notion that 397312 is a good result and that other values indicate an issue with the antivirus software that should be investigated.

Unfortunately, viruses aren't the only malware. You also need to determine the status of your antispyware software.

TECHNIQUE 114   **Testing antispyware status**

Spyware does exactly what it says. It spies on what you're doing, recording information about your activities and reporting to ... someone. This information could just identify websites visited, or it could be actual keystrokes, in which case your passwords are exposed. Many antivirus products also function as antispyware, but there are also independent antispyware products, such as Windows Defender.

PROBLEM
The antispyware product on your systems needs to be checked to determine if it's working correctly and that it's up to date.

SOLUTION
You can adapt listing 14.7 to produce the following listing. The same test for computer operating system version is performed as in the original listing, and depending on the result, the `AntiSpywareProduct` class is used in the appropriate namespace.

Listing 14.8 Get antispyware status

```
function get-antispyware{
[CmdletBinding()]
param (
 [parameter(ValueFromPipeline=$true,
   ValueFromPipelineByPropertyName=$true)]
 [string]$computername="$env:COMPUTERNAME"
)
PROCESS{
 $os = Get-WmiObject -Class Win32_OperatingSystem `
 -ComputerName $computername

 if ($os.BuildNumber -ge 6001 ) {
  $aspys = Get-WmiObject -Namespace 'ROOT\SecurityCenter2' `
  -Class AntiSpywareProduct -ComputerName $computername
 }
 else {
   $aspys = Get-WmiObject -Namespace 'ROOT\SecurityCenter' `
   -Class AntiSpywareProduct -ComputerName $computername
 }

 foreach ($aspy in $aspys) {
   $aspy | select displayName, instanceGuid, pathToSignedProductExe,
     pathToSignedReportingExe, productState
 }

}}
```

There could well be multiple results from this listing, so you use `foreach` to iterate through the set of results. Each instance of antispyware software is piped through `Select-Object` and the desired properties are displayed.

DISCUSSION
The `productState` property has the same meaning as discussed in listing 14.7. I recommend double-checking the result against a known healthy instance of your antispyware software to determine the value to look for.

It's very possible that you may acquire other WMI functionality through the installation of a specific antivirus product. This could cover both antimalware and the firewall.

Testing antimalware status

The ROOT\Microsoft\SecurityClient namespace is installed by Microsoft Forefront Endpoint Protection 2010. It supplies the following classes:

- `ProtectionTechnologyStatus`
- `FirewallState`
- `AntimalwareHealthStatus`
- `AntimalwareInfectionStatus`
- `Malware`
- `AntimalwareDetectionStatus`

Using the `ProtectionTechnologyStatus` class is equivalent to using the `Antimalware-HealthStatus` and `FirewallState` classes. Hopefully you'll never have to use the `AntimalwareInfectionStatus` class, because its job is to report on the status of infections and pending cleanup operations.

We'll concentrate on the health status of the antimalware software and the firewall.

PROBLEM

You're using Forefront Endpoint 2010 as your antivirus software, and you want to discover more about its health than is shown by listings 14.7 and 14.8.

SOLUTION

The `AntimalwareHealthStatus` class can be used for this. The following listing demonstrates how it's used.

Listing 14.9   Antimalware health check

```
function get-antimalwarehealth{
[CmdletBinding()]
param (
 [parameter(ValueFromPipeline=$true,
   ValueFromPipelineByPropertyName=$true)]
 [string]$computername="$env:COMPUTERNAME"
)
PROCESS{
 Get-WmiObject -Namespace 'ROOT\Microsoft\SecurityClient' `
 -Class AntimalwareHealthStatus -ComputerName $computername |
 select AntispywareEnabled, AntispywareSignatureAge,
 AntispywareSignatureUpdateDateTime, AntispywareSignatureVersion,
 AntivirusEnabled, AntivirusSignatureAge,
 AntivirusSignatureUpdateDateTime, AntivirusSignatureVersion,
 BehaviorMonitorEnabled, Enabled, EngineVersion,
 IoavProtectionEnabled, LastFullScanAge, LastFullScanDateTimeEnd,
 LastFullScanDateTimeStart,  LastFullScanSource,
 LastQuickScanAge, LastQuickScanDateTimeEnd,
 LastQuickScanDateTimeStart, LastQuickScanSource,
 Name, NisEnabled, NisEngineVersion, NisSignatureVersion,
 OnAccessProtectionEnabled, ProductStatus,
 RealTimeScanDirection, RtpEnabled

}}
```

A single parameter takes the computer name, which is used in the `Get-WmiObject` call. The namespace and class are given as part of the call. `Select-Object` is used to filter the properties you need returned. The useful information is buried in amongst a lot of properties you don't need. The properties related to signature update times, scan times, and ages will be most useful. One advantage of wrapping these WMI calls in a function is that you only have to type out the property selection once.

DISCUSSION

There is a property called `PackedXML` that returns the data in XML format. It has been excluded from the display.

Dates look like this:

```
2011-05-16T04:49:41.000Z
```

This can be translated as Year-Month-Day, followed by a `T` to signify time, which is displayed as Hours:Minutes:Seconds. The `Z` indicates that the time is given as Coordinated Universal Time (UTC). UTC is also known as GMT or Zulu time (military), which is where the `Z` comes from. The time zones and their corresponding letter codes can be found here: http://wwp.greenwichmeantime.com/info/timezone.htm.

The time can be put into `Get-Date` (or the .NET `DateTime` class) to resolve to local time as shown in figure 14.2. There's a difference between the input and output of one hour due to the clock's advancement for daylight saving time at the time of writing (I'm UK-based, so this figure is based on GMT).

We've considered the status of the antimalware software in a number of ways. We need to consider the firewall next.

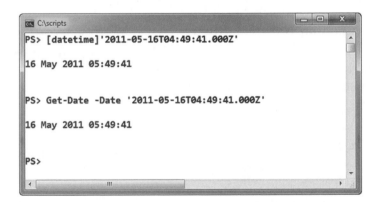

Figure 14.2 Working with dates from the `AntimalwareHealth-Status` class

TECHNIQUE 116   Testing firewall status

Modern versions of Windows ship with a software-based firewall. This will default to on or off depending on the version of Windows. The `FirewallProduct` class in the ROOT\SecurityCenter* namespaces doesn't seem to report in versions of Windows later than Windows XP.

PROBLEM

The firewall status needs to be checked across your systems.

SOLUTION

The following listing solves the problem by using the FirewallState class. The class can be found in the ROOT\Microsoft\SecurityClient namespace.

Listing 14.10   Get firewall status

```
function get-firewallstate{
[CmdletBinding()]
param (
 [parameter(ValueFromPipeline=$true,
   ValueFromPipelineByPropertyName=$true)]
 [string]$computername="$env:COMPUTERNAME"
)
PROCESS{
 Get-WmiObject -Namespace 'ROOT\Microsoft\SecurityClient' `
-Class FirewallState -ComputerName $computername |
 select Name, Enabled, FirewallServiceRunning

}}
```

The only useful properties in this class are the name of the firewall product and Boolean values that indicate if the firewall is enabled and if its service is running.

DISCUSSION

This class also has a PackedXML property, as explained in listing 14.9.

The state of the firewall is important, but the firewall settings are also vital to the security of your systems.

TECHNIQUE 117   **Listing firewall settings**

There's another namespace that you can use to investigate the firewall settings—ROOT\Microsoft\PolicyPlatform\WindowsFirewallConfiguration. This namespace, also from Forefront Endpoint 2010, contains the following classes:

- Firewall_PredefinedRuleGroup
- Firewall_Profile_Parameters
- Firewall_Profile_Public
- Firewall_Profile_Private
- Firewall_Profile_Domain
- Firewall_PredefinedRuleGroup_Baseline

With Windows Vista and later, networks are categorized as being one of three types:

- Public
- Private
- Domain

Separate firewall rules can be created for each type of network. The `Firewall_Profile_*` classes relate directly to the network type.

PROBLEM

You want to investigate the firewall settings on your system to ensure that you aren't inadvertently blocking a critical application.

SOLUTION

The following listing provides one solution to this problem. The computer name is the only parameter to this function.

Listing 14.11 Get firewall settings

```
function get-firewallsetting{
[CmdletBinding()]
param (
 [parameter(ValueFromPipeline=$true,
   ValueFromPipelineByPropertyName=$true)]
 [string]$computername="$env:COMPUTERNAME"
)
PROCESS{
 Get-WmiObject `
 -Namespace 'ROOT\Microsoft\PolicyPlatform\WindowsFirewallConfiguration' `
 -Class Firewall_Profile_Parameters -ComputerName $computername |
select __Class, AllowedIcmpTypes, BlockAllInboundTraffic,
DefaultInboundActionIsDeny, DefaultOutboundActionIsAllow,
DisableInboundNotifications, DisableUnicastResponsesToMulticastBroadcast,
EnableFirewall, LocalLegacyAppRulesMergeAllowed,
LocalLegacyPortRulesMergeAllowed, LocalRulesMergeAllowed

}}
```

This function calls the `Firewall_Profile_Parameters` WMI class and uses `Select-Object` to filter the properties you want to display.

> **WARNING** The classes in this namespace require PowerShell to be started with elevated privileges.

DISCUSSION

The `Firewall_Profile_Parameters` class calls the three profile classes we discussed earlier. If you only want settings for a particular network, you can use one of these classes as appropriate:

- `Firewall_Profile_Public`
- `Firewall_Profile_Private`
- `Firewall_Profile_Domain`

This completes our look at users and security settings. I've attempted to pick the properties I think will be most useful. You should investigate the classes further to determine whether there's any information vital to your needs that I haven't mentioned.

14.4   *Summary*

Users and security go hand in hand. Sometimes you're protecting the users from themselves, and other times you're protecting them from external threats.

WMI enables you to work with local user accounts and local groups. You can't create new accounts but you can do several other things:

- Discover the local accounts and groups on a system, and delete them if necessary
- Check the group membership of local accounts
- Discover other information, such as profile and desktop settings
- Test the membership of powerful groups, such as the local administrators group

Protecting users from external threats includes installing a firewall and antimalware software. There are WMI classes to do the following:

- Test the status of antivirus and antispyware software
- Check that the signature data is up to date
- Test the firewall status
- List firewall settings

You don't get many opportunities to directly administer these products through WMI but you can easily test their functioning. This can be a very useful test when checking for possible problems.

The next chapter continues our investigation of our systems and looks at using WMI to work with event logs, scheduled jobs, and performance counters.

15

Logs, jobs, and performance

This chapter covers

- Discovering event log sources
- Backing up event logs
- Managing simple scheduled jobs
- Investigating performance counters, system assessment reports, and stability indices

Things go wrong even in the best-run IT operations. When they do, you need to be able to investigate and troubleshoot the problem. One of the first places to look is the event logs. These logs record information (events) from a number of sources across the system. WMI can be used to access and manage the logs, but in many cases the PowerShell event log cmdlets are easier to use. We'll look at how you can use PowerShell and WMI to discover some information that the cmdlets don't return and how to back up the logs.

The ability to schedule jobs, which are also known as *scheduled tasks*, to run at a specified time has been available in Windows for a long time. But a change to the scheduled jobs infrastructure was introduced with Windows Vista. As you'll discover, you can still create, access, and manage the older, simpler job types through WMI and PowerShell.

If there is one certainty in IT, it's that users will complain about the performance of their systems. It doesn't matter what you do, they'll claim its running slower! We'll look at how you can view performance information on remote systems using WMI classes.

System performance is closely related to the installed hardware. In the final section of this chapter, we'll look at techniques for using PowerShell and WMI to access this information. The information provided by these techniques may indicate an area of hardware that's causing problems. The other thing we'll look at is the stability of the system. The latest Windows versions provide stability indices that can be accessed through WMI. These indices are a good starting point for getting a general overview of the system's health.

I've spent a lot of time investigating the contents of event logs over the years. They're an invaluable resource for discovering what's happening on your systems, especially when troubleshooting, so they're the logical place to start.

15.1   *Event logs*

Event logs used to be simple. You had the `Application`, `System`, and `Security` logs. But new logs have been introduced in the later versions of Windows, and now a standard installation of Windows 7 will have nine event logs. Nine classic-type event logs, that is. If you include the entire collection of new-style event logs introduced with Windows Vista, you get up to a total of 166 event logs on a standard install of Windows 7.

In the days of VBScript you had to use WMI to work with event logs. This changed with the introduction of PowerShell v1, which included a `Get-EventLog` cmdlet for reading events from the log. Much easier and simpler to use! This support ramped up a level when PowerShell v2 arrived. A suite of cmdlets was made available, as listed in table 15.1. Their purposes should be clear from their names, apart from possibly `Show-EventLog`, which displays the event log viewer GUI application, and `Limit-Eventlog`, which is used to configure event log settings.

Table 15.1   Event log cmdlets

Clear-EventLog	Get-EventLog	Limit-EventLog
New-EventLog	Remove-EventLog	Show-EventLog
Write-EventLog		

All of these cmdlets can access event logs on remote computers. The following code can be used to test for the presence of a `ComputerName` parameter.

```
Get-Help *eventlog -Parameter computername | sort name
```

> **TIP**   These cmdlets and WMI only work with the original, classic-style event logs.

The event logs available on a machine can be discovered using a cmdlet:

```
Get-EventLog -List | select -f 1 | fl *
```

This code shows that the properties listed in table 15.2 are available (-f is a short form of -first; PowerShell will accept shortened forms of parameter names as long as they're unambiguous). These properties can be configured using Limit-Eventlog or the Win32_NTLogEventLog WMI class.

Table 15.2 Event log properties

LogDisplayName	Log	MachineName
MaximumKilobytes	OverflowAction	MinimumRetentionDays
EnableRaisingEvents		

Don't forget to check the new Windows Vista–style event logs. Use this code:

```
Get-WinEvent -ListLog * | select -f 1 | fl *
```

Staying with the classic event logs, you can retrieve a lot more useful information with WMI:

```
gwmi Win32_NTEventlogFile | select -f 1 | fl *
```

This produces the property list seen in table 15.3. The Name property gives the full file path to the event log file. The other really useful property is Sources, which displays the identities of the event sources writing to the log.

Table 15.3 WMI properties of event logs

LogfileName	Name	Archive	Caption
Compressed	CreationDate	CSName	Description
Drive	EightDotThreeFileName	Encrypted	Extension
FileName	FileSize	FileType	FSName
Hidden	InstallDate	LastAccessed	LastModified
MaxFileSize	NumberOfRecords	OverwriteOutDated	OverWritePolicy
Path	Readable	Sources	System
Writeable			

One use of event logs that's often overlooked is using them to log script usage. A call to Write-Eventlog can be used to write data about specific scripts as they run. Either the Application event log or a specific event log can be used.

But before you can write to an event log, you need to discover some information.

TECHNIQUE 118   **Discovering event log sources**

When you write to an event log you need to know which source to use. A source is effectively a label and a route to use when writing. Try this snippet to see some examples of the sources available:

```
Get-EventLog -LogName Application |
Format-Table TimeGenerated, Source, Message -AutoSize
```

Source information isn't available using the event log cmdlets, but you can discover it using WMI.

PROBLEM

You want to discover the event log sources available on a server. Sources are event log–specific, so you need to be able to recover data for all event logs or for a specific event log.

SOLUTION

Listing 15.1 illustrates a solution to this problem using the `Win32_NTEventLogFile` class. The function can take a computer name as a parameter as well as an optional event log name. The `-computername` parameter is aliased to `CN` or `Computer` as an example of how to use this advanced function attribute.

Listing 15.1   Listing event log sources

```
function get-eventlogsource{
[CmdletBinding()]
param (
[parameter(ValueFromPipeline=$true,
   ValueFromPipelineByPropertyName=$true )]
   [Alias("CN", "Computer")]
   [string]$computername="$env:COMPUTERNAME",

   [string]$logname
)
PROCESS{                                                    ❶ Get
if ($logname) {                                               data
 $logs = Get-WmiObject -Class Win32_NTEventlogFile `
 -ComputerName $computername -Filter "LogfileName = '$logname'"
}
else {
 $logs = Get-WmiObject -Class Win32_NTEventlogFile
 -ComputerName $computername
}                                                          ❷ Loop through
foreach ($log in $logs) {                                     logs and sources
 $logsource = New-Object -TypeName PSObject
 $logsource |
 Add-Member -MemberType NoteProperty -Name Computer
 -Value $computername -PassThru |
 Add-Member -MemberType NoteProperty -Name Logfile
 -Value $log.LogfileName

 $i = 1
 $log | select -ExpandProperty Sources | foreach {
```

```
    Add-Member -InputObject $logsource `
    -MemberType NoteProperty -Name "Source$i" `
    -Value $_
    $i++
  }
  $logsource
}
}#process
}
```

❸ **Output data**

The log file information is retrieved ❶ for all log files or for a single log file, depending on whether the -logname parameter has been used.

You create an empty object and add the computer name and log name for each event log ❷. You can then loop through the sources for that event log and add their names as a unique property on the object. The object is added to the PowerShell pipeline at the completion of processing ❸.

DISCUSSION

Once event logs are created, there is usually very little to be done in terms of configuration. Any changes, such as modifying the maximum file size, can be achieved using Limit-EventLog or through WMI:

```
Get-WmiObject -Class Win32_NTEventLogFile -Filter "LogFileName='Scripts'" |
Set-WmiInstance -Arguments @{MaxFileSize=40MB}
```

A particular event log is selected and passed to Set-WmiInstance. A hash table of the properties to be changed and their new values is used as the argument.

> **WARNING** This snippet needs to be executed when PowerShell is running with elevated privileges.

Multiple properties can be set simultaneously. Applying a standard set of changes to the event logs when a server is created is a very efficient way to make those changes.

Protecting and collecting the data held in the event logs is a necessity if an organization needs to be able to investigate historic events on a server.

TECHNIQUE 119   Backing up event logs

There are two ways you can approach the backing up of event logs. The first, more complicated, way would be to read the events using Get-Eventlog and then write the information into a SQL Server database. This has the advantage of bringing the logs for a number of machines together for further analysis.

The second, simpler, technique is to perform a backup of the event log. You can then search the backup file using the PowerShell event log cmdlets.

PROBLEM

Your organization has created a policy that states event logs must be backed up to prevent information being lost when the logs cycle round as they fill up. You also need to be able to clear the event log when the backup has been performed.

SOLUTION

Listing 15.1 can be amended to create a solution for this problem, as shown in the following code. You add parameters defining a destination folder for the backup files and an optional switch that enables you to clear the log files.

Listing 15.2 Backing up event logs

```
function backup-eventlog{
[CmdletBinding()]
param (
[parameter(ValueFromPipeline=$true,
   ValueFromPipelineByPropertyName=$true )]
   [string]$computername="$env:COMPUTERNAME" ,

   [string]$logname,
   [string]$destination="C:\Backup",
   [switch]$clear
)
PROCESS{                                              ❶ Get
if ($logname) {                                          data
 $logs = Get-WmiObject -Class Win32_NTEventlogFile `
 -ComputerName $computername -Filter "LogfileName = '$logname'"
}
else {
 $logs = Get-WmiObject -Class Win32_NTEventlogFile `
 -ComputerName $computername
}
foreach ($log in $logs) {                            ❷ Create
 $filename = Join-Path -Path $destination `            filename
 -ChildPath "$($log.LogFileName)-$((Get-Date -Format 's').
   ➥ Replace(':','-')).evt"

 Write-Debug $filename                               ❸ Perform
 $log.BackUpEventLog($filename)                         backup
 if ($clear){$log.ClearEventLog()}
}
}#process
}
```

WMI objects representing the log, or logs, are created ❶. You can then loop through the collection of logs. A filename is formed that incorporates the destination folder, the name of the log file, and the date ❷. The file is given an extension of .evt. An example file name would be C:\Backup\Application-2011-06-03T11-30-42.evt.

> **TIP** The colons (:) are removed from the time portion of the date because that character isn't allowed in filenames.

The filename is written out to screen when the function is executed with the -debug switch. Win32_NTEventlogFile has a BackUpEventLog method that you can use to perform the backup ❸. It takes the filename of the backup file as its argument.

The function will use the ClearEventLog method to wipe the contents of the event log if required. If you're using these methods in your own scripts, double-check that you use them in the correct order. It's very embarrassing to clear the log file before performing the backup!

DISCUSSION

You could use `Clear-EventLog` to perform the data removal, but it's more efficient to use the WMI method because you've already invested the computer resources in creating the WMI object.

A possible refinement to the function would be to delete backup files that are older than a given period. If the organization's policy was to keep log information for 30 days, you could add this line to the function:

```
Get-ChildItem -Path $destination |
where {$_.CreationTime -lt (Get-Date).AddDays(-30)} |
Remove-Item
```

The backup files can be read in a similar way to reading the event log. The only difference is that you use the `Get-WinEvent` cmdlet. To read a backup file of the Application log you'd use code similar to this example:

```
Get-WinEvent -Path c:\backup\application-2011-06-03T11-30-42.evt -Oldest
```

Running backups manually is acceptable if it's an ad hoc process. In a production environment you need a way to be able to schedule this type of task.

15.2 Scheduled jobs

The `Win32_ScheduledJob` class only shows those tasks created with the `AT` command or WMI. It doesn't work with tasks created in the GUI or with the COM objects introduced in Windows Vista. If a job is accessed or modified through the GUI, it isn't accessible using WMI anymore.

> **NOTE** We're discussing operating system scheduled tasks, not PowerShell background jobs, though it's possible to start a PowerShell job through a scheduled task.

You can manage the lifecycle of creation, discovery, and deletion through WMI starting with creation.

TECHNIQUE 120   **Creating a scheduled job**

There are a large number of utility commands available that you can use within a scheduled job. If you want to run a PowerShell script through a scheduled task, you need to investigate the PowerShell startup parameters. This can be achieved by typing `powershell /?` at the PowerShell prompt.

To start a PowerShell session and run a script, you can do this:

```
powershell -nologo -noexit -file "c:\scripts\test.ps1"
```

The `-noexit` parameter can be dropped if your script creates an output file and you don't want PowerShell sessions remaining open. Alternatively, `Stop-Process` can be used to shut down the sessions.

PROBLEM

You need to create simple scheduled jobs on the local and remote machines. Which commands are executed should be an option within the script.

SOLUTION

The parameters in listing 15.3 are an interesting mixture. The standard computer name parameter is present, and the remainder relate to the scheduled job. The default is running a `dir` command on the root of the C: drive if a command isn't presented. This is a safe command that won't do any damage. Alternatively, you could make the parameter mandatory to force the user to present a value.

Listing 15.3   Creating a scheduled job

```
function new-scheduledjob{
[CmdletBinding()]
param (
[parameter(ValueFromPipeline=$true,
   ValueFromPipelineByPropertyName=$true )]
   [string]$computername="$env:COMPUTERNAME",

   [string]$command="cmd /K dir c:",

   [ValidatePattern("[0-9]{1,2}:[0-9][0-9]")]
   [string]$time="12:30",
   [bool]$repeat=$true,
   [int]$day = 1,
   [int]$monthly = 0,
   [bool]$interact=$false

)
PROCESS{
$tz = Get-WmiObject -Class Win32_TimeZone -ComputerName $computername
if ((Get-Date).IsDaylightSavingTime()) {$bias = $tz.DaylightBias}
else {$bias = $tz.StandardBias}

switch ($bias.ToString().Length) {
 1 {$bias = "+000"}
 3 {$bias = $bias.ToString().Insert(1,"0")}
 default {$bias = $bias.ToString()}
}

$start =  "********$($time.Replace(':',''))00.000000$bias"

Invoke-WmiMethod -ComputerName $computername `
-Class Win32_ScheduledJob -Name Create `
-ArgumentList $command, $monthly, $day, $interact, $repeat, $start
}#process
}
```

The time of day when the job is to be run is validated by a regular expression. There are so many ways to present a time that it's best to pick one and force compliance. When turning this into a production script, add some help that explains the format.

The `-day` parameter represents the day of the week, and the `-month` parameter represents the day of the month. You want the job to run repeatedly and you don't want to interact with it while it's running.

The `Win32-TimeZone` class on the system is interrogated to discover the time zone bias, which is the offset from GMT. There is a standard format to the start time of a scheduled job. You use string substitution to add the time and the bias into the string.

`Invoke-WmiMethod` can be used directly on the `Win32_ScheduledJob` class with the required arguments.

DISCUSSION

The `-day` parameter is a numeric value to designate the days of the week on which the job should be run. The values are rising powers of 2: Monday = 1, Tuesday = 2, Wednesday = 4, and so on. If you want to run the job on multiple days, use a binary OR to derive a composite value.

In a similar manner, the days of the month are based on powers of 2 from day 1, which has a value of 1, to day 31, which has a value of 1073741824. Binary OR is again used to create a composite value for running the job on multiple days of the month.

> **TIP**   In order to make these parameters easy to use, I have provided `new-day` and `new-monthday` functions in the code download for the chapter. These will calculate the correct values for you.

It's possible to create a WMI object for the `Win32_ScheduledJob` class and call the `Create` method on that, rather than using `Invoke-WmiMethod`. By doing so, the following code,

```
Invoke-WmiMethod -ComputerName $computername `
-Class Win32_ScheduledJob -Name Create `
-ArgumentList $command, $monthly, $day, $interact, $repeat, $start
```

is replaced with these two lines:

```
$newjob = [wmiclass]"\\$computername\root\cimv2:Win32_ScheduledJob"
$newjob.Create($command, $start, $repeat, $day, $monthly, $interact)
```

You can see in these two examples that the order in which the arguments are presented is different. This is one of the delightful quirks built into PowerShell and WMI just to keep you awake.

There's a way you can discover the order of the arguments. If `Invoke-WmiMethod` fails with the argument list as presented in the documentation, try running these two commands (modified for the appropriate WMI class and method):

```
([wmiclass]"Win32_ScheduledJob").Create.OverloadDefinitions
```

```
([wmiclass]"Win32_ScheduledJob").GetMethodParameters("Create")
```

In both cases, the order of the arguments will be shown. The first method (using `OverloadDefinitions`) presents the arguments in the same order as the documentation. This is the order you should use to create a WMI object and call the method on the object.

The second method (using `GetMethodParameters`) presents the parameters in the order expected by `Invoke-WmiMethod`.

Table 15.4 summarizes the results of running the previous two commands. It presents the parameters required by the Create method of Win32_ScheduledJob. The parameters are listed in the order in which they must be used if you're creating a WMI object and using the Create method directly (in the method 1 column) or if you're using Invoke-WmiMethod (the method 2 column).

Table 15.4   Parameter order for the Create method

Order	Method 1	Method 2
1	Command	Command
2	StartTime	DaysOfMonth
3	RunRepeatedly	DaysOfWeek
4	DaysOfWeek	InteractWithDesktop
5	DaysOfMonth	RunRepeatedly
6	InteractWithDesktop	StartTime

You now have two code options for creating scheduled jobs. It's time to check whether there are any other jobs on your systems that you might not know about.

TECHNIQUE 121   Discovering scheduled jobs

A large part of any administrator's time is spent checking the configuration of systems or investigating them to discover the cause of problems. One aspect that's often overlooked is the time of day when scheduled jobs are executed.

PROBLEM

One of your servers is having intermittent performance issues. The users are complaining that periodically the applications hosted on that server will slow down. You need to determine whether there are any scheduled jobs running at those times.

SOLUTION

The following listing can produce a report of all scheduled jobs, or a specific job if you know its JobId.

Listing 15.4   Discovering scheduled tasks

```
function get-scheduledjob{
[CmdletBinding()]
param (
[parameter(ValueFromPipeline=$true,
   ValueFromPipelineByPropertyName=$true )]
   [string]$computername="$env:COMPUTERNAME",
   [int]$jobid
)
PROCESS{
if ($jobid) {
 $jobs = Get-WmiObject -Class Win32_ScheduledJob `
```

```
 -ComputerName $computername -Filter "JobId = $jobid"
}
else {
 $jobs = Get-WmiObject -Class Win32_ScheduledJob `
 -ComputerName $computername
}

foreach ($job in $jobs){
 $job | select Status, JobId, JobStatus,
 ElapsedTime, StartTime, Owner, Caption, Command,
 DaysOfMonth, DaysOfWeek, Description,
 InstallDate, InteractWithDesktop, Name,
 Notify, Priority, RunRepeatedly,
 TimeSubmitted, UntilTime
}
}#process
}
```

The required job information is recovered using Win32_ScheduledJob. Each of the
WMI objects for the retrieved jobs is passed through Select-Object to filter the
desired properties for output.

DISCUSSION

The daysofmonth and daysofweek properties are based on powers of 2, as discussed in
technique 120. If the script is run on days 1, 5, 9, and 26 of the month, a value
of 33554705 will be returned in the daysofmonth property. This can be decipher-
ed using this code:

```
$value = 33554705
1..31 | foreach {
 $calc = $value -band [math]::Pow(2, $($_ -1))
 if ($calc -ne 0 ){$_}
}
```

The values 1 to 31 are input into the PowerShell pipeline. Each value is used to create
a power of 2 value and then a band (binary and) is performed using the value from the
daysofmonth property. If you get a result that's nonzero, you output the day value.
This code also works for the daysofweek property.

   If you do find jobs that shouldn't be running you need a method to delete them.

TECHNIQUE 122   Deleting scheduled jobs

Were you continually told to tidy up as a child? The same applies to server administration. You'll be continually pressured to fix somebody's problem or to get a new application into service. Do you have the time to clean up old applications, data, or even
scheduled jobs?

PROBLEM

It has been discovered that a number of scheduled jobs that are no longer required
still exist on your servers. They should have been removed when an application was
retired. These jobs are scheduled to run during the working day and are consuming
resources best devoted to other applications.

SOLUTION

The following listing will perform this cleanup task in an efficient manner.

Listing 15.5   Removing scheduled task

```
function remove-scheduledjob{
[CmdletBinding()]
param (
[parameter(ValueFromPipeline=$true,
   ValueFromPipelineByPropertyName=$true )]
   [string]$computername="$env:COMPUTERNAME",
   [int]$jobid
)
PROCESS{
if ($jobid) {
 Get-WmiObject -Class Win32_ScheduledJob `
 -ComputerName $computername -Filter "JobId = $jobid" |
 Remove-WmiObject
}
else {
 Get-WmiObject -Class Win32_ScheduledJob -ComputerName $computername |
 Remove-WmiObject
}
}#process
}
```

The function can accept a -jobid as an optional parameter. The WMI object for the specific job is retrieved, or by default all jobs are retrieved. Remove-WmiObject is used to perform the deletion.

DISCUSSION

The Win32_ScheduledJob class does have a Delete method if you'd prefer to use that. I think it's better, and safer, to use Get-WmiObject and pipe into Remove-WmiObject, because it's easier to test that the correct objects have been selected. Remove-WmiObject also has the -WhatIf parameter for further safety. I used both of these techniques as I developed and tested the function.

In technique 121, we discussed the possibility of unnecessary scheduled jobs impacting system performance. We need to look at how you can measure the performance of your systems and at what we actually mean by *performance*.

15.3   *System performance*

Measuring system performance has traditionally involved looking at the performance counters. These can be accessed through the performance monitor (sysmon for those who remember earlier versions of Windows) and they can be saved as required. You can also use the Get-Counter cmdlet (which works against remote machines), or you can use the WMI Win32_Perf* classes, as you'll see in technique 123.

Windows Vista introduced the system assessment report. This rates a number of system hardware components, including memory, CPU, disk, and graphics, to produce an overall rating for the system. The higher the score, the better the system should perform.

I'm often asked about system stability. The number of unscheduled restarts is one way to measure stability. Later versions of Windows calculate a stability index on an hourly basis. This is calculated based on failures and changes, with recent events being more heavily weighted. The maximum possible score is 10.

Performance counters are still required to dig into individual aspects of the system.

TECHNIQUE 123   Reading performance counters

If you've spent any time investigating system performance you'll know that there's a huge list of available Windows performance counters. The problem of finding the correct counter to use is increased when you consider that applications such as SQL Server, IIS, and Exchange add their own raft of counters. WMI enables you to access some, but not all, of the counters.

You can see which counters are available on a specific system like this:

```
Get-WmiObject -List Win32_PerfFormattedData* | select name
```

Here's an extract from the results:

```
Win32_PerfFormattedData_PerfDisk_LogicalDisk
Win32_PerfFormattedData_PerfDisk_PhysicalDisk
Win32_PerfFormattedData_PerfOS_PagingFile
Win32_PerfFormattedData_PerfOS_Processor
Win32_PerfFormattedData_PerfOS_Memory
```

You should use the `-Recurse` parameter when searching for these classes as they won't necessarily be added to the default WMI namespace.

> **TIP** The `Win32_PerfFormattedData` class is a superclass that will call the other performance formatted data classes. There will be a lot of data to wade through.

There are also related classes that return the raw performance counter data. These classes are difficult to use, because each value has to be processed through a calculation to derive a meaningful result. It's easier to use the formatted WMI classes or `Get-Counter`.

PROBLEM
You need to monitor the processor performance of one of your systems. The server has multiple processors (or cores), and you need to display the information for each processor core and the total to ensure that the application is using the processor resources in an optimum manner.

SOLUTION
The following listing presents a function that takes a computer name and a number as parameters. The number determines how many times you'll sample the processor information.

Listing 15.6   Accessing performance counters

```
function get-cpucounter{
[CmdletBinding()]
param (
[parameter(ValueFromPipeline=$true,
   ValueFromPipelineByPropertyName=$true)]
   [string]$computername="$env:COMPUTERNAME",
   [int]$number=1
)
BEGIN{
$source=@"
public class CPUcounter
{
    public  string  Timestamp  {get; set;}
    public  string  Name        {get; set;}
    public  ulong PercProcTime  {get; set;}
}
"@
Add-Type -TypeDefinition $source -Language CSharpversion3
}#begin
PROCESS{
1..$number | foreach {

$date = (Get-Date).ToString()

Get-WmiObject -Class Win32_PerfFormattedData_PerfOS_Processor `
 -ComputerName $computername | foreach {
    $value = New-Object -TypeName CPUCounter -Property @{
        TimeStamp = $date
        Name = $_.Name
        PercProcTime  = $_.PercentProcessorTime
    }
    $value
}

Start-Sleep -Seconds 1
}
}#process
}
```

❶ Create class

❷ Create object and set properties

❸ Pause execution

Some inline C# code is used to create a new .NET class to store your results ❶. The class defines three properties—a timestamp, the name of the processor, and the percentage processor time (how much it was used during the measurement period). This is compiled using Add-Type. Creating a class in this manner enables you to strongly type the properties, which supplies another level of error checking.

The range operator (..) is used to put the required series of numbers onto the pipeline. PowerShell will process each value, and for each of them retrieve the processor performance data using Win32_PerfFormattedData_PerfOS_Processor. One object per processor, plus one for the total, will be returned. You create an object using your specially created .NET class, populate its properties ❷, and output it. A one-second pause is activated before you start again ❸.

On my development system, using this code,

```
1..10 | foreach {Measure-Command -Expression {Get-WmiObject
  ➥ -Class Win32_PerfFormattedData_PerfOS_Processor  }}
```

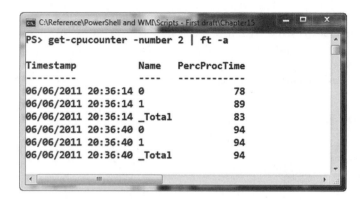

Figure 15.1   CPU performance counters

shows that the Get-WmiObject command takes about 300 milliseconds to retrieve the data. The function could be altered to change the delay, or you could even make it a parameter.

DISCUSSION

Figure 15.1 displays the results from using this function. The results show that processing is relatively equally distributed across the two cores. I wouldn't expect to see the values being identical across all processors or cores all of the time.

> **TIP**   In case you're wondering how I managed to drive processor performance so high, I set a few continuously looping recursive directory listings going. They're a good way to tax the system without spending a lot of money on simulation tools.

Each of the WMI performance counter classes will need to be investigated to determine the properties that you need to record. For example, the class used here also returns information regarding interrupts.

One common scenario that you'll get is users claiming a difference in performance between two systems. You can use the Windows system assessment report to provide a high-level comparison between the hardware of the two systems.

TECHNIQUE 124   Windows system assessment report

The assessment report was introduced with Windows Vista. It examines a number of hardware components to determine an overall score for the system.

> **TIP**   The overall score is determined by the lowest of the individual component scores. Always examine the full report to determine whether a single component is adversely affecting performance.

Accessing this information for the local machine through the GUI is acceptable, but you need a way to perform this action remotely as well.

PROBLEM

You need to create Windows system assessment reports for a number of remote machines. This will enable you to determine which machines should be refreshed and which are worth reusing.

SOLUTION

The following listing utilizes the `Win32_WinSat` class to solve this problem. A hash table lookup is created to decode the assessment state property.

Listing 15.7   System assessment information

```
$satstate = DATA {
ConvertFrom-StringData -StringData @'
0 = StateUnknown
1 = Valid
2 = IncoherentWithHardware
3 = NoAssessmentAvailable
4 = Invalid
'@
}

function get-systemassessment{
[CmdletBinding()]
param (
[parameter(ValueFromPipeline=$true,
   ValueFromPipelineByPropertyName=$true )]
   [string]$computername="$env:COMPUTERNAME"
)
PROCESS{
 Get-WmiObject -Class Win32_WinSat -ComputerName $computername |
 select CPUScore, D3DScore, DiskScore, GraphicsScore,
 MemoryScore, TimeTaken,
 @{N="AssessmentState"; E={$satstate["$($_.WinSATAssessmentState)"]}},
 @{N="BaseScore"; E={$_.WinSPRLevel}}

}#process
}
```

The function returns the data from the WMI class and uses `Select-Object` to output the properties and two calculated fields. One calculated field decodes the assessment state and the other renames the overall score.

DISCUSSION

This report shouldn't be taken in isolation when looking at system performance. The age of the system and any remaining warranty should also be considered.

Proving the stability of a system is more complex than simply measuring how long it has been running.

TECHNIQUE 125   **Stability index data**

System stability is a measure of a number of factors, including up-time, changes, and environmental factors. You can't measure the environmental factors directly but you can look at the internal system stability.

PROBLEM

You need to measure the stability index for your Windows systems. The index value can range from 1 to 10, with 1 being set immediately after a reboot and 10 being returned when the system has run continuously for 30 days with no restarts or changes. This metric will be used as part of your periodic reporting on the health of your systems.

SOLUTION

The WMI class `Win32_ReliabilityStabilityMetrics` is used to solve this problem in the following listing. You can retrieve this information for the local or remote systems.

Listing 15.8 Retrieving stability index data

```
function get-stabilityindex {
[CmdletBinding()]
param (
 [parameter(ValueFromPipeline=$true,
   ValueFromPipelineByPropertyName=$true)]
 [string]$computername="$env:COMPUTERNAME "
)
 Get-WmiObject -Class Win32_ReliabilityStabilityMetrics `
 -ComputerName $computername |
 select @{N="TimeGenerated";
   ➥ E={$_.ConvertToDatetime($_.TimeGenerated)}},
 SystemStabilityIndex
}
```

The returned object has two properties of interest—the stability index and the time at which it was generated. You need to convert the date information from WMI format to your normal format. The results of running the function are illustrated in figure 15.2.

DISCUSSION

Over a year's worth of data is retained, even though Windows only uses the last 28 days' worth of events to compute the index. You may need to restrict the results, especially if you're only interested in recent data. You can pull back a full month's data like this:

```
get-stabilityindex |
where {$_.TimeGenerated -lt ([datetime]"1 June 2011")
   ➥ -and $_.TimeGenerated -ge ([datetime]"1 May 2011")}
```

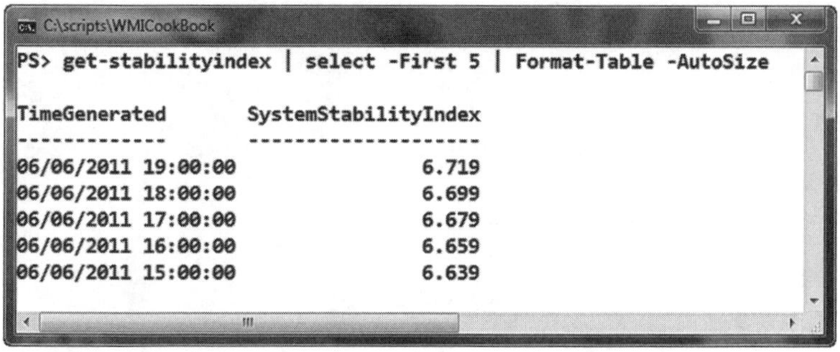

```
PS> get-stabilityindex | select -First 5 | Format-Table -AutoSize

TimeGenerated          SystemStabilityIndex
-------------          --------------------
06/06/2011 19:00:00                   6.719
06/06/2011 18:00:00                   6.699
06/06/2011 17:00:00                   6.679
06/06/2011 16:00:00                   6.659
06/06/2011 15:00:00                   6.639
```

Figure 15.2 System stability index results

Alternatively, you could calculate an average value across the month:

```
get-stabilityindex |
where {$_.TimeGenerated -lt ([datetime]"1 June 2011")
    ➥ -and $_.TimeGenerated -ge ([datetime]"1 May 2011")} |
Measure-Object -Average SystemStabilityIndex
```

This concludes our look at event logs, scheduled tasks, and system performance, but there's always more to discover. The techniques presented in this chapter will be a good foundation for your investigations.

15.4 Summary

Working with event logs, scheduled jobs, and performance indicators is an essential part of the administrator's role. PowerShell and WMI provide a number of tools to help you in these tasks:

- Event log discovery and configuration
- Backup and clearing of event logs
- Lifecycle management for scheduled jobs, including creation, discovery, and deletion
- Retrieval of data from performance counters
- Production of system assessment reports and stability index data

These techniques enable you to gather data for possible forensic investigations, perform out-of-hours tasks through scheduling jobs, and determine how your systems are performing in real time and with a historic perspective.

In the next chapter, we'll look at managing Hyper-V through WMI both directly and using the PowerShell Hyper-V library.

Administering Hyper-V
with PowerShell and WMI

This chapter covers

- Creating and configuring virtual machines
- Controlling virtual machines
- Starting a sequence of virtual machines
- Administering virtual disks

Virtualization technologies have caused a major change in the way we deliver and administer server-based infrastructure to our users. Virtualization provides a way for us to run multiple servers on the same hardware and maximize the use of that hardware.

Robert Heinlein frequently has his characters quote, "There ain't no such thing as a free lunch." This is also true in IT. The fact that we can run multiple servers on a single piece of hardware doesn't make our jobs any easier. In fact, they become harder:

- We have more servers to administer (the hosts always seem to be forgotten when adding up the number of servers).
- The risks increase. With 6, 12, or more servers running on a single piece of hardware, a failure in that hardware means more servers offline, more downtime, and more potential loss of business for the organization. Managing the high availability requirements increases the complexity.
- A virtual server doesn't have a power button we can press to start it or a cover we can take off to add more memory. We need tools to enable us to administer these servers.

Hyper-V is Microsoft's virtualization platform. Introduced in Windows Server 2008, it was refined in Windows Server 2008 R2 (which is the version I recommend until Windows Server 8 becomes available). There are a number of options for automating the administration of virtual machines running under Hyper-V:

- *Hyper-V cmdlets in Windows Server 8*
- *System Center Virtual Machine Manager (VMM) cmdlets*—These cmdlets supply a set of canned functionality. The drawback is that it costs extra to buy System Center VMM.
- *Hyper-V Management Library*—This is similar to the preceding option, in that the library (available from www.codeplex.com) provides a wrapper around the raw WMI by supplying a large number of functions. The functions are supplied as a PowerShell module and behave in a similar way to cmdlets.
- *WMI*—This is the most complex option because you have to create all of the functionality yourself. You've seen in previous chapters that using WMI with PowerShell is easier, but it still involves a lot of work

These options are illustrated in figure 16.1. At the bottom of the diagram, you're accessing PowerShell and WMI directly—this approach provides the minimum ease of use. At the next level up, you're using modules (or snap-ins) to make life easier. At the top of the diagram, you use scripts to call the modules, which gives you ease of use and the means to extend, and adapt, the functionality to meet your exact needs.

One thing you mustn't forget is administering the host systems. Hyper-V is a Windows feature, which means you can use the techniques you've already learned to perform the administration tasks. You'll be reusing a number of functions developed in earlier chapters.

In this chapter, we'll look at using the Hyper-V Management Library by James O'Neill. It's got great functionality and it's

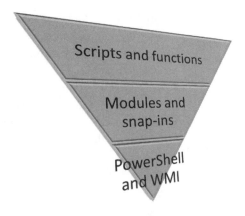

Figure 16.1 PowerShell, modules, and scripts

free! It wraps the WMI calls to make them easier to use. The code is worth examining to see how you could put something like this together. The library supplies 122 functions that are ready to use, and if you don't use VMM I very strongly recommend that you use this library. As you'll see throughout the chapter, it saves a lot of effort.

After you have Hyper-V up and running, your first task will be to create virtual machines. You'll also learn to configure them by adding (or removing) resources such as CPU, memory, disks, or network adapters.

Controlling the virtual machines is the next requirement. Stopping them is easy, but learning how to start them involves some work on your part. You can then move on to the more complex situation where you want to start a number of machines in a certain order.

Virtual disks are a major component of the Hyper-V infrastructure. You'll discover how to monitor, check usage, and compact as required.

First, though, you need to create a virtual machine.

16.1   Creating and configuring virtual machines

Creating a new virtual machine is a trivial task, but it becomes nontrivial when you realize that all you get is an empty shell. You need to configure the virtual machine with CPUs, memory, disks, and network adapters. Some configuration items are added automatically, but most you'll have to add explicitly.

> **TIP**   Remember that the virtual machine must be switched off for configuration items to be applied. We aren't at the hot-plug device quite yet.

Once you have your virtual machine configured you need to install an operating system. You could use an automated install process or add a file containing an image of installation media (an .iso file) to the virtual DVD drive. Starting the virtual machine then initiates the installation process. Once you've installed the operating system you can use the techniques in chapter 13 to configure the server.

Let's start on this journey by looking at how to create a virtual machine.

TECHNIQUE 126   Creating a virtual machine

Using the wizard in Hyper-V Manager to create a virtual machine isn't too painful, but you can make life easier for yourself by creating a function to do all the hard work. When I create a machine, I always add a network adapter and at least one disk. The amount of memory and the number of CPUs are more variable.

PROBLEM

You need to create a virtual machine. Ideally, the method you choose should be repeatable and should ensure that the machine matches your organization's standards.

SOLUTION

Listing 16.1 presents a solution to this problem. The first thing to notice is the name of the function—new-pawVM. The noun is still VM—I'm just adding a prefix.

TIP   Add a prefix to the noun in your function name if you need to distinguish it from another function with the same name. You can use the `-prefix` parameter in `Import-Module` to do this at load time.

The parameters set the Hyper-V host and virtual machine names, the path to the folder that contains the files comprising the virtual machine, the number of CPUs, and the amount of memory to be allocated to the new virtual machine.

Listing 16.1   Create a standard virtual machine

```
function new-pawVM{
[CmdletBinding()]
param (
    [string]$hvhost="$env:COMPUTERNAME",
    [string]$vm,
    [string]$path = "D:\Virtual Machines\",

    [ValidateRange(1,4)]
    [int]$cpu,
    [long]$ram
)
BEGIN{
 $vswitch = "Local Area Connection - Virtual Network"
}

PROCESS{

$vpath = Join-Path -Path $path -ChildPath $vm
New-Item -Path $path -Name $vm -ItemType Directory

$newvm = New-VM -Name $vm -Path $vpath -Server $hvhost

Set-VMCPUCount -VM $newvm -CPUCount $cpu `
-Server $hvhost -Force

$hostram = (Get-WmiObject -Class Win32_ComputerSystem `
    -ComputerName $hvhost).TotalPhysicalMemory
if($ram -gt ($hostram/4) ){$ram = math::Truncate($hostram/4)}

Set-VMMemory -VM $newvm -Memory $ram `
-Server $hvhost -Force

Add-VMNIC -VM $newvm -VirtualSwitch $vswitch -Server $hvhost -Force

Add-VMNewHardDisk -VM $vm -VHDPath "$vpath\$vm.vhd" `
-ControllerID 0 -LUN 0 -Size 125GB `
-Server $hvhost -Force

Add-VMDrive -VM $vm -ControllerID 1 -LUN 1 `
-OpticalDrive -Server $hvhost -Force
}}
```

❶ Create virtual machine

❷ Add CPUs

❸ Add memory

❹ Add disks

The command to set the virtual switch, specifying which network you want the virtual machine to join, is in the `BEGIN` block. It could be part of the `PROCESS` block if it was likely to become a parameter.

The name of the new virtual machine is joined to the path to the virtual machine storage area. You can then create the virtual machine shell ❶. The number of CPUs is also set ❷. I can set a maximum number of 4 on my host machine, and this is tested in the -cpu parameter validation. Change this value to match the capabilities of your host.

The total amount of physical memory in the host server is obtained, and if you're attempting to give the virtual machine an amount of memory that's more than 25 percent of the host's memory it's scaled back to the 25 percent mark. The memory of the virtual machine can then be set ❸. A virtual network card (NIC) is added to the virtual machine using the virtual switch defined earlier.

A virtual hard disk ❹ and virtual DVD drive are added to complete the virtual machine's configuration. The virtual disk size is hard-coded, but this could be parameterized if more flexibility is required.

DISCUSSION

Here's an example of using this function:

```
new-pawvm -vm Test51 -cpu 2 -ram 2GB
```

It's a very simple command to create a fairly complex object. The function could be modified to standardize the machines even further. These lines,

```
[ValidateRange(1,4)]
[int]$cpu,
[long]$ram
```

could be changed to

```
[ValidateSet(1,2,4)]
[int]$cpu
```

In the body of the function you could change these lines

```
$hostram = (Get-WmiObject -Class Win32_ComputerSystem `
   -ComputerName $hvhost).TotalPhysicalMemory
if($ram -gt ($hostram/4) ){$ram = math::Truncate($hostram/4)}

Set-VMMemory -VM $newvm -Memory $ram -Server $hvhost -Force
```

to this:

```
switch ($cpu){
 1 {Set-VMMemory -VM $newvm -Memory 1GB -Server $hvhost -Force}
 2 {Set-VMMemory -VM $newvm -Memory 2GB -Server $hvhost -Force}
 4 {Set-VMMemory -VM $newvm -Memory 4GB -Server $hvhost -Force}
}
```

The amount of memory in the machine is standardized based on the number of CPUs.

When a new virtual machine is created, IDE controllers 0 and 1 are added automatically. Each has two disk logical units (LUNs), labeled 0 and 1. I deliberately created the hard disk and DVD drive on different controllers and LUNs to emphasize this. The final configuration is shown in figure 16.2.

Over the lifetime of the virtual machine you may need to modify the amount of memory and number of CPUs allocated to the machine. Adjusting memory is straightforward using the Set-VMMemory function from the Hyper-V module (it's possible to check the total amount of physical RAM in the machine to ensure that you

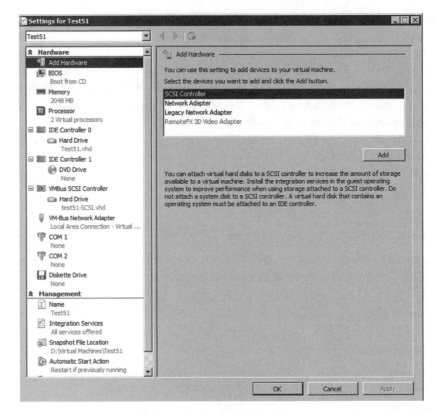

Figure 16.2   Properties of the new virtual machine

don't overcommit). For modifying the number of CPUs you need to ensure that you don't breach the limits set for virtual machines.

TECHNIQUE 127   Adding extra CPUs

It isn't possible to allocate more virtual CPUs than there are physical cores in the host system. You checked the number of CPUs at creation (in technique 126), but you also need to test the number when modifying.

PROBLEM

A test is needed to compare the number of virtual CPUs being allocated to a virtual machine against the maximum number that can be allocated.

SOLUTION

Listing 16.2 uses a `ValidateRange()` test on the `-cpu` parameter to test that the number of CPUs that you propose to add is valid for that host. I've hardcoded that number into the test in this listing, but it would be possible to use `ValidateScript()` to test against a WMI call to get the number of cores (see technique 4 in chapter 5).

Listing 16.2   Set the number of virtual CPUs

```
function set-pawCPU{
[CmdletBinding()]
param (
    [string]$hvhost="$env:COMPUTERNAME",
    [string]$vm,

    [ValidateRange(1,4)]
    [int]$cpu
)
BEGIN{}

PROCESS{

$count = (Get-VMCPUCount -VM $vm).VirtualQuantity
Write-Host "Current CPUs = $count"

Set-VMCPUCount -VM $vm -CPUCount $cpu -Server $hvhost -Force

$count = (Get-VMCPUCount -VM $vm).VirtualQuantity
Write-Host "New CPUs = $count"

}}
```

You then get the current number of virtual CPUs allocated to the machine, make the changes, and display the new number of CPUs.

DISCUSSION

If you need to know how many virtual CPUs have been allocated to the virtual machines on your host you can use this snippet:

```
Get-VM |
Get-VMCPUCount |
Measure-Object -Sum VirtualQuantity
```

You'll receive a count of the number of virtual machines and the total number of virtual CPUs allocated.

You now have a virtual machine, but before you can do anything with it, you need to install an operating system.

TECHNIQUE 128   **Attaching an .iso image to a DVD drive**

When you created your virtual machine in listing 16.1, you didn't attach an .iso image to the DVD drive. If you attach the operating system image and start the virtual machine it will kick straight into the install routine.

PROBLEM

You need to be able to add .iso files (DVD images) to the DVD drive so that you can install software and operating systems.

SOLUTION

The following listing shows how this is accomplished. The virtual machine to which you'll attach the image, and the image to be attached, are specified in the parameters. It's assumed that there's only a single DVD drive allocated to the virtual machine.

Listing 16.3   Attach an .iso image

```
function add-pawiso{
[CmdletBinding()]
param (
    [string]$hvhost="$env:COMPUTERNAME",
    [string]$vm,

    [ValidateSet("W2K8R2")]
    [string]$source
)
BEGIN{}

PROCESS{

$dvd = Get-VMDisk -VM $vm -Server $hvhost |
where {$_.DriveName -eq "DVD Drive"}

switch ($source) {
"W2K8R2" {$file = (Get-ChildItem -Path "C:\Source\Window
  ➥ 2008R2\*.iso").Fullname}
}

Write-Debug $file
Add-VMDisk -VM $vm -ControllerID $($dvd.ControllerID) `
-LUN $($dvd.DriveLUN) -Path $file -OpticalDrive

Get-VMDisk -VM $vm -Server $hvhost | where {$_.DriveName -eq "DVD Drive"}
}}
```

The .iso image to attach is defined by a short code. After you create an object representing the DVD drive you use a switch statement to find the full name of the .iso image file. The image is attached using Add-VMDisk, and the function uses Get-VMDisk to show that the file image is attached.

DISCUSSION

The function is used as follows:

```
add-pawiso -vm test51 -source w2k8r2
```

The length of the .iso image's name for Windows Server 2008 R2 (92 characters) means you likely won't want to type it out! Other codes can be used to point to other images (put one per directory for simplicity). If an invalid code is used the function will throw an error and present you with the list of valid codes.

The following function can be used to remove the image once the software installation has occurred:

```
function remove-pawiso{
[CmdletBinding()]
param (
    [string]$hvhost="$env:COMPUTERNAME",
    [string]$vm
)
PROCESS{
Get-VMDisk -VM $vm -Server $hvhost |
where {$_.DiskPath -like "*.iso"} |
```

```
foreach {
 Remove-VMDrive -Diskonly -VM $_.VMElementName `
 -ControllerID $_.ControllerId -LUN $_.DriveLun -Force
}

Get-VMDisk -VM $vm -Server $hvhost |
where {$_.DriveName -eq "DVD Drive"}
}}
```

The function is used like this:

```
remove-pawiso -vm test51
```

You may need to add complete new disks as well as .iso images, depending on what you want your virtual machine to accomplish.

TECHNIQUE 129   Adding a virtual disk

There are a number of reasons for adding another hard disk to a system. You may need the extra storage for files, or you may want to separate a particular part of the functionality, such as Exchange log files or SQL Server tempdb.

PROBLEM

An extra hard disk must be added to the virtual machine. This will be the first SCSI disk attached to the virtual machine, so you also need to add a SCSI controller.

SOLUTION

The new-pawSCSIdisk function in the following listing takes a Hyper-V host and a virtual machine name as arguments to the parameters. Get-VMDisk is used to discover the path to the folder containing the machine's virtual disks.

Listing 16.4   Add a SCSI disk

```
function new-pawSCSIdisk{
[CmdletBinding()]
param (
    [string]$hvhost="$env:COMPUTERNAME",
    [string]$vm
)
PROCESS{
 $disk = Get-VMDisk -VM $vm |
 where {$_.DiskName -eq "Hard Disk Image"} |
 select -First 1
 $path = Split-Path -Path $disk.DiskPath -Parent

 Add-VMSCSIController -VM $vm -Server $hvhost -Force
 Add-VMNewHardDisk -VM $vm -VHDPath "$path\$vm-SCSI.vhd" `
 -ControllerID 0 -LUN 0 -Size 125GB -SCSI `
 -Server $hvhost -Force

}}
```

A virtual SCSI controller is added, followed by a new virtual disk. Compare the statement in this function with that in listing 16.1 to see that the -SCSI parameter is used to create a SCSI disk rather than the IDE disk created earlier.

DISCUSSION

This function is called as follows:

```
new-pawSCSIdisk -vm test51
```

You can add further disks by wrapping this function in a wrapper function that then tests to see which LUNs are available.

When you created the first hard disk for the virtual machine, the assumption was that the disk would be formatted when the operating system was installed. Additional hard disks have to be explicitly formatted—see technique 30 in chapter 6.

The other piece of virtual hardware you need to consider adding is a network adapter.

TECHNIQUE 130 **Adding a network adapter**

I normally create virtual machines with a single network adapter, which gives connectivity to my virtual environment's internal network. When I've finished configuring the machine, I add another network adapter to give me internet access for Windows product activation. I use Network Address Translation (NAT) to span the virtual machines onto my host's wireless adapter.

PROBLEM

A new network adapter must be added to the virtual machine so that it can link to the internet.

SOLUTION

The following listing shows how you can accomplish this task. After accepting a host and virtual machine name, the function defines the virtual switch to use and creates an object representing the virtual machine.

Listing 16.5 Add a network adapter

```
function new-pawNIC{
[CmdletBinding()]
param (
    [string]$hvhost="$env:COMPUTERNAME",
    [string]$vm
)

PROCESS{

$vswitch = "New Virtual Network for Wireless"          Start virtual  ❶
                                                             machine
$target = Get-VM -Name $vm -Server $hvhost

Add-VMNIC -VM $target -VirtualSwitch $vswitch -Server $hvhost -Force

start-pawvm -hvhost $hvhost -vm $vm

Write-Host "Waiting for 3 minutes"
Start-Sleep -Seconds 180

$nic = Get-WmiObject Win32_NetworkAdapterConfiguration          ◁  Get new
-ComputerName $vm |                                             ❷ adapter
```

```
where{$_.DHCPEnabled -and $_.IPAddress[0].ToString() -like "169.254*"}

$ping = Test-Connection $vm -count 1
$nets = $ping.IPV4Address.IPAddressToString -split "\."
```
❸ Get IP address

```
$ipaddress = "192.168.2.$($nets[3])"
$subnet = "255.255.255.0"

$nic.EnableStatic($ipaddress, $subnet)
$nic.SetGateways("192.168.2.1", 1)
$nic.SetDNSServerSearchOrder("192.168.2.1")
```
❹ Configure adapter

```
Get-WmiObject Win32_NetworkAdapter -ComputerName $vm `
-Filter "DeviceID=$($nic.Index)" |
Set-WmiInstance -Arguments  @{NetConnectionID='Virtual Wireless LAN 99'}

}}
```

A virtual network adapter is added and the virtual machine is started ❶. The start-pawvm function is defined in listing 16.6 in the next technique. When the machine has started you can discover the new adapter ❷ (an address that starts with 169.254 is taken by an adapter that's configured to use DHCP but that can't find a DHCP server).

Test-Connection is used to find the IP address on the internal network ❸. The last octet of the address is taken to use in the address to be configured on the new adapter. A subnet mask is defined, and the adapter configured ❹. The appropriate default gateway and DNS server are applied. The network connection ID is changed as the last act of the function.

> **WARNING** The name that's used for the NetConnectionID must not have been used before. If it has, you'll see a COM exception if running locally or an error about the number arguments if running against a remote machine.

DISCUSSION

The function can be used like this:

```
new-pawNIC -vm Win7
```

A number of actions can be performed directly on the adapters of the various virtual machines on the host. You can view all adapters or select some properties of interest:

```
get-vmnic
get-vmnic | select VMElementName, SwitchName
```

You can test whether the adapter belongs to a particular switch:

```
get-vmnic |
where {$_.SwitchName -like "Local Area Connection - Virtual Network"}
```

Alternatively, you can get all adapters not on a given switch:

```
get-vmnic |
where {$_.SwitchName -notlike "Local Area Connection - Virtual Network"}
```

Finally, you can remove all adapters associated with a virtual switch prior to the removal of that switch:

```
get-vmnic |
where {$_.SwitchName -notlike
  ➥ "Local Area Connection - Virtual Network"} |
Remove-VMNIC
```

Once the virtual machine has been created and configured you have to learn to control it.

16.2 *Controlling virtual machines*

Virtual machines are no different from physical machines in that your control at the machine level is generally restricted to starting and stopping virtual machines. You can safely stop a virtual machine using the `Stop-Computer` cmdlet or a WMI shutdown command as in listing 13.3. Starting a virtual machine can't be done directly from PowerShell, so you need to use the Hyper-V library.

In my test environment I have two Exchange servers, but I need a domain controller to start first. A similar situation exists with SharePoint and SQL Server, where the database server must start before the SharePoint server. Starting machines in a predetermined order is an interesting problem that you'll solve in technique 132.

Also, if virtual machines are offline for an extended period of time, the patch levels will become out of date. The ideal solution is to have an automated solution that periodically brings virtual machines online, ensures that the patches are applied, and then closes down the machines.

A quick test you can apply to determine the state of a virtual machine is to use the `Get-VM` cmdlet. If you only want to see which machines are running you can use this:

```
Get-VM -Running
```

You can now determine which machines to start because you know which ones are currently active.

| TECHNIQUE 131 | **Starting a virtual machine** |

Starting physical machines is easy—you press the power-on button. Virtual machines don't have buttons, so you need to send the virtual host a command to start the machine.

PROBLEM

You need to be able to start a virtual machine on a remote host. The function you use should report the progress and let you know when the virtual machine is up and running.

SOLUTION

The following listing solves this problem. It accepts a Hyper-V host and virtual machine name as parameters and loads the Hyper-V module if it's not already loaded.

Listing 16.6 Start a virtual machine

```
function start-pawVM{
[CmdletBinding()]
param (
    [string]$hvhost="$env:COMPUTERNAME",
```

```
    [string]$vm
)
PROCESS{
if (-not(Get-Module -Name hyperv)){Import-Module -Name hyperv -Force}

$machine = Get-VM -Name $vm -Server $hvhost
if ($machine.EnabledState -eq 3){
 Start-VM -VM $vm
 do{
  Write-Host "System $vm starting $(get-date -Format T )"
  if (-not (Test-Connection -ComputerName $vm -Count 1 -Quiet)) {
    Start-Sleep -Seconds 5
  }
  else {
    Write-Host "System $vm started $(get-date -Format T )"
    break
  }
 }until(1 -gt 2)
}
else {
 write-Host "$vm is not stopped. Check Status"
}
}}
```

You get an object representing the virtual machine and test its status. If the status is 3, it means the machine is stopped so you can start it. If the status isn't 3, you output a message saying that the machine's status needs to be checked—this includes the situation where the machine is running.

Assuming that the status is correct (it's stopped), you issue a Start-VM command. A do loop is used to write a message stating that the machine is starting and giving the date and time. Test-Connection is used to determine connectivity to the virtual machine. If you don't get a result it means that the machine is still starting, in which case the function pauses for five seconds before processing the loop again.

> **TIP** Setting the until condition on the do loop to be impossible forces the loop to run indefinitely.

If you do get a response from Test-Connection it means the machine is available, so you send a message to that effect and break out of the loop.

DISCUSSION

When you use the Start-VM command you receive a message that a background job has started. These jobs can be viewed as follows:

```
Get-WmiObject -Namespace root\virtualization -Class Msvm_ConcreteJob
```

One drawback to this approach is that the Msvm_ConcreteJob WMI class doesn't tell you to which machine the job is related.

Starting a single machine is useful. Starting multiple machines in the correct order with a single command is even more useful.

Starting multiple machines

There are multiple scenarios where you may want to start multiple machines in a particular order, such as starting one domain controller and two Exchange servers. Alternatively, you may just need to start multiple machines in a sequential manner so that you can control resource usage on the host.

PROBLEM

There's a relationship between the functionality of a number of virtual machines, which means you have to start the machines in the correct order for them to work correctly.

SOLUTION

The following listing demonstrates a solution to this problem. The first parameter is the Hyper-V host, as seen previously.

Listing 16.7   Start multiple virtual machines

```
function start-pawVMset{
[CmdletBinding()]
param (
    [string]$hvhost="$env:COMPUTERNAME",
    [string[]]$vmset
)
PROCESS{
if (-not(Get-Module -Name hyperv)){Import-Module -Name hyperv -Force}

foreach ($vm in $vmset){
  start-pawVM -hvhost $hvhost -vm $vm
}
}}
```

The second parameter shows a coding syntax you've not seen often: `[string[]]$vmset`. Read this from the inside out. `String[]` represents a string array, which means that the parameter expects an array (multiple virtual machine names). An array containing a single name is acceptable.

You loop through the list of machines in that array and call the `start-pawVM` function (from listing 16.6) for each one.

DISCUSSION

The function is used in this manner:

```
start-pawVMset -vmset dc02, exch07, exch071
```

In this case, my domain controller is up and running before my Exchange servers start. This ensures that the Exchange servers can contact the domain controller, and there won't be any problems with the Exchange services starting.

The function can also be used to start a set of unrelated machines; for instance, I could start all of my SQL Server systems in one pass.

Starting machines is a good idea, but sometimes you have to stop them as well.

Stopping virtual machines

There are a number of methods available for stopping virtual machines. A brute force approach is to stop the host, but that will probably leave you with more work tidying up the state of the virtual machines when you want to start them again. You can shut down all running virtual machines like this:

```
Get-VM -Running | Stop-VM -Force
```

Alternatively, either of the following examples will close down a single machine:

```
Stop-VM -VM dc02 -Force
Stop-computer dc02
```

The drawback to these approaches is that you don't get any reporting on progress.

PROBLEM

A function is needed that will shut down, in a controlled manner, one or more virtual machines. The close-down procedure must report progress and inform you when the virtual machine is completely shut down.

SOLUTION

The solution to this problem can be found by adapting the code in listing 16.7 as shown in the following listing. The parameters are the virtual host and the set of machines you wish to close down.

Listing 16.8 Stop a virtual machine

```
function stop-pawVMset{
[CmdletBinding()]
param (
    [string]$hvhost="$env:COMPUTERNAME",
    [string[]]$vmset
)
PROCESS{
if (-not(Get-Module -Name hyperv)){Import-Module -Name hyperv -Force}

foreach ($vm in $vmset){
 $machine = Get-VM -Name $vm -Server $hvhost
 if ($machine.EnabledState -eq 2){
  Stop-VM -VM $vm -Force
  do{
   $machine = Get-VM -Name $vm -Server $hvhost
   if ($machine.EnabledState -eq 3){
     Write-Host "System $vm stopped $(Get-Date -Format T )"
     break
   }
   else{
     Write-Host "System $vm stopping $(Get-Date -Format T )"
     Start-Sleep -Seconds 2
   }
  }until(1 -gt 2)
 }
 else {
```

```
    write-Host "$vm is not running. Check Status"
  }
 }
}}
```

The function iterates through the set of machines and for each machine tests that the machine is running and then calls Stop-VM. The machine state is tested periodically during the close-down process (every 2 seconds in the code, but this can easily be changed to allow for latency on really remote machines). When the machine state reaches 3 (stopped) a message is written out confirming that the machine is stopped, and the function breaks out of the loop.

DISCUSSION

The function can be used directly:

```
stop-pawVMset -vmset exch071, exch07, dc02
```

Alternatively, you can predefine the list of machines in a variable:

```
$close = "exch071", "exch07", "dc02"
stop-pawVMset -vmset $close
```

Virtual machines consist of one or more virtual disks. You need to be able to administer those virtual disks.

16.3 *Managing virtual disks*

The final area to be covered in this chapter is virtual disks. These are files on the host that the virtual machine treats as disks. You've already seen how to create virtual disks as you create the machine and how to add virtual disks to an existing machine. We now need to turn our attention to managing virtual disks.

You need to be able to view the status of the virtual disks attached to a virtual machine, determine how much free space is available within your virtual disk, and compact the virtual disk to save space and make the disk more efficient.

The first job is to test the status of the virtual disk.

TECHNIQUE 134   **Testing virtual disk status**

Understanding the status of the virtual disks in your system can go a long way when troubleshooting problems. If the disks have problems you'll definitely see those problems show up in the virtual machine, which could affect a business-critical application.

PROBLEM

You need to be able to determine the status of the various virtual storage devices attached to your virtual machine. This includes DVD drives and virtual hard disks. You also need the option to display information about disk usage.

SOLUTION

The following listing presents a solution to the problem. Two parameter sets are presented to make the selection of DVD or hard disks mutually exclusive options. A further parameter enables you to discover further information about the virtual hard disk.

Listing 16.9 Test virtual disk status

```
function test-pawVHD{
[CmdletBinding()]
param (
    [string]$hvhost="$env:COMPUTERNAME",

    [parameter(ParameterSetName="DVD")]
    [switch]$dvd,

    [parameter(ParameterSetName="HD")]
    [switch]$hd,

    [parameter(ParameterSetName="HD")]
    [switch]$info

)
$vmdisks = Get-VMDisk -Server $hvhost

switch ($psCmdlet.ParameterSetName) {
 "DVD" {$disks = $vmdisks |
        where {$_.DriveName -eq "DVD Drive"} |
        select @{N="VMname"; E={$_.VMElementName}},
        ControllerName, DriveName}

  "HD" {$disks  = $vmdisks |
        where {$_.DriveName -eq "Hard Drive"} |
        select @{N="VMname"; E={$_.VMElementName}},
        ControllerName, DriveName, DiskPath

        foreach ($disk in $disks) {

     $tp = Test-Path -Path $disk.DiskPath
     $disk | Add-Member -MemberType NoteProperty `
     -Name "PathFound" -Value $tp

     if($tp -and $info){
     $vhdinfo =  Get-VHDInfo -VHDPaths "$($disk.DiskPath)"
     $disk |
     Add-Member -MemberType NoteProperty `
     -Name "FileSize" -Value $vhdinfo.FileSize -PassThru |
     Add-Member -MemberType NoteProperty `
     -Name "MaxSize" -Value $vhdinfo.MaxInternalSize -PassThru |
     Add-Member -MemberType NoteProperty `
     -Name "Inuse" -Value $vhdinfo.Inuse -PassThru |
     Add-Member -MemberType NoteProperty `
     -Name "InSavedState" -Value $vhdinfo.InSavedState -PassThru |
     Add-Member -MemberType NoteProperty `
     -Name "Type" -Value $vhdinfo.TypeName
}
  }
 }
}
$disks

}
```

You start by retrieving all of the virtual disks defined on the host. A switch statement determines whether you're working with DVDs or hard disks based on the parameter set. Using parameter set names makes the choices mutually exclusive. Virtual DVDs have the virtual machine name, controller name, and drive name selected.

The processing for a hard disk is slightly more complicated. You select the same information as for DVDs but add the path to the virtual disk file. `Test-Path` is used to determine whether the file exists. If the file exists and you've selected the option for more information, you add properties to the object you're creating to hold disk size, usage, and status.

DISCUSSION

The following examples illustrate how to use the function:

```
test-pawVHD -dvd
```

The preceding example displays the DVD devices allocated to virtual machines. If you want to display the information about virtual hard disks you'd use this syntax:

```
test-pawVHD -hd | ft -a
```

The choice between displaying information on DVD or hard disk is mutually exclusive, as can be illustrated by trying this:

```
test-pawVHD -hd -dvd
```

It generates an error.

Finally, using this syntax,

```
test-pawVHD -hd -info
```

generates output in the following format for every virtual hard disk on every virtual machine on the host:

```
VMname          : Exch071
ControllerName  : IDE Controller 0
DriveName       : Hard Drive
DiskPath        : C:\Virtual Machines\Exch071\Exch071.vhd
PathFound       : True
FileSize        : 22241793536
MaxSize         : 136365211648
Inuse           : FALSE
InSavedState    : FALSE
Type            : Dynamic
```

The file sizes are in bytes but you could easily convert to MB or GB. Examples of such conversion can be found in earlier chapters, such as listing 6.2 in technique 21. Alternatively, you could use the following technique.

TECHNIQUE 135   **Examining virtual disk usage**

Virtual disks have storage limitations in exactly the same way as physical disks. An important part of administering the virtual machines is testing their storage capacity.

PROBLEM

You need to be able to check on the free space of the virtual disks in your environment. This will feed into the capacity-planning reports you need to maintain.

SOLUTION

There are two ways you can solve this problem. If a virtual machine is running you can use technique 27 from chapter 6 to determine the disk space information. The following listing will work for virtual disks connected to machines that are either running or switched off.

Listing 16.10 Determine virtual disk usage

```
function get-pawdisksize{
[CmdletBinding()]
param (
    [string]$hvhost="$env:COMPUTERNAME",
    [string]$vm
)
PROCESS{

Get-VMDisk -VM $vm -Server $hvhost |
where {$_.DriveName -eq "Hard Drive"} |
foreach {
 Get-VHDInfo -VHDPaths $($_.DiskPath) |
 select Path,
 @{N="MaxSize"; E={[math]::round(($_.MaxInternalSize / 1GB), 4)}},
 @{N="Size"; E={[math]::round(($_.FileSize / 1GB), 4)}},
 @{N="PercFree"; E= {100-(($_.FileSize / $_.MaxInternalSize)*100)}},
 Type
}
}}
```

The function takes the usual host and virtual machine names as parameters. `Get-VMDisk` is used to retrieve the disk information, with `Where-Object` used to restrict the returned information to virtual hard disks (you filter out DVD drives).

The pipeline is completed by piping the disks into `Foreach-Object`, where the `DiskPath` property is used in `Get-VHDInfo` to discover the disk capacity information. The usual calculations are performed to convert the results from bytes to more meaningful gigabytes.

DISCUSSION

The calculations round to four decimal places to ensure that new disks register. This could be altered to two decimal places if preferred (new disks will register as 0 used space).

Knowing the available capacity of a virtual disk is one part of the puzzle. You also need to know if the space allocated to the virtual disk is being used efficiently.

TECHNIQUE 136   **Compacting virtual disks**

Virtual disks are files in the host's storage system (the specification of .vhd files is available from Microsoft if you want to dig deeper). All disks, physical or virtual, suffer from fragmentation. This was discussed in detail in chapter 6 (technique 31).

When physical disks are defragmented the file fragments are made contiguous, but no allowance is made for moving white space to the end of the disk. You can compact virtual disks to remove the white space and make more efficient use of the host's storage.

PROBLEM

You need to be able to compact virtual hard disks to optimize the host's storage. The option should be presented to defragment the virtual disk at the same time.

SOLUTION

The function presented in the listing 16.11 solves this problem.

> **NOTE**   The defragmentation and compaction require the virtual machine to be offline.

The parameters are the virtual machine whose disks you'll compact and an optional switch to prevent defragmentation. By default defragmentation will occur.

Listing 16.11   Compact a hard disk

```
function compress-pawVHD{
[CmdletBinding()]
param (
    [string]$vm,
    [switch]$nodefrag
)
PROCESS{
if (-not(Get-Module -Name hyperv)){Import-Module -Name hyperv -Force}
if (-not(Get-Module -Name Chapter06)){
 Import-Module "C:\Scripts\PowerShell-WMI\Chapter06\Chapter06.psm1" `
 -Force
}

$dl = get-nextdriveletter          ❶ Get drive letter
$pn = get-nextpartition

if (-not $nodefrag) {              ❷ Mount drive

 Get-VMDisk -VM $vm    |
 where {$_.DriveName -eq "Hard Drive"} |
 foreach {
  Mount-VHD -Path $($_.DiskPath) -Partition $pn -letter $dl

  $mount = Get-VHDMountPoint -VHDPaths $($_.DiskPath) |
  where {$_.VolumeName -notlike "System Reserved" }    ❸ Defragment drive

  Write-Verbose "Defragging disk $($mount.DeviceID)"
  $def = invoke-defraganal -drive $($mount.DeviceID) -defrag

  Dismount-VHD -VHDPaths $($_.DiskPath) -Force
 }
}

Write-Verbose "Compacting disks for $vm"      ❹ Compact drive
Get-VMDisk -VM $vm    |
where {$_.DriveName -eq "Hard Drive"} |
foreach {
 Compress-VHD -VHDPaths $($_.DiskPath)  -Wait
}

}}
```

The function loads this chapter's module and also the module from chapter 6 if it's not already loaded. You also need to mount the virtual disk as part of the host's filesystem if you want to perform a defragmentation. In order to achieve this you need the next drive letter and partition number ❶. The two functions used for this are shown in listings 16.12 and 16.13 respectively.

If you're performing a defragmentation ❷ (the default action and recommended), you get the virtual hard disks. Note I've had to use a double negative in the logic! It's not a best practice but it works.

Each virtual hard disk associated with the virtual machine is mounted using Mount-VHD. The virtual disk is mounted as two disks (one small System Reserved disk and the main disk). You can use Get-MountPoint to discover the main disk's DeviceId, which you feed into the invoke-defraganal function (from chapter 6) ❸. Once the defragmentation is complete you can dismount the virtual disk.

The virtual hard disks associated with the machine are presented to compress-VHD to perform the compaction and reclaim the space ❹. The -wait parameter shows a progress bar for the compaction.

DISCUSSION

The function is easy to use:

```
compress-pawVHD -vm W08R2SQL08 -verbose
```

I recommend using the -verbose switch so you receive more information regarding the function's progress.

> **WARNING** Performing a defragmentation can take a long time and you don't get any information regarding its progress.

The defragmentation option is the default for this function. If you want to perform a compaction without defragmentation use the -nodefrag switch:

```
compress-pawVHD -vm Win7 -nodefrag
```

Compaction is a much quicker process than defragmentation.

> **WARNING** Fragmented .vhd files may throw an error when you're attempting to compress them. The host filesystem needs to be defragmented in this case.

The function to discover the next drive letter simply gets the currently used drive letters, sorts them in descending order, and then calculates the next letter, as shown in the following listing. A test is performed to determine whether you've already used Z, in which case you have a problem and another solution is required.

Listing 16.12 Get next drive letter

```
function get-nextdriveletter {

$disk = Get-WmiObject -Class Win32_LogicalDisk |
sort DeviceId -Descending |
```

```
select -First 1 -Property DeviceID

$letter = ($disk.DeviceID).Substring(0,1).ToUpper()
if ($letter -eq "Z"){
 Write-Host "No more drive letters available"
}
else {
 $nextletter = [char](([byte][char]$letter) + 1)
 $nextletter
}}
```

The next partition index is calculated in a similar manner, as shown in the next listing This is an easier calculation because you're dealing with integers.

Listing 16.13 Get next partition index

```
function get-nextpartition {

$disk = Get-WmiObject -Class Win32_DiskPartition |
sort Index -Descending |
select -First 1 -Property Index

$nextindex = ($disk.Index) + 1
$nextindex

}
```

This concludes our examination of the Hyper-V library and how you can use it. There's a lot more you can do with these functions—the more you experiment with them, the more functionality you'll discover.

16.4   *Summary*

Virtualization is an essential part of most organizations' infrastructure. Being able to automate the administration of the virtual environment is an increasingly important ability. Hyper-V is a Windows feature, which means you can use the same techniques to administer your virtual machines and their hosts.

These are some common tasks that you've automated in this chapter:

- The creation and configuration of virtual machines
- Controlling individual machines and groups of machines
- Testing virtual disks and determining their remaining capacity
- Defragmenting and compacting virtual disks to improve performance

At the heart of these techniques is the PowerShell Hyper-V library. This free-to-download PowerShell module will prove to be of great assistance as you develop further techniques for automating the administration of your virtual environment.

The topic of the next chapter is working with WMI directly through Windows Remote Management, rather than using the remoting capabilities of PowerShell or the WMI cmdlets.

Part 3

The future:
PowerShell v3 and WMI

WMI has always been a first-class citizen in the PowerShell universe. Its importance has increased immensely with the introduction of PowerShell v3. But before we dive into the new functionality, we'll look at using WMI over the WSMAN protocol in chapter 17. WSMAN increases in importance in PowerShell v3, so a sound grounding in the protocol is a must.

> **WARNING** The last two chapters of the book are based on a beta release of PowerShell v3. Changes could occur before the final versions of PowerShell v3 and Windows 8 are released.

PowerShell v3 introduces a number of improvements to WMI usage:

- New WMI namespaces and classes
- A new API for accessing WMI locally and remotely
- A new set of cmdlets (CIM) for working with WMI
- Creation of cmdlets from WMI classes

Many of the new cmdlets introduced with PowerShell v3 are created from WMI classes. In chapter 18, we'll look at how you can create your own cmdlets from WMI classes (including legacy classes). The creation of format and type files to control the display will also be demonstrated. This is a technique with general application in PowerShell.

Chapter 19 starts by showing how you can create cmdlets from WMI methods. We'll then look at the new CIM cmdlets, compare them with the WMI and

WSMAN cmdlets we've already seen, and close with a look at the capabilities for remote administration introduced with the CIM API and cmdlets.

WMI has always been viewed as powerful, and these enhancements take it to a completely new level. It's going to be a fun time as these techniques evolve.

WMI over WSMAN

17

This chapter covers

- WSMAN protocols
- Using WMI through WSMAN
- Using CredSSP
- Comparing WSMAN and other remoting techniques

In the previous chapters, we've looked at using the capabilities built into the WMI cmdlets to provide access to remote systems. Using the -ComputerName parameter is a simple method of creating a connection to a remote machine, and this is the approach we've used in the majority of the techniques explored in previous chapters. But there are a number of scenarios where this approach isn't enough:

- WMI uses Distributed COM (DCOM) to connect to a remote machine. This may not be available or may be blocked by a firewall.
- You may want to run multiple WMI commands against the same machine—this involves creating and destroying multiple connections. It would be more efficient to create one session and run multiple commands. Some information about the connection is cached, but it's still quicker to create one session and run multiple commands.
- You may need to perform out-of-band hardware management (accessing the hardware by dedicated management links that aren't used by general users) or access non-Windows machines.

Where DCOM isn't available, you'll need to use PowerShell remoting (section 2.8 in chapter 2) or, if remoting isn't available, use WSMAN protocols to directly access the WMI resources. We'll investigate the full PowerShell remoting options and look at how the WSMAN protocols can be used to directly access resources on a remote machine.

NOTE This chapter will look only at working with the WMI provider through WSMAN.

The WSMAN configuration is exposed as a PowerShell drive enabling you to configure WSMAN settings on local and remote machines.

By using WSMAN directly, you can perform three distinct types of tasks:

- Information discovery
- Modification of WMI objects
- Removal of WMI objects

One potential issue with any remoting scenario is trying to directly access one or more other machines from the remote machine. This is blocked by default, but the use of the Credential Security Support Provider (CredSSP) enables this restriction to be overcome by delegating the user's credentials from the local to the remote machine. This capability was introduced to PowerShell with the release of PowerShell v2 in Windows 7 and Windows Server 2008 R2.

After we review the remoting protocol and WSMAN and CredSSP usage, the chapter closes with a review of the options for accessing remote machines and some recommendations for their use.

We'll start by looking at the options available to you.

17.1 Remoting protocols

PowerShell has a number of protocols that can be used to connect to, and work with, remote machines. In this section, we'll review these protocols so that using WSMAN can be put into context and to determine the best approach for working in a particular scenario.

You've seen throughout the book that the WMI cmdlets can access remote computers directly. As an example, the following command returns information about the logical disks on a computer called DC02:

```
Get-WmiObject -Class Win32_LogicalDisk -ComputerName DC02
```

WMI uses DCOM to access the remote machine, which requires the COM- and DCOM-related services to be running on the remote system. It also requires that any firewalls be configured to allow this traffic.

An alternative is to use PowerShell remoting. This can be achieved as a one-off command using Invoke-Command or by creating a session to the remote machine. If you use Invoke-Command, the WMI command is modified to use this syntax:

```
Invoke-Command `
-ScriptBlock {Get-WmiObject -Class Win32_LogicalDisk} `
-ComputerName DC02
```

Each returned object has a property that shows the computer name that was accessed. It's of this form:

```
PSComputerName : dc02
```

To do this, you need to have enabled the PowerShell remoting functionality on the remote machine using `Enable-PSRemoting` run in a PowerShell console with elevated privileges.

A third option is to communicate directly with the WinRM service and access the data:

```
Get-WSManInstance -ComputerName DC02 `
-ResourceURI wmicimv2/Win32_LogicalDisk `
-SelectorSet @{DeviceId='C:'}
```

> **TIP** Try running these commands in your environment to see the differences in the results. They can be run on the local machine, but you'll need to start PowerShell with elevated privileges for the WSMAN example.

There are differences between the data returned by `Get-WmiObject` and that returned by PowerShell remoting or by using WSMAN:

- `Get-WmiObject` returns objects from local or remote machines. These are live objects with methods and properties that can be manipulated as allowed by the WMI class.
- PowerShell remoting returns inert objects that have just the properties available.
- WSMAN cmdlets return XML renderings of the object. These are inert, meaning that methods don't work and properties can't be modified.

You need to understand the differences and similarities of using full PowerShell remoting compared to using WSMAN.

17.1.1 PowerShell remoting

Remoting was probably the most eagerly awaited addition to PowerShell when version 2 was released. It's based on the WS-Management (Web Services Management, usually abbreviated to WSMAN) protocols established by the Distributed Management Task Force (http://dmtf.org/). WSMAN is a SOAP-based protocol for the management of servers, devices, applications, and web services.

Microsoft implemented WSMAN as the Windows Remote Management (WinRM) service. The architecture is illustrated in figure 17.1.

A PowerShell session on the local machine passes the commands to the PowerShell remoting protocol on the local machine. The protocol is installed as part of WinRM. The remoting protocol communicates via SOAP with the WinRM service on the remote machine. The commands are then passed to a PowerShell session for execution. The results are passed back via WinRM.

The communication between the machines is performed using HTTP or HTTPS (if the appropriate certificate is installed). Configuration is performed by

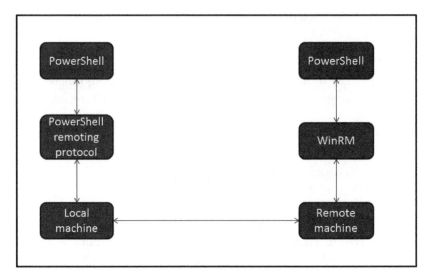

Figure 17.1   The PowerShell remoting architecture, showing the information flow from a PowerShell session on the local machine through the PowerShell remoting protocol to WinRM on the remote machine and terminating at a remote PowerShell session

`Enable-PsRemoting` in the first instance and then by the WSMAN cmdlets or provider if any fine-tuning of the WSMAN/WinRM configuration is required.

Individual commands can be run on the remote machine using `Invoke-Command`, or you can create a PowerShell session to the remote machine and work through that. Using a session is more efficient if you'll be running multiple commands on the remote machine. This was described in detail in section 2.8.

17.1.2   *WSMAN*

When you use WSMAN, you access the resource directly from the WinRM service, as shown in figure 17.2. You don't need to access PowerShell on the remote machine. This means that you could administer remote machines that don't use the Windows operating system, assuming that they have an instance of WSMAN running and have a CIM (WMI) provider.

In the introduction to section 17.1, you saw how to access a WMI resource using `Get-WSManInstance`. The `-SelectorSet` parameter is analogous to the `-Filter` parameter in `Get-WmiObject`, but it uses the WMI class key as its filter. For instance, this works:

```
Get-WSManInstance -ComputerName DC02 `
-ResourceURI wmicimv2/Win32_Service `
-SelectorSet @{Name='WinRm'}
```

But this code doesn't:

```
Get-WSManInstance -ComputerName DC02 `
-ResourceURI wmicimv2/Win32_Process `
-SelectorSet @{Name=
    'Microsoft.ActiveDirectory.WebServices.exe'}
```

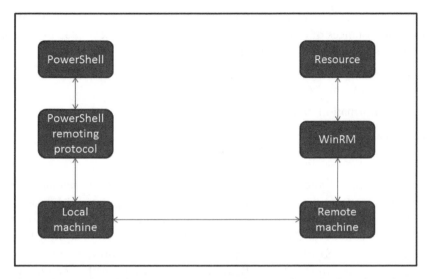

Figure 17.2 Using WinRM to access resources. The local PowerShell session talks through the local PowerShell remoting protocol to the remote WinRM service, which accesses the resources directly.

You need to use this format:

```
Get-WSManInstance -ComputerName DC02 `
-ResourceURI wmicimv2/Win32_Process `
-SelectorSet @{Handle=1420}
```

Section 3.2.4 shows how to discover the WMI key for a class. Review that section if you didn't read it earlier.

You can perform other administration tasks in addition to discovering information. These other tasks require you to be familiar with the WSMAN cmdlets.

17.1.3 WSMAN cmdlets

The WSMAN cmdlets can be discovered using `Get-Command`:

```
Get-Command *wsman* -CommandType cmdlet |
Select name
```

They're listed for convenience in table 17.1. We'll be working mainly with `Get-WSMan-Instance` and `Invoke-WSManAction` in this chapter. These cmdlets can be compared to `Get-WmiObject` and `Invoke-WmiMethod` respectively.

Table 17.1   Cmdlets for working directly with WSMAN

Connect-WSMan	Disable-WSManCredSSP	Disconnect-WSMan
Enable-WSManCredSSP	Get-WSManCredSSP	Get-WSManInstance
Invoke-WSManAction	New-WSManInstance	New-WSManSessionOption
Remove-WSManInstance	Set-WSManInstance	Set-WSManQuickConfig
Test-WSMan		

The `Get-WSManInstance` cmdlet has an `-Enumerate` parameter. It's used when there are multiple instances of a particular resource and the `-SelectorSet` parameter isn't used. To see all of the logical disks on a remote system you'd use this syntax:

```
Get-WSManInstance -ComputerName DC02 `
-ResourceURI wmicimv2/Win32_LogicalDisk -Enumerate
```

If you want information on a particular disk, you'd use this:

```
Get-WSManInstance -ComputerName DC02 `
-ResourceURI wmicimv2/Win32_LogicalDisk `
-SelectorSet @{DeviceID='C:'}
```

`New-WSManInstance` and `Remove-WSmanInstance` are used to manage resources, such as WSMAN listeners. They can't be used to manipulate WMI-based objects. `Set-WSManInstance` can be used to perform some changes to WMI-based objects as well as WSMAN resources. The `*CredSSP` cmdlets are explained in section 17.3.

Connect-WSMan and Disconnect-WSMan enable you to connect to the WinRM service on a remote machine. The configuration information for the remote machine is then available through the WSMAN provider.

17.1.4 WSMAN provider

PowerShell provides access to data stores through providers. The providers expose the data store in a similar manner to the filesystem. A well written provider should supply access to the data store through the core cmdlets, such as `*Item` and `*ItemProperty` (see `Get-Help about_core_commands` for the full list).

A quick overview of the properties exposed in the provider can be found like this:

```
Get-ChildItem -Path wsman: -Recurse | ft Name, Value -a
```

The top-level containers for the provider are shown in figure 17.3.

There are a number of default settings:

- Port 5985 for HTTP and 5986 for HTTPS.
- Machine names, not IP addresses, identify remote machines.
- Credential delegation through CredSSP is disabled.
- Nondomain machines must be in the trusted hosts list.

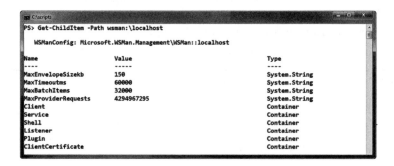

**Figure 17.3
Top-level containers
in the WSMAN drive**

These defaults (apart from the last one) can be changed, though nondomain machines can be added to the trusted hosts list.

> **TIP** I don't recommend changing the ports or any other of the default settings unless there's a security imperative in your organization that mandates the change.

If changes have to be made, they can be performed using code like this:

```
Set-Item -Path wsman:\localhost\listener\listener*\port `
-Value 8080

Set-Item -Path WSMan:\localhost\Client\DefaultPorts\HTTP `
-Value 8080
```

The first line changes the port that WinRM listens on, and the second line makes it the default.

> **TIP** If you have to change the ports, be consistent across your environment to avoid troubleshooting problems.

The WSMAN provider connects to the WinRM service on the local machine:

```
PS> dir wsman:

   WSManConfig:

ComputerName                              Type
------------                              ----
localhost                                 Container
```

If you use the `Connect-WSMan` cmdlet, you can create a connection to the WinRM service on a remote machine:

```
PS> Connect-WSMan -ComputerName dc02
PS> dir wsman:

   WSManConfig:

ComputerName                              Type
------------                              ----
localhost                                 Container
dc02                                      Container
```

The WinRM settings can be configured on the remote machine using the provider. The connection can be destroyed using `Disconnect-WSMan -ComputerName dc02`.

You've seen what the WSMAN protocol is and how you can configure it. It's time to put it to work.

17.2 Using WSMAN

Any administration tool is only as good as the tasks you can accomplish with it. Using the WSMAN cmdlets enables you to perform similar tasks to those you could do by using WMI directly without the use of DCOM.

In this section, you'll discover how you can use aliases for the WSMAN resource URIs and how to test that the WSMAN protocols are available.

TIP   This is also a good test when troubleshooting PowerShell remoting or the CIM cmdlets in PowerShell v3.

The bulk of your administrative work likely involves discovering information about a machine or managing the resources on that machine. We'll investigate how those tasks can be accomplished using WSMAN—specifically, how you can discover, modify, and delete WMI objects.

17.2.1 *WSMAN URIs*

In the examples you've seen so far, the code using the WSMAN cmdlet has contained a Uniform Resource Identifier (URI), which has been stated like this:

```
-ResourceURI wmicimv2/Win32_LogicalDisk
```

That coding is an alias for this URI:

```
http://schemas.microsoft.com/wbem/wsman/1/wmi/root/cimv2/Win32_LogicalDisk
```

The full URI consists of three parts:

- *A root*—http://schemas.microsoft.com
- *A namespace*—wbem/wsman/1/wmi/root/cimv2
- *A class*—Win32_LogicalDisk

The aliases are a lot easier to use and involve a lot less typing than using the full URI (and they reduce the chances of error). Table 17.2 lists the available aliases and their corresponding full URIs.

Table 17.2   WSMAN URI aliases

Alias	Full resource URI
wmi	http://schemas.microsoft.com/wbem/wsman/1/wmi
wmicimv2	http://schemas.microsoft.com/wbem/wsman/1/wmi/root/cimv2
cimv2	http://schemas.dmtf.org/wbem/wscim/1/cim-schema/2
winrm	http://schemas.microsoft.com/wbem/wsman/1
wsman	http://schemas.microsoft.com/wbem/wsman/1
shell	http://schemas.microsoft.com/wbem/wsman/1/windows/shell

Before you can get into using these aliases, you need to make sure that the WinRM service is up and running.

TECHNIQUE 137   **Testing WSMAN**

It is always a good idea to test the tools you'll be using, and the WSMAN protocols are no exception. You could use the Get-Service cmdlet to determine whether the WinRM service was running on a remote system, but you need a little bit more to be sure you can communicate with the service.

PROBLEM

You need to perform an end-to-end test to ensure that the WSMAN communication is configured correctly. It's only necessary to test the remote machine to determine that you can communicate with it, but testing the local machines supplies information that may be useful in troubleshooting.

SOLUTION

The function takes the usual -computername parameter to identify the remote machine, as shown in the following listing. When using WSMAN, this has to be a name by default, not an IP address.

Listing 17.1 Test WSMAN links

```
function test-wsmanlink{
[CmdletBinding()]
param(
  [string]$computername
)

"Testing local machine: $env:COMPUTERNAME"
Test-WSMan -ComputerName "localhost" -Authentication default

"Testing remote machine: $computername"
Test-WSMan -ComputerName $computername -Authentication default

}
```

The Test-WSMan cmdlet submits an identification request that determines whether the WinRM service is running on a local or remote computer. If the tested computer is running the service, the cmdlet displays the WSMAN identity schema, the protocol version, the product vendor, and the product version of the tested service.

The -Authentication default statement is added to the command to ensure that the product version information is displayed; without that, you'd just get zeros.

DISCUSSION

One interesting point is that $env:COMPUTERNAME is used to identify the local machine when returning information. You can use localhost in the Test-WSMan call, but it doesn't tell you which machine you're on!

The output from Test-WSMan for the remote machine looks like this:

```
Testing remote machine: dc02
wsmid           : http://schemas.dmtf.org/wbem/wsman/
  ➥               identity/1/wsmanidentity.xsd
ProtocolVersion : http://schemas.dmtf.org/wbem/wsman/1/wsman.xsd
ProductVendor   : Microsoft Corporation
ProductVersion  : OS: 6.1.7601 SP: 1.0 Stack: 2.0
```

Now that you know that WSMAN is working, how can you use it to get at the data?

TECHNIQUE 138   Retrieving WMI data using WSMAN

One of the primary uses for WMI is to retrieve data from remote systems. You can duplicate this action using WSMAN. The code becomes a little more complex, but the relationship to Get-WmiObject is readily discernible.

PROBLEM

You want to determine which network adapters in your machines have TCP/IP enabled and what their IP properties are. This could be performed using ipconfig.exe for the local machine, but you need to be able to access remote systems as well.

SOLUTION

The following listing shows how you can solve the problem using the Get-WSManInstance cmdlet. You'll be using the Win32_NetworkAdapter and Win32_NetworkAdapterConfiguration classes in listing 17.2. These classes will be used in a similar way to when you solve the problem directly with WMI.

Listing 17.2   Retrieve IP configuration with WSMAN

```
function get-ipinfo{
[CmdletBinding()]
param (
[parameter(ValueFromPipeline=$true,
   ValueFromPipelineByPropertyName=$true)]          ❶ Get
    [Alias("CN", "Computer")]                           parameters
    [string]$computername="$env:COMPUTERNAME"
)

Get-WSManInstance -ResourceURI wmicimv2/* -Enumerate -Dialect WQL `
 -Filter "SELECT * FROM Win32_NetworkAdapterConfiguration WHERE
   ➥ IPenabled='$true'" -ComputerName $computername  |     ❷ Get
foreach {                                                      adapters
$nic = Get-WSManInstance -ResourceURI wmicimv2/* `
-Enumerate -Dialect Association `
-Filter "{Object=Win32_NetworkAdapterConfiguration?
   ➥ Index=$($_.Index);ResultClassName=
   ➥ Win32_NetworkAdapter}" `                           ❸ Get
-ComputerName $computername                                 configuration

 $output= New-Object -TypeName PSObject -Property @{
  NICCardName = $nic.NetConnectionId
  DHCPEnabled = $($_.DHCPEnabled)                        ❹ Output
  IPAddress = $($_.IPAddress)                              results
  SubnetMask = $($_.IPSubnet)
  Gateway = $($_.DefaultIPGateway)
  DHCPServer = $($_.DHCPServer)
  DNSDomain =  $($_.DNSDomain)
  DNSDomainSuffixSearchOrder = $($_.DNSDomainSuffixSearchOrder)
  DNSServerSearchOrder = $($_.DNSServerSearchOrder)
 }
$output
}
}
```

The usual -computername parameter is used to provide access to remote machines. The parameter is provided with two aliases as a reminder of how to code parameter aliases ❶.

You start with a call to Get-WSManInstance that accesses the Win32_NetworkAdapterConfiguration class ❷. The resource URI is coded as wmicimv2/*, which means you're looking at WMI's root\cimv2 namespace. The -Enumerate parameter is used because you expect (or even just suspect) that there's more than one WSMAN instance involved.

The -Filter parameter performs the selection for you. It uses the same syntax you'd use in a WMI query. The command could be rewritten like this:

```
Get-WmiObject -ComputerName $computer `
-Query "SELECT * FROM Win32_NetworkAdapterConfiguration
    ➥ WHERE IPenabled='$true'"
```

You pipe the results into ForEach-Object. Each of the adapter configurations has the corresponding Win32_NetworkAdapater class retrieved ❸. The -Dialect parameter informs the cmdlet you're looking for associations, and the -Filter defines the current object using the Index property (its key) and the class you're looking for—in this case, Win32_NetworkAdapter.

An object is created using New-Object and the -Property parameter ❹. The properties are defined and populated, and the object is output at the end of the processing.

DISCUSSION

There's little difference between using WMI directly or through WSMAN when retrieving information.

The fact that you get an inert object returned isn't an issue because you're only looking to read the data. It does become an issue when you want to modify or remove an instance.

TECHNIQUE 139   Modifying WMI instances through WSMAN

Changing the configuration of your systems is something you can't get away from. Ideally you'd create a server, install the applications, and it would remain unchanged from that time until it was decommissioned. Unfortunately, it doesn't work that way, and you need to be able to make modifications. You've seen throughout the book how to use WMI directly to achieve this. Now we'll look at using WSMAN as the transport mechanism.

PROBLEM

A new disk has been added to the server. The junior administrator (what would we do without them to blame?) has allocated an incorrect drive letter to a removable disk. You need to change the drive letter to bring the system into compliance with your organization's standards.

SOLUTION

The function provided in the following listing will change the drive letter associated with a volume. A computer name, for accessing remote systems, and a new drive letter are the function's parameters.

Listing 17.3   Change a drive letter

```
function set-driveletter{
[CmdletBinding()]
param (
[parameter(ValueFromPipeline=$true,
   ValueFromPipelineByPropertyName=$true)]
   [Alias("CN", "Computer")]
   [string]$computername="$env:COMPUTERNAME",
   [string]$olddrive,
   [string]$newdrive = "Z:"
)
Get-WSManInstance -ResourceURI wmicimv2/* -Enumerate -Dialect WQL `
-Filter "SELECT * FROM Win32_Volume WHERE DriveType=2
   ➥ AND DriveLetter = '$olddrive'" -ComputerName $computername |
foreach {
 Set-WSManInstance -ResourceURI wmicimv2/Win32_Volume `
 -SelectorSet @{DeviceID=$($_.DeviceID)} `
 -ValueSet @{DriveLetter=$newdrive} -ComputerName $computername
 }
}
```

The function uses Get-WSManInstance to discover those volumes with a drive type of 2 (removable media—in this case, USB drives). A similar syntax to listing 17.2 is used, with the work being performed by the WQL statement defined in the -Filter parameter. This is the equivalent of

```
Get-WmiObject -Query "SELECT * FROM Win32_Volume WHERE DriveType=2"
```

The result from Get-WSManInstance is piped into ForEach-Object. A call to Set-WSManInstance is used to perform the change of drive letter. The -SelectorSet parameter is used to identify the exact volume. The DeviceID (the key to the Win32_Volume class) is obtained from the information on the pipeline.

> **TIP**   It would be possible to modify the function to accept a DeviceID as a parameter instead of discovering it.

Set-WSManInstance has a -ValueSet parameter, which defines the new values of the properties that are going to be changed. It accepts a hash table so you can change multiple properties at once. Here's an example:

```
-ValueSet @{DriveLetter=$newdrive; Label="MyNewUSBdrive"}
```

This would change the drive letter and the volume label in one pass.

DISCUSSION

The function does assume that there's only one volume that will meet the filter criterion specified in Get-WSManInstance. Identifying the correct resource is the primary issue when attempting to perform modifications through the WSMAN cmdlets. I've found it easier to develop the functions by identifying the correct instance using Get-WSManInstance and then piping the results to the change process. Many of the pure WMI functions in the rest of the book work in a similar manner.

Discovery and modification will form a large part of your interaction with WMI objects. But at some stage you'll be called upon to delete objects.

TECHNIQUE 140 **Deleting WMI instances through WSMAN**

When you're working directly with WMI, you can use the `Remove-WMIObject` cmdlet to delete WMI objects. Remember that not all WMI-related objects can be deleted; for instance, deleting the `Win32_OperatingSystem` object would not be a good idea.

Using the WSMAN cmdlets, you have to be a little less direct in your processing approach as the `Remove-WSManInstance` cmdlet will only work on WSMAN configuration items.

PROBLEM

Your junior administrator has been at it again and has left a large number of instances of notepad.exe running on a server. You need a way to delete those instances remotely.

SOLUTION

The following listing provides an answer to this problem. When dealing with WSMAN instances, you have to work with the WMI class key if you want to use the `-SelectorSet` parameter. This constrains your function to a structure of discovery and action that you've used in previous listings in this chapter.

Listing 17.4 Delete objects through WSMAN

```
function remove-notepad{
[CmdletBinding()]
param (
[parameter(ValueFromPipeline=$true,
   ValueFromPipelineByPropertyName=$true)]
   [Alias("CN", "Computer")]
   [string]$computername="$env:COMPUTERNAME"
)
Get-WSManInstance -ResourceURI wmicimv2/* -Enumerate -Dialect WQL `
-Filter "SELECT * FROM Win32_Process WHERE Name='Notepad.exe'" `
-ComputerName $computername  |
foreach {

Invoke-WSManAction -ResourceURI wmicimv2/Win32_Process `
-Action Terminate -SelectorSet @{Handle=$($_.Handle)} `
-ComputerName $computername

}
}
```

The function has a computer name as a parameter. You can then use `Get-WSManInstance` to discover the instances of the Notepad.exe process running on the remote machine. Alternative ways to retrieve this information are available, such as the following:

```
Get-Process notepad -ComputerName $computer

Get-WmiObject -Class Win32_Process `
-Filter "Name='notepad.exe'" -ComputerName $computer
```

`Get-WSManInstance` results are piped into `ForEach-Object`, where a call to `Invoke-WSManAction` is made. This uses the `Handle` property of the pipeline object to identify the individual instance of Notepad. The `-Action` parameter defines the WMI method to call, which in this case is `Terminate`, which stops and deletes the process.

DISCUSSION

The process followed here is analogous to the one you employed when using the WMI cmdlets; namely, get the object and pipe it to `Invoke-WmiMethod`. It's slightly more cumbersome to code, but in my opinion a lot safer, as the "get" process can be tested during development to ensure that the correct objects are being accessed.

All of the PowerShell remoting techniques are designed to connect the local computer to a remote computer. You may connect to multiple computers simultaneously, but the tasks are performed on the machine to which you connect. There are times when this causes problems and you need to run a command on a remote machine that accesses a third machine.

17.3   *Using CredSSP to access remote machines*

If you access a machine remotely through PowerShell you can run commands on that machine. If you attempt to run a command that needs a direct connection to a third machine it will fail; for example, running a job on the third machine, accessing a share on a remote machine, or running a cmdlet with the `-ComputerName` parameter to perform an action against the third machine. This is a deliberate security device built into the Windows operating system to prevent malicious software or people performing actions across the domain if a machine is compromised.

As an illustration, suppose you have two remote machines, dc02 and web01. Both are configured for PowerShell remoting, meaning that you can run commands against both machines, as illustrated in figure 17.4.

```
C:\scripts                                                              _ □ ×
PS> invoke-command -ComputerName dc02, web01 -ScriptBlock {get-service p*}

Status    Name              DisplayName                      PSComputerName
------    ----              -----------                      --------------
Stopped   PerfHost          Performance Counter DLL Host     dc02
Stopped   pla               Performance Logs & Alerts        dc02
Running   PlugPlay          Plug and Play                    dc02
Stopped   PolicyAgent       IPsec Policy Agent               dc02
Running   Power             Power                            dc02
Running   ProfSvc           User Profile Service             dc02
Stopped   ProtectedStorage  Protected Storage                dc02
Stopped   PeerDistSvc       BranchCache                      web01
Stopped   pla               Performance Logs & Alerts        web01
Running   PlugPlay          Plug and Play                    web01
Running   PolicyAgent       IPsec Policy Agent               web01
Running   ProfSvc           User Profile Service             web01
Stopped   ProtectedStorage  Protected Storage                web01

PS> _
```

Figure 17.4   Executing remote commands against two machines

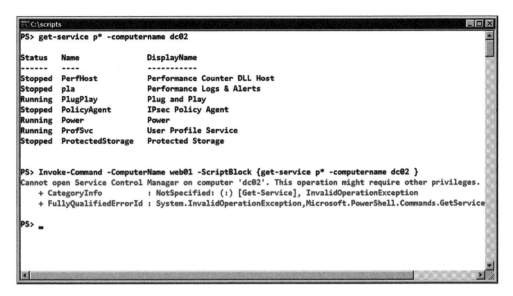

Figure 17.5   Error when attempting double-hop access

If you attempt to run a command on one machine that accesses another you'll get an error, as shown in figure 17.5. Attempting to access a third machine from a remote machine is known as a *double hop*.

> **NOTE**   If the remote machine is a domain controller and you have domain administrator rights (or higher), some double-hop commands will work, but not all.

The error occurs because your credentials aren't available on the remote machine. You're attempting to access resources for which you can't be authorized.

There's a mechanism to overcome this restriction, known as the Credential Security Support Provider (CredSSP). This enables you to delegate your credentials to a remote machine so that it can access other remote machines on your behalf. The default CredSSP settings are illustrated in figure 17.6.

You can enable credential delegation by running this command on the local machine:

```
Enable-WSManCredSSP -Role client -DelegateComputer web01 -Force
```

Figure 17.6   Default CredSSP response

The following has to be run on the remote machine (in this example, web01):

```
Enable-WSManCredSSP -Role server -Force
```

Both commands must be run from a PowerShell prompt with elevated privileges. The first command enables the delegation of credentials, and the second enables the remote system to receive delegated credentials. You need to use -Authentication CredSSP and the -Credential parameter when calling Invoke-Command, as shown in figure 17.7.

The user's credentials must be presented to Invoke-Command. The easiest way is to save them in a credential object for multiple re-use. Remember to include the domain or you'll get local credentials that won't work in this scenario. Invoke-Command can be called as shown. The *WSManInstance cmdlets can also use the CredSSP mechanism to perform double-hop access.

When the need for delegated credentials has ceased, remember to use the following commands:

```
Disable-WSManCredSSP -Role client
Disable-WSManCredSSP -Role server
```

These are run on the local and remote machine respectively to stop delegation.

> **WARNING**   The use of CredSSP is *not* recommended as an everyday practice. It should be reserved for a situation in which there is no other way to access the remote machines. CredSSP should *not* be permanently switched on.

The need to access remote machines to enable CredSSP makes using it more difficult. CredSSP can't be enabled using PowerShell remoting techniques because the remote

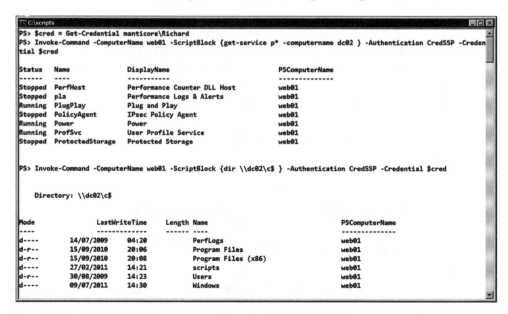

Figure 17.7   Using CredSSP to access a system via a double hop

session doesn't run with elevated privileges. It's possible to use a scheduled job to perform this action, but that could be viewed as a security risk.

This completes our examination of using WSMAN directly. Before we close the chapter, let's review the various remoting mechanisms.

17.4   *How to choose between WMI, remoting, and WSMAN*

This chapter raises the question of how you should access remote machines. You've seen three mechanisms:

- Using DCOM via the WMI cmdlets
- Using PowerShell remoting via `Invoke-Command` or PowerShell remote sessions
- Using WSMAN cmdlets

The obvious question is, "Which approach should I use?" The answer, as always, is, "It depends." A comparison of the techniques is presented in table 17.3.

Table 17.3   Comparison of remote access techniques

Mechanism	Pros	Cons
DCOM and WMI cmdlets	Simple Understood and obvious Returns live objects	Needs DCOM available Not firewall-friendly
PowerShell remoting	Uses HTTP so firewall-friendly Can enter the session	Needs to be enabled Returns "inert objects" Needs PowerShell v2
WSMAN	Uses HTTP so firewall-friendly	Syntax is complicated Not well understood Returns XML

The bulk of the functions presented in this book have used the first option (DCOM and the WMI cmdlets). This is a simple to use, powerful, and well-understood mechanism, but it isn't firewall-friendly. I still recommend it for use within the domain.

PowerShell remoting is one of the "big things" in PowerShell v2, and as such it's getting a lot of attention. GPOs can be used to configure remoting in a domain environment. I would use remoting when I need to access the same machine multiple times in a single session.

WSMAN is the weakest of the three mechanisms at the moment, and I would only use it when conditions prevent other mechanisms from working. I strongly recommend learning how it works, as it offers the potential of access to non-Windows systems, which gives you a single administration tool that can be used across a heterogeneous environment.

Microsoft is making PowerShell functionality available through web services, such as Exchange 2010 and Active Directory in Windows Server 2008 R2. At the moment, this seems to be the preferred direction, which means learning how to use WSMAN could be advantageous. Knowledge of WSMAN will definitely be useful when it comes to using the CIM cmdlets and CIM sessions introduced in PowerShell v3, as you'll see in chapters 18 and 19.

17.5 Summary

The major efficiency to be gained from using PowerShell is the ability to administer remote servers. You can use the WMI cmdlets to perform this action directly as long as the DCOM-related services are available and not blocked by a firewall. If DCOM isn't available, you'll need to use one of the following:

- PowerShell remoting
- WSMAN

The WSMAN cmdlets can be used to retrieve information, modify WMI objects, and remove WMI objects. In a remoting scenario, you can't directly access a third machine from your remote server. This restriction can be overcome using CredSSP, but there are security implications that must be observed.

The recommended approach to accessing remote machines is to use the WMI cmdlets for single access. If multiple commands will be run against a remote machine, use PowerShell remoting.

WSMAN should be learned, because it provides the potential for out-of-band hardware management, for accessing non-Windows systems, and for use with the CIM cmdlets in PowerShell v3.

Your own WMI cmdlets

18

In the previous 17 chapters of the book, you've seen how to use the WMI cmdlets provided in PowerShell v2. PowerShell v3, introduced with Windows 8, enables you to take this a step further and create your own WMI cmdlets! The ability to create cmdlets directly from the WMI classes will radically alter the way we work with WMI in the future. This functionality is referred to as *cmdlets-over-objects*—you create a cmdlet directly from the WMI object. The use of WMI and CIM is massively expanded in the Windows 8 product line. In fact, much of the new PowerShell functionality introduced in the Windows 8 family is cmdlets produced directly from WMI classes.

In one respect, this makes our job easier, because we have a lot of new functionality out of the box, but in another respect it makes things more difficult, as we have new technologies and concepts to learn. This chapter and the next will show how it all works, when you should use the new options, and when you should stick with the traditional ways.

442

Figure 18.1   Using the `Win32_OperatingSystem` class to display data, including boot time

WARNING   This material is based on beta versions of PowerShell v3, and there may be changes between the time of writing and the release of Windows 8 and PowerShell v3.

We looked at retrieving information about your operating system in technique 14 (chapter 5). This was based on the `Win32_OperatingSystem` class, as shown in figure 18.1.

Figure 18.1 demonstrates using WMI to fetch information about the operating system using this code:

```
Get-WmiObject -Class Win32_OperatingSystem |
Format-Table CSName, Caption, ServicePackMajorVersion,
OSArchitecture,LastBootUpTime -AutoSize
```

You call the `Win32_OperatingSystem` class and use `Format-Table` to control the display. This is standard PowerShell that you've seen many times now. But wouldn't it be nice (no I'm not singing that) to use a cmdlet instead, with the option of searching using parameters, as shown in figure 18.2.

The cmdlet `Get-Win32OperatingSystem` displays information about the operating system that's similar to what the `Win32_OperatingSystem` class offers. At this point you may well be jumping up and down shouting, "He's using an advanced function!"

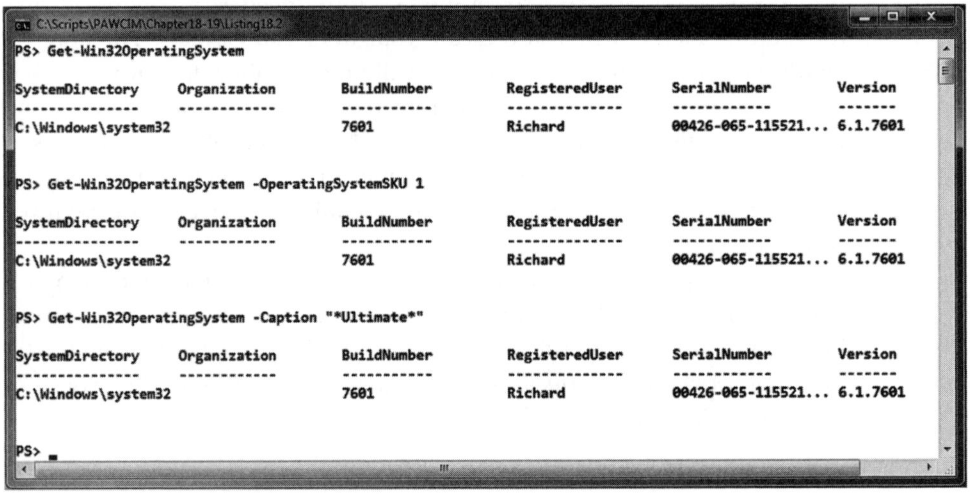

Figure 18.2   Using the `Get-Win32OperatingSystem` cmdlet used to display information

Nope. I'm not. I'm using a module created directly from the WMI class. How this works is the subject of this chapter.

We'll start by examining how to create a cmdlet from a WMI class. The `Win32_OperatingSystem` class will be used in these examples, and we'll look at the examples first. The tools that can be used to make this even easier will be discussed later in the chapter.

WMI provides many properties as integer codes. In earlier chapters we used hash tables or .NET enumerations to decode these values. The cmdlet will be extended to decode the `OperatingSystemSKU` property as an example.

> **NOTE**   These examples are based on the CIM cmdlets and the new API for using WMI that's introduced in PowerShell v3. This is detailed in chapter 19.

A single cmdlet is good, but a module of cmdlets is even better. The second section of the chapter introduces a cmdlet based on the `Win32_ComputerSystem` class and also explains how you can load both cmdlets as a single module.

WMI classes have default display formatting, as you've seen. The penultimate part of the chapter covers adding a format file and a type file (to add extra properties to the objects you produce). The chapter closes with an overview of a tool that makes creating cmdlets from WMI classes much easier.

We'll start looking at all of this new functionality by showing you how to create a cmdlet from WMI.

18.1   Creating a WMI cmdlet

In this section, you'll use the `Win32_OperatingSystem` WMI class to create a cmdlet. The initial version will provide an alternative means of retrieving the operating system data. You'll then enhance it by creating a number of search parameters based on property values. One of the property values will involve the decoding of an integer-coded property as an example.

TECHNIQUE 141   **Creating a simple cmdlet**

In the first two parts of the book, you used a PowerShell cmdlet to access a WMI class:

```
Get-WmiObject -Class Win32_OperatingSystem

SystemDirectory : C:\Windows\system32
Organization    :
BuildNumber     : 7601
RegisteredUser  : Richard
SerialNumber    : 00426-065-1155216-86881
Version         : 6.1.7601
```

The output is a default set of properties, as shown. You can provide wrapper functions to control the output, provide input parameters, and process flow control. These can also be combined into modules as demonstrated in chapters 5–16. The next evolution in this process, introduced with PowerShell v3, is to create the cmdlet directly from the WMI class.

PROBLEM

The functions you're using to retrieve operating system information need to be updated to work with the Windows 8 generation of operating systems. You need to convert the functions to PowerShell cmdlets based on the WMI class.

SOLUTION

The core of the solution is contained in an XML file shown in the following listing. That's right—XML. The bad news about this functionality is that you have to work with XML. The good news is that it's relatively easy.

Listing 18.1   Simple WMI-based cmdlet

```xml
<?xml version="1.0" encoding="utf-8"?>
<PowerShellMetadata xmlns:xsi=
➥ "http://www.w3.org/2001/XMLSchema-instance"
xmlns:xsd="http://www.w3.org/2001/XMLSchema"
xmlns="http://schemas.microsoft.com/cmdlets-over-objects/2009/11">
  <Class ClassName="root\cimv2\Win32_OperatingSystem">          WMI ❶
    <Version>1.0.0</Version>                                     class
    <DefaultNoun>Win32OperatingSystem</DefaultNoun>
    <InstanceCmdlets>                                           Cmdlet
      <GetCmdletParameters                                    ❷ noun
➥ DefaultCmdletParameterSet="ByName">
        <QueryableProperties>                                  Cmdlet
          <Property PropertyName="Name">                    ❸ parameters
            <Type PSType="System.String" />
            <RegularQuery AllowGlobbing="true">
              <CmdletParameterMetadata PSName="Name"
➥ Position="0"
➥ ValueFromPipelineByPropertyName="true"
➥ CmdletParameterSets="ByName" />
            </RegularQuery>
          </Property>
        </QueryableProperties>
      </GetCmdletParameters>
    </InstanceCmdlets>
  </Class>
</PowerShellMetadata>
```

The first two lines are standard and will be used in all examples in this chapter and chapter 19 relating to this technology. They define the XML schema you'll use so that the XML can be checked when you build the cmdlet.

Next, the WMI class is defined ❶. The WMI path, including the namespace and class, has to be provided. The default noun for the cmdlet is required ❷. The noun will become more important in chapter 19 when you use the class methods. The remainder of the XML defines the way parameters are presented to the cmdlet ❸. This information should be familiar from the parameter options in PowerShell advanced functions, such as `Position="0"`.

The ultimate definition of your module will be a folder on the module path. The module path can be found using this line:

```
$env:psmodulepath -split ";"
```

PowerShell v3 automatically loads all modules it finds on the module path when a PowerShell console or the ISE is started. This isn't something I want to occur while I'm developing modules, so I create the module in a development folder and move it to the module path when I'm happy it's working properly.

The XML file shown in listing 18.1 is saved as Win32OperatingSystem.cdxml. The .cdxml extension is new to PowerShell v3 and means "Cmdlet Definition XML." Once you have the file saved, you can import it into your PowerShell session by changing the location to the folder in which you created the file, and then typing

```
Import-Module ./Win32OperatingSystem.cdxml
```

Alternatively, the full path to the file can be supplied.

The module loads and you can use the standard commands, such as `Get-Module` and `Get-Command`, on it, as shown in figure 18.3.

Notice that the module type is shown as `CIM`, and `Get-Command` shows the `Capability` as `CIM`. These are indicators that you're dealing with cmdlets-over-objects—cmdlets created from WMI classes.

> **NOTE** The download code for chapters 18 and 19 is combined, with a subfolder for each stage of development. The final version is also available in a subfolder called SystemInfo that can be copied directly into your module path.

The important thing to note is that you have a single .cdxml file that you can directly import as a module. Think of it as a .psm1 file for cmdlets-over-objects.

Now that you've built it and loaded it, how do you use it?

DISCUSSION

When the `Get-Win32OperatingSystem | Format-List *` command is used, the result is almost identical to running this command:

```
Get-WmiObject -Class Win32_OperatingSystem | Format-List *
```

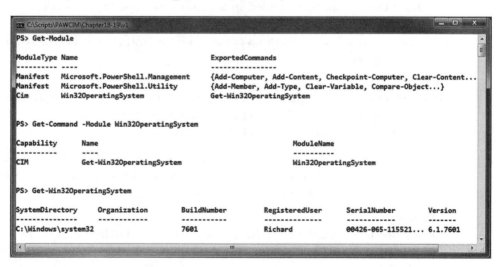

Figure 18.3 Performing standard PowerShell actions on your module

These are the slight differences:

- No system parameters are displayed—those are the properties with the double underscore (__) prefix.
- Dates are converted from the WMI format to a normal format. This is equivalent to using the ConvertToDateTime() method.

The date formatting means that you'll see is this:

```
InstallDate       : 16/03/2011 19:10:44
LastBootUpTime    : 06/09/2011 18:46:20
LocalDateTime     : 06/09/2011 19:30:52
```

The following is what you'd see with a direct call to the WMI object using Get-WmiObject:

```
InstallDate       : 20110316191044.000000+000
LastBootUpTime    : 20110906184620.919125+060
LocalDateTime     : 20110906193539.192000+060
```

These changes alone, especially the conversions of dates, are a major productivity gain. The other fundamental change is that the object type is now

```
Microsoft.Management.Infrastructure.CimInstance#
  ➥ ROOT\cimv2\Win32_OperatingSystem
```

rather than the type you're used to seeing, which is

```
System.Management.ManagementObject#root\cimv2\Win32_OperatingSystem
```

The differences between these two types are discussed further in chapter 19, where the CIM cmdlets are covered.

We can now look at extending the functionality of your basic cmdlet.

TECHNIQUE 142   Extending the cmdlet

The basic cmdlet can be extended in a number of ways. In this section, you'll add more parameters to make searching easier. You could also extend the module by creating cmdlets to utilize the methods available on the WMI classes. This more advanced feature will be added in chapter 19.

PROBLEM

Your basic cmdlet is the equivalent of using the WMI class in Get-WmiObject. You need to add extra parameters to filter on the operating system type (the Caption property) and the SKU (the OperatingSystemSKU property).

> **NOTE** Any property could be used in this manner. You could, for instance, create a cmdlet that looks for computer systems with more than a certain amount of physical memory (see technique 143).

SOLUTION

The solution involves enhancing the XML file you created in listing 18.1. The resultant file is shown in the following listing. The description will concentrate on the additions to the XML file.

Listing 18.2   Extended WMI-based cmdlet

```xml
<?xml version="1.0" encoding="utf-8"?>
<PowerShellMetadata xmlns:xsi=
    "http://www.w3.org/2001/XMLSchema-instance"
xmlns:xsd="http://www.w3.org/2001/XMLSchema"
xmlns="http://schemas.microsoft.com/cmdlets-over-objects/2009/11">
  <Class ClassName="root\cimv2\Win32_OperatingSystem">
    <Version>1.0.0.0</Version>
    <DefaultNoun>Win32OperatingSystem</DefaultNoun>
    <InstanceCmdlets>
      <GetCmdletParameters DefaultCmdletParameterSet="ByName">
        <QueryableProperties>
          <Property PropertyName="Name">
            <Type PSType="System.String" />
            <RegularQuery AllowGlobbing="true">
              <CmdletParameterMetadata PSName="Name"
                  Position="0"
                  ValueFromPipelineByPropertyName="true"
                  CmdletParameterSets="ByName" />
            </RegularQuery>
          </Property>

          <Property PropertyName="Caption">
            <Type PSType="System.String" />
            <RegularQuery AllowGlobbing="true">
              <CmdletParameterMetadata PSName="Caption"
                  Position="1"
                  CmdletParameterSets="ByCaption" />
            </RegularQuery>
          </Property>

          <Property PropertyName="OperatingSystemSKU">
            <Type PSType="OperatingSystem.OperatingSystemSKU" />
            <RegularQuery>
              <CmdletParameterMetadata IsMandatory="false"
                  CmdletParameterSets="BySKU" />
            </RegularQuery>
          </Property>
        </QueryableProperties>
      </GetCmdletParameters>
    </InstanceCmdlets>
  </Class>

  <Enums>
    <Enum EnumName="OperatingSystem.OperatingSystemSKU"
        UnderlyingType="uint32">
      <Value Name="UltimateEdition" Value="1" />
      <Value Name="StandardServerEdition" Value="7" />
      <Value Name="DatacenterServerEdition" Value="8" />
      <Value Name="EnterpriseServerEdition" Value="10" />
    </Enum>
  </Enums>
</PowerShellMetadata>
```

❶ Add caption parameter

❷ Add Operating-SystemSKU parameter

❸ Add enumeration

The XML file starts off identical to listing 18.1. The `caption` parameter is added by defining an additional property ❶, because you're creating these parameters directly from the properties of the class. The parameter is set as second by using `Position=1`.

Another parameter, OperatingSystemSKU, is added in a similar manner ❷. The point to note here is that the property type is set as OperatingSystem.OperatingSystemSKU. Don't go searching for this in .NET as you won't find it—you have to create it yourself.

You've seen enumerations used many times in the code you've created in previous chapters. They're a simple data structure to store a preset suite of values. They normally hold an integer value that's associated with a string value. The enumeration to hold the operating SKU values is defined after the properties ❸. The numeric values don't have to be consecutive. It's possible to define multiple enumerations at this stage.

> **WARNING**   Ensure that the string part of your enumeration doesn't contain any spaces. If it does, an error will be thrown when you try to create the cmdlet. For example, "UltimateEdition" will work, but "Ultimate Edition" will fail.

The file is saved as Win32OperatingSystem.cdxml, as you did in technique 141. I use individual folders to separate the versions.

DISCUSSION

These additional parameters give you more options and ways to use the cmdlet. For example, these are all valid ways to call the cmdlet:

```
Get-Win32OperatingSystem
Get-Win32OperatingSystem -OperatingSystemSKU 1
Get-Win32OperatingSystem -OperatingSystemSKU "UltimateEdition"
Get-Win32OperatingSystem -Caption "Microsoft Windows 7 Ultimate "
```

> **NOTE**   There's a space at the end of the value passed to the Caption property in that last cmdlet call! It has to be exactly right!

The OperatingSystemSKU parameter will accept the numeric or string value of the enumeration for maximum flexibility. The last example is equivalent to this:

```
Get-WmiObject -Class Win32_OperatingSystem `
-Filter "Caption = 'Microsoft Windows 7 Ultimate '"
```

The additional parameters enable you to use the cmdlet to perform queries. These are WMI queries under the hood, but you don't have to write the queries yourself. The hard work is done when you create the cmdlet. This is part of the increased ease of use that is brought to WMI by creating cmdlets from the WMI classes.

In the Caption parameter, the AllowGlobbing option is set to true so you can do this:

```
Get-Win32OperatingSystem -Caption "*Ultimate*"
```

Globbing is shorthand for saying you allow the use of wildcards.

You now have a very useful cmdlet, so it's time to find it a friend and work out how to build multiple cmdlets into a module.

18.2 *Creating multiple cmdlets*

You need to be able to extend the functionality of section 18.1 with the eventual goal of having a suite of cmdlets that can supply all the information you're likely to need about your systems. Technique 143 shows how to create a cmdlet that retrieves computer system information using the `Win32_ComputerSystem` class. This will result in the creation of a second .cdxml file and therefore another module. An overarching super-module is required if your intention is to combine the functionality from different WMI classes. The creation of such a super-module is demonstrated in technique 144.

TECHNIQUE 143   Creating cmdlets from multiple WMI classes

You've created modules of advanced functions in chapters 5–16, but they've all been created on the basis of one function equals one file. This level of granularity makes the functions easy to maintain and troubleshoot.

PROBLEM

The overarching task is to create PowerShell functionality to use for system configuration recording and reporting. The operating system information you can find using the cmdlet from the previous technique is a start. Your next job is to add a cmdlet that will report on computer system information.

SOLUTION

You have to create another XML file because you can't have multiple class statements in a single XML file. This leads to the production of the following listing.

Listing 18.3   Add a computer system cmdlet

```xml
<?xml version="1.0" encoding="utf-8"?>
<PowerShellMetadata xmlns:xsi=
  "http://www.w3.org/2001/XMLSchema-instance"
xmlns:xsd="http://www.w3.org/2001/XMLSchema"
xmlns="http://schemas.microsoft.com/cmdlets-over-objects/2009/11">
  <Class ClassName="root\cimv2\Win32_ComputerSystem">
    <Version>1.0.0.0</Version>
    <DefaultNoun>Win32ComputerSystem</DefaultNoun>
    <InstanceCmdlets>
      <GetCmdletParameters DefaultCmdletParameterSet="ByName">
        <QueryableProperties>
          <Property PropertyName="Name">
            <Type PSType="System.String" />
            <RegularQuery AllowGlobbing="true">
              <CmdletParameterMetadata PSName="Name"
                Position="0"
                ValueFromPipelineByPropertyName="true"
                CmdletParameterSets="ByName" />
            </RegularQuery>
          </Property>
          <Property PropertyName="TotalPhysicalMemory">
            <Type PSType="System.UInt64" />
            <MaxValueQuery>
              <CmdletParameterMetadata PSName="MaxSize"
                CmdletParameterSets="BySize" />
            </MaxValueQuery>
            <MinValueQuery>
              <CmdletParameterMetadata PSName="MinSize"
```

1 WMI class

2 Noun

3 Filter parameter

```
       ➥ CmdletParameterSets="BySize" />
              </MinValueQuery>
          </Property>
        </QueryableProperties>
      </GetCmdletParameters>
    </InstanceCmdlets>
  </Class>
</PowerShellMetadata>
```

One of the good things about using an XML format is that the schema provides the framework in which you work. In this case, you can take listing 18.1 as a template and make the required changes. The first change is to the WMI class. You need to use the `Win32_ComputerSystem` class ❶. The default noun is changed to `Win32ComputerSystem` ❷.

In this case, you want to be able to test for systems that have a defined range of physical memory ❸. The `Win32_ComputerSystem` class has a `TotalPhysicalMemory` property. It's a 64-bit integer (uint64) that records the physical memory in bytes. You can add the query metadata that allows you to search for minimum or maximum amounts of memory. Save listing 18.3 as Win32ComputerSystem.cdxml.

Adding other parameters is a simple case of adding the XML using the existing code as a template, and then rebuilding the module. The small amount of XML required to add a lot of powerful functionality makes this process very cost effective.

DISCUSSION

The really great thing about creating modules like this is that you can test each piece of functionality separately. Navigate to the folder where you saved the Win32ComputerSystem.cdxml file and run this:

```
Import-Module .\Win32ComputerSystem.cdxml
```

The following commands will give it a good workout, though I recommend that you modify the memory values to bracket what's installed in your systems:

```
Get-Win32ComputerSystem
Get-Win32ComputerSystem -MinSize 1gb
Get-Win32ComputerSystem -MaxSize 2gb
Get-Win32ComputerSystem -MaxSize 3gb
Get-Win32ComputerSystem -MaxSize 1gb
```

Examine the output of these carefully. On my test machine, the last example doesn't return anything because the filters are based on greater-than or equals (`MaxSize`) or less-than (`MinSize`) rather than a direct equality.

Next, we need to look at how you can load multiple cmdlets.

TECHNIQUE 144   **Building a super- module**

With all new technologies, there are challenges around how to implement it and how to use it to make our lives as administrators easier. The ability to create cmdlets from objects (WMI classes) is going to be very useful, but importing the modules and sub-modules individually could be painful.

Submodules? So far you have two modules: Win32OperatingSystem.cdxml and Win32ComputerSystem.cdxml. It's time to create a super-module that calls the others as nested modules.

PROBLEM

Your organization is determined to derive the maximum benefit from PowerShell v3, so you'll be investing heavily in creating modules from your WMI classes. You need a process to create the modules and import the super-module that calls them all.

SOLUTION

One of the great things about PowerShell is that there are usually multiple ways to perform a task. This is true of turning XML definition files into cmdlets. The way I've chosen to do it is presented in the following listing. It enables you to add extra submodules with minimum effort.

Listing 18.4   Build multiple cmdlets

```
Import-Module ./Win32OperatingSystem.cdxml
Import-Module ./Win32ComputerSystem.cdxml
```

It really is that easy. Put all of your .cdxml files into a folder on your module path. Call the folder SystemInfo. Add a SystemInfo.psm1 file with the contents of listing 18.4 to that folder. I know it's only two lines of code, but I wanted to emphasize how easy this is.

DISCUSSION

It would be possible to use a module manifest file (.psd1) instead of the .psm1 file in listing 18.4, but they're more complicated to code and they create complications when you get to the format and type files in the next section.

This system is easily extendable by creating other `.cdxml` files using the `Win32_Processor` class or the disk classes, for example, and adding the appropriate lines to listing 18.4. Once you have the basics, as presented in sections 18.1 and 18.2, in place, the rest is easy because you already have XML files to use as templates. This is why I think creating your own cmdlets will become *the* way to work with WMI.

Retrieving the data is the first step. Presenting that data is the second step, for which you need to create format and type files. This is next on the agenda.

18.3   *Creating format and type files*

Many PowerShell cmdlets produce objects with more properties than can be sensibly displayed on screen. `Get-ChildItem $pshome` shows a number of files with formats or types in their name. These are used to control the default display of cmdlet output.

Figure 18.4 shows the default output produced by the `Get-Win32OperatingSystem` cmdlet you've created. This isn't necessarily the set of information you want by default. Suppose you actually want your default display to be the equivalent of

```
Get-Win32OperatingSystem |
Format-Table ComputerName, Caption, ServicePackMajorVersion,
OSArchitecture, LastBootUpTime
```

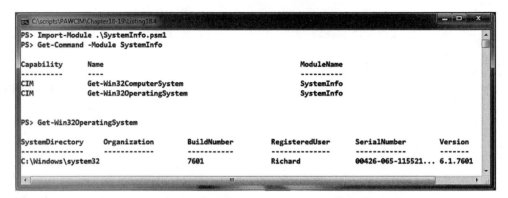

Figure 18.4   Default formatting for the `Get-Win32OperatingSystem` cmdlet

Getting this information displayed doesn't involve changing the properties on the object that's produced—you're only changing the data that's displayed by default.

> **WARNING**   Don't change the format files supplied by PowerShell. This will cause problems. Create new format files and load them using a module or `Update-FormatData`.

The change in default format for the output can be achieved by creating a format file and loading it when the module loads. Format files are XML-based and can be easily created using existing files as a template. You can also modify the output by adding members to the object using a type file. This has the same effect as the actions in previous functions using `Add-Member`, but the work takes place as the object is generated.

TECHNIQUE 145   **Adding a format file**

A common question for newcomers to PowerShell and WMI is, "Why do I only see a few properties when I get a WMI class?" The answer is that a default format file is controlling the output. If you want to change the default, you need to work with format files.

PROBLEM

The default output produced by your `Get-Win32OperatingSystem` cmdlet doesn't meet your needs. You could use `Select-Object` or a format cmdlet to control the output, but it's more efficient to change the default display format.

SOLUTION

The solution to the problem involves producing a format file, as shown in listing 18.5. It's saved as Win32OperatingSystem.format.ps1xml in the folder where you create the XML definition files for your cmdlets. You'll need to modify the SystemInfo.psm1 file to load the new format file.

Listing 18.5   Create a format file

```
<?xml version="1.0" encoding="utf-8" ?>
<Configuration>
<ViewDefinitions>
```

```
<View>
 <Name>Formatting For Win32_OperatingSystem
   ➥ (Table View)</Name>                                        ◁─┐  Table
   <ViewSelectedBy>                                              ❶  view
     <TypeName>Microsoft.Management.Infrastructure.
     ➥ CimInstance#root/cimv2/Win32_OperatingSystem</TypeName>
 </ViewSelectedBy><TableControl><TableHeaders>
   <TableColumnHeader><Label>OS</Label><Width>30</Width>        ◁─┐  Column
   </TableColumnHeader>                                          ❷  header
   <TableColumnHeader>
     <Label>SP</Label><Width>2</Width><Alignment>right</Alignment>
   </TableColumnHeader>
   <TableColumnHeader><Label>Arch</Label><Width>6</Width>
   </TableColumnHeader>
   <TableColumnHeader><Width>19</Width></TableColumnHeader>
 </TableHeaders>
 <TableRowEntries><TableRowEntry>                             New ❸
  <TableColumnItems>                                      property
   <TableColumnItem><PropertyName>SKU</PropertyName>           ◁─┘
   </TableColumnItem>
   <TableColumnItem>                                          ◁─┐
     <PropertyName>ServicePackMajorVersion</PropertyName>       │
   </TableColumnItem>                                           │
   <TableColumnItem><PropertyName>OSArchitecture</PropertyName> │
   </TableColumnItem>                                           │
   <TableColumnItem><PropertyName>LastBootUpTime</PropertyName> │
   </TableColumnItem>                                           │
   </TableColumnItems>                                          │
   </TableRowEntry></TableRowEntries></TableControl>    Column  │
</View>                                                  contents ❹
<View>
 <Name>Formatting For Win32_OperatingSystem
   ➥ (List View)</Name>                                        ◁─┐  List
   <ViewSelectedBy>                                             ❺  view
     <TypeName>Microsoft.Management.Infrastructure.
     ➥ CimInstance#root/cimv2/Win32_OperatingSystem</TypeName>
 </ViewSelectedBy>
 <ListControl><ListEntries><ListEntry><ListItems>
 <ListItem><PropertyName>Caption</PropertyName></ListItem>
 <ListItem>
 <PropertyName>ServicePackMajorVersion</PropertyName>
 </ListItem>
 <ListItem><PropertyName>OSArchitecture</PropertyName></ListItem>
 <ListItem><PropertyName>LastBootUpTime</PropertyName></ListItem>
 </ListItems></ListEntry></ListEntries></ListControl>
</View>
</ViewDefinitions>
</Configuration>
```

The format file may seem complicated, but it breaks down into a set of easy to understand components. It may be beneficial to refer to figure 18.5, where the output resulting from this format file is shown.

Format files can be used to define both table and list displays. In this case, you start with the table display ❶. This means that in the absence of any other formatting commands you'll get a table display. The object type that this format will be applied to is defined.

The table itself is defined as a number of column headers ❷, where items such as the label (such as SP for the ServicePackMajorVersion property), width, and alignment can be defined. In the absence of a label, the property name will be used. The contents of the table columns are defined as either new types added to the object ❸, or existing properties ❹. The addition of the SKU property is covered in the next section.

After defining a shiny new format for table type displays you can't ignore lists, so you define the properties that will appear in the default list view ❺. This format can also be overridden by explicit selection of properties via Select-Object or a format cmdlet.

DISCUSSION

You have to be careful when loading format files as part of a module. Using a module manifest (.psd1) file appends the new format data to any formatting data that exists for the type. This doesn't matter if the type is being created in the module, but it does become an issue when you're modifying an existing type because your formatting won't be used by default. The SystemInfo.psm1 file that was created in listing 18.4 is modified to become the following:

```
Import-Module ./Win32OperatingSystem.cdxml
Import-Module ./Win32ComputerSystem.cdxml
Update-FormatData -PrependPath ./Win32OperatingSystem.format.ps1xml
```

This forces PowerShell to use the new formatting information first. The drawback is that the format information isn't removed if you unload the module.

Choosing to change the default formatting in this manner has a number of consequences:

- Get-Win32OperatingSystem will use the new format.
- Get-CimInstance will use the new format (see chapter 19) if the module is loaded.
- Get-WmiObject will ignore the new format because it's a different .NET type.

You need to complete your definition of the new format by defining the SKU type.

TECHNIQUE 146   Adding a type file

PowerShell has been designed to be extremely extensible. This extensibility ranges from adding extra cmdlets to adding properties to the objects you're working with. The most efficient way to add properties that are always available to an object is to create a type file. If this module will be used on multiple machines the format and type files need to be available on those machines.

> **WARNING** Don't change the type files supplied by PowerShell. This will cause problems. Create new type files and load them using a module or Update-TypeData.

Type files are also XML-based, but as with format files, if a template is followed the creation becomes simpler.

PROBLEM

The default formatting for the `Get-Win32OperatingSystem` cmdlet requires the operating system name to be displayed. This information is contained within the `Caption` property, but it's very verbose. A shorter name will enable you to display more information.

SOLUTION

The solution is shown in the following listing, where you create a type file for the `SKU` property. This is a new property that you're adding to the object.

Listing 18.6 Create a type file

```
<Types>
 <Type>
   <Name>Microsoft.Management.Infrastructure.CimInstance#
    ➥ root/cimv2/Win32_OperatingSystem</Name>
   <Members>
    <ScriptProperty>
       <Name>SKU</Name>
        <GetScriptBlock>
         [Microsoft.PowerShell.Cmdletization.GeneratedTypes.
          ➥ OperatingSystem.OperatingSystemSKU] [System.uint32]
          ➥ $this.OperatingSystemSKU
        </GetScriptBlock>
    </ScriptProperty>
   </Members>
 </Type>
</Types>
```

The XML starts by defining the existing object type to which this file applies. You then have a script block that defines the property name and how the value is defined. The value is derived from the `OperatingSystemSKU` property using the enumeration you created in listing 18.2.

The type file is saved as Win32OperatingSystem.types.ps1xml in the folder with the format file and XML cmdlet definitions. The SystemInfo.psm1 file (listing 18.4) is modified as follows:

```
Import-Module ./Win32OperatingSystem.cdxml
Import-Module ./Win32ComputerSystem.cdxml
Update-FormatData -PrependPath ./Win32OperatingSystem.format.ps1xml
Update-TypeData ./Win32OperatingSystem.types.ps1xml
```

DISCUSSION

The format and type files you've created are automatically loaded when your module is imported into PowerShell. They function in the background and don't require any intervention by the user. When you use the `Get-Win32OperatingSystem` cmdlet you now receive the data in the default format you've defined, as shown in figure 18.5.

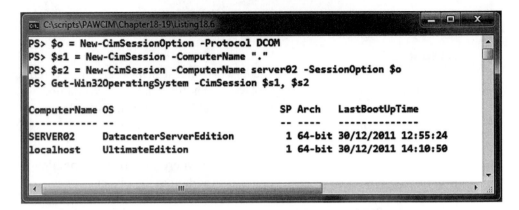

Figure 18.5   The cmdlet accessing multiple machines with the desired default output

The New-CimSession cmdlet provides access to remote machines (similar to remoting and the WSMAN cmdlets) and is explained in chapter 19. Notice the date format. The other big thing is that the cmdlets you're creating will work over DCOM or WSMAN. PowerShell v3 brings some big bonuses for ease of use.

You've now seen how to create the following types of XML files:

- *Cmdlet definition files*—.cdxml
- *Format files*—.format.ps1xml
- *Type files*—types.ps1xml

You don't have a tool to create the format and type files easily, but there's help for creating the cmdlet definition files.

18.4   *Using the CIM IDE*

In sections 18.1 and 18.2 you've created a number of versions of the cmdlet definition file (Win32OperatingSystem.cdxml). It's possible to create these files by hand using an XML editor or even Notepad—I used Notepad to create the first versions of these files. The advantages of using a simple editor are that it's cheap and always available, but the drawback is that it makes the work of producing .cdxml files harder.

There's a tool available that can ease the effort involved in creating a cmdlet definition file. It's called the CIM IDE, and it's available from MSDN at http:// archive.msdn.microsoft.com/cimide. Download and install the CIM IDE following the instructions in the Installation.txt file.

> **NOTE**   The CIM IDE is a plugin to Visual Studio 2010. You'll need Visual Studio installed before you can use the IDE.

Once you have the CIM IDE installed, open Visual Studio and create a new project. Two new templates are available under a CIM folder—CIM Authoring and CIM Providers. You'll be using the CIM Authoring template here.

Figure 18.6   Using the CIM IDE

Next, you'll need a MOF file of the WMI class you want to work with. I've included MOF files for `Win32_ComputerSystem` and `Win32_OperatingSystem` in the download code. Drag the MOF file onto the module name in the Solution Explorer pane at the right side of the IDE, as shown in figure 18.6.

Right click the `Win32_OperatingSystem` node in the CIM Explorer (at the left side) and select PowerShell metadata. This enables details such as version number, default noun, and filename to be set. A skeleton `.cdxml` file (visible in Solution Explorer) and the PowerShell metadata (visible in CIM Explorer, marked with the PowerShell icon) are generated.

The main working area is the PS Metadata Details tab shown in the middle pane. If it isn't visible double-click the metadata file in CIM Explorer. The PS Metadata Details tab supplies functionality to add the following:

- Query parameters, as in section 18.1
- Instance cmdlets utilizing the WMI class methods, as in section 19.1

When you're adding a query parameter, the GUI provides a simple technique for defining the parameter metadata:

- The property name and type can be selected.
- The parameter name defaults to the property name but can be overridden.
- Aliases can be defined for the parameter.
- The parameter sets to which the parameter belongs can be defined.
- Parameter options can be set:

- Mandatory
- Accept pipeline input
- Validate not null
- Allow empty string or collection
- Validation parameters, such as maximum or minimum counts, a range or set of values
- The use of wildcards (globbing)

The `Instance Cmdlets` option enables you to access the methods of the WMI class. Click Add New and the dialog box shown in figure 18.6 appears, where you can do the following:

- Select the method
- Define the verb and noun for the cmdlet and any aliases
- Set `Result` to `Interpret as error code`
- Set the `impact` parameters (`-WhatIf` and `-Confirm`)
- If the method requires parameters use the `Parameters` option to provide their definitions (in a dialog box to the one for query parameters in figure 18.6)

Once the cmdlet definition file has been produced it can be copied from the Visual Studio project folder to your PowerShell module folder and it's ready to use.

Visual Studio can also be used to edit format and type XML files, though there are no templates to assist with that.

18.5   *Summary*

This chapter has introduced the new functionality in PowerShell v3 that enables the creation of cmdlets from WMI classes. This is a huge change in working with PowerShell and WMI. It will make you much more productive and make using WMI much easier.

You've seen how to create multiple cmdlets, build a module, and modify the default display formatting. In chapter 19 we'll show you how to extend this further by utilizing the methods available on WMI classes and we'll look at the new administration opportunities presented by the new APIs for using WMI and the CIM cmdlets.

CIM cmdlets and sessions

This chapter covers

- Using WMI methods in cmdlets created from WMI objects
- Demonstrating the PowerShell v3 CIM cmdlets
- Using CIM sessions to access remote machines

In this chapter, we're going to continue our investigation of the CIM API introduced in PowerShell v3. In chapter 18, you saw how to create cmdlets directly from WMI classes. In this chapter, you'll learn how to extend the use of PowerShell v3's cmdlets-over-objects functionality to utilize the methods presented by WMI classes. You'll create additional cmdlets to provide a mechanism to utilize those methods. WMI methods may or may not require parameters. You'll learn how to work with both of these scenarios.

NOTE This chapter builds on chapter 18 and should be read after that chapter.

The CIM cmdlets are analogous to the WMI cmdlets that you've been using in PowerShell v2, but there are some subtle differences in the way you can access information. These differences provide a great opportunity to brush up on WQL. I strongly advise mastering WQL, as the changes introduced with PowerShell v3 will ensure it becomes an important part of your administration toolset.

WMI has always had great support for working with remote machines. The only snag is that it has required you to use the DCOM protocol. The CIM cmdlets continue to support DCOM, but you can also use WSMAN in a much simpler way that's similar to the way you use PowerShell remoting sessions.

We'll open the chapter by showing you how to create cmdlets to use WMI methods.

19.1 *Using WMI methods*

In chapter 18, you saw how to use the PowerShell cmdlets-over-objects functionality to create cmdlets based on WMI classes. This provides an abstraction layer that makes the WMI classes easier to use (which is the whole purpose of this book!). It's highly unlikely that you'll end up with all WMI classes being wrapped in cmdlets, but performing this task for your commonly used WMI classes (or those critical to your role) will make life easier. This process had already started in PowerShell v2 with `Test-Connection` and `Get-HotFix` acting as wrappers for WMI classes. In fact, many of the new PowerShell modules introduced with Windows Server 8 are created from WMI classes. They make a great reference source.

The cmdlets that you've created up to now return information. This is great, but you need to be able to do stuff to your servers. Otherwise the boss won't believe you're worth keeping around. When you use `Get-WmiObject`, the PowerShell object that's returned gives you access to most, if not all, of the methods available to that WMI class. That's how you get things done, as you saw in part 2 of this book.

You can extend the XML source files that you created in chapter 18 to provide access to the WMI classes' methods. One difference in the way you use WMI in PowerShell v3 as compared to v2 is in the way that the methods of a WMI class are accessed. You won't add methods to the objects your cmdlets return. You'll create another cmdlet, in the same module, to execute the method!

You'll start by utilizing simple methods that don't take parameters (technique 147) and then extend this to methods that need one or more parameters (technique 148). When we deal with parameters, we'll also look at how to validate the data input to the parameter.

TECHNIQUE 147   Adding a method

The first type of method we'll consider is one you'll meet in various scenarios and WMI classes. It's a simple method that doesn't require any further input. You just call it and it does its stuff.

PROBLEM

Your `Get-Win32OperatingSystem` cmdlet (from chapter 18) enables you to retrieve information about remote systems. Due to application changes, there's a requirement to reboot remote systems on a periodic basis. This functionality needs to be produced quickly and be firewall friendly.

NOTE For this technique, we'll assume that there isn't a native PowerShell mechanism to accomplish this task. PowerShell v3 betas have a `Restart-Computer` cmdlet, but it's possible that it may be removed, as happened in PowerShell v2.

SOLUTION

The `Win32_OperatingSystem` class has a `Reboot` method that's used in the following listing to solve the problem. The listing is identical to listing 18.2 in the early sections (these sections are truncated to concentrate on the new section of code). The listing in the download is complete.

Listing 19.1 Add a restart operating system method

```xml
<?xml version="1.0" encoding="utf-8"?>
<PowerShellMetadata xmlns:xsi=
   "http://www.w3.org/2001/XMLSchema-instance"
xmlns:xsd="http://www.w3.org/2001/XMLSchema"
xmlns="http://schemas.microsoft.com/cmdlets-over-objects/2009/11">
  <Class ClassName="root\cimv2\Win32_OperatingSystem">
    <Version>1.0.0.0</Version>
    <DefaultNoun>Win32OperatingSystem</DefaultNoun>
    <InstanceCmdlets>
      <GetCmdletParameters DefaultCmdletParameterSet="ByName">
            .. as listing 18.2

      </GetCmdletParameters>

      <Cmdlet>                                          ❶ Method
        <CmdletMetadata Verb="Restart"                    definition starts
           Noun="Win32OperatingSystem"
           ConfirmImpact="None" />
        <Method MethodName="Reboot">                    ❷ Method name
          <ReturnValue>
            <Type PSType="System.UInt32" />             ❸ Return type
            <CmdletOutputMetadata>
              <ErrorCode />
            </CmdletOutputMetadata>
          </ReturnValue>
        </Method>
      </Cmdlet>

    </InstanceCmdlets>
  </Class>

  <Enums>
    .. as listing 18.2
  </Enums>
</PowerShellMetadata>
```

To generate a cmdlet representing the `Reboot` method, you put the XML between `<Cmdlet>` tags ❶. The cmdlet verb is defined—in this case we use `Restart`. The method name is `Reboot` ❷, but if you use that as the verb, PowerShell will throw a warning when you import the module, because `Reboot` isn't an approved PowerShell verb.

TIP Use `Get-Verb` to view the list of approved verbs. The warning can be suppressed by using the `-DisableNameChecking` parameter of `Import-Module`.

A return code is defined to be an integer value ❸. That's all you have to do. You still have a single file—Win32OperatingSystem.cdxml—but it now supplies two cmdlets! The Listing 19.1 folder in the download code contains these files:

- SystemInfo.psm1
- Win32ComputerSystem.cdxml
- Win32OperatingSystem.cdxml
- Win32OperatingSystem.format.ps1xml
- Win32OperatingSystem.types.ps1xml

Import the module and test the contents:

```
PS> Import-Module .\SystemInfo.psm1
PS> Get-Command -Module systeminfo

Capability     Name
----------     ----
CIM            Get-Win32ComputerSystem
CIM            Get-Win32OperatingSystem
CIM            Restart-Win32OperatingSystem
```

One very powerful feature of working with this functionality is that as well as the default common parameters, the query parameters you created for `Get-Win32Operating-System` are automatically added to your `Restart-Win32OperatingSystem` cmdlet:

```
PS> Get-Help Restart-Win32OperatingSystem

NAME
    Restart-Win32OperatingSystem

SYNTAX
    Restart-Win32OperatingSystem [[-Name] <string[]>]
    [-CimSession <CimSession[]>] [-ThrottleLimit <int>]
    [-AsJob] [-PassThru] [<CommonParameters>]

    Restart-Win32OperatingSystem [[-Caption] <string[]>]
    [-CimSession <CimSession[]>] [-ThrottleLimit <int>]
    [-AsJob] [-PassThru]   [<CommonParameters>]

    Restart-Win32OperatingSystem
    [-OperatingSystemSKU <OperatingSystemSKU[]>
    {UltimateEdition | StandardServerEdition
    | DatacenterServerEdition | EnterpriseServerEdition}]
    [-CimSession <CimSession[]>] [-ThrottleLimit <int>]
    [-AsJob] [-PassThru]   [<CommonParameters>]

    Restart-Win32OperatingSystem -InputObject
    <CimInstance#Win32_OperatingSystem[]>
    [-CimSession <CimSession[]>]
    [-ThrottleLimit <int>] [-AsJob] [-PassThru]   [<CommonParameters>]
```

That's a massive return on the few lines of code you wrote.

DISCUSSION

The use of the new cmdlet is illustrated in figure 19.1.

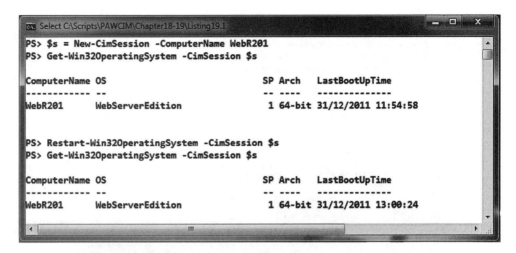

Figure 19.1 Using the `Restart-Win32OperatingSystem` cmdlet

Remote systems are accessed by creating a CIM session (analogous to a Power-Shell remoting session). These are covered in detail in section 19.3. The code in the figure starts by creating a session to a computer called WebR201 and uses `Get-Win32OperatingSystem` to display the `LastBootUpTime`, among other details. `Restart-Win32OperatingSystem` is used, and another call to `Get-Win32OperatingSystem` shows the revised boot time. Notice that there was no need to reestablish the CIM session. It automatically reconnects. There is an appreciable delay (up to a few minutes) once the target system has rebooted while the session is reestablished, but the reestablishment will happen.

CIM sessions to remote machines use WSMAN by default, but they can be constrained to use DCOM as shown in figure 19.2.

> **NOTE** Connectivity to systems by the CIM cmdlets, including `New-CIMSession`, always uses WSMAN by default if the `-ComputerName` parameter is used, even if the computer name supplied is the local machine. If the `-ComputerName` parameter isn't used, then a COM connection is made to the local machine.

A session option to use the DCOM protocol is created. This is used to create a CIM session to a machine called Win7. The difference between this system and WebR201, used in figure 19.1, is that this system is running PowerShell v2 and version 2.0 of the WSMAN stack. In this case, you need to use DCOM.

`Get-Win32OperatingSystem` is used with the session to retrieve the `LastBootUpTime`. A call to `Restart-Win32OperatingSystem` causes the system to reboot. Once it comes back online, you can attempt to use `Get-Win32OperatingSystem` again. This results in a nasty, big error message. The error's meaning isn't obvious from the message, but it actually means that the session link to the remote machine has been broken and needs to be reestablished.

Figure 19.2   Using DCOM with CIM sessions

TIP   WSMAN-based sessions automatically reconnect, but DCOM sessions don't.

Once you have reestablished the CIM session, you can use `Get-Win32OperatingSystem` again. The flexibility of the CIM cmdlets is shown at the bottom of the figure, where WSMAN and DCOM sessions are used together.

That's the simple type of method dealt with, but real admins need methods with parameters.

TECHNIQUE 148   **Adding a method that uses parameters**

Many of the methods to be found on WMI objects require one or more parameters. So far you've seen how to add a method that doesn't require parameters. There are many methods on WMI classes that don't require parameters, enabling you to build a set of functionality very simply. Eventually, though, you'll come across a method that does require parameters.

An example is the `Win32Shutdown` method of the `Win32_OperatingSystem` class. It can take the values shown in table 19.1 and perform different actions depending on the value. If you can harness this type of method, you can easily add powerful functionality to your module.

Value	Meaning
0	Log off
4	Forced log off
1	Shutdown
5	Forced shutdown
2	Reboot
6	Forced reboot
8	Power off
12	Forced power off

Table 19.1 Values for the `Win32Shutdown` method

Technique 147 demonstrated how to restart a remote system, but there are times when you'll need to shut down the remote system completely.

PROBLEM

The functionality of your module needs to be expanded by adding the capability to shut down a remote machine. This could be achieved using the `Stop-Computer` cmdlet, but you want to ensure that potential firewall issues don't interfere by using the WSMAN protocol.

SOLUTION

Listing 19.2 extends listing 19.1 by adding the functionality to use the `Win32Shutdown` method. The listing has been compressed by removing statements that have been shown in previous listings so that we can concentrate on the new items. The full listing is available in the download code that accompanies the book.

Listing 19.2 Add a method with parameters

```
<?xml version="1.0" encoding="utf-8"?>
<PowerShellMetadata xmlns:xsi=
  "http://www.w3.org/2001/XMLSchema-instance"
xmlns:xsd="http://www.w3.org/2001/XMLSchema"
xmlns="http://schemas.microsoft.com/cmdlets-over-objects/2009/11">
  <Class ClassName="root\cimv2\Win32_OperatingSystem">
    <Version>1.0.0.0</Version>
    <DefaultNoun>Win32OperatingSystem</DefaultNoun>
    <InstanceCmdlets>
      <GetCmdletParameters DefaultCmdletParameterSet="ByName">
            .. as listing 19.1
      </GetCmdletParameters>
```

```
    <Cmdlet>
      <CmdletMetadata Verb="Restart" />
          .. as listing 19.1
    </Cmdlet>

    <Cmdlet>
      <CmdletMetadata Verb="Stop"
        ➥ ConfirmImpact="High" />
      <Method MethodName="Win32Shutdown">
        <ReturnValue>
          <Type PSType="System.UInt32" />
          <CmdletOutputMetadata>
            <ErrorCode />
          </CmdletOutputMetadata>
        </ReturnValue>
        <Parameters>
          <Parameter ParameterName="Flags">
            <Type PSType="System.Int32" />
            <CmdletParameterMetadata PSName="Flags">
              <ValidateNotNull />
              <ValidateSet>
                <AllowedValue>4</AllowedValue>
                <AllowedValue>5</AllowedValue>
                <AllowedValue>6</AllowedValue>
                <AllowedValue>12</AllowedValue>
              </ValidateSet>
            </CmdletParameterMetadata>
          </Parameter>
        </Parameters>
      </Method>
    </Cmdlet>
  </InstanceCmdlets>

</Class>
<Enums>
  .. as listing 19.1
</Enums>
</PowerShellMetadata>
```

❶ **Cmdlet start**

❷ **Method name**

❸ **Return value**

❹ **Parameter name**

❺ **Validation**

The XML file is identical to listing 19.1 until you get to the point where you want to add the cmdlet that uses the `Win32Shutdown` method. The new cmdlet is assigned the verb `Stop` ❶, and it's linked to the `Win32Shutdown` method ❷. A return value is defined ❸.

This method has a single parameter ❹. It's given the same name that's used in the WMI documentation, but that isn't mandatory. A different name could be used if preferred. My recommendation is to conform to the WMI documentation for ease of maintenance. The type of data to be input through the parameter (in this case an integer) is also defined.

When you used PowerShell advanced functions in chapters 5–16 you utilized the input validation techniques when defining parameters. You can do exactly the same with the cmdlets you create from WMI objects ❺. The code will test that the parameter isn't null and that it contains one of the allowed values taken from table 19.1.

DISCUSSION

Once the module has been imported, you'll find that it contains three cmdlets:

- `Get-Win32OperatingSystem`
- `Restart-Win32OperatingSystem`
- `Stop-Win32OperatingSystem`

You created the `Get` cmdlet in chapter 18, and the `Restart` and `Stop` cmdlets were added in this section. Building functionality in this granular manner makes development and testing easier and more efficient, as it's a simple matter to isolate the new aspects of the module.

You can use the `Stop-Win32OperatingSystem` cmdlet as follows:

```
$cs = New-CimSession -ComputerName WebR201
Stop-Win32OperatingSystem -CimSession $cs -Flags 6
```

Creating CIM sessions is covered in section 19.3. The cmdlet is used with the appropriate `Flag` value to trigger the desired action. If you input a value for the `-Flags` parameter that isn't in the allowed set you'll get an error message:

```
PS> Stop-Win32OperatingSystem -Flags 9
Stop-Win32OperatingSystem : Cannot validate argument on parameter 'Flags'.
    The argument "9" does not belong to the set "4,5,6,12" specified by the
    ValidateSet attribute. Supply an argument that is in the set and then
    try the command again.
```

The system very helpfully informs you of the values the cmdlet will accept.

> **TIP** If you need to discover the acceptable values for a parameter, input an incorrect value and the error message will supply the correct set.

Some methods require more than one parameter, in which case the information between the `<Parameter>` and `</Parameter>` tags needs to be duplicated and modified as required. You could extend the module to cover the other methods on the `Win32_OperatingSystem` module:

- `SetDateTime`
- `Shutdown`
- `Win32ShutdownTracker`

As these are similar activities, I'll just supply the code in the final version of the module, to be found in the SystemInfo folder of the chapter 18–19 code download.

When you incorporate a method from a WMI object into your code, you generate an extra cmdlet to perform the action. Some methods require parameters, as you've seen. Adding multiple parameters is equally easy.

This provides a very granular method of adding functionality to modules. You can quickly get the functionality into production as it becomes available, allowing the module to repay the investment in development sooner than if development were slower.

In this section, and in chapter 18, you've seen and used a number of the CIM-related cmdlets. It's time to investigate these in depth and see how they relate to the WMI cmdlets you know and love.

19.2   *CIM cmdlets*

The other big WMI-related change with PowerShell v3 is the introduction of the CIM cmdlets. These are analogous to the WMI cmdlets, and they can work with the legacy WMI classes and provide access to the new CIM API. These cmdlets are discussed in section 19.2.2. Windows 8 also supplies a number of new WMI namespaces.

> **WARNING**   On pre-Windows 8 systems, PowerShell v3 won't install the new WMI providers, or namespaces, that are introduced with Windows 8. If the new cmdlets access currently available classes, they will work; otherwise an error will occur.

You need to understand the similarities and differences between the CIM cmdlets and the WMI cmdlets you've been using. The second part of this section will compare and contrast the two sets of cmdlets to illustrate how to best use each set.

Our old friends, the WMI cmdlets, don't get any new parameters and are used in the same manner as in PowerShell v2.

19.2.1   *WMI and CIM objects*

The WMI cmdlets that you've been using in PowerShell v2 remain in PowerShell v3:

- `Get-WmiObject`
- `Invoke-WmiMethod`
- `Set-WmiInstance`
- `Remove-WmiObject`
- `Register-WmiEvent`

The WMI cmdlets are unchanged as far as using them is concerned.

I've mentioned several times that there's a new API for accessing the CIM cmdlets. They also use a different set of .NET classes. Consider the types returned by the WMI cmdlets:

```
Get-WmiObject Win32_OperatingSystem | Get-Member
```

You'd get this type returned:

```
System.Management.ManagementObject#root\cimv2\Win32_OperatingSystem
```

The corresponding CIM cmdlet is as follows:

```
Get-CimInstance Win32_OperatingSystem | Get-Member
```

This returns a completely different type:

```
TypeName: Microsoft.Management.Infrastructure.CimInstance#
    ➥ root/cimv2\Win32_OperatingSystem
```

TIP Remember that the CIM cmdlets return objects that have been deserialized from XML. The classes' methods aren't included on the returned object.

The best way to see the differences is to use `Get-WmiObject` and `Get-CimInstance` against the same class and compare the results. Try this:

```
Get-WmiObject -Class Win32_LogicalDisk -Filter "DeviceID='C:'" | fl *
Get-CimInstance -ClassName Win32_LogicalDisk -Filter "DeviceID='C:'" | fl *
```

The best way to perform the comparison is to use two PowerShell consoles and run one command in each. These are some of the differences:

- The CIM cmdlet doesn't display the system properties (those with a double-underscore prefix).
- The CIM cmdlet has a `ComputerName` property, whereas the WMI cmdlet has a `PSComputerName` property.
- The CIM cmdlet doesn't display the WMI class qualifiers.
- The class and namespace information is different for the two cmdlets.

On a Windows 8 system try this code:

```
Get-WmiObject -Class Win32_LogicalDisk -Filter "DeviceID='C:'"
Get-CimInstance -ClassName Win32_LogicalDisk
```

The new root\standardcimv2 namespace adds a number of additional WMI classes for the modules shipped with PowerShell v3. These can be accessed using `Get-CimInstance`, as well as by the module (many of the new modules in Windows Server 8 are cmdlets created from WMI classes):

```
Get-CimInstance -NameSpace ROOT/StandardCimv2 `
-ClassName MSFT_NetAdapter
```

You can also use `Get-WmiObject` on these new classes:

```
Get-WmiObject -Namespace ROOT/StandardCimv2 -Class MSFT_NetAdapter
```

The classes are accessible on remote systems using the `-ComputerName` parameter:

```
Get-WmiObject -NameSpace ROOT/StandardCimv2 `
-Class MSFT_NetAdapter -ComputerName server8build
```

If you try to access this class on a Windows 7 machine (even though it has PowerShell v3 installed), like this

```
Get-WmiObject -NameSpace ROOT/StandardCimv2 `
-Class MSFT_NetAdapter -ComputerName win7test
```

the following error message will be returned:

```
Get-WmiObject : Invalid namespace "ROOT/StandardCimv2"
```

This is all great. You get more WMI classes to work with, and you can access them using the standard WMI tools that you've seen throughout the book. The only catch is that the new classes are only available on Windows 8 and above.

The big question is what can the CIM cmdlets do for you and how do you use them.

19.2.2 *CIM and WMI cmdlets*

The new CIM cmdlets are listed in table 19.2. Comparing them with the WMI cmdlets and the WSMAN cmdlets (table 17.1 in chapter 17) will show many points of similarity in the names and functionality, as you can see in table 19.3. The cmdlets for working with CIM sessions will be discussed in section 19.3.

Table 19.2   CIM cmdlets

Export-CimCommand	Get-CimAssociatedInstance	Get-CimClass
Get-CimInstance	Get-CimSession	Invoke-CimMethod
New-CimInstance	New-CimSession	New-CimSessionOption
Register-CimIndicationEvent	Remove-CimInstance	Remove-CimSession
Set-CimInstance		

Table 19.3   Comparison of WMI, WSMAN, and CIM cmdlets

WMI cmdlets	WSMAN cmdlets	CIM cmdlets
Get-WmiObject	Get-WSManInstance	Get-CimInstance
Invoke-WmiMethod	Invoke-WSManAction	Invoke-CimMethod
Set-WmiInstance	Set-WSManInstance	Set-CimInstance
Remove-WmiObject	(Remove-WSManInstance)	Remove-CimInstance

TIP   In PowerShell v2, the Remove-WSManInstance cmdlet can only be used to remove WSMAN configuration information.

The best way to compare the WMI and CIM cmdlets is to see them in action (the WSMAN cmdlets were discussed in chapter 17). As usual, notepad.exe has volunteered to be the central part of the examples. You can start an instance of Notepad like this:

```
Start-Process notepad
```

There are a number of ways you can use Get-WmiObject to return information on the Notepad process. The one with the least typing involves using a filter:

```
Get-WmiObject -Class Win32_Process -Filter "Name='notepad.exe'"
```

This is equivalent to using the following WQL query:

```
Get-WmiObject -Query "SELECT * FROM Win32_Process `
WHERE Name='notepad.exe'"
```

Queries and filters can be used in Get-CimInstance to produce the same result:

```
Get-CimInstance -ClassName Win32_Process
  ➥ -Filter "Name='notepad.exe'"
Get-CimInstance -Query "SELECT * FROM Win32_Process `
WHERE Name='notepad.exe'"
```

TIP The -Filter parameter was added in PowerShell v3 CTP 2. Early commentary on PowerShell v3 may state that these cmdlets don't have a -Filter parameter.

Notice that the WMI cmdlets use the -Class parameter, but the CIM cmdlets use the -ClassName parameter. The CIM cmdlets have a -Class parameter, but it's used in a different manner, as you'll see shortly.

One drawback with the WMI cmdlets is that you have to completely refetch the data from the server to refresh the data. The CIM cmdlets provide an easier way to refresh the data. Start by creating a CIM instance. In this case, you'll only be using a single process, but it would work just as effectively if multiple, or even all, processes were selected:

```
$proc = Get-CimInstance -ClassName Win32_Process `
-Filter "Name='System Idle Process'"
```

You can then display the contents of the variable:

```
$proc | Format-Table Name, KernelModeTime -AutoSize

Name                 KernelModeTime
----                 --------------
System Idle Process  183482968750
```

The data is refreshed by simply piping it through Get-CimInstance:

```
$proc | Get-CimInstance |
Format-Table Name, KernelModeTime -AutoSize

Name                 KernelModeTime
----                 --------------
  System Idle Process   183838906250
```

The variable $proc still contains the original data.

You can create a process using WMI:

```
Invoke-WmiMethod -Class Win32_Process -Name Create `
-ArgumentList notepad.exe
```

The Create method of the Win32_Process class is called with the path to notepad.exe being passed as the argument. You don't need the full path because notepad.exe is in Windows\System32, which is on the search path by default.

You can use Invoke-CimMethod in the same way:

```
Invoke-CimMethod -ClassName Win32_process -MethodName Create `
-Arguments @{CommandLine = "notepad.exe"}
```

The only slight difference is that you have to provide the parameter name that the Create method expects (CommandLine).

When it comes to removing WMI objects you have a number of options. When you're dealing with processes, you can get the object and pipe it to `Invoke-WmiMethod`:

```
Get-WmiObject -Class Win32_Process -Filter "Name='notepad.exe'" |
Invoke-WmiMethod -Name Terminate
```

Alternatively, you can pipe it to `Remove-WmiObject`:

```
Get-WmiObject Win32_Process -Filter "Name='notepad.exe'" |
Remove-WmiObject
```

This is my preferred way of removing WMI objects, because I can test the filter before piping to ensure I'm working with the correct object.

You can perform similar actions with the CIM cmdlets:

```
Get-CimInstance -ClassName Win32_Process `
-Filter "Name='notepad.exe'" |
Invoke-CimMethod -MethodName Terminate

Get-CimInstance -ClassName Win32_Process `
 -Filter "Name='notepad.exe'" |
Remove-CimInstance
```

The `-Class` parameter can be used to provide much improved error messages. If you try to use a nonexistent method—for example the "DieYouHorribleProcess" method—you'll get results like the following by default:

```
PS> Invoke-CimMethod -Class Win32_Process `
-MethodName DieYouHorribleProcess `
-Argument @{CommandLine='notepad.exe'}
Invoke-CimMethod : Not found
At line:1 char:1
+ Invoke-CimMethod -Class Win32_Process
-MethodName DieYouHorribleProcess -Argumen ...
+ ~~~~~~~~~~~~~~~~~~~~~~~~~~~~~~~~~~~~~~~~~~~~~~~~~~~~~~~~~~~~~~~~~
~~~~~~~~~~~~~~~~~~~~~~~~
    + CategoryInfo          : ObjectNotFound: (:)
[Invoke-CimMethod], CimException
    + FullyQualifiedErrorId : HRESULT 80041002,
Microsoft.Management.Infrastructure.
  ➥ CimCmdlets.InvokeCimMethodCommand
```

As you can see, the error message here just states that something is not found. Not the most helpful of messages. You can use `Get-CimClass` (similar to using `Get-WmiObject -Class -List`) to get the class definitions:

```
PS> $c = Get-CimClass Win32_Process
```

If you then try using the non-existent method, you'll get the following results:

```
PS> Invoke-CimMethod -Cimclass $c `
-MethodName DieYouHorribleProcess `
-Argument @{CommandLine='notepad.exe'}
Invoke-CimMethod : Method 'DieYouHorribleProcess'
is not declared in class 'Win32_Process'.
At line:1 char:1
```

```
+ Invoke-CimMethod -Cimclass $c
-MethodName DieYouHorribleProcess
-Argument @{Comm ...
+ ~~~~~~~~~~~~~~~~~~~~~~~~~~~~~~~~~~~~~~~~~~~~~~~~~~~~~~~~~~~~~~~~
~~~~~~~~~~~~~~~~~~~~~
    + CategoryInfo          : NotSpecified: (:)
[Invoke-CimMethod], ArgumentException
    + FullyQualifiedErrorId : System.ArgumentException,Microsoft.Management.
➥ Infrastructure.CimCmdlets.InvokeCimMethodCommand
```

You receive a much more helpful message stating that the method isn't declared in the `Win32_Process` class.

In chapter 3, we looked at documenting WMI namespaces and classes. `Get-CimClass` can aid this process. The following example shows how you can expand the information for properties, methods, and qualifiers:

```
Get-CimClass -ClassName Win32_Process | foreach {
 $_ | select ClassName, SuperClassName, Namespace | Format-List

 "Methods"
 $_ | select -ExpandProperty Methods | Format-List

 "Properties"
 $_ | select -ExpandProperty Properties | Format-List

 "Qualifiers"
 $_ | select -ExpandProperty Qualifiers | Format-List

}
```

I recommend using this cmdlet as a tool for investigating WMI. It's much simpler than the scripts you've had to use in the past.

19.2.3 *Jobs and events*

The WMI cmdlets in table 19.3 have an `-AsJob` parameter that enables you to run the cmdlets asynchronously:

```
Get-WmiObject -Class Win32_ComputerSystem -AsJob
Get-Job
Receive-Job -Id 2
```

The CIM cmdlets can't be started directly as jobs, but you can overcome this by using `Start-Job`:

```
Start-Job -ScriptBlock {
Get-CimInstance -ClassName Win32_ComputerSystem}
Get-Job
Receive-Job -Id 4
```

The same end result is achieved, because you've performed the task within a job. The execution methods are different, but by using the standard job cmdlets you retain consistency with other cmdlets and, in my opinion, have a simpler environment.

WMI has excellent event support. You've seen numerous examples of accessing events in the chapters in part 2. The CIM cmdlets can also be used to access events. In WMI you've used the system event classes:

```
Get-WmiObject -List __Instance*event* | select Name

Name
----
__InstanceOperationEvent
__InstanceModificationEvent
__InstanceCreationEvent
__InstanceDeletionEvent
```

The CIM cmdlets utilize similar classes:

```
Get-CimClass -ClassName *modification | Select ClassName

ClassName
---------
CIM_ClassModification
CIM_InstModification
```

When working with WMI events through the CIM cmdlets you start by defining a WQL query in exactly the same way as when working with the WMI cmdlets. Here's an example:

```
$q = "SELECT * FROM CIM_InstModification WHERE `
TargetInstance ISA 'Win32_LocalTime'"
```

An event registration is performed using the query:

```
Register-CimIndicationEvent -Query $q
```

The events can be viewed using `Get-Event`. Because they're triggered every second, it's more meaningful to just view the timestamp on the event:

```
Get-Event | select TimeGenerated
```

The event system is cleaned up in the usual way:

```
Get-Event | Remove-Event
Unregister-Event *
```

As you can see, the CIM cmdlets are analogous to the WMI and WSMAN cmdlets. The biggest difference is the way that the WMI and CIM cmdlets connect directly to remote machines using the `-ComputerName` parameter. When using the WMI cmdlets, this is performed over the DCOM protocol. The CIM cmdlets use the WSMAN protocols, but they can also use DCOM via CIM sessions, which make them more powerful and flexible.

19.3   *CIM sessions*

In PowerShell v2, you have three ways to access a remote system using WMI:

- Use the `-ComputerName` parameter on the WMI cmdlets to access the remote system via DCOM.
- Use PowerShell remoting via WinRM and PowerShell on the remote system. This can be used for a single command or to establish a session to the remote machine for repeated use.
- Use the WSMAN cmdlets to access the WMI providers directly from the WinRM service (which was the subject of chapter 17).

PowerShell v3 retains all of these options and adds another—the use of CIM sessions.

> **BIG WIN** This option will prove to be one of the big wins for administrators in PowerShell v3, as it enables us to access systems running Windows 8 operating systems and older legacy versions of Windows without needing to upgrade them to PowerShell v3.

In this section, we'll examine the theory behind CIM sessions and then look at how to use them. This discussion follows the lifecycle of creating, accessing, and removing CIM sessions.

19.3.1 CIM sessions explained

I'll briefly explain the structure of the environment I used to test this functionality because it's important to understanding the following sections. The systems I used are detailed in table 19.4.

Table 19.4   Systems involved in testing CIM sessions

Machine	Type	Operating system	PowerShell version
Server02	Physical—Hyper-V host and domain controller	Windows Server 2008 R2 SP 1	PowerShell v2
Win7Test	Virtual	Windows 7 SP 1, 64-bit	PowerShell v3
Server8BUILD	Virtual	Windows Server 8	PowerShell v3
Win8BUILD32	Virtual	Windows 8, 32-bit	PowerShell v3

The important point regarding CIM sessions is that they use a completely new application programming interface (API), which is made available through new .NET classes introduced with PowerShell v3. This new API is referred to as the Management Infrastructure Client API, abbreviated to MI. The API enables the following:

- Standards-based and -compliant access to any CIM Object Manager (CIMOM). WMI is Microsoft's implementation of CIMOM, but you now get access to CIM on non-Windows machines, such as Open Pegasus (www.openpegasus.org) on Linux systems.
- Support for all the standard operations supported by the WS-Management (WSMAN) protocols. A set of cmdlets are provided that are analogous to the WSMAN cmdlets (see table 19.1).
- Use of the WS-Management protocol, which is an industry standard and firewall-friendly protocol. This is implemented as the WinRM service in a Microsoft environment. WinRM provides the basis of PowerShell remoting, WSMAN remote access, and CIM sessions.
- Access to a full range of classic Windows operating systems through DCOM when PowerShell v3 isn't installed.

In short, you can now access WMI over the WinRM service and still drop back to using DCOM if you need to access legacy systems. It's this flexibility that provides the power of the new API. The combinations can get a bit confusing, but the summary presented in table 19.5 puts them into context.

Table 19.5   Protocols and parameters for remote access mechanisms

Access by	Protocol	Parameters
WMI cmdlets	DCOM	`ComputerName`
`Invoke-Command`	WSMAN	`ComputerName` `Session`
`PSSession` cmdlets	WSMAN	`ComputerName` `Session`
CIM cmdlets	WSMAN DCOM	`CimSession` or `Computername` `CimSession` or used without `Computername`

The next step is learning how to create CIM sessions.

TECHNIQUE 149   Creating a CIM session

Table 19.2 shows that you have four cmdlets to use when working with CIM sessions:

- `New-CimSession`
- `New-CimSessionOption`
- `Get-CimSession`
- `Remove-CimSession`

The `New-*` cmdlets are used when creating sessions. The `Get-` and `Remove-CimSession` cmdlets are used to enumerate and destroy sessions respectively.

Creating a `CimSession` appears to be straightforward:

```
PS> New-CimSession -ComputerName Server8BUILD

Id           : 1
Name         : CimSession1
InstanceId   : 5ed6fca5-df1f-4767-be7a-c4db9569333e
ComputerName : Server8BUILD
Protocol     : WSMAN
```

Notice that the protocol defaults to WSMAN. If you use this syntax to connect to a machine running Windows Server 2008 R2 and PowerShell v2, you'll get an error, as follows:

```
Get-CimInstance : The WS-Management service cannot process the request. A
    DMTF resource URI was used to access a non-DMTF class. Try again using a
    non-DMTF resource URI.
```

The same error will be returned if you try to use this syntax:

```
Get-CimInstance -ClassName Win32_OperatingSystem
⇒ -ComputerName server02
```

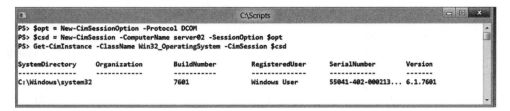

Figure 19.3 Using the New-CimSessionOption cmdlet to force a CIM session to use the DCOM protocol

The way to resolve this is to force the CIM session to use DCOM, as shown in figure 19.3.

Start by creating a CIM session option. The option forces use of the DCOM protocol. A session connecting to Server02 is created using that option. You can then access the session to retrieve data.

This just leaves one tiny problem. You need to know the configuration, operating system, WSMAN version, and PowerShell version before you create the session. Or do you?

PROBLEM

The cmdlets you created from WMI objects in chapter 18 and section 19.1 don't have a -ComputerName parameter. They use CIM sessions to access remote computers. The Win32_OperatingSystem and Win32_ComputerSystem classes are available on both Windows 8 and earlier versions of Windows. The only available access mechanism for CIM cmdlets in earlier versions of Windows is DCOM. Windows 8 and above can use WSMAN. You need a mechanism to create CIM sessions that takes into account the configuration of the remote machine and that utilizes the appropriate protocol.

SOLUTION

The following listing demonstrates how you can build on your knowledge of the WSMAN cmdlets to determine which protocol to use. Refer to technique 137 in chapter 17 for an in-depth explanation of the Test-WSMan cmdlet.

Listing 19.3 Set CIM session protocol

```
function set-cimsession {
[CmdletBinding()]
param (
 [string]$computername="$env:COMPUTERNAME"        ❶ Set default
 )                                                    computer name
BEGIN {
 $opt = New-CimSessionOption -Protocol DCOM        ❷ Create DCOM
}                                                      option

PROCESS {
switch ($computername){
 "."        {$computername="$env:COMPUTERNAME" }
 "localhost" {$computername="$env:COMPUTERNAME" }
}
```

```
if (-not (Test-Connection -ComputerName $computername -Quiet -Count 1)){
  Throw "Computer: $($computername)
  ➥ could not be contacted"
}
```
◁─┐ **Test connection**
❸ **to computer**

```
$twsman = Test-WSMan -ComputerName $computername `
-Authentication Default
$pva = $twsman.ProductVersion -split ": "
$stack = $pva[-1]
Write-Debug $stack
```
◁─┐ **Test WSMAN**
❹ **stack**

```
switch ($stack){
 "2.0" {$ncs = New-CimSession -ComputerName $computername `
         -SessionOption $opt }
 "3.0" {$ncs = New-CimSession -ComputerName $computername }
 default {Throw "Error - could not
    recognize WSMAN stack for $computername"}
}
```
◁─┐ **Create**
❺ **session**

```
$ncs
} # end process
}
```
◁─┐ **Return**
❻ **session**

The function takes a single parameter—the name of the remote computer to which you wish to connect ❶. The function will convert "." or "localhost" to $env:COMPUTER-NAME. This is because Test-Connection throws an error when "." is used.

> **TIP** $env: is a shortcut to using the environmental variables via the Environment provider and PowerShell drive. The full list of environmental variables can be viewed using Get-ChildItem -Path env:.

The only CIM session option to be configured is the protocol, and that's set using New-CimSessionOption ❷. WSMAN is the default protocol, and your option is to use DCOM instead. The function starts by testing that the remote machine can be pinged using Test-Connection ❸. The -Quiet parameter ensures that a Boolean (True or False) result is returned. If a result of False is returned—meaning the remote machine isn't contactable—an error is thrown and the function terminates.

Test-WSMan is used to determine the version of the WSMAN stack on the remote machine ❹. The -Authentication Default parameter is used to ensure that the version information is returned. A split of the ProductVersion property is performed, and the last item is allocated to a variable ($stack).

Switch is used to test the value of the $stack variable ❺. If version 2.0 (PowerShell v2) is found, DCOM is set as the protocol using the option you created earlier (at ❶). Version 3.0 (PowerShell v3) can use WSMAN as its protocol.

The function finally returns the created session to its caller. The variable is returned by placing it on a line by itself ❻. If the function is used in a standalone manner, the details of the session are displayed on screen.

DISCUSSION

The problem originally appeared to involve a number of possible variables that had to be checked, including operating system version, PowerShell version, and the version of the WSMAN stack. But only the version of the WSMAN stack is a determining factor for the protocol you can use.

When you run `Test-WSMan`, Server02 (Windows Server 2008 R2 SP 1) returns this data:

```
ProductVersion  : OS: 6.1.7601 SP: 1.0 Stack: 2.0
```

Win7Test (Windows 7 SP1 with PowerShell v3) returns this:

```
ProductVersion  : OS: 6.1.7601 SP: 1.0 Stack: 3.0
```

The important difference is in the `Stack` version. PowerShell v3 uses version 3.0. This provides the differentiator. If further stack versions are introduced, the `switch` statement can be extended to accommodate them.

The hard work of creating a CIM session has been accomplished. You can sit back and enjoy yourself for a while. Oh, hang on, you haven't figured out how to use the session yet.

TECHNIQUE 150   Accessing CIM sessions

You have a shiny new cmdlet created from a WMI class, and you have a CIM session. You can put the two together like this (as you've seen in the examples in chapter 18 and earlier in this chapter):

```
$cs7 = set-cimsession -computername Win7test
Get-Win32OperatingSystem -CimSession $cs7
```

Does this seem familiar? Think of creating PowerShell remoting sessions and using `Invoke-Command`, and you have the correct comparison.

You can also be a little sneaky and take advantage of the fact that PowerShell will treat an expression in parentheses as an object:

```
Get-Win32OperatingSystem -CimSession
  ➥ (set-cimsession -computername Win7test)
```

In this example, the `(set-cimsession -computername Win7test)` expression is evaluated first to produce a CIM session object that's used by the cmdlet.

You can create sessions to multiple computers as follows:

```
$cs = New-CimSession -ComputerName server02, win7test
```

All sessions will default to WSMAN in this case.

Ideally you'll want to automate some, or all of the session creation process.

PROBLEM

When accessing remote systems using the `*CIMInstance` cmdlets, or cmdlets you've created yourself, you need to be able to reuse sessions without having to remember which machines you've created sessions for. The session protocol should be determined automatically as part of the creation process.

SOLUTION

The following listing shows how you can solve this problem by building on the function you created in technique 149. This function pulls together a lot of the ideas you've seen throughout the chapter.

Listing 19.4 Access CIM sessions

```
function get-systeminfo {
[CmdletBinding()]
param (
 [string]$computername="$env:COMPUTERNAME"
 )
BEGIN {
 Import-Module systeminfo -Force
}

PROCESS {
switch ($computername){
 "."          {$computername="$env:COMPUTERNAME" }
 "localhost" {$computername="$env:COMPUTERNAME" }
}

if (-not (Test-Connection -ComputerName $computername -Quiet -Count 1)){
  Throw "Computer: $($computername)
    ➥ could not be contacted"
}

if (-not(Test-Path -Path variable:\"cs_$computername")){
  New-Variable -Name "cs_$computername" `
   -Value (set-cimsession -computer $computername)
}

Get-Win32OperatingSystem `
-CimSession (Get-Variable -Name "cs_$computername").Value |
Out-Default

Get-CimInstance -ClassName Win32_ComputerSystem `
-CimSession (Get-Variable -Name "cs_$computername").Value |
Out-Default
} # end process
}
```

❶ Force module import

❷ Test connection

❸ Test variable existence

❹ Use your cmdlet

❺ Use PowerShell cmdlet

The function takes a computer name as a parameter, with the name of the local computer taken from the environmental variables acting as a default value. You're using the systeminfo module created in chapter 18, so it's imported ❶. The -Force parameter ensures that the import occurs even if it's already loaded.

> **TIP** Many cmdlets have a -Force parameter to ensure that restrictions can be overcome. If your syntax isn't working, check to see if the cmdlet is a Jedi and can use the force.

The remote system is pinged to determine if it's contactable ❷. If it is, the function then uses Test-Path to determine whether the variable cs_$computername is present ❸. If not, the variable will be created (note that the variable name doesn't have a $ prefix) with a value set to a CIM session created using set-cimsession from technique 149. Test-Path is normally seen used on the filesystem, but it should function on any correctly written provider.

You can then use your session with a WMI object-based cmdlet ❹ or a PowerShell CIM cmdlet ❺. In both cases, the CIM session is set by using (Get-Variable -Name "cs_$computername").Value.

DISCUSSION

When accessing a single remote machine, the function can be used like this:

```
get-systeminfo -computername win7test
```

If multiple machines are to be accessed, you can put the names into a CSV file and pipe them into the function:

```
Import-CSV myfile.csv |
 foreach {get-systeminfo -computer $_.ComputerName}
```

Closing your PowerShell session will remove the CIM sessions, but you should be a bit better organized and be able to clean up after yourself.

19.3.2 *Removing CIM sessions*

Removing CIM sessions is a simple matter of using `Remove-CimSession`. The fun bit comes in identifying the correct session to close. The existing CIM sessions can be discovered using `Get-CimSession`. Each session returns information like this:

```
Id           : 1
Name         : CimSession1
InstanceId   : 5c95e7ad-f347-4409-a644-65ce9f726b55
ComputerName : win7test
Protocol     : WSMAN
```

You can remove sessions using a number of criteria. For example, you can remove individual sessions based on `Id`:

```
Remove-CimSession -Id 1

$cs = Get-CimSession -Id 2
Remove-CimSession -CimSession $cs

Get-CimSession -Id 3 | Remove-CimSession
```

Or, you can remove all of the sessions associated with a particular computer:

```
Remove-CimSession -ComputerName server02
```

Alternatively, you can remove all sessions:

```
Get-CimSession | Remove-CimSession
```

`Get-CimSession` also allows you to select sessions based on computer name, instance ID (GUID), or name. Selections based on any of these criteria could be piped to `Remove-CimSession`.

19.4 *Summary*

The cmdlets that you create from WMI objects can be extended to utilize the WMI object's methods. This creates an additional cmdlet in the module for each method you include, providing a very granular and simple way to access the functionality. You can use these cmdlets across CIM sessions, which gives you an instance remoting capability that can bypass some of the issues with DCOM and firewalls.

The CIM cmdlets are analogous to the WMI and WSMAN cmdlets, but they have some subtle differences that could cause problems if you forget them. You can use these cmdlets to access the new WMI classes as well as the legacy ones.

CIM sessions are an additional tool for accessing remote machines. You can use them with the CIM cmdlets as well as the cmdlets you create from WMI classes. They can access systems using DCOM or WSMAN to provide maximum flexibility. Just remember that these sessions return XML-based objects, which means you have a different way to utilize WMI methods. It's not difficult, just different.

Afterword
This is not the end

You've come a long way since you started on this journey. You've learned how to use PowerShell and WMI to manage many parts of your environment, including the following:

- Computer systems and hardware
- Performance counters and stability measures
- Filesystem, event logs, and page files
- Printers and scheduled jobs
- Disk systems
- Network configurations
- IIS, DNS, and Hyper-V
- The registry
- Local accounts and groups

Is this the end? Very definitely not! WMI is constantly changing as new versions of Windows and applications are released. You need to keep on top of the changes to ensure that you can manage your systems as efficiently as possible and that you find all the new toys to play with. The real fun in all of this is getting something new to work.

The third part of this book opened the door to some of the most exciting developments of all, with the CIM APIs released in PowerShell v3 and Windows 8. With these you can create your own cmdlets from WMI objects and finally break free of the restrictions of DCOM. WMI has always been a powerful tool for performing management tasks remotely, and it has taken a huge step forward in capability with these new releases.

Having said all that, there's still much to investigate. I deliberately didn't include any content on working with clusters or NLB in this book. A lot of WMI is used in the System Center family of products, and it's waiting for an intrepid explorer to investigate and publish the details. The classes that lurk in the root\wmi namespace need investigating and documenting. And that's just the tip of the iceberg.

When Windows 8 arrives, there will be a number of new namespaces to investigate. Some of these can be accessed via the modules that are provided, but there will still be activities where you're better off dropping back to WMI or CIM and using the classes directly. The CIM APIs also provide an opportunity to manage non-Windows devices with PowerShell and WMI. This will provide many new opportunities.

Creating your own WMI providers has become much easier with PowerShell v3 and Windows 8. I haven't determined the exact scenarios, but I have a few possibilities in mind.

The enjoyment produced by writing a script (or module) to solve a unique problem is very real. I've produced over 150 scripts for this book alone, not to mention those created for my blogs and work. Savor it and then move on to the next problem. PowerShell and WMI, like all skills, need constant practice. Don't be too upset looking back on scripts you created six months ago when you were just beginning with Power-Shell and WMI. Think instead of the things you've learned and how much you've accomplished with those scripts.

I said at the beginning of the book that there's a fantastic PowerShell community. Join it. Bring your scripts and problems and share them with the community. If you get really excited about something you've discovered, I and many others are always looking for speakers for User Group meetings. Help build a bigger and better Power-Shell community.

The closing words of this book belong to Jeffrey Snover, the man who invented PowerShell:

"Experiment! Enjoy! Engage!"

RICHARD SIDDAWAY

appendix A
PowerShell reference

This appendix supplies a number of templates, syntax formats, and other useful information that you can use when creating your PowerShell scripts.

A.1 *Automatic variables*

There are a large number of variables that PowerShell automatically creates. The list can be seen by using

```
Get-Help about_Automatic_Variables
```

Reviewing the contents of this help file is highly recommended.

A.2 *Calculated fields*

Use calculated fields to create new properties or to perform calculations:

```
Get-WmiObject -Class Win32_OperatingSystem |
select @{Name="BootTime";
Expression={$_.ConvertToDateTime($_.LastBootUpTime)}}
```

A.3 *Flow syntax*

The if and switch statements are used to control flow:

```
if (<condition>){ .. statements .. }
elseif (<condition>){ .. statements .. }
else { .. statements .. }

switch (variable or pipeline) {
  value { .. statements .. }
  {expression} { .. statements .. }
  default { .. statements .. }
}
```

In the switch statement, use break in each statement block to prevent further processing.

A.4   *Function template*

The following listing provides a template for advanced functions, containing all validation options as well as comment-based help options.

Listing A.1   Advanced function template

```
function verb-noun{
[CmdletBinding(SupportsShouldProcess=$true,
    ConfirmImpact="Medium Low High None",
    DefaultParameterSetName="XXXXX")]
param (
[parameter(Position=0,
    Mandatory=$true,
    ParameterSetName="YYYYYYYYY",
    ValueFromPipeline=$true,
    ValueFromPipelineByPropertyName=$true,
    ValueFromRemainingArguments=$true,
    HelpMessage="Put your message here" )]
    [Alias("CN", "ComputerName")]
    [AllowNull()]
    [AllowEmptyString()]
    [AllowEmptyCollection()]
    [ValidateCount(1,10)]
    [ValidateLength(1,10)]
    [ValidatePattern("[A-Z]{2,8}[0-9][0-9]")]
    [ValidateRange(0,10)]
    [ValidateScript({$_ -ge (get-date)})]
    [ValidateSet("Low", "Average", "High")]
    [ValidateNotNull()]
    [ValidateNotNullOrEmpty()]
    [string]$computer="."
)
BEGIN{}#begin
PROCESS{

if ($psCmdlet.ShouldProcess("## object ##", "## message ##")) {
    ## action goes here
}

}#process
END{}#end

<#
.SYNOPSIS

.DESCRIPTION

.PARAMETER   <Parameter-Name>

.EXAMPLE

.INPUTS

.OUTPUTS

.NOTES

.LINK

#>

}
```

A.5 Hash tables

Create hash tables from here strings:

```
$arch = DATA {
ConvertFrom-StringData -StringData @'
0 = x86
9 = x64
'@
}
```

A.6 Loops

PowerShell supplies a number of looping mechanisms. The syntax of these mechanisms is summarized in the following examples:

```
1..10 | foreach-object {$_}
1..10 | foreach {$_}

$xs = 1..10
foreach ($x in $xs){$x}

for ($i=0; $i -le $($xs.length-1); $i++){$xs[$i]}

$i = 0
while ($i -le $($xs.length-1)){$xs[$i]; $i++}

$i = 0
do {$xs[$i]; $i++} while ($i -le $($xs.length-1))

$i = 0
do {$xs[$i]; $i++} until ($i -gt $($xs.length-1))
```

A.7 Operators

PowerShell uses a wide variety of operators. These are listed in table A.1. Operators are case-insensitive by default. The c and i prefixes create case-sensitive and case-insensitive versions of the operators.

Table A.1 PowerShell operators

Type	Operators
Arithmetic	+ - * / % is modulo operator
Assignment	=, +=, -=, *=, /=, %=
Bitwise	-band, -bor, -bxor
Comparison: Equality	-eq, -ceq, -ieq
Comparison: Inequality	-ne, -cne, -ine
Comparison: Greater	-gt, -cgt, -igt; -ge, -cge, -ige
Comparison: Less	-lt, -clt, -ilt; -le, -cle, -ile

Table A.1   PowerShell operators *(continued)*

Type	Operators
Contains: Wildcard match	`-like, -clike, -ilike; -notlike, -cnotlike, -inotlike`
Contains: Regex	`-match, -cmatch, -imatch; -notmatch, -cnotmatch, -inotmatch`
Contains	`-contains, -ccontains, -icontains; -notcontains, -cnotcontains, -inotcontains`
Logical	`-and, -or, -xor, -not` `!` is alternative to `-not`
Pipeline	`|` pipeline symbol `$_` current object on the pipeline
Range	`..`
String	`-replace, -creplace, -ireplace; -split; -join`
Type	`-is, -isnot, -as`
Unary	`-, +, --, ++, [<type>]`
Special	`&, -f, $(), @(), @{},` Note: `,` as a unary operator creates an array.

A.8   *PowerShell install folder*

In case you were wondering how find the PowerShell install folder, there's an automatic variable that will give you this information:

```
PS> $pshome
C:\Windows\System32\WindowsPowerShell\v1.0
```

A.9   *Size constants*

There are a number of size constants defined in PowerShell as shown in table A.2.

Table A.2   PowerShell constants

Constant	Meaning	Usage	Size
KB	Kilobyte	`1kb =`	1,024
MB	Megabyte	`1mb =`	1,048,576
GB	Gigabyte	`1gb =`	1,073,741,824
TB	Terabyte	`1tb =`	1,099,511,627,776
PB	Petabyte	`1pb =`	1,125,899,906,842,624

A.10   *Type shortcuts*

A number of type shortcuts or accelerators have been mentioned throughout the book. They are used as shortcuts for .NET types. You can use the shortcut instead of typing the whole name of the type. The most commonly used are probably [adsi] for System.DirectoryServices.DirectoryEntry and the datatype shortcuts [int] and [string] for integer and string respectively.

A full list does not seem to have been published, but Oisin Grehan, a PowerShell MVP, has shown how to obtain the list from PowerShell itself on his Nivot Ink blog (http://www.nivot.org/). The full list for PowerShell v2 is shown in table A.3.

Table A.3   PowerShell type shortcuts (accelerators)

Shortcut	.NET type
adsi	System.DirectoryServices.DirectoryEntry
adsisearcher	System.DirectoryServices.DirectorySearcher
array	System.Array
bool	System.Boolean
byte	System.Byte
char	System.Char
decimal	System.Decimal
double	System.Double
float	System.Single
hashtable	System.Collections.Hashtable
int	System.Int32
ipaddress	System.Net.IPAddress
long	System.Int64
powershell	System.Management.Automation.PowerShell
pscustomobject	System.Management.Automation.PSObject
psmoduleinfo	System.Management.Automation.PSModuleInfo
psobject	System.Management.Automation.PSObject
psprimitivedictionary	System.Management.Automation.PSPrimitiveDictionary
ref	System.Management.Automation.PSReference
regex	System.Text.RegularExpressions.Regex
runspace	System.Management.Automation.Runspaces.Runspace

Table A.3   PowerShell type shortcuts (accelerators) *(continued)*

Shortcut	.NET type
runspacefactory	System.Management.Automation.Runspaces.Runspace Factory
scriptblock	System.Management.Automation.ScriptBlock
single	System.Single
string	System.String
switch	System.Management.Automation.SwitchParameter
type	System.Type
wmi	System.Management.ManagementObject
wmiclass	System.Management.ManagementClass
wmisearcher	System.Management.ManagementObjectSearcher
xml	System.Xml.XmlDocument

appendix B
WMI reference

This appendix supplies a collection of WMI-related reference material to help you when writing PowerShell scripts that use WMI.

B.1 Useful WMI namespaces

There are a number of WMI namespaces that you'll often use. These are collected in table B.1.

Table B.1   Useful WMI namespaces

Namespace	Comments
Root\cim2	Default WMI namespace; contains the majority of the Win32 classes
Root\wmi	Contains many hardware-related classes but is mainly undocumented
root\MicrosoftDNS	DNS server management
root\virtualization	Hyper-V management
Root\MSCluster	Cluster
Root\MicrosoftNLB	NLB management
Root\webadministration	IIS management
root\StandardCimv2	New classes introduced with Windows 8; drives many of the new modules
root\Hardware	Hardware-related data
root\Microsoft\Windows\dns	PowerShell v3 DNS client configuration and utilities
root\Microsoft\Windows\PowerShellv3	Information on PowerShell modules
root\Microsoft\Windows\Storage	Windows storage server management
root\Microsoft\Windows\Smb	SMB management

B.2   *Useful classes*

The list in table B.2 doesn't include classes from specific providers, such as DNS or IIS. Those namespaces should be investigated directly. All classes are in the root\cimv2 namespace unless stated otherwise.

Table B.2   Useful classes

Component	WMI class	Chapter
Computer make and model, computer type, domain role	`Win32_ComputerSystem`	Chapter 5
Chassis type	`Win32_SystemEnclosure`	Chapter 5
Motherboard	`Win32_BaseBoard, Win32_OnBoardDevice`	Chapter 5
Buses	`Win32_Bus`	Chapter 5
CPU	`Win32_Processor, Win32_CacheMemory`	Chapter 5
BIOS	`Win32_BIOS`	Chapter 5
Memory	`Win32_PhysicalMemoryArray, Win32_PhysicalMemory`	Chapter 5
Display settings	`Win32_DesktopMonitor, Win32_VideoController`	Chapter 5
Input device	`Win32_Keyboard, Win32_PointingDevice`	Chapter 5
Hardware ports	`Win32_ParallelPort, Win32_SerialPort, Win32_USBHub, Win32_USBController, Win32_1394Controller, Win32_1394ControllerDevice`	Chapter 5
Battery	`Win32_Battery`	Chapter 5
Battery status, test power source	`root\wmi\BatteryStatus`	Chapter 5
Power plans	`root\cimv2\power\Win32_PowerPlan`	Chapter 5
Operating system, service pack, boot time	`Win32_OperatingSystem`	Chapter 5
Hotfix	`Win32_QuickFixEngineering` (see `get-hotfix` also)	Chapter 5
Bootup configuration	`Win32_BootConfigurations`	Chapter 5
Recovery configuration	`Win32_OSRecoveryConfiguration`	Chapter 5
System time	`Win32_LocalTime, Win32_UTCTime, Win32_TimeZone`	Chapter 5
Installed software	`Win32_Product`	Chapter 5
COM applications	`Win32_COMApplication`	Chapter 5

Table B.2 Useful classes *(continued)*

Component	WMI class	Chapter
Disk controller	`Win32_IDEController, Win32_SCSIController`	Chapter 6
Physical disk	`Win32_DiskDrive`	Chapter 6

Disk partition	`Win32_DiskDriveToDiskPartition,`
	`Win32_DiskPartition,`
	`Win32_LogicalDiskToPartition`
		Chapter 6

Logical disk	`Win32_LogicalDisk`	Chapter 6
Mount point	`Win32_MountPoint`	Chapter 6
Volume	`Win32_Volume`	Chapter 6
CD drive	`Win32_CDROMDrive`	Chapter 6
Registry: file data	`Win32_Registry`	Chapter 7
Registry: access data	`root\default:StdRegprov,` `root\cimv2:StdRegprov`	Chapter 7
Files	`CIM_DATAFILE`	Chapter 8
Folder	`Win32_Directory`	Chapter 8
File security	`Win32_LogicalFileSecuritySetting`	Chapter 8
Shares	`Win32_Share`	Chapter 8

Page file	`Win32_PageFileUsage, Win32_PageFile,`
	`Win32_PageFileSetting,`
	`Win32_PageFileElementSetting`
		Chapter 8

Services	`Win32_Service`	Chapter 9
Service load order	`Win32_LoadOrderGroup,` `Win32_LoadOrderGroupServiceMembers`	
Process	`Win32_Process`	Chapter 9

Printers	`Win32_Printer, Win32_PrintJob,`
	`Win32_TCPIPPrinterPort,`
	`Win32_PrinterDriver`
		Chapter 10

Network adapters	`Win32_NetworkAdapter,` `Win32_NetworkAdapterConfiguration`	Chapter 11
Network connections	`Win32_NetworkConnection`	Chapter 11
Network protocols	`Win32_NetworkProtocol`	Chapter 11
Client software	`Win32_NetworkClient`	Chapter 11
Routing table	`Win32_IP4RouteTable`	Chapter 11

Table B.2   Useful classes *(continued)*

Component	WMI class	Chapter
System activation	`SoftwareLicensingProduct,` `SoftwareLicensingService`	Chapter 13
Local user account	`Win32_UserAccount, Win32_LoggedOnUser`	Chapter 14
Local groups	`Win32_Group,`	Chapter 14
	`ROOT\SecurityCenter2\AntiVirusProduct,` `ROOT\SecurityCenter2\AntiSpywareProduct`	Chapter 14
Event logs	`Win32_NTEventlogFile`	Chapter 15
Scheduled jobs	`Win32_ScheduledJob`	Chapter 15
System stability	`Win32_WinSat`	Chapter 15
System reliability	`Win32_ReliabilityStabilityMetrics`	Chapter 15

B.3   *WQL*

Tables B.3 through B.5 summarize the WQL query language, focusing on keywords, operators, and wildcard characters respectively.

Table B.3   WQL keywords

Keyword	Meaning
`AND`	Combines two Boolean expressions and returns `TRUE` when both expressions are `TRUE`.
`ASSOCIATORS OF`	Retrieves all instances that are associated with a source instance.
`__CLASS`	References the class of the object in a query.
`FROM`	Specifies the class that contains the properties listed in a `SELECT` statement. Can only query one class at a time.
`GROUP Clause`	Causes WMI to generate one notification to represent a group of events. Use this clause with event queries.
`HAVING`	Filters the events that are received during the grouping interval that is specified in the `WITHIN` clause.
`IS`	Comparison operator used with `NOT` and `NULL`. The syntax for this statement is the following: `IS [NOT] NULL` (where `NOT` is optional).
`ISA`	Operator that applies a query to the subclasses of a specified class.
`KEYSONLY`	Used in `REFERENCES OF` and `ASSOCIATORS OF` queries to ensure that the resulting instances are only populated with the keys of the instances, which reduces the overhead of the call.
`LIKE`	Operator that determines whether or not a given character string matches a specified pattern.

Table B.3 WQL keywords *(continued)*

Keyword	Meaning
NOT	Comparison operator that's used in a WQL SELECT query.
NULL	Indicates that an object does not have an explicitly assigned value. NULL is not equivalent to 0 or blank.
OR	Combines two conditions. When more than one logical operator is used in a statement, the OR operators are evaluated after the AND operators.
REFERENCES OF	Retrieves all association instances that refer to a specific source instance. Use this statement with schema and data queries. The REFERENCES OF statement is similar to the ASSOCIATORS OF statement, but it doesn't retrieve endpoint instances; it retrieves the association instances.
SELECT	Specifies the properties that are used in a query.
TRUE	Boolean operator that evaluates to -1.
WHERE	Narrows the scope of a data, event, or schema query.
WITHIN	Specifies a polling or grouping interval. Use this clause with event queries.
FALSE	Boolean operator that evaluates to 0.

Table B.4 WQL operators

Operator	Description
=	Equal to
<	Less than
>	Greater than
<=	Less than or equal to
>=	Greater than or equal to
!= or <>	Not equal to
LIKE	Matches a pattern

Table B.5 WQL/WMI wildcards

Character	Description
[ ]	Any one character within the specified range ([a=f]) or set ([abcdef]).
^	Any one character not within the range ([^a=f]) or set ([^abcdef]).
%	Any string of zero or more characters.
_ (underscore)	Any one character. Any literal underscore used in the query string must be escaped by placing it inside square brackets ([]).

appendix C
Best practices

Best practice is a topic that can, and will, cause arguments, especially among the many passionate members of the PowerShell community. Many people, including myself, have a view of what constitutes best practice. In this appendix, I'll present some suggestions that distill both my observation of and my experience with Power-Shell. These suggestions are based on using PowerShell for over six years, writing and speaking about it, talking to many PowerShell users, and observing the scripts that are available.

> **WARNING** Some the functions in the book do not follow all of these suggestions. This is to reduce the length of the examples (for readability) and to concentrate on the working parts of the functions.

The contents of this appendix are not meant to be prescriptive but to provide a framework for you to adopt or adapt to suit your needs. Be prepared, and know when to step outside of these best practices to solve the problem you have right now. These best practices cover the majority of cases but not necessarily every case.

The first section covers PowerShell in general and the second section extends to WMI.

C.1 PowerShell best practices

This list of tips and suggestions for using PowerShell provides a framework of best practices that will help you produce better scripts in a shorter time. Always remember that your particular situation may cause you to ignore them—getting the job done is the important point.

- Don't use aliases in scripts and functions. Don't create new aliases unless you publish them with your module.
- Use full parameter names.

- If you use proxy functions, ensure they are published with your module.
- Read the help files. There's a mass of useful information, especially in the examples, that will help you overcome problems.
- Use the pipeline. It reduces code, passes objects directly between cmdlets, and lets PowerShell work in the way it's designed.
- Use advanced functions. The validation methods and the -debug and -whatif parameters all become available to your function for a few lines of code that can be put in a template (see appendix A). Don't waste time reinventing the wheel.
- Advanced functions should be like cmdlets—small pieces of functionality that perform a single job.
- Create objects for output. The output can then be filtered, displayed, or even passed to other PowerShell commands (functions, scripts, or cmdlets). Some scripts in the book may not adhere to this rule, but that's to reduce repetition and conserve space.
- Use string substitution and multiplication. It's much easier and simpler than using string concatenation.
- Use the built-in constants. Don't divide by 1024—use 1MB! Remember that kb, mb, gb, tb, and pb are all recognized by PowerShell.
- Use remoting sessions. If you are accessing a remote machine once, use the computername parameter (on a cmdlet or via Invoke-Command). If you are accessing multiple machines or the same machine multiple times, use Power-Shell remoting.
- Use PowerShell jobs for long-running tasks.
- Use standard verbs, and always use a verb-noun syntax for functions that are exposed. Hidden helper type functions do not have to follow this convention, but it will make maintenance easier if they do.
- Test-Path is often overlooked. It should be used to check on a file's existence before attempting to read the file.
- Add help files to modules and functions. Comment-based help is the easiest to add.
- Use Write-Debug and Write-Verbose to comment your functions rather than simple comments. Write-Warning can be used to pass information back to the console.
- Filter early and format late. In other words, restrict the data set you're working on as soon as is practicable, but don't format for display until the end of your script. Better still, output objects and format independently for maximum flexibility.
- Use double quotes for strings *unless* you are sure you will never want to substitute into the string. WMI filters (see listing 11.1) and WQL queries (see listing 3.3) will modify this behavior, as demonstrated in the listings.
- Be careful with code downloaded from the internet. Always ensure that you understand how it works, and always, always test it very carefully.

- Use code-signing techniques to ensure that your code has not been changed.
- Restrict access to production code. Only those who need to use it should have access. Be even more careful about who has permission to modify production code.
- Keep the logic simple. For instance, avoid double negatives in `if` statements.

C.2   *WMI best practices*

These tips bring together the things you need to remember when using WMI. The technology has some quirks, but if you keep these tips in mind when writing your scripts, you shouldn't meet too many problems.

- Use `Test-Connection -ComputerName $computer -Count 1 -Quiet` to test the availability of a remote machine before using WMI.
- Ensure that DCOM is working and the firewall is opened for WMI on remote machines.
- Ensure that WinRM is running on remote machines for access via WSMAN or CIM cmdlets.
- WMI filters are quicker to type than WQL queries. The results are the same, but you get there quicker. Save queries for WSMAN, WMI events, and WMI associations.
- Wrap WMI in functions for ease of use. In PowerShell v2 use functions, but in PowerShell v3 use the "cmdlet from object" functionality to create a module for the class (see chapters 18 and 19).
- Use WMI cmdlets ahead of WSMAN cmdlets if possible. In PowerShell v3, use the CIM cmdlets.
- Use the WMI and CIM cmdlets rather than .NET code.
- When running against a remote machine, reducing the amount of data returned by using `-Filter` or `-Query` is much quicker than returning all instances of a WMI class and then filtering with `Where-Object`. There is no appreciable difference in performance between using `-Filter` or `-Query`.
- Test the return codes from WMI methods. A return code of 0 is good. Any other value is bad.
- Many WMI classes can only be accessed when PowerShell is running with elevated privileges. The `-EnableAllPrivileges` parameter is also sometimes required. The page file classes on Windows 7 and above are a good example where both are required.
- Use `Get-WmiObject -List *network*` or similar to get all classes containing a particular string in their name.
- If you are using `-Query` and `-ComputerName`, you may see error messages unless you put the `-ComputerName` parameter first. This is an intermittent error.
- Credentials should be created before being used. Attempting to create a credential as a subexpression in the WMI cmdlets can lead to errors if the WMI

connection is made before the credential is available, because the connection will use the user's security context.

- Use `Get-WmiObject | Remove WmiObject` when deleting. It allows you to see what is going to be removed and allows more testing using the `-WhatIf` parameter on `Remove-WmiObject`.

- Make sure WinRM is running on remote machines to use WSMAN connectivity. Enabling PowerShell remoting is the simplest way to configure the service and firewall.

- CIM sessions using WSMAN will reconnect if the remote machine restarts. Those using DCOM need to be re-created.

- Remember that a WMI method's parameter order can change when using `Invoke-WmiMethod`. Use `([wmiclass]"<class name>").GetMethodParameters ("<method name>")` to discover the correct order.

- If you are making a change that may break the link to the remote machine, put the code into a PowerShell job. This allows the network timeout to occur in the job so that your main script can keep working.

- Be prepared for a lack of WMI documentation. The only way around this it to perform internet searches to determine if someone else has information or has experimented with it.

- Remember the `ASSOCIATORS` and `REFERENCES` keywords in WQL. These can reduce the effort in linking classes.

appendix D
Useful links

These are the links that I've found useful during my investigations of PowerShell and WMI. I consulted many of them during the writing of this book.

D.1 WMI

WMI SDK
http://msdn2.microsoft.com/en-us/library/aa394582.aspx

WQL
http://msdn.microsoft.com/en-us/library/aa394606(VS.85).aspx

WMI .NET CLASSES
System.Management.ManagementObject:

http://msdn.microsoft.com/en-us/library/
system.management.managementobject.aspx

System.Management.ManagementClass:

http://msdn.microsoft.com/en-us/library/
system.management.managementclass.aspx

System.Management.ManagementObjectSearcher:

http://msdn.microsoft.com/en-us/library/
system.management.managementobjectsearcher.aspx

WINDOWS SCRIPTING GUIDE
http://www.microsoft.com/technet/scriptcenter/guide/
sas_ent_qpyo.mspx?mfr=true

WMIEXPLORER
http://thepowershellguy.com/blogs/posh/archive/2007/03/22/
powershell-wmi-explorer-part-1.aspx

D.1.1 Forms for WMI questions

THIS BOOK'S FORUM
http://www.manning-sandbox.com/forum.jspa?forumID=719&start=0

MY FORUM
http://powershell.com/cs/forums/217.aspx

USING POWERSHELL AND WMI
http://powershell.com/cs/forums/78.aspx

D.2 Microsoft MSDN .NET

.NET FRAMEWORK
http://msdn.microsoft.com/en-us/library/w0x726c2.aspx

.NET FRAMEWORK CLASS LIBRARY
http://msdn.microsoft.com/en-us/library/ms229335.aspx

D.3 PowerShell blogs

This isn't meant to be an exhaustive list, but it represents a good cross section of the PowerShell community. These blogs will include links to many other areas of the PowerShell community.

RICHARD SIDDAWAY
Richard Siddaway's Blog (my primary blog):

http://msmvps.com/blogs/RichardSiddaway/Default.aspx

PowerShell and Windows Admins (this one concentrates on PowerShell and WMI):

http://itknowledgeexchange.techtarget.com/powershell/

PowerShell Admin Modules (many of the code examples from my blogs will be published as PowerShell modules):

http://psam.codeplex.com/

POWERSHELL TEAM BLOG
http://blogs.msdn.com/PowerShell/

WMI TEAM BLOG
http://blogs.msdn.com/b/wmi/

MICROSOFT SCRIPTING GUY
http://blogs.technet.com/b/heyscriptingguy/

JEFFERY HICKS
http://jdhitsolutions.com/blog/

DON JONES
http://www.windowsitpro.com/blogcontent/seriespath/
powershell-with-a-purpose-blog-36

JAMES O'NEILL
http://jamesone111.wordpress.com/

DMITRY SOTNIKOV
http://dmitrysotnikov.wordpress.com/

LEE HOLMES
http://www.leeholmes.com/blog/

THOMAS LEE
http://tfl09.blogspot.com/

SHAY LEVY
http://blogs.microsoft.co.il/blogs/ScriptFanatic/

Shay also has a PowerShell IE toolbar download available with many useful links.

JONATHAN MEDD
http://www.jonathanmedd.net/

MICROSOFT PERFORMANCE TEAM
http://blogs.technet.com/b/askperf/

D.3.1 Other PowerShell downloads

POWERGUI
http://www.powergui.org

Check on a regular basis for new power packs.

POWERSHELL PLUS
http://www.idera.com/Products/PowerShell/

POWERSHELL MANAGEMENT LIBRARY FOR HYPER-V
http://pshyperv.codeplex.com/

D.4 Code sources

CODEPLEX
http://www.codeplex.com/

Check CodePlex on a regular basis for new PowerShell and WMI projects.

TECHNET SCRIPT CENTER
http://technet.microsoft.com/en-gb/scriptcenter/default.aspx

Code examples can be found here.

GOOD POWERSHELL CODE REPOSITORIES
PowerShell.com:

www.powershell.com

PowerShell Code Repository:

www.poshcode.org

D.5 Podcasts

POWERSCRIPTING
http://powerscripting.wordpress.com/

GET-SCRIPTING
http://get-scripting.blogspot.com/

D.6 User groups

POWERSHELL COMMUNITY GROUPS
http://powershellgroup.org/

index

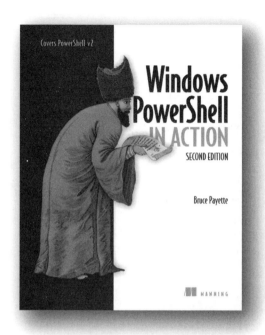

Windows PowerShell in Action,
Second Edition

by Bruce Payette

ISBN: 978-1-935182-13-9
1016 pages
$59.99
May 2011

PowerShell in Practice

by Richard Siddaway

ISBN: 978-1-935182-00-9
584 pages
$49.99
June 2010

For ordering information go to www.manning.com

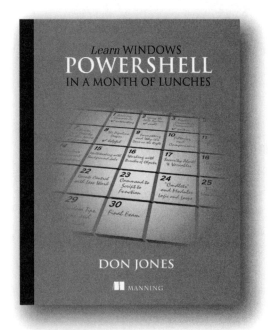

SQL Server MVP Deep Dives

Edited by Paul Nielsen,
  Kalen Delaney, Greg Low,
  Adam Machanic, Paul S. Randal,
  and Kimberly L. Tripp

ISBN: 978-1-935182-04-7
848 pages
$59.99
November 2009

SQL Server MVP Deep Dives, Volume 2

Edited by Kalen Delaney, Louis Davidson,
  Greg Low, Brad McGehee,
  Paul Nielsen, Paul Randal,
  and Kimberly Tripp

ISBN: 978-1-617290-47-3
688 pages
$59.99
October 2011

For ordering information go to www.manning.com

SQL Server 2008 Administration in Action

by Rod Colledge

ISBN: 978-1-933988-72-6
464 pages
$44.99
August 2009

Learn SQL Server 2012 in a Month of Lunches

by Grant B. Fritchey

ISBN: 978-1-617290-66-3
325 pages
$44.99
Fall 2012

For ordering information go to www.manning.com